THE PRACTICE OF
Macro Social Work

Nelson-Hall Series in Social Work

Consulting Editor: Charles Zastrow
University of Wisconsin—Whitewater

THE PRACTICE OF
Macro Social Work

William G. Brueggemann

Former Director
Social Work Program
Fresno Pacific College

NELSON-HALL PUBLISHERS • CHICAGO

Project Editor: Dorothy Anderson
Design/Production: Tamra Phelps
Photo Researcher: Nicholas Communications
Printer: Courier Companies
Typesetter: E.T. Lowe
Illustration: Corasue Nicholas
Cover Painting: Untitled, by Patrick Miceli Lawrence

Library of Congress Cataloging-in-Publication Data

Brueggemann, William G.
    The practice of macro social work / by William G. Brueggemann.
      p.   cm.
   Includes bibliographical references and index.
   ISBN 0-8304-1368-5
   1. Social service. 2. Social service—United States. 3. Social
workers—United States. 4. Macrosociology. I. Title.
HV41.B76   1996
361.3'2'0973—dc20   95-30670
                                        CIP

Reprinted 1997

Manufactured in the United States of America

10 9 8 7 6 5 4 3 2

DEDICATION

For my Native American great grandparents, whose communities were destroyed, but whose spirit has survived.

To those who raised my mother, Blanche Lena Clarke, in Otterbein Orphan Home, Springfield, Ohio; and those who took in my father as a stranger from Germany.

To Americans of Japanese ancestry, interned in concentration camps during World War II, grandparents, uncles and aunts of Lorraine Luri Inaba Brueggemann,

And to all who care for orphans and widows, who take in the stranger, and who seek justice for the oppressed.

CONTENTS IN BRIEF

CONTENTS

PART I
Solving Social Problems and Making Social Change

CHAPTER 2 / Social Problems: The Challenge of Being a Macro Social Worker   23

CHAPTER 3 / Methods of Solving Social Problems   47

CHAPTER 4 / Leadership: The Hallmark of Macro Social Work   71

PART II
Social Work Practice with Communities

CHAPTER 5 / Communities   107

CHAPTER 6 / Becoming a Macro Social Work Researcher   129

CHAPTER 7 / Becoming a Community Developer   153

CHAPTER 8 / Becoming a Social Activist   177

PART III
Social Work Practice with Organizations

CHAPTER 9 / Modern Complex Organizations   211

CHAPTER 10 / Becoming a Social Planner:
Making the Good Society   233

CHAPTER 11 / The Social Worker as Program Developer   257

CHAPTER 12 / The Macro Social Worker
as Administrator   283

CHAPTER 13 / Becoming an Organization Developer   311

PART IV
Societal Social Work

CHAPTER 14 / Social Work at the Societal Level: Social Policy and Politics   343

CHAPTER 15 / The Future of Macro Social Work   367

FOREWORD

by John L. Erlich
Professor of Social Work
California State University, Sacramento

Many of us have been searching for high-quality, comprehensive practice texts for as long as we have been teaching macro practice. For the most part, what has been available was either too narrow or superficially and inconsistently broad. At the same time, these texts tended to be either overly theoretical and have few or inadequate illustrations, or they had extremely detailed illustrations held loosely together (if at all) by theory.

What is needed is a book that covers the major areas of macro practice: community development and planning; organizing; management and administration; and policy-making. We need a text that offers clear, reasonably detailed illustrations. It should also present a coherent theoretical approach or set of approaches that give the material both explanatory power and an intervention framework that permits evaluation of the strategies and tactics described. And, as any student will tell you, it has to be readable.

William Brueggemann's *The Practice of Macro Social Work* does all of these things. Moreover, there are a number of valuable items here beyond those just noted. One is a richly detailed biography of an important practitioner in each arena. A second is suggested exercises related to "live" situations in each practice arena. In addition, key concepts, questions for discussion, and additional readings are proposed. Perhaps most importantly, Brueggemann provides lists of resources for those wishing to become involved, especially in those areas not readily accessible to many students.

Historically, my students have regularly complained about their practice texts. One of their typical concerns focuses on theories and concepts delivered in a way that makes them feel they are being treated with condescension. Or the same material is often delivered in a fashion that makes students say they have received an intellectual display that demonstrates the author's brilliance rather than addressing their learning needs. Another criticism has to do with a general lack of relevance to the practice world in which the students are field placed and work.

I believe that Brueggemann has responded to these concerns better than most authors; I think student readers will find him straightforward and relevant to their needs and interests. His action design, for example, is not a full-blown, take-it-or-leave-it theoretical model. It is a work in progress to which both students and teachers can add or subtract. It conveys the sense of a shared journey to master complex material for use in the real world.

We have come a long way since macro practice was the core of the social work profession in the early part of this century. The resurgence of broad interest in macro practice in the late 1960s and early 1970s did little to counter the long-term trend away from social work involvement in change at the community, organizational, and societal levels. In part, this book is a plea not to abandon this proud and often distinguished tradition.

What, then, is the basis on which we may hope to be involved in change at these levels? One of the important things that Brueggemann does—right at the beginning of *The Practice of Macro Social Work*—is to address the fundamental question of how we know what we know. He considers the currently predominant systems and social ecological designs, notes some of their limitations, and proposes an action model grounded in symbolic interaction theory. The centrality of a socially constructed reality to this perspective is especially useful in fueling a practice that is ethnically sensitive, empowering, and builds on strengths. It also provides ample room to celebrate both our commonality and our diversity.

Another important contribution that Brueggemann makes is to set forth a social problems context in which to view the promise of macro practice. This runs counter to the current tendency to deliver macro material as an adjunct to micro practice. No doubt this is partly a response to the limited job market and to social work curriculum designs that loudly honor but quietly undermine the commitment to meaningful change. Among other things, Brueggemann's perspective challenges us to address root causes of problems as well as their consequences.

Brueggemann also looks at what being a macro social worker entails in a social problems context and how this context relates to problem solving. This is followed by a particularly thoughtful consideration of leadership as a key ingredient in macro practice—something that is often lacking in even the most widely used macro texts. While stimulating us to think about practice in each of the eight arenas addressed, the author does not shy away from hard data. For example, in drawing our attention to the level of violence in the United States as part of an exercise, he notes some comparative statistics on violent deaths by handgun in 1988. For America, 8,915 were killed, compared to only 53 people in Switzerland, 19 in Sweden, 8 in Canada, and 7 in the United Kingdom. Clearly, this is one of the stark realities of American life that demands our attention. And given the global realities, it is one where positive change efforts might well bear fruit.

One of the many significant things this book reminds us of is the vital nature of the connections we make with each other. These connections are part of the core on which macro practice builds. In an era of lowered expectations, rampant downsizing, restricted entitlements, and taking our small miracles one at a time, *The Practice of Macro Social Work* reminds us that it is still possible to "think big," which means being the best we can be in contributing to progressive social change and helping and stimulating our human service organizations to do the same. It also encourages us, where possible, to join with potent strategies that will impact our social, political, and economic systems to make this country a better place for us all.

PREFACE

The times they are a changin'—BOB DYLAN

Looking back over the past century, it is obvious that our society has made significant progress in many areas. The list of technological advancements in the past one hundred years outstrips our imagination. We have moved from the horse and buggy to landing men on the moon and exploring outer space. We have probed the inner space of the atom, releasing its energy and creating new elements. In biology, we have discovered the genetic code of life itself, creating new life and conquering disease. Computers have revolutionized the way we solve problems. Nearly every day one can read about another medical advance or scientific breakthrough in our newspapers. We have developed mass organizational systems, the most sophisticated human tools ever devised, many of which span the globe, and whose budgets are sometimes larger than those of some entire nations. Our global society is becoming more complex and interrelated.

The shining areas of scientific light and technological advancement of our present age, however, while brilliant in disclosing the wonders of nature, pale in comparison to the difficulties in the social sphere that lie before us. While some progress has been made, there are indicators that, as Anne Schaef says, our society "is deteriorating at an alarming rate."[1] Even in these enlightened and modern times the issues that fill our newspapers, compel our attention, and provoke our conversation are social concerns such as violence and criminality, homelessness and poverty, civil rights violations, war, famine, and human rights abuse.

The field of social work was born because of concerns such as these. Growing out of the Progressive Era (1890–1910), a period of massive political and social reconstruction, social workers were involved in the major social struggles of the day—the suffrage movement after the Civil War, child welfare reform and juvenile criminal justice movements at the turn of the century, the pacifist movement during WWI, the labor movement during the Great Depression, and the Civil Rights Movement of the 1960s. Social champions such as Dorothea Dix, Charles Loring Brace, Jane Addams, Harry Hopkins, Michael Harrington and others had a major impact on helping our society to become more healthy, humane, and just.

However, while social workers have challenged our society to live up to its expectations, in recent decades the social work profession has retreated from its emphasis in the macro social arena of practice. Our cities are in disarray, crime is on the increase, poverty continues to abound, and human rights and civil rights abuses still plague us even after years of legislation.

This book is intended to reclaim for social work its rightful place as the profession whose mandate is the welfare of our society as a whole. I hope to inspire and inform all social workers who read it about the array of opportunities and needs for this important field of practice and in so doing, assist in the process of social change.

Acknowledgments

This book could not have been written without the valuable contributions of many individuals. I want to thank the people at Nelson-Hall who worked with me to ensure a quality text. In particular, I want to acknowledge the many hours of hard work put in by Dorothy Anderson—from manuscript to bound book. I also want to thank Steve Ferrara and Richard Meade for their enthusiasm and support about the first draft of the manuscript, and Libby Rubenstein for her responsiveness to my concerns and her helpful suggestions.

The following reviewers contributed time, expertise, and excellent ideas that significantly enhanced the quality of the text: Marvin D. Feit of the University of Akron and Martin Sundel of the University of Texas at Arlington.

CHAPTER 1

Introduction to Macro Social Work

Entire groups of people are impoverished economically, socially, educationally, and spiritually because of social conditions of racism, indifference, greed, and violence.

The world is so much larger than I thought. I thought we went along paths—but it seems there are no paths. The going itself is the path.
—C.S. LEWIS, *PERELANDRA*

The dogmas of the quiet past are inadequate to the stormy present. The occasion is piled high with difficulty, and we must rise to the occasion. Just as our case is new, so we must think anew and act anew.
—PRESIDENT ABRAHAM LINCOLN, ANNUAL MESSAGE, DECEMBER 1862

IDEAS IN THIS CHAPTER

Death Comes to Francisco

Francisco Martinez is dead. He was one of many faceless and insignificant laborers in our country. His passing will scarcely make a ripple in the course of world affairs. But "when his friends chew over the events of that morning, they taste the bile of being strangers in a strange land, the mules pulling agriculture's plow," writes Alex Pulaski.[1] To his friends Francisco's death is symbolic of the hypocrisy of American culture. Searching for a better life, Francisco, a young Triqui Indian, came to America from the state of Oaxaca, Mexico. As Filemon Lopez, an advocate for the Mixteco Indians, said, "the end of all this, for many, is death."[2]

Each year, the numbers of Mixteco Indians swell in California when summer farm work calls. The many who remain in the United States often must live in caves or in the open. Francisco, however, was more fortunate than most. Part of a vine-pruning crew, he was one of fourteen men, their wives, and their children who shared an unheated brick shed owned by rancher Russell Scheidt.

On the morning of January 17, 1993, Francisco's fortunes changed. Waking for work at about 5:00 A.M., Augustin Ramirez found Francisco on the floor, his breathing labored, appearing near death. Augustin woke two of Francisco's friends, who ran to the ranchhouse to ask Scheidt if they could use the phone. Rousted out of bed, Russell Scheidt was exhausted, having just returned at midnight from a vacation in Jamaica. Mario Ramirez told him in Spanish that Francisco was dying and that they needed to call the police. Scheidt's response, according to Ramirez, was that they had cars, and they could take him to the hospital if they wished. Then he shut the door in their faces. Later, Scheidt said, "I can't really remember what I told them . . . I was kind of incoherent, to tell the truth."

Desperate for help, Francisco's friends sped into Kerman, a nearby town. Stopping at a service station, they talked an attendant into calling the Kerman police. They explained their problem to the officer who asked several questions and then called the Sheriff's Department. The friends waited for twenty-two minutes for the sheriff's deputies to arrive. Wasting more precious time, the deputies drove to the shed, where they found Francisco, at 6:15 A.M., already dead. Finally, they called the ambulance.

Francisco died of acute alcohol poisoning, which caused his brain to shut down his lungs. Tom Stoeckel, manager of the Valley Medical Center's emergency unit in Fresno, said that paramedics can revive victims of alcohol poisoning by simply giving them oxygen. However, death can result if the supply of oxygen to the brain has stopped for even a few minutes. The official report makes no mention of Scheidt or his refusal to allow the workers to call an ambulance. It stated that Francisco was already dead when the worker's found him that morning.

The afternoon Francisco died, Scheidt returned with a translator and told the Mixteco men, women, and children to leave. The translator reportedly told them that housing inspectors were coming, and the shed was not fit for human habitation. Scheidt said later that the men had finished their work and were basically squatters.

Francisco was buried February 17, 1993, a victim of human indifference, powerlessness, and poverty. His friends, now unemployed and homeless, gave him the best funeral they could buy with the $861 they collected. Four of his friends attended the service. Russell Scheidt did not bother to come.

Introduction

Francisco Martinez died a victim of alcoholism. But more importantly, his death was ultimately brought on by social conditions of poverty, exploitation, racism, indifference, greed, and violence against an entire group of people. Even in America, many are impoverished economically, socially, educationally, and spiritually for the benefit of a few. When social abuse occurs in this fashion, the entire society is diminished and degraded.

Macro social workers are professionals who want to make a difference in people's lives where oppression, intolerance, and insensitivity exist. They try to correct social conditions that cause human suffering and misery. They struggle to get at the root of social problems by calling attention to injustice, finding out where human needs exist, and working to improve communities and organizational systems.

They work to develop new programs and change social policies.

This chapter describes macro social work and why this field is important, and challenges you to consider your own role as a macro social worker. As you read this chapter, think about how macro social work and its particular methods could have made a difference to the Triqui Indians and others like them in our world.

What Is Macro Social Work?

Macro social work is the practice of solving social problems and making social change at the community, organizational, and societal levels. Let's look at this definition in more detail.

Solving Social Problems

Many social work practitioners help individuals, couples, and groups who have been affected by, and who bear the scars of, *personal problems*. While healing and helping damaged individuals is important, it is a wider social concern that distinguishes social work from other helping professions. This wider concern involves *social problems*—those conditions of society that create personal troubles and that are often embedded in the premises and institutions on which our society is based. Among these social problems are racism, sexism, urban decay, economic injustice, and dysfunctional political systems.

Macro-level social workers apply a method called the "rational problem-solving process" to conditions that cause social problems. Rational problem solving was conceived of as a way of implementing social change over four hundred years ago and was gradually applied to economic, policy, and organizational decision making. Rational problem solving was adopted by macro social workers as early as the turn of the century. Since then it has become known as the "generalist social work method." Chapter 2 deals with social problems, and chapter 3 covers rational problem solving as a method of macro social work change.

Making Social Change

People who make social change are called change agents. Change agents come from a variety of disciplines and many have numerous interests. Change agents may be everyday people working voluntarily for change in their own communities. For example, volunteers working to rid communities of drug dealers or abusive gangs are change agents. Ministers engaged in issues of social justice or scientists involved in protesting against nuclear war are change agents. Environmentalists are change agents working to save the earth and its ecosystems from destruction. Sociologists who do research on social problems and political scientists who try to improve social policies are change agents, as are public administrators working with or through complex organizations to improve social conditions.

While change agents may come from many walks of life and any number of professions, there is one profession that claims change agent practice as its own. This is the profession of social work. Social workers need to understand how macro social systems work in order to design systems that are better,

fix them when they become dysfunctional, challenge those models that are failing, and infuse those that are unethical with integrity and goodness. No other helping profession claims for itself so broad a social mandate as social work.

The heart of social change is leadership. To some extent, every macro social worker needs be a social leader. Social work leadership is the focus of chapter 4; it is the basis for each arena of social work practice that follows.

The Spectrum of Macro Social Work

Engaging social change by means of macro social work practice is the heritage, the present responsibility, and the future promise of the social work profession. It is social work's commitment to social betterment at all levels that insures its continued impact in our world today. Social workers see communities, organizations, and society as the arenas of their concern and involvement.

The heart of social change is leadership.

Community Social Work

Next to the family, communities are the most basic and necessary social systems. When communities begin to erode, people's social bonds become weak. When communities become dysfunctional, their members fail economically, emotionally, or socially.

For years many of our communities have been neglected. Others are in disarray. As a result, these communities are rife with violence, poverty, or drug abuse. Instead of oases of hope, enlightenment, and meaning, they are deserts of despair, ignorance, and alienation.

One of the most important roles of macro social workers, therefore, is to help build communities. Macro social workers who treat ailing communities are called *community developers.* Community developers work not only in the ghettos, slums, barrios, migrant work camps, reservations, and "housing projects" of America but also in war-torn, poverty-stricken areas of Guatemala, Somalia, Thailand, India, and other developing countries.

Some community social workers are *social activists* working to empower the powerless, challenge injustice, and fight oppression. Social activists are reformers who remind us about the best that our society can be. Community social workers need to be perceptive observers of society; *social researchers* gathering information about the causes and conditions of community problems. Part Two is devoted to community social work. Chapters 5, 6, 7, and 8 explore the community as a needed social system and the fields of social work research, community development and social action.

Organizational Social Work

Robert Presthus and others have observed that we live in an organizational society.[3] Modern complex organizations have become the referent of social life at large, replacing human communities. Almost everyone in our society is intimately connected with and draws his or her sustenance from complex organizations. Most social workers, for example, work in organizations such as departments of social services, hospitals, service systems for developmentally disabled or mentally ill, or criminal jus-

One of the most important roles of macro social workers is to build communities of people.

tice. We are all influenced, for better or worse, by the organizational values and premises of these systems.

Macro social workers are becoming increasingly concerned about how organizations are transforming the community into social structures that are completely new and how this phenomenon is changing the nature of our social/cultural milieu. Organizations and their defects are one reason many social problems exist, but they are the means by which these problems can be resolved as well.

While community social work continues to be a needed arena of macro social work practice, social work with complex organizational systems is rapidly becoming even more important. Macro social workers need to be vigorously involved in organizational social change. *Social planners,* for example, assess human needs and work with the infrastructure of different organizations, assisting those who are at the mercy of the social machinery of their communities. A social plan evolves out of coordination, communication, and improved organizational networks, often resulting in the establishment of a new service program. Social planning often leads to *program development,* a second arena of organizational social work. Program developers create social agencies, which in turn require skilled *social work administrators* to implement change over the long haul. When social agencies or other organizations fail to adapt to their rapidly changing social environments, administrators often call upon management consultants, called *organization developers,* who treat the organization as a client and bring the system back to effective functioning. How social workers can use these often impersonal power systems in solving the complex human problems of our day is explored in Part Three, chapters 9 through 13.

Societal Social Work

Social change, no matter how well intended, may be vitiated unless that change is instituted by new social policy. *Social policy analysts* work with the political system, gathering facts, writing legislation, lobbying, giving testimony before state legislative bodies and Congress, and working as watchdogs over regulatory commissions to insure that laws, once enacted, are carried out. *Social ethics* are the heart of social policy. We want policies that help us arrive at a society that is not only prosperous but also truly good and humane. All social workers need to have a vision of how to apply personal values to helping achieve a good society. Macro social workers must understand the past, make changes in the present, and have a vision for society's *future*. In Part Four, chapters 14 and 15 look at societal social work and explore social policy and ethics, and the future of social work, and make recommendations about macro social work practice and the role you might play in it.

Conclusion

Understanding the workings of our social world and intervening in it are crucial to the repertoire of every social worker. While all social workers need to be engaged in macro social work to some extent, there are others for whom macro social work will become a full-time endeavor. I hope that this book may inspire some of you to become interested in macro social work practice as a professional goal in itself. It is probably safe to say that those social workers who engage in macro practice will have a lasting impact on our social environment, helping make fundamental changes in the way we live and guiding the future direction of our society.

KEY CONCEPTS

macro social work
solving social problems
making social change
community social work
community
social work research
community development
social action
organizational social work
organization
social planning
program development
social work administration
organization development
societal social work
social policy analysis
social values
social ethics

QUESTIONS FOR DISCUSSION

1. It has been asserted that the trend of the social work profession in the past thirty years has been to concentrate on clinical helping—individual counseling, family therapy, and group work rather than macro level helping.[5] If this is a fair statement, social workers tend to serve people who have already been damaged by the effects of social problems, rather than working toward the eradication of the causes and conditions of social decay itself. In this sense, social work is reactive rather than proactive. Do you believe this assessment is correct? Why or why not? If you believe it is true, comment on the implications of this trend for the practice of social work today.

2. Macro level social workers must often take a moral or ethical stance against people or social systems that perpetrate injustice. Is this stance similar to or different from the ethical stance that micro social workers take? Explain your perspective.

EXERCISES

EXERCISE 1:
Solving a Social Problem

Indifference to the plight of others allows "man's inhumanity to man" to thrive. When we become bystanders, spectators not actors in human affairs, we avoid our social responsibility and retreat into a world of individualism, exploitation, and greed. We become socially and ethically numb, giving tacit assent to a host of social ills that eat at the heart of our social well-being. Macro social workers are people who insert themselves actively in the lives of others and do not allow social ills to go unnoticed or unchallenged.

Imagine for a moment that you are a macro social worker involved with migrant farm workers in Kerman, California. The news of the death of Francisco Martinez reaches you. The plight of the Mixteco Indians is all too familiar to you: wrenching poverty, oppression, prejudice, powerlessness, miserable living conditions, lack of educational opportunities for children, alcoholism, language barriers, health problems, and long hours of backbreaking labor in fields where temperatures often pass 100°F for days on end.

This chapter has described briefly eight different arenas of macro social work: community development, social action, research, social planning, program development, administration, organization development, and social policy. How would you address the problem of the Triqui Indian laborers? Which method or combination of macro social work methods would you employ? What specific steps would you take?

Outline your methods and then discuss them in class. It is very likely that you already have an intuitive grasp of how to go about social change. Explore your ideas with your instructor and come to some consensus. Keep your answers. Later, when you read chapter 3, Methods of Solving Social Problems, and later chapters you will discover more completely how they can be brought to bear on social problems.

EXERCISE 2:
Developing Commitment

There are a number of ways that you can confirm, individually or as a class, your own impressions about the role of being a macro social worker, find out directly what it's like, and explore questions you might have. Choose one or more activities from the following list and report back to class.

1. Visit local agencies or organizations that are involved in social problem solving: Habitat for Humanity; organizations working with the homeless; abortion groups, either pro-life or pro-choice; gay rights groups; political party organizations; human rights commissions; local county boards of supervisors or city councils; environmental action groups; civil rights organizations, such as NAACP, Mexican-American community action groups; women's rights organizations, such as NOW; and B'nai B'rith Jewish Anti-Defamation League.
2. Bring macro social workers to

class who can tell you directly about what they are doing. For example, you could invite people involved in setting up programs, social planners, social activists, management consultants, administrators, community developers, social policy analysts, or others.
3. Interview a macro social worker who is well known in your community or one who is doing the kind of work that attracts you. In class, share what you have learned about the change agent you interviewed.
4. Read articles in current magazines or watch videos about particular community social action issues.
5. Read a book that describes a social change or that has been instrumental in social change. Listed below are books written by macro social workers, social activists, novelists, journalists, and "muckrakers." Your instructor may have others to suggest. Choose one to read and report on it to your class.

Community Development

Jane Addams. *Twenty Years at Hull House.* New York: Macmillan, 1910.
Jane Addams. *The Second Twenty Years at Hull House.* New York: Macmillan, 1930.

Civil Rights

Martin Luther King, Jr. *Stride Toward Freedom: The Montgomery Story.* New York: Ballantine Books, 1958.

(continued next page)

EXERCISES

EXERCISE 2 (continued)

John M. Perkins. *Let Justice Roll Down*. Glendale, CA: G/L Books, 1976.

W.E.B. (William Edward Burghart) Dubois. *The Writings of W.E.B. DuBois*. New York: Crowell, 1975.

Social Action and Social Justice

Saul Alinsky. *Reveille for Radicals*. New York: Vintage Books, 1969.

Saul Alinsky. *Rules for Radicals*. New York: Random House, 1971.

Upton Sinclair. *Cry for Justice: An Anthology of the Literature of Social Protest*, rev. ed. E. Sagaren and A. Teichner, eds. New York: Lyle Stuart, 1963.

Social Ethics

Jane Addams. *Democracy and Social Ethics*. Boston: Harvard University Press, 1964.

Richard L. Means. *The Ethical Imperative: The Crisis in American Values*. Garden City, NY: Anchor Books, 1970.

Racial Intolerance

Oscar Handlin. *The Uprooted: The Epic Story of the Great Migrations That Made the American People*. New York: Grosset and Dunlap, 1951.

Cary McWilliams. *Brothers Under the Skin*. Boston: Little, Brown, 1951.

Cary McWilliams. *Prejudice, Japanese Americans: Symbol of Racial Intolerance*. Hamden, CT: Archon Books, 1971.

Oppression and Injustice

Cary McWilliams. *Factories in the Field: The Story of Migratory Farm Labor in California*. Santa Barbara, CA: Penguin, 1971.

Frank Norris. *Octopus: A Story of California—The War between the Wheat Grower and the Railroad Trust*. New York: Bantam Books, 1958.

Jacob Riis. *Children of the Tenements*. New York: Macmillan, 1903.

John Steinbeck. *Grapes of Wrath*. New York: Viking Press, 1939.

John Steinbeck. *Cannery Row*. New York: Viking Press, 1945.

Political Corruption

Walton Bean. *Boss Reuf's San Francisco: The Story of the Union Labor Party, Big Business and Graft Prosecution*. Berkeley: University of California Press, 1952.

Frank Norris. *The Pit: A Story of Chicago*. New York: Doubleday, 1903.

Social Policy

Rachel Carson. *The Silent Spring*. Boston: Houghton Mifflin, 1962.

Michael Harrington. *The Other America: Poverty in the United States*. Baltimore, MD: Penguin Books, 1962.

Richard Harris. *A Sacred Trust: The Story of Organized Medicine's Multi-Million Dollar Fight Against Public Health Legislation*, rev. ed. Baltimore, MD: Penguin Books, 1969.

Social History

Henry Steele Commager. *The American Mind: An Interpretation of American Thought and Character since the 1880's*. New York: Bantam Books, 1950.

Richard Hofstadter. *The Age of Reform: From Bryan to F.D.R*. New York: Vintage Books, 1955.

Richard Hofstadter. *The American Political Tradition and the Men Who Made It*. New York: Vintage Books, 1954.

Social Leaders

P. David Finks. *The Radical Vision of Saul Alinsky*. New York: Paulist Press, 1984.

Dorothy Clark Wilson. *Stranger and Traveler: The Story of Dorothea Dix, American Reformer*. Boston: Little, Brown, 1975.

EXERCISE 3:
The Journey of a Macro Social Worker

Macro social workers are people who are committed to improving society and correcting its defects. I will tell you the story of my own journey into macro social work. After I tell you my story, I would like you to consider your own motivation in the field of macro social work practice by exploring some questions and then filling out a checklist.

Along with her three sisters, my mother, a part Cherokee Native American, was raised in Otterbein Home, an orphanage operated by the Evangelical and Reformed Church in Southern Ohio on property that was originally a Shaker Colony. My father migrated to this country from Germany just before the Great Depression hit in 1929, the same year my mother graduated from the Otterbein Home high school. For nearly ten years, just as many Americans, my parents existed on jobs wherever they could be found. My mother became a

EXERCISES

nanny and my father traveled America as a laborer and cook for a Wild West show. Eventually, he settled in Cincinnati, Ohio, where he had relatives and where a large German American population existed. A year after I was born, America declared War on Japan and Germany.

The next five years were difficult ones for my father and other German Americans. His brothers, who had remained in Germany, became soldiers or officers, fighting against my father's adopted country. My father's German accent, attendance at German gatherings, associations with other German-Americans, and activities as a union organizer marked him as a person warranting investigation by the FBI. I learned from him what it was like to be an alien in one's own country. My mother, who had no family of her own, taught me to respect people of all backgrounds, particularly those who did not have the same opportunities as others.

When I was about eight years old, an event occurred that was to make these values real to me. One day I saw a new boy in my school who was strange looking. In an unthinking and unfeeling way I began to make fun of him. I still remember the look of hurt and confusion on his face. That look made me deeply ashamed. He did not attend any of my classes, but sometimes, when I saw him on the playground, I would talk to him. Over the years, he became one of my closest friends.

In high school, this boy, whose name was Jackie, invited me to his home. When I went away to Concordia College, Milwaukee, Wisconsin, and Concordia Senior College, Ft. Wayne, Indiana, to pursue a ministerial career, Jackie and I continued to write to one another, and we visited when I came home on vacation. We were both very proud when he graduated from high school, a great achievement for a young man who was mentally retarded.

While in high school and college I expressed my interest in working with people by finding a number of part-time jobs: As a group worker at the Silverspring Neighborhood Center, Milwaukee, Wisconsin; as a summer camp counselor at Camp Sidney Cohen, Delafield, Wisconsin; as a training director for Dan Beard Scout Reservation, Cincinnati, Ohio; as a Gray-Y leader for Fort Wayne YMCA; and as a recreation leader for the Fort Wayne State School for Mentally Retarded.

These experiences helped me confirm that I wanted to become a group social worker. In my last year of college, I was accepted at the school of social work, University of Hawaii, a school that met my interests in ethnic diversity. After graduating with an MSW degree in 1964, I returned home for a visit. Jackie, my friend, was working full time. In a few days, I was to begin my first full-time job as a social worker at Bethesda Lutheran Home, Watertown, Wisconsin, a facility for the developmentally disabled.

Wanting to round out my skills in individual counseling, I attended the University of Wisconsin, Madison, Department of Counseling and Behavioral Studies, for a year. Then, I returned to Hawaii where I worked as a clinician, performing individual, family, and group psychotherapy at Catholic Social Services, Honolulu.

After several years of clinical practice, I married. I accepted a supervisory position in group social work at Potrero Hill Neighborhood House in San Francisco. The late 1960s and early 1970s was a time of social ferment over the war in Vietnam and the Civil Rights Movement. Many social workers, including myself, became engaged in social action activities such as protest marches and active resistance to the war, as well as advocacy in civil rights demonstrations. I became involved with helping different community groups and neighborhood associations on Potrero Hill struggle with issues of racism, housing, youth gangs, and drug abuse.

After a number of years as supervisor and director at the Neighborhood House, I decided to begin a small agency for the developmentally disabled. I wrote a grant proposal and obtained funding. As administrator of the Potrero Hill Social Development Center, I became actively involved in social planning, serving on several planning boards in health and developmental disabilities and performing needs assessments. Out of these research efforts, it became clear that social development center programs needed a broader base of support. As a result, I formed a coalition group of four small social development centers, writing and obtaining a federal grant, developing the board, and helping the new organization get started.

I accepted a position at Loma Prieta Regional Center for Developmentally Disabled in San Jose, California, beginning as a senior counselor. As the agency grew larger, I became its first community resource developer, a position that included social planning, research, and program development. Later, I became a supervisor managing several different offices.

During this time I became more and more fascinated with broad-based social problems and began

(continued next page)

EXERCISES

EXERCISE 3 *(continued)*

reading widely in the field of social policy. I grew more concerned with the social problems I saw in our society. After taking several courses in administration, I found a field in which the strands of my various interests in social planning, policy, research, and program development came together. I began to pursue doctoral studies at the University of Southern California, School of Public Administration. At the same time, I became involved in practicing organization development with local churches and began teaching public administration at the University of San Francisco.

After I received my degree, I became a full-time faculty member directing the social work program and teaching administration at Fresno Pacific College, Fresno, California. I joined other faculty members to establish a small family care home for developmentally disabled in a residential neighborhood over the strenuous protests of some community members. Later, along with several of my social work students and other faculty, I began a plan to include developmentally disabled adults on our college campus. Today, developmentally disabled adults attend classes, engage in work training projects, participate in college events, and at graduation walk across the stage in full graduation garb just as any other college students and receive a certificate of completion. My friend Jackie would have been proud. It is one more installmant in repayment for that day on the playground in Cincinnati, Ohio.

Now that you have read my story, let's explore the kinds of patterns that shaped my interest in macro social work. My parent's ethnic backgrounds and the milieu in which my mother and father were raised provided a powerful underlying context that shaped my life, my motivation as a social worker, and my interest in macro social work. What kinds of backgrounds do your parents and grandparents come from that may have affected your values, what is important to you, and your own interests in social work?

My father's arrival in the United States and my mother's graduation from high school the same year that the Great Depression occurred, my birth at the beginning of World War II, my entry into social work in the midst of the Civil Rights Movement and the protest against the war in Vietnam affected my interest in the poor and oppressed, my response to social problems, and my commitment to ethnic diversity. What sorts of historical and political situations have you or your parents experienced? How have these experiences affected your concern for social problems, your view of the world and the role that social work can play in making it a better one?

My religion provided an underlying foundation and motivation in choosing a career. Perhaps it is important for you as well. What role can religion play in heightening one's sensitivity to people who are oppressed, to the "orphan and widow," and to the strangers in our midst?[4]

Sometimes one particular incident can have a lasting impact in one's life. For me, that incident was my en-

counter with Jackie. Has there been an occurrence in your life that brought you to an awareness of the kind of career that is right for you? What kinds of personal experiences have you had that affected your interest in social work or in macro social work?

My career path in social work, as for many social workers, began with clinical practice. In a short time, however, I moved from being a clinician to supervision and administration. From there I became involved in community development, program development, research, social planning, social action, and organization development. I became interested in social policy and eventually became involved in teaching and writing. Programs I began are still in existence. There are people whose lives I have affected; organizations I helped change for the better, communities that are more healthy because of my input, and systems that I helped lead. Each of these aspects of social work practice required me to use different problem-solving and leadership functions, demanded new skills, and required growth and learning.

What role do you see yourself playing in social work? Envision yourself after graduation. Let yourself feel the excitement. What kinds of clients do you see yourself working with?

Now imagine yourself five years after graduation. What will you be doing then? In what kind of setting do you see yourself? What kind of social work do you see yourself involved in? Finally, envision yourself ten years after graduation. As you envision your career, what sort of macro social work do you see yourself doing?

CHECKLISTS

CHECKLIST 1: Exploring Motivation

The following checklist will give you a chance to explore your motivation to become a macro social worker. Read each question and circle the number on a range of "strongly agree" to "strongly disagree" that reflects your interests.

1. I get concerned when I hear about an injustice perpetrated on others.
   Strongly Agree   1   2   3   4   5   6   7   Strongly Disagree

2. I have feelings for people who generally are the underdogs or who have been disadvantaged.
   Strongly Agree   1   2   3   4   5   6   7   Strongly Disagree

3. I want to take up the cause of people who have been wronged.
   Strongly Agree   1   2   3   4   5   6   7   Strongly Disagree

4. I am attracted to social issues or problems I feel should be solved.
   Strongly Agree   1   2   3   4   5   6   7   Strongly Disagree

5. I feel that everyone ought to try to get involved in his or her community.
   Strongly Agree   1   2   3   4   5   6   7   Strongly Disagree

6. I feel particularly hopeful that there is something important for me to do in my neighborhood or community—that I can really make a difference.
   Strongly Agree   1   2   3   4   5   6   7   Strongly Disagree

7. I feel I have a role to play in social change—in making life better for others.
   Strongly Agree   1   2   3   4   5   6   7   Strongly Disagree

8. I want to become involved in something bigger than myself, larger than my own self-interest.
   Strongly Agree   1   2   3   4   5   6   7   Strongly Disagree

9. I get excited about the idea of being engaged in social renewal and transformation.
   Strongly Agree   1   2   3   4   5   6   7   Strongly Disagree

10. I feel I have creative ideas and can see possibilities for change that others may miss.
    Strongly Agree   1   2   3   4   5   6   7   Strongly Disagree

Look over your answers. Do your answers generally lean toward "strongly agree" or in the direction of "strongly disagree"? Do they hover around the center? What does that say about your motivation for macro social work?

Are there specific areas where you strongly agree and others in which you strongly disagree? What prime motivators lead you to be interested in social change? What detracts you from interest in being a macro social worker?

How will you use macro social work skills in generalist practice? In clinical practice? Do you want to make macro social work a career? With which arenas of macro practice do you feel most comfortable? Least comfortable?

CHECKLISTS

CHECKLIST 2: The Stance of a Macro Social Worker

Within the field of macro social work are a number of particular arenas of practice. This checklist will help you discover where your particular strengths may lie.

Look over the following list. At the end of the list are four columns. On a scale of 1 to 5, with 1 being the lowest and 5 the highest, score each sentence, placing the score in the column next to the number of the sentence.

It is important for me to:

1. Take part in a movement to bring an end to injustice.
2. Become involved with a community and help mold the destiny of a people.
3. Use my vision to look for possibilities in the future.
4. Shape a system in the here-and-now over the long term.
5. Gather information and facts to correct dishonesty or deceit.
6. Develop relationships strengthening communities or organizations.
7. Exert my creativity and ability to see the big picture to try out something new.
8. Fix a broken system by applying my technical skills.
9. Help the underdog obtain redress, and empower the powerless.
10. Engage others in forging social bonds.
11. Be a part of something positive that is larger than myself.
12. Make a tangible contribution by implementing concrete decisions today.
13. Get involved in social action and social justice.
14. Get involved in building community or neighborhood.
15. Get involved in developing new programs, plans, or projects.
16. Get involved in making things happen by implementing the details of decisions.

Place your scores for each sentence in the following columns. Add up your answers at the bottom.

A	B	C	D
1 _____	2 _____	3 _____	4 _____
5 _____	6 _____	7 _____	8 _____
9 _____	10 _____	11 _____	12 _____
13 _____	14 _____	15 _____	16 _____
_____	_____	_____	_____
SA/SP	CD/OD	PD/PL	AD/R

If you scored highest in column A, you may have an interest in either social action or social policy analysis. If you scored highest in column B, you may have an aptitude in the areas of community or organization development. If your score in column C is highest, you might have an interest in either program development or social planning. Finally, those of you who are highest in column D could be best at either administration or social research.

What do your scores say about your motivation and stance as a macro social worker? Compare your rankings with those of others in your class.

EXERCISES

EXERCISE 4:
Contracting Trios

One way of insuring that you learn is to develop a set of learning objectives for yourself. First, describe the learning you want to achieve, what you need to do to acquire that learning, the behaviors from your classmates/instructor that will either enhance or detract from that learning.

1. What are the most important things I want to learn from this course?
2. What are the things that I need to do to achieve these learnings?
3. What are the behaviors or activities of my classmates and the instructor that will enhance my learning?
4. What behaviors or activities of my classmates or the instructor will disrupt my learning?

After you have finished your lists, form triads. First, compare the personal learnings you want to achieve. Combine and rank them in order. These become your *learning objectives*. Then look at the things you need to do to accomplish your objectives; these are your *learning tasks*. Discuss your learning tasks and combine them. Finally, examine the *learning behaviors* that will help or detract from your learning. Develop a list of positive behaviors and activities and negative behaviors and activities.

While you are organized in triads, the instructor will make four columns on the board. After your group is finished, write your learning *objectives* in the first column, your *learning tasks* in the second column, your *positive behaviors* in the third column, and your *negative behaviors* in the fourth column.

As a class, look at column 1, your learning objectives. See how congruent they are with the course objectives described by your instructor. Come to a joint agreement about the goals for the class as a whole. These will become your *class objectives*.

Then look at your learning tasks. These become your *individual commitments* to the class. Finally, look at both positive and negative class/instructor activities. After discussing them, make an agreement that those positive behaviors will become the *rules or norms of behavior* in the class. the negative activities or behaviors will become behaviors to be avoided.

These combined lists become your *class contract*. Have someone from the class write them down. Each of you should commit to achieving your personal objectives, your class goals, learning tasks, and class norms and behaviors. Each person should type his or her own learning contract form:

I _____ agree to
       (Name)
work toward the following:

1. Individual Objectives:

2. Course objectives:

3. Learning Tasks:

4. Maintain the following positive behaviors:

5. Avoid the following negative behaviors:

The contracts should be signed and kept. Give a copy of your individual contract to your instructor. Midway through the course you can review the contract for progress and renegotiate it. At the end of the course, use the contract to reflect on the extent to which you and your classmates have met your objectives and goals, worked on learning tasks, and maintained your learning behaviors.

PART I

Solving Social Problems and Making Social Change

The original mission and vision of social work is the perfectibility of society: to deal with the enormous social problems under which our society staggers—the social isolation of the aged, the anomie experienced by youth, the neglect and abuse of children, hopelessness, drug addiction, and the problems of those who suffer from AIDS.

—HARRY SPECHT AND MARK COURTNEY,
UNFAITHFUL ANGELS[1]

Competent social work practice should always be based on solid theory. A good social theoretician looks for better ways of understanding, for reasons why things are as they are. Social work theory for the most part is derived from the social systems and/or social ecology models of society. This section describes the systems and social ecology models and how they are applied to social work. A different social work model, known as the action model of social work (on which this book is largely based), is also described. Finally, the way the action model relates to Part One is offered.

SYSTEMS THEORY

The systems model is based on a theory of society derived from the physical sciences. Society is composed of a series of systems and subsystems that work together like a gigantic machine. Every system has four components: (1) *inputs,* which provide energy, information, or resources; (2) a *processing mechanism,* in which the energy or information is used; (3) *outputs,* which are the result of systems processes; and (4) *feedback* from the outputs to the input, which helps the system adjust to its environment. All systems operate on principles such as inertia, feedback, entropy, and homeostasis. *Inertia* means that once a system is set in motion it tends to keep going in the same direction. *Entropy* means that every system is prone to eventually wear out or break down. *Homeostasis* "suggests that most living systems seek a balance to maintain and preserve the system."[2]

SOCIAL ECOLOGY THEORY

The social ecology model applies systems theory to living organisms. In addition to being subject to the laws of physics, biological systems experience growth, adaptation, and interaction with their environment.[3] Individuals, families, and groups are social systems that exist in a social environment.

SOCIAL WORK THEORY

The systems and social ecology concepts are very useful in social work. They "give us a method of conceptualizing a great deal of complexity."[4] Social ecology, for example, is a basis for the model known as the "person-in-the-social-environment." By understanding individual, family, and group life cycles and the ways social systems interact, one can develop interventions to improve social functioning. Systems theory is also the basis for the social pathology theory of social problems. This theory asserts that when a system or subsystem fails to adapt to changing conditions in its environment, it may become dysfunctional. Social workers, using systems concepts, attempt to heal the pathological system and restore it to full functioning.

The method of applying systems theory to solving social problems has been called the systems approach. Charles Zastrow asserts that there is an "increasing acceptance by social workers to use a systems analysis approach to social work practice."[5] This approach is also called rational problem solving. It forms the basis for what we now call the generalist social work method.

Social workers, according to Pincus and Minahan, engage four kinds of systems in making social change: a change agent system, a client system, a target system, and an action system. A change agent is a social worker who intentionally attempts to bring about social change.[6] The client system includes the people who are beneficiaries of the social service, who ask for help, and who engage the services of the change agent.[7] In collaboration with the client system, the change agent "establishes goals for change and determines the specific people—the targets—that will have to be changed if the goals are to be reached."[8] This client system may be individuals, communities, organizations, or society as a whole.

Social work change agents do not work alone in changing social systems. They must engage others in cooperative and collaborative efforts, which is where the action system[9] enters the picture. The systems approach is used in clinical social work practice.[10] It has been applied with success in family therapy as well.[11]

LIMITATIONS OF SOCIAL SYSTEMS AND SOCIAL ECOLOGY

Despite their importance and utility, the social systems and social ecology theories have limitations for social work. In both the systems and social ecology models, humans are seen as passive and determined beings who lack control over their own social processes. Gibson Winter, for example, asserted that when social scientists adopt a systems model of human association, people begin to be treated "like the subject matter of physical science. . . . Man ceases to be a subject and becomes an object of calculable forces external to him."[12] In the same way, when social science becomes subject to biological models, humans are seen as simply another category of living organism that operates by impersonal laws of social evolution. Systems that are successful survive; others are eliminated. Ultimately, the physical and biological science models place the most important dimensions of humanity, such as shaping community, ethics, and even reason beyond human capacity.[13]

People are viewed as passive objects whose futures are by and large determined by system processes that "shape our mentality, control our life chances, and define our humanity."[14] Social problems are defined as defects in systems function rather than in the particular values, goals, decisions, or culture of the people who comprise those social systems. While the systems approach to problem solving is efficient and can be effective, it tends to be value neutral and mechanistic. It may leave out or overlook nonquantifiable values and relationships that are often at the heart of social change.

ACTION MODEL OF MACRO SOCIAL WORK

There is another model of society that overcomes the limitations of the social systems and social ecology models. This model is called the *action model of macro social work* and is based on the work of symbolic interactionists. The roots of symbolic interactionist theory go back to Soren Kierkegaard and those existentialists who pondered questions about the meaning of existence and good and evil. They were highly skeptical of reliance on certain social processes that they viewed as being inherently destructive of the human condition. Among these was the adoption of a highly scientific, technological, and bureaucratic stance toward life. They believed that this stance ultimately results in a tendency toward alienation and dehumanization.[15]

In the United States, a group of social scientists, inspired by existentialism, became concerned about social science models derived from physical science or biological science instead of from human interaction. Sociologists such as Charles Horton Cooley, George Herbert Mead, and Alfred Schutz conceptualized a model of man as a meaning-creating creature. This model purports to accurately reflect people's active social nature. According to these theorists, people *consciously* construct social reality through symbols such as ritual and language, social attachments, and their day-to-day experiences. Because they viewed symbols and human engagement as necessary in forming the self and society, these sociologists came to be known as symbolic interactionists.

The action theory of social work is based on the work of symbolic interactionists and contains the following principles:

1. *Social:* At his or her roots, the person is "a social structure which arises out of social experience."[16] One becomes a "self" only in society[17] by interaction with "the people in one's environment."[18]

   > The self, which receives its meaning from the response of the other, is likewise a social structure created through the social process. I am who I am through the view of my self which is furnished by others. I have a self only as I am conscious of my self as an object.[19]

   > A model of humans as individualistic, isolated, and atomistic is essentially erroneous. A person is always a "social self."[20]

2. *Active:* Humans, as social beings who find selfhood in community and society, are active and creative agents in the construction of social reality.[21] People are not passive recipients of forces beyond their control that determine their fate. Humans consciously conceive and shape their own social milieu, infuse it with values, and derive meaning from it. Eric Voegelin, one of the seminal thinkers of our age, asserts:

   > Human society is not merely a fact or an event in the external world to be studied by an observer like natural phenomenon. Though it has externality as one of its important components, it is as a whole a little world. [It is] a cosmion, illuminated with meaning from within by the human beings *who continuously create and bear it as the mode and condition of their self-realization.*"[22] (Emphasis added)

3. *Interdependent:* The social self is interdependent with others. The social self exists in what Alfred Schutz called the "we-relation" in which "interdependence rather than dependence characterizes the self's relation to society."[23] This mutual engagement with many people is what Schutz and others mean by "intersubjectivity."

   > We depend on each other in the "We-relation" for the confirmation of our being-in-the-world. The possibility of actualization as self-in-the-world depends upon the intersubjective experience of self and other in the "We-relation."[24]

   The self becomes real only as a person interacts with others.

4. *Community:* Community is a valued, primary, and necessary social context by which people find meaning, relationships, and healing, and without which people could not exist. Community is *the* means by which healthy, active social beings are formed. The self becomes valid and actualized only in relation to others in the community.

> The self comes into being as [a] reflection of the attitudes, approvals, and meanings of the community. [In this way,] the "me"—my self as social or seen from the perspective of significant others and the community in general—comes to be.[25]

A reciprocal relationship occurs in the creation of the self and community. Just as the self finds its center and being in community, the many selves that constitute the community are continually in the process of informing and creating community.

5. *Diversity:* The heritage of each ethnic community is a cherished and needed component of humanity. The diversity of these traditions enriches and affirms everyone and helps expand human consciousness and values. Roles played by kinship patterns, social and leadership networks, religion, language, and the economic and political configurations within each ethnic community are formative elements of the human family, all of which add to the richness of life.[26]

6. *Rationality:* Not only does an individual receive his or her selfhood from engagement with others, but consciousness and human reason occur as the self discovers itself in and through its relationship with others. "Rationality . . . rests upon the arousal in the individual of the response which he is calling out in the other—a taking the role of the other, a tendency to act as the other person expects one to act."[27] Human reason is a social structure, resting on a variety of aspects of human consciousness.

7. *Wholistic:* Limiting reason to purely empirically based factual understanding of the world by means of calculative, instrumental rationality deprives macro social workers of the full use of all of their rational functions in solving social problems. According to Carl Jung, intuition, feeling/valuing, and sensing are important and necessary components of human reason in addition to thinking. Each of these problem-solving functions needs to be validated and used in macro social work. Heus and Pincus call this "whole-mind thinking."[28]

8. *Problem solving.* An action method of social change, therefore, will use conventional cognitively based rational problem solving, known as the generalist social work method. It will also include decision making using the other personality functions, along with community-centered engagement with others in the process of constructing society.

9. *Social problems.* Social problems are caused not only by impersonal social forces acting on people but also by the intentional actions of individuals and the values and presuppositions built into social systems.

10. *Value laden.* Social workers are not neutral about social systems or social processes. Action-oriented social workers assert their values in helping society move in a direction that they perceive is better for all people.

11. *Social critique.* Social workers must be engaged in social critique. Social critique is a cornerstone of action theory, in which a macro social worker asserts his or her values, challenges social decisions and policies that are unjust, and recommends alternatives that are better.

12. *Responsible.* Just as people are active in creating social systems, they are also responsible for changing them. The active social self is a responsible self.

> This means that people have a measure of autonomy in determining their actions, which are at the same time bound up by a social context . . . and focused on subjective meanings that people attach to their own actions and to the actions of others.[29]

A responsible self actively engages in making the community a healthy social milieu and works to bring about a just society. A responsible self seeks social involvement and exerts leadership in bringing about social change.

13. *Ethical.* The responsible self must also be an ethical self. In relationship to others, the ethical self works to transform inferior inclinations to a good embodied in the community and also informs and shapes that community according to a vision of a good society.[30]

PLAN OF PART I

In Chapter 2, social problems are explored from a conventional approach, including social systems perspectives. The chapter presents an action approach to understanding and diagnosing social problems. You are encouraged to use your own critical thinking skills to assess those models.

Chapter 3 explores rational problem solving, the generalist social work method, and an action model of social work based on an expanded view of human reason developed by Carl Jung.

A social worker is a leader who has a vision of community empowerment and helps people move toward that shared vision. Chapter 4 describes conventional leadership theory and an action model of leadership, and shows how this model can be used in helping communities grow.

ADDITIONAL READING

Churchman, C. West. *The Systems Approach.* New York: Dell Publishing Co., Inc., 1968.

Epstein, Laura. *Helping People: The Task Centered Approach,* 2nd edition, Columbus, OH: Merrill Publishing Co., 1988.

Martin, Patricia Yancey, and Gerald G. O'Connor. *The Social Environment: Open Systems Applications.* New York: Longman, 1989.

Schon, Donald A. *Beyond the Stable State.* New York: Norton, 1971.

Von Bertalanffy, L. *General Systems Theory: Foundations, Development and Application.* New York: George Braziller, Inc., 1968.

———. *Perspectives on General Systems Theory.* New York: George Braziller, Inc., 1975.

Von Gigch, J. P. *Applied General Systems Theory.* New York, Harper and Row, 1978.

CHAPTER 2

Social Problems: The Challenge of Being a Macro Social Worker

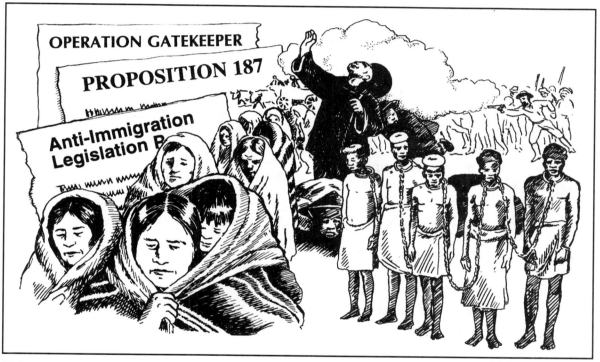

Enslavement, physical violence, relocation, and exclusion are but a few examples of ethnic intolerance in United States history.

Let us not forget, when we talk of violence, that the death of a young mother in childbirth is violent; that the slow starvation of the mind and body of a child is violent; let us not forget that hunger is violent, that pain is violent, that oppression is violent, that early death is violent; and that the death of hope is the most violent of all.

The organizer brings hope to the people.
—Si Kahn[1]

In the final analysis, however, we must realize that social injustice and unjust social structures exist only because individuals and groups of individuals deliberately maintain or tolerate them. It is these personal choices, operating through structures, that breed and propagate situations of poverty, oppression, and misery.
—Pope John Paul II, San Antonio Texas,
September 13, 1987

IDEAS IN THIS CHAPTER

Ethnic Intolerance: The History of a Social Problem

The first English settlement in America began in April 1607 with the landing of three ships in Chesapeake Bay. The men from these ships laid out the colony of Jamestown and claimed the territory as English soil. By 1619, the colony of Virginia comprised no more than two thousand people.[2] In that year, however, two events occurred that were to set a pattern for the emerging life in America throughout the next several centuries. On July 30, the first legislative assembly on the continent met, initiating representative government in America. In August, a Dutch ship arrived with African slaves, twenty of whom were sold to the settlers.[3]

These two contradictory impulses—freedom, independence, and democracy for some; slavery, exploitation, and even extermination for others—were to run like scarlet threads through the American experience. While beginning with Africans and Native Americans, exploitation and subsequent fear of immigrants and strangers waxed and waned with the particular insecurities and instabilities of the times. The foreigner and the stranger, especially but not exclusively nonwhites, were often victimized and blamed for conditions brought on by the greed and ambition of the majority population. Antiforeign sentiment began with the French, continued with the Irish in the East and the Germans in the Midwest, and spread to the Chicanos in the Far West. It was directed at Chinese and Japanese at the turn of the century, against the Germans during World War I, and culminated in the forced imprisonment of over 100,000 Japanese Americans during World War II. It was pervasive against African Americans throughout America.

Eastern Native Americans

Early settlers of America were guided by one overriding motive—self-interested pursuit of wealth. To that end they appropriated with impunity land that had been the domain of Native American inhabitants for the previous ten thousand years. These early frontiersmen presumed that the continent was not yet possessed by anybody at all. It was theirs for the taking "to exploit and despoil or to use to build a new society."[4] Native Americans were a mere impediment to the inevitable process of colonization and exploitation of the wilderness. The solution was extermination or removal of these undesirables.

As early as 1637, the Pequot War in New England ended in the complete destruction of the Pequot Tribe inhabiting the Connecticut Valley. The conflict between Virginia settlers and Powhatan's tribes resulted in the annihilation of the Native Americans in the northeastern United States.

In the fall of 1794, on the heels of American Independence, "Mad Anthony" Wayne defeated Tecumseh's followers at the Battle of Fallen Timbers on the Maumee River, not far from present day Ft. Wayne, Indiana. In the same year, in one of the most "bloodcurdling wars with the Creeks in the South, Andrew Jackson won a bloody victory."[5] Later, the Seminoles were slaughtered in the Florida swamps.

The Black Hawk Wars were particularly brutal affairs. Under threat of force to relinquish his claim to 50 million acres of prime forest in the Midwest, Black Hawk and his tribes, the Sauk and Fox Indians, withdrew from their traditional corn farming lands in Illinois to the west bank of the Mississippi. Suffering from hunger, they recrossed the river to join the friendly Winnebago in Wisconsin to grow their corn there. They were immediately attacked. Black Hawk retreated, making offers of peace, which were ignored by the two thousand militia. Driven mercilessly through southern Wisconsin to the Mississippi, Blackhawk and his followers were slaughtered as they tried to cross the river. "Although they were of the savage enemy," wrote one rifleman, "it was a horrid sight to witness little children, wounded, and suffering the most excruciating pain" as they were gunned down.[6]

Hungry for land, claiming unfettered rights to exercise their own interests, the white settlers

> constantly encroached on Indian lands in defiance of treaties, . . . destroyed the game on which the Indians depended for food and clothing; and many were ready to slay any redskin on sight. When the Indians tried to defend themselves, war ensued.[7]

An "Indian Country" was established beginning at the Mississippi and running from Canada to Texas. This area, part of the Great Plains and including the "bad lands" of the Dakotas, was thought to be worthless and uninhabitable by white men. The entire Native American population was to be removed, forcibly if necessary, with little consideration about how these people, who were forest hunters and farmers, would survive in the plains and hills of the West.

The "Five Civilized Tribes"—the Creeks, Choctaws, Chickasaws, Cherokees and Seminoles— offered stubborn resistance. They loved their homeland, and "many of them, especially the Creeks and Cherokees, had learned to be thrifty farmers, built good homes and towns, acquired herds of cattle, erected gristmills, and educated their children in missionary schools. They clung to their lands to the last."[8] Between 1838 and 1842, they were brutally rounded up by soldiers at gunpoint and herded on foot from Georgia and Florida across the Mississippi. About half of the Creek Nation died, and many members of the Cherokee Nation, particularly the children and women, failed to survive this removal along the "trail of tears." Captive Native Americans continued to be expendable. Tribes were removed again and again to even less desirable areas. Between 1829 and 1866, the Winnebago, for example, were forced to move six times.[9]

French, German, and Irish Americans

Native Americans were not the only group to experience hostility in early America. In 1798, a pathological xenophobia against French Americans resulted in the passage of the Alien, Sedition, and Naturalization Acts, giving the president a blank check to repress "dangerous aliens" by fines, deportation, or imprisonment, particularly recent immigrants who opposed him politically or criticized the government.

Xenophobia appeared in Eastern cities directed at the German and Irish Americans and increased in the 1840s and 1850s. During this time, restrictions on immigration were called for. Marked by the burning of an Irish convent in New England and "beer riots" against German Americans in Columbus, New York, and Louisville, this period was the most violent in terms of abuse of immigrants in our nation's history. One result was residence requirements of *twenty-one* years before citizenship could be obtained and severe restrictions against holding political office.

Mexican Americans

As early as 1503, the first Mexican settlers in America, many of whom were Catholic missionaries, had staked a claim to the land of the Southwest. They established the first towns and cities in this country, predating those on the East Coast. They developed a living culture, including farming and ranching, and for the most part a peaceful relationship with the Native American population. In 1848, when America acquired the Southwest, the Treaty of Guadalupe Hidalgo was signed guaranteeing citizenship, personal property rights, and religious freedom. Shortly after the Civil War, however, settlers from the East, hungry for California gold, rescinded the rights of Mexican Americans to vote.[10] Mexican Americans, who had called the Southwest their home for nearly three hundred fifty years, were treated as interlopers who had no rights or entitlements to the territory on which they had lived for generations.

African Americans

By 1765, slavery existed in law and fact in each of the thirteen colonies. Out of a population that numbered 1.85 million, 400,000 were African Americans, fully seven-eights of whom lived in the southernmost colonies. In South Carolina, African Americans outnumbered the white population by two to one.[11] Hardly considered human, slaves were the machinery that drove the economy of the south, and until the days of the Revolution, this was considered "natural."[12]

[Slavery] exalted a few whites, degraded many more, permitted sinfully wasteful agriculture, created a miasma of fear in areas where [African Americans] were plentiful, hardened class lines, stunted the growth of the Southern middle class, cheapened respect for labor, and dehumanized man's sympathy for man in an age already inhuman enough. . . .

As for the slave himself, the sin against him was so colossal as to give most Americans the chills even to this day. . . .[13]

By 1800, most northern states had ended slavery, but the antislavery movement was generally weak and "conciliatory to the master."[14] In 1831, however, agitation against slavery began to grow. William Lloyd Garrison, a young native of Newburyport, Massachusetts, published the first issue of the *Liberator,* a rabid antislavery newspaper. The very next year, the New-England Anti-Slavery Society was founded, and by 1833, delegates from several states founded the American Anti-Slavery Society, which was dedicated to immediate emancipation. In 1837, the abolitionists began to agitate for social legislation by circulating petitions directed at Congress.[15] Speakers were recruited to spread the message of abolition and inspired the "formation of town, country, and state antislavery groups. By 1838, the Anti-Slavery Society claimed a membership of 250,000 with over 1,300 auxiliaries."[16]

The success of the movement, however, inspired active and vengeful retaliation. In 1835, a mob in Charleston, South Carolina, broke into the post office and stole and burned antislavery publications. President Andrew Jackson applauded the riot along with southern and a few northern public officials.[17] In the same year, rioters in Boston led Garrison through the streets on a rope, and two years later, Elijah Lovejoy, an antislavery editor, was murdered while defending his press in Alton, Illinois.

From 1850 onward, events began to escalate. The Fugitive Slave Act required northerners to assist in capturing and returning ex-slaves. African Americans resisted and protested slavery by escaping from bondage, by day-to-day resistance, and by staging occasional insurrections.[18] Engaging in civil disobedience, African Americans and abolitionists alike fought slave-catchers. They rescued fugitives from courtrooms and jails, inspiring the single most effective piece of antislavery propaganda, *Uncle Tom's Cabin* by Harriet Beecher Stowe, published in 1852.

In 1857, in spite of the moral and human rights issues involved, the U.S. Supreme Court rendered the Dred Scott Decision, ruling that ownership of people was constitutional and that Congress had no authority to ban it from the territories. In October 1859, John Brown, an antislavery supporter from Kansas and a small band of African American and abolitionist followers attacked the federal arsenal at Harper's Ferry, Virginia.

A little over a year later, on December 20, 1860, South Carolina seceded from the Union over the issue of slavery, and the Civil War began, the bloodiest conflict this nation has ever experienced. By its end in 1865, almost 500,000 Americans had died in the struggle, and hundreds of thousands more were maimed for life.

Even though the Emancipation Proclamation ended slavery in the United States, state governments throughout the South instituted the infamous "Black Codes," the most repressive measures this country has ever seen, denying African Americans equal rights and equal justice in nearly every area of life. African Americans continued to be slaves in all but the strictest sense. In 1896, in *Plessy vs. Ferguson,* the Supreme Court concluded that the Fourteenth Amendment could be interpreted as maintaining "separate but equal" facilities, particularly schools. In one stroke, the Supreme Court insured that segregation was not only tacitly permitted but enforcable as the law of the land. Schools and other facilities for African Americans were separate, and they would also become unequal. Discrimination became the official policy in the United States.

Effectively excluded from the mainstream of American culture and opportunity, African Americans, for all intents and purposes, remained socially, economically, and politically enslaved. Even the Constitution was used against them. The institution of racism would exist in fact and as the policy of our country for the next fifty-eight years.

Native Americans

By 1851, the policy of maintaining "one big reservation" for the Native Americans in the desert badlands and the Great Plains had ended. White settlers, hungry for more and more land, came into increasing conflict with the Indians. Native Americans were pushed onto ever-shrinking sites, across which the government was permitted to build roads and railroads.

The Great Plains, which had been the traditional home of the Plains Indians, was carved up into ranches. The buffalo were slaughtered, in part to make way for cattle and sheep but primarily to de-stroy the food supply of the Native Americans, forcing them to give up their freedom and succumb to a life of dependency on government aid. The prairie sod was plowed so that wheat and corn could be planted. The ecology of the great American plains, which had existed as a self-sustaining system for tens of thousands of years, supporting animals, plants, as well as humans, was completely destroyed in a period of about four decades.

Following the Civil War, the U.S. Cavalry turned its attention to exterminating the remaining Native Americans of the western plains or rounding them up and forcing them onto reservations. Desperate to maintain their freedom, Native Americans engaged the cavalry in hundreds of battles between 1865 and 1880. On June 25, 1876, for example, General George Custer made his "last stand" against Crazy Horse and Sitting Bull at the Battle of the Little Big Horn. However, Native American victories were rare. The last of the free Native Americans, led by Geronimo, a Chiraquahua Apache, finally surrendered in 1886.

Chinese Americans

Actively recruited by many large American companies, particularly the railroads, Chinese males were imported in large numbers in the 1840s to perform the most grueling and dangerous labor imaginable, labor that even Irish Americans refused. They worked hard for pitiful wages, often losing their lives or becoming maimed for life blasting tunnels and carving roadbeds from the sides of California's Sierra Nevada mountains. When the economy soared during the gold rush of 1848–1850 in California, Chinese were sought to provide a variety of menial tasks in mining and logging camps—such as cooking and laundering. By 1860, over fifty thousand Chinese, mostly men, were living in California.[19]

When prosperity began to wane after the Civil War, and the need for gold, mercury, lumber, and other goods lessened, "the Chinese were cavalierly blamed for job shortages."[20] In the election of 1867, anti-Chinese sentiment emerged as a major California campaign issue. The Chinese were treated with suspicion, distrust, and even hatred by those who had previously benefitted from their labor. Angry men formed Anti-Chinese Coolie Associations and actively protested the Burlingame Treaty of 1868, which allowed Chinese immigration.[21] What made these protests so irrational was that neither the railroads nor San Francisco's mining industries would have been developed as quickly as they were without the labor of Chinese Americans, since they performed tasks that others were unwilling to do.[22]

By the 1870s, violence directed at Chinese Americans was intensified by an economic depression. A frenzied Los Angeles mob shot and killed twenty Chinese Americans in one incident alone on October 24, 1871.[23] While a grand jury indicted one hundred fifty men, only six stood trial. By 1880, seventy-five thousand Chinese Americans were living in California, over half of whom were concentrated in San Francisco. The San Francisco Board of Supervisors, in response to demands of Anti-Coolie Associations, *taxed* Chinese immigrants for the privilege of performing backbreaking and dangerous work in California's mines. They were denied citizenship and suffrage, and they were restricted in their use of courts and schools.[24] Governor William Irwin, a keynote speaker at one anti-Chinese rally, claimed that the Chinese were the enemy of American civilization.[25]

Anti-Chinese agitation became so powerful that in 1882 the federal government persuaded China to surrender her most-favored-nation status and to agree to the exclusion of her nationals from the United States. Congress enacted the Chinese Exclusion Act preventing Chinese immigration and effectively isolating and disenfranchising those Chinese people who had chosen to live in America.

In 1890, the California legislature was authorized to protect the state from "dangerous and detrimental aliens," a euphemism for Chinese Americans. Chinese Americans were not to be employed on public works or by corporations. The legislature discouraged immigration and delegated power to cities and towns to remove Chinese Americans or locate them "within prescribed areas,"[26] reminiscent of treatment of Native Americans. The result was the establishment of "Chinatowns" throughout California.

This forced segregation required Chinese Americans to fall back on their own resources for mutual support and self-protection. They formed their own cultural and social groups, carrying with them their own traditions, language, and religion. In 1892, the Chinese Exclusion Act was renewed, and in 1902 it became permanent.[27]

Japanese Americans

The ink was barely dry on the Chinese Exclusion Act, cutting off this source of cheap labor, when large agribusinesses were soon looking for another labor source. Like the Chinese, Japanese males were actively recruited by large companies to work on the sugar and pineapple plantations in Hawaii and in the fields of California. Lured by promises of good wages and working conditions, about two hundred thousand Japanese came to the United States as laborers between 1890 and 1924.

Little thought was given to the social climate into which these Asians were being imported or the impact that immigration would have on them. Unlike the experience of the Chinese, for whom females were not part of the labor force, migration of young Japanese women was encouraged. As a result, the industrious and hard working Japanese began to raise families and save money. Many Japanese quietly began to cultivate areas of the Sacramento–San Joaquin Valley, becoming prosperous farmers.

Anti-Japanese sentiment, however, began to show up almost immediately. By 1911, a variety of proposals to exclude Japanese immigrants had been introduced to Congress by Californians. In 1912, a wave of hysteria was touched off by the news that a group of Japanese-American immigrants was about to buy land in Baja, California. Other newspapers carried headlines such as "Jap Puts on Airs" and "Yellow Peril in College Town" when Japanese Americans, after careful saving, had the temerity to purchase homes or attempt to buy land on which to farm.[28] Fully thirty-four bills curbing Japanese rights were introduced into the 1913 California state legislature, resulting in the Alien Land Act. Not only were "aliens ineligible for citizenship," but it became illegal for them to purchase land in California. Land could be leased for only three years, and land already owned or leased could not be willed to other persons, preventing parents from passing farms to their own children, a law which remained in effect until 1952.

The hysteria that occurred against the Japanese in the years before World War I was renewed with a vengeance after the bombing of Pearl Harbor on December 7, 1941. Executive order 3906 gave permission for the mass removal of nearly the entire Japanese-American population to "relocation camps," a euphemism for concentration camps, on the pretext that the Japanese Americans, many of whom had become established as farmers in California's Central Valley, were sympathetic to Japan and were potential or even actual spies.

Not only was there no evidence that any Japanese Americans committed an act of treason against the United States during the war, but Japanese-Americans went to extreme lengths to demonstrate loyalty. Hundreds of young men volunteered as translators and interpreters in the Pacific, helping to intercept Japanese messages. The famed 442 Regiment of the 100th Battalion became the most decorated regiment in the war. While their parents were imprisoned in concentration camps, these *nisei* (second generation Japanese Americans) suffered more casualties than any other battalion, accomplishing feats of bravery that were unmatched by any other American combat group.

Introduction

> Social problems . . . take a toll and a dreadful one. People's lives are diminished or destroyed. Society is disrupted by the behavior of those who no longer care, or are so damaged that they cannot function in acceptable ways. Our society continues to suffer from serious problems, some of them long standing and others more recent.—Ronald C. Frederico[29]

All social workers should be involved in solving social problems such as racism, sexism, economic injustice, urban decay, and dysfunctional political systems. H. Wayne Johnson has commented that "social work may be thought of as a profession concerned with social problems, their remedy and control."[30] We must have the ability to understand and diagnose social problems and take a stance. This chapter is intended to help you define social problems and understand their complexity.

Defining Social Problems in America

It is important that you, as a macro social worker, have a working definition of "social problems." C. Wright Mills, in *The Sociological Imagination,* commented that

> perhaps the most fruitful distinction with which the sociological imagination works is between "the personal troubles of milieu" and the "public issues of social structure." This distinction is an essential tool of the sociological imagination and a feature of all classic work in social science.[31]

The distinction between personal problems and social problems is important. Exercise your own "sociological imagination" and develop your own definition using your critical thinking skills. Develop your own ideas about what distinguishes social problems from personal problems that people have by reflecting on the short history of ethnic intolerance described earlier—injustices perpetrated against the Native Americans, the French, the Germans, the Irish, the Africans, the Chicanos, the Chinese, and the Japanese. Was ethnic intolerance caused by decisions that these groups made or by their behavior? Who was to blame for the ethnic intolerance to which these groups were subjected?

Sometimes people profit by the misery of others. Was ethnic intolerance caused by agribusinessmen, miners, ranchers, corporate leaders, or politicians who often gained from the labor of certain ethnic groups? Were ordinary citizens who benefitted by the low cost goods or services produced by certain ethnic groups the cause of intolerance?

Purely personal problems usually affect a limited number of people. Was the problem of ethnic intolerance limited to those against whom intolerance was directed, or did it spread beyond them? If it spread, how did it spread, and who were the people affected by it?

In the past, for many people in America, issues of ethnic intolerance were not problems at all. If anything, they were necessary conditions without which the development of America could not have oc-

Social problems often have long-term serious consequences. In July 1935, near Ft. Lauderdale, Florida, mob fury cost the life of Rubin Stacy. More than a hundred masked men seized him from sheriffs deputies and hanged him.

curred. The Alien and Sedition Acts directed against the French, for example, were seen as necessary to prevent treason. Slavery was claimed to be a necessary and important economic institution in the South without which the development and prosperity of the South would not have occurred. The extermination and forced confinement of Native Americans on reservations was viewed as a necessary precondition for the settlement of the West. The subsequent importing of Chinese and Irish to build railroads was seen as necessary for expansion and development. The imprisonment of Japanese Americans during World War II was deemed essential for winning the war with Japan. In these and other instances of ethnic intolerance, who decided that the oppression of a group of people was necessary for the nation's development and preservation?

Personal problems can often be solved by counseling or some form of specific treatment aimed at the particular person affected. For example, if a person has trouble managing money and is constantly in debt, a curative measure would involve counseling and training in money management skills. Can social problems be resolved by aiming treatment at the particular people who are the focus of the problem? For example, can the problem of ethnic intolerance be solved by applying some method of treatment to the ethnic group? In the case of social problems, to whom do socially curative measures need to be directed?

Interventions applied to personal problems are usually limited in scope to one or two procedures aimed directly at the locus of the problem. For example, if a person is addicted to tobacco, treatment may simply consist of helping "break the habit" by drugs, hypnotism, will-power, or avoidance. Are there one or two curative procedures that one can apply to resolve a social problem? How many mechanisms may be required to bring about resolution to social problems? How many strategies, for example, have been employed in responding to the problem of ethnic intolerance?

Personal problems may often be resolved fairly quickly, as briefly as two or three hour-long counseling sessions or at most up to a year or two of individual or family psychotherapy. Can social problems be solved in a relatively short time span? How long has it taken to resolve the problem of ethnic intolerance in the United States? Has it been resolved today?

Finally, resolving a personal or family problem is relatively inexpensive, or at least the costs are usually borne by the family members themselves. Figuring out the costs of social problems and who pays for them, however, is another matter entirely. Try to estimate the cost of ethnic intolerance. In your answer consider, for example, the social costs that slavery created in the lives of both African Americans and slaveholders. Add to this the financial costs of the Civil War. Then calculate the costs of the war in terms of lives lost, families destroyed, and ill will generated. After this, add up costs engendered by the destruction of the culture and forced relocation of Native Americans and the forced internment of Japanese Americans. Once you have done this, include in your sums the costs of broken families, human potential wasted, oppression, and the poverty that racism has perpetuated among Chicanos and other Latin Americans, Chinese Americans, Puerto Ricans, Filipino Americans, Korean Americans, and Southeast-Asian Americans, among others. Would you consider these costs expensive or inexpensive? Who bears the costs of ethnic intolerance? Is it born by the victims only, or does everyone pay the price?

EXERCISES

EXERCISE 5:
Defining Social Problems

Write out your own definition of a social problem. Reflect on who is affected by social problems, who decides what social problems are important, how long it takes to resolve them, what kinds of strategies should be employed, and the social costs they bring. After you come up with your definition, you will have a chance to compare it with a conventional definition.

Conventional Definitions of Social Problems

Sullivan and Thompson state that a "social problem exists when an influential group defines a social condition as threatening its values, the condition affects a large number of people, and it can be remedied by collective action,"[32] a definition echoed by Charles Zastrow.[33] Robert K. Merton and Robert Nisbet, two highly influential sociologists, have defined social problems as "the substantial, unwanted discrepancies between what is in a society and what a functionally significant collectivity within that society seriously . . . desires to be in it."[34] Social problems have the following components:

1. The problem must have *social* causation rather than be an issue of individual behavior.
2. It must *affect* a large number of people.
3. It must be judged by an *influential* number of people to be undesirable.
4. It must be *collectively* solvable by the community rather than by individual action.

A mark of a good macro social worker is to be responsibly critical of existing knowledge. This means using your own ideas and insights to challenge things that may not seem right. How did your own definition compare with the ones developed by other theorists and thinkers? How did those of your classmates compare with yours? Can you come up with a composite definition that is even better for macro social work practice than one that is conventionally accepted? Later in this chapter I will give my own definition of social problems. Compare your definition with this one as well.

Assumptions about Social Problems

In addition to a definition of social problems, macro social workers need to have an overall perspective of the social order and the status of social problems generally. There are three ways to view the origin of social problems in society. Some see social problems as issues of personal moral deviance. Others see them as correctable social defects that are products of social growth. Another group sees them as inherent defects in the social order.

Moral Deviance Model

Perhaps the most prevalent way of thinking about social problems begins with the idea that the cause of social problems lies not in society or its structures but in the character of individuals who refuse to conform to social rules. These are socially deviant individuals who interfere with the normal workings of society and restrict its progress.[35] Social problems are seen as caused by entire classes of people who are inherently unwilling or unable to contribute to the welfare of society as a whole. The moral deviance paradigm places the source of these problems in defects in individual character and will.[36]

According to this model, poverty is caused by persons who are lazy, undisciplined, and lack motivation. The poor are seen as individuals who tend to be selfish, immature, and irresponsible. They are viewed as less intelligent or as possessing few skills. Many times their parents were poor. They are assumed to prefer to remain dependent on society's help.

Social Pathology Model

Another view, proposed by a group of sociologists called "structural/functionalists," assumes that while society is generally good and healthy, it sometimes develops defects, which, like illnesses, can make the social body sick. These theorists view the social system as composed of structures and functions, each of which needs to be congruent with the other. Problems occur in one part or another in the total system as society adjusts to growth and to changing conditions in its environment. When this happens it is the role of people such as business leaders or politicians to realign those structures and functions.[37]

According to Robert Merton, there are two different kinds of social problems.[38] One is manifest problems, and the other is latent social problems. Manifest problems are those that are clearly apparent when things in society get out of order. Often, the feedback loops break down or the automatically self-regulating devices cannot respond quickly enough to change. One of the causes of the Great Depression, for example, was the belief that government ought not play a role in regulating the economy. When the economy went into a tailspin, government had few tools at its disposal to diagnose and prevent market failure. Since then, the government has changed its philosophy and regularly institutes many ways to adjust for inflation and recession.

Structural functionalists assume that particular groups have the function of defining officially what social problems will be recognized and how those problems will be addressed. For example, in an informal sense, social problems are often defined by those who are in positions of influence to shape our opinions: writers, newscasters, religious leaders, journalists, politicians, even actors, musicians, or sports figures. Those who are publicly charged with defining social problems in a practical sense are policymakers and legislators. Ultimately, manifest social problems are those that politicians place on their agendas. Legislators often react to problems that are most pressing or those concerning a majority of their constituents.

Sometimes, however, things go wrong, because we simply do not understand the consequences of our decisions.[39] These latent social problems occur because we lack information or because we cannot predict all of the possible outcomes of a decision. Sometimes the rapidity of social change or progress outstrips the ability of society to adjust and does not allow us time to forecast all of the possible outcomes of decisions. This occurs today with the rapid changes that technology imposes on our system. Alvin Toffler described this phenomenon as "future shock."[40] For example, the demands that people "keep up" with change often mean that today both partners in a marriage must work. This puts pressure on families, often contributing to divorce and family breakdown. As society progresses, it simultaneously creates the conditions for breakdown, the "unintended consequences" of social decisions.

Technological advances have created unintended consequences or latent dysfunctions. For example, because of improvements in technology, people's job skills become outmoded. This puts pressure on society to continually provide the means for people to upgrade their abilities and adjust to changing job markets. If this does not happen, pools of unemployed and unemployable people will become a drain on the economy.

Medical science is increasingly able to decrease infant mortality. We are now able to save many more premature infants, but at the same time these infants are more subject to birth defects and genetic disorders. Our medical ability to save lives is now contributing to an increase in children with birth defects and handicapping conditions.

Social problems, then, are "growing pains" of society or malfunctions that occur as the stresses in adapting to new and changing social situations are encountered. Social problems are to some extent inevitable, but they are also correctable. In fact, the presence of social problems may be a healthy sign that society is changing and developing. They are warning signs that tell us where we need to focus our efforts in decision making and problem solving.

Society as Inherently Defective

The final view claims that society can be best understood as a consciously planned construct of people's minds. We intentionally create social situations out of our common understandings about meaning and truth and our own social laws and the systems by which those laws operate. We are not helpless or determined beings molded by natural societal forces to which we are subject or over which we have little control. Rather, as the social pragmatists argue, "although [a person's] situation confronts him with limitations and problems, he is the one who struggles to understand his situation, to master it, and to utilize it for the realization of his interests."[41]

Society therefore reflects the key ideologies and ways of thinking that were built into it in the first place—the outcomes of which become exactly what were intended.[42] The origin of these ideologies can be easily seen in the writings of social and political philosophers such as Thomas Hobbes, John Locke, Adam Smith, and James Madison,[43] who propounded its various notions that were legitimized in our Constitution.[44] Among these notions are self-interest and individualism. "They frankly proclaimed" for example, "that a society was wanted in which everyone would be committed to the rational pursuit of self-interest,"[45] resulting in radical, possessive individualism,[46] and an ideology that abstains "from

imposing an ideal pattern of life"[47] onto political life. In this self-interested, individualistic society "an explicit concern for the community as such could be dispensed with."[48]

> The era of individualism . . . coincides with the era when urban people have little sense of a common value or goal. It is no accident that the age of self-interest rather than duty, of narrow and personal goals, is also an age when community is so rare.[49]

Social problems, according to this model, are not the result of moral deviance or of social sicknesses that can be healed, but are the result of foundational social principles or premises that are wrong. Our ways of thinking are defective, our values and ethics are misplaced, and our perception of time and history is misguided. Frank M. Coleman says:

> The social failures of American political institutions are not like an oversight, corrected after a second look, but are a permanent blindness fixed in the nature of the institutions and the social philosophy used to design them.[50]

As a result, "propensities toward violence, unattended social problems, and a tendency toward petty corruption" are "manifested in characteristic and unvarying ways related to the American constitutional philosophy."[51] In practice, therefore, overcoming our social problems becomes enormously difficult to resolve, because they are *built into the very fabric of our social order.* Furthermore, our social, political, and economic systems become self-sustaining and self-reinforcing, resisting solutions that could mitigate the problems they are creating. Henry Kariel says that "as the force of their revolutionary thrust has been exhausted," the liberal political philosophers and the founding fathers

> left a legacy of ideas which today block the emergence of alternative social policies. *An ideology originally designed to vindicate private interests now serves to legitimate the maintenance of the established equilibrium of interests.*[52]

Upsetting this equilibrium of radical individualism, self-interested pursuit of profit, and the dehumanization that our technological organizational society supports will not be easy. It will require a new consensus about the importance of human life and social justice. It will also entail painful and controversial decisions to redistribute resources and opportunities from those who are most privileged in our society to those who are at its fringes . . . a change we have yet to make. Eliminating poverty and increasing social justice will require very different choices than those we have made in the past.[53]

The elimination of many of our social problems requires, according to this view, that we change our values, adapt our ways of thinking, shift our ideologies, modify many of our structures, and even give up some of our wealth to others who have less.

Violence in America

There are two kinds of violence in America. On the one hand, there is violence that is overt and acted out in crime and destruction. The second kind of violence is more subtle and less overt. It is the kind of violence that results in poverty and oppression. America is among the most violent nations in the world by almost any standard. Former U.S. Surgeon General C. Everett Koop determined "violence in America to be a public health emergency."[54]

Murder

In the United States, 8.4 murders are committed for every 100,000 people, the highest murder rate in

EXERCISES

EXERCISE 6: Assessing Social Assumptions

The assumptions you make about social problems will determine the kind of stance you take in trying to correct them. What is your assessment about social assumptions that underlay social problems in American society?

1. Are social problems caused by the "deviant behavior" of individuals who operate by values other than those that are traditionally accepted in our society?
2. Are social problems the inevitable result of a nation in the process of making adjustments in an otherwise sound social system?
3. Are social problems a permanent blindness built into the fabric of our social order, as Coleman asserts, that will require a redefinition of the premises of our social order to solve?

See how closely your own assessment coincides with the description in the text of violence in America today.

EXERCISE 7: A Contingency Approach to Social Problems

After reading the section on violence in America, in EXERCISE 6, it may have occurred to you that social problems exist in a continuum and operate in different ways under different circumstances. Some social problems are the result of the collective behavior of people who react to the social situations in which they find themselves; others may be the result of societal growing pains; and some are inherent in our social order. Some social problems may be and often are a combination of all three assumptions simultaneously reinforcing one another.

A contingency approach to solving social problems means that the social solution is adjusted to fit the

particular complexities of the social problem that you are trying to solve.

One way of understanding the complexity of social problems is to examine one social problem that occurs at each of these three levels. Then figure out what systematic processes exist in society to routinely recognize, assess, treat, and pay for the resolution of each of those social problems. Try this out in class with the help of your instructor.

EXERCISE 8: Critiquing Models of Social Problems

One of the skills of a macro social worker is to critique models in order to decide which model or which aspect of various models is correct. Take some time and critique either the moral deviance or the social pathology model. With what parts do you agree? With what parts do you not agree? Share your critique with others in class and with that of your instructor. Then, add your critique to the ones that follow.

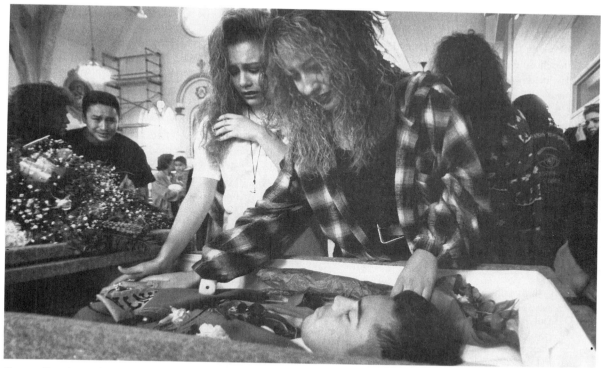

Everett Koop's assertion that "violence in America is a public health problem" becomes a reality as gang members grieve at the funeral of a fellow gang member.

the world—80 percent more than Canada, which has a rate of 5.45 murders per 100,000 people. In 1991, 24,020 people were murdered in the United States, the highest number ever recorded up to that point.

Violence to Women

Women are particular targets of violence. The United States has the distinction of being the world leader in rapes: 37.2 women are raped per 100,000 citizens in America, more than double the number in Sweden, which reports 15.70, over three times as many as Denmark, which counts 11.25, and four times the next highest country, Germany, which reports 8.60 rapes per 100,000 people.[55]

When attempted rapes are added, the figures go much higher. The U.S. Justice Department reports that in 1990 there were 60 rapes and attempted rapes per 100,000 people in the United States, and in 1991, the number climbed to 100 women assaulted per

100,000 people, an estimated 207,610 rapes, up 59 percent from 1990.[56]

"Domestic violence," according to an August 1990 article in the *Journal of the American Medical Association* (JAMA), "has become a nation wide problem. . . . It is the most common cause of injury to women." Studies in the JAMA report show that 34 percent of all female homicide victims sixteen years or older died at the hands of a partner. Battering by a partner outranks automobile accidents, muggings, and rapes combined.[57]

Handguns

One indication of violence in America is our addiction to handguns. According to Wolff, "the 200 million privately owned firearms in the U.S. could arm almost every man, woman, and child in the country. Of those weapons, nearly 70 million are handguns."[58] American citizens are the most heavily armed people in the world. In the United States, 29 percent of households own handguns, double that of Switzerland, in which only 14 percent own guns, and four times as many as Germany and Finland, 7 percent of whose citizens own guns.[59]

Every day, on average, a child under fourteen is shot dead, 25 adults are murdered, 33 women are raped, 5,765 people are robbed, and 1,116 threatened.[60]

In comparison with other countries, the number of violent deaths by handguns in the United States is astronomical. In 1988, 8,915 persons in America were killed with handguns, compared to only 53 persons in Switzerland, 19 in Sweden, 8 in Canada, and 7 in the United Kingdom.[61]

WHEN TAPS SOUND AGAIN
Saul Pett

Since its birth, little more than 200 years ago, the United States has fought 11 wars, less than one every generation. In all, from Concord to Kuwait, 38,290,000 Americans have gone to war and 1,153,541 have not come back. Their graves stretch across the country and around the world. More than 100,000 other Americans are still missing in action, lost at sea, vanished in distant jungle, desert sand, or alien mountain top.

But what is most astounding is that we have killed more of our own than have been killed by any single foreign foe. In the Civil War almost one half million Americans lost their lives, more than any other war before or since, surpassing even World War II, in which 406,000 died, and more than all other wars combined up until that time.

116,000 Americans died in WWI, 58,000 in Vietnam, 54,000 in Korea, 13,000 in the Mexican War and 4,000 in the Revolutionary War. In the Spanish-American War, 2,400 died, 2,000 in the War of 1812, 1,000 in the Indian Wars, and 141 in the Persian Gulf.

1,153,541 lives ended too soon, most before they could become husbands or fathers, teachers or doctors, builders or engineers. Were there composers among them whose music we never will hear? Thinkers whose ideas we shall never know? Was there one among them who might have found a cure for cancer?

The answers are beyond us now. We are only left with the cemeteries, lots of cemeteries: 129 of them in 39 states and 24 others in 12 foreign countries.

Source: Saul Pett, When Taps Sound Again, *The Fresno Bee,* May 31, 1991. Reprinted with permission of Associated Press.

Violence to Children

Gunfire is the second-most-frequent cause of death for teens aged fifteen to nineteen, outdone only by traffic accidents. Among African American teens, gunfire is the leading killer.[62]

In 1990, according to the Children's Defense Fund in Washington, DC, over thirty-six hundred California children died and nine thousand more were wounded by guns. A report prepared by the Center for the Study of Social Policy found that between 1988 and 1989 the teen death rate rose 11 percent, driven almost entirely by a rise in suicides and homicides.[63]

In addition to overt violence, covert violence in the form of poverty and lack of services also affects children. African-American babies are twice as likely as white babies to die in their first year of life. In 1991, while about 18 percent of all white children in the United States did not have any form of public or private health insurance, nearly 25 percent of African-American children and almost 35 percent of Hispanic children were not covered. At the beginning of the 1990s, over 20 percent of the nation's youth were living in poverty, a 22 percent increase from the 1980s.[64]

The figures are even worse in California, the most affluent state in the nation, a state which, if it were an independent nation, would rank sixth or seventh richest in the world. According to a 1990 study conducted by the Children Now organization, California ranked worst in its treatment of children compared to other states. Nearly twenty-one hundred children killed themselves in California alone. Nearly ten thousand youngsters died from malnutrition and other effects of poverty. More than sixty-five thousand were victims of abuse and neglect. Over a million saw their parents divorce. Close to eighty thousand children were arrested for drug abuse or possession and another one hundred sixty thousand were arrested for drinking or drunk driving.[65]

Think about these various kinds of violence. Are they the result of moral deviance, social pathology, or inherent social defects? Based on your assessment, develop three solutions to the problem of violence in America. After you have developed these solutions discuss them in class.

Critique of Deviance Theory

Deviance theory divides the world into those who are socially appropriate and those who are assumed to be inherently bad or dysfunctional. The Charity Organization Society movement is a good example of the deviance theory applied to problems of poverty.[66] This group saw poverty primarily as a personal problem of deviant individuals, not as one that emanated from society as a whole. The COS movement was motivated by a desire to "reform" or assist individuals who were unable or unwilling to provide for themselves. Assistance most often took the form of moral education, advice, and instruction in character building as well as job referrals and in some cases minimal financial assistance.

The motivation of the COS movement was to correct the personal defects of a few so as to create a better and more perfect society, or as the Reverend Steven Humphreys Gurteen, founder of the COS movement, said, "All avoidable pauperism would soon be a thing of the past, and an age of good will soon be ushered in, when the poor would regard the rich as their natural friends, and not, as now, fair objects of their deceit and position."[67]

Today, proponents of the deviance paradigm claim that by *not* blaming the perpetrator or holding each deviant personally accountable for his or her actions we are doing a disservice to the deviant individual and to society as a whole. Individuals will tend to evade personal responsibility for their actions. Rather than providing them with a convenient excuse, deviant individuals need to be singled out and required to conform to socially acceptable behavior.

In this way, society, which was seen as basically good, would be assisted in its progressive evolution toward perfection here on earth both for the good of the deviants themselves as well as for society as a whole.

Even with its good intentions, deviancy theory tends to *misallocate* the locus of social problems. By locating the root of social problems in individuals, it denies that people's troubles are primarily or at least to a large extent the result of social conditions that need remediation. Because deviance theory refuses to recognize that social problems are often the result of such things as public social policies or private

business enterprise, the deviance paradigm actually may contribute to and entrench the very problems described.

Deviance theory tends to be moralistic and judgmental. Critics of the deviance paradigm conclude that society itself sometimes victimizes the so-called deviant and fails to allow or at least makes it difficult for that person to have opportunity to enter the mainstream. We tend to "blame the victim"[68] for problems beyond his or her control and punish that person for being deviant. The idea, for example, of placing groups of children in special classes because they are "culturally disadvantaged" is simply a way of holding children to blame for the fact that the school system has failed them.

The deviance paradigm maintains the social status quo. Deviancy is based on the validity of current social norms or values. Society has an obligation to "cure" those individuals or otherwise treat, socialize, induce, or shape them so that they conform to those social norms. Those who define deviancy and what is socially acceptable, therefore, have power to exact conformity to the norms they consider desirable. The novel *One Flew Over the Cuckoo's Nest* by Ken Kesey, in which "Big Nurse" finally treated the irascible McMurphy by destroying his mind, is a good example of this approach.

In other cases, those in power have used the deviancy paradigm to suppress individual freedom. The "Red scare" of McCarthyism during the early 1950s is an example of singling out as social deviants people who were alleged to be "Communists" and "black listing" them. Jailing people because of political or even religious beliefs is another example.

Deviancy theory is expensive. Modern deviance theorists focus on problems one at a time. Treating each individual who becomes deviant is extremely costly. It has been claimed that it is often more costly to incarcerate a person for four years than to send that individual to one of the best universities. Because it is expensive, there is understandable reluctance to spend public money on treatment. But because deviance is the prevailing paradigm, social-policy makers are captured in an untenable position. They cannot avoid the social costs of crime, drug abuse, poverty, and other social ills. But at the same time, they want to keep taxes low. Therefore, even though they are committed to dealing individually with "deviants," they are loath to spend any more money than the minimum. Welfare recipients get by on subsistence allowances and receive no real treatment or help in getting off welfare. Criminals are housed in correctional facilities but receive little rehabilitation. Because deviance theory is unable to conceive of alternative solutions, welfare roles do not decrease and jails remain full.

Deviancy does not officially exist until a person has become deviant or has done something deviant. Even though some individuals may be identified at an early age as being potential criminals, there is little one can do until they actually become criminals, and by then it is too late.

Deviance theory leads to failures in social policy. For example, proponents of the deviance paradigm might oppose gun control on the basis of the slogan "Guns don't kill, people do." In other words, violence attributed to the use of guns in our society should not be resolved by any social policy dealing with the availability of guns themselves. Instead, violence attributed to the use of guns is a personal problem of those few deviant persons who misuse guns. Rather than limit or ban the use of handguns, society should apprehend and punish deviant individuals and allow law-abiding citizens the right to protect themselves.

People who are social deviates tend to be labeled, for example, as an "ex-convict," as "retarded," or as "delinquent." Critics of the deviance paradigm claim that labeling tends to strengthen deviance rather than reduce it. When so-called deviant individuals are labeled, they may be stigmatized, and the deviant behavior may be reinforced. For the rest of his or her life, for example, a person who has been convicted of a crime will have to label him- or herself as an ex-criminal on job applications, making it more difficult to obtain a job, find acceptance in society, and become self-supporting. This not only continues to stigmatize an individual, but also blocks his or her rehabilitation and access to opportunities. Sometimes the label becomes self-fulfilling.[69] The ex-offender, finding it impossible to escape his or her label, returns to a life of crime.

The deviance paradigm tends to be self-defeating. Treating, jailing, or rehabilitating individuals after they have become affected and damaged by social conditions is ruinous to society. Instead, it is more rational to correct the social conditions that cause problems rather than try to change individuals after the fact. In other words, the ultimate antidote to the social deviancy paradigm is prevention, but according to deviance theory, we are incapable of preventing deviancy in general, and it is impossible to identify everyone who may become deviant.

Critique of Social Pathology Theory

Conceiving of social problems as located in the structures of society "permits going beyond explaining these problems exclusively in psychological terms."[70] Many social problems are seen as the result of unintended consequences of progress.

Sociologists who are functionalists pride themselves on looking at social systems "objectively." They want to see the system the way it really is. But such allegiance to objectivity may also lead to a value-neutrality and moral blindness. They may be blind to the fact that social systems and their designers are not ignorant of the consequences of the systems at their command.[71] For example, in Nazi Germany, the prevailing social values were Aryan supremacy, the restoration of Germanic "homelands," the subjugation of Europe, and the total annihilation of Jews, Gypsies, homosexuals, and other so-called deviants. Those who opposed such values became "problems" to be dealt with.

While the Nazis may be an extreme case, there are many other modern examples. The totalitarian regime of Argentina, the racist nation of South Africa, the abysmal conditions of Haiti under "Papa Doc" Trujillo, and Uganda under Idi Amin are only a few examples. Any society that values racism, totalitarianism, sexism, militarism, and imperialism would view equality, democracy, peace, and nonaggression as social problems. Structural functionalists who accept the social values of decision makers and the institutions they create as pre-given and therefore not open to challenge may tend to allow moral blindness to infiltrate their thinking.[72]

On the other hand, some social theorists propose

that what may appear to be mere "latent" consequences of social systems design may actually be intentionally constructed components of the system. Charles Perrow, for example, raises the question that once a social system is in place, does it sustain the values and goals of those in control of that social system? In our society, those in positions of power are intentionally rational and goal-maximizing. They mobilize their values and seek advantage by calculating the benefits and costs of achieving their goals. In other words, the powerful intentionally create the conditions under which they operate and are well aware of the consequences of the social systems they command: "The outputs of the organization may be just what they planned."[73] For example, ecological problems such as pesticide poisoning in our water supply or air pollution are not unintended consequences of technology that occurred as well-meaning businesses provided us with goods and services. Social costs such as pollution or their consequences such as fines, taxes, and penalties are calculated into the costs of doing business. The claims that social problems occur because something goes wrong with otherwise well-intentioned decisions or that social problems are the result of the failure of benign social systems in adjusting to social conditions beyond their control[74] may often be simple denial or an attempt to evade responsibility.

Perceived from this vantage point the social pathology model may tend to provide a rationalization for the existing status quo and justify institutionalized oppression. The values and premises inherent in these systems are seen as beyond reproach simply because we cannot do without the benefits they provide for us. The refusal of some sociologists to take a stand about issues they are describing betrays a certain moral numbness that tends to reinforce the conditions they explore and a tacit approval for those who would use social science to reinforce social control at the expense of others.

The challenge for macro social workers using a social pathology model of social problems is to be sensitive in observing whom the system serves and protects. Is the system serving a latent function that gives the advantage to some at the expense of others? Is there an implication in the theory that the system is its own justification and is beyond criticism? Is there a self-justification for oppression such as "it has always been that way"? Will helping a social

system function more effectively reinforce exploitation, oppression, and injustice perpetrated on some at the expense of others? How does your critique of the social deviance and social pathology models compare with the one above? Can you think of issues in support of these models? Can you think of other problems with them? Are there times when these models are useful?

An Action Model: Redefining Social Problems

Earlier, I asked you to critique the conventional definition of social problems and develop your own definition. Now I will give you my definition based on an action model of social work:

A social problem is one experienced by a group or community of people, often caused by a source external to the community, that harms their welfare in identifiable ways and can be resolved only by common or public action.

Compare this definition with the one you and your classmates came up with. In what way is it the same? How is it different?

While traditional social science, because of its value-neutral stance, tends to avoid making recommendations about what society "ought" to do about social betterment, an action model of macro social work takes a highly value-laden, critical stance. It is informed by social critique, in which you as a macro social worker apply your own innate sense of the rightness of things to the conventional wisdom of the day, judging it not only by means of cognitive thought but with your intuition, your emotions and most of all with your own sense of what is right— *your values.*

Every macro social worker must be a perceptive social critic. While the action worker develops a macro social work practice out of past theories, she or he is always in process of generating new theories based on lived experience and interactions with others. Workers actively reflect on the assumptions, definitions, theories, and processes with which they attempt to make social systems better rather than accept them as "givens."

A critique of the conventionally accepted definition of a social problem would therefore find it to be defective in two ways. First, it is ruled by a *quantitative criteria of size*. A social problem must affect a "large" number of people. In reality, many social problems are more than likely to be experienced by relatively small groups of people. If the process of defining what is or is not a social problem is limited to large powerful groups, the very people affected by or who experience the problem may be excluded. The problem may be ignored, misperceived, viewed in terms that benefit the powerful themselves, or skewed to maintain the status quo.

Second, the conventional definition is ruled by a *qualitative criteria of "influence."* An "influential" group of people is required to judge whether an issue is a social problem. For the most part, social problems are experienced by people who are not at all influential. Placing the control of defining what is or is not a social problem in the hands of the influential or powerful not only excludes the very people who experience the problems but also keeps them in a subordinate position, denying them the opportunity of defining their own life situations for themselves.

Social problems affect people regardless of whether they are recognized or acknowledged by those who are influential or powerful or by anyone else. Groups experiencing social problems may at one time or another include women, persons with handicapping conditions, persons with nonheterosexual orientations, diverse ethnic groups, the elderly, and the poor.

The action model of macro social work maintains that those experiencing injustice, intolerance, economic, or political oppression need to define their own issues on their own terms, regardless of the perceptions or approval of the majority of the population.

> It is . . . self-evident that man makes the greatest use of his several capacities and endowments when none of these are subordinated or sacrificed to others, and when none of the persons who variously personify these capacities are subordinated.[75]

Anyone who suffers injustice and unequal treatment can find strength in refusing to be subordinated to others. This first step means defining and assessing one's social situation for oneself, not leaving it in the hands of others to define. That definition comes from one's lived experience of poverty, racism, violence, or disability. Action-oriented macro social workers, therefore, leave the definition of "social problem" in the control of those who are *immediately affected* by the issues involved, regardless of the size of the group or its influence.

Furthermore, an action orientation to social problems asserts that while communities or groups often reflect in their behavior the effects of social problems, the locus is often, if not entirely, external to them. It is the role of action-oriented macro social workers to help those affected to recognize those forces in the social environment by placing the locus of the problem where it belongs and identifying its effects.

The action model asserts that in the process of taking action against social problems, people not only gain power and mastery but also engage themselves in the self-defining and self-creating process of community making. An action model of macro social work places the recognition and definition of social problems in the hands of those who experience these problems and recognizes their capacity to resolve them. When people work together to solve their common problems, they forge community and in the process forge a life-world for themselves. The community becomes an arena of healing and nurture.

Finally, when social problems become so massive that they overwhelm communities of people, macro social workers call on the sense of justice of society-at-large through public action using social protest and the political system to seek redress.

Escape to Illusion: Answers That Won't Work

The strategies people use to deal with social problems may delude, blind, and prevent people from solving them. Those illusions are so pervasive that people, especially those in positions of power, often condone or perpetuate the very problems they pretend to solve.

Action-oriented macro social workers must seek answers that work. They must learn to recognize these escapes to illusion: denial, avoidance, blaming, moralizing, and the quick fix.

Denial and Its Modes

Denial takes many forms. We refuse to acknowledge the existence of social problems. When we do admit their existence, we look at them as "personal" problems instead of "social" problems. We deny their existence by excluding problem people from our lives.

Refusal to Admit the Problem Exists

A major form of denial in our society is refusal to admit that social problems exist. We declare that problems such as welfare, crime, and racism exist because of deviant individuals who refuse to conform to societal norms, who let others carry them, or who engage in illegal or immoral behavior. Poverty, for example, is caused by persons who are lazy, undisciplined, unmotivated, selfish, immature, and irresponsible.[76] Rather than contribute to society, these deviants interfere with social progress.

Personalizing the Problem

By trying to solve social problems on a person-by-person, one-by-one basis, we create the illusion that we are solving them. In reality, we are applying Band-Aids, patching up people who may already be so severely damaged as to be beyond repair. We concentrate on the social deviant but fail to look at the conditions that cause people to become deviant.

Excluding Reality

When we personalize social problems it becomes easy for us to exclude reality by shutting away those with whom we do not want to deal. Excluding reality operates by the maxim "Out of sight, out of mind." What we do not see and experience is not part of our reality and therefore not our problem.

We relocated Native Americans to reservations, Chinese to Chinatowns, Japanese Americans to concentration camps. We effectively banished developmentally disabled people from our awareness by placing them in large institutions. Segregation in the South before the Civil Rights Act attempted to use this form of denial as a way of dealing with race relations.

Rationalizing

Rationalizing is a form of the "Yes, but" game.[77] Some rationalizations are: "*Yes,* gangs are rampant, *but* more social programs will not make them go away." "*Yes,* there are few services for children, *but* throwing more money at social problems is not the answer." "*Yes,* our cities are deteriorating, *but* we tried community development in the sixties and we still have the problem." "*Yes,* poor people need medical care, *but* a national health care system will only make the problem worse."

Avoidance

We tend to avoid responsibility for social problems because it may be in our own interests to do so. We believe that they are too difficult to face, or we ourselves are implicated in the social milieu that creates or condones them. There are a number of ways of avoiding social problems. Sometimes we ignore them, hoping they will go away or waiting until people adjust to their condition. If all else fails, we can simply rationalize our avoidance.

Avoiding Responsibility

Business corporations tend to see themselves not as a cause of poverty but as a cause of prosperity. The political system sees itself not as preventing change but as developing solutions to society's problems. However,

> the political system in America is marvelously well designed to enable actors to evade responsibility for events such as energy waste and widespread pollution, even when these events are the products of decisions they have made. . . . For example, it has long been the genius of American industry to produce private affluence and public squalor, to promote a fetish for personal hygiene and general filth, all at the same time.[78]

Society Heal Thyself

Ignore problems and eventually they will go away. It is easy to delude ourselves that by waiting long enough social problems will either diminish on their own or become someone else's problem. This laissez-faire approach to social problems expects the powerless to commit their fate to a benevolent social system, which will ultimately work things out in their interests.

Time Heals all Wounds

In time, the naturally self-correcting mechanisms of the social body will solve social problems. While there may be short term pain or difficulties for certain groups, if we have faith in economic and political systems, everything will work out in the long run.

Social Adaptation

A more subtle variation of the time-heals-all-wounds strategy is the idea that the longer society puts things off, the more people will adapt and accept their lot. They will eventually forget injustices and learn to live with their social condition. As they adjust, they become subservient, forming a culture of victims in which powerlessness becomes part of their milieu. The more people act the role of victims, the more they reinforce their stereotyped roles, becoming unwilling or unable to gain resources for themselves. Delaying and avoiding dealing with social problems always works in favor of those in power.

Blaming

Blaming others is a way of deflecting responsibility from those who are actually responsible for creating social problems to those who bear their effects. Those in power have often honed this strategy to a fine point. There is no dearth of targets of blame. We can blame the victim, we can blame the providers, we can blame the system. It is a strategy that always results in a dead end.

Blaming the Victim

The strategy of blaming the victim, popularized by William Ryan, is a way of shifting responsibility and making the victims seem like the perpetrators of problems. According to this view, the problem of poverty in America is caused not by an economy that advantages some at the expense of others but by the person who is laid off and cannot find work or a di-

vorced mother who must apply for welfare because her ex-husband refuses to pay child support.

Blaming the Providers

People charged with the responsibility of solving problems are blamed for their cause. "We have too many bureaucrats." "There is too much inefficiency, too much red tape, too much regulation, too much interference, too much government." All of these complaints beg the question of the real locus of social problems.

Blaming the Reformers

Social change agents are blamed for causing social problems. Socialists, pacifists, anarchists, union organizers, social activists, community organizers, and civil rights activists have all been vilified as malcontents and subversives, who tend to disturb social stability and undermine the social order. Many social activists have been harassed, jailed, and even murdered.

Passing the Buck

Sometimes those who want to exonerate themselves or further their own ambitions use social problems as a means to their ends. Crime, welfare, and racial intolerance often become the focus of political campaigns. One politician blames another for being "soft on crime" or for the "welfare mess." The president blames Congress or Congress blames the president. One political party blames the other. Social problems become political footballs. After an election, however, and one politician or political party gains power, concern for resolving the social problem often evaporates.

Scapegoating

A social group is blamed for the existence of social problems even when the group members are the victims. The Chinese, for example, were brought to the United States as laborers to blast roads and tunnels for railroads in the Sierra Mountains and then were blamed for displacing other workers during recessions. No responsibility was placed on owners of the mines and railroads who brought them here and paid poor wages. The Chinese who could not read, write, or speak English were easy targets of scapegoating and racial hysteria.

Blaming Ignorance

Sometimes those in control of social systems play the "ignorance" game. For example, the tobacco industry has consistently claimed that tobacco smoke does not cause cancer or other health problems. Often, however, complex organizations are intentionally constructed systems with consequences that are clearly planned and controlled by their owners.

Moralizing

People who do not meet the moral standards of those in power "do not deserve help." The poor, for example, are divided into the "deserving" poor and the "undeserving" poor. Those who are considered deserving receive help; those who are undeserving receive little or nothing.

Retribution

The retribution game is a refinement of blaming the victim and moralizing. Those enmeshed in social problems are made to pay. Welfare recipients are punished by reducing payments, passing residency requirements, and increasing restrictions—incentives for people to get off welfare. Criminals are punished with longer, harsher sentences. Once freed, they are labeled so that they will find it difficult to get a job.

The Quick Fix

Most social problems are perpetuated by years of reinforcement, neglect, and denial. Those who propose one-shot, short-term, stop-gap solutions and expect an immediate turnaround set up social change efforts for failure. President Johnson's War on Poverty in the 1960s, dismantled by the Nixon administration after only a few years, is still blamed for problems plaguing our cities. The illusion that long-standing social problems can be solved quickly ultimately leads to discouragement and anger.

Conclusion

Social problems such as drug abuse, crime, inadequate housing, alcoholism, AIDS, teen pregnancy, and underemployment affect us all. Not only has the lack of resources for combating these problems impacted the poor and ethnic minorities most heavily but the growing national debt has served conservative forces well as an excuse for not meeting the urgent need to expand services.[79]

Social problems afflict particular communities and specific people. These problems may be manageable and solvable if communities do not allow themselves to be captured by

> a system of ideological control which aims to make issues seem remote from the general population and to persuade them of their incapacity to organize their own affairs or to understand the social world in which they live without the tutelage of intermediaries.[80]

To help communities solve their social problems, macro social workers need to understand the history of the problems. They must have an adequate understanding of society's role in creating social problems and not be naive about the ways that decision-makers justify, minimize, evade, deny, and even perpetuate them. Answers that work, a commitment to resolution, and a will to eradicate social problems are the means to their solution.

KEY CONCEPTS

social problems
moral deviance
social pathology
society as inherently defective
contingency approach
unintended consequences
action model
refusing to admit problems exist
personalizing problems
excluding reality
rationalizing
avoiding responsibility
society heal thyself
time heals all wounds

social adaptation
blaming the victim
blaming providers
blaming reformers
passing the buck
scapegoating
moralizing
retribution
quick fix

QUESTIONS FOR DISCUSSION

1. Why do social problems persist?
2. Ann Schaef says that society is deteriorating at an alarming rate. Do you agree or disagree? If you agree, to what do you attribute this deterioration?
3. Some social philosophers claim that our ability to solve our social problems has not progressed much beyond the Middle Ages, when poverty, war, famine, and disease plagued the world. Is this a fair statement? Why or why not?
4. Eric Voegelin claims that society is both progressing and regressing at the same time. Do you agree with this assessment? In what areas are we progressing? In what areas are we regressing?
5. While we have become masters at scientific techniques for solving problems in the areas of physics and biology, we still tend to solve our social problems by violence, greed, and self-interest rather than by reason. Do you agree or disagree? What are the ways our society tends to resolve social problems?

ADDITIONAL READING

Social Problems

Manis, Jerome G. *Analyzing Social Problems.* New York: Praeger, 1976.
Mills, C. Wright. *The Sociological Imagination.* London: Oxford University Press, 1959.
Seidman, Edward, and Julia Rappaport, eds. *Redefining Social Problems.* New York: Plenum Press, 1986.

Deviance Model

Means, Richard L. *The Ethical Imperative: The Crisis in American Values.* Garden City, NY: Anchor Books, Doubleday, 1970.
Winslow, Robert. *The Emergence of Deviant Minorities, Social Problems and Social Change.* San Ramon, CA: Consensus Publishers, 1972.
Ryan, William. *Blaming the Victim.* New York: Vintage Books, 1976.

Social Pathology

Lemert, Edwin. *Social Pathology: A Systematic Approach to the Theory of Sociopathic Behavior*
Hofstadter, Richard. *Social Darwinism in American Thought, 1860–1915.* Boston: Beacon Press, 1959.

Society as Inherently Defective

Coleman, Frank M. *Hobbes and America: Exploring the Constitutional Foundations.* Toronto: University of Toronto Press, 1977.
Reik, Charles A. *The Greening of America.* New York: Bantam Books, 1970.

Special Problems

Allport, Gordon. *The Nature of Prejudice.* Reading, MA: Addison-Wesley, 1954.
Billingsley, Andrew, and J. Giovannoni. *Children of the Storm: Black Children and American Child Welfare.* New York: Harcourt Brace Jovanovich, 1972.
Freedman, Jonathan. *From Cradle to Grave: The Human Face of Poverty.* New York: Atheneum, 1993.
Kozol, J. *Rachel and Her Children: Homeless Families in America.* New York: Fawcett Columbine, 1988.
Myrdal, Gunnar. *An American Dilemma.* New York: Harper, 1944.
Reiman, Jeffrey. *The Rich Get Richer and the Poor Get Prison: Ideology, Crime and Criminal Justice.* 4th ed. Boston, MA: Allyn and Bacon, 1990.
Riis, Jacob. *Children of the Tenements.* New York: Macmillan, 1903.

EXERCISES

EXERCISE 9:
Diagnosing Social Problems

Described below are three social problems. First, come up with a diagnosis of the social problem. Then discuss what role, if any, professional social workers ought to take in trying to solve each of these social problems.

1. *Violence toward Children.* Child physical abuse, child sexual abuse, serial murders of children, and child theft occur with regularity. It is estimated that 375,000 babies were born to mothers who used drugs in 1990.[81] In 1992, 1,261 children in the United States died because of child abuse,[82] and 2,428 children were murdered.[83] In California, 175,200 cases of child abuse were reported in 1980. By 1992, that number had risen to 615,602, a 350 percent increase.[84] In 1992, 4,650 fifteen-to-twenty-four-year-olds took their own lives.[85]

2. *Racial Discrimination.* Long-standing systematic racial discrimination continues to exist. The Urban Institute recently concluded that when equally qualified for jobs, African Americans are still three times less likely to be hired than white candidates. Inner cities are pockets of despair and poverty, abandoned by businesses and rampant with drug abuse.

3. *Poverty.* The gap between rich and poor is increasing. In 1987, for example, 5 million children under the age of six, almost one child out of every four, lived in poverty in the United States, according to the Columbia University National Center for Children in Poverty. At the same time, however, "the total amount of dollars in salaries funneled to the rich soared in the 1980s as did the rich themselves."[86] In the 1980s, the salaries of people earning more than $1 million increased by 2,184 percent, and the number of people earning between $200,000 to $1 million increased by almost 700 percent. By 1991 the combined wealth of the richest four hundred Americans hit $288 billion, an average of $720 million per person, the highest ever recorded in our nation's history.[87] "It was," Bartlett and Steele comment, "a phenomenon unlike any America has seen in this century."[88]

EXERCISE 10:
The Illusion Game

Choose a social problem that is current. Ask yourself what illusions we as a society hold about the problem that prevents us from solving it: for example, what illusions do people hold about welfare? Do we indulge in illusions of denial? Do we avoid the problem, blame or moralize about it? Develop a list of potential illusions about the social problem you chose. Then, talk to people, read newspaper editorials and letters to the editor, listen to talk shows, watch TV news, and try to spot instances of avoiding, blaming, moralizing, or quick fixes.

In class, form a "fishbowl," with one group of members seated in a circle and the rest of the members seated outside the circle. Members of the inner circle choose one or more of the "escapes to illusions." Focusing on a current social problem, each member discusses a solution in terms of that illusion. The outer circle observes the process and gives feedback. Then the two groups reverse positions and choose a different set of illusions to act out. After both groups have had a chance to interact and give feedback, the entire class reassembles and discusses their reactions to the exercise.

EXERCISE 11:
Choosing a Social Problem

This exercise is intended to help you decide on a social problem to solve and to get you started working on it. Think of the kind of issues on which you want to work. One way is to choose a problem that is "hot," one that is current and on which you can obtain information. The problem you choose should be one that you and your class can work on.

Ask yourselves, How far do we want to go? Do we want to make a proposal or do we want to move the problem into its first stages? Do we want to work on something from scratch or do we want to join in on something that is already going on? List all of the constraints that you can think of.

Once you have considered these factors, think about the kinds of problems that are possible choices. Following are some categories you may consider.

1. *Community Development.* A number of community development organizations exist in most communities. One is Habitat for Humanity. Perhaps your local community also has organ-

(continued next page)

EXERCISES

EXERCISE 11 (continued)

izations aimed at improving neighborhoods by eradicating gang graffiti, planting trees, cleaning neighborhoods, or getting better community services. Try to get involved not only in working on a project but also in the planning and decision-making processes by which it is developed.

2. *Social Action.* There are any number of social issues around which people are organizing today: abortion, gun control, AIDS, women's rights, gay rights, environmental issues, pollution, and so on. You can also get involved in your local political party organization to work on a local issue of importance to you.

3. *Program Development.* Is there an unmet need in your commu- nity or at your college or uni- versity? Agencies and action groups in your community may be working on developing a shelter for battered women, a residence for the homeless, pro- grams to eradicate drug abuse, or a center for runaway teens. If a local community group is al- ready developing a program, your class might assist in the project.

4. *Social Planning.* Social plan- ning organizations dealing with mental health, developmental disabilities, aging, and human rights, among other issues, are active in most communities. Visit some of these organiza- tions. There may be a planning project in which your class could participate.

5. *Administration.* Your college may have a project in the works for which your class could pro- vide administrative assistance— gathering facts, developing al- ternative solutions, or making recommendations. Perhaps you can even work on implementing your own solution to the social problem that inspired the project.

6. *Organization Development.* Ev- ery organization has problems or dysfunctional areas. What dysfunctions have you observed in your own college community or in an organization that you know well? Work with the ad- ministration of the organization to help develop a solution.

7. *Social Policy.* Social policy is- sues abound. Abortion, gun control, euthanasia, legalizing drugs, welfare policy, and capi- tal punishment are only a few. Choose one of these policy problems or some other problem and come up with a solution.

CHAPTER 3
Methods of Solving Social Problems

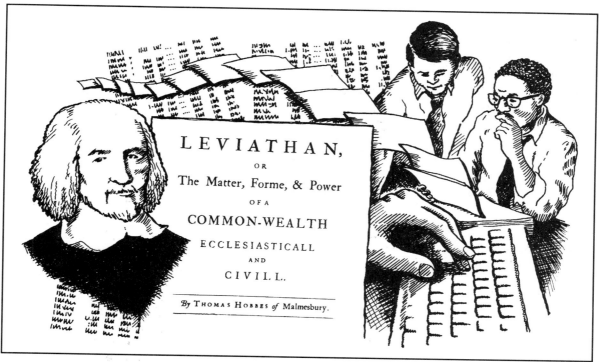

Sophisticated modern techniques of social-problem solving are indebted to the tenets of rationality set forth in Thomas Hobbes' Leviathan.

When a man *reasoneth* he does nothing else but conceive a sum total. . . . For reason, in this sense, is nothing but *reckoning,* that is, adding and subtracting of the consequences . . . agreed upon. The use and end of reason is not finding the sum and truth of one, or a few consequences . . . but to begin at these and proceed from one consequence to another.

—THOMAS HOBBES, *LEVIATHAN,* 1651[1]

IDEAS IN THIS CHAPTER

Thomas Hobbes and Modern Reason

Sitting at his desk in an upper room in Paris, 1650, golden light streaming through the window, Thomas Hobbes contemplated the destructive turmoil of social and political relationships since the dawn of history. The natural propensity of people to fight over power, quarrel over religious dogma, and dispute over morality, thought Hobbes, had kept humankind in a perpetual "war of all against all,"[2] where "every man is enemy to every man . . . and the life of man, solitary, poor, nasty, brutish and short."[3]

Was there another way that political and social relationships could be ordered that would place society on a less turbulent and more secure foundation? His friend Galileo, whom he had recently visited, suggested that the physical world, based on euclidian geometry, was nothing but a system of interrelated moving parts. Galileo, Roger Bacon, and others were engaged in the exciting task of discovering the laws that governed the physical universe. Hobbes reasoned that since society also was nothing more than a system of interrelated components,[4] were there not similar laws by which political relationships were determined? By applying rational calculation, could not humankind devise ways of regulating and ordering human relationships?[5]

Published in 1651, Hobbes's *Leviathan* attempted no less than to remake the entire world of thought up to that time.[6] In a single stroke was born the idea of modern reason,[7] systems theory,[8] and the fields of political and social science. Hobbes believed that humans were not at the mercy of irrational emotions, dogma, or metaphysics. By applying reason to relationships, people could construct social systems to achieve the rational self-interested pursuit of their goals, laying the groundwork for the framers of the American Constitution, modern democracy, and capitalism.

Rooted deeply in scientific culture, rational problem solving has become the way we think about our modern world. It is the form of reasoning used in solving the most complex problems of our day. Political scientists use it in their search for understanding about public policy decisions. Decision-making tools utilizing complex computers are based on this approach. Economists using rational problem solving apply many economic forecasting tools. Rational problem solving is the generalist method that social workers use to help clients solve problems in counseling and therapy. Macro social work change agents apply rational problem solving to social problems that occur in communities, organizations, and societal issues as a whole.

Introduction

Macro social work is a highly personal venture, one that depends on you and your own mix of perceptions, personality functions, and ability to apply yourself to making a better society. There is no one rigid model, nor is there a right or a wrong way of making social change. While there are skills to be learned, macro social work cannot be reduced to a bag of tricks or techniques. What you decide to do and how you decide to do it is a complex matter of immersing yourself in the social environment in which you are working, understanding the social dysfunctions that are occurring, and engaging people in efforts to bring about conditions that are more wholesome, healthy, and virtuous.

The "method" of solving problems, therefore, does not exist independently of you, the practitioner. To be effective, any model you use must fit you and your own way of thinking. It must be natural to you and make sense. Furthermore, it must be of practical value. Your method must work so that you can see its results in practical, tangible ways. Finally, it must be congruent with the kinds of problems with which you are dealing.

Before we explore one such problem-solving model, I invite you to take a test adapted from David Kolb's Learning Style Inventory and based on Jungian personality functions that will help you understand how you go about solving problems (see EXERCISE 12 and figure 3.1).

The Four Personality Functions

Each of us has a way of presenting ourselves to others, our way of "being-in the world." Carl Jung ob-

---

EXERCISES

EXERCISE 12: Problem-Solving Inventory

In the following inventory you will complete ten sentences. Each sentence has four endings intended to help you discover how you go about solving problems. Try to think of a situation in which you were faced with a problem you had to solve. In the spaces provided mark the ending that fits your problem-solving style best with the number 4, the ending that fits next best with a 3, and so on to the one least like your style. Put a different ranking in each space.

For example:

I solve problems best when I
a. _3_ explore what is good.
b. _1_ anticipate options.
c. _4_ use logic.
d. _2_ engage in practice.

4 = most like you
3 = second most like you
2 = third most like you
1 = least like you

1. I solve problems best when I
   a. ___ use my values.
   b. ___ grasp the future.
   c. ___ think things through.
   d. ___ do something.

2. I decide by
   a. ___ using my feelings.
   b. ___ using my intuition.
   c. ___ using my mind.
   d. ___ using my practicality.

3. When I problem solve I consider
   a. ___ others.
   b. ___ all the possibilities.
   c. ___ only the facts.
   d. ___ effectiveness.

4. When I decide I pride myself on
   a. ___ my caring attitude.
   b. ___ my creative insight.
   c. ___ my ability to assemble data.
   d. ___ how I get things done.

(continued next page)

EXERCISES

EXERCISE 12 (continued)

5. The best kind of problem solvers
   a. ___ are compassionate.
   b. ___ have vision.
   c. ___ rely on ideas.
   d. ___ have common sense.

6. When faced with a problem I rely on
   a. ___ how it affects others.
   b. ___ my hunches.
   c. ___ logic.
   d. ___ what has worked before.

7. A problem solver needs to be
   a. ___ enthusiastic.
   b. ___ imaginative.
   c. ___ analytical.
   d. ___ down to earth.

8. Problem solving requires
   a. ___ a warm heart.
   b. ___ inventiveness.
   c. ___ a tough mind.
   d. ___ hands-on action.

9. Problem solvers should depend on
   a. ___ experience.
   b. ___ insight.
   c. ___ theories.
   d. ___ models.

10. Problem solvers should always attempt to discern
    a. ___ the meaning a situation holds.
    b. ___ opportunities a situation presents.
    c. ___ what the facts say is right.
    d. ___ what is workable.

Total the scores for all the *a* answers. Then total the scores for all the *b, c,* and *d* answers.
   a. ___ (F)
   b. ___ (N)
   c. ___ (T)
   d. ___ (S)

served that people have four general ways of relating to their environment and making decisions. These are intuiting, sensing, thinking, and feeling.

Intuition and sensing are ways people have of *perceiving* the world or *obtaining* information. When you obtain information by means of experiencing the world primarily through your senses, such as seeing, hearing, touching, or tasting, you are using your sensing function. On the other hand, when you relate to the world by means of your imagination, which goes beyond sense perception, you are using your intuition.

Thinking and feeling are ways people have of *making decisions* or *processing the information* provided by their senses and intuition. When you process information by means of thinking cognitively, you gather facts and analyze them. On the other hand, you may base your decision making on your feelings and values.

While all of us have these four functions at our disposal, each person gradually adopts one dominant way of perceiving the world and of making decisions. The choices you make depend on any number of factors such as your genetic predisposition, your family upbringing, conditions in your environment, or circumstances that you encounter in your life.

For example, a person may perceive the world either as a "senser" or an "intuiter." The opposite function, while still important, becomes a supplementary way of relating to the world. People also choose to process information by means of either their thinking function or their feeling function. The opposite becomes a subsidiary way of decision making.

Sensing Function

People who are dominant in using their sensing functions see, smell, hear, and touch to explore and understand the world about them. If you have high sensing function you are probably a down-to-earth, pragmatic realist who enjoys doing rather than conceptualizing or imagining. You won't mind getting your hands dirty, tinkering with the machinery of life, or getting immersed in fixing things. Proficient at assessing current reality, sensers enjoy working with details and facts and can face present troubles realistically.

Figure 3.1

Understanding Your Personality Functions

Each of the four groups gives an indication of one aspect of the personality functions problem solvers use. These functions are Feeling—group *a* (F); Intuiting—group *b* (N); Thinking—group *c* (T); and Sensing—group *d* (S).

On the diagram below, place a dot on the scale corresponding to your T, N, F, or S scores in EXERCISE 12. Connect the lines. You will get a kite-like shape. The shape and position of your scores will show which of the functions you prefer most and which you prefer least.

Thinking (T)
40
38
36
34
32
30
28
26
24
22
20
18
16
14
12

Sensing (S)   **Intuiting (N)**
40 38 36 34 32 30 28 26 24 22 20 18 16 14 12 10   10 12 14 16 18 20 22 24 26 28 30 32 34 36 38 40
10
12
14
16
18
20
22
24
26
28
30
32
34
36
38
40
Feeling (F)

By looking at how you scored on the four functions, you can get an idea about where your problem-solving strengths lie. The strongest areas are those that you will tend to use most often and with the most ease. The ones on which you score lowest are areas that you will need to work harder to use or will use less frequently.

Sensers are present-day oriented rather than future oriented. They may tend to learn by doing and easily move to take action to accomplish something. They might be called "hands on" persons who value getting the job done and seeing the results of their action in tangible programs and services. If you are a highly developed senser, however, you may become so engrossed in the present-day details that you lose sight of the big picture and cannot envision the future. You may see the trees but not the forest.

Intuiting Function

Intuiting, or using one's intuition, is a way of delving into one's unconscious, bringing ideas together, making connections, and seeing relationships beyond information from one's senses. Intuiters are able to make leaps of insight, are imaginative, and seek inspiration. If you are an intuiter, you will tend to be creative, envisioning possibilities and opportunities that others may not see. A visionary, you dream about future directions, are hopeful and forward looking, and usually can see numbers of options and ideas. You rely on your hunches and may see beyond empirical facts to gain insight into situations.

If you are one-sided in using your intuition, however, you will not tend to be detail oriented, to look hard at current reality, or to be involved in the day-to-day practicality of things. You may see the forest but not the trees.

Thinking Function

Thinking is one way of making decisions using information gathered by your senses and your intuition. If you are more comfortable in deciding by means of thinking you will tend to look logically and analytically at things, using your intellect to understand situations. Thinkers are interested in what is objectively right or wrong and do not falter when the facts point to unpleasant or uncomfortable realities. Thinkers are critical, seeing the consequences of decisions, even when they are unpleasant to deal with. Thinkers can be tough, firm, and hard headed. They want to be treated with fairness and honesty and get

particularly concerned when others are dishonest and treat people unfairly.

Thinkers prize justice. They stand against opposition by using logic and analytical skills to hold to a position they are convinced is right, particularly if supported by the facts. They like to develop theories and use their ideas to solve problems. The downside of being a highly developed thinker, however, means that one may tend not to be conciliatory, open to compromise, or sensitive to other's feelings.

Feeling Function

People who decide by means of their feeling function emphasize values, beliefs, and relationships. If you are a feeling type you will tend to put your feelings and values first when making decisions. Your subjective perceptions about how your decisions affect others and yourself will tend to win out over or color the objective facts of a situation. People who rely on their feeling function look for meaning implicit in facts, are open to possibilities that facts may only imply, and are adaptable to change.

Unlike thinkers, feelers tend not to be judgmental or critical but value other people's opinions, seek consensus, build relationships, and bring people together on issues. They tend to be persuasive, are good at working on common projects, enjoy ceremony and ritual, and are able to arouse enthusiasm in others.

If you have developed your feeling function more than your thinking function, however, you may tend to loose sight of your own viewpoint and get enmeshed in feelings. You may be sensitive to criticism and as a result overlook people's weaknesses or failings. Unlike thinkers, you may have a hard time being in situations where you have to pass judgment on or evaluate others.

Problem-Solving Style

While you may see yourself as having some functions that are more dominant than others, it is likely that no single function describes your problem-solving pattern completely. This is because the functions work in pairs. Each of us has a dominant or primary a way of grasping information about problems and a supplemental way of transforming it into decisions or solutions. For example, if you grasp information by your intuitive function, you will process that information either by thinking or feeling.

Calculating Your Problem-Solving Preference

Use the scores from your personality functions F, T, S, and N in EXERCISE 12 to do the following subtraction problems.

$$\underline{\qquad}_{F} - \underline{\qquad}_{T} = \underline{\qquad}_{F-T}$$

$$\underline{\qquad}_{S} - \underline{\qquad}_{N} = \underline{\qquad}_{S-N}$$

A positive score on F–T means that you are a feeling type who takes feelings and values into consideration when making decisions. A negative score on F–T means that your thinking functions are stronger than your feeling functions. A thinker, you decide objectively on the basis of the facts, not feelings.

A positive score for S–N means that you tend to decide by means of your senses rather than intuition, and that as a senser you are more down-to-earth and practical than future oriented. A negative score on S–N means that you are an intuiter. You tap into your intuition to decide, dreaming and envisioning the future rather than concentrating on day-to-day details of implementation.

You can now figure out what combination of functions work for you. In figure 3.2, find the place on the vertical axis where your F–T score falls and mark the place. Then, move across the vertical axis and mark where your S–N score lies. Find the point inside the quadrant where each of the two meet. This quadrant is your problem-solving preference. For example, if your F–T score is –6 and your S–N score is +15, you would fall into the S/T quadrant. Your dominant problem-solving preference would be as a senser/thinker.

Take a moment and consider your own problem-solving preference. What combination describes you best?

- *Sensing Plus Thinking.* Senser/thinkers tend to like to look at everyday realities and make decisions by objective analysis. They are practical and analytical. Because they need to have all the facts at their disposal and are action oriented, they are effective in situations where they can gather information and solve practical problems on a day-to-day basis. This is the kind of formal problem solving that is congruent with complex organizations. Senser/thinkers tend to become good administrators and planners.
- *Sensing Plus Feeling.* Senser/feelers also look at everyday reality but do so by means of meaning and relationships. They are action oriented and want to see issues turned into practical solutions. When they experience a problem they see it in relation to how it will affect people directly. They use their sensing/feeling skills to envision and create policies and programs, becoming program developers or social policy analysts.
- *Intuiting Plus Thinking.* Intuiter/thinkers look at future possibilities but do so by means of logic and analysis. They often become good social planners, forecasting the future using their technical skills and logical analysis. They also can become competent social researchers. An intuiter who is stronger in thinking may become a social activist, using his or her sense of justice and the facts to mobilize people to strive for his or her vision of the future.
- *Intuiting Plus Feeling.* Intuiter/feelers are visionaries who enjoy gathering people together, inspiring others, and engaging people in social causes. They tend to enjoy problem solving in situations where relationships are important. Intuiter/feelers obtain satisfaction from engaging others in solving problems at the level of feelings, meaning, and envisioning future possibilities. Intuiter/feelers tend to be drawn to community development or organization development.

As you reflect on the meaning that your own problem-solving style has for you, look back to chapter 1, CHECKLIST 2: The Stance of a Macro Social Worker. The checklist helped give you an idea about what kinds of macro social work might be most appealing to you. Compare that assessment with your problem-solving style. Are they congruent? If not, what macro social work arena of practice is most appealing to you? Does your own problem-solving style fit that? If not, your own perceptions about your strengths and interests is your best guide.

Problem-Solving Cycle

David Kolb describes apprehending the world as "grasping" ideas and skills and then "transforming" them into concepts or meaning that we can use.[9] We

---

Figure 3.2
Your Problem-Solving Preference

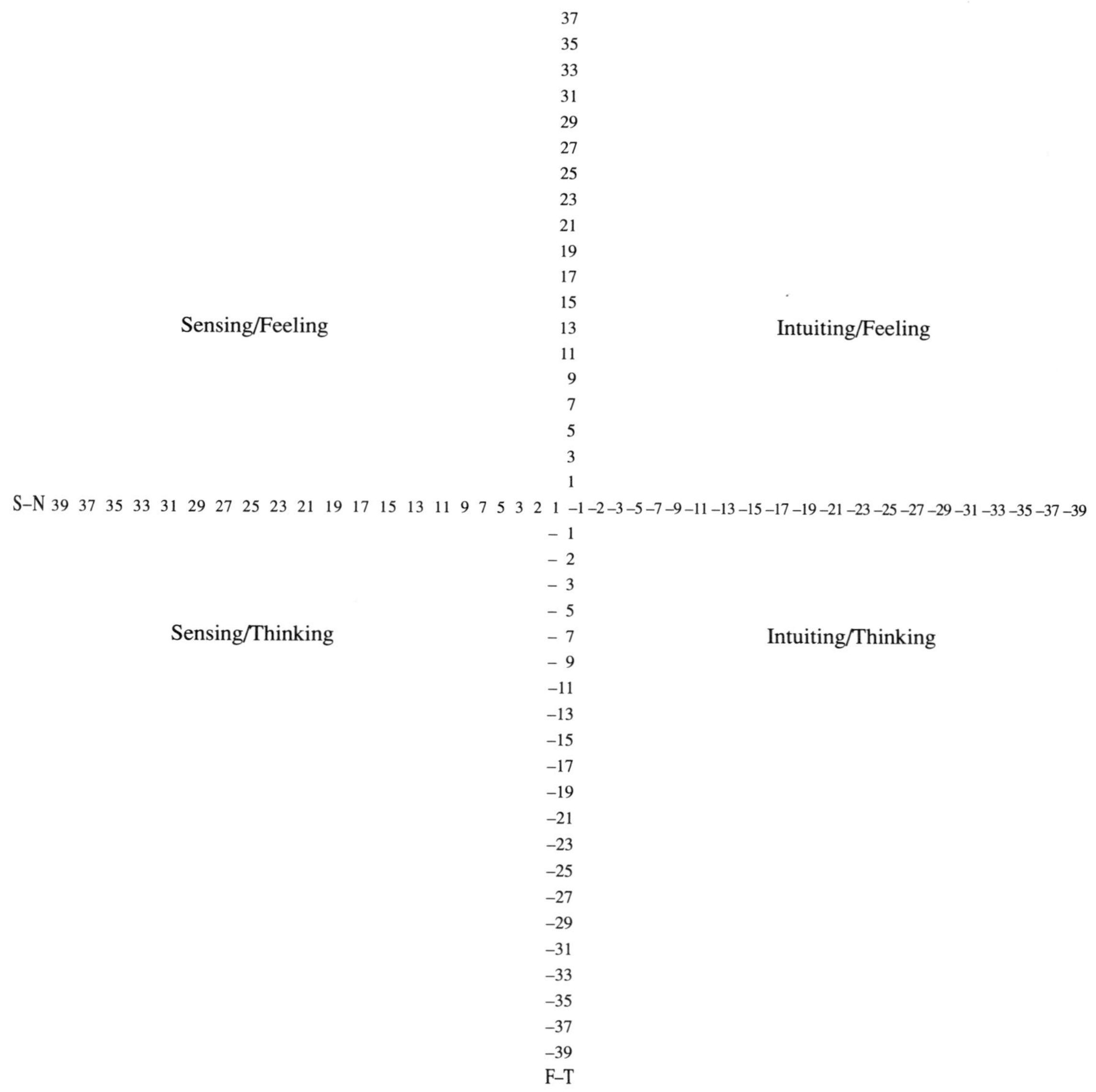

```
                                              37
                                              35
                                              33
                                              31
                                              29
                                              27
                                              25
                                              23
                                              21
                                              19
                                              17
                                              15
     Sensing/Feeling                          13            Intuiting/Feeling
                                              11
                                               9
                                               7
                                               5
                                               3
                                               1
S–N 39 37 35 33 31 29 27 25 23 21 19 17 15 13 11 9 7 5 3 2 1  –1 –2 –3 –5 –7 –9 –11 –13 –15 –17 –19 –21 –23 –25 –27 –29 –31 –33 –35 –37 –39
                                             – 1
                                             – 2
                                             – 3
                                             – 5
     Sensing/Thinking                        – 7           Intuiting/Thinking
                                             – 9
                                             –11
                                             –13
                                             –15
                                             –17
                                             –19
                                             –21
                                             –23
                                             –25
                                             –27
                                             –29
                                             –31
                                             –33
                                             –35
                                             –37
                                             –39
                                             F–T
```

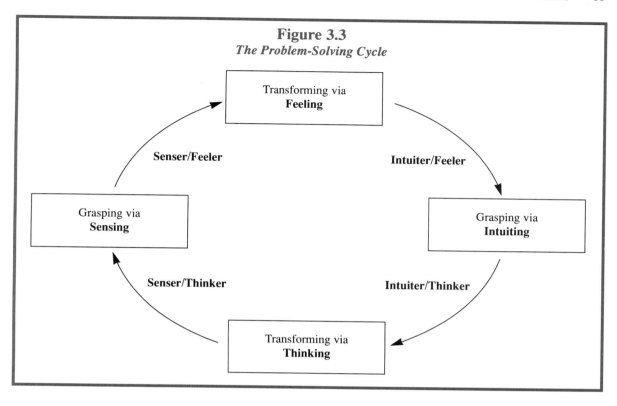

Figure 3.3
The Problem-Solving Cycle

grasp the world by our senses and intuition and transform these perceptions by thinking and feeling to make sense of our world. For example, we recognize chocolate ice cream immediately through our senses without the need for understanding. However, these sensory perceptions become meaningful for us as we transform them into an experience that adds meaning to our lives. In the same way, an intuiter/thinker will generally grasp information with his or her intuition and transform that information by means of his or her thinking function. A senser/thinker will grasp information by means of his or her sensing function and transform that information into something meaningful by his or her thinking function.

Generalist Social Work Method

The problem-solving process is similar to the generalist social work method. Take a moment and consider how you have learned to solve problems with a client. The first thing you do is begin a relationship.

You use your feeling function. At the same time you probably reach out intuitively to try to understand what the client implies or infers. This has sometimes been called using your "sixth sense" or listening with your "third ear." As you begin to ask questions you employ your thinking function. When you reflect on the information you have gathered, you plug in the information to your intuition and come up with a diagnosis. The ideas you have about the problem, however, lead you to consider how to solve that problem in the real world. You add your sensing function to your thoughts to develop a solution, which becomes a treatment plan. Your sensing function helps you put the plan into action.

Of course, as others have pointed out, the process is not one directional but is interactive, holistic, and reciprocal.[10] Sometimes parts of the process occur simultaneously. For example, as you use your feeling function to reach out to your client, you also gather information by your intuition and by gathering facts. You may begin thinking of solutions and acting in a therapeutic way even as you engage the client's situation. Your actions cause the client to disclose

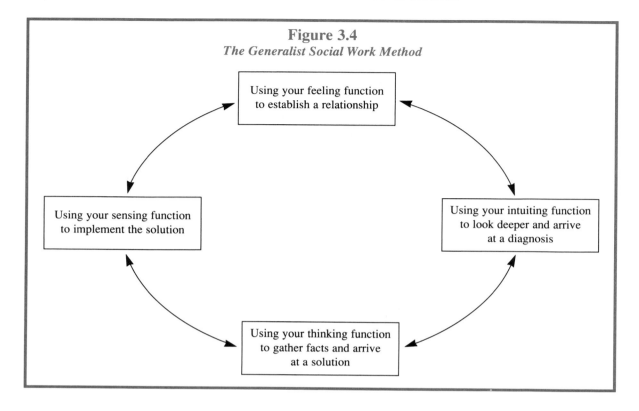

Figure 3.4
The Generalist Social Work Method

more of him- or herself, which gives you more clues, confirms your hunches, and leads to more ideas.

The generalist social work method, also known as a problem-solving method,[11] is "a common approach to intervention [that] has emerged over the last decade."[12] Popularized by Helen Harris Perlman in 1957 as a social casework method, the problem-solving approach became widely used. In 1958, Lippitt, Watson, and Westley examined the work of a variety of social workers, psychiatrists and organization consultants and concluded that most change processes pass through the following seven phases:

1. Development of a need for change
2. Establishment of a change relationship
3. Clarification or diagnosis of the client's systems problem
4. Examination of alternative routes and goals, establishing goals and intention of action
5. Transformation of intentions into actual change efforts
6. Generalization and stabilization of change
7. Achievement of a terminal relationship[13]

Not only was the generalist social work method commonplace in micro social work practice, but "it was soon recognized that social workers involved in organizing, planning and administering use the same basic steps in their work."[14] Rational problem solving, or the generalist social work method, is a model that can be used for changing social systems and helping people reach their goals effectively. Compton and Galaway, for example, state:

> For anyone or for any social system, effective movement toward purposive change, or altering something that one wishes to alter, rests on the ability of the system or of the professional helper to engage in rational goal-directed thinking and to divide this cognitive activity into sequential stages.[15]

What Is Rational Problem Solving?

Imagine that you are an airplane pilot. You choose a destination (goal), then gather all the facts you need to help you accurately calculate how to reach this goal. You need to know at what time you must arrive at your destination. In order to arrive at that time you need to know at what altitude you will be flying, the wind velocity and direction at that altitude, the airspeed at which you will be flying, and weather conditions you may encounter. Once you have all that information, you determine the best among various alternative routes (solutions to the problem of reaching the goal). Usually the shortest, most direct route is best. You calculate how long the trip will take and how much fuel you will need. Given this information, you can determine the time of your departure.

But, if you leave out a crucial piece of information or it is not available to you, your calculations may be wrong.

Rational problem solving depends on fairly stable environmental conditions. In the example, if conditions in the environment are turbulent and change suddenly, you may not arrive on time or you may be forced to change your goal. Rational problem solving also requires an unimpeded path since it is on a linear model. For example, if something occurs that interferes with an airplane's flight, such as cloud cover or fog, the trip may need to be cancelled or the plane may crash.

Finally, rational problem solving is predicated on a *consistent* goal. For example, after you are airborne, it would not be rational to change your mind and decide that instead of heading for Cincinnati you prefer to go to Tampa, Florida. Your calculations will not take you to Tampa, and furthermore, your fuel supply may not last. Once you are heading for a certain goal, changing directions may be difficult, inefficient, or even disastrous.

While rational problem solving has been appropriated by micro social work practitioners, it has been a model in use for hundreds of years. It was first conceived by Thomas Hobbes in 1650 and described by John Dewey in his 1933 book *How We Think*.[16] Rational problem solving was described as the basis for administrative decision making by Herbert Simon in 1943,[17] for political and policy change by Graham Allison,[18] and in planning by Churchman.[19]

Applied to macro social work, rational problem solving refers to a process by which a social problem is examined, broken down into its parts, and a resolution attempted. The rational problem-solving process involves the following steps:

1. Deciding on a problem
2. Gathering information about the problem
3. Generating a number of alternative solutions
4. Assessing and comparing alternatives
5. Selecting the best or most cost-beneficial solution
6. Developing a strategy or plan of implementation
7. Carrying out or implementing the solution
8. Evaluating the results[20]

Rational problem solving can be used for changing social systems and helping people reach goals effectively.

Based on efficiency, rational problem solving can enable you to calculate how to reach a particular goal in the shortest amount of time and at the least cost. Rational problem solving is logical and simple, straightforward and direct. It is empirical. It deals with facts, and as a result, easily lends itself to issues that can be quantified or that are clearly defined. It is systematic and sequential. You know that you will not miss crucial issues or skip over things that need to be considered.

This logical model is useful in a number of macro social work contexts, particularly those in which you have some degree of control over the environment, over information, and over the goals or destination of the project. For example, rational problem solving is very useful in macro social work research because you decide on the kind of research problem you want to solve, the amount of information you need, the amount of money and time available to you, and the environment in which the research will take place. Rational problem solving is commonly used by managers of organizational systems who have access to lots of information and have clear goals, and who can mobilize resources to arrive at those goals efficiently.[21] It is commonly used in calculating administrative decisions and is very useful in social planning and in program development. Once you have mastered its steps, you have a powerful tool at your disposal, which you can adapt to any number of situations. (See figure 3.5.)

Deciding on a Problem

Deciding on a social problem is the most important part of the problem-solving process. It is also the most lengthy. There are two parts to deciding on a social problem: recognizing the problem and identifying it.

Recognizing the Problem or Issue

A social issue, as troublesome and painful as it may be, is not a "problem" until someone recognizes and labels it as such. Many times social pain and dysfunction exist, but people ignore or deny their existence. Racial discrimination of African Americans, for example, has existed since the first slaves were imported to this country. However, racism was ac-cepted as a normal way of life among many members of society until the strife of the Civil War and was perpetuated even after that until the community of African Americans decided to actively resist. In the same way, the problem of drunken drivers was not a nationally recognized issue until the mother of a child killed by a drunk driver organized MADD— Mothers Against Drunk Drivers.

Identifying the Problem

Social problems tend to be large in scope. Once you recognize that a problem exists, the group with which you are working needs to identify what specific problem or issues are important. Make a list of these problems or issues. Then compare your list with the following guides[23] and narrow your choice to one.

1. *Resolve successfully.* Choose an issue that the group has a good chance of resolving successfully. Consider the amount of energy, time, and money you have available. Do not choose a problem that is beyond the resources or the limitations of your group. Rather than a large problem, choose a smaller one that the group has a good chance of solving.

A problem-solving task group works to choose a problem it can resolve successfully.

2. *Legitimacy.* Choose a problem over which the group has some legitimacy. Community problems are so broad that most of them can be seen as legitimate ones that you can address. However, if you are dependent on an agency, make sure that your work falls under the agency's umbrella. Otherwise, you will find your source of support disappear, or else you will be in conflict with your agency. Sometimes the problem being addressed crosses the boundaries of several agencies. In this case it may be helpful to develop a coalition in which agencies and groups from a number of arenas may join together in the change effort.

3. *Under your control.* Select a problem that is potentially under the control of your group or one

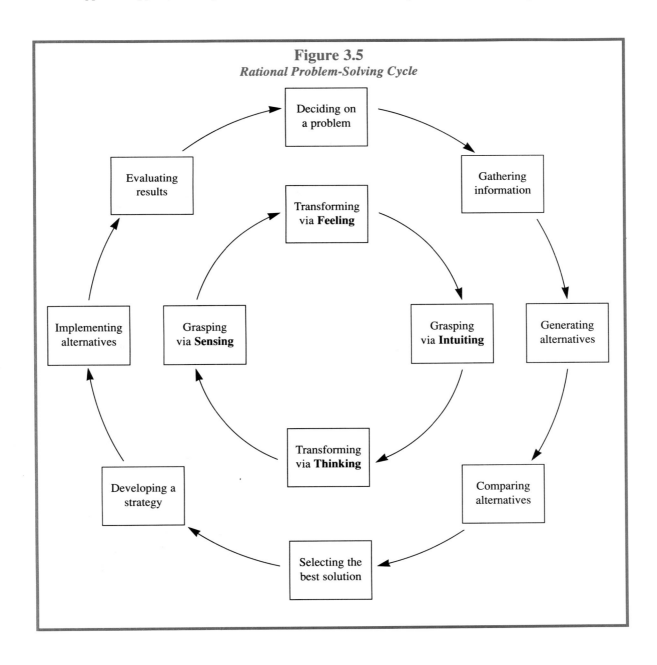

Figure 3.5
Rational Problem-Solving Cycle

in which control needs to be established. Consider, for example, a group of low-income residents concerned about the inadequate schooling their children are receiving. They have little control over the school board or its policies. They have no input into the amount of funding available for their children in comparison to other, more affluent school districts. This does not mean that they cannot become empowered to gain control or change school policies. They can strategize to gain seats on the board or put pressure on local governments to make funding more equitable.

4. *Meaning.* Choose a problem that is pressing and current. It should have meaning to the group members, be deeply felt, and be one that can excite and energize them. Its solution should be important to the community as a whole, and the community should have a vested interest in having the situation resolved.

5. *Beneficial effects.* Finally, select a problem that, when resolved, will have far-reaching beneficial effects. By changing one piece of a problem, you may begin a process that can bring changes in an entire system. In this way, you can initiate a series of events that can cause an entire facade to crumble. At the very least you can prevent future problems from occurring. Make sure that what you are attempting will have a major impact. The effort and energy you and your group expends should pay off.

If your group has misgivings about any of these issues, resolve them before you commit yourself. Your group needs to be fully invested in the issue on which it will be working. After you have identified the problem on which you will work, write down a tentative statement of the problem as it appears to your group.

Gathering Information about the Problem

There are a number of ways of gathering data about the problem. The people of the community or organization are the best source of information about what is wrong, and you will spend lots of time talking to them. On a more formal level, however, you

can administer surveys to community or organization members or interview key leaders. You may also collect information about the problem from agency records, newspapers, or other sources. Macro social workers often bring speakers together to discuss the problem from various points of view. Chapter 6 "Becoming a Macro Social Work Researcher," provides details about these specific methods of gathering data about the problem.

Regardless of the method you use, however, there are a number of questions that you will need to ask. These are who, where, when, why, and how the problem occurred.

Asking Why: Observing Patterns

Asking why gets at causation, helping you form a social diagnosis of the problem. Once you understand why a social condition exists you have some control over it. Look at your problem definition and then ask "why" until you can go no farther. Suppose, for example, you are working with a community on lack of police protection. Ask yourself, Why is there lack of police involvement? Because the city's priorities are elsewhere may be the answer. Why are they elsewhere? Because neighborhood residents lack input to decision making. Why do they lack input? Because they have no effective voice in the process. Why do they have no voice? Because they are not organized effectively. Asking "why" questions this way helps you focus on one possible cause and allows you to see patterns that you can use to correct the problem.

Where: Locating the Pain

While you might want to track down the cause of a social problem, practically speaking, this may be a waste of time. Like the ripples in a pond, one problem creates multiple effects, each of which spread out from its source, touching more and more systems. Furthermore, the ultimate cause of a social problem, even if known, may be irrelevant to its effects. The series of events leading up to the Civil War in the United States, for example, began with the importation of the first slave into this country. Knowing this fact adds nothing to resolving the eventual conflict and resultant racial discrimination that the act set in motion.

Causation cannot be undone, but the effects of causation can be understood and dealt with. Spend your time understanding the effects of social problems and discovering *where* in the system the problem is most acute. The problem of "where" may be a physical location. Where in a city or community do the homeless congregate, for example? Where are immigrants collecting or slums developing?

The social pain may not be located in a geographical place but may be in particular groups of people who become victims. In the past, for example, very few services nationwide were provided for persons who were developmentally disabled. Uniting together, parents, friends, and professionals identifying themselves as a community pressed for changes in education, housing, and access. Bit by bit, attitudes changed and services improved.

Who: The People

By asking "who," you pinpoint victims and perpetrators. Victims are those who are damaged by a social problem. They are the poor, the dispirited, the alienated. For example, a bank may have an unwritten rule to not approve home loans within a certain area of the city that it assesses as risky—usually areas high in minorities or low-income residents. Such policies, called red-lining, tend to discriminate against minority neighborhoods, making it next to impossible for people to obtain home loans or even to improve homes, resulting in run-down neighborhoods. In these kinds of communities, almost everyone is a victim.

Perpetrators are those who cause, condone, or provide the conditions "enabling" the social problem to exist. It is the individual acts of specific leaders, businesses, or organizations that formalize and institutionalize problems in our social systems. Target the individuals in charge, the leaders, administrators, policymakers, executives, or others who have control over and can make changes in the system. If redlining policies exist, for example, who are the particular bank employees, officers, and trustees who formulate and carry out those policies? The process of identifying those responsible for instigating, creating, perpetuating, or condoning social problems provides the victims of social problems with tangible, personal targets.

When: The Time Frame

When did the problem arise, and how did it develop over time? Has the problem been increasing over the last six months or year? What specific events triggered the problem, and when did they occur? Answers to these questions help your community understand the history, severity, and patterns of the problem.

How: The Development of the Problem

Devising a chronology of the problem will tell you about decisions that were made, who made them, and perhaps why they were made. If you can understand the reasons that things are the way they are, you have come a way toward changing them. You may find out that decisions that once made sense are now outmoded. A system has failed to adjust to changing conditions. Or, mistakes were made that have not been corrected, and a defective system is being perpetuated. When decision-makers defend the current system by saying "We've always done it this way," there is a good chance that systems inertia is carrying them along. Understanding the history of policies and practices can help extricate people from dysfunctional patterns.

On the other hand, you may find that a conscious and planned series of events were construed to deprive people of power, control, or resources and to keep them in a position of subservience for the benefit of others. Knowing this history can uncover patterns of systematic abuse and provide you with evidence you can use in your struggle to restore justice.

Generating Alternative Solutions

After a problem is selected and defined, and you have gathered as much information about it as you can, you are ready to consider potential solutions. If the problem has been well researched, generating solutions should be relatively easy. They should flow naturally from the data. Generate as many alternative solutions that can legitimately solve the problem as you can.

There are some hazards in developing solutions, however.[24] For example, there is a tendency to jump to solutions before you have explored the problem in depth. If you do this you may be fitting the problem to your solution. Sometimes people have pet solutions that they use for any situation, or they may have a tendency to accept the first solution that comes to mind. Try to avoid these pitfalls, because you will be limiting your search for the solution or solutions that will best help you remediate the social problem.

One way of opening up the group to consider all possible alternatives is to list every possible aspect of the problem that should be changed. Each potential solution should help accomplish at least some of your goals.

Assessing and Comparing Alternatives

After you have generated several alternative solutions, decide which one is best. Assess each alternative in terms of particular criteria that will give you some indicator of success. One way of doing this is by means of a *force field analysis.* Force field analysis was developed by Kurt Lewin and is based on the idea that in every change situation there are *restraining forces,* also called disadvantages or costs incurred in a solution, and *driving forces,* also called advantages or benefits.[25] For example, you may decide that for your situation some of the constraints are the time, money, and manpower that each alternative requires. These can be considered the costs of implementing that particular solution. You and your group will discover that some solutions are more costly or time consuming, or require more manpower than others. You need to estimate the strength of the restraining forces on a scale. In the example in figure 3.6 I have used a scale of 0 to 5.

After you look at the costs, consider the driving forces or benefits. Some solutions may give a higher payoff than others in terms of meeting the quantity of services, quality of services, or solving the problem more effectively. Once you have calculated the strengths of both the restraining and the driving forces, array them on a scale such as the one in figure 3.6.

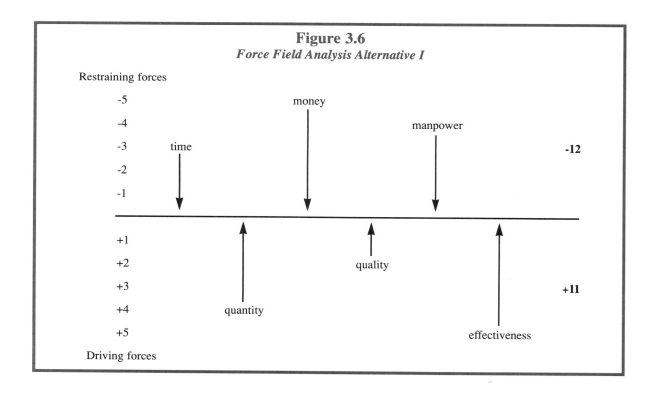

Figure 3.6
Force Field Analysis Alternative I

Choosing the Best Solution

Add up the driving forces and subtract this number from the total restraining forces. The alternative with the highest number will give you an indication of which solution has more power. By comparing each alternative solution you can see which ones will have more potential for success. Force field analysis is a way of deciding rationally on the best solution. In the force-field diagram in figure 3.6, would the alternative be one to seriously consider? Why or why not?

Developing a Change Strategy

Deciding what to do about the solution is called a *strategy for change*. In many cases the change strategy will flow directly from the problem solution and almost be self-evident. However, there is a more formal way of developing a strategic plan. Here are the various steps that your action group can take to develop a change strategy.

Goals

Planning for action begins with setting goals. Begin with ultimate or long-range goals. More than likely there will be only one or two ultimate goals. On a chalkboard or large pad of newsprint, place a long-range goal on the far right. Work backwards identifying intermediate goals and immediate, short-term objectives. List all of the events that should occur that might precede accomplishing each long-range goal.

Objectives

What specific things need to be accomplished in order to reach the mid-range goals? These become objectives. Each objective should meet three criteria. It should be (1) time limited, (2) specific, and (3) measurable. For example, an objective might be: "The police department will provide one additional patrol officer on Elm Street by June 1, 1996." Branch these objectives off from the mid-range goals. You may have several objectives preceding each goal.

Tasks

Break down each objective into tasks required. Tasks are specific duties or steps group members must take to reach objectives. Tasks may be printing information, calling and attending meetings, contacting the media, and meeting with perpetrators, among others.

Tactics

Tactics tell you how to carry out tasks, especially confrontations, activities that are politically sensitive, or those that are complex and require coordination of members. Tactics of social action include leafletting, picketing, and sit-ins. When deciding on specific tactics, be sure that group members give thought to the kinds of resistance that they might expect from power figures and how they might overcome resistance.

Targets

Your tactics will often include identifying specific targets. Targets are those individuals or groups that are the key power figures that you want to influence, change, or co-opt, or whose support is crucial to the project.

Reviewing Your Strategy

Review your strategy. Look for duplications. Some issues may be irrelevant or subsidiary. New ideas may have occurred to your action task group. Revise the plan. Develop a backup or *contingency plan*. Try to anticipate what could go wrong with your strategy. For example, what if you do not meet your objectives? What alternative objectives are there? What if your tactics backfire? What other tactics or targets should be considered? Be prepared to think through these issues so that you will not be caught off guard or surprised if things do not go the way that you expect.

Now you are ready to finalize the plan. Decide on the sequence of events that need to be orchestrated in order to accomplish your group's goals. Do certain events, tasks, and activities need to precede others? Which things do the members need to do first, second, or third? Create time lines. Then assign individuals to tasks and get commitments from the members to carry them out. Make a list of their assignments and deadlines.

Implementing the Solution

Implementation means carrying out the project or the program that you have decided upon. Members of your group become the nucleus around which the community becomes organized. Community meetings, for example, inform people about the problem and the proposed solutions. Members also promote community involvement, assist you in soliciting help from community members, and begin organizing the change effort. Your group members may chair committees or lead other task forces committed to carrying out the goals of the project, or even become a formal organization.

Evaluating the Results

Throughout the change process you need to evaluate your progress. Perhaps the easiest, most useful, and most immediate evaluation is feedback. After meetings, or at least periodically, the task force should spend time "debriefing." Debriefing gives the group a chance to share stories, let off steam, get recognition, enjoy triumphs, and obtain support from each other when things have not gone well.

Debriefing empowers the group and provides a learning tool for the members. Members learn about change and the change process by sharing. Learning takes place as people talk about problems, share perceptions, and wrestle with what to do next. The social situation becomes a problem to be solved, a puzzle to be figured out.

Debriefing also allows the task group to regroup and plan where to go from here. After an attempt at implementation, your task group has acquired information about resistance, system dynamics, and power structures. Debriefing helps you and the task group determine whether predictions about what would happen were correct. Armed with this information, your group can reassess the situation, modify its strategy, plan, and move ahead.

In addition to debriefing, more formal evaluation processes may also be used. For example, keep-ing records of meetings and activities and referring back to them, particularly progress toward objectives and goals, will help you shift strategy, keep track of events, and make sense of what has occurred. Keep a log or a journal about the project. Writing often helps you develop ideas and gain insights. This information can also be helpful in developing a history of your change effort.

An Action Approach to Problem Solving

As valuable as it is, the rational problem-solving process may have considerable limitations. Community social workers require approaches that center on the history, values, and aspirations of a particular community culture within a political milieu and framework of human values. In the long run, these are more important than quantifiable data, because they are the key elements by which a community is formed and healed. While social policies can be rationally decided upon, the turbulent environment of politics requires the mobilization of the differing preferences of several contending actors. Rational problem solving will often need to give way to bargaining and negotiation between these actors. In addition, rational problem solving may be useless in working with ethnically diverse populations who prize traditional community values, relationships, and methods over rational choice.

Rational problem solving needs to be supplemented with other ways of deciding. One of these is the action model[26] of decision making. Action is defined by Michael Harmon as "a concept that directs attention to the everyday meanings people give to their actions."[27] Action theory is based on a model of man that "focuses on the study of subjective meanings that people attach to their own actions and the actions of others."[28] It begins with and is centered in the needs and perceptions of community members themselves, not in an external goal that a decision-maker imposes on the community. It is nonlinear and fluid.

Drawing on your intuitive function, you as a macro social worker immerse yourself in the hopes and dreams of the community members. You imagine their future. Then, focusing on the values and beliefs of that community, you develop an understanding of the truth as they see it and values from their historical experiences. Then you apply traditional rational problem solving, using thinking and sensing as a way of making the dreams real and their values come alive.

Community Focused

You always begin in the community where people are and follow the lead of the people you serve. It is not you who charts the direction or calls the shots. It is the group of oppressed people in the community that you serve who determine the content of the action. It is, after all, their future and their process. You can help direct the action, but it is they who carry it out and bear the brunt of its failure or its success in their lives and culture.

When actors mutually decide on a course of action based on common or shared values, they are empowered because it is the community's values which are being furthered, not some outsider's. Community members have a commitment to the process because they are actively engaged in its formulation. By using the very human

> material in the turbulent action setting, for example, people can unrandomize variables and literally create their own constraints. By means of action itself, the environment [or situation] is altered, including the stock of information that may inform future action . . . [and] it may sometimes be more sensible to act, in an "experimental mode," and *then* observe, than to make decisions about whether to act *after* information is gathered and predictions are made about the likely success of actions based on that information.[29]

Nonlinear

The action model is nonlinear. The shortest route may not be the best way, nor is efficiency always the highest value in solving problems. When working in communities, for example, you will often find no single preferred ordering of goals. You may need to work on multiple goals simultaneously, some of which may aim at short-term gains while others seek long-term solutions.

Because of the multiplicity of goals and strategies, you may not be able to start the problem-solving process at the beginning. Sometimes you begin in the middle of a situation and work backward to discover what has happened and sort out things before you can proceed with generating alternative solutions. You may need to use your feeling function or sensing function at different points. You may work backward or forward or do several parts of the process at once. Sometimes you may need to shorten or even eliminate steps, returning to them later as you assess what has happened.

A clear understanding of the problem and its causes may come only *after* you have tried to work on a solution. Simply trying something out may help test the "lay of the land," giving you and the group ideas about what might work and what may not work. In this case you have begun at the "end" and have worked backward toward the beginning.

Intuitive

While rational problem solving relies almost exclusively on sensing and thinking, the action model also makes use of intuition—people's dreams and visions, hope and faith. While visions and dreams are non rational and non quantifiable, they are often the substance on which community is built. You intuitively grasp the hopes of people and then with faith you help make those dreams real. The wisdom literature of the Hebrews recognized this truth: "Where there is no vision, the people perish."[30]

> It is a common experience that before action, a human being visualizes a desired result. He visualizes the future and undertakes to bring it about. People whose purposes cannot be understood appear to us enigmatic, dangerous and frequently disturbed. Human beings try to understand one another by believing to understand their purposes. Human behavior is therefore presumed to be wish relevant . . . to seek out purpose behind apparent purposelessness. To make sense out of nonsense seems to be a basic human need . . . to establish one's similarity with others by ascribing to them purpose because we experience purpose ourselves. The assumption of purpose as an element of human behavior thus expresses a need for community with others.[31]

Value Centered

Rational problem-solving tends to be value neutral. It views emotions as unreliable and values antithetic to objective fact gathering.[32] Rational problem solving is a purely "technical calculation of means and ends; it contributes nothing substantive to the grasp of ends or values."[33] It accepts the ends of decision-makers or those in power as they are given and is incapable of evaluating the goodness or badness of those goals or ends. This is why rational problem solving is *"instrumental . . . it functions to map out terrain and achieve goals."*[34] In contrast, the action model specifically includes values such as shared decision making, moral responsibility, and creativity.

Classical rational decision making tends to alienate and fragment people. It separates those who make decisions from those who carry them out. Rational decision making assumes that there are two classes of people: managers who decide and functionaries who carry out the decisions. In social work this leads to a dichotomy between professionals who are the actors and clients who are acted upon.

The action model dissolves these differences because it is based on mutual decision making. "The motive or normative expression of our sociality is mutuality in primary face-to-face relationships, [and] the motives underlying responsible action is a function of the *commitment* of one person to the other—as persons."[35] Those who carry out decisions to effect changes in the social environment are also those who are the decision-makers. They not only bear responsibility for their own actions but also benefit from the power of deciding and accepting the consequences of those decisions. By taking charge of their own destiny, by deciding *and* doing, community members actively engage those in power who impose functional and dependency-creating roles on them. They challenge the assumption that they cannot or ought not decide and act on their own behalf and for their own welfare.

African Americans, for example, decided that they would not allow themselves to be degraded by accepting an inferior status position. By so doing and suffering threats, jail, and punishment, they captured the moral imagination and conscience of the American people as a whole.

The action model demands that people take moral responsibility for their decisions. "Actors are agents who must bear the moral brunt of their actions, rather than shift the blame or responsibility to other people or external standards of correctness."[36] Actors are not mere functionaries carrying out the decisions or commands of others, but see themselves as responsible for the consequences of their actions.[37] The action model does not allow people to escape responsibility by blaming others, society, or to external standards of correctness such as laws or even institutionally acceptable moral codes. Such excuses as "I was only following orders" or "I had no choice because these are the rules" are unacceptable because they condone personal irresponsibility.[38]

As community members engage in issues of shared decision making, they begin to define for themselves standards of right and wrong that transcend or broaden the moral confines of society. Action theory thrives on differences and so allows for innovation in problem solving. People themselves, not external goals or objective criteria, are the content of solutions. Community members form the solution, and they *are* the solution. "Face-to-face interaction enables decisions to be desegregated and permits the formulation of unique decision for unique circumstances."[39] This is the opposite of rational problem solving, which often resists innovation and tends to keep shooting for certain goals even though the situation may have changed.

While action oriented problem solving is innovative, it is also centered in certain values that it holds to be absolute. Among these values are justice and human dignity. When these values come into conflict with established norms, the established mode of operation and conventional values may be shaken up by placing community members at the center of moral conflicts and dilemmas. The result may be decisions that may be viewed as irrational by traditional society. Community members sacrifice their own self-interest for the interests of others. They join together in a common cause out of concern for justice against all odds of succeeding. They place the good of the community above their own survival.

Conclusion

We use rational problem solving in a context of human needs, interests, and aspirations, within a milieu of politics and the framework of democracy. Rational problem solving tends to be based on objectivity, prediction, and control and assumes that we can know the real world in its raw and uncontaminated state. If we understand this world, we can make decisions that reflect a measure of truth about the systems we observe. Rational problem solving is a "thought" process, not a rigid model. Once you have mastered its steps, you have a powerful tool that you can adapt to any number of situations. Process is a tool, not a master. One learns a particular process in order to gain mastery. It should not be done for its own sake. Like any other tool or process, therefore, rational change must be molded and adapted to the contours of the people with whom and for whom one is working.

It is important to understand that solving social problems remains a value-laden and very human enterprise. Therefore, rational problem solving has some major limitations. Action theory of problem solving, based on the "lived experience" and "active-social" model, supplements rational problem solving by placing people at the center of the problem-solving process and recognizing that values and relationships are central to any social problem solution.

KEY CONCEPTS

personality functions
thinking
intuiting
feeling
sensing
problem-solving cycle
generalist social work method
rational problem solving
deciding on a problem
gathering information
generating alternative solutions
analyzing and comparing alternatives
selecting the most cost-beneficial solution

developing a change strategy
carrying out a solution
evaluating results
rational problem-solving cycle
force field analysis
goals
objectives
tasks
techniques
contingency plan
action approach to problem solving

QUESTIONS FOR DISCUSSION

1. What are the restraining forces and the driving forces in these social problems: homelessness; poverty among children; and lack of sufficient health care?
2. Discuss the action approach and the rational problem-solving approach to the social problems listed in question 1, or other problems.

ADDITIONAL READING

Learning Theory

Kolb, David. *Learning Style Inventory.* Boston, MA: McBer and Company, 1981.

———. *Experiential Learning.* Garden City, NJ: Prentice Hall, 1984.

Kolb, David, and R. Fry. "Toward an Applied Theory of Experiential Learning." In C. Cooper, ed., *Theories of Group Processes.* London: Wiley, 1975.

Lewin, Kurt. *Field Theory in Social Sciences.* New York: Harper and Row, 1951.

Piaget, Jean. *Play, Dreams, and Imitation in Childhood.* New York: Norton, 1951.

Jungian Personality Theory

Myers, Isabel Briggs. *Introduction to Type.* Palo Alto, CA: Consulting Psychologists Press, 1987.

———. *Gifts Differing.* Palo Alto, CA: Consulting Psychologists Press, 1980.

Rational Problem Solving

Allison, Graham T. *The Essence of Decision: Explaining the Cuban Missile Crisis.* Boston, MA: Little, Brown, 1971.

Hobbes, Thomas. *Leviathan: Or the Matter, Forme, and Power of a Commonwealth Ecclesiastical and Civil.* Introduction by Richard S. Peters. Michael Oakeshott, ed. New York: Collier Books, 1962. Ch. 5, pp. 41–45.

Simon, Herbert. *Administrative Behavior: A Study of Decision-Making Processes in Administrative Organization,* 3d ed. New York: Free Press, 1976. Pp. 41, 61–109.

Watzlawick, Paul, J.N. Weakland, and R. Fisch. *Change: Principles of Problem Formation and Problem Resolution.* New York: Norton, 1974.

Weber, Max. *The Theory of Social and Economic Organizations.* A.M. Henderson, trans. Talcott Parsons, ed. Glencoe, IL: Free Press, 1947. Pp. 115–18.

CHECKLISTS

CHECKLIST 3: Group Problem-Solving Skills

The following checklist will help you assess your problem-solving skills. Mark those items that you do often, sometimes, or never. Is there a pattern in the issues you have marked? What do these patterns say about you and your problem-solving skills? What areas would you like to improve?

1. I am the kind of person who generally can see larger solutions/problems quickly.
   Often ___   Sometimes ___   Never ___

2. I like to focus on one aspect of an issue and nail it down.
   Often ___   Sometimes ___   Never ___

3. I get stuck with my own perception of a problem and find it hard to let go of it.
   Often ___   Sometimes ___   Never ___

4. I usually go along when the group moves off in a direction that I feel is wrong or bad.
   Often ___   Sometimes ___   Never ___

5. I am able to present my position clearly and succinctly.
   Often ___   Sometimes ___   Never ___

6. I tend to ramble and talk around subjects.
   Often ___   Sometimes ___   Never ___

7. People usually listen and respond to me when I present my ideas.
   Often ___   Sometimes ___   Never ___

8. When I talk, people simply wait until I'm finished and then move on.
   Often ___   Sometimes ___   Never ___

9. I find myself jumping to conclusions before the group is ready.
   Often ___   Sometimes ___   Never ___

10. I find myself looking at details and sometimes discover that I have missed the larger situation.
    Often ___   Sometimes ___   Never ___

EXERCISES

EXERCISE 13:
Solving a Social Problem

Take one of the problems you have chosen in chapter 2. Outline how you would use the rational problem-solving process to solve it. Try to be as specific as possible.

1. Give your definition of the problem.
2. What facts would you need to obtain? Where would you get those facts? How would you collect them? Who would you need to contact?
3. How would you decide on alternative solutions?
4. What kind of criteria would be useful for ranking alternative solutions to your problem?
5. What strategies can you think of?
6. How would you implement your plan?
7. How will you know whether you have achieved success?

EXERCISE 14:
Examining Modern Reason

Read the following critique of modern reason. Then answer the questions.

Critique of Modern Reason

Even though rational problem solving is so much a part of us, it is not without its critics. It is important to understand these criticisms from the outset. One stream of criticism comes from a group of philosophers and is called the philosophical attack on modern reason. This group of philosophers comprise various off-

shoots of the Frankfort School. Essentially the argument runs that while modern reason "works," it has become so pervasive that it has all but eliminated another way of thinking entirely.

In fact, this other way of thinking has a claim to be the more authentic and appropriate way of thinking about things. This way of thinking is called "substantive reason" as opposed to "instrumental" or "functional rationality," as modern reason is also called. While functional reason is scientific in that it is empirical and factual, substantive reason or classical reason is value-infused. It taps into the intuitive and moral side of thinking and challenges humans to reach for ethical constructs that are good and true in and of themselves, whether or not they can be empirically demonstrated.

The philosophical argument says that acceptance of pure instrumental reason is the "triumph of technique over purpose."[40] It allows one to reach goals faster and more efficiently, but it avoids the issues of what goals and whose goals, and the important question, "Are those the right goals?" Only by infusing modern reason with ethics can we be assured that our social policies are good or proper.

The second argument against modern reason comes from practical realists. Their argument with modern reason is not that it doesn't work but that it doesn't work well enough. This attack comes from various sources all centering around the role of the individual in problem solving. Herbert Simon, for example, says that the problem with instrumental reason is that it requires near omniscience[41] and the accumulation of near perfect information, and places nearly impossi-

ble demands on the human intellect. As a result, it has "little discernible relation to the actual or possible behavior of flesh and blood human beings."[42] Instead, says Simon, "human behavior is intendedly rational, but only limited"[43] because "administrative man can make his decisions with relatively simple rules of thumb that do not make impossible demands upon his capacity for thought."[44]

Because the individual human being cannot possibly be fully rational, there needs to be another kind of system into which he can be integrated that allows humans to reach full rationality. This system is the *organization*. According to Simon, the "organization permits the individual to approach reasonably near to objective rationality."[45] This is so because "the behavior patterns we call organizations are fundamental . . . to the achievement of human rationality in any broad sense. The rational individual is, and must be, an organized and institutionalized individual."[46] Therefore, for Simon, modern reason is no longer a function of the individual but the organizational context in which the individual is embedded. The more integrated the individual in the organizational milieu, the more nearly he or she can attain complete rationality.

The third attack on modern reason is leveled by Aaron Wildavsky and William Morrow, who assess "politics" in organizational life.[47] The political attack claims that organizational systems are themselves not really rational either. In fact, while organizations pretend to be fully rational, they are highly "irrational." Far from being rational, say these writers, decisions are really made by any number of factors in organiza-

(continued next page)

EXERCISES

tions, few of which are "rational." They are made on the basis of expediency, survival, self-interest, and short-term gains. While calculation occurs, it is often "used" not for lofty goals or for the achievement of principle but rather for the specific interests of people who are out to further their own particular agendas.

Therefore, rationality is rarely a smooth process in which agreed-upon goals are easily achieved in a linear fashion. Instead, there is pulling in all sorts of directions as individuals in positions of power seek to have their own preferences ratified by means of the political process. In this game, any number of strategies are employed that will guarantee success. Therefore, there are many political actors, each applying pressure to extract concessions from public organizations in an atmosphere of bargaining and negotiation.

Formaini takes a normative attack in rejecting rationality in the change process. He says that scientifically based (i.e. *justified*) public policy is a dream that has grown ever larger since the Enlightenment and that, perhaps, has reached its apogee now at the close of our own century. It is a myth, a theoretical illusion.[48] Formaini makes the point that while science can supply information and facts, inevitably those facts are often disputable, subject to distortions, and will always be used by decision-makers who will apply their own norms or values to them. In the last analysis

it doesn't matter what the "facts" are. What really matters is that "eventually someone has to decide the issue on purely normative grounds."[49]

In the United States that normative model is the democratic process, a system of checks and balances, combined with adherence to certain rights.[50] In spite of its weaknesses, among which is a majoritarian system of decision-making rules, Formaini says that "there is no better way to decide such issues. Reliance on tradition, whether cultural or legal, is unworkable. . . . It is the virtue of a democratic political system that its mechanisms for change are available to those who wish to organize and use them."[51]

1. Social work, and society in general, has tended to adopt premises of rational problem solving as the means by which decisions are made. While this chapter claims that rational problem solving has considerable utility, it also points out its weaknesses. Additional criticism is leveled in EXERCISE 14. What is your assessment of the utility and importance of rational problem solving?

2. Some writers have claimed that modern reason is, in reality, a truncated or partial way of thinking primarily because it does not allow for ethics to emerge in problem solving? Is this a fair criticism? Is there a way of overcoming this defect?

3. Herbert A. Simon claims that in-

dividuals are not fully rational but that rationality is provided extraneously to people by organizational systems without which humans would remain only "intendedly" rational.[52] Is Simon right or wrong? What are the implications of his assessment?

4. Aaron Wildavsky[53] and William L. Morrow[54] attack modern reason because they suggest that decision making is ultimately "irrational," at least in the political arena. Is problem solving ultimately "irrational"?

5. Formaini[55] claims that, given that rational problem solving is a myth, procedural democracy is the best available system we have for solving our social problems. What is your opinion of this assessment?

6. Can you think of some difficulties in applying modern reason to social issues? For example, modern reason assumes one has complete knowledge of the consequences of alternative decisions. Is this ever possible? How does this assumption relate to Robert Merton's assessment in chapter 2 that many social problems are the result of unintended consequences of our decisions?

7. If modern reason is the best way of thinking about and solving social problems, why is it that some social problems seem to continue to evade resolution? If rational problem solving is not the best way, what alternatives are there?

CHAPTER 4

Leadership: The Hallmark of Macro Social Work

Laura Jane Addams, macro social worker, was without a doubt one of the great social leaders of our time. . . . Wherever there was a need, she was open to experiment, establishing programs, building relationships, improving neighborhoods, and forging community.

Leaders take us on journeys to places we have never been before.
— Jim Kouzas and Barry Posner

These are the hard times in which a genius would wish to live. Great necessities call forth great leaders.

—Abigail Adams, Letter to Thomas Jefferson, 1790

IDEAS IN THIS CHAPTER

Jane Addams, Social Leader

Year after year during her lifetime she was voted the greatest woman in the United States, the greatest in the world, and on one occasion, the greatest in history.[1] Even today, in a survey of one hundred professors of history she was ranked second only to Eleanor Roosevelt as the most influential woman of our century. Publicist and persuader, social reformer, crusader, and social activist in the causes of progressive education, housing reform, child-labor legislation, criminology, labor organizing, recreation, direct democracy, feminism, treatment of the immigrant, pacifism, and more, she was vitally engaged in almost every important issue of her day.[2]

She was Laura Jane Addams, one of the pioneers of the progressive era in American history, winner of the Nobel Peace Prize and macro social worker. Born on September 6, 1860, two months before Abraham Lincoln was elected to the presidency, she became valedictorian and president of her senior class at Rockford Female Seminary in an era when there were no clearly defined roles for young college-educated women. Most women became homemakers. Jane Addams was clearly out of the mainstream. Intensely sensitive, wealthy, and a born leader, but with no clear arena in which to expend her gifts, she entered a period of seven years of deep personal suffering, incapacitating back pain, and depression. Except for a brief period in medical school, these apparently fruitless and painful years were a period of gestation, in which her character, determination, and sense of mission and purpose were being formed.

Restless and unhappy, Jane Addams had no thought of entering social work when she landed in England at Southampton three days before Christmas 1887. She had come into direct contact with the poor for the first time on an earlier trip to Europe. Now, she and her companion, Ellen Starr, investigated social work in the slums of London and met Canon Samuel A. Barnett, founder of the first Settlement House, Toynbee Hall. She lived at Toynbee Hall for six weeks—it was an experience that would change her life.

Like Barnett, she saw how the absence of leadership in the poorer districts had allowed local government to fall into disrepair. Guilt at the desertion of duty by those who had been trained to lead impelled her to absorb the milieu of Toynbee Hall and its philosophy, ideals of service, leadership, community, and culture in the face of massive urban disorganization and poverty. It was this experience that ended her desperate years of struggle. Jane Addams had found her mission in life. She not only conceptualized a new way of life but also lived it.

Upon arriving back in the United States, Jane Addams and Ellen Starr bought Hull House, a building in a poor section of Chicago, and turned it into a social settlement. For the next forty years she lived not as an observer of social causes but as a resident of a Chicago slum. She engaged people where they were. Unafraid to get her hands soiled by the squalor around her, she determined to learn from the homeless poor, immigrants, working-class women, children, and the elderly. She learned from experience, from trying things out. Wherever there was a need, she was open to experiment, establishing programs, building relationships, improving neighborhoods, and forging community. "She had the kind of mind which could tolerate and even thrive on uncertainty and new experiences."[3]

Jane Addams was a visionary, a part of the radical tradition in America. Ahead of her time, she planted the seeds of reform, many of which were to bear fruit years later. "The poor were poor," she said, "because of misconstructed social environment, not because of a defect in themselves."[4] Americans, in general, proved resistant to this idea.

She advocated for the rights of women and laborers, and was "concerned with the poor, immigrants, and children simultaneously; and she seemed to regard all of them as sources of the social salvation which she continuously sought."[5] She was convinced that with those who were the outcasts of society she could "bring to reality the social vision which she had been formulating. . . . She wanted to enfold the poor, immigrants, children, blacks, and women to full participation in American life, not only because as a matter of right they deserved it, but because all of society would be redeemed by their inclusion."[6]

Concrete experience and envisioning the future, however, were only the beginning. As she reflected on the misery she saw around her, Jane Addams "effectively convinced Americans . . . of the seriousness of the problems the nation faced, and of the

need for change."[7] A publicist for almost every social cause of her time, author of twelve books and hundreds of articles and speeches, she became a master at persuading people to take up the cause of reform.

But more than simply reflecting and writing about human misery, she put her words into action, clearly pointing the direction these changes should take. As a leader of the settlement house movement, Jane Addams was instrumental in developing day care, kindergartens, adult education, group work and recreation, immigrant education, sanitation, public health and labor research, unions, child welfare and child labor legislation, programs to combat juvenile delinquency, neighborhood playgrounds, probation services, food safety, the eradication of sweat shops, and improvement of sewage disposal. She supported and was active in the Illinois Equal Suffrage Association, the Christian Socialists, the Chicago Peace Society, the National Consumer's League, the Legal Aid Society, the Juvenile Protective Association, and many labor unions. She had a vision of "an America in which women not only had the vote but . . . would aspire and have opportunity to become college professors, legislators, policymakers in the executive departments of government."[8]

Even before World War I Addams was a fervent advocate for women's suffrage and peace, nearly destroying her reputation and credibility. Her unwavering efforts were finally recognized in 1931, when she was awarded the Nobel Peace Prize. She died in 1935 in the midst of the great reforms of Franklin D. Roosevelt and Harry Hopkins, each of whom followed her legacy—that the role of government in social welfare was not only practical but necessary.[9] Laura Jane Addams, macro social worker, was one of the great social leaders of our time.

Introduction

The hallmark of macro social work practice is *leadership*.[10] A leader helps communities of people take risks and envision a better future for themselves, encourages commitment, and helps people move ahead along a path to accomplish their goals. Leadership comes from innate personality characteristics and, more importantly, how abilities are used. Like Jane Addams, each step of a leader's personal journey is a challenge in exercising his or her thinking, intuiting, feeling, and sensing functions.

Social work has been a profession of social leaders. Our heritage is full of people who

> manifested leadership both within and outside the profession. We have had leaders of great significance to the development of the profession and of professional expertise, and we have had some who achieved a prominent place in the community at large. . . . Jane Addams, Edward T. Devine, Florence Kelly, Edith Abbot, and Harry Hopkins . . . earned reputations beyond the social work community, influencing the course of social welfare and the quality of life in our country in a broader sense.[11]

A leader helps people take risks and envision a better future for themselves. Here, Dr. Martin Luther King, Jr., addresses a crowd in Washington, D.C., August 1963.

In spite of this history, however, the "role assigned to leadership by the social work profession has declined in recent years," according to Burton Gummer.[12] The de-emphasis of social work leadership has been the result of an intraprofessional "struggle for primacy between individual intervention and social change to improve the quality of life."[13] The resultant retreat of social work leadership is "in sharp contrast to fields like business and public administration, where the preparation of graduates to assume leadership positions is given high priority."[14] There is a great need for the social work leaders to recapture "the profession's vision of social welfare and social justice."[15]

In this chapter you will learn about a variety of theories of leadership and have an opportunity to explore what leadership is and how your own particular mix of personal qualities can help you find a leadership style and role. Much of what is called leadership today is actually management and has grown out of the attempts of organizational psychologists to understand how managers of large, complex organizations can operate more effectively and efficiently. You need to understand at the outset that there is a discrepancy between leadership, which is helping people get where they want to go or empowering them to develop a better future for themselves, and management, which is the process of inducing people to accomplish the goals of others, namely owners of large, complex organizational systems. One of the implications of this shift in meaning is that leadership, classically conceived of as a process of personal engagement with community, has become the domain of formal organizational systems and organizational theorists. As a result, when you read about leadership today, substitute the word *management,* because unless the writer qualifies the term this is what he or she is talking about. Conventional leadership (management) is based on a functional idea of human relations in which the person in charge applies techniques to attain a level of behavior and performance that leads to goal accomplishment. It is most commonly used in developing social programs, in social planning, in administration, and in improving organizational functioning.

After describing conventional leadership theory, I will apply the action theory described earlier to leadership and show how you can use action-oriented leadership to improve your own practice and, deepen the quality of leadership in social work.

Conventional Leadership Theories

Since the 1920s, leadership theorists have tried to find the elusive ingredient by which some people can influence others. I will trace this history to its current point, situational leadership theory, and then go beyond it to a theory I call group life-cycle theory of leadership. Then, I will show how you can apply the group life-cycle theory of leadership to macro social work.

Trait Theory

Early psychologists attempted to define leadership by means of personality traits.[16] Hundreds of traits were thought to be associated in some way with leadership. However, no definitive listing was agreed upon nor was there a clear positive relationship between specific traits and leadership ability. Eugene E. Jennings concluded, "Fifty years of study have failed to produce one personality trait or set of qualities that can be used to discriminate leaders and nonleaders."[17]

The Leadership Triad

In 1938, one of the single most influential studies of leadership was conducted by Kurt Lewin, R. Lippett, and R. White.[18] Of the hundreds of traits that seemed to characterize good leadership, Lewin et al. identified three clusters of traits, each forming a leadership style.

One style was *authoritarian*. Here, the leader was directive and did not allow much participation. The *democratic* leader encouraged group discussion, sharing, and decision making. The *laissez-faire* leader was highly nondirective. He or she provided very little overt direction to the group. In order to test these styles, the researchers instructed volunteer leaders to adopt one of these styles in leading groups of ten-year-old boys. Each of these styles was experimentally manipulated to under-

stand how it affected such variables as satisfaction and frustration-aggression.

While the results overall were inconclusive, the study did suggest that different styles did produce different reactions among the group members. Groups having autocratic leaders generated high degrees of hostility or apathy in members. Laissez-faire leaders also produced aggressive reactions in members. Leaders displaying democratic leadership, however, generally produced fewer negative reactions than either autocratic or laissez-faire leaders.

The Lewin, Lippitt, and White study provided an advance over the trait theory. Reducing traits to several clearly defined styles provided a model that was simpler and easier to understand. The idea of "style" implied that leadership is not a fixed characteristic of one's personality but is more fluid. A style is something that one can "put on" and adapt. One's leadership style affects group members in varying ways that can be predicted. Finally, democratic leadership style was seen as the "best" style, at least for some groups. The extremes of either laissez-faire permissive leadership or autocratic domineering leadership were seen as less effective.

McGregor's Theory X and Theory Y

In 1960 Douglas McGregor wrote what is perhaps one of the most influential books in the field of leadership, *The Human Side of Enterprise*,[19] in which he proposed two theories of leadership based on the nature of man and work. One of these he called Theory X and the other, Theory Y.

Theory X assumes that the average human has an inherent dislike of work and will avoid it. Individuals must be coerced, controlled, directed, or threatened to produce. People avoid responsibility and take the route of least resistance.[20]

Theory Y, on the other hand, asserts that people want to accept responsibility, learn, and work. External inducements, punishment, and coercion are not always effective. Instead, people have the capacity for self-direction, growth, independence, and self-reliance. Commitment results from people being rewarded for their achievements.[21]

Theory X tends to be pessimistic, static, and closed. Theory Y is optimistic, growth oriented, open, and humanistic. While McGregor emphasized that these two theories are not polar opposites, most managers accepted the implicit message that " 'good leadership' is generally described as democratic rather than authoritarian, and employee-centered rather than production-centered, concerned with human relations rather than with bureaucratic rules."[22]

McGregor's concepts, therefore, lent themselves to a further refinement of leadership theory, the notion that there are two different leadership variables that are basic to and underlie leadership. These two aspects are people orientation, expressed in Theory Y, and task or productivity orientation, expressed in Theory X.

McGregor's concept was empirically validated by Rensis Likert of the University of Michigan's Institute for Social Research, who attempted to understand those characteristics that led to success as a line supervisor. He found that high-performing supervisors focused their attention on the "human aspects of their subordinates problems, and on endeavoring to build effective work groups with high performance goals."[23] Likert called these supervisors "employee-centered" (Theory Y). Supervisors who kept constant pressure on production, whom he called task or "job-centered" (Theory X), were more often found to have low-producing sections.[24]

While Likert believed his research showed that "employee centered" supervision was the "best" leadership style, it also showed that there was some inconsistency between the two styles.

Curiously, one out of eight of the job-centered (Theory X) supervisors developed high-producing groups while three out of nine employee-centered (Theory Y) supervisors ended up with *low*-producing sections. In other words, 15 percent of job-centered supervisors whose Theory X style was theoretically supposed to result in poor performance actually created high performance, and 30 percent of employee-centered (Theory Y) supervision that should have produced high performance resulted in poor productivity.

The conclusion was that while the employee-centered style did work much of the time, there were conditions under which it was not effective, and while job-centered supervision was less effective much of the time, there were situations in which it was superior to an employee-centered leadership style.[25] While people/employee-centeredness and job/task-centeredness were empirically verified to be key components of leadership, more was going on than a simple cause-effect relationship between them. It was left to theorists at Ohio State University and to Robert R. Blake and Jane S. Mouton to refine our understanding of how these two variables interacted.

Ohio State Studies

Long before Likert and McGregor, researchers at Ohio State University had been toying with the

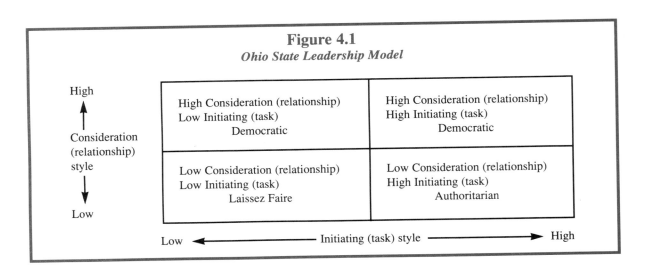

Figure 4.1
Ohio State Leadership Model

High ↑ Consideration (relationship) style ↓ Low	High Consideration (relationship) Low Initiating (task) Democratic	High Consideration (relationship) High Initiating (task) Democratic
	Low Consideration (relationship) Low Initiating (task) Laissez Faire	Low Consideration (relationship) High Initiating (task) Authoritarian

Low ◄——————— Initiating (task) style ———————► High

idea of a task/relationship leadership dichotomy. By observing the actual behavior of leaders in a wide variety of situations, they found that they could classify most of the activities of leaders into two behavioral categories: "initiating structure" (task/job-centered, or Theory X) and "consideration" (relationship/people-centered, or Theory Y).[26]

In agreement with Likert, they verified that leadership styles vary considerably from leader to leader. Some leaders liked to structure activities of followers in terms of task accomplishments, others concentrated on providing socio-emotional support by means of personal relationships, while still others provided little structure. No one style appeared dominant. Thus, they concluded, "task and relationship are not either/or leadership styles as the authoritarian-democratic-laissez faire continuum suggests."[27] Instead, these styles can be considered as "typologies" and plotted on two separate axes, where one axis represents consideration (task) style and the other initiating (relationship) style. (See figure 4.1).

The Ohio State study assumed that there were four leadership styles. Low Consideration (relationship)/High Initiating (task) was an authoritarian style, while Low Consideration (relationship)/Low Initiating (task) was equivalent to a laissez-faire leadership sytle. The two middle-range styles, High Consideration (relationship)/High Initiating (task) and Low Consideration (relationship)/High Initiating (task), were different types of democratic leadership styles.

Blake and Mouton's Leadership Grid

In 1964, Robert R. Blake and Jane S. Mouton, utilizing the typology developed by the Ohio State group, refined the definitions of consideration and initiating structure into concern for task or productivity and concern for people.[28] Task behavior is the extent to which a leader structures leader/member relationships, defines member roles, and establishes well-defined structures, roles, boundaries, channels of communication, and ways of getting the job done. Relationship behavior is the extent to which a leader is likely to maintain personal relationships between him- or herself and the members

of the group, provide socio-emotional support, characterized by friendship, mutual trust, and respect for followers' ideas.[29] Each of these behavioral leadership factors should be combined. The best leaders may be *both* people oriented and task oriented at the same time! Figure 4.2 shows the Leadership Grid.

While Blake and Mouton recognized the interaction between relationship and task behavior, they felt that a relationship/people orientation and a task/productivity orientation were qualities inherent in leaders. A leader who has low people orientation and low productivity orientation (1,1) would be effective under conditions where little leadership effort is required. A leader with high people orientation and low production or task orientation (1,9) would be able to sustain relationships. A leader who possessed low people orientation and high task or production orientation (9,1) would be effective when human elements interfere with accomplishing tasks. Finally, a high people and high task orientation leadership style (9,9) would be useful under conditions in which people need to be independent and goal or task oriented. While each of these styles may be productive under certain circumstances, Blake and Mouton, still wedded to finding the *best* leadership style, recommended that leaders attempt to adopt the high-relationship/high-task-orientation style as the preferred one.

A.K. Korman and One Best Way

Writing two years after Blake and Mouton published *The Managerial Grid,* A.K. Korman, in 1966, gathered and published some of the most convincing evidence dispelling the idea of a single "best" style of leadership.[30] Korman suspected that both task and relationship were not independent variables inherent in leaders, but were *affected by something else as situations changed.* It was this something else that was the key determinant of leadership, not leadership style itself.

Korman reviewed all of the studies examining the relationship between the two leadership dimensions—task orientation (production, initiating structure, Theory X) and relationship orientation (concern for people, consideration, Theory Y)—as well as a variety of intermediate variables such as salary, performance under stress, absenteeism, turnover, and so on.

While Korman did not definitively discover the missing variable, he did show that there was no "best" style. There may be any number of effective leadership styles. Korman decisively destroyed the quest for a "best" leadership style. The field was now open to find the elusive variable around which both relationship and task leadership revolved.

Fiedler's Contingency Theory

From 1951 to 1966, Fred Fiedler, an organizational psychologist, struggled to create a model that could verify the relationship between people orientation and task orientation.[31] Finally, in 1967, Fiedler inverted the whole leadership paradigm that had been accepted until then.[32] People- and task-oriented leadership styles are not constants that apply, as

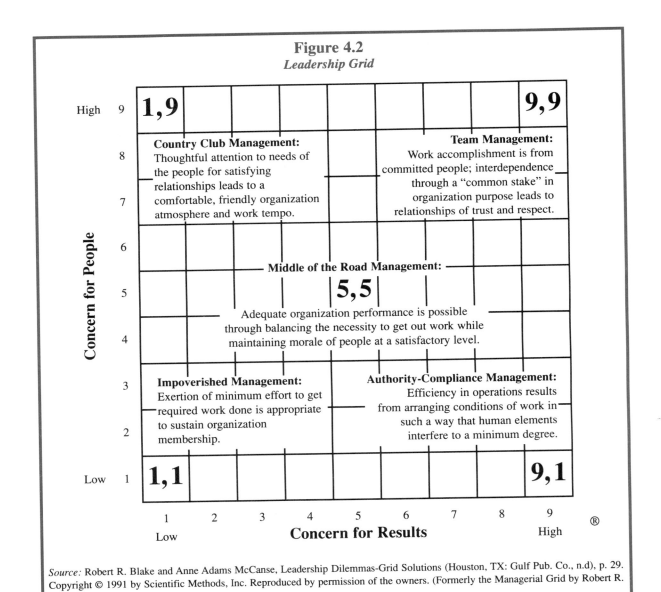

Figure 4.2
Leadership Grid

Source: Robert R. Blake and Anne Adams McCanse, Leadership Dilemmas-Grid Solutions (Houston, TX: Gulf Pub. Co., n.d), p. 29. Copyright © 1991 by Scientific Methods, Inc. Reproduced by permission of the owners. (Formerly the Managerial Grid by Robert R. Blake and Jane S. Mouton.)

Blake and Mouton thought, to any group. Instead, an appropriate leadership style must be adapted to the "situation." While one style may work for one group situation, as soon as the situation changes, that style may become dysfunctional. Leadership, therefore, is not an independent variable on which "followership" depends. Leadership is contingent on and should vary depending on nonleadership variables, such as needs of the group and its climate.[33] Fiedler "demonstrated that the 'climate' of the group had substantial impact on the effectiveness of leadership styles."[34] Therefore, *"different leadership situations require different leadership styles"*[35] (emphasis in original).

For example, a high-task/low-people-oriented style would be effective under certain situations. For other group situations, a leader must be high-task and high-people oriented. In yet others, a leader would be most effective if he or she were low-task oriented and high-people oriented, and finally, other group situations require a leader with a high-task/high-people-oriented style. Fiedler assumed that personal leadership styles were fixed in an individual's personality and that it would be easier to find a correct fit by placing a leader in a situation that matched his or her own leadership style, rather than expect the leader to adapt his or her style to each new leadership situation.[36] Fiedler's theory, therefore, explained in part why Lewin, Lippitt, and White and Likert found differing degrees of effectiveness when using autocratic, democratic, and laissez-faire leadership styles. Fiedler, however, was not able to demonstrate how leadership varied with group climate or to define *climate* in a way that showed what kinds of groups matched the variety of leadership styles. In addition, because his theory assumed that each group situation was static, as was a leader's style, Fiedler did not see that adapting one's leadership style to differing situations inside a group was possible.

Situational Leadership

In 1969 Paul Hersey and Kenneth Blanchard, two organizational psychologists, building on the Ohio State Studies, developed a leadership model that they called "Life Cycle Leadership Theory,"[37] later termed "Situational Leadership." Following Fiedler, Hersey and Blanchard showed that leadership is based on the behavior of a leader in relation to followers, not on the followers in relation to the leaders. In contrast to Fiedler, however, Hersey and Blanchard believed that leadership was not inherent in the personality of the leader and therefore was changeable. With training, people could adapt their own leadership styles to the follower's needs. Also, looking at groups from a behavioral perspective, they claimed that leader effectiveness was determined by adjusting to the readiness *level* that followers exhibit in performing specific tasks.[38] Member readiness or maturity was the missing variable on which leadership style depended.

Hersey and Blanchard assumed that individuals in groups go through various phases of development. As people develop, their needs change. A successful leader will adapt his or her style to these changing phases. Hersey and Blanchard concluded that a leader must modify his or her guidance and direction (task behavior) and the amount of socio-emotional support (relationship behavior) he or she offers depending on the task or readiness level of members. They defined four levels of member readiness. Members who are unwilling (lack motivation) and unable (lack skills) will display low readiness to successfully complete a task, engage in group problem solving, or work on a community project. A leader who is working with people with low readiness will require a high-task/low-relationship leadership style (HT/LR), a "telling" stance that is a characteristic of an autocratic leader.

Group members who are willing but who lack skills or who have the skills but need motivation will be moderately successful in completing a project. As they become increasingly motivated and skilled, the leader's style should shift to a high-task/high-relationship style (HT/HR) and take a "selling" or "coaching" stance of a democratic leader. Members will often experience a stage when their skills have progressed yet the follower needs reassurance and encouragement, or high relationship/low task (HR/LT) from the leader. Group members who are highly engaged, who have strong motivation coupled with good capabilities, will be likely to work on and successfully complete a project independently. The most effective leader of people who are highly capable and self-motivated will be one who takes a low-relationship/low-task (LR/LT) delegating style similar to that of a laissez-faire leader.[39] Having developed this model, Hersey and Blanchard adapted it to Blake and Mouton's Leadership Grid (figure 4.3).

Situational Leadership with Task Groups

Hersey and Blanchard were psychologists; they were looking at the behavior of individuals in groups. They assumed that a leader would work individually with members and bring the members along as a whole. However, while they finally located the elusive missing variable in the readiness of followers, they did not give attention to the fact that the group itself acts like a unit and develops, as Fiedler realized, a group "climate."

Every system goes through a cycle of change. Groups are no different. Toseland and Rivas explain that "four properties of the group as a whole influ-

ence how leadership emerges in the group, including (1) the size of the group, (2) the time limit in which the group is expected to accomplish its goals, (3) group dynamics, and (4) the stages of a group's development."[40] Work needs to be done in applying the factors that Toseland and Rivas have identified to group leadership. For example, I developed a model of group leadership based on the stages of the group's development that I call the "Group Life Cycle Theory" of leadership. I will describe that model in part to show how you can take an existing theory and extend it one step beyond its current state.

First, I postulated that there are four stages of the group life cycle. I generated these stages from the work of Tuckman, but modified them based on my own observations and work with groups as well as other developmental theory. The "Forming" stage occurs in the beginning of group life; the "Norming" stage and "Storming" stage are middle stages of group life; and the "Performing" stage occurs when group members are fully functioning.[41] As I observed groups and how leaders interacted with them, I discovered that groups do not move through these stages in a lockstep fashion. Instead, some groups skip a stage, others move through some stages slowly or very quickly. A group may work at several stages at the same time. Another group may move through issues involving several stages in one meeting. Some groups resolve issues at one stage only to return to those issues again later. Finally, groups vary according to their purpose, their size, and time constraints, as well as the particular mix of individuals in the group and pressures from their external environments. These and other characteristics interact and affect the life cycle of a group and the choice of leadership styles. While I feel that the group life-cycle model is an accurate one, it remains for you or someone else to investigate the relationships between these variables and group leadership.

Group Life Cycle Theory

Figure 4.4, adapted from and building on Hersey and Blanchard's model, illustrates the group life cycle theory of leadership. One of the keys to effective group leadership is assessing the level of readiness and skills of members at each stage of the

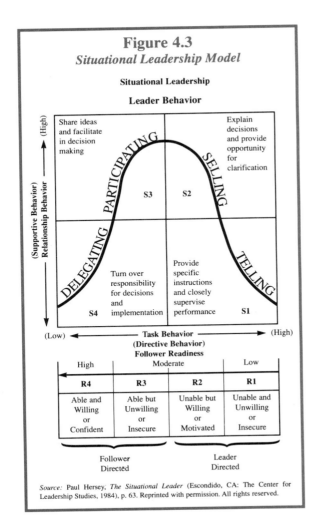

Figure 4.3
Situational Leadership Model

Source: Paul Hersey, *The Situational Leader* (Escondido, CA: The Center for Leadership Studies, 1984), p. 63. Reprinted with permission. All rights reserved.

group's life. The survey in CHECKLIST 4 will help you make such an assessment.

Each section in CHECKLIST 4 relates to a different stage of the group. Section I is the Forming stage, Section II is the Norming stage, Section III is the Storming stage, and Section IV is the Performing stage. Compare scores from each section. A low score of 7 to 14 indicates that a particular member is not operating at that stage. A medium score of 15 to 21 indicates that a member is in transition from one stage to another. A high score of 22 to 28 indicates that a member is clearly operating at this stage.

When scoring for the group as a whole, ask whether members received low, medium, or high scores for each section. Do most members rank higher in one or two sections than in the others? This will tell you at what stage the group is operating and what issues the leader needs to resolve before moving to the next stage.

If some members score high on one section and others score high on a different section, the group as a whole is operating at different levels. This tells you that members are experiencing differing levels of maturity. If members are evenly split, the leader should aim his or her style at the higher level, expecting that the less-ready members will catch up. If the group is mixed, they may need to engage in some exercises or learning experiences until all the members are operating at about the same level. Or take a look at the mix of the membership and establish a group in which most members are operating at approximately the same stage.

It is probably a good idea to have some members at a lower stage and others at a higher stage so that the higher level members can assist lower level members. However, if several members are two or more stages ahead or behind the others, the higher stage members may feel bored and out of place, or the least mature members may appear to be a drag on the group.

Stages of Task Groups

Macro social workers use task groups in solving social problems. Task groups are used in management teams, work groups, committees, and problem-solving groups. At the beginning of a group, members tend to be anxious and uncertain. The leader may not know the members as well as members know one another. Members may not have a clear understanding of their tasks and roles, know the rules and boundaries, or know what behaviors are expected of them. Task group members may be unsure about whether or not they will be personally accepted by others or by the leader, or whether their abilities will be recognized or utilized. They are unfamiliar with the processes they will be using. Although they may come with skills and experiences that are relevant to the group, they may have little concept about how to use them.

The Forming Stage

In the forming stage of a task group, members do not know what to do and how to do it. They are not able to take full responsibility for carrying out tasks or directing their own actions.[42]

As a result, the most effective stance for a task group leader is to be structured, organized, and di-

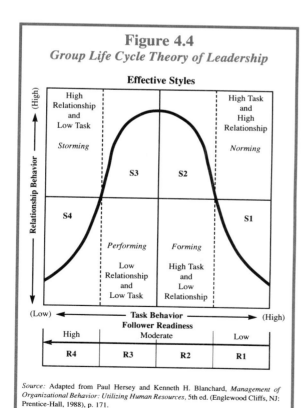

Figure 4.4
Group Life Cycle Theory of Leadership

Effective Styles

High Relationship and Low Task

Storming

High Task and High Relationship

Norming

S3   S2

S4   S1

Performing
Low Relationship and Low Task

Forming
High Task and Low Relationship

Relationship Behavior (High) / (Low)

(Low) ← **Task Behavior** → (High)
Follower Readiness

High	Moderate		Low
R4	R3	R2	R1

Source: Adapted from Paul Hersey and Kenneth H. Blanchard, *Management of Organizational Behavior: Utilizing Human Resources*, 5th ed. (Englewood Cliffs, NJ: Prentice-Hall, 1988), p. 171.

CHECKLISTS

CHECKLIST 4: Group Life Cycle Assessment

This assessment survey will help you identify the stage of the development of a group. Answer as honestly as you can to help the leader and members understand at which level the group is functioning. Circle one of the following that most closely matches your feeling about each statement:

1. Strongly Disagree   2. Disagree   3. Agree   4. Strongly Agree

If you agree with only part of a question, mark it "Disagree." After you have finished a section, add up the points to find the score.

Section I

a. I need to know what is expected of me in this group.
   1. Strongly Disagree   2. Disagree   3. Agree   4. Strongly Agree

b. I need to understand what this group is supposed to accomplish.
   1. Strongly Disagree   2. Disagree   3. Agree   4. Strongly Agree

c. I need to know when the group is supposed to accomplish its goals.
   1. Strongly Disagree   2. Disagree   3. Agree   4. Strongly Agree

d. I need to get to know members of this group.
   1. Strongly Disagree   2. Disagree   3. Agree   4. Strongly Agree

e. I need to know what the members of this group are supposed to do.
   1. Strongly Disagree   2. Disagree   3. Agree   4. Strongly Agree

f. I need to know how to proceed in this group.
   1. Strongly Disagree   2. Disagree   3. Agree   4. Strongly Agree

g. The leader of this group needs to give us clear directions about how this group is to go about its business.
   1. Strongly Disagree   2. Disagree   3. Agree   4. Strongly Agree

Score: _____

Section II

a. I know what is expected of me but am not sure how to do it.
   1. Strongly Disagree   2. Disagree   3. Agree   4. Strongly Agree

b. I am uncomfortable about some of the procedures in this group.
   1. Strongly Disagree   2. Disagree   3. Agree   4. Strongly Agree

c. I disagree with some of the rules in this group.
   1. Strongly Disagree   2. Disagree   3. Agree   4. Strongly Agree

d. I am sometimes confused about the direction the group is going.
   1. Strongly Disagree   2. Disagree   3. Agree   4. Strongly Agree

e. I think we are wasting time in this group.
   1. Strongly Disagree   2. Disagree   3. Agree   4. Strongly Agree

f. I don't think we are accomplishing everything we could.
   1. Strongly Disagree   2. Disagree   3. Agree   4. Strongly Agree

CHECKLISTS

g. I dislike the way the leader is conducting the group.
   1. Strongly Disagree   2. Disagree   3. Agree   4. Strongly Agree

Score: _____

Section III

a. This group has internal conflicts it needs to work out.
   1. Strongly Disagree   2. Disagree   3. Agree   4. Strongly Agree

b. I find myself disagreeing with members in this group.
   1. Strongly Disagree   2. Disagree   3. Agree   4. Strongly Agree

c. Some members in this group need to be more forthright.
   1. Strongly Disagree   2. Disagree   3. Agree   4. Strongly Agree

d. Some members in this group dominate discussions.
   1. Strongly Disagree   2. Disagree   3. Agree   4. Strongly Agree

e. Some members in this group tend to get off track.
   1. Strongly Disagree   2. Disagree   3. Agree   4. Strongly Agree

f. Some members in this group waste too much time.
   1. Strongly Disagree   2. Disagree   3. Agree   4. Strongly Agree

g. The leader needs to help group members work through interpersonal issues.
   1. Strongly Disagree   2. Disagree   3. Agree   4. Strongly Agree

Score: _____

Section IV

a. Members of this group demonstrate that they know what to do and are able to do it.
   1. Strongly Disagree   2. Disagree   3. Agree   4. Strongly Agree

b. Rules in this group are jointly worked out with everyone.
   1. Strongly Disagree   2. Disagree   3. Agree   4. Strongly Agree

c. This group is well on its way to accomplishing its goals.
   1. Strongly Disagree   2. Disagree   3. Agree   4. Strongly Agree

d. The procedures in this group are clear and workable.
   1. Strongly Disagree   2. Disagree   3. Agree   4. Strongly Agree

e. Leadership in this group is shared by all the members.
   1. Strongly Disagree   2. Disagree   3. Agree   4. Strongly Agree

f. Conflicts in this group are resolved internally.
   1. Strongly Disagree   2. Disagree   3. Agree   4. Strongly Agree

g. Members need only occasional assistance from the leader.
   1. Strongly Disagree   2. Disagree   3. Agree   4. Strongly Agree

Score: _____

rective. Members generally need a leader on whom they can depend for direction, who can explain what to do, how to do it, and when and where to do it. They need someone to answer questions and provide the structure needed to get the job done. Members look to the leader to get things started and for guidance along the way until they get enough experience to begin functioning on their own.

As the leader, you introduce the general purpose of the group, welcome members, and help members become acquainted with each other. You provide structure, often by handing out an agenda or telling members what should be accomplished. Explain the purpose of the group and go over the goals that will help the group accomplish its purpose. Members need to feel excited and motivated. They need to share a vision and see how they can make a real difference in making social change.

Suggest procedures by which the group can accomplish its purpose. For example, brainstorming or round-robin techniques can be used to stimulate input of ideas. As you explain your vision, you help the group stay focused. If the group gets off track, redirect the discussion by restating the group's purpose and the direction the group should be going.

Work to obtain commitment by asking members to structure the agenda for the next meeting and to decide on the next steps in accomplishing the group's purpose. Ask members to accept assignments for specific tasks and set up time lines for accomplishing the group's purposes. At the end of the meeting, summarize the meeting's accomplishments, the task assignments, and the goals of the next meeting and its time and place.

The Norming Stage

At the norming stage, members know the rules, the boundaries, and their roles intellectually. However, before members can be fully functioning, they need to test the boundaries, rules, norms, and structure of the group for themselves to integrate them into their own experience and to make sure that they are practical. The norming stage is one in which members make the group their own. Members are still dependent on the leader, but they are struggling against their own dependency in their desire for mastery. They want to perform, but they may not know how to do it successfully. They know something about what to do but may not be able to do it.

In order to feel completely comfortable with the structure that the leader has provided, members need to make sure the task environment is secure and stable. In the norming stage members ask lots of questions to clarify their roles and to understand the group's boundaries and its procedures.

The most effective stance you can take as leader of a group in the norming stage is to remain task oriented but supportive as members express their feelings of unsureness or lack of understanding. You respond to the needs of members for more information, clarity, or structure. Your goal is to help members gain greater experiential understanding about the boundaries of the group task, the ways that the group will accomplish those tasks, and the style by which the leader will help them meet their goals.

Members will test themselves against the leader to assure themselves that she or he is firmly in charge. It is important that you expect and even welcome this testing, because it is an indication that members are ready to take on ownership of the group and need to challenge the leader before they can make the group their own. They will observe how you respond to questions and pressure. The way you respond to group challenges at this stage will set the tone for much of the life of the group.

Welcome questions from members and look for any indicators of unsureness or uncertainty. Look for verbal and nonverbal cues that indicate misunderstanding, anxiety, or unwillingness on the part of members. As members ask questions, affirm them and validate the importance of openness in questioning. Answer the questions that members pose, but at the same time ask members for their suggestions or ideas. Listen carefully for themes or patterns of unclarity, and suggest an exercise to help the group as a whole come to terms with the issues around when they are struggling.

While you explore the boundaries of the problems that face the group, be clear and consistent about the group's purpose and goals. Explain the reasons for those goals and give opportunity for clarification, helping group members understand and accept the task and the process. Acknowledge misgivings members may have. Assist members see "the relevance and importance of issues as they are brought before the group."[43]

Ask the group to begin working on decision making and problem resolution. At this stage, members make mistakes, because they still lack skills and ability. They may go too far in one direction or another. Give encouragement and affirm them and, at the same time, remind them about the purpose of the group and its goals to help keep them on track. Raise questions and help critique ideas or suggestions to ensure they are consistent with what the group is to accomplish. As you clarify, explain, encourage, and validate, members will gain confidence as well as skills in discussion and generating ideas.

The Storming Stage

Once group members have accepted the tasks, boundaries, and goals of the group, they tend to work hard at trying themselves out within the group structure. In their efforts to accomplish a group task, they work to adapt their skills and abilities to the task. Members will try to find their own style of working, discover how their style fits with others in the group, and accommodate their own personality functions to those of the leader and other members of the group. As a result, members may come into conflict with one another as they try to solve mutual problems and as they increasingly become dependent on one another for information and for mutual support. The storming stage is one in which member's roles become clear and internal conflicts and relationships are resolved.

As they work on problem-solving tasks, members discover that they have personal differences with one another and with the styles of other group members. For example, those who rely mainly on their thinking function and focus on facts may not be comfortable with members who emphasize feelings and want to make decisions based on relationships or meanings behind the facts. Intuiters who look at the big picture may become impatient with sensers who get involved with details of issues. Some members may be overly dominant or subservient. Others may disclose too much or withhold information.

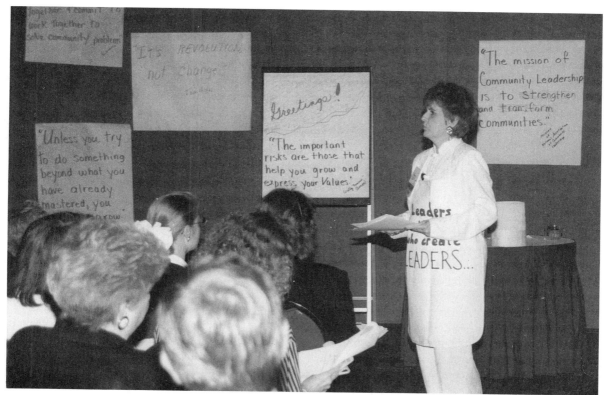

A leader provides training and information so that group members can understand what is possible.

Welcome differing viewpoints as opportunities for members to gain greater understanding of one another. Validate the importance of various problem-solving functions and encourage those with different functions to work with one another. "Help members share information, thoughts, and feelings with one another."[44]

Ensure that everyone is included in the decision-making process. Help members learn good problem-solving skills. One way to do this is to encourage members to keep comments brief, to listen attentively to what others are saying, to wait until the speaker is finished, and to always include silent members. Make sure that everyone has time to present his or her ideas fully and that all ideas are counted. Build on suggestions, affirming individual contributions. Work toward a clear understanding of the topic. Summarize progress, frequently check for understanding on issues that need clarification, and review issues that were not fully discussed.

When conflicts occur, help develop a conflict-resolution process. Ask members to elaborate on thinking that led to their positions. Ensure that members listen carefully and ask questions before they react. Help members refrain from evaluating ideas or suggestions until all ideas have been generated. As members respond, point out areas of consensus and mutual interest as they arise.[45] Build on agreements rather than disagreements, promoting consensus rather than discord.

Help members learn good communication skills. Encourage them to use "I" statements so that people assume responsibility for their own ideas and feelings rather than "you" statements, which tend to be judgmental, block communication, and often project blame. Perception checking—asking for clarification about another person's position—is another technique. In perception checking, one person tries to paraphrase what another person said. Miscommunication may be avoided by using this technique.

The results of navigating through the channels of the storming stage are that group members accept member differences, learn to use those differences in problem solving, develop skills in problem solving, conflict resolution, and communication skills, and grow in their ability to work independently.

The Performing Stage

The final stage is the performing stage. Members are now willing and capable. A formal leader has emerged who directs the meetings. Members understand the task and know what to do and how to do it. They have skills, experience, and confidence in their abilities. They own the group and have made its rules and boundaries their own. They have developed working relationships with one another and have resolved conflicts that may have gotten in the way of accomplishing their task. They have learned skills in problem solving, in group process, and in interpersonal relationships. They are working as a cohesive unit with high motivation and morale.

A good strategy for a leader of highly independent and motivated members is to assume a "hands off" laissez-faire style of leadership. A successful leader for members in the performing stage delegates and facilitates. The leader observes and monitors but does not try to give directions, persuade, or interfere with the group process. She or he will "give them the ball and let them run with it."[46] Members take responsibility and implement decisions on their own.

Attend carefully to the group and its members, listening, often remaining silent but involved with the process. Maintain eye contact, express interest, and offer support and encouragement. Give input when asked, and then in a way that avoids taking sides but raises questions, clarifies, or summarizes. Take notes and keep track of the process so that important ideas or decisions are not forgotten.

As the group struggles with communicating openly and resolving conflicts, and works toward shared decision making and equal participation, dysfunctional patterns may emerge. If members avoid issues that they must face, point this out. If they are reverting to dysfunctional behaviors in the struggle for adaptation, point out this pattern and help members deal with it.

If members need information, resources, or assistance, help them figure out how they can obtain it without doing it for them. Give the formal leader support and encouragement, and after meetings, meet with him or her to review and critique the process so that he or she is more effective.

Situational Leadership and Communities

Situational leadership can be useful in working with communities as well as with groups. The place to begin is to diagnose the level of readiness of the community to solve community problems. You can gauge the readiness of members of a community by assessing their willingness (motivation) to engage in community-related problems and by their ability to do so (skills). CHECKLIST 5, Community Leadership Analysis, will help you diagnose the level of willingness and ability of community members and assist you in determining an appropriate leadership style.[47]

CHECKLISTS

CHECKLIST 5: Community Leadership Analysis

1. To what extent are community members aware of community needs, problems, and issues?
   4 ___ High awareness   3 ___ Moderate awareness   2 ___ Little awareness   1 ___ No awareness

2. To what extent are community members aware of available resources, services, or programs that can be used to address community problems?
   4 ___ High awareness   3 ___ Moderate awareness   2 ___ Little awareness   1 ___ No awareness

3. To what extent do people have the capacity or skill to make use of resources, services, or programs that can be used to address community problems?
   4 ___ High capacity   3 ___ Moderate capacity   2 ___ Little capacity   1 ___ No capacity

4. To what extent do community members express interest in mobilizing to resolve community problems?
   4 ___ High interest   3 ___ Moderate interest   2 ___ Little interest   1 ___ No interest

5. To what extent are community members willing to act on the problems?
   4 ___ High willingness   3 ___ Moderate willingness   2 ___ Little willingness   1 ___ No willingness

6. To what extent are community members able to establish rules, procedures, and assign tasks to resolve community problems?
   4 ___ High ability   3 ___ Moderate ability   2 ___ Little ability   1 ___ No ability

7. To what extent are community members able to resolve conflicts among themselves in setting goals and implementing plans?
   4 ___ High ability   3 ___ Moderate ability   2 ___ Little ability   1 ___ No ability

8. To what extent do community members engage one another in mutual problem solving?
   4 ___ High engagement   3 ___ Moderate engagement   2 ___ Little engagement   1 ___ No engagement

9. To what extent do community members coordinate their efforts independently?
   4 ___ High coordination   3 ___ Moderate coordination   2 ___ Little coordination   1 ___ No coordination

10. To what extent do community members share leadership and task accomplishment?
   4 ___ High sharing   3 ___ Moderate sharing   2 ___ Little sharing   1 ___ No sharing

Total Score:

Telling for Low Readiness

Low scores on CHECKLIST 5, between 10 and 15, mean that community members are generally not aware of community needs, do not know what the services or programs the community offers, do not look to the community as a resource in meeting their needs, and do not see community issues as important to them. Community members at this level tend not to be highly motivated to become involved in trying to make their community a better place or improve its services. If community members have few abilities, little knowledge, or weak skills in group process, decision making, or problem solving, they need direction from a leader so they can make a contribution to community improvement tasks. People may feel helpless to do anything or they may be so engrossed in just trying to survive that they have little energy or interest in wider community concerns.

Faced with these issues, a macro social worker needs to give information about what is possible, to inspire hope, and to mobilize people's anger, pulling them into engagement with one another to make changes on their own behalf. A leader will need to be active in stimulating and motivating apathetic community members. Appealing to people's sense of pride and justice may be necessary to heighten the sensitivity of those who are most directly affected by the problem.[48] Providing information about what others have done and what is possible, training in processes by which they can accomplish their goals together, and providing an arena of safety may stimulate otherwise alienated people to become motivated to action. A high task/low relationship (HT/LT) stance tends to be the most effective one with community members at this level of readiness.

While you stimulate and motivate community members to action, avoid reinforcing hopelessness, despair, alienation, and a sense of "victimization." The tendency of individuals to dwell on misery or to simply complain about personal situations may be strong. A leader avoids supporting members in these kinds of fruitless and self-defeating topics, focusing instead on what is possible.

Selling

If community members score between 16 and 25 on the Community Leadership Analysis Checklist, they are engaging one another, or they may be willing to try but are still reluctant. Their lack of experience may keep them from moving. They may still not have a clear idea about what to do or how to do it or may need help in understanding what they can contribute.

Focusing on the tasks, you provide training and information. Maintain a high task/high relationship (HT/HR) orientation so that members understand what is possible and at the same time help members with their legitimate anxiety about task accomplishment. As people begin to try things on their own, give validation and space to try harder. If they try but fail, acknowledge their efforts, critique what went wrong, and encourage them to try again.

In general, restrain yourself from giving direction or controlling the agenda but encourage and support people as they begin to do this on their own. Respect the rights of community members to make their own decisions, no matter how small. The more steps they take, with your support, the stronger they become. They will begin to generate their own ideas and establish roles and rules.

Coaching

If community members score between 26 and 35 on CHECKLIST 5, they will be motivated, but their skills need to be tested and tried before they are completely comfortable with their abilities. They need the opportunity to experiment, to try and fail, if necessary, knowing that the leader will be there to help and assist if needed. Community members are ready to put the plans they have generated into action. You understand that the challenge is theirs, just as the risks are theirs, and the victory is theirs as well. Watch, encourage, and support, but do not do things for them. You are like a coach who takes a high relationship/low task orientation (HR/LT), helping and encouraging from the sidelines while the members themselves take control of the action. When their efforts fail, when they do not accomplish all they have wished, help them critique what has happened. Give advice and support for strategizing and regrouping. Mediate disputes, assist members to see the larger picture. Assist them in streamlining their roles and smoothing conflicts generated out of disagreements over strategy or intense feelings because of the importance that the cause has taken and the seriousness with which community members have become involved.

Consultation

Community members who score 36 or more on the checklist will be those who have experienced struggle together, claimed some victory, and own some defeat. Out of this they have grown in hope, courage, and understanding. They realize that forging a community takes a long time and is a gradual process. Leaders have emerged. Members have gained skills, capabilities, and techniques. They have learned how to work together, developed closer relationships, and worked through their differences. They are both willing to continue the process on their own and are able to do this independently. The members need only occasional assistance. Under these conditions

> it is quite appropriate to use a collaborative strategy when there is consensus that a problem exists or a proposed solution will work. . . . The practitioner or planner might play an enabling or facilitator role serving as a guide or catalyst or, a convener, a mediator, a consultant or even a coordinator. . . . The presumption would be one of goodwill, of complementary of objectives. The practitioner, staff developer, or planner would perform most effectively as an orchestrator of that consensus.[49]

Situational Leadership and Action Theory

Hersey and Blanchard's situational leadership model is adaptable to working with groups within an organization or in a community. It can also be adapted to diagnosing community readiness and helping you adopt a leadership style with the community-as-a-whole. The situational leadership model, however, has limitations. While it may tell you something about what kind of leadership style you ought to adopt and suggests techniques, it presumes that the goals and direction of the task group are already clear and appropriate. This is because management goals are handed to people. The organizational manager, except at the very top, does not decide the inner content of goals but is simply con-

cerned with how to induce members to reach them efficiently and effectively. The situational leadership model, as all management theory, presupposes that members simply carry out decisions made elsewhere. Management, therefore, tends to be empty leadership. The organizational manager often uses leadership devoid of substance and reduced to mere technique.

Macro social workers, however, do not impose goals on people. They assume people can and should make the decisions that affect their lives. Macro social work leadership assists people in carrying out the goals they have designated. Social work leadership, therefore, is "substantive." Substantive leadership is full of content or substance, not empty like that of management. Macro social work is value-infused leadership. As a leader, you want to make sure that the ends you are working toward are ethical. Leadership in macro social work, therefore, may use managerial leadership techniques but will do this only when members are included and involved. A theory of macro social work leadership that is substantive and value laden, concerned with ends as well as means, is the action model of leadership.

Action Model of Leadership

The action model of leadership is a "process" oriented model in which a leader helps a community or organization solve problems, meet needs, and move in a direction that its members want to go. Such a model "leads to a concern with *increasing the power of others* rather than seeking their submission."[50] A leader cannot influence others, McClelland argued, unless he or she expresses "vivid goals" that the others want. The role of the leader

> is to strengthen and uplift, to make people feel that they are the origins, not the pawns of . . . the system. . . . His message is not so much: "Do as I say because I am strong and know best . . . ," but rather, "Here are the goals which are true and right and which we share. Here is how we can reach them. You are strong and capable. You can accomplish these goals."[51]

The action model is based on a paradigm of mutuality and "intersubjectivity"[52] in which the community and even organizations are seen as arenas in which and by which people find their identity, meaning, and values. The leader has a firm commitment to people as active and creative agents who form social meaning for themselves and who have "the capacity to make choices about where, and what kind of action or response is called for."[53] The leader understands that social reality "is 'constructed' rather than existing independently of people's conception of it."[54]

> The active view holds that people act from the basis of rules of their own devising, rather than being driven solely by forces beyond their control. Further, their actions are mediated by the subjective meaning that they attach both to past experiences and explorations leading to future experience.[55]

An action-oriented social worker engages people in a mutual relationship out of respect for their ability to develop their own meanings, rules, values, and processes. You help in that development. The macro social worker in either an organization or community, therefore, does not apply leadership *to* people, as does a manager or a boss, but proceeds with them on a journey in which all walk together.

In this process, you as leader use all your personality functions, applying them to your leadership style just as you did in applying them to solving social problems using the action model of problem solving (chapter 3). Therefore, before we examine the content of the action model of leadership, do EXERCISE 15, which will help you apply the four personality functions to leadership.

EXERCISES

EXERCISE 15:
Leadership Preferences Inventory

The leadership preferences inventory is based on a Jungian personality typology. As you recall from action oriented problem solving, each of us has four different personality functions that in combination become our dominant leadership style. We can use and modify those styles if we understand them. This inventory will help you understand your leadership role, the different mix of your own style preferences, and your strengths, and help you be a more effective leader and be able to change your style when appropriate.

Complete the following sixteen sentences. There are four endings for each sentence. Rank each of the endings according to how much it resembles you.

4: most resembles you
3: second most like you
2: third most like you
1: least like you

Example:

1. I like leaders who are strong in:
   a. _3_ thinking (second most like you)
   b. _1_ imagining (least like you)
   c. _4_ feelings (most like you)
   d. _2_ doing (third most like you)

1. I like leaders who are strong in
   a. ____ thinking.
   b. ____ imagining.
   c. ____ feeling.
   d. ____ doing.

2. As a leader I would
   a. ____ conduct an impersonal analysis of the situation.
   b. ____ explore all of the options.
   c. ____ weigh how deeply I care about the issue.
   d. ____ apply the facts.

3. I admire a leader who is full of
   a. ____ justice.

   b. ____ hope.
   c. ____ mercy.
   d. ____ service.

4. I like a leader who above all is
   a. ____ fair.
   b. ____ original.
   c. ____ friendly and kind.
   d. ____ down to earth.

5. If I were a leader I would focus on
   a. ____ reason.
   b. ____ experience.
   c. ____ relationships.
   d. ____ accomplishments.

6. I appreciate a leader best who is
   a. ____ logical and systematic.
   b. ____ stimulating and creative.
   c. ____ warm and caring.
   d .____ practical and realistic.

7. When in doubt as a leader I would
   a. ____ stand firm.
   b. ____ look at the ultimate purpose.

EXERCISES

c. _____ conciliate.

d. _____ get involved in the here-and-now situation.

8. As a leader I would speak from
   a. _____ my head.
   b. _____ my dreams and visions.
   c. _____ my heart.
   d. _____ my actions.

9. I admire leaders who
   a. _____ find flaws in something in advance.
   b. _____ bring up new possibilities.
   c. _____ appreciate values such as what is good and right.
   d. _____ keep track of essentials.

10. I feel that the best leaders show interest in
    a. _____ rational thought.
    b. _____ envisioning the future.
    c. _____ convictions.
    d. _____ concrete things in the here-and-now.

11. I enjoy leaders who
    a. _____ explain things logically.

b. _____ stimulate my imagination.

c. _____ relate to me personally.

d. _____ give a concrete demonstration.

12. In my leadership role I like to
    a. _____ analyze and predict the logical outcomes of choices.
    b. _____ conceive of a plan and dream about its future.
    c. _____ see the effects of choices on people.
    d. _____ have details of a program and carry them out.

13. I relate best to a leader who is
    a. _____ analytical.
    b. _____ imaginative.
    c. _____ sympathetic.
    d. _____ sensible.

14. I would rather lead
    a. _____ a decision-making group that solves a problem in a logical way.
    b. _____ a brainstorming group

that tries to come up with all of the possibilities.

c. _____ a support group that deals with feelings and personal issues.

d. _____ a task group that deals with the here-and-now.

15. I work best when I
    a. _____ am treated fairly.
    b. _____ can learn new skills.
    c. _____ get occasional praise.
    d. _____ focus on the immediate job.

16. What I appreciate about a leader is (are) his or her
    a. _____ ideas and theories.
    b. _____ invention of future possibilities.
    c. _____ feelings and values.
    d. _____ ability in practical application.

Total the scores in each letter group.
    a. _____ (T)
    b. _____ (N)
    c. _____ (F)
    d. _____ (S)

The Action Leadership Process and the Four Functions

One task of an action-oriented social work leader is to discover what is wrong with a social system. This requires using one's thinking function and gathering facts. The leader uses his or her thinking function to confront what has been done before and challenge what is possible in the future.

Once you have a firm grasp on what you want to do, add your intuiting function to inspire that vision of the future in others. To be successful in inspiring others, use your feeling function to develop relationships, form members into an organization or

community, and make decisions on how issues affect the members of your group. Finally, help the organization or community move to action using your sensing function to seek tangible results with practical, day-to-day skills of organizing.

What follows is a model of action leadership based on research that a number of current leadership theorists have developed, among them Burt Nanus, Warren Bennis, Barry Posner, Jim Kouzas, and Edgar Schein. While the action leadership model is presented as a cycle, in reality, you may begin anywhere along in this cycle and move backwards or forwards depending on the isuues that confront you in building organization or community and solving social problems.

Using Your Thinking Skills to Confront the Past

When you use your thinking function, you confront the way things have been done in the past that create troubles in the present. You challenge the way things are done today, so as to bring about a better tomorrow. The action-oriented social work leader uses his or her thinking function and facilitates that of the members to be single-minded and challenge injustice in society.

Being Single-Minded

Your thinking function and that of your members helps you become "single-minded" or purpo-

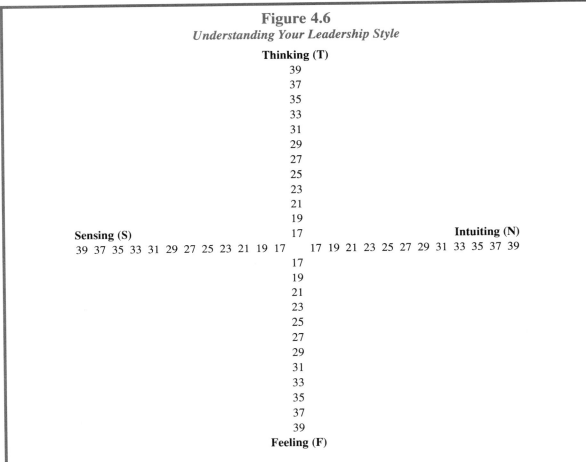

Figure 4.6
Understanding Your Leadership Style

Each of the four groups gives an indication of one aspect of leadership functions: Thinking (T)—group *a;* Intuiting (N)—group *b;* Feeling (F)—group *c;* and Sensing (S)—group *d.* Just as you did when you explored your problem-solving functions, place a dot on the scale corresponding to your T, N, F, and S leadership scores. Connect the lines. You will get a kite-like shape. The shape and position of your scores will show which of the four leadership functions you prefer most and which you prefer least.

By looking at how you score on the four leadership functions, you can get an idea about where your leadership strengths lie. The strongest areas are those that you will tend to use most often and with the most ease. The ones on which you score lowest will be areas that you will need to work harder to use or will use less often.

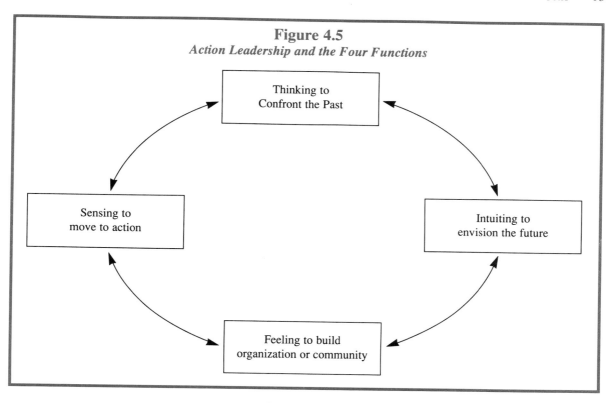

Figure 4.5
Action Leadership and the Four Functions

sive. When you use your thinking function, you infuse people with a sense of mission that can shape and improve their lives. People want leaders who have a clear sense of direction.

> People who present clear and convincing arguments for taking action in situations where knowledge is limited or absent will be influential in shaping the thinking and behavior of others. Their influence, moreover, comes from their intense convictions and strongly held beliefs, qualities that people wish to identify with in ambiguous and amorphous situations . . . [the] ability to convey . . . beliefs about what should be done about baffling and complex problems. . . . Individuals who can act forcefully not only when they know what is the right course of action, but when—in the absence of knowledge—they *believe* in a course of action, will be looked to for leadership.[56]

The best leaders use thinking to help members develop a set of intentions, outcomes, goals, and directions. Your thinking function helps you become confident in your ability to make things happen[57] and

helps you access member's confidence as well. You know what results you and your group's members are trying to accomplish.

Action-oriented leaders who are firm in their thinking function stand up for their beliefs and assist group members to firm up their beliefs as well. They practice what they preach and show others by their own example that they live by the values that they profess. They are not simply committed to truth and justice in the abstract; they exemplify these ideas in the way they live. "While their position gives them authority, their behavior earns them respect. It is consistency between words and actions that build leaders' credibility."[58] Your thinking function helps you focus yourself and in doing so members gather strength and confidence in using their thinking function.

Confronting Injustice

The thinking function helps you and your group members gather information, analyze facts, think things through, assess what is wrong, and make decisions about what to do. Members gain a sense of the injustices that have been perpetrated against them and then see what can be done.

Using Your Intuition to Inspire a Shared Vision

Henry Kissinger once said, "The task of the leader is to get people from where they are to where they have not been. The public does not fully understand the world into which it is going. Leaders must invoke an alchemy of great vision. Those leaders who do not are ultimately judged failures, even though they may be popular at the time."[59] While you help group members exercise their thinking functions and become single-minded and purposeful, and gain a vigorous sense of justice, allow your visionary, intuiting sense to come into play. To effect social change means having a vision and leading people toward that vision. An action-oriented leader is "one who commits people to action, who converts followers to leaders and who may convert leaders into agents of change."[60] The Reverend Theodore Hesburgh, president of the University of Notre Dame, said, "Vision is the key to leadership. Unless you have a vision of where you are going, you are not going to get there."[61] "Begin with imagination and with the belief that what is merely an image can one day be made real."[62] Accept people as they are, damaged and hard pressed, and envision them as they might be. "Every organization, every social movement begins with a dream. The dream or vision is the force that invents the future."[63] This dream gives shape and meaning to people's lives. As you use your intuition to become a dreamer, your members will also begin to dream dreams and have visions about what is possible.

Martin Luther King challenged injustice with a vision:

> [He] envisioned the future "gazing across the horizon of time" and imagined that greater things were ahead. [He] foresaw something out there, vague as it might appear from the distance, that others did not. [He] imagined that extraordinary feats were possible, . . . that the ordinary could be transformed into something noble.[64]

The vision is seen though the eyes of the leader, who reflects it back to the people so that they see themselves. In seeing themselves, they see their common future and what they can be and do. The community becomes the vehicle by which the shared vision is transmitted.

Using Your Feeling Function to Create Community

As you single-mindedly hold to your sense of justice, share a vision with group members about what is possible, you tap into your feeling function to form a community out of individuals who may be alienated and distrustful of one another.

Action-oriented leaders reach out, touch others, and bind people together. They go out into the neighborhoods, listen to people's difficulties and disappointments, gather their hopes and dreams, and help them unite into a community.

> Leaders find that common thread that weaves together the fabric of human needs into a colorful tapestry. They seek out the brewing consensus among those they would lead. In order to do this, they develop a deep understanding of the collective yearnings. They listen carefully for quiet whisperings in dark corners. They attend to subtle cues. They sniff the air to get the scent. They watch faces. They get a sense of what people want, what they value, what they dream about.[65]

Not afraid to show emotion, an action-oriented leader is full of passion and lets this passion show. "Managers," on the other hand, value being neutral and impersonal, often treating themselves and others as objects. Having passion for a cause and setting a tone of engagement and accessibility, an atmosphere in which people depend on and reach out to one another, is essential.

This process is not simply a technique of forming community. Instead, it is something that comes from within yourself and something that you develop in the process of doing it. And as you begin to realize community with others, they will feel what it is like to be in community with one another. You enable and encourage people to respond to one another with commitment and cohesion. The encounters between people and the feelings that are elicited put substance onto the dream so that it is not only a vision but a reality. Leaders "act as channels of expression between the down-to-earth followers and their other worldly dreams,"[66] not only communicating but *creating* meaning as well.

Using Your Sensing Function to Move to Action

Armed with facts and a vision, the leader uses the sensing function and "commits people to action, . . . converts leaders into agents of change."[67] Together, the leader and the community propose programs, develop plans, engage in activities, and carry them out. An action-oriented leader is a social architect.[68] By developing tangible services and programs, the community discovers its strengths. Relationships take shape as people meet the real needs of those who are in need.

Developing programs requires particular skills, such as doing research, planning, writing proposals, seeking funding, developing an organization, and carrying out services. People discover talents they did not realize they had, and they put those talents to use in meaningful work that contributes to the common good. The leader keeps an eye on the larger picture, and the community moves ahead one step at a time. Larger problems are broken into small units, and small wins are accomplished. "The magic in small wins is the experimentation process or setting up little tests that continually help you learn something."[69]

The action leadership process now comes full circle. You challenge injustice with your thinking function, use your intuition to hold onto your dream in the face of challenges, draw upon your feeling functions to strengthen the community in times of stress, and use your sensing functions to immerse yourself in strategizing and planning.

Conclusion

Rosabeth Moss Kanter has observed that "powerlessness corrupts and absolute powerlessness corrupts absolutely."[70] People who have little power tend to hoard what little power they have and "lord" it over others. Good leaders enrich and empower their followers. They "use their power to transform their followers into leaders."[71]

Action-oriented leaders give of themselves so that their followers can move ahead on a journey to find their dreams. In struggling and working together, they learn to overcome obstacles, achieve goals, become the kind of people that they want to become, and construct their own social reality.

Action-oriented "leaders make heroes of other people."[72] It is the people who hear the call, make the commitment, endure the struggles, face the trials, move through transitions, and undertake a journey toward a common goal.

KEY CONCEPTS

trait theory
leadership triad
authoritarian leadership
democratic leadership
laissez faire leadership
theory X
theory Y
people orientation
task orientation
initiating structure
consideration structure
managerial grid
task behavior
relationship behavior
one best way
contingency leadership theory
situational leadership theory
member maturity
telling leadership style
selling leadership style
coaching leadership style
consulting leadership style
group life cycle leadership theory
forming stage of the group
norming stage of the group
storming stage of the group
performing stage of the group
action model of leadership

QUESTIONS FOR DISCUSSION

1. Have you ever exerted leadership? What did you do? What did you learn about yourself? What did you learn about leadership?

2. What leadership opportunities do you have around you?

3. Do you have a vision for something that could change—in your school, work, church, or community? How would you go about it?

4. Review the story of Jane Addams at the beginning of this chapter. What leadership preferences did she exhibit? What does this tell you about macro social work leadership?

5. At the beginning of this chapter, Kouzas and Posner say, "Leaders take us on journeys where we have never been before." How does this statement relate to the action model of leadership? Does a community go on a journey? How does that journey inform the community members? How do the personal journeys of community members inform the larger community? Are members of a community also its leaders?

6. Burton Gummer, one of the influential writers in macro social work, asserts that social work leadership has declined in recent years. What is your opinion about this statement? Is social work leadership on the decline? If so, to what do you attribute this? Is this something about which social workers ought to be concerned? What can be done to inspire social workers to greater leadership roles in today's society?

ADDITIONAL READING

Leadership

Bennis, Warren G., and Burt Nanus. *Leaders: Strategies for Taking Charge.* New York: Harper and Row, 1986.

Bethel, Sheila. *Making a Difference: Twelve Qualities That Make You a Leader.* New York: Putman, 1990.

Burns, James MacGregor. *Leadership.* New York: Harper and Row, 1978.

Flores, Ernest. *The Nature of Leadership for His-panics and Other Minorities.* Saratoga, CA: Century Twenty-One, 1981.

Gardner, John. *On Leadership.* New York: Free Press, 1990.

Greenleaf, Robert K. *Servant Leadership: A Journey into the Nature of Legitimate Power and Greatness.* New York: Paulist Press, 1977.

Hersey, Paul. *The Situational Leader: The Other 59 Minutes.* New York: Warner Books, 1985.

Hitt, William. *The Model Leader: A Fully Functioning Person.* Columbus, OH: Battelle Press, 1993.

Kouzes, James, and Barry Posner. *The Leadership Challenge: How to Get Extraordinary Things Done in Organizations.* San Francisco, CA: Jossey-Bass, 1987.

Kouzes, James, and Barry Posner. *Credibility: How Leaders Gain It and Why People Demand It.* San Francisco, CA: Jossey-Bass, 1993.

Oakley, Edward, and Douglas Krug. *Enlightened Leadership: Getting to the Heart of Change.* New York: Simon and Schuster, 1993.

Followership

Bellman, Goeffrey. *Getting Things Done When You Are Not In Charge: How to Succeed from a Support Position.* New York: Simon and Schuster, 1992.

Kelly, Robert. *The Power of Followership: How to Create Leaders; People Who want to Follow and Followers Who Lead Themselves.* New York: Doubleday, 1992.

Small Group Leadership

Cartwright, Dorwin, and Alvin Zander. *Group Dynamics: Research and Theory.* 3d ed. New York: Harper and Row, 1968.

Forsyth, Donelson R. *Group Dynamics.* 2d ed. Pacific Grove, CA: Brooks/Cole, 1990.

Toseland, Ronald W., and Robert F. Rivas. *An Introduction to Group Work Practice.* 2d ed. Boston: Allyn and Bacon, 1995.

Tubbs, Stewart L. *A Systems Approach to Small Group Interaction.* 4th ed. New York: McGraw-Hill, 1992.

Zander, Alvin. *Making Groups Effective.* San Francisco, CA: Jossey-Bass, 1983.

CHECKLISTS

CHECKLIST 6: Leadership Development Inventory

This inventory will give you a chance to explore more deeply leadership skills connected with your functions and discover which ones you may need to work on. First, read through the following inventory and decide which items you need to do more of or less of. Keep in mind that thinkers need to be balanced by feeling, and sensers need to be balanced by intuition. After you have finished the inventory, break into groups of four or five and share what this exercise says about your skills.

	Okay	Need to do more	Need to do less
Thinking Functions			
Making up my mind firmly			
Organizing myself	_____	_____	_____
Being consistent	_____	_____	_____
Relying on my logic	_____	_____	_____
Reaching objectives on schedule	_____	_____	_____
Making tough decisions	_____	_____	_____
Facing unpleasant tasks	_____	_____	_____
Being efficient	_____	_____	_____
Living by the rules	_____	_____	_____
Holding to my principles	_____	_____	_____
	_____	_____	_____
Intuitive Functions			
Conceiving new possibilities			
Using my imagination	_____	_____	_____
Enjoying being good in many areas	_____	_____	_____
Looking to the future	_____	_____	_____
Looking forward to challenges	_____	_____	_____
Interest in growth	_____	_____	_____
Enthusiasm for projects	_____	_____	_____
	_____	_____	_____
Feeling Functions			
Needing approval			
Being sensitive to others	_____	_____	_____
Being loyal to others	_____	_____	_____
Valuing harmonious relations	_____	_____	_____
Persevering	_____	_____	_____
Being conciliatory	_____	_____	_____
Concerned with quality	_____	_____	_____
Raising ethical questions	_____	_____	_____
	_____	_____	_____
Sensing Functions			
Focusing on the here-and-now			
Good at practical application	_____	_____	_____
Going step-by-step	_____	_____	_____
Good at details	_____	_____	_____
Dealing with facts	_____	_____	_____
Enjoying hands-on work	_____	_____	_____
Following plans	_____	_____	_____
	_____	_____	_____

CHECKLISTS

This chapter has pointed out that leadership depends on the maturity of the members. Membership requires skills as does leadership. CHECKLISTS 7 and 8 will help you assess your leadership and membership skills. Mark those items that you do often, sometimes, or never. Is there a pattern in the issues you have marked? What do these patterns say about you? What areas would you like to improve?

Look over your lists and choose some areas about which you would like to get feedback. Your instructor will help your class form dyads. One person shares an item and the other person gives feedback. Then reverse roles. Share as many items as time allows.

CHECKLIST 7: Leadership Skills

1. I try to be the leader in groups or situations.
   Often ____   Sometimes ____   Never ____
2. I wait for others to take over.
   Often ____   Sometimes ____   Never ____
3. People follow my ideas.
   Often ____   Sometimes ____   Never ____
4. People ignore my ideas.
   Often ____   Sometimes ____   Never ____
5. It is easy for me to let others take the lead.
   Often ____   Sometimes ____   Never ____
6. Is it hard to let go of the lead.
   Often ____   Sometimes ____   Never ____
7. It is easy for me to accept responsibility in a group.
   Often ____   Sometimes ____   Never ____
8. I resist doing things in a group.
   Often ____   Sometimes ____   Never ____
9. I have been elected to an office in a group.
   Often ____   Sometimes ____   Never ____
10. I avoid trying out for an office.
    Often ____   Sometimes ____   Never ____
11. I end up taking over in groups whether I want to or not.
    Often ____   Sometimes ____   Never ____
12. I do not take over in groups even when I want to.
    Often ____   Sometimes ____   Never ____
13. I need to have others recognize what I am saying.
    Often ____   Sometimes ____   Never ____
14. I need to have people in a group like me.
    Often ____   Sometimes ____   Never ____
15. I am persistent in getting something done.
    Often ____   Sometimes ____   Never ____
16. I tend to let nature take its course.
    Often ____   Sometimes ____   Never ____

CHECKLISTS

CHECKLIST 8: Membership Skills

1. I feel exposed in a group.
   Often ___   Sometimes ___   Never ___
2. I am in control of my thoughts and ideas in a group.
   Often ___   Sometimes ___   Never ___
3. I am the first person to break a silence in a group.
   Often ___   Sometimes ___   Never ___
4. I hold back until everyone else has spoken.
   Often ___   Sometimes ___   Never ___
5. I can't wait to get things off my chest in groups.
   Often ___   Sometimes ___   Never ___
6. I have difficulty speaking my mind in groups.
   Often ___   Sometimes ___   Never ___
7. I over disclose at the beginning of a group.
   Often ___   Sometimes ___   Never ___
8. I underdisclose in group meetings.
   Often ___   Sometimes ___   Never ___
9. I am comfortable "fitting" in with others.
   Often ___   Sometimes ___   Never ___
10. I feel that I compromise myself in group situations.
    Often ___   Sometimes ___   Never ___
11. People seem to enjoy me in groups.
    Often ___   Sometimes ___   Never ___
12. I seem to be a problem to others in groups.
    Often ___   Sometimes ___   Never ___
13. I generally include myself in groups.
    Often ___   Sometimes ___   Never ___
14. I tend to be on the fringe in groups.
    Often ___   Sometimes ___   Never ___
15. I am comfortable with the role that I play in a group.
    Often ___   Sometimes ___   Never ___
16. I feel that I get stuck with a role that I don't like.
    Often ___   Sometimes ___   Never ___

EXERCISES

EXERCISE 16:
Qualities of Good Leaders

Following is a list of some qualities of good leaders. Read this list. Are there qualities missing that you feel are important? What do you think are the most important ones? How difficult are these qualities to achieve? Discuss what makes a good leader.

1. Good leaders enable people to feel and become empowered. Members feel significant and are infused with purpose. Each person can make a difference.
2. Good leaders inspire values of caring. In such a caring community, each person has meaning. A community is judged to be good to the extent that it prizes and values its weakest members.
3. Good leaders insure that learning and competence matter. In communities that prize learning, there is no failure, only mistakes that give feedback and tell people what to do next so they can learn and grow.
4. Good leaders, particularly those in administration, create an atmosphere where work is stimulating, challenging, and fun. People are self-motivated. Good leaders pull; they don't push. They pull people by attracting and energizing them with an exciting vision of the future.
5. Good leaders help people feel a sense of unity. They develop a community in which everyone is welcome and has a role to play, and they ensure that everyone is wanted and needed.
6. Good leaders help members develop a sense of security and trust not only in the leader but also in one another.
7. A good leader displays reliability and integrity. Reliability means constancy. Everyone knows where the leader stands.
8. A good leader is honest and trustworthy, and has integrity. Integrity means that the leader has an allegiance to higher values and standards. He or she does not compromise these values for mere expediency.

EXERCISE 17:
What Kind of Leader Am I? A Feedback Exercise[73]

This exercise requires some self-disclosure, skill in communication, active listening, and feedback. Review active listening skills and how to offer feedback.

First, think of the person who is the most admired leader that you have ever known. Picture that person in your mind. Now think of all the characteristics that you admire about that leader. Write down at least five of those traits that you admire most.

When you have finished, think of a leader that you disliked or felt was the worst leader you have ever known. Write down five of the characteristics of that leader in a second column.

These lists give a rough idea of the qualities in leaders that you value and that are important to you. Look over your lists. What do they say about your own leadership values?

Compile the lists of the members of your class. You now have an overview of the leadership qualities that your class values and those that are not valued. What patterns are there?

The next phase of this exercise involves both positive and negative feedback. Choose someone in class with whom you are comfortable in sharing feedback. Write down three items from each list that describe positive and negative leadership traits of your partner.

After each of you has written down the traits, solicit feedback from each other. First do the positive characteristics. Spend some time discussing why the traits were chosen. How similar were the traits you and your partner chose? Now that you have shared positive characteristics, move on to the negative ones. What did you learn about your leadership style?

EXERCISE 18:
Matching Leaders and Social Work Action Arenas

Listed below are some of the arenas of macro social work as well as some prominent social leaders and change agents. How many leaders can you associate with a field of macro social work? If these leaders are not immediately recognizable, look them up in the Encyclopedia of Social Work or a general encyclopedia. Some may be associated with several fields of macro social work.

1. Community Development
2. Social Action
3. Program Development
4. Research
5. Administration
6. Social Policy

Jane Addams
Saul Alinsky
Sir Robert Baden-Powell

EXERCISES

Canon Samuel Barnett
William Booth
Charles Booth
Charles Loring Brace
Mary McLeod Bethune
Dorothea Dix
Michael Harrington
Harry Hopkins
Harriet Tubman
Benjamin Franklin

George Wiley
Roy Wilkins
George Williams
Florence Kelly
Homer Folks
Lilian Wald
Grace Abbott
Mary Simkhovitch
Clifford Beers
St. Frances Cabrini

Clara Barton
Rev. John Perkins
Caesar Chavez
W.E.B. DuBois
Booker T. Washington
Dorothy Day
Paul Kellog
Sojourner Truth
St. Elizabeth Ann Seton

PART II

Social Work Practice with Communities

Somewhere in the Deep South, on the road that runs from New Orleans to Atlanta, an eighty year old woman is living alone in a shack by the roadside. If you are driving along that road, you can sometimes see her going painfully along in the long grass beside the highway. She is looking for Coke bottles the motorists throw out the windows of their cars as they go past at 70 miles an hour. Tomorrow a child will come by her shack to collect the bottles and bring them to the grocery downtown, and will bring the 3 cents a bottle she gets back to the woman to buy food.

Or if you were walking the dirt streets of a town not far from there some six months ago, you might have seen a child playing in the road. He is throwing his toy into the air, chasing it, picking it up, throwing it, and chasing it again. You come closer. It is a dead bird.

Make no mistake. Organizing is not about strategies, about analyses, about tactics. Organizing is about people, about the old woman with her Coke bottles, and the child with his dead bird. Organizing is about the "welfare cheats," the "deadbeats" on unemployment, the "white trash," the "niggers"—and everybody else this society locks out and shuts in.

—SI KAHN, "HOW PEOPLE ACT"[1]

Traditionally, social work practice at the community level has been called "community organization." According to Rubin and Rubin, "community organizing means bringing people together to combat shared problems and to increase their say about decisions that affect their lives."[2]

Until our modern era, communities of people were not in need of such organizing. Communities were contiguous, cohesive, strong, and self-sufficient. They were *the* building blocks of society. Communities were based on a common economy and had a religious or cultural foundation that supplied meaning to their members. It was out of these natural human associations that society was formed.

The community, however, has become vulnerable in today's modern world.[3] While many viable communities still exist, community social systems in general are becoming formless and decaying. What were once the centers of our society are now in need of help. People on the fringes of today's modern social systems, for example, lack power, control, resources, and opportunities. They exist in remnants of communities that are weakened enclaves in the larger society—little islands, lacking economic resources, leadership, goals, structure, and purpose.

Environmentalists warn us that modern technology is destroying the ecosystems that make our planet habitable. In the same way, our modern social systems and technologies are destroying the fabric of our social environment, which makes our society habitable. Just as there are "signal" species that warn us that entire ecosystems are in danger of dying, so too the destruction of inner city communities in East Los Angeles, the Bronx, Hunter's Point, and countless others signal us that entire populations of our people have been "lost." Wynetta Devore, a community social worker, sees communities no longer as places of support for families, but rather as places of danger.

> It is difficult for families to feel a sense of community that defines shared history, mutual expectations, roles, values or norms. The city as a community is no longer a haven for families. They appear to be trapped in a dangerous environment, at significant risk in the economic and social areas of their lives.[4]

Even as many social workers attempt to retrieve individuals and families by means of various therapeutic interventions, the community basis of those lives is dissolving. Some social workers, however, continue to uphold the banner of community as the central focus of social work. Hans Falck, for example, asserts that "community social work *is* social work."[5] And yet,

> many clinical social workers acknowledge that community social work is an integral component of social work almost as an afterthought. And, indeed, community social work appears to be of interest to dwindling numbers of social workers and students.[6]

The result of social work abandoning community is not only family breakdown and individual dysfunction, which psychotherapy cannot hope to prevent, but also the tendency to facilitate the destruction of people's lives even as micro social work attempts to rescue them.

> The demise of authentic community results in people being uncertain and uninformed about policy opportunities and consequences, yet believing that others "know better"; cynical about the promise of their own participation and deferential to those with expert, official, or investor status, consenting through deference about participation; doubting their own social and community capacities for cooperation, and trusting instead in the good faith of professionals or the hidden hand of market advocates; and confused about and distracted [about] options that could address social needs in more than a "trickle down" fashion.[7]

When community betterment as *the* focus of social work is abandoned, social work itself contributes to feeding the disengaged and disenfranchised to the social machinery that grinds them up in its onward search for prosperity and progress.

Remnants of community still exist, particularly among the ethnically diverse members of our society. It is in the traditions and culture of African Americans, Japanese Americans, Chinese Americans, Mexican and Latin Americans, Southeast Asian Americans, Native Americans and others that solidarity and hope for community exists today.

> Part of what made [communities] places of identity and empowerment were elements of ethnic solidarity. Aspects of religion, similarity of economic status, and life situation contributed to this solidarity. The contempt of more affluent surrounding communities also contributed to defensive, but supportive efforts of mutual aid.[8]

It may well be that it is the few social workers who retain the vision of a nation of healthy communities who work among the marginalized and people of color who can show us what authentic community is. Following in the footsteps of Jane Addams and Harry Hopkins, they can lead us back to what social work is all about.

This section deals with the vision of community as a cherished social system, one that is slowly becoming extinct. The idea of community and a description of three different kinds of communities are presented in chapter 5. Developing community begins with research. Macro social workers need to evaluate a community's functions, assess its needs, and understand its problems. Chapter 6 describes how to conduct social work research. Community development, a method of helping restore modern, ontological, and third world communities, and searching for a new and modern role for the community[9] is the focus of chapter 7. Social action, which deals with oppressed communities, is described in chapter 8.

ADDITIONAL READING

Anderson, Walt. *The Age of Protest*. Pacific Palisades, CA: Goodyear Publishing Co., 1989.

Betten, Neil, and Michael Austin. *The Roots of Community Organizing: 1917 to 1939*. Philadelphia, PA: Temple University Press, 1990.

CHAPTER 5

Communities

For the citizens of Le Chambon, memories of their own persecution made it only natural to offer shelter within their community to other victims of social injustice.

We must delight in each other, make other's conditions our own, rejoice together, mourn together, labor and suffer together, always having before our eyes our community as members of the same body.

—JOHN WINTHROP (1588–1649),
FIRST GOVERNOR OF MASSACHUSETTS BAY COLONY[1]

IDEAS IN THIS CHAPTER

Le Chambon

In 1940, France fell to Nazi Germany, and by 1941, the puppet Vichy government began the systematic deportation of the Jews. The Nazis appeared triumphant. The people of the area of Le Chambon sur Lignon in southwestern France, however, refused to give up. Here, in the course of four long years, five thousand Jews were sheltered by five thousand Christians.[2]

Outwardly the people of Le Chambon, a poor farming community 350 miles south of Paris, were much like those of any other small French village. Most were peasants and villagers descended from Huguenots, the first Protestants in Catholic France. Once they too had been persecuted for their beliefs, their rights abolished, their men deported to slave in galleys, and their women imprisoned in towers. The persecution Huguenots called "the wilderness" lasted for one hundred years.

In spite of this, the people of Le Chambon clung to their beliefs, their land, and their community. The memory of their past was the key to their survival. In every challenge there would be an echo of their forefathers faith and struggle. It was not only their religious beliefs, it was the persecution they endured that made them different.

At the turn of the century when industry exploited women and children in mass numbers, Le Chambon welcomed the sickly working-class women and children from neighboring cities and took them in. In the 1930s, they sheltered refugees from the Spanish Civil War, and in 1940 they took in "guests" offering them hospitality because "it was only a natural thing to do."

In the beginning, only a few Jews made their way to this tiny corner of the world. At great risk to themselves, villagers cared for the Jewish people. The Jews kept coming, and the people of Le Chambon took them in: individuals, couples, families, children, the elderly, those who could pay and those who could not—doctors, merchants, intellectuals, and homemakers from Paris, Warsaw, Vienna, and Prague.

One day during a church service a man came into the congregation. "I have," said he, "three old testaments," meaning there were three Jews who needed shelter. Without hesitation, an old farmer raised his hand. "I'll take them," he said. Never once did the people of Le Chambon ask if the strangers were Jews, even though they knew they were. To them it did not matter. They took in the strangers and protected them, helping them on their way.

The day before the people of Le Chambon were threatened with occupation by the Nazis, Reverend Trocme delivered a sermon that exemplified their resolve and the roots of their resistance. "The duty of Christians is to resist the violence that will be brought to bear on their consciences through the weapons of the spirit. We will resist whatever our adversaries demand of us contrary to the orders of the Gospel. We will also fear, but without pride and without hate." It was a conspiracy of compassion.

The people of Le Chambon started schools for the refugees, and even helped them observe their own religious services. They began a center for forging documents, identification cards, and passports, giving the Jews false identities. Even when Nazis occupied Le Chambon, they continued to hide the Jews, once in a hotel directly across the street from where soldiers were bivouacked. Le Chambon became a center of the French resistance.

The community of Le Chambon and the Jewish people were anchored in community. The Nazis, on the other hand, considered themselves the epitome of progress, modernity, and technological efficiency. How they despised and attempted to destroy community! And yet, the community of compassion and resistance survived, while the Third Reich was destroyed in only a few years.

Introduction

Each of us has a notion of what is meant by community. We all live in a community defined as a geographic locality. Some communities are based on economic status or social condition. Persons who are developmentally disabled and their families form associations that can be seen as communities sharing common needs and purposes. In the same way, people who have encountered difficulties or who have special needs, interests, or purposes form communities. Alcoholics Anonymous, for example, is such a community, as are the numerous other twelve step groups.

People of different religious or ethnic backgrounds form what are called "ontological" communities, or communities of meaning. Churches, temples, and synagogues are authentic communities building on a history stretching thousands of years into the past whose rituals, traditions, and literature continue to inform and suffuse people of today with a sense of *koinonia*, or fellowship, and *shalom*, or unity in God's presence. Diverse ethnic groups form communities of meaning to maintain, promote, and keep alive the heritage, religion, history, culture, and traditions of a people.

Humans are genetically predetermined to be social beings. We cannot exist without one another.[3] Communities are a component of the human condition, not just a particular historical era, place, or time. Neither are communities unique to one racial, national, or cultural group. Deeply rooted in man's nature, community may be said to be a universal phenomenon, not contingent on circumstances. Wherever humans exist they will seek and form community. We all live in and identify with the "community" in which we live.

Macro social workers assist communities of people and help develop community. It is important, therefore, to understand what is meant by the idea of community.

This chapter presents the two most important theoretical models of community: the social ecological model and the social systems model. Because these models are integral to social work, you need to be able to assess their usefulness. A third model, an action model of community, is also presented.

There are three different kinds of community with which social workers concern themselves: modern communities, ontological communities or "communities of meaning," and traditional communities. We will explore community social work in each of these types of communities and then explore some ideas about community social work in the future. At the end of this chapter are several exercises that will help you better understand community.

What Is Community?

Bellah et al. define *community* as :

A group of people who are socially interdependent, who participate together in discussion and decision making, and who share certain *practices* that both define the community and are nurtured by it.[4]

Community is an "inclusive whole celebrating the interdependence of private and public life, and of the different callings of all"[5] that "attempts to reproduce the entire institutional complex of a functioning society."[6] Among its components is "a solidarity based on a responsibility to care for others because that is essential to living a good life"[7] and an interconnection of economic and social relations that are "visible and, however imperfectly, morally interpreted as parts of a larger common life."[8] Such a "caring community of empathic sharing"[9] is not quickly formed. It almost always has a history defined in part by its past and its memory of its past[10] that "exists before the individual is born and which will continue after his or her death."[11] Community

> encompasses all forms of relationship which are characterized by social cohesion, and continuity in time. . . . Community is a fusion of feeling and thought, of tradition and commitment, of membership and volition.[12]

Communities, therefore, are natural human associations based on ties of kinship, relationship, and/or shared experiences in which individuals voluntarily attempt to provide meaning in their lives, meet needs, and accomplish personal goals.

Theories of Community

Just as social systems and social ecological models have been applied to theories of social problems, they have also been applied to community social work. These models provide conceptual handles that help us understand communities. Models are useful because they can give us simplified versions of how complex phenomena such as communities operate. Whenever you use a model as a representation of the real thing, however, you must understand its limitations. No model is an exact replica of the real thing. Sometimes models are even deceptive. In other words, there may be hidden agendas implicit in models that may not be apparent at first. Rather than merely accepting a theory or idea as true simply because it is handed to you, apply your own intuition and thinking functions to get at underlying premises on which theories or models are based. Once you have examined the model critically, you can either accept or reject it because you have thought about its meaning for you. Ask yourself the following questions:

1. The social systems model borrows concepts from physical mechanics and applies them to humans. The social ecology model borrows concepts from biology and applies them to humans. Are there logical fallacies implicit in this conceptual borrowing? If so, what do you think those might be?
2. What role does the individual play in the social systems and social ecological models?
3. Are important elements of community excluded from the social systems and social ecological models? If so, what elements do you think these might be?
4. How would you apply the social systems model to changing communities? If you were to adopt the social ecological model, how would you apply it to improving communities?

Ecological Model

Using concepts borrowed from biology to understand and explain the dynamics of human community, Carel Germain and Alex Gitterman popularized the "ecological perspective" in social work. "Ecology," according to Germain, "is the study of organisms: environmental relations."[13] It is "a form of general systems theory."[14] The ecological perspective sees the community as an organism that has a boundary and that engages in transactions with its environment. A transaction is a reciprocal exchange in which each part of a social organism gives and receives in a symbiotic relationship with other parts. The outcome of this exchange is a homeostatic balance in which the biosystem is held in equilibrium. A healthy social organism is one in which all of the different components fit together with one another and that has adapted to its environment. "Adaptedness refers to the fit between person and environment, the adaptive balance between needs, capacities, rights, and goals, *and* the qualities of the social and physical environment within a given culture."[15]

One factor that affects social organisms' ability to adapt is stress. Biological organisms experience stress in their ecosystems because of changes in their environment. Temperature changes and lack of food or water, for example, cause stress. Stress in the social environment is the "lack of perceived control over events because of insufficient internal and external resources, and threats to self-esteem arising from devaluation and rejection by others."[16] Examples of negative stressors in the social environment are poverty, unemployment, loss, and devaluation by others likely to have long-term consequences resulting in a "vicious cycle of internal and external messages."[17]

Just "as in plant and animal ecology, a pattern of interdependence develops among humans who share a common habitat."[18] A *habitat* is a

> place where the organism is found, the dwelling place, home range, and territory. In the case of human beings, the physical and social settings such as dwellings, buildings, rural villages, and urban layouts must support the social settings of family life, social life, work life, religious life and so on, in ways that fit with life-styles, age, gender, and culture.[19]

In order to improve the human habitat, social ecologists are interested in "predictable patterns of land use and spatial distribution"[20] and concern themselves with the condition of housing, streets, lighting, transportation, and schools so as to make the social environment habitable for people.[21] Crowding or distance, for example, are issues that affect an individual's sense of personal space. Overcrowding tends to stress people. On the other hand, where there is too much space, people become socially isolated.[22]

Communities, like biological organisms, are assumed to develop niches in their social habitat. Niche refers "metaphorically to the status occupied in the social structure by a particular group or individual and is related to issues of power and oppression."[23] While many people have the opportunity to carve out niches for themselves and gain an abundant supply of desirable commodities, others are "forced to occupy niches that do not support human needs and goals—often because of sex, age, color, ethnicity, social class, life-style, or some other personal or cultural characteristic devalued by society."[24] Social workers must be concerned about the existence of unhealthy niches into which people are forced, such as slum conditions, poverty, and low-status position.

In addition to social niches and habitats, the ecological perspective focuses on "population characteristics of a community (size, density, heterogeneity), the physical environment (land use), the social organization or structure of the community, and the technological forces in the community."[25] Because the ecological perspective focuses on community "social geography, distribution of people and organizations in space,"[26] an ecological perspective allows a social worker to map the community and to observe "changes in the use of space, the distribution of people, and the movements of people over time."[27]

Armand Lauffer asserts that "the use of ecomapping tools provides you with a visual framework for assessing the balance between an organism and its environment.[28] Such techniques can be used "to examine current or anticipated relationships and to explore the ramifications of moving from where we currently are to where we want to go. Like any map, they describe relationships in space and can be used for guiding us in our movements through that space."[29]

Finally, a social organism needs to have a variety of social "nutriments that release and sustain people's potentialities . . . including biological, cognitive, sensory-perceptual, emotional, and social stimuli."[30] Among these are "environmental properties of opportunity, social respect, and power."[31] Like plants and animals, the social organism is affected by social pollution of its environment. Among these pollutants are "poor housing, inferior schools, inadequate health care, poor systems of income security, and inadequate juvenile and criminal justice systems,"[32] as well as "abuse of power, and the oppression of population segments based on race, ethnicity, gender, sexual orientation, disablement, and age."[33] Social ecologists attempt to rid the social environment of these social pollutants.

Social Systems Model

The social systems perspective, according to Phillip Fellin, adopts a "structural/functional model of communities."[34] A community is composed of a series of interrelated parts each of which serves a specific function in the community structure. In other words, each component of a community exists for a purpose. The structure of the community system reveals the particular function each of its units serves. Bronislaw Malinowski, a cultural anthropologist, said:

> The functional view of culture insists upon the principle that in every type of civilization, every custom, material object, idea, and belief fulfills some vital function, has some task to accomplish, represents an indispensable part within a working whole.[35]

Like social ecologists, advocates of the social systems perspective see communities as composed of "locality relevant" functions of the social system. Among these functions are the production, distribution, and consumption components of the economic system of the community.[36] The socialization function is the responsibility of schools and community agencies that comprise the educational system. The social control function is carried out by government, which makes laws through the political system and enforces them by means of the criminal justice system. Social participation functions are provided by voluntary associations, social agencies, and religious groups, which are components of the social system of a community. Finally, mutual support functions are the purview of hospitals and social agencies, the health and welfare systems.[37]

All systems are comprised of particular elements such as inputs, outputs, boundaries, processes, and feedback. Each community needs inputs in the form of resources to ensure its functioning. Resources can be seen in terms of money, people, raw materials, and information. For example, communities try to attract businesses because businesses generate jobs and bring income to the community. Communities also try to attract people, particularly those with skills that the community needs for its growth. Communities that have rich sources of raw materials are able to exploit them to their economic advantage. Land, water, minerals, and forests are all raw materials that can be used by communities.

Communities use inputs to create living conditions, cultures, and relationships, which can be defined as outcomes of community processes. Children are educated and socialized. People engage in professions, earn a living, and raise families. They engage in social, religious, and recreational activities.[38]

Communities are defined by their boundaries, particularly as they exist in specific geographic localities or take the shape of territory defined by the town or city limits. Furthermore, processes by which the economic, political, social control, and other functions operate ensure that all the parts of the community remain in a homeostatic balance and all the parts function smoothly. Feedback comes from social indicators such as population growth, unemployment figures, crime statistics, housing starts, median income levels, rainfall, tax revenue, SAT scores for school children, and so on.

Critiquing Social Ecology and Social Systems Models

Ask yourself how adequate the social ecological and social systems theories of community are for you. For example, do you see any logical fallacies in borrowing from physical or biological sciences and applying them to communities? What role does the individual play in these models, and are elements excluded from these models? What practical application of these models to community social work are there?

Misplacement of Concepts

The social ecological model and social systems perspective borrow ideas and terminology that are appropriate for the biological or physical sciences and apply them to the human social sphere. While there is some utility in this kind of borrowing, when it occurs with little qualification the result may be a logical fallacy called "misplacement of concepts." Misplacement of concepts may have deceitful implications that tend to undermine the human content that the theory purports to describe.

It is true that humans obey biological and physical laws, and to that extent we can apply these principles to our own activities. However, these models begin to break down when it is assumed that human action tends to be determined by natural processes and laws without regard to the meaning that the human actors themselves give to those processes and functions.

The social ecology model is based on biological concepts and finds its roots in the writings of the William Graham Sumner, particularly his famous work *Folkways*.[39] Sumner

> examined social customs and interpreted their emergence as the environmental adaptation of highly developed organisms. The work of the (social) sciences was to formulate the laws of this adaptive process. . . . Evolutionary process thus furnished the model for human sciences—defining human social evolution through laws of social adaptation.[40]

In the theory of biological evolution plants and animals exist in an ecological environment in which principles of survival of the fittest, natural selection, and evolution operate.[41] Nature promotes survival of those that are the fittest by a process of natural selection. Those species that are less adaptable to changing environmental conditions or that cannot compete for resources tend to die off and are replaced by others who fill evolving ecological niches.

It is proper to consider plants or animals as being subject to biological laws of nature since they "have no opinion regarding the merits of their own survival."[42] However, the "treatment of persons, if only by implication, as the functional equivalent of lungs or kidneys"[43] obscures the realization that people in contrast to animals make conscious decisions about the ways they associate together.

The transferal of concepts of biological evolution into the social human sphere is known as Social Darwinism. Social Darwinism proposes that

> society is not made by man; society develops like any other organic process—evolving according to laws of nature. Society's problem is to recognize the course which nature is taking and to conform to it.[44]

According to this view, communities of people who appear less capable, incompetent, less intelligent, or who cannot compete in modern society will fail to adapt and survive, providing room for the more competent individuals or groups to survive, grow, and adapt to new ecological niches in the social environment. Taken to its logical conclusion, the social ecology perspective could breed antagonism toward allegedly "less highly developed" groups or

communities of the poor, mentally ill, developmentally disabled, immigrants, and certain ethnic groups because it would not be the interests of society to support or encourage their continued existence.

Social ecological models, for example, are implicit in the notion that some nations are "underdeveloped" in contrast to modern Western society. Less-developed communities or nations must adapt and accept Western attitudes or values.

Subjugation of community to biological laws of nature provides justification for the indifference of people to the fate of communities as a cherished social form of human existence. The dominant social system today, in contrast to community, is the complex organization, which penetrates and replaces community.[45] Under constraints of social ecology, if community as a living social system does not survive, there would be no reason to mourn its loss, because its demise would be seen as inevitable. Having failed to adapt to the demands of a naturally evolving organizational society, community could simply be discarded as an extinct social species. This, in fact, is already beginning to happen.

> Many traditional sociologists, writers, and social observers will say that communities no longer exist. They characterize communities as inventions of primitive and prehistoric people. We are even taught that a desire to belong to a community is an outdated need not entertained by sophisticated people who are socially or physically mobile.[46]

While social ecology utilizes premises drawn from biological sciences to explain human affairs, the systems model appropriates laws of physical mechanics and applies them to society, furnishing

> a scientific calculus of the social process comparable to the laws of mechanics in physical process. . . . Calculation of the laws of social life gave sociology a role in society comparable to that of physics in its dealing with physical nature.[47]

Humans are viewed as nothing more than component parts of an artificial mechanism, a concept that originated with Thomas Hobbes over four hundred years ago.[48] Because matter and energy inevitably obey laws of physics such as the law of gravity, we can accurately predict and ultimately control those physical forces. This gives us lots of power over nature. This power enables humans to create technologies that can add to the quality of life. But when concepts that are true of physical objects are translated into the social realm, as in systems theory, humans are assumed to operate as bits of social matter that are inexorably determined by social laws.

> When the subject matter of social science is handled like the subject matter of physical science, knowledge of social laws becomes a knowledge of laws which control man's activity. Knowledge of society reveals man's enslavement to societal forces. Man ceases to be a "subject" and becomes an "object" of calculable forces external to him.[49]

Humans are treated as components of social systems just like mechanical parts of a machine. Forces such as motivators are applied to them externally to induce them to greater productivity. They are socialized to function according to the goals of those who control the system. People become a means to an end. Their worth is determined by their utility to produce.

Social work relies heavily on social systems and social ecological models. However, care must be exercised in the extent to which we rely on these models because they may give us a distorted conception of the human condition and undermine our efforts to change social situations.

Passive/Atomistic Model of Man

Both ecological and systems theory presume a model of man that is passive and atomistic. On the one hand humans are considered to be "passive, conformed and adapted."[50] Rather than creating and controlling social systems, the masses of ordinary people are viewed as acted upon by irresistible biological and mechanical forces beyond their control. A person has little choice but to "discover himself to be the passive object of forces playing upon him."[51]

In addition, systems and ecological models tend to see people as atomistic rather than as social beings.[52] Atomistic means that people are much like atoms, autonomous bits of social matter that interact with other atoms according to physical laws. In the social realm the atomistic conception of the self is individualism. Individualism "lies at the very core of

American culture."[53] The idea of individualism originated with Thomas Hobbes, who viewed individuals as discrete components of the larger social mechanism.[54] John Locke, in agreement with Hobbes, asserted that "the individual is prior to society, which comes into existence only through the voluntary contract of individuals trying to maximize their own self-interest."[55]

One might assume that the social work profession clearly considers humans to be social rather than atomistic. Social workers, however, tend to be ambivalent about humans as primarily social creatures. If anything, the "tendency of individualism to exclude adequate attention to social factors"[56] has prevailed in the history of the social work profession. This individualistic rather than social focus is perhaps one reason that social work has welcomed the ecological and systems models, which assume that people are atomistic, isolated, and separated.[57]

The Charity Organization Society movement in 1877, for example, took an individualistic, person-by-person approach to problems of poverty. It was influenced by Mary Richmond, who "shaped the business of friendly visiting into the professional practice of social work."[58] The trend toward an "individualist view of human nature"[59] continued with the identification of social work as a psychotherapeutic profession.[60] This "therapeutic attitude reinforces the traditional individualism of American culture."[61] To the extent that social work adopts systems and ecological models, and conceives of practice mainly in psychotherapeutic terms, "the primary work of social work is individualizing."[62]

During the social ferment of the 1960s, the social work profession was challenged to return to its social roots, bringing to a head two contradictory impulses. In practice, social work centered on individual treatment, but ideologically it was still social in nature. In an attempt at rationalizing this split, "social systems theory . . . was seized on as an organizing framework" providing theoretical justification for thinking of people as subsystems of increasingly larger systems.[63] Later, Carel Germain softened the mechanism of systems theory by casting people as living organisms in an environment.[64]

This tendency of "splitting the human condition into individuals and environments fits the historic main current in social work theory building,"[65] resulting in "a series of unexamined, nonempirically based statements about individuals and environments."[66] Both systems and social ecology models, for example, resolve the problem of individual versus social by simply adding them together,[67] resulting in the "person-in-the-social-environment" view of the human condition. The individual remains either an atomic particle (systems) or a cell (social ecology) responding to social forces in an environment into which he or she is embedded. These bits of physical or biological matter, then, are assumed to interact as do atoms or cells.

The "person-in-the-social-environment" idea does little to amplify understanding of the social aspects of the human condition. In fact, it tends to add to the confusion. For example, while the social worker builds on the premise of client self-determination—that "people are to be respected as individuals regardless of circumstances"[68]—the person is left as a being determined by forces around him or her, "overwhelmed, powerless, disenfranchised and, therefore, in need of social work help."[69]

Michael Harmon and others cite this kind of theory as "conspiracy." "By conspiracy is meant the inclination of those with specialized knowledge to enhance their power to manipulate, control, or confuse their clients."[70] Specifically, "systems theories, which are usually based on either mechanistic or organismic metaphors,"[71] are conspiratorial because they erroneously assume that humans and communities are passively under the control of social forces external to them and are irrevocably subservient. If we assume that human freedom is dependent on atomistic individualism, then "each person is rendered vulnerable and weak, and each person [is] left to negotiate his or her own 'contracts' in the marketplace."[72] Systems and social ecology models, therefore,

> postulate the idea that the human person is an island unto him- or herself and that this condition of "aloneness" is the natural and preferred state. They deny and negate the tenacity of the human community and the inventiveness of people to sustain themselves within social groupings that meet their needs, and they promote the destructiveness of human communities by devaluating all forms that do not meet some traditional norm.[73]

Humans, according to social systems and ecological theory are passive atomistic creatures responding in predetermined and predictable ways to stimuli or forces beyond their control. They "behave"; they do not act. And individual "behavior" is conditioned by the requirements of the market. "It makes [the person] responsive to the sales appeals that activate him as a consumer and by assuming that his attitudes and actions will not differ widely from those of his neighbors, keeps him firmly in place as a member of the mass market."[74]

Missing Elements

Because the systems view tends to see the social components as interacting parts, it highlights only those parts that are directly observable, measurable, and therefore subject to prediction and control. Systems and ecological models do not tend to include less tangible aspects of community such as values, meaning, or commitment.[75] In the social ecological model "people are bound together not by sentiment but by utilitarian considerations, cooperating through their mutual interdependence caused by the division of labor, but at the same time competing in matters of common desire, but scarce satisfactions."[76]

Passive atomistic individuals collect in niches, engaging one another by reciprocal transactions in a kind of giving-and-getting social exchange.[77] "In this imagery of exchange, the self stands apart from what it does, and its commitments remain calculated and contingent on the benefits they deliver."[78] Community, therefore, becomes simply "an aggregation of people competing for space . . . in a competitive situation."[79]

Missing in this competitive striving and continual adaptation are the very qualities that make a community social—feelings, relationships, beliefs, mutuality, and commitments. The people who inhabit such communities tend to be transient, to lack permanence, to indulge in self-interested pursuit of goals, to be wedded to the present, and constantly seek to adjust to a fluid environment in which adaptability is the key to survival. Social systems and social ecology models of community tend to exclude the qualities of permanence, support, cooperation, and relationship.

Community, as perceived by systems theorists and social ecologists, tends furthermore to be restricted to a physical location or a habitat that fills a particular niche in the social environment. This restriction excludes communities of people who, while not living in a contiguous location or habitat, continue to see themselves as a community, sharing culture, history, meaning, and social reality. On the other hand, simply because people inhabit the same territory or because functional systems operate side by side is no guarantee that a locality constitutes a real community. People may live close to each other and function together, but not be a community.

A conception of community as an aggregate of institutions, functions, structures, or various organic components leaves a community "external and soulless."[80] Under these assumptions a community becomes not an integrated whole but simply an amalgam of parts. In the systems and social ecology models, therefore, people

> work together but for diverse reasons, and so the life they jointly lead is external, not infused with mind. . . . They imagine themselves to be brought together as a matter of convenience. It is to their mutual advantage to work together—each is enabled to earn a living in this way, or to amuse himself. But these are private and personal aims. By entering into activity for such reasons the participants reduce the activity to the status of means. There is then nothing in the activity which can unify them, no basis for community.[81]

Competitive atomistic individuals striving for a social niche from which they can pursue their interests are a covey of persons devoid "of a sense of social responsibility."[82] If, say Bellah et al.,

> the aggregation of atomistic selves are defined by their preferences, but those preferences are arbitrary, then each self constitutes its own moral universe, and there is no way to reconcile conflicting claims about what is good in itself. All we can do is refer to chains of consequences. . . . In the absence of any objectifiable criteria of right and wrong, good or evil, the self and its feelings become our only moral guide. What kind of world is inhabited by this self, perpetually in progress yet without any fixed moral end?[83]

There is little vision of what constitutes a good community, because a community is simply an aggregate of individuals inhabiting a social environment, each pursuing his or her individual interests. The social ecological model of community is therefore "essentially a negative one: it offers not the re-

alization of an ideal, but simply the elimination of certain conditions—slums, blight, congestion, and sprawl that are deplorable. The negativity and plurality of this approach could not be expected to elicit the same enthusiasm as positive efforts toward achieving a unified ideal."[84] There is a tendency with both the ecological and systems perspectives, therefore, toward an "implicit bias in favor of conservative, that is, system-maintaining values."[85] Sheldon Wolin points out that

> in the systems approach, the category of "input" reduces heterogenous issues to a single homogeneous item. For instance, the term *input* stands "equally for a civil rights protest, a deputation from the National Rifle Association, and a strike by the UAW."[86]

"Systems theorists," Wolin remarks, "make it possible to talk about an entire political system without ever mentioning the idea of justice, except in the distorted form of its contribution to system maintenance."[87]

Practice Limitations

In practice, it would be nearly impossible to gather atomistic, passive, and competitive individuals together to work in their own common or the public interests.[88] The most effective way to work with people based on the presuppositions of systems and social ecology models is on a one-to-one basis. The systems and social ecological models, therefore, while claiming to be "integrated approach[es] to social work practice [are], on the whole, individual-client oriented."[89] A community model of social work practice based on systems and social ecology theories will probably not occur.

Systems and ecological models are models of homogeneity and similarity, not diversity, creativity, or innovation. Community

> derived from the social ecology perspective in sociology [is based on] an assumption that people who are basically similar will tend to live and interact with each other—while those that are dissimilar will not, that they will seek out similar groups. Therefore, a community is probably present where a goodly percentage of people share key social and economic characteristics.[90]

This conventional model of community is what Victor Thompson[91] and R. M. MacIver call "associations,"[92] and Bellah et al. call "life-styles enclaves" or "communities of interest."[93] Life-style enclaves are not authentic communities but are pseudo or surrogate communities that "bring together those who are socially, economically, or culturally similar . . . the chief aim [of which] is the enjoyment of being with those who share one's life-style."[94] A neighborhood habitat is simply a "residential enclave chosen as a place in which to pursue appropriate private life-styles, [each of which] is no different from thousands of other American suburbs."[95]

Such homogeneity of interests is necessary because a system, by definition, cannot operate effectively if its components are different and carry values, culture, and ideas that disrupt the homeostatic balance the system attempts to achieve. Both the ecological and systems models tend to smooth out diversity and differences, and to see community only as people that place themselves into enclaves. In these social niches, "the different, those with other life-styles, are not necessarily despised. They may be willingly tolerated. But they are irrelevant or even invisible in terms of one's own life-style enclave."[96]

Social work practice using the systems and ecological vision of community will have difficulty including ethnically diverse populations, the poor, or the marginal as integral parts of the whole. These groups will tend to be seen as deviant or in the case of a "nonconforming system unit, as 'dysfunctional.'"[97] These components will need to be adjusted or treated to bring them into conformity with the overall social ecology of society. Social work practice utilizing systems and social ecology theories can be expected to be treatment oriented rather than emphasizing prevention, to be oriented toward system maintenance inducing people to conform to system values and processes, to work toward smoothing rather than celebrating differences and to create a homogenous rather than a culturally or ethnically diverse culture.

The social systems and social ecology models based on structural functional premises[98] have, in fact, found a secure place in social work theory. These models are powerful tools because they work. However, simply because "they work" does not make them entirely valid. Alberto Guerreiro-Ramos claims that such theories are "naive." By this he means that these

> descriptions of behavior are not necessarily wrong: they are simply insufficient. . . . They are naive in the sense that they uncritically accept conclusions drawn from sensory observations without reflecting about the basic assumptions which underlay those observations.[99]

The interconnection between social systems and social ecology models, individualism, and the predominance of clinical therapeutic technique in social work has left "only an impoverished language in which to think about [unifying the] individual's life story with the community's ideals of a good life."[100] "For the therapeutically inclined, [therefore] community is something hoped for, something yearned for, something sadly missing most of the time, and, when found . . . something that therapeutic language cannot really make sense of."[101]

An Action Theory of Community

> Not only man's action towards external objects but also the relations between men and all social institutions can be understood only in terms of what men think about them. Society as we know it, is, as it were, built up from concepts and ideas held by the people; and social phenomena can be recognized by us and have meaning for us only as they are reflected in the minds of men.—Friedreich A. Hayek[102]

The action model of social work reestablishes community as centering around the sentiments that unite people. It includes community as the arena in which humans find their identity as social beings who are active agents in the creation of social reality. Community is the medium in which people meet their common social needs, communication, relationship, meaning, and ritual.

Active/Social Model of Man

A community is more than a social habitat in which people fill ecological niches. The community becomes the bearer of the self. In a community "one gives oneself to learning and practicing activities that in turn define the self, entering into the shape of its character."[103] We become selves by means of our relationships and interactions with others. And, we form our values and our character by means of the influence others have had on us.

The goal of selfhood is to contribute to the development of the community, providing a sense of social responsibility by contributing to the life of the whole and thereby enriching one's own self. People form community with one another as an expression of the human needs for substance, purpose, and identity.

In a community we are expected to take others into account by providing support, healing, and helping to those in difficulty and trouble. Our humanity is extended when we provide a milieu of safety and protection to those least able to care for themselves. Exemplary communities become warm, nurturing and supportive environments in which personal growth and development take place.

One of the most common descriptions of community comes from the German sociologist Ferdinand Toennies, writing in the 1870s. He observed that a phenomenon was occurring in which one form of human association or "*gemeinschaft*" was giving way to another form of social relations which he called "*gesellschaft*." *Gemeinschaft* is what we commonly call community characterized by warm, intimate, natural, face-to-face relationships. These relationships include sentiment, affect, and loyalty.[104] For Toennies,

> *Gemeinschaft* was not a local community, but rather a type of relationship that could permeate any level of society . . . a relationship focused around sentiment and emphasizing common ties and feelings and a sense of moral interdependence and mutual obligation.[105]

Max Weber, in his essay "Some Categories of a Sociology of Understanding," expanded on Toennies' ideas. *Gemeinschaft* for Weber was defined as social action or "action based on mutual understanding."

> Action is social insofar as, by virtue of the subjective meaning attached to it by the acting individual (or individuals), it takes account of the behavior of others and is thereby oriented in its course.[106]

When I "act" I attach some sort of meaning to my action. But action does not occur as I act individually but as I take into account the meaning that other people attach to my actions. "When I so design my actions that I take into account how others might react, I have begun to transform action, with its purely personal meaning, into social action."[107] When two or more people attempt to direct their actions toward each other, they engage in a social relationship.

Another way of looking at social action is the idea of we-relations expressed by phenomenologist Alfred Schutz. "In the pure we-relationship I create my social life with others who have intentions similar to mine."[108] Furthermore,

> what makes social life appear human is a kind of intimacy I gain from interacting in depth with my consociates—the members of the little world whose center I am and which I enlarge by including you in the we-relationship. In fact, the more I make an effort to understand you in your complexity and the closer to you I feel, the more meaningful and satisfying life in the social world appears to me.[109]

For Weber, *gemeinschaft* as the kind of social relationship is also "communal action," or *Gemeinschaftshandeln*,[110] which exists in and forms the basis for community. Personal face-to-face relations are the frame of reference in which life occurs in community. The shared perceptions and meanings are the glue that holds communities together. People "become communities only with this sense of community, this *Gemeinschaft*."[111] According to Martin and O'Connor:

> From this view, a community exists because of values, sentiments, feelings of identification, and commitment that are held in common by a collective of individuals. This can occur in a locality, such as a town or city, but can also occur independently of locale . . . The defining quality is that the members share common sentiments that unite them.[112]

A community "is above all a network of friends. Without civic friendship, a city will degenerate into a struggle of contending interest groups unmediated by any public solidarity."[113] Friendship was an important component of early American communities. "In such small communities, it was obvious that people not only helped one another and enjoyed one another's company but also participated mutually in enterprises that furthered the common good."[114]

Social action or "we-relations" are the means by which community comes together. The human condition is active in the sense that people themselves construct society. It is social in the sense that people construct society out of "we-relationships."

Meaning

People in community have common memories that give meaning to their lives. In community, we begin to get a sense of our history.[115] This history shapes our experiences and provides us with our particular heritage. Communities develop stories that become legends and myths, distilled from collective endeavors, successes, failures, conflicts, victories, and defeats. These memories of shared suffering, of heroism and of deceit, of struggles to overcome adversity, make up traditions that "contain conceptions of character, of what a good person is like, and of the virtues that define such character."[116]

The stories of the collective past form the substance that guides a community into the future. People learn from their successes, failures, cooperation, and conflicts. They confront the dilemmas of existence in the context of the history, traditions, and customs of their community, and as they relate to other communities they discover other missions, purposes, and alternative histories. In so doing, they develop an understanding of "truth." Out of these shared experiences individuals come to see themselves as a community and ultimately as human. Community is *the* means by which solitary, isolated human beings are transformed. Even the difficulties by which people in community overcome adversity provide them with meaning.[117] When people struggle to solve common problems, they express those things that they cherish and they struggle for what is best and good, noble and excellent.

Finally, communities bear the "truth" of a group of people by means of culture and symbol. People acknowledge that truth by commemorating important events and celebrating common bonds with ritual, ceremony, and celebration.

> The communities of memory that tie us to the past also turn us toward the future as communities of hope. They carry a context of meaning that can allow us to connect our aspirations for ourselves and those closest to us with the aspirations of a larger whole and see our own efforts as being, in part, contributions to a common good.[118]

In this way community prepares the way for *ethics* to emerge in human life as a collaborative effort of a group of people devoting themselves to a heritage of truth but continually aiming themselves toward a future and a vision.

Ethical Ideals

The action model of community is informed by an ethical ideal. This ideal includes "solidarity based on a responsibility to care for others because that is essential to living a good life."[119] It is a process of *social involvement*, stemming from a life of active civic consciousness and engagement.

In an action model of community, relationships are not private activities but public ones. The private interests of community members are infused with a sense of purpose, meaning, and commonality; the good of all becomes a unifying whole with public spirit as its center.

> It will become a community when their purpose in participating in each of these varied institutional affairs becomes one with the public purpose served by the institution itself . . . When the public outcome of the activity is the aim of the participants, this outcome becomes a unifying and mutually held purpose. The fact that their efforts are centered on a common project draws the participants together into a community.[120]

The means by which people establish public purposes and goals and discourse about ethics is called *politics*. The word *politics* comes from the Greek work for community, *polis*. Politics is reserved for community. Community politics is decision making by means of the shared values, feelings, meaning, and perceptions that enhance the life of the people who compose the community. Community is founded on "an ethics of duty, on the idea of the good life, but also on the ideas of discipline, responsibility and obligation."[121] The individual centers his or her life on something outside of him- or herself, toward which efforts are directed. Community not only constitutes a way of being in the world, of mere existence, but also a "way of life" as individuals actively engage one another. An ethical community

> is, simply, one whose structure encourages such a life in every way possible. It provides an environment which grasps the good; it is so designed that a good life is on all sides the natural outcome of the way affairs are conducted. . . . The good life for the individual is one wherein he develops his powers harmoniously to the fullest extent.[122]

Community is invested with social ideals, a conception of what it means to be *good*, an appreciation for the "public good" as opposed to purely private good, and ultimately to a normative standard for what it means to be a good community or a good society.

Diversity

An action model of community is innovative and creative and prizes difference and diversity. A community needs people of differing ages, backgrounds, history, and personality. However, each community must be held together by a common bond that unites the diversity of individuals into a cohesive unit. Then the differences can be used and appreciated.

There is not just one model of community or one community ideal. Rather, each community is seen as a unique blend of the people of whom it is composed. Insofar as a community is based on ethical ideals, it can be a model for others. The more communities that come into existence, the more opportunities there are for people to explore alternative ways of being in the world and achieving richness of character.

Kinds of Communities

There are three kinds of communities with which macro social workers become involved: modern communities, ontological communities, and traditional communities.

Modern Communities

Modern communities exist in large urban and rural areas and include neighborhood districts, eth-

nic neighborhoods, planned communities, low-income communities, towns, and villages.

Some older cities still have well-defined neighborhoods that may be called modern communities. In San Francisco, for example, geography and ethnicity play a role in defining communities. Districts bear names that give these neighborhoods specific identities, such as Mission District, Potrero Hill, Twin Peaks, Noe Valley, the Marina, and Bernal Heights. People identify themselves with their neighborhoods and take pride in them.

Many neighborhoods also have an ethnic distinctiveness. San Francisco's Chinatown, for example, is world famous. Everyone in San Francisco knows where Nihon-Machi is located. It is the center of the Japanese American neighborhood. The Mission District has a large percentage of the city's Chicano and Filipino population. Potrero Hill is still the home of San Francisco's Molokon Russians.

In many of our large cities there are areas where people live in planned communities. One kind of planned community for the affluent are townhouse communities, which often are completely enclosed so that only residents or guests can enter. Another kind of planned community is one consisting of mobile homes.

Finally, modern communities may exist in rural areas. Small towns are often pictured as the ideal modern communities. People share a common way of life and often know one another. The economy may be tied to one or two enterprises such as agriculture or a major industry that supports the town.

Many modern communities display symptoms of dysfunction. Dysfunctional modern communities are found throughout America. They exist among the affluent as life-style enclaves. They exist among dispossessed homeless residents of deteriorating inner cities in Washington, D.C., and in the Bronx, New York. They include residents of low-income housing projects in Cabrini Green, Chicago, and in Hunter's Point, San Francisco. They are the communities of Vietnamese, Laotian, or Hmong immigrants who live crammed together in ghettos in San Jose, Fresno, and Los Angeles, California.

Modern communities of the poor exist among migrant workers living in substandard housing with few sanitary facilities along the Rio Grande in Texas and in California's rich Central Valley. They are found in farming or rural areas of Minnesota where

Community has become vulnerable in today's modern world. In a large area cleared for urban renewal, a single building remained in Manhattan's TriBeCa district, New York City.

the economy has become eroded, in once-prosperous mining areas in the hills of Appalachia, or in high unemployment, ex–steel mill towns like Clairton, Pennsylvania. Dysfunctional modern communities exist in every state, in every large city, and in every area of this country. People in these dysfunctional modern communities are alienated, oppressed, and depressed.

Alienation

Even in relatively affluent neighborhoods, residents of many modern communities display alienation—they lack community spirit and exist in relative anonymity. Many do not even know their own neighbors. In many neighborhoods there is not even the possibility of developing real "community spirit." In our mobile society, people come and go frequently. There is no guarantee that people will remain in any of these communities long enough to have a stake in them.

There are few ties that bind these communities together. Many residents do not work in the neigh-

borhood. They commute to a distant place to work. Recreation and social activities are usually conducted outside of the community. If people belong to a religious group, more than likely it too will be located outside their own neighborhood. For many, the only real "center" of such modern communities is the local elementary or middle school. Alienation breeds loneliness, fear, and lack of identity with others.

Oppression

Sometimes modern communities play out a "zero-sum" scarcity game in which there is never enough to go around. One easily identified group in the community is "scapegoated," or systematically oppressed, to the advantage of other segments of the population. People in these communities are often divided into haves and have-nots, winners and losers. Winners, often wealthy and advantaged, may work in central city financial centers and live in lush suburban neighborhoods while in the older parts of the city are communities of the poor who exist in squalor, dirt, and desperation. We isolate poor communities so we do not have to see them. When our encounter with them becomes unavoidable, our blinders go up and denial sets in. We pretend that they do not exist.[123]

Depression

People in dysfunctional modern communities are depressed. Many inner cities have become communities of hopelessness. Services and businesses have moved. What remains is social decay. Runaway children and teenagers are preyed upon. Prostitution and drug abuse is rampant. The chronically mentally ill find few services, the homeless wander the streets, and vagrants exist on the fringes of the community. Those who remain tend to exhibit gross indifference and inattention to people's needs. People are allowed to suffer and are ignored. People feel helpless, unable to do anything to change things.

Ontological Communities

Interspersed within the infrastructure of modern communities are religious, cultural, and civic associations that provide spiritual, emotional, and existential meaning and support. Called ontological communities or communities of meaning, they often symbolize and become the heart and soul of the larger community. A Christian church, for example, is sometimes the center of life of many rural communities. The Japanese Cultural Association is a center of meaning for the Japanese community in many cities, often supported by the Buddhist Temple and sponsoring Japanese schools, evening classes, summer youth programs, and religious and cultural events such as Bon dances, Taiko drum and Kendo demonstrations, all of which keep the spirit and culture of the Japanese community alive. The Sons of Italy provides an arena in which Italian Americans can share and celebrate their culture. The Jewish synagogue is not only a center of religion and worship, but also a cultural, social, and intellectual center of life for the Jewish community. Mosques provide a sense of identity for Muslims.

Ontological communities supplement components of modern life that are missing, providing stable values, rituals, and direction to people's lives. They fulfill people's needs for affiliation, connec-

tion, socialization, and ultimate purpose, which our modern society often lacks.

Ontological communities accept the wider culture as a reality, learning and growing from it while maintaining their own particular values, truths, and distinctions. They neither succumb to or become that

---

EXTERMINATION: A MODERN SOLUTION TO A COMMUNITY PROBLEM

"Everyone is afraid" he said as he fiddled with a piece of plastic tape, keeping his eyes on the table. Sister Beatriz Semiano and a social worker, Wolmer Nascimento, a coordinator for the National Movement for Street Boys and Girls, listened as A.G., a thin, dark boy, one of the ragged legion of street kids who live by their wits in Rio, Sao Paulo, and Reclife, told how death squads hired by local merchants roam the streets exterminating homeless children.

"He was sleeping," A.G. said, "and they filled his face with bullets." Cleiton, twelve, used to steal from stores in a shopping gallery near the center of Duque de Caxias, Brazil, one of the grimy, violent suburbs only a few miles from the swaying palms, elegant hotels, and white sand beaches of Rio de Janeiro. Cleiton's death was not an isolated incident.

Hundreds of children are murdered each year by bands of private security guards, many of them off-duty or former policemen, the very people who should safeguard the children. A.G. said that he had known "a heap" of youngsters killed in Duque de Caxias. One was Luciano, sixteen, picked up by his killers and shot in the head. "He robbed stores," A.G. said of Luciano. Two weeks after Luciano's death, gunmen killed his friend Ademir, sixteen. "He also robbed," A.G. said. There is no doubt, A.G. insisted, about who the killers work for. "The store owners pay them to kill us." A.G. has slept on the streets for eleven of his sixteen years. He said the killers almost got him when he was thirteen.

The merchants treat the children like rats. Kill them and the problem goes away. Sometimes in a shrewd, if twisted scheme, they even pay members of some street gangs to exterminate children in rival gangs.

Sr. Beatriz confirmed the dangers A.G. described. "He lives in the street, he sleeps in the street, and he is threatened with death," she said. "It is a terrible problem in Brazil." The problem, she and others say, has its roots in urban poverty, antiquated laws, police corruption, and ineffective systems for providing child welfare and criminal justice.

wider culture and do not reject or resist it either. Ontological communities are often judged by their altruism, compassion, and caring. Many ontological communities prize justice and stand strongly for their convictions.

Because of their importance, macro social workers become concerned when ontological communities fail to function. When social workers assist these communities they are interested in their leadership, mission, boundaries, organization, and growth problems.

Leadership

Leadership of ontological communities is particularly difficult in today's world. The leader must play several often incongruent roles simultaneously. The leader must, on the one hand, understand and relate the truths, values, and purposes of the community to the world in which it exists. On the other hand, the leader must relate the world and its values to those of the community so that members have a

means to respond to the external culture. The leader must be skilled as a ceremonial figure capable of symbolizing, articulating, and living the community's ideals. He or she is a bridge between both worlds, a model and a teacher showing how both worlds can learn and grow from one another.

In addition, the leader must be an administrator managing an organization. Administration requires attention to detail, skill in delegation, program development, and budgeting required to keep the organization functioning.

A leader who is a good administrator providing efficient organizational structure but who is ineffective in providing modeling will fail to help the community in its basic function. Members may lose their sense of altruism, caring, and compassion. Their values, boundaries, and purpose become weakened. On the other hand, a leader who is a strong charismatic figure but poor in administration will have an organization that flounders because roles are unclear, details are not attended to, communication becomes

Communities of meaning often symbolize and become the heart of the larger community. Here, community members march in support of urban peace and justice in Kansas City, Missouri, May 2, 1993.

muddled, conflicts go unresolved, meetings are poorly run, and functions are not provided for.

Unclarity of Mission

Sometimes problems arise because the mission or purpose of the ontological community is unclear. Is the mission of the community to maintain itself as best it can, serve the needs of its members, or provide services to the culture in which it is embedded? Must that mission remain static, or can the mission of the community change and grow as the needs and requirements of the members change and grow?

Boundary Problems

When ontological communities fail to reevaluate their primary mission or become unclear about their purpose, the boundaries of the community become fluid, and the community loses its strength and firmness. As a result, it fails to uphold the particular truth that it stands for. When ontological communities succumb to the culture around them and fail to maintain their distinctiveness, they become indistinguishable from the wider social environment.

On the other hand, if boundaries become impermeable, some ontological communities may become so rigid about the truth they represent that they become enclaves unto themselves and refuse to accept truths that exist in the wider culture. If this occurs, they fail to infuse the wider culture with their particular truth, alienating their own members by not helping them understand or see the place of the truth of their community in the wider world. They become isolated and alone.

Time Orientation

Ontological communities are, for the most part, based on long-term relationships, stability, and continuity over time. Because our society is increasingly mobile and operates on shorter time commitments, these communities may find it difficult to adapt quickly to changing circumstances.

Lack of Growth

Ontological communities begin failing when they experience lack of growth and loss of members.

CHURCHES AS CENTERS OF COMMUNITY

Overall, the organizing effort for self-help and self-development programs in the Chinese-American communities for the past twenty years have been the establishment of hundreds of churches of all denominations in this country. . . . The congregational development of the church as a strategy and tool of community organization has been considered as a successful event to achieve the concepts of self-help and self-development. It also preserves the ethnic identity of Chinese Americans in a multiethnic society.

Even though the primary purpose of the church is to proclaim the gospel of Christ and to promote spiritual growth, its practical objective is to assist the church members to cope with various psycho-social problems and social adaptation as well as to meet their socio-cultural needs in the ethnic community. Each local church can be considered a community service center even though it may not be staffed with professional social workers or community organizers. . . .

The basic reason for the existence of a church as a community agency is that the church programs are meeting the various needs of its members; otherwise the church will disappear in the community. Most social gospel-oriented churches have developed community service programs for their neighboring communities. They usually provide services to lonely elderly, frustrated women in family crisis, dependent children without parental care, and teenagers without proper supervision, such as the Good Shepherd Formosan Presbyterian Church in Monterey Park. It has provided child care and nursery school for children and youth programs for teenagers. The Cameron House of Chinatown in San Francisco, which was set up for girls about a hundred years ago, has become the cradle for training the Protestant pastors, teachers, community organizers, social advocates, and youth leaders of Cantonese-speaking Chinese Americans in this country. . . . The Protestant churches, Catholic Social Services, and many Buddhist organizations can play a very important role in organizing community resources and providing social services to meet the psycho-social and socio-cultural needs of their followers and the neighboring communities.

Source: Isaiah C. Lee, "The Chinese Americans—Community Organizing Strategies and Tactics," in Felix G. Rivera and John L Erlich, *Community Organizing in a Diverse Society* (Boston, MA: Allyn and Bacon, 1992), pp. 153–55. Reprinted by permission.

Those communities that experience changes in membership or member loss find it difficult to maintain programs and services. Relationships become harder to establish and there may be a tendency to rely on a few of the "old guard" to carry on the core functions of the community.

Traditional Communities

Traditional communities exist side-by-side with modern culture but attempt to maintain their separateness, uniqueness, cultural integrity, and historical identity. They exist at variance with "normal" modern society, which operates on values of speed, efficiency, mass production, increasing technological advancement, wealth accumulation, competition, growth, progress, and individualism.

The mutual relationships, commonality, tradition, ritual, and social bonds distinguish third-world traditional communities from one another. An African proverb, for example, asserts, "It takes a whole village to raise a child." A communal endeavor, child rearing is so important that it cannot be left to parents entirely. The community is the mother and father of its people.

The work and the social relationships of the traditional community tend to be inseparable. Members of traditional communities may interact and relate to society in general, but in a restricted way and often on their own terms. For the most part, traditional values and ways of life are seen as more important than the promises of technology, wealth, or prosperity of modern society.

There are probably only a few remnants of authentic traditional community in America today. Native American nations and tribes that have survived decimation continue to struggle to maintain their own identity. Of these, the Navajo have been most successful, having developed their own system of laws, governance, economy, and social system within the majority culture in southwestern United States. While not every Native American would agree with the following assessment, it does describe a common ideological preference. The chairman of the American Indian Movement (AIM) said in an interview in the *Akwesasne News:*

We can live by what would be considered a poor standard of life by white standards and still have a good life and be happy. That is one of the differences between us and the struggles of other minority groups. We are not concerned with having a $10,000 median income for our people. We are concerned with our people being free and living the way they want to live. . . . We're not looking for the nine to five job, a white-collar job for all our Indian people. We're not looking for upward mobility in the social structure of the United States. We don't need that. We don't want that, we don't want anything to do with that. We're looking for our sovereignty, our ability to govern ourselves, and for every person to live as a free person. To live the way they want to live.[124]

In addition are the communities that are recipients of Western culture but have rejected its forms and values. One example are the Amish, who use horse-drawn carriages in place of cars, and reject other modern technological inventions. Other traditional communities are experimental, utopian communities called "communes" and religious orders, particularly those of the Roman Catholic church, in which the members live and work as a community. In Israel, separate communities or communes are called Kibbutzim. Kibbutzim are small agricultural communities in which work and child rearing are shared along with religious traditions.

Traditional communities also exist in Africa, South America, and southern Asia. Many people in the "developing" nations of Africa and South America suffer the effects of "development" because their own customs, culture, and attachments are alien to that of Western industrialization. Trying to hold on to customs and a way of life that have sustained them for thousands of years, they find themselves an anomaly in the modern world.

Traditional communities exist where drought, war, famine, disease, poverty, and conflict rage. They are found in the jungles of Guatemala, the drought-ridden regions of Northern Africa, in refugee camps in Thailand, in the poverty stricken City of Joy in Calcutta, and in the villages of Haiti.

The difficulties of community life in the United States are mild compared to those experienced by the tribes people and villagers in many places in the world. In barrios, towns, and villages, children with swollen abdomens die of malnutrition or suffer irreparable brain damage. In the garbage dumps of Manila, children forage for food. By drinking water from rivers and streams in African towns, people become infected with parasites and eventually become blind. Casting their fate to the wind, desperate Haitian and Vietnamese families set sail in unseaworthy boats, hoping to be rescued and given sanctuary.

Conclusion

With few exceptions community has been *the* form of association by which people have related throughout history. Community as a "natural" social system has been giving way to "artificial" social systems dominated by progress, efficiency, and goal achievement. In the same way that industry has systematically decimated natural biological ecosystems, replacing them with highways, factories, cities, and parking lots, so organizations are destroying communities—natural human ecosystems—replacing them with corporations, universities, military machines, banking systems, and hundreds of complex organizations.

Just as environmentalists attempt to preserve the remnants of failing ecosystems, community social workers are "social ecologists," helping people in community develop countervailing structures, power, and strategies to counteract the deleterious effects of modern organizational life.

The predisposition to community insures that people will meet their basic needs and develop culture and ethical values, which are difficult for single, isolated individuals to accomplish alone. However, because individualism is a major ideology today, people often develop an ambivalence to community as a social ideal and as a social model. The result is a paucity of theory and a lack of practice principles on which to build community. Current ideology tends to undermine community and at the same time make people yearn for it.

Social work is a field in which relationships are the key ingredient in treating social ills. The common good as opposed to purely private good is the desired outcome of the macro social worker's concern for people's welfare and the healing of society. According to Robert Greenleaf, the word *healing* means "to make whole."[125] The community has traditionally been a source of healing of the self. Social work has tended to reduce the importance of community by its emphasis on treating individuals and by its theoretical models. The psychotherapeutic process "attempts to cure people by detaching them from society and relationships. All other forms [of healing] . . . bring community into the healing process."[126]

Community can be the means by which people develop a sense of who they are. Without this, they become prone not only to dysfunctional behaviors, but to moral and ethical disease as well. Community is the context in which healthy selves develop. Without community, the social bonds and relationships that give purpose and meaning to life, and friendships that fulfill the need for affiliation and connectedness with others, are not formed.

KEY CONCEPTS

community
ecological model of community
transaction
homeostatic balance
adaptedness
stress
habitat
niche
ecomapping
social nutrients
social systems perspective of community
structural/functional model
locality relevant functions
socialization function
social control function
social participation function
mutual support function
community resources
community boundaries
community processes
community feedback
misplacement of concepts
Social Darwinism
passive model of man
atomistic model of man
social exchange
life-style enclave
action model of community
active model of man

social model of man
gemeinschaft
communal action
community of memory
community politics
diversity
modern community
ontological community
traditional community
planned community
alienated communities
oppressed communities
depressed communities

QUESTIONS FOR DISCUSSION

1. Le Chambon sur Lignon is an example of a modern community. Compare it with the components of communities described in this chapter. Which components does it have? Which components does it lack?
2. This chapter makes a point that communal social systems, much like ecosystems, are slowly being eroded by the encroachment of modern technology. What is your opinion about this observation?
3. Can a case be made that the social arrangement we call community has, for the most part, outlived its usefulness, and that we should allow it to die off as social systems evolve?

ADDITIONAL READING

Community

Bellah, Robert N., Richard Madsen, William M. Sullivan, Ann Swidler, and Steven M. Tipton. *Habits of the Heart: Individualism and Commitment in American Life.* New York: Harper and Row, 1985.

Bernard, J. *The Sociology of Community.* Glenview, IL: Scott, Foresman, 1973.

Fellin, Phillip. *The Community and the Social Worker.* Itasca, IL: Peacock, 1987.

Haworth, Lawrence. *The Good City.* Indianapolis: Indiana University Press, 1966.

Koenig, Rene. *The Community.* London: Routledge & Kegan Paul, 1968.

Sanders, I. *The Community: An Introduction to a Social System.* 3d ed. New York: Ronald Press, 1975.

Toennies, Ferdinand. *Community and Association.* London: Routledge & Kegan Paul, 1955.

Warren, Roland L. *The Community in America.* Skokie, IL: Rand McNally, 1963.

Social Ecology

Germain, Carel B., ed. *Social Work Practice: People and Environments—An Ecological Perspective.* New York: Columbia University Press, 1979.

Germain, Carel B., and Alex Gitterman. *The Life Model of Social Work Practice.* New York: Columbia University Press, 1980.

General Systems Theory

Berrien, K. *General and Social Systems.* New Brunswick, NJ: Rutgers University Press, 1968.

Bertrand, A. *Social Organization: A General Systems and Role Perspective.* N.p.: Davis, 1972.

Boulding, Kenneth. "General Systems Theory: The Skeleton of Science." *Management Science* (1956), pp. 197–208.

Hearn, G. *The General Systems Approach: Contributions Toward an Holistic Conception of Social Work.* New York: Council on Social Work Education, 1969.

Leighninger, R. "System Theory." *Journal of Sociology and Social Welfare,* 5 (1978):446.

Stein, I. *Systems Theory, Science and Social Work.* New York: Scarecrow Press, 1974.

Person-in-the-Social-Environment

Anderson, R., and J. Carter. *Human Behavior in the Social Environment: A Social Systems Approach.* 2d ed. New York: Aldine, 1978.

EXERCISES

EXERCISE 19:
The Ideal Community

This exercise gives you a chance to design an ideal community. Think of communities you have known or have read about. What qualities constitute a human environment that not only provides for meeting needs but also inspires people to reach for excellence? After you have thought about the components of your ideal community, consider what it would take to actually implement it.

Compare your vision with those of your classmates. What are the qualities that make up an ideal community? What are the difficulties in constructing such a community?

EXERCISE 20:
The Future of Community

Social work needs to refine and develop alternative models of community and advocate for social policies and programs that support community in the face of increasing anomie, alienation, loneliness, and social despair. The traditional view of community as existing in a particular locale is an anomaly, and social work viewed as "locality development" is out of step with modern realities. For example, a Census Bureau analysis released December 12, 1994, indicates that "more than 2 in 10 of all the nation's households moved in the 15 months before the 1990 census."[127] Furthermore, the study "found that fewer than 1 in 10 households had been ensconced in the same house since Dwight Eisenhower was president. . . . Pittsburgh and two New York City suburbs—Long Island and northern New Jersey—were the only major metropolitan areas in the nation where people who moved in the 15 months before the census were outnumbered by people who had lived in the same house since 1959."[128]

Community conceived of as occurring in specific locales is, therefore, less and less likely to remain a reality. Neighborhoods today are simply places people are housed, not where people commune together. What alternative forms of community can you conceive of by which people can retain social relationships and adapt to our highly mobile and technologically sophisticated society?

CHAPTER 6

Becoming a Macro Social Work Researcher

Charles Booth's seventeen-volume Inquiry into the Life and Labour of the People in London *was the culmination of extensive social research aimed at bringing poverty under control.*

The government is very keen on amassing statistics. They will collect them, add them, raise them to the nth power, take the cube root, and prepare wonderful diagrams. But you must never forget that every one of those figures comes in the first instance from the village watchman, who just puts down what he pleases.

—SIR JOSIAH STAMP, INLAND REVENUE DEPARTMENT, ENGLAND (1896–1919)

IDEAS IN THIS CHAPTER

Charles Booth, Social Researcher

More than any other person of his time, Charles Booth was able, by means of his *Inquiry,* to change the course of the development of the society in which he lived.[1] The father of scientific surveys,[2] he applied the modern research methods of the natural sciences to solving the social problems of an industrial society.[3] Not only a great sociologist and social statistician, but an outstanding social work researcher as well,[4] Charles Booth ultimately struggled with issues of "social change and the discovery of methods of bringing it under control."[5]

Booth demonstrated that, by understanding and identifying causes of social conditions, people could control them and not be victims. "He showed not only that human vice and misery could be brought under control,"[6] but that by using certain methods he could examine and remediate those problems. His work led to a fresh definition of poverty to be used by governments to establish the field of social welfare, to implement new programs, and to develop a renewed role of government in social policy.

A contemporary of Sir Robert Baden-Powell, founder of the Boy Scouts, George Williams, founder of the YMCA, Samuel Barnett, founder of the Settlement House Movement, William Booth, founder of the Salvation Army, and Charles Dickens, author and social commentator, Booth was, in the words of Beatrice Webb, "perhaps the perfect embodiment of . . . the mid-Victorian time and spirit— the union of faith in the scientific method with the transference of the emotion of self-sacrificing service from God to man."

Beginning his career as a merchant, shipowner, and manufacturer, Booth volunteered to walk the precincts of the rowdiest and most corrupt part of all Liverpool to fight for the Liberal cause in 1865. Gaining first hand knowledge of the poor convinced him that "poverty . . . was an evil for which no possible justification could be advanced. His reaction was forthright and immediate, an experience which never left him."[7]

The sense of guilt and shame with which he had been troubled, overflowed in a passion of resentment against both the poverty of the poor and hypocrisy of those who countenanced it. . . . Comparing and contrasting his own way of life with that of the crowded streets of the dockside of south Liverpool, he was miserably conscious that there existed among those who were presumed to be his inferiors "a brand of Christianity much more in keeping with the religion that is read each Sunday in our Churches" than anything ever achieved in his own class.[8]

If the human misery he observed all around him was only an isolated instance of social breakdown, he could have dismissed it. However, the pervasiveness of poverty presented itself as fundamental to the times. It was something he could not ignore. The only alternative was to attribute its existence to the greed of man. As the implication of this conclusion became clear to him, it placed upon Booth a burden of personal responsibility for the welfare of others, which was at once so weighty and so unwelcome that he shrank from its acceptance.[9]

Finally, making a decision to remedy this misery, Booth helped organize wards among the Irish immigrant dockworkers of South London, supported land reform, and helped set up a political association by which the dock workers could find representation. While his party failed to win a seat in the election, Booth's interest in the labor union movement grew, and he worked to secure support for the trade unionists in the settlement of disputes. This also failed, but later, he threw himself with renewed energies into a campaign for a system of universal education. While many people agreed that universal public education for the poor was a good thing, Protestants feared their taxes might be spent on Catholics, and Catholics feared taxes that would benefit Protestants. The proposal to provide nonsectarian education died.

These were sobering experiences for young Booth. Exhausted from his efforts at community organizing and social action, he retreated to the calmer world of commerce and built up his various business enterprises. Slowly, however, Booth's interest in social questions revived.[10] During a visit to Canon Samuel Barnett in Whitechapel, founder of the Settlement House movement, Booth realized that all too many proposals for dealing with the poor had been prepared without regard to the facts. Lacking basic information, no one knew the truth about how the poor lived. What did the poor really want? How could their condition be relieved? Having no satis-

factory answers, Booth concluded that "what was required was a means of influencing public opinion for good, based on a knowledge of science and the natural laws governing human behavior." He decided that "the most hoped for form of social service was the craft of the social investigator," the application of the scientific method to solving social problems.[11]

The winter of 1885 brought renewed distress to the poor, crystallizing Booth's determination to devise, singlehandedly and with his own resources, a means of securing information on the extent and real conditions of poverty in London, and then to make recommendations for their cure. So began the great seventeen volume *Inquiry into the Life and Labour of the People in London,* completed in 1903, eighteen years later. He worked at his businesses during the day and on the project at night and on weekends. The task to which he set himself was no less than to classify every family by economic status on every single street, court, and block of buildings in the entire metropolitan London area. "It was an epoch-making event in the history of the social sciences, as significant for the field of social planning and social policy as it was in survey research."[12]

Volume one was published in April 1889. "Its appearance was greeted with 'wondering admiration,' demonstrating that human society could be analyzed and described by means of a combination of statistics and observation."[13] The first part of the *Inquiry,* called the Poverty Series, developed and applied a new method of fact finding and statistical analysis[14] called the Poverty Survey, which was to become the foundation of the survey method of social science research that we use today.

Booth challenged the conventional wisdom of his day—that the poor were poor because of "God's will" or because of personal immorality, laziness, or indolence. "It was," he concluded, "transparently plain that . . . the existence of poverty . . . was to be attributed directly to the working of some 'natural' law whose nature it was the function of science to reveal."[15] Booth examined the relationship between employment, earnings, and human needs, confirming the fact that the economic system of the nineteenth century had failed to provide a secure basis for family life regardless of the morals of individual men and women[16] and laying the foundation for the phenomenon now referred to as the "cycle of poverty."

Another of Booth's innovations was the concept of the "poverty line," a predictive tool still in use today. Developing the first operational definition of poverty, Booth provided the means by which the truth or falsehood of his hypotheses could be tested experimentally.[17] The accuracy of these hypotheses have withstood verification by independent studies.

Booth demonstrated a link between fact and theory, between pure and applied research, and between hypothesis and application of ideas to social policy and practice. Old age assistance, unemployment insurance, health insurance, trade unions, the machinery for minimum wage laws, the breaking up of the restrictive and punitive measures of the Poor Law, the development of factory inspection and social legislation are all direct results of the work of Charles Booth.

By analyzing the factors that contributed to poverty, Booth made a cure of the disease possible and, more importantly, showed that much of it could be prevented.[18] Never the detached scientist, his ultimate aim was to bring about an improvement in the conditions of the people[19] in whose midst he found himself. He laid the moral and practical foundation for social research, establishing it firmly not only for collecting information for its own sake but also for solving social problems and finding answers to the pressing social questions of his day.

Introduction

Like Charles Booth, macro social workers need to have information about the social problems they address, and they have to be expert at getting it. Community social workers, for example, examine the settings they are about to enter. Social planners spend a good deal of their time gathering data to perform social needs assessments. Program developers collect information to write grant proposals. Organization developers evaluate organizational dysfunctions, and social work administrators scan the external and internal environment of their agencies to ensure that their service plans are effective. Social policy requires quantitative research using benefit cost analysis in decision making. All of these processes require gathering and analyzing information.

Just as Charles Booth discovered, making recommendations for social change is often useless unless you have first found answers to questions about the social problem and have developed solutions based on that research. Research is a key to all macro social work practice. This chapter describes the kinds of questions macro social workers must ask and explores various ways they go about finding the answers.

What Is Macro Social Work Research?

Research, as Robert Grinnell states, is composed of two syllables, *re,* which means to do again, and *search,* which means to look closely and carefully for something.[20] Research, therefore, is to look again carefully and closely for something. It is a logical process centered in gathering information by means of our senses that can be empirically tested and measured and thus objectively and publicly verified.

While social scientists are generally interested in information and generating theory for its own sake,[21] macro social workers conduct research to obtain information they need to carry out their work to bring about a better society. Research in macro social work is applied research.[22] For example, if you are engaged in helping a community that lacks resources and services, you will want to find out as much as you can about this community to discover how those conditions came about and what can be done to develop resources and services. If the issue is planning for homeless mentally ill, you will want to know how many people have this problem, where they are located, and what their service needs are. If you are studying an organization in terms of its effectiveness, you will ask what symptoms of organizational dysfunction are being exhibited, where breakdowns occur, and how they affect the functioning of the organizational system. If you are an analyst interested in developing policies on child abuse, you will need to know how extensive the problem is, what its effects are, and what can be done to remedy it.

The history of social work in America finds its origins in social research. Perhaps the best example of research in aiding social reform and development of programs is that of Dorothea Dix, who worked for the betterment of conditions for people with mental illness. She began each campaign with patient, careful research. "Before starting out, she read widely on the subject and then, wherever she went, studied antiquated and impractical commitment laws, inspected buildings, talked with and observed the patients and their overseers."[23] Today, we would label these methods as using existing data, ethnographic research, focused interviews, and participant observation. She wrote reports on her findings, and "armed with numerous case studies and statistics depicting the extent and nature of the problem, she made her appeal,"[24] giving testimony before state legislatures and Congress. So successful were her methods that between 1843 and 1853 she "became personally responsible for the founding of state hospitals of mental patients in nine states . . . and quite a few others around the world."[25]

During the Progressive Era, social work made a major contribution to social reform by means of the introduction of systematic social surveys to the study of social problems. For example, the Pittsburgh Survey of 1907–1908, directed by Paul Kellogg, a social worker and assistant editor of *Charities and the Commons,* was "the first major attempt to survey in depth the entire life of a single community, . . . and covered wages, hours, conditions of labor, housing, schooling, health, taxation, fire and police protection, recreation, (and) land values."[26] Social research also was a major weapon of the National Child Labor Committee at the turn of the century.[27]

Research Questions

Research begins with a problem, question, or puzzle to be resolved. There are three major kinds of questions that social work change agents ask: questions that ask "what," or *descriptive* questions; questions that ask "why," or *predictive* questions; and questions that get at "how," or *prescriptive* questions.

Descriptive Questions

Social work change agents often begin with "what" questions. When you go into a community or an organization, the first thing you want to know is

what this setting is like. You need to get to know its people and understand its character. You want to get a feeling for its culture and a sense of its social dynamics, and you need to know its structure, size, demographics, power, needs, and services. You should become acquainted with its politics, its financial base, and its social milieu. As you engage the social setting, you want to know as much about it as possible.

Predictive Questions

After you understand "what," you begin to ask "why?" Asking "why" questions sometimes leads you to fundamental issues causation. Usually these kinds of "why" questions are the domain of social scientists. Social scientists such as sociologists, social psychologists, or political scientists are interested in what social conditions exist and in discovering why they came about. For example, a sociologist may ask why poverty exists or try to understand why crime rates are increasing. If a scientist can come up with a theory, then he or she may be able to predict and eventually offer a solution to control those social problems.

While macro social workers generally do not perform pure social science research, they are interested in answers to specific problems so they can discover how to solve them or to change social situations for the better. For example, if you have discovered gaps in services, dysfunctions, unaddressed needs, or major social problems, you will want to understand why these particular conditions have occurred. Once you know why a situation exists, you have some confidence that you are solving the real problem and not something else. You can then decide the extent to which you want to try to get at root causes, take a piece of the problem, or go after symptoms. You can do this only if you know "why."

"Why" questions lead social scientists to predict and eventually control phenomena in the real world. As a macro social worker, you will also want to be able to accurately predict the results of interventions that you make. If you cannot predict that an intervention you use will bring about a positive result, then people would have a right to question why you are using it. Systems theorists, for example, claim that once a part of a system is changed, other parts of the system will also change. Sometimes those changes occur in unanticipated ways.[28] The more you know about what will happen as a result of a change strategy, the more confidence you can have that you are helping to cure a social problem.

In addition, you can learn important lessons from social scientists who are engaged in predictive theory. For example, social scientists attempt to be very objective. This means that they try to avoid making value judgments that could prejudice them in their search for truth. Social scientists often try hard to remain value neutral and unbiased. They do not want to impose their own values or ideas about how things ought to be. They just want to know what is—the facts.

As a macro social worker, you must be careful to not let your own preconceptions, biases, or values color your perceptions of the social setting before you understand it. You need to withhold your tendency to jump to conclusions. Let the data speak to you about what is causing the social problems in the community or organization. That way you know that you are examining the situation as it really is and not one colored by your past experience or previous understandings.

Prescriptive Questions

Predictive questions lead to prescriptive ones. For example, once you have come to some assessment of why certain conditions exist, you will want to ask, "How can I improve or change them?" Prescriptive questions are "how" questions.

How questions are prescriptive because they lead you to look for prescriptive cures, to answers that will solve social problems. Your how question includes not only the direction of change but also the way you choose to engage in change, or your strategy. Strategies are plans, and you will want strategic plans that work. Prescriptive questions are practical because they can lead you to examine the kinds of techniques that will bring about change.

Research can help us understand "what interventions really help or hinder the attainment of our noble goals."[29] If you can do adequate research, you can become a self-conscious professional who can offer help with some confidence in its effectiveness.[30] Research can help you understand what really works so that you can make use of this information

to improve your practice. Grinnell, for example, says that

> we have no business intervening in other people's lives simply on the assumption that our *good* intentions lead to *good* outcomes. Although we may mean well, our good intentions alone do not ensure that we really "help" our clients. . . . Truly professional social workers never solely rely on their good intentions, intuitions, subjective judgments, and practice wisdom. They use the research process to *logically guide* their interventions and assess their effectiveness.[31]

Action Research

Macro social workers use descriptive, predictive, and prescriptive questions to develop "principles and strategies of action."[32] The term for applied research aimed at improving social conditions in an action setting is "action research."[33] Action research is an outgrowth of the action model of macro social work practice.

Rubin and Rubin define action research as *the systematic gathering of information by people who are both affected by a problem and who want to solve that problem.*[34] Action research has much in common with other kinds of research. It is logical and analytical. You use your thinking function to ask what and why questions. Action research "helps you structure the information-finding process and leads you to making decisions about the kinds of interventions that may be warranted."[35] Action research is practical and seeks solutions to here-and-now questions using your sensing function.

Action research, however, differs in several ways from other kinds of research. It is research conducted in the midst of a turbulent social milieu. It actively engages members of the community in both formulating and conducting the research. Action research is holistic. It utilizes not only your thinking and sensing functions, but also your feeling function and intuition. It is both self-critical and self-conscious in its methods.

The Turbulent Action Setting

Unlike the social scientist, the macro social worker does research in an action setting that is the target of change. While the generalist social work method is an ideal model based on assumptions that rarely exist in the real world, the world of social work research is a turbulent one in which social settings rarely remain static long enough to allow you to examine them under controlled, stable conditions.

Social settings change continuously as they are affected by the conditions in their environments. For example, as soon as you begin to engage a community you change it by your very presence. Members of social settings such as communities and organizations continually enter and leave the social setting. The environment of the setting makes demands on it, and the setting reacts, adapts, or copes with those demands. Therefore, even as you begin to examine the milieu of your change effort, that milieu is shifting. Unlike the laboratory in which all the variables of your research environment can be controlled, in action research you have little or no control over the conditions you are investigating. As a result, you may not be able to follow the pattern of traditional social science research in a lockstep, rigid fashion.[36]

Community Engagement

Social science researchers choose problems out of an attempt to understand social settings and to develop social theory. With action research, control of defining the issues or problems is in the hands of those affected by the social problems because "people won't work to solve the problem unless they feel it is important."[37] But more importantly, because social work is relational and social in character the focus of macro social work action research is the "face-to-face encounter,"[38] which places social work research in a context of "concrete experience and is, therefore, the most elemental—and, in a sense, real—unit of human interaction."[39] Action research "focuses on the study of the subjective meanings that people attach to their own actions and the actions of others."[40] Because social facts "have no existence other than as artifacts of shared agreements among people,"[41] action researchers maintain that knowledge of the social world is "a social product, a result of either tacit or explicit agreement among people."[42] Action research that accepts the subjective meanings of people and places people at the center of construction of social reality validates the way that so-

cial constructs occur. Macro social work research, therefore, is not "an autonomous form of knowledge, or an autonomous discipline"[43] that operates one step removed from people and is something that occurs to others. It is instead intimately involved *with* and *for* others.

Action research attempts to bring to light the social conditions people want to change and to devise ways of changing them. In macro social work "people are not objects and a neighborhood is not a laboratory; facts don't speak for themselves."[44] Action research assumes that the people affected by social problems are not simply passive recipients of a fate-entangled existence but can actively take part in determining their own futures.

Rubin and Rubin assert, for example, that action research "not only finds out what community members feel the problems are, but what in particular about the problems disturbs them, and what they hope to accomplish by solving them."[45] Action research, therefore, is not a process conducted out of a social worker's research interests, or for the purpose of building theory, or in the splendid isolation of the research laboratory. Instead, it is based on the needs and concerns of the community, it is practical, and it involves members of the community in its efforts.

> By involving others in the assessment process, you will also be sharing with them the responsibility for programming. You will be energizing them and stimulating their further involvement in problem solving. You will also provide them with a structure through which they can make decisions based on the facts they have uncovered.[46]

Action research not only attempts to explain or describe social phenomena but also is intimately related to social work because it mobilizes people as they "learn they share the problem."[47] It is a "capacity-building endeavor as people work to solve the problem."[48]

Intuition

In addition to using a researcher's thinking and sensing functions, action research engages the researcher's intuition. Traditional social science research tends to be skeptical about the usefulness of intuition. Grinnell, for example, warns against relying solely on intuition in evaluating social work practice. He says that

> (1) intuition and reality do not always mesh; (2) intuitive judgments may lead to superstitious behavior and complacency; (3) intuitive judgments vary dramatically from person to person; and (4) intuition is susceptible to bias.[49]

Sole reliance on only one of the problem-solving functions is questionable when carrying out macro social work, whether it is problem solving or research. For example, one could raise arguments about the sole reliance on thinking and logic as a way to understand social settings or how to engage humans in helping resolve social problems. People are not always logical nor are the issues with which they struggle amenable to rational understanding.

Sometimes, therefore, understanding people can occur by immersing oneself in the culture and the significance that people attribute to their own history, and with intuitive insight come to an awareness of the meaning behind the facts of social situations. Often in macro social work, where situations are complex and turbulent, one needs to rely on one's intuition function, as well as thinking and sensing functions.

Values

Conventional social science research tends to be scrupulously value free. Researchers work hard to insure that their own values do not color the facts that they are observing. They want the facts to speak for themselves, without bias. As a result, they hold their own feeling function in abeyance.

One's feeling function, you may recall, is that personality component that imputes meaning and values onto facts. Value-neutral social researchers, therefore, may be able to accurately describe social settings, but they are often unable to critically assess those social systems. They generate a great deal of knowledge *about* people.

Action researchers take a different approach to understanding social phenomena. They accept their feeling function and use it as a research tool, rather than attempt to suspend their feeling and values. In this way, they enter into a social setting using subjective feelings in a conscious way as they experience the setting first hand. An action researcher wants to know *about* people as does a conventional researcher, but more importantly, he or she wants to *know* people. The action researcher can know people only by direct, face-to-face experience.[50] When this happens, the researcher enters into the subjective world of the people. The researcher can begin to understand the meaning people attribute to their own lives, to their community, and to society as a whole.

Furthermore, action researchers are not neutral about the settings they are evaluating. They will actively assess those systems in terms of what is good or right. Questions of what is good and right are normative questions. Macro social workers not only want to know what can be done but what *ought* to be done to improve the quality of life and to make things better for people. Macro social workers want to know how to change things for the better. What direction should you go in? What decisions are the right ones? These kinds of questions are not value free. Normative questions are "should" questions. Action research, therefore, looks to what is best—norms, values, and behaviors that you want to change.

Self-Conscious and Self-Critical

Action-oriented macro social work research is both self-conscious and self-critical. It is self-conscious because researchers are aware and clear about the particular values that they seek to further in trying to change systems. It is also critical, because they do not accept information, facts, or even theories simply because they are handed to them. The stance of macro social workers should be one of "dialogue and critique rather than passive acceptance"[51] in relation either to the social settings in which they operate or the theories that support those systems. John Lambert calls this research style "ideology critique" in which the researcher treats critically the "taken-for-granted assumptions and definitions" and criticizes positively "plans, proposals and ideas for the neighborhood . . . so that he can say in whose interest such proposals are made."[52]

While researchers must understand and use predictive, descriptive theory, they do so with a careful understanding of the premises or fundamental assumptions on which the facts and theories emanating from that research are based. "In utilizing social science theories, then, community workers need to evaluate them in terms of what overall view of the social sciences they are based upon."[53]

When critiquing social systems and social theory, macro social work action researchers apply their values and ethical judgments to settings and methods. They realize that social settings are not simply objects that they can assess dispassionately. Social settings are human creations that are infused with meaning, value, and social substance. Action researchers recognize this and use their own values in decisions about what kinds of issues to address, how to address those issues, and evaluating the techniques that are appropriate.

The Action Research Process

Macro social work practice and research follow the generalist or rational problem-solving process[54] described in chapter 3. The process of identifying a problem, gathering facts about it, analyzing and developing alternative solutions to the problem, and evaluating the results of the intervention are all components of social work research.[55]

While rational social work problem solving begins with engaging the client, macro social work research begins with engaging the social setting. Both macro social work research and rational social work problem solving recognize and identify a problem to be solved. Rational problem solvers try to arrive at a social diagnosis; macro social work researchers generate hypotheses. Rational social work problem solvers develop a series of alternative solutions called a treatment plan; macro social work researchers arrive at a research design or plan of attack. Rational social work problem solvers implement a treatment plan that, if successful, will resolve the client's problem, while macro social work researchers carry out the design by gathering data, interpreting it, and coming up with an answer to the research problem.

Finally, a rational social work problem solver evaluates the results of social treatment; a macro social work researcher assesses the strengths and weaknesses of research and recommends areas for further research. Both rational social work problem solving and macro social work research follow the same steps.[56] You cannot, in fact, conduct macro social work practice without doing research.

Entering the Setting

Just as macro social workers use a combination of questions to get at social problems in the action setting, they also use a combination of a number of research methods to understand the truth of those settings. For example, before a community activist enters a community or an organization consultant walks into an organization, he or she needs to know something about the social system with which he or she will be working. A wealth of *statistical information,* called existing data, is available to help the consultant understand the setting as well as obtain a perspective on problem areas that concern you. *Rates under Treatment* (RUT) and the *Social Indicators* approach are ways to use existing data in discovering particular information about the community.

Statistical Information

Social scientists and social workers working for government agencies have already collected statistical information that you can use. World statistics are available through the United Nations. Its *Demographic Yearbook* presents vital statistics such as births and deaths, and other population data. A wealth of statistical information can be found at most libraries in the annual *Statistical Abstract of the United States* published by the U.S. Bureau of the Census, U.S. Printing Office, Washington, D.C. This volume can be purchased from government bookstores or commercially under the name *The U.S. Fact Book: The American Almanac,* published by Grosset and Dunlap. Local census data can give you an overview of demographic data of a neighborhood. City or county *planning departments* have a wealth of statistics that update or amplify census data. Local universities often have extensive research programs and data banks.

All public welfare, mental health, and criminal justice agencies keep records of their client populations and prepare reports on their respective areas of interest. Almost always this information is stored on computers. For example, you can obtain information on the number of people receiving public assistance, abuse cases reported, children and teenagers living in group homes, persons being treated in drug abuse and alcohol facilities, admissions to state hospitals, and the incidence of violent crime.

If you are involved in organizational development, almost certainly you will want to examine the agency's records. Board minutes will give you a quick, if formal, review of the history and processes through which the organization has been going. The agency's budget, procedures manual, statistics, and annual reports as well as various historical documents offer invaluable sources of information.

Finally, client case files may be of great help in conducting program evaluation research. If the records are computerized, it may be a fairly simple task to access the statistics. If not, you can select a sample portion of the files of the agency to obtain information.

Rates under Treatment

Rates under treatment (RUT) is a special way of using existing data from social and health agencies. RUT means the "rate" or extent to which services (treatment) are being utilized in a community. RUT can tell you a lot about the incidence of particular problems and something about the distribution of problems demographically in a community, the types of services used, and the quality of services available.

"Incidence" means the extent to which the problem occurs. People living in communities that are less affluent may have less access to services and experience a higher incidence of social problems. For example, discovering how often mental health services are utilized in certain areas of the city compared to others will tell you where to concentrate your efforts. The crime rate for rape, murder, or other violent crimes may differ from one part of town to another. In addition, RUT can give a picture of the kinds of programs and services available to the client population. It can show where the strengths or weaknesses are in the service continuum and where there are gaps in services.

Rubin and Babbie point out that a disadvantage of rates under treatment "is that the records and data . . . may be unreliable or biased."[57] For example, "agency accurate record keeping may be a low priority . . . Also, many agencies may exaggerate the number of clients served or their needs for services in order to look good to funding sources."[58] You may need to make allowances for such weaknesses in accepting data from agencies.

Social Indicators Approach

Social indicators are "inferences of need drawn from descriptive statistics found in public records and reports."[59] They are "markers" by which macro social workers can spot underlying social issues. Emile Durkheim's classic study of suicide, for example, used a social indicators approach. Using available statistics, Durkheim collected official government statistics from a number of different countries in Europe on the incidence of suicide. He observed that the countries had radically different suicide rates that seemed to remain stable over long periods of time. The rate in Saxony (eastern Germany) was about ten times higher than that of Italy, for example. By correlating the incidence of suicide with the religion of those countries, Durkheim found that suicide was more prevalent in Protestant countries than Catholic ones. Also, suicide increased during times of social instability. Durkheim hypothesized that suicide may have something to do with what he called "breaches in social equilibrium."[60] In times of social upheaval people lose their social moorings. Because Catholic countries provided people with a greater coherence and stability than more socially fluid Protestant countries, Catholic countries experienced less suicide. This observation led Durkheim to hypothesize that suicide is connected with the phenomenon of *anomie,* or normlessness. The incidence of suicide, therefore, was an indicator of the extent of anomie in society.

A wealth of information exists to help you discover such indicators of social problems in your community. Public health services both locally and nationally collect data on the incidence of diseases and the health of the population, including mental health, disabilities, aging, alcoholism, and drug abuse. The Department of Housing and Urban Development (HUD) collects information on housing and homelessness. Social workers are interested in and on the alert for these social indicators. Today, we are experiencing a rise in violence of all kinds. What does this indicate about underlying conditions in our society?

While "using social indicators is unobtrusive and can be done quickly and inexpensively," Rubin and Babbie caution that "this must be weighed against potential problems in the reliability of a particular data base . . . and the degree to which the existing indicators can be assumed to reflect future service utilization patterns accurately."[61]

Identifying the Problem

As you use your research tools to understand social problems, you will discover ways of helping those people who are affected by the problem gain power and control over the forces in the social environment that are causing them trouble. The social problem that you wish to remedy and the research question you want to answer are interrelated and come out of the issues felt by the people in need. For example, the problem of unemployment caused by a plant closing or the slowing down of the economy is a social problem, but it is felt personally by each person who is laid off.

By guaranteeing that community members are involved in problem identification, you ensure that research reflects what is important to the community. Placing the members of the social setting at the center of problem identification removes the possibility that they are treated as passive "objects" of research. The members of the setting become active participants in an endeavor that increases their self-understanding and their control of a process that can help give direction to their lives. Action research means empowerment.[62]

When people take charge of defining problems for themselves, they gain skills and reduce their reliance on technical experts who frame problems for them. Community members will have more trust in the outcomes of research if they have a hand in framing the problem and in carrying out the research themselves.[63]

Problem identification helps sharpen thinking by forcing you and the community members to be clear about the question. If your questions are focused, the means of gathering information to answer those questions become much clearer. "The first step in action research," therefore, "is to learn what problems people want to solve and how community members interpret given problems."[64] Ways of finding out about the social setting can be done by ethnographic analysis, focused interviews, focus groups, surveys, and needs assessments.

Ethnographic Analysis

The culture of a community or an organization is the "shared values, beliefs, assumptions, perceptions, norms, artifacts, and patterns of behavior" that the members of these systems have constructed, a kind of "social energy that moves people to act."[65] J. Steven Ott says that "culture is to the organization what personality is to the individual—a hidden, yet unifying theme that provides meaning, direction, and mobilization."[66] It is the shared meanings that make a social setting what it is. Understanding these meanings helps you "get into" the community or organization and recognize where the failures of its culture have occurred. Terrence Deal says that you begin at the surface and proceed inward toward the system's "unconscious."[67] When you do this you are conducting ethnographic analysis. Ethnography includes examining the physical character of the setting, what the setting says about itself, its social networks, how the community treats strangers, and how people spend their time.

1. *Examine the physical character of the setting.* First, look at the physical setting. The buildings and geography of a community or organization make up the public face that it presents to the world. A community that is proud and confident and has an integrated culture will reflect pride in the way it appears. What about consistency? Are the streets in affluent sections broad, in good repair, and lined with trees while poorer sections have streets that are narrow, full of holes, and lack trees and grass? Are people of color clustered in poorer sections of the community? Discrepancies in the quality or quantity of community services and attention for different classes or ethnic groups is a sure sign of a weak or fragmented community culture.

2. *Discover what the setting reveals about itself.* Does the community have a motto or logo that

portrays its character? With what qualities does the community identify itself? Is the motto or logo posted prominently on billboards or signs? Local newspapers describe what is important to a community's members. Communities with strong cultures recognize and take pride in the accomplishments of its citizens. What stories do the members tell about themselves? Who are the community's heroes? What is its history? If a community is concerned only about its economy and critical of its less-distinguished members, it may be fragmented and divided.

Strike up conversations with people you meet on the street corner, in restaurants, or in stores. Ask what kind of a community this is? Is it a good place to live? You will find out about the qualities people admire. Ask people about the history of the community and what their role is in it. Find out about important rituals, events, and activities that characterize the people.

Ask about the good things in this community. This will give you a picture of the sorts of things people prize and in what they take pride. Ask what kind of people live there. Who has met with success? This will tell you about the values of the community.

3. *Look at social networks.*

What kind of civic organizations exist and what kinds of communities of meaning such as churches and synagogues have a central place in the community? What is the diversity of these community components? Are the social service networks both public and private? The number and variety of nonprofit social service organizations and agencies will tell you about the civic-mindedness of its citizens. Do religious groups interact and engage one another or are they insular and disengaged?

How are schools maintained and where are they located? What is the racial and economic balance in the schools? Do some schools have rich resources and better students while other schools have fewer resources and poorer students? This will tell you a lot about how resources are allocated, what values are important, and the engagement of citizens in a community.

Are businesses locally owned and oper-

ated and is there a variety of them or are there a few large companies whose owners live outside the community? How engaged are businesses in the community? Do they invest effort in the community or simply take its resources for profit?

4. *Look at how the community treats strangers.*

Are there social networks for people who are new to the community or those with few connections? Wander into stores and see how you are greeted. Are the clerks friendly or do they ignore you? Pretend that you need assistance—ask for directions, for change to use a phone, or use of a restroom, and observe the response you get. Do people ignore you or go out of their way to assist you?

5. *Ask about the stability of the population.*

How long do people stay? A community where people have roots and tend to remain will be different from a community where people are continually on the move. Is the population rising or falling?

6. *Signs of a community in trouble.*

How do you recognize a community in trouble? Communities with weak cultures have no clear values or beliefs about what is important or their values may be contradictory. For example, a "lifestyle enclave"[68] is a type of insubstantial community in which people "express their identity through shared patterns of appearance, consumption, and leisure activities which often serve to differentiate them sharply from . . . others."[69] These kinds of communities often develop subcultures that become ingrown and exclusive, have restrictions on membership, and arbitrarily exclude particular kinds of people. Communities with weak cultures, furthermore, have few rituals that give meaning and shape to the community or to memories of their history. Those rituals that do exist are either disorganized (everybody is doing their own thing) or contradictory (different facets of the community work at cross purposes).

Care of strangers, the helpless, and the dependent are inadequate, and people express indifference to strangers or even resentment of those who are helpless. Communities in trouble have members who don't care about the community or who act out against it. Communities with numbers of children who join gangs, or children who run away from home may indicate a culture that fails to support family life. Extensive behavior problems such as crime, vandalism, and violence are indicators of a culture that is losing its boundaries. Community leaders in fragmented cultures are oppressive, corrupt, or self-serving, and fail to build a common understanding about what is important.

Focused Interviews

One of the first tasks of macro social work research with communities or organizations is to get to know people who are involved in the change effort of the community or organization. Focused interviews, or what Wahrheit et al. call the key informant approach,[70] accomplish this and at same time help you understand people's perceptions about their community and its problems. The key informant approach is "a research activity based on information secured from those in the area who are in a position to know the community's needs and utilization patterns."[71]

A researcher will use key informants in different ways depending on his or her focus. A community developer, for example, selects grassroots community members who can give information about how the community developed, how problems came about, what has or has not been done to solve them, and important groups that constitute the community.

A social work planner, on the other hand, uses formal agency leaders or those representing organized community interests in gathering information. For example, a planner for the homeless mentally ill will interview key members of the local mental health association, support groups for the mentally ill, psychiatric hospitals and clinics, county mental health departments, and departments of social services. Organization developers will interview key administrators, supervisors, line staff, and board members of organizations to obtain a general idea about the structure, leadership, organizational culture, and its milieu of the organization experiencing problems.

A focused interview tends to be *semi-structured;* it "centers on selected topics but specific items are not entirely predetermined."[72] Keep a notebook to jot down names and phone numbers of key people you meet as well as names of others that may

be important to you. It is frustrating to meet key people and not be able to follow up because you can't remember their names or phone numbers. Keep a journal, and as soon after the interview as possible write down the things you want to keep in mind, questions you want to ask, names and addresses of other people to contact, and items to track down.

As you talk to people, you will learn about others who are involved in issues. This is called *snowball sampling.* In action research, this is an important way of discovering key people in the community. Because people tend to give you names of people they know who share their views on issues, however, the information you receive may be *biased* and provide the views of a fairly narrow section of the community.

If you talk only to people who are sympathetic to the issues on which you are working, you may have ignored a large number of people who oppose those issues. If you talk only to those who have reached top positions in agencies, you miss the important grass-roots individuals who can provide you with a different perspective. If you confine your interviews to affluent, white, able-bodied adults, you will not hear the views of the poor, the people from ethnically diverse backgrounds, or nonvocal groups such as developmentally disabled, elderly in nursing homes, or children.

Make sure you include a variety of key individuals in your study to ensure that you have heard all sides of community opinion. One way to do this is to get names of people who share other points of view, who are leaders of groups who would block or even fight against issues that some groups consider need change. For example, if you discover that unemployment is a problem, talk to the head of the local chamber of commerce, the heads of large businesses or factories, union leaders, social workers, vocational counselors, equal opportunity agencies, and private industry councils.

If you find that certain groups meet you with skepticism or rejection, try to discover why they feel this way. Talking with these people is crucial, because they may give you valuable insights about restraining forces or issues in the community of which you were not aware. They will broaden your perspective and help you get a feeling for the opposition you may be facing.

There are a few things to keep in mind when

you do focused interviewing. First, remember the principles of ethnographic studies. Wherever you go think like a researcher and get a feeling for the culture, values, beliefs, and meaning of the setting you are in.

Second, as you interview people, you will not only get information about the problems that people see, but you will also be developing relationships with those people and gathering insights into the kinds of services that exist. Let people know that you will be using the information they give you to bring about positive changes and to work on the problems in the community that *they* feel are important. You may want to ask these people to help you in your change efforts. Key community leaders can be very important in opening up doors and in using their influence and power to help you accomplish your goals. Everywhere you go, you should be a person who builds bridges, makes connections, and develops relationships.

Third, prepare yourself for your interview with a series of questions you want to ask. Try to ask these questions in about the same way with each person you interview so that you can compare answers. If you ask completely different questions of different people, you will get incomplete or fragmented information.[73] However, while you want to cover the same ground with all your respondents, be flexible enough to go into more depth when the opportunity presents itself. An advantage of focused interviews is that you may obtain unanticipated information that interviewees offer that will help you define the problem.[74]

Tell people how many questions you will ask and how long the interview will take. Because people tend to be busy, this will give them some assurance that you will not keep them from their activities. Let people know that what they tell you will be confidential, and that you will not quote them or otherwise misuse their information. This will help them be open and honest with you. Generally, you should use a "funneling" technique, going from the general to the specific.[75] For example, you may ask whether a respondent is aware of the drug problem in the Hillcrest neighborhood. If the person answers yes, go deeper and ask questions such as whether they have personally been affected by the problem, if it is an important issue to them, and what things they think might help alleviate it.

As you interview people, keep your eyes open for nonverbal clues such as a raised eyebrow, an unexplained smile, a laugh that may seem out of place, the tone of voice, or hesitation about answering. All of these clues may open the door to more information.[76]

Focus Groups

Usually key informants are people who have a vested interest in the problem and will want to hear what you have found out. Warheit et al. recommend that you bring key informants together in a meeting or series of meetings to present findings and discuss implications.[77] As you get them together, you build community around the issue, open up channels of communication, develop relationships, and begin an exchange of ideas that will stimulate a process of problem solving.

Focus groups or community forums are "series of public meetings to which community residents are invited and asked to express their beliefs about the needs and services of the community."[78] Focus groups not only help you build community around problems, but also help you gather additional information.

Meetings should be small enough that people can relate to one another but large enough that information can be shared and task groups established. Churches, businesses, and civic organizations are places where you may have access to groups of people. You may get permission to meet with church members after services or with employees during lunch breaks. Sometimes you could obtain an invitation to a board meeting of a civic organization. Senior centers and community centers are good places to talk with groups of people, or you could meet in someone's home. This provides an informal atmosphere and centers the group in the community.

Start with a brief introduction about the purpose of the group, and briefly have each person introduce him- or herself. Then present the issue that prompted you to call the meeting. You want to find out what are issues of concern to the members of this particular group. One way is to toss out a general question about the kinds of problems they are facing or those that are most important. For example, you might say, "You have all had a lot of difficulties with getting service from the police department, but no one has talked about the amount of crime in the area. Is that a problem?" People will probably talk for a while and then "converge on a topic that creates great enthusiasm."[79]

Sometimes a few people dominate and others are less likely to express disagreement. You may need to stop the process and ask these people for their ideas and opinions. Often you find that there are disagreements on the extent, cause, or importance of certain problems. Point out these inconsistencies. You may discover differences of opinion or perceptions about underlying problems.

Spend time eliciting people's perceptions of the problem. Write down all of the ideas and perceptions on large sheets of newsprint. If solutions are suggested, write them down separately, but try to keep the group talking about their ideas. If time runs out, get a commitment from members to meet again.

Ideally, community forums should lead to activities for which members can volunteer. Make sure you get the names and addresses of people who attend the meeting. After the meeting, follow up with a letter thanking people for their help and letting them know of follow-up meetings or what the next steps might be.

Surveys and Needs Assessments

Surveys or needs assessments are ways of following up on issues that have been raised in ethnographic studies, focused interviews, or focus groups. A survey is a systematic inquiry of perceptions or attitudes about problems that affect an entire population or a sample of that population. Surveys give you the opportunity to quantify information and to ask specific questions. They can be used to "explore, describe, or explain respondents' knowledge about a particular subject, their past or current behavior or their attitudes and beliefs concerning a particular subject."[80]

Sometimes "for state and national organizations, a survey might be the only practical way of finding out about the feelings of the organization's widely scattered membership."[81] For example, you may be interested in the perceptions of members of the YMCA regarding adolescents' needs for socialization and whether the Y should have a role in providing those needs. A survey is one way of discovering those attitudes.

Because surveys ask specific questions, however, the responses will be brief and not in depth. Therefore, surveys are most useful when you want to narrow down the issues, ask respondents to rank the importance of particular concerns, or give you an indicator of a range of preferences among items. This can be very important for a community because it gives specific information members can use in making decisions about the direction in which they should go.

Needs assessments are surveys that focus on gaps in service and unmet needs. In social planning, for example, you may study the lack of services for people with developmental disabilities, people with AIDS, immigrants, or migrant laborers. Often needs assessments are required if you are going to write a grant proposal to fund a project, because funding sources want to ensure that the "need" your project will serve is real.

Performing useful surveys involves wording the questions correctly, field testing the questionnaire, and choosing your sample carefully if you are giving your questionnaire to only a portion of the population. If you are going to assess only a sample of the population, you will need to analyze your data statistically to ensure that the data you develop is statistically significant. All of these components of using surveys can be technically complicated. Refer to texts that deal specifically with these issues. Several are listed at the end of this chapter.

Three factors are important in designing a survey or needs assessment: when—the time frame; who—the population you wish to survey; and how—how the survey will be accomplished.

WHEN—THE TIME FRAME. The time frame of your research is important. There may be any number of deadlines that your community group must meet. If you are applying for a grant from a foundation or a government agency, a needs assessment may be required. Funding sources have deadlines for submitting applications, and you will have to conduct your needs assessment by that deadline.

Communities are often interested in legislation. For example, a bill on gun control is scheduled for a public hearing, and some people in your community have expressed opinions about it. A survey can provide data to support your community's position, but you need to have it ready in time for the hearing. A highway is being proposed that would run directly though a low-income area of your community. A planning commission meeting will be held, and you know that a survey of resident's perceptions could have an important impact on the decision. But the survey must be completed and the data analyzed before the meeting.

WHO—THE SURVEY POPULATION. Usually you survey those people who are directly affected by or who have a vested interest in the problem and in the outcomes of your change efforts. Sometimes you survey all of the individuals involved in the issue being investigated. But often the number of people to survey is so large that you cannot reach all of them. Your time frame and costs are limited, and you need to reduce the number of people you survey. In this case a small number of the total population, called a "sample," must be used.

If you are surveying a sample, it is important to select the subjects using a valid sampling procedure to assure that the sample is *representative,* that is, it accurately reflects the composition of the entire population involved in the issue. The size of the sample that you use is significant. There are formulas that can help you determine a sample size that will give you a level of accuracy as high as 99 percent.[82] However, as a rule of thumb, try to use as large a sample as possible, because the larger the size of your sample, the smaller the error. Guy et al., for example, recommend that "for most research endeavors, samples will be adequate if they are within the limits of 30 and 500. Samples of less than 30 are usually too small, while samples greater than 500 are seldom necessary."[83]

Four kinds of sampling procedures are common: simple random sampling, systematic sampling, stratified random sampling, and cluster sampling.

1. *Simple random sampling.* One way to do simple random sampling is to put everyone's name in a hat and pick out one-third of them. If a computerized listing of an entire population is available, the computer can assign random numbers to each name and choose a sample of the size you want.
2. *Systematic sampling.* A simpler and in some ways better method is systematic sampling. First, compile a list of the names of all the people in the population you wish to sample. Then, beginning with a name chosen at random, count down every xth name. For example, for a population of 1,000 people you decide that a sample of 100 people, or 10 percent of the population, is the number of respondents you have time and resources to survey. You obtain a list of the names of the 1,000 people. You choose a place to begin, and count down every tenth name to obtain 100 names.
3. *Stratified random sampling.* It is important to make sure that your sample includes every subgroup in proportion to its actual representation in your population. For example, in a college population, there may be a number of Asians, African Americans, and Hispanics. A simple random sample may not give you an accurate representation of them. One way to make sure that your sample includes a representative number of such small groups is to "stratify" your sample.

    First, calculate the percentage of subgroups such as African Americans, Hispanics, and Asians in the population you are sampling. Then sample each of these populations separately by randomly drawing out respondents until you reach the proportionate amount. For example, suppose you are going to take a total sample of 100 people, and you know there are 20 percent Hispanic, 15 percent African Americans, and 5 percent Asians in the population. Separate the names of African Americans, Hispanics, and Asians from the total population to be studied. Out of the group of Hispanics, randomly draw twenty names; from the population of African Americans, draw fifteen names; and from the group of Asians, draw five names. From the remaining names, draw sixty. You now have a representative sample with exactly the same proportion of African Americans, Hispanics, Asians, and others as are reflected in the total population.
4. *Cluster sampling.* Sometimes you have many different groupings of people such as families, schools, or businesses from which to obtain a sample. In this case you can do a cluster sample. Assume, for example, you are conducting a survey of religious group members in your town. First, define a "religious group" for your purposes. Then, cluster the groups into cate-

gories depending on the purpose of your research. Take a stratified sample of each group to ensure you get an accurate count of both large and small ones. You now have a representative list of the specific religious groups. Obtain a membership listing from each religious group selected and take a systematic or simple random sample of names from each. In this way your survey will accurately represent the membership of religious groups in your town.

HOW—ACCOMPLISHING THE SURVEY.   Surveys use questionnaires, which can be administered by means of an interview in person or by telephone, or by mail. When you decide how you will conduct the survey, your community group will need to consider its resources of time, energy, and money. Interviewing one hundred people in person is time consuming and takes a lot of energy, particularly if the people are spread out over a large geographical area. Your group will also have to deal with not finding people home.[84] In addition, face-to-face interviewing requires skill, so time must be invested in training interviewers.[85]

On the other hand, doing interviews face-to-face ensures that you will get the information you need. Rubin and Babbie state that a good face-to-face interview will obtain a completion rate of at least 80 to 85 percent, which is usually required if you are conducting a survey funded by the federal government.[86] A face-to-face interview decreases the number of "don't know" answers, and the interviewer can sometimes help clarify survey questions that are vague.[87]

Mailing questionnaires is popular, because they "reach sample respondents living in widely disbursed geographical areas at relatively low costs."[88] However, a major problem with mail-out questionnaires is the response rate. Rubin and Babbie state that for mail-out questionnaires "a response rate of at least 50 percent is usually considered adequate for analysis and reporting. A response rate of at least 60 percent is good, and a response rate of 70 percent is very good."[89] However, the response rate for mailed questionnaires may be "well below 50 percent."[90] Therefore, a mailed questionnaire may not give you enough data. You can overcome this by following up—sending out a reminder or making phone calls to nonresponders.[91]

The third method of conducting surveys is by telephone. Telephone interviews can "greatly reduce the cost and inconvenience of reaching and personally interviewing respondents."[92] Telephone interviewing eliminates the problem of the physical appearance of the interviewer affecting the answers given by respondents.[93] Telephone interviews also allow researchers to operate in comfort and safety, which is particularly important if the survey is being done in areas of the city that may offer a threat to their safety.[94] A disadvantage of telephone interviewing is the tendency of people to refuse to talk because of the numerous calls they get from solicitors. However, if the interviewer introduces the issue as one that is of interest or concern to the respondent and if the questionnaire is short, telephone interviewing can be effective.

PREPARING THE QUESTIONNAIRE.   Whether your survey is face-to-face, mail out, or by telephone, you must prepare a questionnaire. It is important that your questionnaire helps you get information about the kinds of problems you and the community want to resolve. The questionnaire should be clear, easy to administer, and not too long.

Doing interviews face to face ensures that you will get the information you need.

Review the information you have already gathered from your ethnographic study, focus interviews, or focus groups. With help from the community group with whom you are working, determine what you need to know to decide what direction to take. For example, if your group is working on economic development in a highly industrialized community where there is high unemployment, you will want to know the numbers of people who are out of work, the kinds of skills required to get new jobs, and the kinds of training people might need.

Brainstorming can help you elicit the kinds of questions you need to ask. Group members give as many questions as they can without discussion. Write down each of them. When no more questions are forthcoming, the group looks over the responses. Some of them may be redundant, vague, or have more than one idea in them. Continue this process until you feel you have enough questions to obtain the information you need from your survey.

When you develop questions for your questionnaire, there are a few rules to follow.

1. Don't ask for more information than you need. Keep your questionnaire short and to the point and make sure the answers are necessary in planning action.[95]
2. Aim your questions at the level of education and background of your respondents.[96] Rubin and Babbie tell of a survey conducted in the Appalachian Mountains. In this area the term "very" means "fairly" or even "poorly." When people responded to a question asking whether they felt "very well" their response meant that they were not in good health but were just getting along, exactly the opposite of what the framers of the survey interpreted the answer to mean.[97]
3. Avoid jargon. For example, you may talk about "delinquent" while your respondents may talk about "being in trouble."
4. Do not ask two questions at once. Asking a double-barreled question will cause confusion. For example, "Should the government reduce the amount it pays to welfare recipients and spend it on education instead?" is a double-barreled question. One respondent may agree with reducing welfare but not that money should be spent on education. Another may want to increase spending on education but not at the expense of reducing welfare. Yet another may disagree with both parts of the statement, wanting neither to reduce welfare nor to increase educational spending. Whenever the word "and" appears in a question, check to see if it is a double barreled question and, if so, break it apart into separate questions.
5. Make sure your questions are clear. Consider the following example:

    What is your level of education?
    a. grade school
    b. high school
    c. college
    d. graduate school

    A person may have attained all these levels and therefore could circle every category. It is also not clear whether "level of education" means that a person graduated or simply attended at that level. A clearer question is: "Circle the highest level of education from which you have graduated."
6. Do not ask "leading" questions. Leading questions are those that presuppose an answer or skew the answer in a certain direction. For example, "Delinquent teenagers should be placed in institutions: ____Yes ____ No" is a leading question because it biases the response towards a yes answer and gives only two choices.
7. Avoid long items that may confuse the respondents.
8. Avoid negative terms. In answering the question "Carrying guns should not be allowed on our streets," some people may overlook the word "not" and answer on that basis.
9. Try to use a mixture of both "closed-ended" and "open-ended" questions. Closed-ended questions are those in which a respondent can answer with a yes or a no. Another kind of closed-ended question is a listing from which a respondent is to choose a response. Closed-ended questions are easy to quantify but give limited information.

    Open-ended questions, on the other hand, allow flexibility in response but are harder to quantify. Often you may follow a closed-ended question with an open-ended one. For example,

"In your opinion, is President Clinton doing a good job as president? Yes____ No____" is a closed-ended question. If you then ask, "Why or Why not?" you are following it up with an open-ended question that gives you more information.

SCALES AND RANKINGS.   A common way to get a range of responses is to ask respondents to answer questions on a scale. One common scale is the Likert scale. A Likert scale looks like this:

1	2	3	4	5
Strongly disagree	Disagree	Neutral	Agree	Strongly agree

Ranking asks respondents to make choices among a range of answers. For example:

On a scale of 1 to 5, with 1 being the highest and 5 the lowest, rank the community services that are most important to you.

_____ education
_____ employment
_____ health
_____ police
_____ recreation

WRITING A COVER LETTER AND INTRODUCTION. Give your questionnaire a title, and write out an opening paragraph or script that you or the interviewer will use in describing the purpose of the research. Include a statement on confidentiality. In the case of a mail-out questionnaire, this will take the form of a cover letter. Emphasize the importance of the research and the need for accurate and truthful answers. Assure the respondents that their answers will be anonymous and will not be divulged to anyone not involved in the survey.

Tell how many questions the questionnaire contains and how long it will take to answer them. Explain how the questionnaire is to be filled out. For example, if you are using a scale, explain how it is to be scored.

PRETESTING THE INTERVIEW QUESTIONNAIRE.   It is important to pretest the questionnaire. Pretesting gives you "the opportunity to discover unforeseen problems of administration, coding, and analysis."[98] Select a number of people from your population and try out the interview schedule on them. Pretesting helps you answer the following questions: Does the questionnaire give you the information you need? Are the questions worded correctly? Are they clear and unambiguous? Is the length of the questionnaire appropriate? Is it easy to administer?

After you have pretested the questionnaire, meet with your community group and revise the questionnaire using the information from the pretest.

Analyzing and Presenting Data

Count the number of responses to each question, and calculate percentages of people responding to each question. If you have a large number of respondents, arrange your data in graphs or tables rather than describing the data in narrative form only. Computer programs are available that can automatically convert raw data into graphs and tables without the laborious process of hand calculations and drawing graphs, which this used to require. One such program is called SPSS. Follow up tables or graphs with a narrative explanation or interpretation highlighting the points that you want to make. Summarize the data as you go along. Be sure that you have fully answered the questions you have posed.

Every sample has some built-in error. Formulas can help you determine the degree of confidence that readers can have in the survey and the degree of sampling error that may exist. Computer programs can also be helpful in this area, enabling you to avoid doing the complex mathematics involved in using statistics.

Writing the Report

The style and formality of a research report will vary depending on the uses to which it will be put. For example, if you are gathering data for your own use in community development work, your report will be informal. If you are presenting information to your task group, you will write a more formal report but aim it at the level of the members of the group. If you are preparing a proposal for a grant or present-

Dr. Donald Pryor, director of Human Services Analysis at the Center for Governmental Research, uses a computer program to convert information from hundreds of interviews into tables and graphs.

ing to a funding agency, your report will be much more formal in nature. Finally, if you are submitting your research for publication, you will use a stylized format acceptable to the academic world. Keep in mind that your report may vary depending on the degree of formality that serves the purposes of your project.

The following format is formal. Once you understand this model, you can adapt it to less formal situations. The format for a formal research report includes:

Title Page and Table of Contents
Chapter 1. Introduction
Chapter 2. Review of Literature
Chapter 3. Research Design
Chapter 4. Data Collection
Chapter 5. Data Analysis
Chapter 6. Recommendations
Chapter 7. Conclusion

Title Page and Table of Contents

Written reports always begin with a title page and a table of contents, which lists the chapters and appendix material.

Chapter 1—Introduction

The first chapter introduces the reader to the research problem, describes the process, and gives the conclusion. In this way the reader will know exactly what to expect and be able to assess the quality and competency of the report. In some research reports this information is in the form of an *abstract,* or summary, which precedes the report itself. The first chapter is usually the last one you write, because this chapter is the one that introduces the reader to the entire research process and gives the conclusion reached by the researcher.

Begin this chapter with an introduction and a general description of the setting or problem area. Then, narrow the field to the specific problem you are studying. State the primary research problem along with subsidiary or secondary problems. Then, in summary form, explain what will occur in chapters 2 through 6, and state the conclusion that will be reached.

Chapter 2—Review of Literature

In formal research reports a review of literature is mandatory. It assures the reader that the researcher has covered the topic under consideration and is pushing the field ahead. It is also necessary in applied action research to know what specific information exists in the field and to describe in more detail what others have to say about the topic under consideration.

Chapter 3—Research Design

The research design, also called the research methodology, is the strategy by which you plan to discover answers to your research question. It is the blueprint for doing the research. In your research design, you describe where, when, and how you will conduct the research. (Once you have written chapters 1, 2, and 3, you can convert them into a research proposal that you can use to submit to a funding agency or for writing a grant.)

Chapter 4—Data Collection

In this chapter you describe how the data was collected, how this differed from the proposal, and any issues relating to the confidence one should have in the results. This essentially is a story of how the research process actually occurred. In particular, if you used a sample of the population, you tell how you selected the sample. If you used key informants, your readers should know how you selected them and why. If you used existing data, you should inform the reader where you obtained the data, how much data you used, and what sampling techniques you employed. Finally, if you engaged in ethnographic analysis you should inform the reader about the techniques you used.

Chapter 5—Data Analysis

In this crucial chapter you present and assess the data you have collected and answer your research questions. In addition to the data itself, you describe the limitations of the study. Limitations are cautions that the reader must take in interpreting the data. For example, if a study is performed in a certain geographical area, then caution must be exercised in applying that data to other geographical areas.

Chapter 6—Recommendations

This chapter may also be titled "Implications" or "Problem Solutions." Here is where you bring the weight of your research to bear on the problem and tell what you think needs to be done about it. Come up with as many recommendations as you think are necessary, rank them, and then assess them. You can even describe how you would implement your recommendations, so that your research will not only be informational but also reach for practical solutions.

Chapter 7—Conclusion

End with a short conclusion, usually no longer than two or three paragraphs that repeat the purpose, the problem, the process, and recommendations.

Conclusion

Macro social work research is a key to solving social problems. Research helps you see the problem you are trying to correct more clearly and understand its origins and its size. It gives you and your community group ideas about how to correct social problems. Use research to understand the setting in which you will be conducting your change effort. Before you go into a community or organization, you need to gather facts about it. Macro social workers use ethnographic studies, focused interviews, focus groups, and surveys or needs assessments to gather these facts. Every macro social worker needs to be a skilled researcher.

KEY CONCEPTS

applied research
descriptive questions
predictive questions
prescriptive questions
objective
value neutral
action research
intuition
value laden

subjective
self-conscious
self-critical
action research process
statistical information
rates under treatment (RUT)
social indicator approach
ethnographic analysis
focused interviews
snowball sampling
key informant
focus groups
survey
needs assessment
sample
representative sample
simple random sample
systematic random sample
stratified random sample
cluster sample
questionnaires
face-to-face interview
mail-out questionnaires
telephone interviews
leading questions
double-barreled questions
open-ended questions
closed-ended questions
Likert scale
ranking
cover letter
pretesting
tables
graphs
research report

QUESTIONS FOR DISCUSSION

1. What we now call social science research was born out of and is derived from macro social work research. The field of social work itself was, in large measure, founded by and based on research conducted by Charles Booth and research connected with the Settlement House Movement. What is the role of social work research in our society and in the field of social work today?

2. What does the process of conducting social work research have in common with the generalist social work method, or rational problem solving?

3. What is the difference between pure social science research and macro social work research?

4. Why is research an essential component of macro social work? Is research important for micro social work?

ADDITIONAL READING

Babbie, Earl. *The Practice of Social Research,* 4th ed. Belmont, CA: Wadsworth, 1986.

———. *Survey Research Methods,* 2d ed. Belmont, CA: Wadsworth, 1989.

Campbell, Donald T., and Julian C. Stanley. *Experimental and Quasi-Experimental Designs for Research.* Chicago, IL: Rand McNally, 1963.

Grinnell, Richard M., Jr. *Social Work Research and Evaluation,* 3d ed. Itasca, IL: Peacock, 1988.

Kerlinger, Fred N., *Behavioral Research: A Conceptual Approach.* New York: Holt, Rinehart and Winston, 1979.

Kidder, Louise H., and Charles M. Judd. *Research Methods in Social Relations,* 5th ed. New York: Holt, Rinehart and Winston, 1986.

Lofland, John. *Analyzing Social Settings: A Guide to Qualitative Observation and Analysis.* Belmont, CA: Wadsworth, 1971.

Mills, C. Wright. *The Sociological Imagination.* London: Oxford University Press, 1959.

Rubin, Allen, and Earl Babbie. *Research Methods for Social Work.* Belmont, CA: Wadsworth, 1989.

Tripodi, Tony, Phillip Fellin, and Henry J. Meyer. *The Assessment of Social Research: Guidelines for Use of Research in Social Work and Social Science,* 2d ed. Itasca, IL: Peacock, 1983.

Weiss, Carol H. *Evaluation Research: Methods of Assessing Program Effectiveness.* Englewood Cliffs, NJ: Prentice-Hall, 1972.

EXERCISES

EXERCISE 21:
Research as a Tool for Action

Read the following example of macro social work research. Then answer the questions at the end.

Two years ago, Dr. Julio Morales was hired by the Bridgeport school system as a consultant/researcher to study why Puerto Rican youngsters drop out of school. Dr. Morales reported:

> As an organizer, I knew that if the research was to lead to changes, a strong and diversified community team, to which I would be accountable, had to be organized. Fortunately, the Ford Foundation, sponsor of the study, insisted on broad community participation. A collaborative team, with heavy Puerto Rican representation, was formulated. Reporting directly to them and actively seeking their involvement in all aspects of the research process empowered the team. They were encouraged to develop all research instruments and were trained to interview Puerto Rican youngsters who had dropped out, Puerto Rican youngsters that were at-risk of dropping out, and youngsters who were underachieving. Parents, teachers, administrators, counselors, social workers, and other staff were also interviewed in order to get the broadest level of participation, as well as raise awareness and obtain support. All questionnaires addressed community and school factors attributed to students and their families. Numerous community forums were organized to share findings and obtain more input on problems and solutions. The collaborative "owns" the study, continues meeting, advocates for programs flowing from the study's recommendations, and monitors them. Programs addressing school policies, teacher training, and a Puerto Rican studies curriculum have been initiated as a direct result of the study.[99]

Using what you learned about social work action research in chapter 5, assess what aspects of action research this example portrays. What aspects are left out? Is this a good example of social work research? Why or why not?

EXERCISE 22:
Designing a Research Project

Think of a social problem that your class might be interested in working on. Try to define the problem. Then list the kinds of information you would need to solve it.

CHAPTER 7

Becoming a Community Developer

By restoring buildings and traditions of their Finnish heritage, citizens of Embarrass, Minnesota, revived their town and sense of community.

Social change isn't going to come as quickly as any of us would like it to come. Building a community is a subtle, delicate, long-term process.

—SAM BROWN, COMMUNITY ORGANIZER[1]

Each person in a community must do his part. All have gifts and an area to do. Together we can accomplish great things. Where there is no vision, the people perish. If we don't continue with that vision before us, then in essence our community will perish.

—MARGARET KINAANEN, COMMUNITY LEADER,
EMBARRASS, MINNESOTA

IDEAS IN THIS CHAPTER

A Town Called Embarrass

Embarrass, population 822, is a mining town in northern Minnesota. One hundred years ago immigrants from Finland worked the open pit iron mines near Embarrass. They worked for the lowest wages, took the dirtiest, most backbreaking jobs, and helped each other build houses, barns, and saunas. As the ore was used up, however, the jobs disappeared. In 1982, the Reserve Mining Company, the largest single employer in the area shut down. Unemployment rose to 80 percent. Some families were forced to move away to find work. In the month of August 1984 alone, eight families of teachers and community leaders moved away. The only people who kept their jobs were independent farmers, loggers, and merchants.

The people who stayed looked for some way to make a living, but it was not easy for the community to come to terms with the situation. Many felt that the situation was only temporary, that things would improve on their own. Others did not believe things would change and began to look at who they were and to decide what their community meant.

John Kousta, a community development consultant from the Minnesota Project, says that the underlying issue facing the people of Embarrass was what they had to do as a community to survive. The local people had to make their own analysis, make their own decisions as to what was critical for their own community and buy into it. One idea was to have the local high school, a building that had stood empty for the past ten years, declared a national landmark. The National Trust for Historic Preservation said no to the school but was interested in the old Finnish houses and barns. The local volunteer fire department had been routinely burning down these old Finnish homesteads so they wouldn't become fire hazards. To the National Trust, however, these were "diamonds in the field." With backing from the Trust and the Minnesota Project, town leaders began work on renovating and stabilizing the Gable house-barn—the only one of its kind in the United States. Their vision was a renewed town based on tourism.

However, major skepticism still existed, but despite the drawbacks, Margaret Kinaanen and other leaders pushed on with their vision. The town drafted an economic development plan to restore the Finnish architecture and the heritage of Embarrass, forming an organization called the SISU Heritage Project. *Sisu* is a Finnish word variously translated as stubbornness beyond reason, blind determination, foolhardy perseverance, or simply as "guts." As one community member said, "Finland lost forty-six wars with Russia, but she kept her independence. That is *sisu*."

The leaders of SISU applied to the state for help but did not receive it. They went to the federal government but were turned down. Then SISU applied to Finland, and the Finns responded by sending foreign aid to the American town of Embarrass. As a result, 165 log buildings have been discovered, putting Embarrass on the map as a kind of Finnish Williamsburg and creating a market for Finnish home-based crafts and businesses. The townspeople of Embarrass are discovering all sorts of skills and abilities they never realized they had: woodcarving, sculpture, painting, restoration, and weaving. But most of all, they have discovered their community and their heritage. They have found one another, and that discovery is the key to their survival and their future.

Introduction

Like the town of Embarrass, modern communities in rural America and in the inner cities are in trouble and need help. Ontological communities that provide meaning for people—churches, synagogues, mosques, and ethnic community associations—are often in disarray. Traditional communities, such as American Indian tribes, struggle to survive in the modern world. Communities are in trouble in many third world countries. Community development is a method of helping these communities and the people who live in them survive and become healthy. This chapter discusses why community development is so important today, defines community development, and explores how community developers work with modern, ontological, and traditional communities.

Why Community Development?

Social action is appropriate when a social system that is enmeshed in denial, scapegoating, oppression, or injustice needs to be confronted. Sometimes, however, challenging those parts of the social system to do better or be more inclusive will not work because "poor people and their organizations are not able to take over or significantly influence the power structure through persuasion, power tactics, and/or political action."[2] Elected officials simply may not have the resources, skills, ability, or resolve to bring about equity and justice, even if they want to. Rather than applying to the government or to businesses to do something for the community, it may be in the community's own interest to rely on itself, find its own resources, and operate its own programs, at least as a beginning.

What Is Community Development?

Community development is a method by which macro social workers apply techniques, develop resources, and promote networks that enable a community to become a source of social, economic, political, and cultural support to its people. Antonia Pantoja and Wilhelmina Perry define community development/restoration as

> the work with people through which members of an economically dependent and politically disenfranchised community accept to work together with the following purposes:

1. To understand the forces and processes that have made them and keep them in their state of poverty and dependency.
2. To mobilize and organize their internal strength, as represented in political awareness, a plan of action based on information, knowledge, skills, and financial resources.
3. To eradicate from individuals and from group culture the mythology that makes them participants in their own dependency and powerlessness.
4. To act in restoring or developing new functions that a community performs for the well-being of its members—starting with the economizing function.[3]

Community development aims at the creation "of economic and social progress for the whole community with its active participation and the fullest possible reliance on the community's initiative."[4] Community developers treat the community-as-a-whole as a client.

Community developers assist rural and urban economically depressed communities to enter the mainstream of prosperity and progress. They work to improve the functioning of ontological communities that are failing. In third world "underdeveloped" nations, they help restore and rebuild traditional communities that have been damaged by modernization, war, drought, famine, and economic dislocation.

BENJAMIN FRANKLIN: COMMUNITY DEVELOPER

One of the early leaders of the Revolutionary War, Benjamin Franklin visualized an ideal of economic freedom that would also insure political liberty. He advocated a "gospel of industry, frugality, and sobriety as a way of achieving individual freedom." So strongly did he believe in changing the social order to insure a free society that he sold his printing business at age forty-two and devoted the rest of his life to public service.

He began a socialization group, which later became involved in community projects, and establishing a library. He developed a plan for neighborhood improvement including paving, lighting, and cleaning the streets of Philadelphia and a plan for the development of a police department.

He organized his neighbors into a Volunteer Fire Company. Concerned about health care, he helped establish the Philadelphia Hospital. Wanting to assist in education, he helped found an academy that later became the University of Pennsylvania. He believed in the power of communities to assist themselves, self-help, and the importance of neighbors working together.

Source: Robert H. Bremner, *American Philanthropy* (Chicago, IL: University of Chicago Press, 1960), p. 18. Reprinted by permission.

A Short History of Community Development in America

Early in our nation's history, groups of immigrants banded together to assist each other and develop communities. Such community-oriented associations were established by immigrants from Holland in 1609 and from Scotland as early as 1656. In 1754, fifty-four Boston Anglicans founded the Episcopal Charitable Society. Thirteen years later, the Charitable Irish Society of Boston was born, along with the German Society of New York and the French Benevolent Association.[5] Even now, such community associations flourish. Jewish citizens, for example, have the B'nai B'rith; Mexican Americans have the Mexican American Citizens Association (MACA); African Americans have the National Association Colored People (NAACP); and Japanese Americans have the Japanese American Citizen's League, (JACL).

By the end of the Civil War, populations of the cities were growing. Immigrants flooded into American cities, and the country experienced cycles of inflation and depression. Urban squalor was rampant, as were public health problems. Homeless and abandoned children roamed the streets, and sweatshops exploited women and children.

A variety of utopian community experiments were conducted. The Shakers, the Amish, the Oneida colony, and others attempted to maintain community values in opposition to the encroachment of urban industrialized society.

Social reformers became concerned about problems of the cities. In his book *Progress and Poverty,* published in 1879, Henry George described the social consequences of private profit in land sales. He asserted that "land values were *created by the growth and needs of the community rather than by efforts of the owner*"[6] (emphasis in original). He criticized landlords for appropriating for their private use "socially created value of land . . . [which] properly belonged to the community as a whole."[7] Walter Rauschenbusch, a Baptist minister and theologian, working in New York's Hell's Kitchen, called for a renewed Christian response to the poor. This theology of social involvement, called the Social Gospel, stimulated churches to become engaged in community development and social reform.

Various other efforts, many of which were motivated by the slum conditions of England and the massive dislocations created by industrialization, became important components of developing healthier communities. Among these efforts were the YMCA and YWCA, the Boy Scout and Girl Scout movements, and the Salvation Army, all of which attempted to develop groups and communities to counter the social fragmentation of industrialization and urban life.

Among the most notable of these efforts was the Settlement House Movement, which transplanted upper- and middle-class social workers and students to the slums of New York, Chicago, St. Louis, Pittsburgh, and Cincinnati. Settlement workers developed programs and tried to meet the needs of community residents. They attempted to improve education and the family and social life of the community by a variety of craft programs, theater productions, discussion groups, and clubs. "The founders of the settlements believed that broad social and economic reforms would result from the experience, the thinking, and the joint action of the whole population of a neighborhood."[8]

During the Great Depression, community development efforts were expanded and ratified by the federal government. One of these was the Public Works Administration, administered by social worker Harry Hopkins, whose goal was not only to give unemployed people jobs but to put people to work on projects of community improvement and

Community development aims at the active participation of community members and the fullest reliance on the community's initiative.

betterment. Hopkins pioneered the development of the Civilian Conservation Corps (CCC), which "employed young men whose families were on relief in various projects planned by the Department of the Interior[9] such as improving parks and beautifying communities. One of the most famous community development projects of all time was the Tennessee Valley Authority (TVA).

Community development efforts took another leap ahead with President John F. Kennedy in the early 1960s. President Kennedy captured the imagination of young people with the establishment of the Peace Corps, an international community development program in which volunteers were assigned to assist third world communities.

When Lyndon Johnson became president, he continued and expanded community development efforts in his Great Society programs. Among these was a series of programs designed to assist communities on a variety of fronts. For example, the Demonstration Cities and Metropolitan Development Act, better known as the Model Cities Program, enacted by Congress in 1966, was the most "ambitious and comprehensive effort by the federal government to aid America's blighted urban areas."[10] The act provided grants and technical assistance to help cities plan, develop, and execute programs to improve both the physical and social environment of neighborhoods. Grants were to be used for coordination, education, training, and enhanced delivery systems aimed at changing "the total environment of the target area."[11]

The Economic Opportunity Act (EOA) passed in 1964, often called the War on Poverty, was aimed at improving and uplifting inner-city communities. It initiated a series of programs including the Volunteers in Service to America, or VISTA (a domestic Peace Corps program), a Job Corps program for school dropouts, a Neighborhood Youth Corps for jobless teenagers, Upward Bound (a program encouraging slum children to go to college), and Operation Head Start, a project of preschool training for children.[12]

Community Action Programs (CAP) attempted to engage community residents directly in the development of locally based programs. They were

based on the belief that people who lived in poverty and with discrimination were damaged and made ap-

athetic by their lack of political and social power, by their lack of opportunities to participate in controlling their own lives and the community decisions that affected them.[13]

Projects were funded by "either public or private agencies" and included day-care centers, recreation centers, and health centers[14] in inner-city areas.

Among the innovative and progressive pieces of community development legislation during the Johnson presidency was the Housing and Urban Development Act of 1968, "the culmination of the federal government's attempts to provide housing and assistance programs for poor and moderate-income families. . . . Johnson called the act the 'Magna Carta to liberate our cities,' putting into motion over seven hundred planning grants, water and sewer funds, flood insurance, model cities funds, and urban mass transit."[15]

Stimulated by this federal legislation, community development efforts grew in the 1960s, including an increase in local neighborhood development groups and social action organizations in North Avondale near Cincinnati, in the Hillside Terrace Housing Project in Milwaukee's north side, in the Near North area of Chicago, in the Mission District of San Francisco, the Lower East Side of New York City, in the Woodlawn neighborhood of Chicago, and in Newark, New Jersey, Syracuse, New York, Roxbury, Massachusetts, Austin, Texas, and others. The 1960s also witnessed a movement of increased interest in the formation of cooperative associations, alternative communities called "communes," and a wide variety of alternative self-help groups based on a renewed sense of community.

In the 1970s, community development saw additional neighborhood organizations springing up in Birmingham, Brooklyn, Oakland, Stockton, San Diego, Cleveland, and Wichita, among others. Neighborhoods U.S.A. (NUSA), is a national organization begun in 1975, whose goal is to build and strengthen the nation's neighborhoods by developing partnerships among residents, elected officials, and professionals by sponsoring conferences bringing people together on community development issues.[16] The Neighborhood Reinvestment Corporation (NRC), a nonprofit public corporation devoted to stimulating the creation of local partnership efforts, was organized to improve the quality of life in older neighborhoods. Today it provides residents with comprehensive housing rehabilitation services.[17]

During the Nixon and Ford administrations community development programs were reduced in scope. In 1973, President Nixon declared a moratorium on funding urban development programs. In 1974, President Ford signed the Housing and Community Development Act, replacing model cities, urban renewal, and neighborhood facility grants with a single community development block grant program.[18] This bill was a setback for neighborhood organizations because "unlike the Great Society legislation which had forced local officials to share power with neighborhood community organizations, [the act] limited citizen participation to purely an advisory role."[19]

When Jimmy Carter became president in 1977, the act was amended to allow for more citizen participation and required citizen involvement in the planning, execution, and evaluation of the program. As a result, "new community organizations have been stimulated and have become agents for citizen participation in the local community."[20] During the Carter administration, "the tireless efforts of those involved in the neighborhood movement to bring the needs and potentialities of the nation's neighborhoods to the attention of federal policymakers" bore fruit with the passage of the National Neighborhood Policy Act of 1977.[21] This act created the National Commission on Neighborhoods to investigate the state of the nation's neighborhoods and to recommend appropriate public policy directions."[22] The report, titled *People, Building Neighborhoods,* made numerous recommendations including "a system of neighborhood human services, establishment of neighborhood advocacy posts, training, and technical assistance" to neighborhoods.[23] The report "remains a well-developed blueprint for improving our communities."[24] Unfortunately, the commission's report came too late in Jimmy Carter's presidency for implementation. The Reagan administration ignored the commission's findings.

Extending President Carter's interest and commitment to community and neighborhood development, "federal interest in neighborhood-based programs grew: One of these was the Neighborhood Self-Help Development Act of 1978, which recognized "the neighborhood to be a national resource which . . . deserved to be conserved and revital-

ized."[25] The act fostered the implementation of projects by encouraging partnerships with local government and other public agencies and with private agencies.

Finally, during the Clinton administration in the 1990s, interest in community development and volunteerism was renewed with the National Service Corps, in which young people are assigned a variety of community development projects. Private community development programs were stimulated. Among these were Habitat for Humanity, in which community groups construct housing for the poor, and locally based housing programs, in which community members take over abandoned buildings in inner cities and, by means of "sweat equity," renovate them to make them habitable.

Action Model of Community Development

An action model of community development promotes both the ideal of community and the role of government in promoting and protecting community. An action model of community development sees an important role for social work in fostering and developing new kinds of community in today's highly technological, individualistic, and impersonal society.

An action model of community development is based on the social work principle of self-determination. Community self-determination means that people are not seduced or coerced into giving up their culture and selfhood as the price of inclusion, survival, or material well-being. The action model recognizes the necessity of all communities, but particularly ethnically diverse communities, to maintain their cultural heritage, language, religion, and other expressions of uniqueness and to engage the larger society on their own terms. It also recognizes the role of government in facilitating this community freedom and independence.

> The goal and substance of social development is the welfare of the people, as determined by the people themselves, and the consequent creation or alteration of institutions so as to create a capacity for meeting human needs at all levels and for improving the qual-

ity of human relations and relationships between people and societal institutions. In this process we have to deal with the fact that human and natural forces are constantly intervening between the expression of needs and the means to attain them.[26]

Community, according to the action model, is the center of the self. Without healthy communities, people tend to become aimless, vulnerable, and displaced, their freedom becomes emptiness. In order for individuals to be authentically free, they must experience and have available to them communities from which they can draw strength. Just as government protects individuals' rights, so an action model of community development recognizes the need for government to protect, nurture, and support the rights of communities of people to establish themselves, to be free from exploitation, and to have the resources by which they can grow. An action model of community development will press government for resources when the community is in danger of being overwhelmed.

Action-oriented community development is based on certain values. Among these are equality, not inequality; cooperation, not competition; and public spirit, not self-interest.[27] Operating within these values, action-oriented community developers stimulate new forms of community so that community can continue to play its needed role in society. (An example of such a model is provided by Harry Specht and Mark Courtney at the end of this chapter.)

Community Development with Modern Communities

Community developers working with modern communities use "democratic work through procedures, voluntary cooperation, self-help, development of indigenous leadership, and educational opportunities" to solve common problems, according to Arthur Dunham.[28] They work to

> inculcate among the members of rural communities a sense of citizenship and among the residents of urban areas a spirit of civic consciousness; to introduce and strengthen democracy at the grass-roots level through the creation and/or revitalization of insti-

tutions designed to serve as instruments of local participation; to initiate a self-generative, self-sustaining, and enduring process of growth; to enable people to establish and maintain cooperative and harmonious relationships; and to bring about gradual and self-chosen changes in the community's life with a minimum of stress and disruption.[29]

Choosing a Community

As a professional community developer, you will usually work for an agency, community organization, or community center, using the social agency as your base and your means of support, direction, power, and legitimacy. Often your agency will have specific purposes and policies that determine the kind of community with which you may work.

Within these limits, however, choose a community in which you have as much in common with the people as possible, so that you can become personally committed to it as well as to the particular problems in which you will be involved.[30] This "lived-in experience" is crucial for doing community development work. Without such experience, a community developer will find it difficult to directly engage a community in all of its history, values, symbols, language, culture, and traditions. This is especially important when working with ethnically diverse communities. "Too often we forget that experiencing racism, economic deprivation, and social injustice are the key relevant politicizing forces in most urban areas."[31]

Rivera and Erlich have devised a three-tiered model based on contact intensity and influence that can help determine an appropriate role for community developers with ethnically diverse communities.[32] At the primary level of involvement, the community developer directly, immediately, and personally engages the community. This is the most intense and intimate level of engagement "where the only way of gaining entry into the community is to have full ethnic solidarity with the community. . . . It is that level that requires racial, cultural, and linguistic identity."[33] Working at the primary level, for example, "would not be possible for a Chinese American in a Vietnamese or African-American area."[34]

One step removed from personal identification

with the community and its problems, for example, "would be a Puerto Rican in a Mexican-American neighborhood or a person identified as Haitian in an African-American area." At this secondary level of involvement, knowledge of the language, although a benefit and a help, is not absolutely mandatory. Community developers function as "liaison with the outside community and institutions and services as a resource with technical expertise based on the culturally unique situations experienced by the community.[35]

The third level of engagement is that of a non–ethnically similar "outsider working for the common interests and concerns of the community. Cultural or racial similarity is not a requirement."[36] Using their technical skills, political connections, and understanding of the outside environment, structures, and systems, non–ethnically similar community developers can play effective roles as advocates and brokers on behalf of the ethnically diverse community.

Even though ethnic and cultural identification with a community is important, this does not guarantee acceptance by them.

> Ultimately in community development work, it is the members of that community who will decide who is with them and who is not. They choose who they will work with and who they want to work with them. Community residents make these choices based on their gut reactions, their ideological views of people, and the demonstrated and informed results of their work together.[37]

Sizing Up the Community

Even before you enter a community, analyze it as well as you can to help you put your work into perspective and understand some of the problems you will have to confront.[38] You can learn about the community by gathering census data, crime statistics, and incidence of poverty from local governmental agencies and the chamber of commerce. Even the phone book can give you a wealth of information about the population, local businesses, and services.

By walking around the community, you will easily see particular situations that need remediation. A housing project may be in danger of being taken over by gangs. A neighborhood may have become a haven for drug pushers, creating fear and even in-

timidation. Another community may be victimized by subtle discrimination and not have equitable city services. Still another may be deteriorating economically. Any of these are good places to start.

Sizing Up the Problem

For the most part you will have the option of defining what particular community issue on which to focus. Sometimes a particular event occurs in a community that you can use as a jumping off place for community involvement. A woman may be raped, a homeless mentally ill person murdered, or a runaway abused. Suddenly the community's attention becomes focused on a common problem. Many women's shelters, for example, have been started because a woman has been murdered by an abusive husband.

On the other hand, you may begin by holding a community meeting. Jane Addams, for example, began her efforts by simply inviting the elderly and other groups of people in her neighborhood to informal meetings. From these meetings she organized clubs, classes, and a variety of services.

Sizing Up Yourself

After you have examined the community and its problems, examine your own concerns, ideological beliefs, and personal strengths. If you can't get excited about or invested in an issue, stay away from it, and choose something else that "grabs you." The community problem should pull at you so that you can engage your emotions and generate compassion for the people involved.

In addition to "gut level" commitment to an issue, your own values must be "in sync" with the values of your community and their culture. "By becoming ideologically clear, your belief system guides you, helping you to support others' basic beliefs more easily, and to draw from that insight a better understanding of whom one can and cannot work with over time."[39]

Having strong beliefs about the value of what you are trying to accomplish will also strengthen you for encounters with those who may challenge your belief system or position. Prepare yourself in advance for those encounters by reading and mastering the ethical and practical implications of the issues with which you are wrestling. You need to become a practical ethicist about the moral and value components the community's problem.

Finally, look at your abilities and strengths. While community development draws heavily on your feeling function—your ability to forge relationships, bring people together, and inculcate culture—the project that you ultimately choose may also require social action, planning a future direction, or developing a program or service using your thinking, intuiting, and sensing functions. Each of these tasks may demand different requirements of you. Before you get too far along, give some thought to whether the problem or problems with which the community is wrestling are congruent with your problem-solving and leadership abilities.

You should not force your feelings, values, or ideas. As much as you can, try to be yourself. Be genuine and have integrity. Remember, you are on your own journey as much as you are helping a community move along on theirs. You do not further your own development or that of the community if you are not true to your own feelings, beliefs, and selfhood.

Living in the Community

When you present yourself to a community, engage its members on their territory and on their terms. Sometimes you must be willing to give up your own life-style and economic attainments to gain the trust, respect, and confidence of the community members. For the most part, this means living in the community. This demonstrates immediately that you are not an outsider but are committed to the community, willing to breathe its air, engage its sights and smells, hear its noises, feel its depression, and endure its helplessness.

Canon Samuel Barnett, for example, was born in 1844 and raised in an upper-middle-class family in Bristol, England. After his education as a clergyman, he was assigned to a parish in the slums of Whitechapel. Coming with no ready-made solutions, but simply living as a resident in one of England's worst districts, he decided to commit himself to bettering the lives of the people of the community.

Barnett and his wife opened up their home to the community and began working to engage people in improving their lives. They were soon joined by others. They met the community on its own terms, establishing the first social settlement house, which they called Toynbee Hall. Out of this emerged a movement that inspired hundreds of settlement houses.

Exploring the Community's Problems

Community development takes a great deal of commitment, interest, and effort. You will probably want to work first on some of the community's most pressing problems, especially those that put people in immediate risk such as lack of food, shelter, and protection. Community problems, however, are usually deep seated and have taken years, even generations, to come to a head. They will not be solved overnight. It may take an entire generation to revitalize one community.

Programs and plans "put together quickly tend to lack the mutual trust and interdependence which give an organization internal strength."[40] You should be interested not only in solving immediate problems but also in reaching long-term solutions. Ultimately your goal is that the community be self-sufficient and socially healthy. Therefore, the organizing that you attempt must be done with care and deliberation.

Developing Relationships

One of the hallmarks of a community developer is an ability to engage people. In the early stages of community development your main job is to get to know the community and to "to make friends with the people there."[41] People talk about the things they know: themselves, their ideas, and their opinions. Talk to them about their lives, about the life of their community, and their feelings about living in this community.

Share with them who you are and be as genuine as you can. Try to express interest in people, their surroundings, hopes, fears, and personal situations. And try to relate their lives with something in your own life. When you develop common ground or rapport, understanding and communication can begin. The more you talk with people and get to know them, the more you become one of them.

Relationships and communication develop trust. Trust is essential in community development. Your influence in a community will depend on the extent to which you are trusted by its members.[42] The fastest way to develop trust is visibility.

> People tend to be most accepting of that which is most familiar. . . . This familiarity is established by spending as much time as possible with people in the community and in places where they spend their time. An organizer's home should be the place where he sleeps and little else. From early in the morning until late at night, an organizer's place is with the people.[43]

Places to "hang out" are places where people congregate. In rural areas it may be the general store. Gas stations are also gathering places, as are cafes, fast-food restaurants, saloons, pool halls, barbershops, and beauty parlors. Any place people in the community gather is a good place for the developer to spend time. Go to special events such as auctions, dances, revivals, drag races, football games, fish fries, chicken suppers, barbecues, farmer's markets, church socials, and local fairs.

Try to become close to several key people. If you can gain acceptance by one or more members of a particular subgroup, you can establish a toehold in that community. Once you have done this, you will be able to expand to other subgroups, because most communities have overlapping networks of relationships.

While, you want to capitalize on these relationships, however, too close a connection with one group may result in your rejection by other groups that may be in conflict with it. Try to become aware as soon as possible of the different factions within a community so that you can avoid too close an involvement with groups that would limit your acceptance by other elements of the community.[44]

Try to take someone with you wherever you go. "Come with me" should be a stock phrase in your vocabulary.[45] The trips you take with others will help you get to know people more intimately, help them identify with you and your mission, and give you a

BANANA KELLY AND THE MID BRONX DESPERADOS

In the 1970s South Bronx, New York, was a desert of abandoned tenements, so decrepit that even the city fathers thought the only way to rebuild was to allow people to burn them down. It wasn't unusual to find three or four fires going at once. The devastation was like that in the bombed-out city of Dresden during World War II. Block upon block of destroyed buildings littered the landscape, until Jenny Brooks began to get involved. Filled with a vision and a desire to be proud of her neighborhood, she went to her neighbors and developed a block group. Together, they began to beautify the neighborhood. They then went to their landlords to restore water and heat and to the city to get increased police protection and to investigate arson. They called themselves the "Mid Bronx Desperados."

At the same time, about two miles east, a group of twenty-one families was forming on banana-shaped Kelly Street to oppose the demolition of three abandoned buildings on their block. They called themselves Banana Kelly. They used their own labor as a down payment, took over the three buildings, and for six months cleared out the rubble. They had stopped the bulldozers. And they kept going.

In the face of conditions that had confounded policymakers at all levels, local community development groups proved that their neighborhoods were not hopeless. They were rapidly evolving into powerful vehicles capable of bringing in outside resources, striking a responsive chord in corporations and foundations. They formed their own sweat equity cooperative, and the city learned that they were capable of shaping their own community. The residents gained experience and became more sophisticated. They learned how to build and organize complex projects.

Ten years later, Jenny Brooks' organization, called the MBD Housing Corporation, had reclaimed or built housing for one thousand residents and redeveloped Charlotte Street into ninety ranch-style houses for middle-income residents. Today, fifteen hundred community development housing groups nationwide have produced more than 200,000 housing units. But 7 million are needed. Instead of national solutions to local problems, we need community developers like Jenny Brooks who can inspire national response to local efforts.

chance to recruit them for possible roles in your community effort. One of your goals it to help move people toward becoming organizers themselves. The more you engage people, the more you can help them learn what you know about community development and assist them in gaining ideas that they can implement.

Group Meetings

As soon as you get to know enough people, invite them to a meeting. Meetings should be informal and held in someone's home. Serve refreshments, and give plenty of time for socializing. Start off with an enjoyable activity that is appropriate to the people you are attempting to organize. Encourage each person to speak his or her mind with a spirit of acceptance, and listen carefully to their ideas, concerns, questions, and issues. As you listen, try to help develop commonality and look for patterns that you can use in helping direct them toward a common goal. At the end of the meeting, the group should come to some sort of decision about a problem that should be worked on, with each person saying his or her piece.

In these kinds of informal meetings, avoid parliamentary procedure. Parliamentary procedure is helpful in large meetings where managing debate and decision making are important. That will come later when the community develops a more formal organization.

Rotate the leadership of meetings. This will give everyone a chance to gain experience and status in the group.

> The key value in decision making within a poor people's organization is not efficiency, but participation. The time required to reach a decision should not be the shortest time required for a small, select group to make the decision, but the amount of time it takes to educate all the members in the meaning of the decision and to involve them in understanding the decision-making process.[46]

Keeping in mind the community-based situational leadership model described in chapter 4, you should rarely act as the formal leader, or chairman, of meetings. This is the role of a community leader.

GETTING STARTED IN A PUERTO RICAN COMMUNITY

In early January 1985, we arrived at our farm in Cubuy. Living in the hills and on a farm was entirely foreign to both of us. We quickly learned that two women living alone would need some help with the heavy work. John Luis, a young man in the area, was a member of a crew of handymen that helped us out. As custom requires, he became like a family member rather than simply a "stateside" handyman. He was unemployed and his prospects for a job were dismal. We began to informally involve him in sessions on entrepreneurship skills. Eventually, he asked whether his friends and family members could join him in these sessions. Before we could proceed to accept his suggestion, John Luis explained that we had to talk with his family and the parents of other youths who would be coming. We visited homes to introduce ourselves and explain the purpose of the youth sessions. Before long, the sessions expanded to formal Saturday morning meetings with eight of his relatives and friends.

Word spread around the small village that two "American" teachers from California had come to live in the area and that they were teaching the children. Within a week, John Luis brought a verbal invitation to present ourselves at a meeting of the local association. Not knowing what to expect, we arrived at the meeting fully equipped, carrying documentation as to who we were. We were seated in a small room opposite eight older gentlemen and one woman who never spoke throughout the meeting. The men were dressed in the true "jibara" style. They wore sparkling clean and ironed "guayaberas." We introduced ourselves and they asked why we had come to their village. We spoke for several hours. At the end, fully satisfied, the association asked us to work with the entire community in solving its serious unemployment problem. We told the association that we needed a planning and action committee. They named a committee, immediately including some of those present and others whom they could notify. Our work began that night. Every Thursday evening we met to plan and create a model of action. As a result of our work, Producir, Inc., an economic and community development corporation, was legally incorporated in June 1986.

Source: Antonia Pantoja and Wilhelmina Perry, "Community Development and Restoration: A Perspective," in Felix G. Rivera and John L. Erlich, *Community Organizing in a Diverse Society* (Boston, MA: Allyn and Bacon, 1992), pp. 224–25. Reprinted by Permission.

Instead, you should work toward playing the role of an enabler or facilitator. "The enabler role is one of facilitating a process of problem solving and includes such actions as helping people express their discontents, encouraging organization, nourishing good interpersonal relationships, and emphasizing common objectives."[47]

Developing a Program

After a period of helping community members talk, organize them around an issue and come up with a plan. The community will begin to move toward implementation. Implementation of change in modern communities includes initiating a community project of volunteer efforts, obtaining a grant for developing a special program, coordinating efforts with other community action projects to form a coalition, and engaging in social action. For example, where there is one major employer,

> it is reasonable to think in terms of strategies designed to produce higher wages, comprehensive fringe benefits, and improved working conditions. In areas, however, where there is no one major employer, solutions must be looked for outside the area—bringing industry in, carrying people out to where jobs can be located, or causing higher levels of authority . . . to assume responsibility for those who, on a national basis, have been left in the economic backwater.[48]

An example of a community organization that is continually engaged in community development is Aid for Retarded Citizens. Composed of individuals who are developmentally disabled, parents, and interested professionals, this self-help group has developed programs, services, and agencies including sheltered workshops, infant programs, camping and recreation, Special Olympics, job programs, education, training, and adult development programs.

One kind of community development self-help project is a cooperative. Cooperatives are projects that people plan, construct, and operate, and then share in the services, profits, and benefits of the project. Community developers have helped develop cooperatively run factories that place control of profits in the hands of workers, cooperative insurance programs that provide low-cost medical and life insurance, cooperative fire departments that provide fire protection where it is not otherwise available, and cooperative housing projects that renovate or take over low-income housing projects and slum tenements.

Community developers have organized credit unions that provide loans at reasonable cost, especially to those who otherwise would not be able to get loans. Cooperative stores have been created in which food, clothing, drugs, and other items are sold to members at low cost, with profits distributed to members in proportion to their purchases. Cooperative educational programs have been formed in which members teach, learn, and engage in fundraising.

Ending the Process

There will come a time when the developer must leave a community. At that time, community members should be able to carry on the programs, implement the vision, and continue the leadership that they have begun. The community should have a sense of itself, and its members should be walking their way together. There should be a sense of accomplishment, and the vision of the future should be clear.

Community Development with Ontological Communities (Communities of Meaning)

In addition to helping modern communities, community developers also work with religious communities, such as churches, synagogues, and mosques, and with cultural and civic associations that provide the spiritual, emotional, and existential meaning and support for a neighborhood or community group. Ontological communities, or communities of meaning, are often the heart of the larger community in which they are embedded.

Developing communities of meaning, because they already have an organizational structure, tends to be a more formal process than working with modern communities. When you work with an ontological community, you establish a relationship with its leaders and the community as a whole, work with a task group to develop solutions, present solutions to the community, implement those solutions, and come to closure.

Ideological Identification

Working with communities of meaning often requires ideological identification with that community. For example, in working directly with a Jewish synagogue, it is best if the community worker is Jewish, in order to provide value and cultural identification with the community. It would be difficult for someone who is not Jewish to develop the kind of identification necessary for effective work. The same is true of providing community development services to members of a Southern Baptist church or a Roman Catholic parish.

Talking with Leaders

At the outset establish a relationship with the primary "gatekeepers" to the community—the pastor, priest, rabbi, officers, executive committee, or board of trustees of the ontological community. Listen actively for areas of dysfunction and pain as you talk with these members. At this point you are assessing whether the problem is one with which you want to work. If you decide you want to work with this community, help the community leaders see that the variety of problems they are experiencing are solvable.

In brief terms describe the process that you will undertake to help resolve the issues. Community development with ontological communities is much like practicing therapy with families or groups. You are going to uncover and break up dysfunctional systems and replace them with new and hopefully better ones. Make sure that the community leaders understand that the process may take up to six months or more and may require considerable commitment from all of the members of the community. They also need to understand that the process includes taking a hard look at themselves and being willing to engage in behavioral change, and that things will more than likely become worse before they will get better.

A commitment to change often means at least one weekly meeting of a select committee of community members, individual meetings with community leaders, and other meetings as needed. Be sure to explain your fee structure and ancillary costs.

Presentation to the Community as a Whole

After the community leaders have "bought into" your plan, present a proposal to the entire community at a special meeting or at the community's annual meeting. Once the entire community agrees to engage in the change process, contract for the entire service or for an initial study.

The Problem-Solving Process

The exploration phase begins with gathering information about the community. Read as much as you can about the community. Find out about its history, its traditions, its values, and its culture. Spend time with the community. Attend its functions and gatherings, talk to its members, and try to discover where the dysfunctions are located. Because ontological communities combine authentic community with aspects of formal organization, you need to discover to what extent the problem lies in the informal communal life of the community, its relationships, and leadership and/or in its formal organizational structure.

1. *Communal problems.* If the problem is in the communal components of the community, begin where the dysfunction is the greatest. Often this may be the formal or informal leadership of the community. Form a group of these leaders and spend time working on better communication, building relationships, and conflict resolution. This may take the form of day-long "workshops" or weekend retreats.
2. *Organizational Problems.* Often problems in community relationships result in organizational problems. When this occurs you need to look at the fit between what the community wants to do (its functions) and the way it has decided to accomplish them (its structure).

Meet with a select committee committed to working on the structural/functional fit with you. This becomes your problem-solving team or task force.

Engage your group in an introductory warm-up exercise to develop cohesion between members. Next, establish the purpose of the group, describe the principles of community growth and process, obtain feedback from the members, and contract with them. Make sure that members understand they will develop solutions and help implement them. Your role is to provide expertise, training, facilitation, and staff support, and to help them function as a working group with shared leadership and decision-making, communication, and conflict-resolution skills.

Help members understand the steps of problem solving, and begin a process of problem recognition. First, brainstorm a list of all of the functions that the community tries to perform, and group them in categories. Then make a list of the ways the community tries to fulfill these functions. There will probably be a number of discrepancies. As you consider the gaps and inconsistencies, make a list of the problems. These might be gaps in service, poor communication, lack of accountability, poor leadership, ineffectiveness in meeting objectives, no objectives at all, poor motivation, or others.

Assist the team to develop alternative solutions that will help solve the problems and create a better "fit" between the community's structure and its functions. At least two, preferably three, proposals should be developed—one of which should be the way things are at present. List the "pros" and "cons" of each alternative. A force field analysis process, described in chapter 3, might be useful to help rank the various proposals.

Presentation of Solutions

The problem-solving team should hold a series of community forum informational meetings to explain the alternative solutions and their pros and cons and to obtain feedback. This feedback input may significantly change some of the alternatives.

After the community forum, the task group should revise and rework the proposals, incorporating the community's suggestions. After this, alterna-

tive solutions should be ready to be presented to the community at large. The entire community should vote on accepting one of the alternative proposals.

Implementation

The original group that developed the change proposal should be disbanded, and a fresh group that has no vested interests in or political aspirations about the project should be chosen to help implement the solution. This group can see the proposal from a new and unbiased perspective. They may see flaws or faults with the proposal and be valuable in assuring that the proposal actually works.

Assessment and Closure

An evaluation component should be designed before the project is implemented. (Program evaluation is presented in chapter 8.) The project should be evaluated at the end of its first six months and first year to assure that it is functioning properly. As your last effort, organize a community party to give recognition to all those involved, help the community celebrate its success, and give closure to the process.

International Community Development: Helping Traditional Communities

International community development has as its target traditional communities in the "third" world areas of Africa, Asia, and South America. While these communities are far removed from our experience, life-style, and culture, and distant from us in space, they deserve our interest, concern, and compassion. International community development can be an opportunity for exceptional caring, giving, and even heroism. The work of Mother Theresa, for example, working with the sick and homeless in the streets of Calcutta, has been an inspiration to the world. Father Damien devoted his life to the lepers of Molokai in Hawaii. Dr. Albert Schweitzer in

Africa and Dr. Tom Dooley in Vietnam are people who have given of themselves to others in the highest tradition of community service.

History of International Community Development

The earliest international community development efforts were church related.[49] The first international community developers were Christian, Hindu, and Buddhist missionaries.[50] The major aims of these missionaries were often "evangelism and conversion, but it was soon realized that the ameliorating of the whole condition of the lives of their converts was inseparable" from religious goals.[51] Thus, "community development efforts of the missions became intertwined with community development efforts of the colonial government."[52]

Western missionaries have often been criticized for trying to destroy tribal culture by superimposing Western values, culture, and religion onto traditional communities. Such criticism, however, has often been too extreme.[53] Roland Oliver, for example, points out that "missions intended to work within the framework of the tribal system . . . evidenced by the missionaries' patient, almost hopeless, study of tribal languages and their insistence that education should be given in the vernacular."[54]

Missionaries pioneered strategies of establishing experimental pilot community development projects in an attempt to discover appropriate methods of assisting people. One of the earliest community development efforts was a mission program begun in 1838 that organized and conducted day schools, model farm schools, and normal schools for emancipated slaves in the British West Indies.[55] The British experience was to "set up in each territory a pilot project to experiment with a comprehensive and intensive program of rural betterment and experiment with a team of technical offices and missionaries to try to combine efforts in a single, unified program."[56]

The experiences of British, German, French, and American missionaries in working with third world communities resulted in a growing under-

International community development targets traditional communities in Africa, Asia, and South America.

standing of community development work. In 1923 an international missionary conference brought together missionaries from several countries to share information and explore community development principles. The result was a report by the Advisory Committee on Native Education in Tropical Africa, "often regarded as the original foundation of modern community development."[57] This committee recommended that community development

> should . . . render the individual more efficient in his or her condition of life, whatever it may be, and . . . promote the advancement of the community as a whole through the improvement of agriculture, the development of native industries, the improvement of health, the training of the people in the management of their own affairs, and the inculcation of true ideals of citizenship and service. It must include the raising up of capable, trustworthy, public-spirited leaders of the people, belonging to their own race.[58]

The term "community development" was originated in 1928 by the International Missionary Council, which defined its methods and its focus. Among these were (1) preserving all of the permanent values in indigenous family systems, renewing and giving major attention to the role of women; (2) fellowshiping, building, and ministering to the whole life of the community; (3) assisting in education by means of local schools; (4) developing economic and social voluntary organizations and training in self-government; and (5) promoting relationships with government.[59] Many of these principles, innovative for their time, are valid for international community development today.

With the demise of colonialism and the increasing self-determination of emerging nations, community development could no longer be left solely in the hands of voluntary religious and civic organizations. With the birth of the United Nations on April 25, 1945, community development work became the responsibility of those nations of the world considered to be the "most developed." The leadership of the United Nations defined community development as a

> process by which the efforts of the people themselves are united with those of governmental authorities to improve the economic, social, and cultural conditions of communities, to integrate these com-

munities into the life of the nation, and to enable them to contribute fully to national progress.[60]

Operating under the auspices of its Economic and Social Council, the United Nations provides community development programs and services to developing nations world-wide in the arenas of information and technical assistance, and in a variety of specialized areas. Information is an important resource in community development efforts. The United Nations is a central repository for social data and statistics from all the member nations. "All organizations in the UN system collect, process, and publish masses of data on the economic and social situation in member countries and in the world generally"[61] for use in community development efforts. In addition, the UN publishes *World Economic Survey, Report on the World Social Situation,* and *State of the World's Children* compiled by UNICEF. This data is complemented by periodical statistical collections such as the *UN Statistical Yearbook* and the monthly *Statistical Bulletin.*[62]

The UN Development Program (UNDP) is a major vehicle for community development in third world communities. It provides expert assistance to developing countries, regional training centers, scholarships, and planning projects for investment.[63] The UN Fund for Population Activities (UNFPA) assists communities in applying knowledge of population dynamics to training and family planning services, and the UN Capital Development Fund (UNCDF) provides grants and long-term, low-interest loans for community development in the least-developed countries.[64] The UN also recruits a corps of volunteers who do community development work. In 1991, for example, the corps consisted of more than two thousand volunteers world-wide.[65]

The UN provides a variety of specialized programs that complement its community development efforts. One of the best-known programs is UNICEF, the United Nations Childrens Fund. Initially established to provide aid to children who had suffered during World War II, it now develops long-term programs for health, social welfare, and teaching. The UN, in addition, continues to provide assistance and protection to refugees who are displaced because of war, famine, floods, and other disasters through the UN Disaster Relief Organization (UNDRO). This agency "is on the scene first to protect the human rights of people outside their own countries and to offer material assistance where forced migrations occur."[66]

The World Food Program was designed to send agricultural surpluses or gifts of food to developing countries.[67] The UN is also involved in health issues, mainly by means of its affiliation with the World Health Organization (WHO). WHO coordinates research and provides a system for informing member nations of outbreaks of infectious diseases. It also assist developing countries in organizing their own public health services and controlling health-related problems such as poor sanitation.[68] The World Bank provides long-term low-interest loans for development and undertakes technical assistance projects exceeding $15 billion annually.[69]

Action-Oriented International Community Development

While community development has had many successes helping third world communities, over the years it has been strongly criticized. The economic development model has been seen as something that can be applied or done to "underdeveloped" third world communities by doling out technology, economic assistance, or foreign aid rather than respecting the self-determination, culture, and history of the people.

Taking a paternalistic, Western view of progress as its base, development sometimes has led to subversion of some of the very goals and values it should have espoused, weakening and disempowering communities even as it seeks to empower them. As a result, community development has often been a vehicle for transporting "modernization" to less-developed nations as a covert means of inducing them to give up their indigenous culture and history in favor of dependence on Western technology.

Sometimes indigenous cultures have become sources of raw materials coveted by industrialized nations. In the name of progress, people have been economically exploited by powerful imperialistic countries. At other times, they have been used by world superpowers who wanted to obtain political, economic, and strategic advantages in the struggle for world dominance.

Action-oriented international community de-

velopment, in contrast, bases its activities on aiding the struggle for the preservation and survival of the integrity of third world communities. It is the "conquest of a small piece of humanity for the common heritage of human kind."[70] Action-oriented community developers assist indigenous peoples to develop power over their own economic resources and to maintain the integrity of their own culture and history. The action model assists the well-being of third world communities on their own terms, not those of other nations. Chau and Hodge assert that

> today's community practice in the third world . . . emphasizes two interrelated features: (1) popular participation and a reliance on the people's initiative; and (2) the provision of services to encourage self-help. It also differs from prior community practice which, often based on educational process, focused on human resource development and neglected institutional change. . . . The adoption of a social development perspective . . . recognizes the importance of creating new institutions or changing existing ones. . . . New community resources and programs are needed to replace or supplement the traditional ones.[71]

The Action Process

As an action-oriented international community developer, keep in mind the three-tiered levels of engagement developed by Rivera and Erlich described earlier. Match yourself as closely as possible with the ethnic and cultural background of the people you are helping. In addition to your own ethnic heritage and cultural background, you have personal skills, interests, and abilities. You need to be firmly grounded in macro social work methods and should have technical skills in economic development, health, education, administration, agriculture, child welfare, relief work, housing, construction, or some other substantive area.

You will also need a particular love and concern for people of other cultures, an appreciation and enjoyment of human differences, and a respect for the integrity and self-determination of people whose history, values, religion, and culture often stretch back thousands of years.

Added to this you will need to have a set of human relations skills to help a community mobilize itself on its own behalf. Finally, you will need the backing and support of an organization such as the Peace Corps, international social work agencies of the United Nations such as UNICEF or UNDP, or some other community development organization. You will work with a larger team that has been established as part of a community development plan providing relief, education, medical, agricultural, or technical assistance to a community.

Orienting Yourself to the Community

Learn about the mores, values, history, religion, and customs of the people. Read as much as you can and/or take courses about the community with which you will be working, and learn the language of the people.

Spend considerable time immersing yourself in the culture and milieu of the community. Just as a counselor needs to develop rapport and see a problem from the point of view of the client, you should begin to see and think and understand from the point of view of the people with whom you are working. While immersing yourself in the community, however, keep in mind that it is always *their* community, not yours. Never let your priorities override or undercut the community's goals.[72]

Engaging the Leaders

If a community leader invites the community developer or an agency into the community, the process of community development is much easier. Leaders of third world communities carry symbolic and personal power. A community developer must be sensitive to the role community leaders play and their place in the community.

However, if you can develop enthusiasm in indigenous leaders even if they did not invite the community development effort, then much of the battle is won. It has been said that a leader's commitment and investment is 70 percent of the problem solution. An indigenous leader can mobilize support and involvement of even a depressed or demoralized community.

On the other hand, indigenous community leaders may be a source of resistance to the community development effort. They may legitimately resent "outsiders" coming in and "taking over." Unless they have been sufficiently involved in the problem-solving process, they will not be emotionally committed to it. It is, after all, their community, their problem, their people.

In addition, indigenous community leaders may feel hopeless about any change efforts. While they may want change, they may fight it at the same time. Change may mean that they must also change, and this may be threatening to them. Give a great deal of attention to understanding culturally acceptable ways of relating to the traditional structure of the people and to its leaders, or your effort will be doomed to failure.

Engaging the People

You must be skilled in working within the history and context of the community as well as in relating to those people important to the change effort. As an action-oriented community developer you want to reduce human suffering such as hunger, disease, or lack of housing. You also want to help the community members to develop self-reliance, mobilize resources, and use decision-making skills so that they can carry out development tasks on a long-term basis and generate solutions that come out of their own interests and culture. What may appear to be the shortest or most rational route to solving a problem in a third world country may not always be the best or the most effective one.

The Development Process

Just as in community work with modern and ontological communities, meet with a group of community members, listen to the issues, and gather information, taking time to talk to key community leaders or simply become a participant-observer in the community itself. A good community developer with third world communities will be keenly aware of helping the community members increase their ability to work together, making use of group processes to develop communication and community awareness. This must be done in relation to tangible, substantive outcomes. The task or end product is the motivating force that brings individuals together.

Community development projects in third world communities include attempts to improve local agriculture and irrigation, encourage rural industry, and found schools; develop public health projects related to sanitation, clean water, and eradication of disease; build homes; do relief work, such as distribute food; and develop day-care centers and youth and women's programs. Community developers help people to establish businesses and jobs and training.[73] It is, according to S. K. Khinduka, "multipurpose and intersectorial."[74]

Community Activism

By strengthening community ties, the community developer can be a major force in preventing the destruction of a third world community by the wider society. This may mean active resistance, political action, and sensitizing society to the problems of the community in danger. Where the integrity of a community is being threatened, a community developer may need to take an activist stance to help protect the community. Be aware, however, that social action in third world countries can result in severe reprisals by political and business leaders who have a vested interest in exploiting the poor. Community developers and missionaries have been jailed, tortured, and murdered when their community development efforts threatened the status quo.

Community-Based Social Care: A New Model of Community Development

Social workers concerned about the universal needs of people to form community must develop models and theories of community that can fit today's fast-paced social environment. The rural town in which people lived their entire lives, had face-to-face relationships with one another, and developed strong social bonds is no longer a reality for most Americans. Today people change jobs and even professions. People are mobile, moving from place-to-place as much as once every several years. They rarely satisfy all of their social needs in the community in which they live. A person may live in one community, work in a setting outside that community, attend religious functions in another location, shop in yet others, and

spend leisure time elsewhere. People communicate more often with others by telephone, E-mail, and internet than face-to-face with their own neighbors.

If people are going to relate in community with one another, community itself must be redefined and models of community developed that can be adaptable to a highly mobile, technologically sophisticated society. Harry Specht and Mark Courtney propose a model of community-based social care[75] that breaks with the traditional view of social work as a primarily psychotherapeutic profession, discards an individualistic conception of the human condition, and rejects the provision of treatment as preferable to prevention. It is based on a wholistic idea of social services as engaging the entire community rather than being only for the poor and marginal.[76] It contravenes the traditional model of social services, which asserts that

> social services should achieve their objectives by eradicating individual weakness, that social services should be provided to people in the most unattractive way possible lest people should like them; and that social services should be controlled by politicians and professional administrators, our modern-day counterparts of overseers of the poor.[77]

The vision of Specht and Courtney is the development of community service centers, founded on the model of the Settlement House Movement at the turn of the century, that are "locality based and utilize adult education, social groups, and community associations as [their] major mode of intervention."[78] Service centers differ from settlement houses, however, in that they would be publicly financed and operated for all members of the community. Leadership would emanate not from professionals helping lower-class citizens but from the community.[79]

> This community-based system of social care will be *universal*—that is, available to everyone; *"comprehensive*—providing on one site all of the kinds of social services required by an urban community; *accessible*—easily reached by all people in the area designated as the service area; and *accountable*—with community residents having a prominent role in making policy for the service and overseeing its implementation.[80] (Emphasis in original)

An advantage of this kind of model is that it places the community, not individuals, at the center of healing. "A community-based social service system . . . brings together all of the families of the community—children and adults—to work out problems and to share meaningful social and cultural experiences."[81] Rather than stigmatizing the poor, universal community-based social service programs would

> meet the normative needs of all community residents: for example, for child care and for advice, assistance and guidance with respect to child rearing, health, and family care. . . . Instead of being considered a "case" (as in social casework), or a "patient," or a "client" (as in psychotherapy), users of center services will be considered "members," or "service users," or "residents."[82]

Social group work would also be a prime modality for delivering services. Such social groups enhance individuals'

> social roles and carry out important social functions relevant to their social status such as being a student, working, and developing a family. The best test of this capacity is the extent to which it is evident in the groups in which individuals participate in everyday life: at school, on the job, and in the family. Social work that builds a wide variety of the social structures that constitute a community—neighborhood associations, play groups, parents' groups, self-help groups, and so forth—is a more direct way of building the community's capacities to help its members.[83]

In such "communal forms of help of the participants, we develop strengths of the participants rather than weakening them by making them dependent on the approval and support of the individual therapist or caseworker."[84]

> In a modern system of community-based social care, we begin with the assumption that the community itself has the capacity to deal with most individually experienced problems through classes, self-help groups, social clubs, recreation groups, special interest groups, and community service organizations. Moreover, we assume that working with community groups is the preferred way to meet social needs because, in addition to solving the individual's problems, we increase the community's overall problem-solving ability.[85]

Such a center would have "a mix of some qualities of a public school, a settlement house, an adult education center, and a community center . . . [and might be located] on the same site as the local elementary school."[86] Specht and Courtney envision service priorities in the following areas:

1. Child care and parent education related to child care.[87]
2. Services for older adults, and a service bureau that would have the task of recruiting volunteers to assist, develop, and operate center programs.[88]
3. A citizen's advice and education bureau offering counseling and making referrals, and the development of child welfare services including foster care, adoptions, and child abuse prevention.[89]
4. A variety of self-help groups, such as Twelve Steps groups like Alcoholics Anonymous, Parents without Partners, adult education, and social groups for teenagers.

Leadership for these centers would be drawn from area residents, representatives of larger units of government, and representatives of voluntary organizations, with policy control for center programs resting in large part in the hands of the residents.[90] Funding would come from establishing an independent district with its own taxing power.[91]

Conclusion

Community development involves helping communities meet their needs. It is helping people develop particular projects to enhance their life chances, opportunities, and progress. It is helping communities of people work together to help themselves.

Community development is much like "grass roots" democracy, in which power is shared in an open forum. It encourages citizen participation in the life of the community, civic pride, and civic consciousness.

Three kinds of communities offer opportunities for development efforts. There is scarcely a modern community that does not have pockets of poverty and groups of mentally ill, homeless, migrants, or others who cry out for help. Macro social workers assist ontological communities as they attempt to provide meaning in today's impersonal world. Finally, macro social workers help third world communities that need assistance in health, social, and economic areas, while respecting their cultural differences and need for self-determination.

Individuals cannot thrive without authentic community. But our modern society is one in which a sense of community is lacking, one in which we can expect personality dysfunctions, greater alienation, lack of identity, and a tendency to ignore those who are marginal. Community development is a macro social work field that aims to remedy that lack. Community development is perhaps the most urgently needed and yet least-recognized arenas of helping in our society today.

KEY CONCEPTS

Community development
Action model of community development
community self-determination
three tiered model of intensity and influence
community development process with modern
    communities
community development process with communities
    of meaning
United Nations Children's Emergency Fund
    (UNICEF)
United Nations Development Program (UNDP)
United Nations Fund for Population Activities
    (UNFPA)
United Nations Capital Development Fund (UNCDF)
United Nations Disaster Relief Organization
    (UNDRO)
World Food Program (WFP)
World Health Organization (WHO)
World Bank
Action oriented international community
    development
community based social care

QUESTIONS FOR DISCUSSION

1. America is often called a "melting pot," meaning that eventually differing cultural, religious, and national groups become assimilated into the wider national culture and lose their identity. Is it healthy for diverse groups to become assimilated, or should they maintain their own boundaries and separateness? What is the role of a community developer in facilitating either assimilation or cultural diversity?

2. Another model of diversity is "pluralism," or the "vegetable stew" model. Rather than everyone becoming the same, as in the "melting pot," the vegetable stew model maintains that each community can and should maintain its own centrality and culture while interacting with the whole. What are the advantages and disadvantages of the pluralistic model? What are it's implications for community development? Should, for example, African Americans, American Indians, the Amish, and other groups maintain their own schools, dress, language, and customs?

3. To what extent should these differences be supported by the larger society by means of taxes? For example, should there be tax-supported schools for African Americans or Native Americans who want to maintain a specific type of education for their children rather than integrating them into the mainstream?

ADDITIONAL READING

Addams, Jane. *Twenty Years at Hull House.* New York: Macmillan, 1910.
——. *The Second Twenty Years at Hull House.* New York: Macmillan, 1930.
Biddle, William W., and Loureide Biddle. *The Community Development Process: The Recovery of Local Initiative.* New York: Holt, Rinehart and Winston, 1965.
Fitzsimmons, Stephen J., and Abby J. Freedman. *Rural Community Development: A Program, Policy and Research Model.* Cambridge, MA: Abt Books, 1981.
Halpern, Robert. *Rebuilding the Inner City: A History of Neighborhood Initiatives to Address Poverty in the U.S.* New York: Columbia University Press, 1995.
Jones, W. Ron. *Finding Community. A Guide to Community Research and Action.* Palo Alto, CA: Freel and Associates, 1971.
Perkins, John. *With Justice for All.* Ventura, CA: Regal Books, 1982.
Specht, Harry, and Mark Courtney. *Unfaithful Angels: How Social Work Has Abandoned Its Mission.* New York: Free Press, 1994.

EXERCISES

EXERCISE 23:
Critiquing "A Town Called Embarrass"

Review the story of the town called Embarrass at the beginning of this chapter. What would you have done if you had been a community developer in this town? Do you think the town was worth saving? Why or why not? What is the value of towns such as Embarrass? Does the field of social work have a responsibility to such communities? If so, what is that responsibility?

EXERCISE 24:
Choosing a Community Development Problem

When visiting Toynbee Hall in England, Jane Addams had a vision of a way to revitalize communities in Chicago. Today, many communities in the United States are faced with problems similar to those Jane Addams confronted. We have communities of immigrants, deteriorating inner cities, increased violence, racial turmoil, and destructive gangs. As you consider the kinds of social problems facing cities and rural areas, think of community development programs or solutions that might solve these problems. Write an essay describing what a community developer might do to deal with one social problem.

EXERCISE 25:
Critiquing Community-Based Social Care

Harry Specht and Mark Courtney have proposed an alternative way of revitalizing not only our communities but also the social work profession. Read their book *Unfaithful Angels: How Social Work Has Abandoned Its Mission*. Critique their proposal for a "Community-Based System of Social Care." Would this alternative work? What are its benefits? What are its costs? What forces of resistance would have to be overcome? What political issues would it encounter? Would it solve the problem of the demise of community in our modern age? Can you think of ways to improve this model? Can you come up with a model of your own?

EXERCISE 26:
Critiquing Action Principles of Community Development

The following principles on which community development models might be based are offered for your analysis. What do you think of these principles? Are there any of these principles that you would *not* choose? Are there any principles that you would add that were left out? How would you prioritize these principles?

1. Shared leadership—everyone participates to the extent they are able and interested. Followership is as important as leadership.
2. Shared information—no secrets here.
3. Shared power—no one commands others. Those who have positions of power are seen as servants of others, not their masters.
4. Shared learning and growth—if members "miss" the mark, make a "mis-take," take a "mis-step," or becomes "mis-placed," the "misses" are acknowledged, and the group goes on from there.
5. Shared experiences, shared joys, shared sorrows, and shared memories—everyone is on the road together. Everyone becomes a hero, and each person's journey is an heroic one.
6. Shared meanings—everyone celebrates and participates in the shared rewards.

EXERCISE 27:
Researching Community Development Models

The Settlement House Movement, the YMCA, the Salvation Army of the 1880s and 1890s, the Civilian Conservation Corps of the 1930s, the War on Poverty of the 1960s, self-help groups, the Civil Rights Movement, the Peace Corps, and the National Service Corps are all models of ways to build communities that change people, give purpose and meaning to people's lives, and enable people to care about one another.[92] Research these models and compare them. What were they trying to accomplish? Is there anything we can learn from them about doing what Specht and Courtney describe as adding purpose and meaning to peoples lives, and enabling us to care about and love one another? Would you recommend reviving and/or expanding any of these models today?

EXERCISES

EXERCISE 28:
Community Development Using a Church as a Base

Read the following vignette. Then respond to the questions at the end.

"I knew that I needed to get people to trust and like me and my singing, and playing my guitar at the services helped a lot," said Ms. Ada Suarez, a young and dedicated second year community organization student at the University of Connecticut School of Social Work. Ada had been raised as a Pentecostal in Puerto Rico and was convinced that organizers can tap into the spiritual mandate that Pentecostals have to do "God's work" and enable the "brothers" and "sisters" to be more effective with their goals for church and community improvements.

The Pentecostal church pastor welcomed Ada's help, seeing her as a nonpaid staff member who also brought university resources. In addition to singing and helping the pastor with clerical duties, Ada visited the homes of people she identified as having leadership potential, met with the church's elders, and played big sister to some of the church's youth. She also distributed questionnaires to members, asking them to provide information about what they felt their needs were. She did this data gathering at youth meetings, meetings of the women

volunteers, prison visiting committees, and so on. She then shared with the congregation what they had identified as problems and gave recommendations for addressing them. "Some brothers and sisters want to read and write better in Spanish, some want to learn English, and others want help in finding work or better jobs. . . . Some committees want help in functioning better at meetings, and others want to know more about how to help people. . . . The youth want to discuss school issues and some church elders wish to learn how to be better leaders in and out of the church."

Ada brought the public school system into the church to teach literacy [in Spanish] and English classes for non-English speakers. She organized leadership training workshops and called on Puerto Rican Studies faculty, community organization students, and community leaders for help. Wherever possible, church members themselves introduced speakers and planned gatherings. Workshops on job training, resume writing, interviewing skills, and eligibility for food stamps were conducted at least twice in one year.

Ms. Suarez also chose to work on some more controversial projects. For example, she organized workshops on AIDS. . . . Ada encouraged young people to talk about their feelings of isolation in school and in the community

due to the strict moral codes of the church (no hard rock music, makeup, movies, smoking, etc.), and some parents were less than comfortable with that. In addition, she facilitated and encouraged the women of the congregation to become more assertive and to be more represented on the Board of Elders.

With sensitivity, she explained to the church members that since they welcomed drug addicts and worked with prisoners, some had expressed interest in knowing more about the AIDS epidemic. . . . She imparted community organization skills to elders and had them prepare flyers, lead discussions on setting agendas, form committees, and select strategies. She utilized videos, films, and other visuals effects when talking about conserving energy, applying for a job, presenting information on AIDS, etc.

1. What kind of processes did Ada use?
2. What kinds of qualities did you observe in Ada?
3. Was Ada successful? Why or why not?
4. Is there anything you would have done differently? Why or why not?

Source: Julio Morales, "Community Social Work with Puerto Rican Communities in the United States: One organizer's Perspective," in Rivera and Erlich, eds., *Community Organizing,* pp. 102–4. Reprinted by permission of Allyn and Bacon.

CHAPTER 8

Becoming a Social Activist

"Fighting Minister" Douglas Roth and others put their lives on the line to demonstrate on behalf of workers thrown out of work by steel mill closings.

Sojourner Truth, a former slave who could neither read nor write, was a fervent activist who could not tolerate slavery nor second-class citizenship for women. One day during an antislavery speech, she was heckled by an old man.

"Old woman, do you think that your talk about slavery does any good? Why, I don't care any more for your talk than I do for the bite of a flea."

"Perhaps not, but the Lord willing, I'll keep you scratching, " she replied.

—MARIAN WRIGHT EDELMAN[1]

Eventually, anyone concerned with the transformation of the individual must engage in social action.

—MARILYN FERGUSON[2]

IDEAS IN THIS CHAPTER

Fighting Ministers

For one hundred years, Duchesne, Pennsylvania, was a thriving steel town. Then, the dream of the good life turned into a nightmare. On Thanksgiving day 1983, fourteen steel mills in Pennsylvania closed, and 250,000 people in the valley lost their jobs. In Pittsburgh, nine out of ten blast furnaces shut down. The steel industry had gone from boom to bust. Suicide and divorce rates skyrocketed.

A group of Lutheran pastors whose congregations were hard hit by the plant closings organized themselves into a group called the Denominational Ministry Strategy, or DMS, to help the unemployed steelworkers. DMS discovered that Pittsburgh's unemployment was not simply the result of fate or a natural downturn in the business cycle but rather the deliberate decision of Pittsburgh's corporations to eliminate heavy industry in the area. Mellon Bank, Pittsburgh's most powerful institution, with $28 billion in assets, much of it in steelworker pension funds, was foreclosing steel mills in Pittsburgh while at the same time loaning money to build mills in another country where labor was cheaper and profits higher. Politicians, the steel industry, and banks colluded in a conscious plan to rid themselves of their own steelworkers. Hundreds of thousands of people who depended for their livelihood on the steel industry were jettisoned like so much excess baggage.

The pastors believed that if they set up a dialogue with the power brokers, help for the unemployed would come. Instead of help, they found deaf ears. When the milltown of Clairton was shut down, the pastors thought that if they petitioned the governor to declare the town an economic disaster area, he would listen, but he turned away from them. They thought that if they went to corporate leaders and showed how people were being destroyed while corporations were making the highest profits in years, the CEOs would listen. But the leaders of industry refused to help.

The Lutheran pastors decided to go to the people. But Pittsburgh's unemployed failed to join the ministers in massive numbers. It had been thirty years since anyone had seen a strike, and the workers had become complacent. The pastors preached on the steps of Mellon Bank, urging customers to take their savings out of Mellon and invest in another bank. They laid the blame for Pittsburgh's unemployment on Pittsburgh's doorstep. Corporate leaders began to retaliate.

While this was to be expected, what was not expected was the reaction from the pastors' own synod. Castigated in a synod meeting, the DMS pastors were declared outcasts. The synod withdrew its support and the DMS pastors were alone.

Then a group of labor leaders who called themselves the Network to Save the Monohio Valley joined the DMS pastors. The pastors and labor leaders banded together and became more militant. They began to stage demonstrations to spotlight Pittsburgh's abandonment of her own workers. They dumped dead fish and skunks in lobbies of corporate offices, scattered coins on the floor of Mellon bank, milled about, and disrupted business.

These nonviolent resistance tactics, however, brought only ridicule and resentment. Trinity Lutheran Church voted to oust the Reverend Douglas Roth of Clairton because of his activism. Having many members of the congregation on his side, he refused to leave. When the synod appointed a substitute minister to take over, the board president refused to allow him to preach. Finally, Roth barricaded himself in the church.

Hiring the same law firm that represented Mellon Bank, the synod filed an injunction against their own minister and directed the county sheriff to arrest the Reverend Roth. He was sentenced to ninety days in jail and fined $1,200. One person commented, "Look at Nazi Germany. Who do they lock up first? The ministers and union leaders. It's a dangerous thing to put a minister in jail for standing up for what he believes in."

The wives of the DMS ministers had struggled for over a year on the side lines. Now, they decided to act as a group by visiting St. John's Lutheran Church, the church attended by the synod bishop and many church administrators. When confronted outside the church by the sheriff and a contingent of armed police officers, the women refused to leave, insisting on their right to worship with their fellow Lutherans. The bishop gave silent assent as the wives of his pastors were arrested and taken away to jail for trying to attend church on Sunday.

When the Lutheran Church in America (LCA) took title to Trinity Church, sealing the church building, a number of church members, union leaders, DMS pastors and their wives barricaded themselves inside. Breaking down a rear door, the sheriff forcibly arrested the entire group. They were all sentenced to thirty to sixty days in jail and fined.

Meanwhile, Douglas Roth, who had been given an extra sixty days in jail for taping sermons and sending them to his parishioners, was finally released after a total of 122 days in jail. He was immediately removed from the clergy roster, the first minister ever to be defrocked by the Lutheran Church in America.

Since the synod had locked them out of the church, members of Trinity Lutheran church-in-exile continued worship in a bus and in warmer weather held services on the sidewalks. Like Martin Luther, who began the Protestant Reformation five hundred years earlier, these Lutheran pastors had taken action against an oppressive system and even against their own church. They gave new meaning to Luther's words, "Here I stand. God help me, I can do no other."

Introduction

Social work as a profession is called to transform society and to create a more just social order. To do nothing in favor of those who are oppressed is to act against them.[3] Social work change agents ought to be "building a world where every man, regardless of race, religion, or nationality, can live a fully human life, free of the servitude that comes from other men and from the incompletely mastered world about him."[4]

Social action is for those social workers who, like the Lutheran pastors, "are deeply troubled by our present world, seek a vision of a society which supports life,"[5] and are committed to a process of social change and an end to violence and human misery. Social action has nothing less as its goal than making fundamental changes in social structures that foster oppression and injustice.

This chapter defines social action and describes its heritage and three stances social activists take. Next, it shows how to go about doing social action and explores how to unfreeze dysfunctional systems, move to action, and refreeze them in healthier ways. Finally, how to terminate the social activist role is discussed.

What Is Social Action?

Social action occurs when oppressed, disadvantaged, or injured people engage in mutual action against an oppressor, aim at redistribution of power at the political or economic levels, reorder organizational alliances at top levels of the bureaucratic apparatus, and ultimately change public policies. According to Saul Alinsky, one of the best-known social activists of our time, the challenge of social action is

> to create mass organizations to seize power and give it to the people; to realize the democratic dream of equality, justice, peace, cooperation, equal and full opportunities for education, full and useful employment, health and the creation of those circumstances in which man can have the chance to live by values that give meaning to life.[6]

Social activists advocate for people who have been victimized by institutionalized racism, economic exploitation, dehumanizing social policies, oppression, injustice, and corruption. They help people pinpoint where oppression has occurred, enable them to take a stand, and strategize for joint community action in confronting the perpetrators of injustice.

Social activists work not only to change oppressive and unjust systems but also to change people's responses to those social systems that are disabling them. By taking charge of their lives, the people of a community can change the conditions of the victimization and gain empowerment.

The Stance of the Social Activist

There are three different stances that social activists take: social prophet, visionary, and confronter. The prophetic stance of social action calls for radical change. The social prophet critiques the defects in current world views, attitudes, values, and policies, proclaiming that the conventional wisdom of the day, the customary way of looking at things, is defective and in need of revision. The activist questions the status quo—things as they are—recognizing that the order of things is often wrong and needs to be reversed. "The new society, the new vi-

sion is an inverted or upside-down way of life in contrast to the usual or prevailing social order."[7]

Michael Harrington, a social work activist, took a prophetic stance in *The Other America*, a book that was instrumental in sensitizing people to the issue of poverty and gave impetus for President Johnson's War on Poverty program. Journalists who expose corruption and call for reform are social prophets.

Social work activists are dreamers and futurists—this is the visionary stance of social action, picturing the future as it might be. They build the future out of a sense of justice and truth, an end to violence and oppression. The old society is left behind; the new society lies ahead. Activists foretell of the new world, and lead people to seek that new world. The work of activists is to learn from the past, and take up the work of creating a better future. They are actively involved in making the future real.

Social work activists challenge the existing order of things by direct action against perpetrators of injustice and social inequity. Through confrontation, activists help people take over or influence the power structure by means of persuasion, political action, or power tactics.

The Heritage of Social Action

Social action deals with some of the most pressing and important issues of our time. Some of the most impressive and long-standing social victories in the human struggle for justice and equality have come from social action. Many of these, such as regulating nuclear arms, protecting the environment, and ending racism, affect all of us.

Social action has been practiced under many names. It has been variously called social reform, social revolution, counter-revolution, social protest, and resistance. It has taken the form of war resistance, cultural resistance, civil disobedience, civil insurrection, and even anarchism.

This nation was peopled, by and large, by the disaffected, outcasts, protestors, idealists, visionaries, dreamers, and religious dissidents who fled their homelands because of persecution. It was founded in protest and finally revolution by those seeking liberty, freedom from oppression, and an end to tyranny by an oppressive monarchy that exploited the colonies for their wealth and resources.

Social activists continued that tradition, fostering the abolition movement, which brought about freedom from slavery, the temperance movement, and the labor union movement, protecting and legalizing the right of labor to organize. Workers in the settlement house movement campaigned for child labor laws, child welfare reform, and health and sanitation laws, and were leaders in the women's suffrage movement and pacifism.

The Abolition Movement

Social activists observed with rising concern the horrors of slavery and racism. They worked in many ways and in increasing numbers to establish the beginnings of the abolition movement. They championed an end to the Black Codes in the South, the establishment of the Freedmen's Bureau, and civil rights legislation after the Civil War.

The Temperance Movement

After the Revolutionary War, whiskey drinking became something of a national pastime for men, women, and children.[8] Between 1800 and 1830, whiskey consumption increased to more than 5 gallons per person per year in the United States. Many people were concerned about the relationship of alcoholism to unemployment, poverty, and family breakdown. Alcoholism caused loss of time from work and physical abuse of wives and children. Ultimately its eradication was seen as a matter of women's and family rights.[9]

In 1826, the American Society for the Promotion of Temperance was founded, motivated by a spirit of religious and humanitarian reform. So successful was this movement by social activists that the annual consumption of whiskey after 1830 dropped from 5 to less than 2 gallons per person per year. In the 1830s and 1840s, thousands of local temperance societies were formed to prohibit the sale of liquor altogether.[10]

By 1860 the temperance movement boasted a membership of more than a million individuals. The members of the movement became more and more politically active. One state, Maine, actually voted for prohibition.

Even though women lacked the right to vote, they entered the political arena when, in 1869, a Prohibition party was formed, along with the Women's Christian Temperance Union (WCTU) and the Anti-Saloon League. Frances Willard, the militant leader of the prohibition forces, carried the battle into the saloons themselves, where women sang hymns, prayed, and at times engaged in acts of protest.

By the turn of the century, seven states had voted to prohibit alcohol. By World War I, two-thirds of the population lived in areas where drinking was outlawed, and in 1919, the Eighteenth Amendment to the Constitution was passed. This amendment completely outlawed the manufacture, sale, import, or export of alcoholic beverages in the United States. Social protest by women against drinking was overwhelmingly effective, but implementation proved to be another matter. Enforcement of Prohibition by interdiction ultimately proved to be impossible, and in 1933, the Eighteenth Amendment was repealed. The problem of alcohol abuse was returned to the states.

Women's Rights Movement

Women have been involved at the very center of important social movements in the United States: the abolition of slavery, temperance, and universal suffrage. "They moved from a concern for the rooting out of individual imperfections that would lead to unhappy family living to a demand for explicit political recognition and power, and then to larger social issues."[11] The temperance movement encouraged women to push for their own political rights. In 1848 the first Women's Rights convention was held in Seneca Falls, New York. Women's suffrage was demanded, and a Declaration of Independence adopted.[12]

While the women's rights movement at this point made limited gains, it set the stage for growing awareness of social activism and the power women could wield in gaining access to social policy making. Women's rights, temperance, and political liberty were not issues that would go away.

In 1900 the National American Woman's Suffrage Association was founded[13] along with a number of other women's groups, among them, the

National Consumer's League, the National Women's Trade Union League, and the Young Women's Christian Association. All these organizations "were at once concerned with matters affecting women as women and the potential of the vote for righting wrongs."[14]

Social workers and social activists such as Carrie Chapman Catt took the fight for women's rights into the streets—demonstrating, marching, and picketing. The Nineteenth Amendment to the Constitution, giving women the right to vote, was approved by Congress on June 4, 1919, and ratified by the states on August 26, 1920. The National American Women's Suffrage Association dissolved but was later revived as the League of Women Voters.[15]

In the late 1960s, the women's rights movement took on renewed vigor. Gloria Steinem spearheaded

Social protest is an important form of social action.

the National Organization for Women (NOW) and the Equal Rights Amendment (ERA) to the Constitution, promoting women's rights to equal pay for equal work and the right of women to have abortions on demand. While the ERA gained momentum in the 1970s and 1980s, it did not obtain the approval of two-thirds of the states, needed for ratification.[16] It did heighten the consciousness of America to women's issues. This movement continued to develop on the political front. Women became increasingly active, gaining two senatorial seats in California in 1992 and many others in the House.

The Settlement House Movement

In 1881 there were six settlement houses in the United States. By 1910, the number had grown to over four hundred. Settlement house workers such as Jane Addams, Lillian Wald, and Florence Kelly were tireless fighters for social justice and social reform in an era that was desperate for social change. Settlement house staff worked on legislation attempting to combat slums and slum conditions. Pushing for municipal reforms, they worked to improve sanitation, sewage disposal, and clean water. They advocated for regulation and inspection of food to prevent disease and illness. They worked to create small neighborhood playgrounds, housing code improvement, reduction of congestion through city planning, and the transformation of public schools into neighborhood social centers.

Jane Addams was instrumental in the creation of state boards of conciliation and arbitration[17] and in establishing the first probation service in Chicago and the Juvenile Protective Association.[18] Hull House workers organized the Immigrant Protective League to ease the immigrant's adjustment to the new world, were active in voter's rights, forming the Municipal Voters League, and worked as advocates for child welfare legislation.[19] One of the notable settlements that engaged in social and political action was Chicago Commons, founded in 1894 by Graham Taylor. Such men as Allen T. Burns and Raymond Robins "made surveys, filed reports, checked for voting frauds, organized political rallies and torch parades, and distributed posters and handbills."[20] While "settlement workers seldom ran for political office . . . they served as campaign managers, advisers on policy, statistics gatherers, and 'brain trusters' for reform administrations."[21]

Sometimes settlement workers *opposed* measures as well as proposing them. One measure they fought against was a "proposed elevated loop that would have connected the Brooklyn and Williamsburg Bridges," because the loop would cause needless blight and congestion.[22] The settlement workers of the Henry Street and University Settlements in New York City

> organized mass meetings, sent out letters to influential people, persuaded newspapermen to present their point of view, and bombarded the city council with letters and petitions.[23]

Settlement staff fought for laws to protect employed women,[24] helped organize the National Women's Trade Union, and picketed with women workers in strikes against sweat-shop owners. Lillian Wald, founder and director of the Henry Street Settlement, and Florence Kelly, a social worker at Hull House, spearheaded a meeting of representatives of thirty-two settlement houses in New York City, mobilizing action to abolish child labor in 1902. In 1903 the Conference of Charities and Corrections determined to build opposition to child labor on national lines, and in 1904 the National Child Labor Committee was organized. Founding members included settlement workers Jane Addams, Florence Kelly, and Lillian Wald.[25]

Both Lillian Wald and Florence Kelly were instrumental in developing the first White House Conference on Child Dependency in 1909, bringing the issue of dependent children before the entire nation. The White House Conference was instrumental in developing the Children's Bureau, established in 1912, the first Child Welfare agency of the Federal Government.[26] Settlement house workers provided national leadership to the General Federation of Women's Clubs, spearheading the women's suffrage movement, which culminated in passage of the Women's Suffrage Amendment to the Constitution in 1919, enabling women to vote.

Settlement house staff, including Jane Addams, contributed to the platform and the organizational work of the Progressive Party in 1912.[27] Jane Addams was a delegate to the first national convention of the Progressive Party and seconded the nomination of Theodore Roosevelt as presidential candidate. In 1915 she founded the Woman's International League for Peace and Freedom and continued to press for peace during World War I.

Workers' Rights Movement

The struggle of workers for decent working conditions, fair wages, and decent hours began as early as 1636, when a group of fishermen in Maine fell "into mutiny" when their wages were withheld.[28] In 1806 the Journeymen Cordwainers of Philadelphia struck for higher wages and were indicted for criminal conspiracy. "What kind of justice is being served," they asked, "when merchants, politicians, and sportsmen could conspire against the worker to promote parties and banquets while the poor laborers organizing against starvation are indicted as criminals?"[29]

Abuse of workers continued unabated in the nineteenth century, culminating at times in major battles. Workers at the Carnegie steel plant, Homestead, Pennsylvania, refused to accept wage cuts, instigating the great Homestead Strike of 1892. The company's general manager, Henry Clay Frick, shut the plant down and hired special deputy sheriffs to guard the buildings. The striking workers ran them out of town, whereupon Frick called in three hundred Pinkerton detectives armed with Winchester rifles to pacify the workers. A battle ensued as the workers opened fire on Frick's private army and attempted to sink their barges with a small brass cannon. Eventually, the detectives ran up a white flag of surrender. Infuriated that seven of their number had been killed, the workers again attacked the detectives, who escaped but had to run the gauntlet of an angry mob of men and women. Six days later, the governor of Pennsylvania mobilized a militia of 8,000 men who took over Homestead and placed it under martial law. Frick brought in "scabs"—nonunion workers hired to take the jobs of the striking workers—and reopened the plant with militia protection.[30]

During this period, metal miners in Coeur d'Alene, Idaho, switchmen in Buffalo, New York, and coal miners in Tennessee walked off their jobs in defiance of their employers. In each instance, the strikes were forcibly broken through the intervention of the state militia.[31] The worst strike of all was the Pullman Strike of 1886 in Chicago. The Pullman Company layed off more than three thousand of its fifty-eight hundred employees and cut the wages of the others from 25 to 40 percent without reducing the rents the workers paid for living in company houses. "In one instance, an employee found that after payment for rent was taken out, his paycheck came to two cents."[32]

The fight for decent working conditions and fair pay, and against exploitation of workers, continued during the early 1900s, prompting bloody confrontations with paid henchmen of wealthy owners and their cohorts in law enforcement. In company after company, activists and organizers fought for worker rights. At times the struggle was brutal and bloody. Workers in the minefields of western states established the Western Federation of Miners in 1897 and engaged in a series of strikes in the gold, silver, lead, and copper mines. In 1903–1904, miners in the Cripple Creek area of Colorado attempted to go on strike and were attacked by strike breakers. The miners fought back. Mineowners hired vigilantes and called in the state militia against the striking miners. Miners sabotaged trains and exploded mines. In retaliation a number of miners were murdered or arrested and imprisoned. Miners' meetings were machine-gunned. The strike was finally crushed by the vigilantes, deputized sheriffs, police, and militia.[33]

It was not until early March 1932 that

a highly significant victory for organized labor as a whole was won through the passage by Congress of the Norris-LaGuardia Act. This measure at long last declared it to be public policy that labor should have full freedom of association, without interference by employers, outlawed yellow-dog contracts and prohibited federal courts from issuing injunctions in labor disputes except under carefully defined conditions.[34]

In 1933, when President Franklin D. Roosevelt assumed the presidency, a shift in attitude toward labor became evident.

For the first time in our history a national administration was to make the welfare of industrial workers a direct concern of government and act on the principle that only organized labor could deal on equal terms with organized capital.[35]

On July 5, 1935, the National Labor Relations Act (NLRA) was passed and signed by President Roosevelt legalizing labor unions, prohibiting employers from interfering with unions or refusing to bargain collectively, and upholding the rights of workers to negotiate for their rights on an equal basis with management.[36] The NLRA established a regulatory agency, the National Labor Relations Board (NLRB), which had sole authority to determine bargaining units and the power to supervise elections, hear complaints of unfair labor practices, issue "cease and desist" orders, and petition the court for enforcement of its orders.[37]

Pacifism

In 1815, David Low Dodge wrote an essay, "War Inconsistent with the Religion of Jesus Christ," and helped found the New York Peace Society.[38] By the early 1820s, there were over a dozen local peace societies.[39] Interest in pacifism waned in the 1850s and nearly collapsed during the Civil War, when many pacifists who also tended to be abolitionists found themselves in a moral conflict. Attempting to resolve the issue, the American Peace Society declared that the war was not a war at all but a rebellion.

During World War I a number of social workers became pacifists, among them Jane Addams. Many religious groups, particularly Quakers and Mennonites, held to their beliefs in nonviolence and were jailed. Out of these efforts, however, conscientious objection to war became recognized as a legitimate right.

The Civil Rights Movement

Not until May 1954 did the Supreme Court, in *Brown v. Board of Education of Topeka, Kansas*, find that segregation of schools in seventeen states was a violation of the Fourteenth Amendment. In September 1957, Little Rock, Arkansas, became the focus of attention when Governor Orval Faubus used the National Guard to prevent nine African-American children from attending school. President Eisenhower sent federal troops to ensure that the children had the right to attend.

A number of activist groups, including the Student Nonviolent Coordinating Committee (SNCC), the Congress of Racial Quality (CORE), and others, promoted nonviolent resistance to segregation and discrimination by means of sit-in demonstrations, picketing, and marches. These young people, both black and white, ministers, social workers, and social activists caught the imagination of the nation. Many were spit on, yelled at, threatened, beaten, jailed, and some even murdered in the cause of civil rights.

Finally, after ten years of protracted effort, the Civil Rights Act of 1964 was passed. This act prohibited racial, sexual, or ethnic discrimination in employment and in public accommodations. It established an enforcement mechanism, the Equal Employment Opportunity Commission to implement the law.[40] As a result of the persistent efforts of activists, Congress also passed a Voting Rights Act authorizing federal registrars to assist African Americans and others in those counties where a majority of persons were not registered to vote.

Protest Against the War in Vietnam

The civil rights movement created an atmosphere of ferment, which translated into the protest movement against the war in Vietnam in the mid-1960s and a general sense of disenchantment with government, large complex organizations, and the values of the "establishment." Student activists organized and led marches, sit-in demonstrations, and symbolic resistance against what they felt was an unjust, unnecessary, and immoral war. Not only were American soldiers dying for a cause that was unclear, but innocent civilians were being killed by napalm, an incendiary plastic-like substance that was nearly impossible to extinguish. In addition, large tracts of rain forest in Vietnam were being defoliated by the use of Agent Orange, later found to cause sterility and cancer in humans.

Protesting these activities, social activists were beaten, tear gassed, jailed, and in one incident at Kent State University, young people were killed when soldiers shot into a crowd of demonstrators. The protest movement against the war ultimately led to American withdrawal from Vietnam.

Social Protest Today

Boycotting lettuce and grapes, Cesar Chavez and other social activists forced growers to alter their use of pesticides, which were harmful to the health not only of farm workers but of consumers as well. The California Coastline Initiative forced government to establish a commission to protect the ecology of the coast. Environmental activists pushed and obtained establishment of the Environmental Protection Agency.

The struggle of the nonwhite population of South Africa, led by Nelson Mandela (and his social worker wife, Winnie), finally brought democracy and an end to the oppressive political regime fostering "apartheid." Continued demonstrations on behalf of the homeless, against the nuclear arms race, for protection of fragile wilderness areas, for decent housing and health care, for migrant farm laborers, and for government involvement in the AIDS epidemic show the viability of social protest today. Social activism has a long and successful history in America and continues to be a strong and viable means of social change.

The Process of Social Activism

The change process, according to Kurt Lewin, is a process of "unfreezing" those systems that are "frozen" in oppressive structures. The activist documents a problem, chooses as a target those who can effect a solution, and symbolizes the issue.[41] This may mean confronting the perpetrators of injustice for which the community seeks redress. Once the system is "unfrozen," the activist moves to action by means of a variety of strategies and tactics to make positive changes in the system. Finally, the activist and the community "refreeze" the change by implementing it. This may mean institutionalizing new laws, policies, and a system of enforcement. Rubin and Rubin, for example, describe how

> a neighborhood group concerned about the safety of school children documents the high accident rate at a particular corner. They target the city council as the group that can put in a stop sign. To symbolize the problem, they circulate a picture of an injured child.

The group appears at a city council meeting to argue for the stop sign. When the plan is approved, group members check that the stop sign has been installed.[42]

Unfreezing the System

Unfreezing the system means defining the problem, engaging the community, empowering the forces of change, and building an action organization.

Defining the Problem

Social work activists try to pinpoint and expose areas of oppression, intentionally focusing on one or more problem situations that are clearly visible. Sometimes the inequities they struggle with come out of their own life experiences. Cesar Chavez, social activist in the farm labor movement, was himself a farm laborer. Martin Luther King, Jr., was an African American who had experienced oppression personally.

In addition to being an issue in which the social worker is passionately and personally involved, however, the problem must be important to the welfare of the community, one that is current and one around which people can be mobilized to action. He or she begins where people are and raises issues of acute concern—lack of police protection, crime, gangs that hang out on street corners, drug abuse, poor maintenance of a housing project, or violence that creates an atmosphere of fear in the neighborhood. In so doing, the social activist "places himself clearly on the side of the people with whom he is working and states as plainly as possible his purpose in the neighborhood, but does not presume to define for them their problems or solutions to their problems."[43]

For example, even though you may feel that other issues are more important and more effective, if the people in a low-income housing project want to begin getting their housing project repaired or welfare checks increased, you help them act on these issues,[44] because you know that whatever action you take will be contested and can be used for action solutions.

AVOIDING ILLUSIONS ABOUT THE PROBLEM.   As you encourage people to engage problems which they personally experience, you must be free from il-

lusions about the world if you are to be successful. "We must work with it on its terms if we are to change it to the kind of world we would like it to be. We must first see the world as it is and not as we would like it to be."[45] This "real world," according to Alinsky, is an "arena of power politics moved primarily by perceived immediate self-interests, where morality is the rhetorical rationale for expedient action and self-interest."[46]

Engaging the Community

Having decided on an issue, the activist engages the community and its people, obtaining an understanding of the community that he or she is attempting to organize, and gaining a feeling for their issues and their plight. This must be done carefully.

> Everything [the activist] does after he arrives in a community will be influenced by the initial impression he makes and by how the community reacts to him. During the entry period, the organizer must make such basic decisions as who his first contacts in the community will be; which parts of the community he will try to communicate with and which, if any, he will try to avoid; where he will live and how he will dress; how he will talk and how he will explain to people in the community what he is trying to do.
>
> He may later change his mind about the way he wants to do some of these things, but for the most part, as far as people in the community are concerned, he will continue to be seen in terms of the initial impression he makes. An organizer has the chance to enter a particular community for the first time only once, and the mistakes he makes will stay with him as long as he is there.[47]

Empowering Forces of Change

Empowering people often means acting like a salesman who is trying to convince people to do something. "He pulls and jolts them into the public arena."[48] According to Haggstrom, the activist convinces people that he or she is "credible [and creates] a convincing picture of what might be, relying on the emotional contagion"[49] that he or she develops as well as on the factual account of what can be done. The social work activist

> listens, describing the meeting or action as it is relevant to the situation of those with whom he is talk-

ing. He appeals to self-interest, builds anger, works along friendship and relationship networks, as well as other formal and informal social structures.[50]

Activists provide people with experiences that appeal to their innate dignity.[51] Haggstrom, for example, tells of a group of residents who, with the help of organizers, went to a district sanitation inspector to appeal for better street cleaning. During the meeting the inspector claimed that there was no point in putting more equipment into such neighborhoods because the residents didn't care whether their streets were dirty or not.[52] When the community heard of the report, they became angry at this affront. Their anger mobilized them to fight the issue.

AVOIDING ILLUSIONS ABOUT THE PEOPLE.   While you accept the people for whom you work, you must not have illusions about their ability or their dysfunctions. People who are victimized are often unwilling participants in an unequal and hurtful system in which they are powerless, just as children are in a dysfunctional family. They may feel that they cannot change the system and react to their abuse by adopting any number of mechanisms that enable them to survive often brutal life circumstances.

Some may *act out* their pain by turning to a life of crime or gangs. Many times people who have been forced to live in abysmal conditions develop negative attitudes and behaviors. When this happens Saul Alinsky reminds us that

> the radical's affection for people is not lessened nor is he hardened against them even when masses of them demonstrate a capacity for brutality, selfishness, hate, greed, avarice, and disloyalty. He is convinced that these attitudes and actions are the result of evil conditions. It is not the people who must be judged but the circumstances that made them that way. The radical's desire to change society then becomes that much firmer.[53]

Others may *get out*—escaping the community and going to a better environment. A very few may *opt out*—rising above poverty and oppression and becoming successful professionals, actors, and businesspeople. There are even a few who *"flake out."* Flake-outs are like children who adopt a clown role in dysfunctional families. They become comedians.

Comedians are those who bring the pain out into the open by focusing it on themselves so people can laugh about it. They play a therapeutic role by helping people release the pain they feel.

For the overwhelming majority of people who live with cultural abuse, discrimination, victimization, and racism, however, these survival mechanisms are neither available nor appropriate. Many cannot get out, and acting out only adds to the problem. Neither can everyone opt out or even flake out. Instead, most victims of oppression *cop out*. Like children who have been abused, they bury their pain and learn to live with an oppressive situation until they become part of the cycle. They perpetuate, unwillingly and often unwittingly, the cycle of victimization because they have no other choice. Julio Morales calls this "self-oppression" or a "colonized mentality," a condition Puerto Ricans have experienced as a result of centuries of oppression and colonization.

> Many Puerto Ricans have internalized stereotypes [and] blame themselves for their fate, not understanding that their poverty is responsible for their alienation and feelings of helplessness or that their poverty is a function of a macro process over which they have little, if any, control.[54]

Conditioned to accept their situation, they believe that they are not as capable, as competent, or as good as others. Some may even believe that they deserve poor services and shoddy living arrangements, and that they should be grateful for anything they get. Some may express "dependency or unwarranted respect for authority and authority figures, making it difficult, at times, to organize" them and hold an "expectation" that leaders and "experts" will solve their problems.[55]

DENIAL.   As a means of survival, victims of oppression will often repress, minimize, ignore, or deny the circumstances that they have to endure. When you begin to encounter the oppressed, they may not want to admit the seriousness of their problems, recognize that their condition is as bad as it is, or that things can ever change. They may not be willing to look clearly at the pain they are experiencing.

Rather than give in to this cycle of hopelessness, the social activist must force the oppressed poor to remember and to face issues that they would rather avoid. Recognizing and accepting the reality of the situation is the first step in recovery. The problems of the community will not be solved until and unless community members recognize them, take a stand, and resist those who exploit them.

REAL-WORLD PROBLEMS.   In addition to overcoming denial, organizers understand that poor people, just like anyone else, are consumed with their own private affairs, personal survival, raising families, making it on the job, and getting along until the next paycheck. Moreover, people in poor, oppressed communities do not have the wealth of resources, support systems, education, and influence that more affluent members of society have, particularly the powerful whom they will be confronting. Even if they recognize the reality of their situation, they are made even more helpless by the poverty and stress with which they live. Julio Morales calls this the "full plate" syndrome, in which problems are compounded so that the poor and oppressed have little time or energy to confront their problems.[56] He says of Puerto Ricans, for example,

> racism, violence, AIDS, drugs, crime, homelessness, alienation from the judicial system, massive underemployment or unemployment, high levels of school dropouts, rivalry among adult leadership, etc., are common ingredients on that crowded plate. Insufficient services to families, inappropriate foster care for Puerto Rican children, lack of school curriculum on the Puerto Rican experience, lack of curriculum aimed at building the self-esteem of Puerto Rican youngsters, and the competing and clashing of cultural values within the larger society add to the full plate. The needs leading to the migration [of many families] to and from Puerto Rico, the different perspectives and levels of acclimating to U.S. society that [people] experience, and intra-community issues such as competition for resources . . . at times fragmentize community efforts.[57]

In spite of all of this, the oppressed have their innate dignity and moral justice on their side. You, as the organizer, bring resources and strength that can help mobilize people even in their weakened condition. You can bring people together, fire up their energies, and mobilize the "rightness" of their cause.

Building an Organization

When enough people in the community are concerned about the problem, the organizer schedules a series of preliminary meetings with them to build an organizational structure for social action. He or she makes sure that people remember the meeting day and time.[58] The organizer may have to arrange transportation and continue to encourage people to come. Once at the meeting, the "organizer concentrates on moving those attending into decision and action."[59] In principle, the "basic orientation has always to be the expression of power through the greatest possible number of members acting together to resolve the central problems of their lives."[60]

Once the structure becomes clear and a decision is made to organize, the social work activist can help community members elect officers and develop preliminary committees, role assignments, strategy, and time lines.

THE ROLE OF THE SOCIAL ACTIVIST.   The activist never imposes him- or herself on the community or tries to manipulate the community. The organizer must always present him- or herself clearly and on a basis "that he [or she] will help build an organization which belongs and will belong to the members."[61] The worker does not build an organization to achieve his or her goals; rather, the organization exists for the people.

The activist's leadership style must fit the situation, changing according to the particular readiness levels of the members (described in chapter 4). In principle, the activist rarely intervenes in the organization directly unless it is absolutely necessary.[62] If there is too much intervention, community members will not see the victories as their victories, and will not acquire knowledge and skills or develop an effective organization.[63] "People provide the content of action. The organizer has the responsibility to create and maintain the effective democratic structure of action."[64] The social work activist continually "allies himself [or herself] with the long-term objective self-interest of the people, building an organization through which they can act effectively."[65] This is done by balancing the depth and amount of interventions so as to continually enable community members to learn skills and to assume more and more responsibility.

Moving to Action

In any social action movement, there will be resistance to change. The entire process of social action may be seen as an attempt to change the direction of a social system to one that is more just and equitable. Any change of direction meets resistance. A number of factors combine to create resistance to change. Among these are inertia and homeostasis, fear of the unknown, disruption of routine, threats to security, and threats to power.[66]

1. *Inertia and homeostasis.* In any system there is a strong tendency to keep moving along in the direction it has been going. This is called inertia. It is very difficult to derail a system once it is moving along a prescribed path. Another tendency that keeps the system from changing is homeostasis. Systems have built-in mechanisms for self-correction that keep them stable; they resist external forces that would disturb their equilibrium.

2. *Fear of the unknown.* On a more personal level, change creates anxiety. It is often easier to keep something old and familiar, even if it is dysfunctional, than trade it in for something that is new and unknown.

3. *Disruption of routine.* People are creatures of habit and routine. Change in the social system tends to upset this routine, disturbing life-styles and often requiring people to change behaviors, thinking, attitudes, and perceptions that have served them over the years. It is difficult for people to adjust to new ways of being and to give up life-styles they have created for themselves and which serve some useful functions even if they are dysfunctional.

4. *Threats to security.* A person's livelihood or job depends on and is a result of fitting into a system, learning and becoming socialized to that organizational setting, putting down roots, and investing time and energy in that effort. Social change may disrupt or threaten one's job, one's family life, one's social situation, and one's place in a community. Environmental legislation, for example, often faces severe opposition simply because it might mean losing a source of income and having to learn new job skills.

5. *Threats to power.* Those people in power want to keep things the way they are, often because they have developed a system that benefits them at the expense of others. They have a vested interest in maintaining the systems over which they have control. Control means that they have freedom to influence policy, pursue their own interests, and develop social tools such as organizations to create wealth and more power for themselves. Social action develops new power bases that disrupt and threaten to usurp this power. Perhaps more than anything else it is the struggle for social, political, and economic power that motivates people in influential positions to resist social change.

Reducing Resistance to Change

There are three different ways to reduce resistance to change. One way is to lessen the resistance so that the forces for change can prevail. Providing information and using nonviolent resistance methods are ways to weaken resistance to change. A second way is to overpower the resistance by direct action, such as public disruptions including "rallies, marches, sit-ins, and vigils as well as slowdowns of services, traffic blockages, and demonstrations."[67] It is possible to move in both of these directions at once. Informational campaigns, for example, "simultaneously mobilize people and pressure the opposition."[68] In community education programs, often used in the environmental movement,

> people learn about environmental problems and then hold community forums that inform concerned neighbors. . . . A frequent side effect is that when confronted by knowledgeable opponents, the opposition shows itself to be ignorant of technical details, which makes them look foolish and denies them legitimacy.[69]

In addition, public disruptions can sometimes

> create news, imply the potential for violence, and tempt the opponents to retaliate in ways that may recreate a climate more sympathetic to protesters. The fear of future social disorders might put some important questions on the public agendas.[70]

Life Cycle of Resistance to Change

While there are many forces that work to resist change, an abiding reality of our modern society is that change is inevitable. Forces for social change often have momentum on their side, particularly those who are aiming toward social betterment and resolving social problems, and who have moral necessity as a guide. Forces against change, on the other hand, particularly those forces that are invested in maintaining the status quo for their own benefit, can engage in postponing and obfuscating change. However, if you understand the life cycle of this resistance, the process of change becomes easier; you can work at it in small increments, measure your progress, and predict eventual victory.

Most change efforts will move through all the phases of the cycle of resistance, but because each change effort is unique, some phases may be shortened or omitted, or there may be regression to previous phases. Inevitably the process is a slow one.

Two factors influence the cycle of resistance: the magnitude of the social problem and the time frame.

1. *Magnitude of the problem.* The greater the extent and pervasiveness of the social problem, the more resistance and the greater the forces that will oppose any change effort. The greater the degree of change that needs to be made, the more difficult it will be to make successful changes.
2. *Time frame.* The longer the history of the problem, the more likely that change will need to proceed slowly and take a longer time period before victory is reached. Often the longer the time frame of the change process, the more successful it will be. Sometimes, however, rapid changes are indicated. The massive social changes that were instituted during the Great Depression and the urgency to end the war in Vietnam are examples of the necessity for speedy change.

PHASE ONE.   At the beginning of the change effort, while people may be in pain and suffering as a result of social problems, the existing state of affairs—the status quo—is solidly entrenched. The status quo benefits those in power, has evolved over time, and has become part of the system's culture and way of operating. Keeping the system going is accepted as the way things are or even should be. In addition, because of many defenses that operate, oppressed people escape into a world of illusions that blind them to accepting the reality of social problems. They are often socialized to condone or may have been intimidated in perpetuating the very systems that oppress them. Only a few may see the status quo as being problem.

In the beginning of the change effort, therefore, social work activists often take a prophetic stance. Like a "voice in the wilderness," they are in the minority. They can expect to be openly criticized, ridiculed, scapegoated, and attacked by whatever means the entrenched interests have at their disposal. Personal attacks on activists and on the members of activist organizations in the form of harassment, intimidation, threats to their security, and even physical attacks may be used to force them to conform to the norm and not disturb the system's equilibrium. Resistance to the change effort appears to be massive. Unless macro social workers and activists understand, prepare for, and are willing to encounter this phase of resistance, the change effort may be overwhelmed.

Harvey and Brown[71] describe, for example, how the environmental movement began with a small group of concerned conservationists, scientists, and young people in the 1960s. Rachel Carson's book, *Silent Spring*, raised the nation's consciousness about the dangers of pesticides, and the first Earth Day was held in 1970. However, because of political forces that emerged during the late 1970s and throughout the 1980s, commitment to environmental concerns waned. Environmentalists were portrayed as alarmists and radicals who were concerned about saving insignificant species at the expense of jobs and progress.

Because resistance is massive at the beginning of a change effort, Rubin and Rubin suggest that, before commencing, every change organization should consider the following issues.[72]

1. How can you obtain the power you need either to overcome opponents or to reduce the forces that resist change?
2. How can your organization achieve legitimacy?
3. What kinds of symbols can you design that will allow the organization to get its issues high on the agendas of those who can influence change?

4. What strategies can the organization develop to increase chances of victory?

5. What can the organization do to maintain people's morale until victories occur?[73]

PHASE TWO.   As the movement for change grows, it encounters the second stage of resistance. Forces for and against change become more clearly defined. Facts are gathered and information increases. As people become more aware of the issues and the consequences, what was at first an insignificant issue begins to be seen as a legitimate social problem that concerns everyone. As people are sensitized to the problem, the initial threat that exposure posed begins to lessen, and forces for change gain understanding and recognition.

During the 1980s, for example, growing bodies of evidence on a number of fronts supported the position of the environmentalists, who persisted through court actions and pressure on elected officials. Research confirmed that pollution was destroying the ozone layer in the atmosphere and that the "greenhouse" effect was a reality. Data on the harmful effects of pesticides not only on wildlife but also on humans was documented.

Information showed that shrinking habitats and decimation of wilderness areas resulted in the extinction of numbers of species of plants and animals. Massive oil spills brought home to people the dangers of technology. The inability of communities to process raw sewage and solid and nuclear waste became national concerns. The extent of danger to the environment could no longer be ignored. In fact, it was becoming an international problem.

PHASE THREE.   At this stage, social workers take a confrontational stance of social action. Lines have been drawn, and there is direct confrontation between forces battling for change and those that are struggling to maintain the status quo. Those fighting against change marshall all of their forces, realizing that they need to take the activists seriously. An all-out attempt is made to destroy the change effort once and for all.

Social activists at this stage refine their strategies, sometimes using direct confrontation tactics such as sit-ins, marches, distributing leaflets, demonstrations and rallies, media exposure, attacking specific perpetrators, and gaining publicity.

In the early 1980s, for example, the environmental movement became increasingly well organized, vocal, and active on a number of fronts. Numerous environmental groups began agitating for change locally as well as nationally. Specific companies that engaged in pollution were targeted. James Watt, secretary of the Interior, one of the most vocal and visible opponents of environmental concerns, became a "lightning rod" for pro-environmental forces such as the Sierra Club and the Wilderness Society.

PHASE FOUR.   If those who support change are successful in their efforts at persuasion and have won decisive battles, people who continue to resist are now seen as stubborn, ignorant, and obstructionist. However, resistance forces can still mobilize enough power to shift the balance. This is a time for activists to shift gears and, using tact, patience, and wisdom, keep their balance and persuade those who, though not openly opposed to change, may not yet be completely convinced about the need for change. Change strategies move from direct confrontation to legal action, negotiation, and policy development. The activist shifts from a confrontive to a visionary stance.

In the environmental movement, for example, the battle shifted to the development of policy, culminating in the Endangered Species Act, the Clean Air Act, the creation of the Environmental Protection Agency, and the development of the Environmental Super Fund. Each piece of legislation meant compromise and bargaining with landowners, farmers, miners, and developers who continued to press for concessions favoring their interests. With each successive victory, however, the environmental movement gained strength and power.

PHASE FIVE.   In the final phase, those who resist change are as few and as alienated as were the social activists in Phase One. For example, even those who were opposed to environmental change jumped on the bandwagon and tried to show how they too were part of forces for change. Today, for example, businesses that had at first been major opponents of the environmental movement take out advertisements showing how they too contribute to cleaning the environment. Being environmentally sensitive is now "politically correct."

However, it is important to understand that battles for social change are never finished once and for all but must be fought over and over. After a period, forces against change may still be mobilized to undermine changes that have been so hard won. For example, the congressional elections of 1994 saw the Republican Party win a majority of House and Senate seats. Conservative forces lost no time in establishing strategies to dismantle as much environmental, social welfare, and other progressive social legislation as possible.

Action Strategies and Tactics

Strategies are broad plans to achieve goals. Tactics are short-term actions designed to carry out a strategy. Each campaign for social justice may require a variation in tactics commensurate with the unique situations that are being confronted.

> A campaign may begin with a confrontation to attract media attention, then proceed to political pressure tactics to make long-term changes. Or, it may begin with mild pressure tactics, and if success is not forthcoming, gradually apply more power, using first legal and finally confrontation tactics. Or, the campaign may run several tactics simultaneously. Community organizations need to know how to combine tactics in an overall strategy to achieve a desired effect.[74]

Saul Alinksy recommends that you "keep the pressure on, with different tactics and actions, and utilize all events of the period for your purpose."[75] Some of the strategies by which social action organizations mobilize change are:

1. *Active non-cooperation with oppression*; resistance to and refusal to participate in the cycle of victimization
2. *Active exposure of perpetrators* and acts of oppression to public scrutiny
3. *Using information to actively challenge misinformation* and distortions of truth where they occur
4. *Public relations* including media coverage to gain public recognition
5. *Legal action* including legislation and lobbying
6. *Satyagraha* or nonviolent resistance, soul force, or truth force

7. *Direct confrontation* and challenging perpetrators of oppression

ACTIVE NON-COOPERATION. One of the key strategies in breaking cycles of victimization is to refuse to participate in self-defeating victimization, not cooperating with required behaviors, and refusing to accept laws, policies, and procedures that are demeaning. For African Americans in the South, this meant sitting in white-only sections of public transportation, using white-only restrooms in defiance of existing practices, and "sitting in" at restaurants, quietly demanding service.

Non-cooperation may also include not acting the role of a victim. A victim may act in stereotyped ways, which reinforce the perception of oppressors that the victim is inferior. Retraining oppressed individuals to develop new skills, habits, dress, appearance, and language helps overcome the stereotype. For example, during the civil rights movement, African Americans mounted campaigns emphasizing Black Pride and education in African American Studies. Many African Americans adopted African names and African dress, hairstyles, and jewelry.

Education, however, means acquiring not only cognitive skills and changes in outward appearance but also the inner social presence and self-presentation skills that stimulate others to treat the oppressed people with respect and dignity. To the extent that oppressed and stigmatized persons no longer act the role of victim, oppressors will have difficulty in relating to them as victims.

EXPOSURE OF PERPETRATORS. Social activists publicly uncover the plight of the disadvantaged and show who is responsible for their plight. Active exposure of perpetrators of oppression is accomplished by giving speeches, making personal appearances, and writing articles, pamphlets, books, newsletters, and flyers. At the turn of the century, for example, a group of journalists and novelists, called "muckrakers," aided social activists in their cause. Carey McWilliams wrote of discrimination with such books as *Brothers Under the Skin*, and John Steinbeck, in *The Grapes of Wrath*, publicized the story of migrant workers in California. Newspaper and TV investigative reporters can be of great help to social activists in exposing injustices. Exposure may mean finding a particular vulnerable spot and exploiting it.

For example, a successful boycott on table grapes by the United Farm Workers union exposed sensitivities of the nation to the plight of farm laborers in California.

INFORMATION CAMPAIGNS. Information campaigns dig up facts and data that oppressors would rather hide or obfuscate in their attempts to keep power and domination. For example, for decades the tobacco industry consistently denied, distorted, and suppressed research that indicated that smoking caused cancer. Once evidence was shown to be irrefutable, they resisted facts that second-hand smoke was also cancer-causing. The exposure of this "disinformation" and evidence of the dangers of tobacco smoke led to laws banning smoking in public places and requiring warning labels on cigarette packages.

Because one of the tools of oppression is misinformation and distortion of the truth, activists "anticipate the attempts of established interests to shape the perceived needs of citizens . . . and work against such needs-shaping rhetoric."[76] Forester, for example, describes a number of ways that activists counter those who shape information to keep people in subservient positions.

1. Counter misrepresentations, distortions, stereotyping of the poor and oppressed by gathering facts and presenting them in newspapers, magazines, and on television.
2. Demand that reports and information about victims of oppression be intelligible to the public and actively explored at public hearings, not simply noted and passed over.
3. Challenge misrepresentations of costs, risks, and available alternatives to social problems by those in power.
4. Temper exaggerated claims.
5. Demystify organizations, bureaucratic, or corporate processes.
6. Encourage and inform the mobilization and action of affected citizens.[77]

PUBLIC RELATIONS. Public relations tactics include all the ways of making headlines in newspapers and TV and obtaining other kinds of publicity. As the activist organization strategizes and maneuvers, it gains media attention, and political leaders become allies in the fight for justice. When the organization becomes better known and wins some victories, it develops a following. The public becomes more and more interested in the outcome, and people begin to take sides.

One of the most powerful tactics of the civil rights demonstrators, for example, was the television exposure of the brutality, anger, and hate aimed at nonviolent resisters as they sought the equal rights and access guaranteed in the Constitution. The media captured national attention by showing that civil rights was a compelling moral cause that could not be denied.

LEGAL ACTION. Legal tactics are ways of forcing a solution by using the court system and existing laws. "Legal action uses the courts to force those in positions of power to live up to their own rules and agreements."[78] By using the legal process, community organizations can ask judges to clarify the responsibility of governmental agencies in cases where vaguely written legislation makes implementation difficult or force governmental officials to faithfully and responsibly carry out laws in situations where they have been pressured by particular interest groups to dilute or not comply with existing laws. For example, courts can order slum landlords to stop evicting people from their homes, order school districts to provide equal educational opportunities, and mandate compensation for damages caused by toxic waste.[79]

Getting an injunction can assist a community in attempts to stop certain practices that are harmful. Injunctions are court orders to stop possibly harmful action until additional facts are gathered.[80] The instant papers are served, the recipient must cease action or risk being in contempt of court. Such tactics place the full weight of the government behind the community, giving the community organization time to rally its forces, gather information, and plan its next tactic.

Another legal tactic is discovery, "the legal procedure that allows lawyers to examine documents germane to the case even if the documents are in the possession of the opponent."[81] Through discovery, for example, community organizations found internal reports of the Department of Interior that showed that public water was being sold far below market cost to large-scale commercial farmers.[82] Discovery gives the activist organization an opportunity to obtain information about their opponents.

A lawsuit is another major legal action communities can take against perpetrators of oppression. A lawsuit can be filed to "right a wrong, claim compensation for harm done, or make a party perform as agreed."[83] A performance suit is a lawsuit that forces a person to live up to a contract. Sometimes administrators deny people rights or benefits to which they are legally entitled. During the Regan administration, for example, many people were wrongly denied Social Security benefits because policies were interpreted too narrowly. Many of these people sued to obtain aid.[84]

Sometimes community groups or regulatory agencies whose legal role is to protect the public file a class action suit. Class action suits are helpful when the overall societal damage is large but the damage suffered by any one person is relatively small, making individual suits prohibitively expensive. Consumer activists have filed class action suits on behalf of citizens who have been overcharged by utility companies and insurance companies, or who have purchased defective products.

Sometimes regulatory agencies—often those whose membership is stacked with vested interest groups from the very concerns they regulate—do not follow their own procedures. In cases in which the "fox is guarding the hen house," community groups can file a procedural suit. Community action groups can greatly improve their bargaining power if they can show that governmental agencies do not follow their rules or adjudicate claims fairly. Community groups and health organizations, for example, have sued the Food and Drug Administration for ignoring scientific evidence and forced them to regulate food additives.[85]

Sometimes city councils illegally hold closed hearings, planning commissions give preferential treatment to developers, and general services agencies do not use sealed bids but give favored treatment to certain contractors. These agencies may begin to follow correct procedures if challenged with a lawsuit.

Legal tactics give communities power because they can be so expensive that the very threat of a lawsuit can lead oppressors to the bargaining table. Builders, for example, can make a profit only when houses are sold and loans are paid off. If a community group gets an injunction against a builder, construction is delayed, costing the builder money on the loans he has incurred. To avoid these expenses, as well as those of a potential court battle that could drag on for months or years, a developer might be willing to negotiate and give the community its demands for a playground, housing for the poor, or other concessions.

Legal action has some disadvantages. Lawsuits may stimulate opponents to file countersuits against the organization or the court system. Suits filed in one state are not valid in other states. And even if the court gives a community organization a victory, it may be only temporary. Laws may be repealed, or past legal actions revoked. Finally, court processes are slow and expensive.

SATYAGRAHA.   Mahatma Ghandi remains one of the foremost change agents of our time. A diminutive man, he challenged the entire British Empire and nearly singlehandedly mobilized colonial India into a massive effort to gain independence. In doing so, he pioneered one of the most compelling principles of social action. This is the principle of Satyagraha, which has been described as "soul force" or "truth force."

Ferguson says that Satyagraha has been misunderstood in the West as "passive resistance" or "nonviolent resistance." Ghandi disavowed these terms, because they suggest weakness, nonaction, or simple passivity in the face of violence and oppression. Educator Timothy Flinders said, "To call Satyagraha passive resistance is like calling light non-darkness: it does not describe the positive energy of the principle."[86]

Satyagraha is a combination of two opposite forces: fierce autonomy and total compassion. It asserts:

> I will not coerce you. But, neither will I be coerced by you. While I will not allow you to behave unjustly toward me, I will not oppose you by violence (physical force), but by the force of the truth and the right—by the integrity of my beliefs and by my commitment to what is just and good.
>
> My integrity shines forth, because I will not compromise my commitment by acting unjustly or falsely or try to overturn violence with violence, humiliation, injury, or subjugation. Instead, I will show my integrity by my willingness to suffer, to pour myself out for my community, to place myself in danger, go to prison, and die if necessary. But I will not

condone, cooperate, or allow by inaction injustice, oppression, or violence to continue.

Ultimately you will feel the moral force of my restraint, see my intention, and sense my compassion and openness. Because I treat myself with intense respect and dignity, you must also treat me with respect and dignity. By my unrelenting commitment to justice, you too must also begin to respect justice.

Satyagraha opens the heart of the adversary and stirs the conscience of the indifferent. Satyagraha requires heroic restraint and the courage to forgive. It removes social action from the arena of confrontation or threat, bargaining or negotiation, deal making, game playing, or pleading. Martin Luther King, Jr. used oppression of African Americans as a moral force with which to confront oppressors. He resisted being oppressed, even submitting to imprisonment. He demonstrated that while oppressors could imprison his body, they could not imprison his "self" or break his spirit. He challenged injustice with demands of justice, he demonstrated justice in every action, and he did not let himself be treated unjustly. He demonstrated to oppressors that injustice was not acceptable, and challenged America to live up to the values it espoused, to become a just nation in its actions as well as its words.

Conflict and Confrontation

Whenever one stimulates neighborhood action, one will inevitably generate conflict.

> When an organizer helps people begin to act on central problems, that is, to make their own decisions about resolving their own problems and to begin to implement their own decisions, by that very fact, the organizer deliberately creates conflict since the problems of low income areas cannot be resolved without negative consequences for . . . [those who are] advantaged.[87]

Conflict and confrontation are integral parts of the social action process. "In a conflict situation, the objective consequences of an act by one side or another or the intentions behind the act may almost be irrelevant. The act is one point around which conflict swirls."[88]

Conflict inevitably means confrontation. Confrontation is often scary and threatening to the par-

ticipants. It is not part of the cultural or psychic milieu of most people. In addition, there are real life consequences for people who engage in direct action confrontation.

When an organization takes to the streets to conduct demonstrations, rallies, marches, strikes, sit-ins, boycotts, leafletting, or picketing the companies, businesses, or offices of those targeted for change, the activist needs to be aware of negative and potentially dangerous outcomes. People can be threatened with intimidation, insults, harassment, physical attacks, jail, or even death. During the civil rights movement of the 1960s, police officials raided homes of African-American militants and killed them, supposedly in self-defense.[89] The entire city of Berkeley, California, was put under martial law and tear gas was used by police during violence surrounding People's Park demonstrations.

Union organizers have been fired from their jobs, threatened, beaten, and murdered.

> Goon squads were used against labor organizers, tactical police against peace protesters, Southern police assisted local hooligans in beating up civil rights workers. Repression against African-American and Native-American militants involved the use of "eavesdropping, bogus mail, black propaganda operations, disinformation, harassment arrests, infiltration, . . . creating suspicion—through spreading of rumors, manufacturing of evidence—that bonafide organization members . . . are FBI/police informers—fabrication of evidence and even assassination."[90]

Don't be so naive as to believe that oppressors will play fairly to keep the distribution of power in their favor. You can expect that the forces of oppression will "make a mockery of the democratic . . . process by misrepresenting cases, improperly invoking authority, making false promises, or distracting attention from key issues."[91] Perpetrators will

very selectively inform and misinform citizens. They may call attention to particular apparent needs and obscure others, whatever the resources available to meet those needs. Appealing to the public trust in their reputation and their record of community service . . . they may stress pressing community problems and their devotion and commitment to addressing them.

They may appear to welcome legitimate, open discussion and public education while simultaneously ignoring the inability of significantly affected populations to join in those discussions. They may omit a careful analysis of public-serving alternatives to the proposed expansion and thus misrepresent the actual planning options.[92]

Sometimes officials of a government agency or corporate managers will even give in during a demonstration but then renege on agreements after everyone has gone home.[93]

"Direct action campaigns must not be undertaken lightly; they require people's time and moral commitment to the issues, and sometimes they involve risk. Only try direct action after a conventional approach has failed, and then do so cautiously by engaging in testing actions that 'continuously explore the protective armor of the power structure.'"[94]

There are five ways that the threatening aspects of confrontation may be diminished. First, carefully consider the issues involved and plan the confrontation carefully, taking into consideration the abilities of the participants, their commitment to the issues, and the effectiveness of the tactic you are using in achieving the ends you are trying to reach. Second, prepare and train participants well. Third, personalize the confrontation. Fourth, anticipate retaliation and strategize for it in advance. Fifth, maintain distance from the threatening aspects of confrontation by conceiving of the action as a "morality drama." Develop a mindset that allows the players to depersonalize confrontations.

PLANNING THE CONFRONTATION.   In planning picketing, organizers must consider many details. Some cities have laws about the materials with which pickets signs can be made to prevent them from being used as weapons. Picketers should be located where they get attention, but if they obstruct traffic or violate private property, they may anger the public and risk arrest. Organizers need to work out a plan to get picketers out of jail.[95] Likewise, an enormous amount of planning is required for a successful march. For example:

> When Dr. Martin Luther King, Jr. led marches in Chicago during the summer of 1966, months of negotiation were required to determine which groups would participate and to ensure that King's overall philosophy of nonviolence would be observed. The choice of which streets to march down were argued

over for weeks because some streets showed the deterioration of housing but other streets better illustrated the effects of discrimination.[96]

TRAINING.   Confrontation tactics must be "planned with an awareness of how far members of the action organization are willing to go in a campaign."[97] They must be rehearsed and participants trained in their use, especially for nonviolent tactics.

> Few people can be beaten and arrested without wanting to defend themselves. People who by temperament are not nonviolent must be kept out of the action. During the Montgomery bus boycotts, there were training schools in nonviolence, and only people trained and experienced in nonviolence were allowed to become Freedom Riders.[98]

Such training has to be done with care because "you don't push a person beyond their [sic] commitment."[99] Saul Alinsky, one of the foremost organizers of his day advised, "Never go outside the experience of your people."[100] Training is also crucial to the "success of picketing and marching. . . . For picketing, volunteers must be willing to carry signs and walk endless miles around a plant or an office. Of equal importance, picketers must be trained not to respond to taunts or unpleasant distractions. Giving in to taunts, the picketers look disorderly and thereby lose legitimacy."[101]

PERSONALIZING THE CONFRONTATION.   Social activists challenge perpetrators of oppression by making demands, giving ultimatums, and delivering messages to them personally even though they may be shielded by layers of bureaucracy and networks of interlocking relationships with others in power, by the right of protection from self-incrimination, and by skillful use of evasion. Make every effort to expose perpetrators to the victims of their oppression, and let those victims see their oppressors. This puts often impersonal, distant, and sanitized oppression where it belongs—at the personal level. Victims gain power as they see their oppressors as real people, not shadowy processes, procedures, rules, or policies. They learn that behind the seemingly impenetrable maze of rules and norms are individuals. This places the victims, often for the first time, on an equal footing with those who have taken advantage of them.

Specific individuals rather than institutions should be the target of the campaign. Who can attack the telephone company or the government? It is far easier to attack the callousness of the president of the company, Mr. Smith, who won't let shut-in elderly people have affordable phones, while he has a telephone in his limousine.[102]

Alinsky puts the point this way: "Pick the target, freeze it, personalize it and polarize it."[103]

ANTICIPATING RETALIATION.   When using direct confrontation, be prepared for retaliation.

When organizations go after important targets and big issues, the enemy almost always strikes back. In its mildest form, the response of targets may only be an attempt to deny the legitimacy of protests. . . . Sometimes, however, those counterstrikes are brutal and may decimate the membership.[104]

Sometimes the opposition "will turn one group against another, exploiting tensions between groups."[105] They may use slander and personal defamation. "Opponents may accuse the group's leader of being a communist, homosexual or lesbian, an embezzler, or a philanderer."[106] They may charge that the protest is un-American or they will mount their own campaigns against social change. Phyllis Schlafly, for example, established a national movement called STOP ERA (the Equal Rights Amendment to the Constitution), and Jerry Falwell of the religious right established the Moral Majority to counteract abortion rights and gay rights activists.[107]

Always expect and try to anticipate counterattacks. Rubin and Rubin alert organizations to expect that "opponents will try to seize the organization's books, records, and mailing lists. They will search for financial irregularities . . . and try to taint the organization with scandal."[108] Make sure that your organization's books are squeaky clean, be aware of skeletons in the closet of organizational leaders, keep books and mailing lists in secure places, and be sure that what is put in writing will not give the appearance of slander.[109] The community organization must be very cautious to avoid the appearance of impropriety because it is trying to be on high moral ground.

Plan what to do in the face of massive assault such as imprisonment of leaders, attempts to demor-alize the membership, and threats or bribes. The more aware and prepared your organization is, the better it will resist counterattacks. Try not to play in a game you don't think you can win, and never take on more than your organization can handle.

There are some tactical advantages to being retaliated against. "Overt repression," for example, "denies the enemy legitimacy and often grants it to protesters. . . . Evoking a response (even a high negative response as with the use of excessive force) from the opposition is a sure indication that a direct action organization has reached and scared its target."[110]

CONFRONTATION AS DRAMA.   You can reduce the threatening aspects of confrontation by carefully orchestrating the action so that it becomes a game or an exciting morality play. In this sense you control the use of confrontation, choosing its timing, its content, and its strength to help stimulate and excite your members, not intimidate them. Do not simply move ahead, letting events control you or the community. Alinsky says, "A tactic that drags on too long becomes a drag."[111]

President Kennedy looked at the political struggles in which he was engaged as a game like football in which he, as quarterback, directed the action. The game metaphor is useful because you can "objectify" the situation, seeing it as an enjoyable experience in which conflict is managed, goals are achieved, and those who have been "losers" have a chance to become "winners."

Likewise, when you conceptualize the confrontation as a drama, you stage the action, each participant plays a particular role, and you act it out as a play. As you do this, both you and the people of the community organization distance yourselves from the action and at the same time gain some control over it.

In such a performance, you stage the drama as a struggle between the underdogs, who are forces of good, and the villains, the powerful forces of evil. You rehearse the roles of your actors, orchestrate their performances, and review their scripts, and the process evolves toward a inevitable climax.

The organizer sees him- or herself as the director of the play, who conducts the conflict which draws to itself the fascinated attention of a large portion of the entire community. The public conflict creates an audience and actors who play to the audience. The actors invent their own lives in a performance not to be repeated.[112]

The wider society is the audience that watches the drama unfold. The spotlight of public attention shines on the villains (the oppressors) and mobilizes the sympathy of the audience. After each act in the drama, you review the performance, help the actors improve their roles, improvising as you go. The oppressed actors begin to anticipate the scenes they will play and outmaneuver the villains. Because you and the actors write the lines and direct the action, the oppressors usually can only react.

In speaking their lines convincingly and communicating their message through actions as well as words, the community of actors begin to demonstrate their ability. Ultimately winning the applause and approval of the audience, the troupe of the oppressed not only learn how to conduct themselves but also often achieve a moral victory that may bring tangible benefits. Confrontation as drama can help give members a sense of empowerment and excitement.

KINDS OF DIRECT CONFRONTATION.   The kinds of direct confrontations are rallies, moral demonstrations, picketing, marches, sit-ins, boycotts, and symbolic demonstrations.

1. *Rallies*. Rallies mobilize numbers of people for a cause, provide supporters and potential supporters with information and a sense of unity, provide an arena for attracting media attention, and make a statement about the issues that are being raised.[113] One of the most impressive rallies in the history of protest was the 1963 March on Washington for civil rights in which the Reverend Martin Luther King, Jr. gave his now legendary speech "I Have a Dream." The rally, seen on national television, had between 200,000 and 500,000 participants.[114]

2. *Moral demonstrations*. Moral demonstrations include voluntary jailing, fasts, and prayer vigils. In these kinds of demonstrations individuals may often become the focus of attention. For example, Mahatma Ghandi placed himself at the center of attention by going on hunger

strikes in his efforts to free the nation of India from British rule. Cesar Chavez's fast during the grape boycott in California gained national attention. This demonstration solidified the strikers, demonstrated the need to continue the grape boycott, and brought Senator Robert Kennedy on the side of the farm workers.[115]

Demonstrators can turn what may seem like ignominious defeat into a victory. Dr. Martin Luther King, Jr., refused bail when jailed, and while incarcerated, he wrote his eloquent moral statement *Letters from a Birmingham Jail*.

Prayer vigils, in which demonstrators silently light candles, demonstrate both moral and spiritual nonviolence. "Unlike the more militant anti-abortion protesters, those supporting 'peaceful prayer walks' do not argue with opponents or interfere with the use of the clinic. They are trying to symbolize their suffering in silence for the unborn."[116]

3. *Picketing and marches*. Picketing "focuses attention on the target of the opposition and is intended to achieve immediate political solutions."[117] "Protesters have picketed nuclear reactors to protest the dangers of nuclear energy, the Love Canal Homeowners Association picketed the governor of New York and President Carter, and demonstrators against the war in Vietnam picketed Vice President Humphrey."[118] Marches demonstrate the power of the organization, provide media attention, and bring organization members together in a show of solidarity.

4. *Sit-ins*. Sit-in demonstrations inconvenience the opponent, obtain media attention, and avoid violence[119] by taking over offices, highways, lunch counters, stairways, lobbies, or other public places. A sit-in puts the protesters on the opponent's turf, and often leads to arrests because those involved are trespassing.[120] Sometimes a sit-in is staged for immediate gains, as when welfare rights activists demand services to which they are legally entitled. Other sit-ins aim at broader issues such as the Native American "capture" of Alcatraz, which publicized the abnegation of Indian treaty rights.[121]

5. *Boycotts*. A boycott is an economic pressure campaign designed to force an immediate solu-

Prayer vigils, in which demonstrators silently light candles, display moral and spiritual nonviolence.

tion to a problem by refusing to purchase a particular product. For example, Cesar Chavez initiated a national boycott of table grapes to force commercial farmers to yield to union demands.[122] Environmentalists organized a boycott of tuna fish caught with nets that endanger dolphins.

Another kind of boycott is the renters' strike, in which people in an apartment building refuse to pay rent until their landlord takes responsibility for repairs or provide services such as adequate heat. Sometimes, however, such boycotts are illegal. For example, in some states it is illegal to withhold rent no matter what the landlord does. In other states, "tenants who claim inadequate services can place funds in an escrow account while engaged in a battle with the landlord."[123] Another tactic is a rent slowdown. Tenants wait until the middle of the month to pay their rent, and the tenant leader gives the landlord all the rent at the same time, demonstrating the power and solidarity of the tenants. Landlords often respond to tenants at this point.[124]

6. *Symbolic demonstrations.* Symbols are powerful ways of demonstrating the goals of protest.

For example, students protesting apartheid in South Africa constructed shantytowns on the lawns of universities as a "visible representation of the horrible living standards facing black South Africans."[125] When Greenpeace protesters surround nuclear naval vessels with small boats, or place themselves between a whaling ship and whales to protest their destruction, the "image is of David taking on Goliath. The action has the immediate effect of stopping the [activity], while the symbolism reinforces the idea of the power of the small but brave."[126] Demonstrators advocating awareness for AIDS research have developed a huge quilt, made up of sections. On each section is the name of a person who died from AIDS placed their by a friend or relative. The quilt is unrolled at demonstrations and rallies and symbolizes the people who have died as their names are read into a microphone.

WHAT IF THE STRATEGY FAILS?   You will not win every battle. When a strategy fails it is important to spend time debriefing to figure out what happened and why. What organizational tactics could have been changed? Was the timing of the campaign poor? Did the opponents capture the symbols that garner public support? Was there too much fragmentation in the organization to bring about a coherent effort? What could be done differently the next time?[127]

BURN-OUT AND DEMORALIZATION.   Because of the stress of confrontation, the long-term nature of the issues, and the strength of the opposition, members may burn out and demoralization may occur, discouraging activists. What occurred in the 1960s may happen with any long-term protest: "The movement no longer satisfied, [it] made too many demands of a depleted self. What arrived was a full-blown crisis of faith."[128] It is difficult to continue a struggle for a long period of time. It is common for social movements to experience "significant collapse, in which activists believed that their movements had failed, the power institutions were too powerful, and their own efforts futile . . . even when the movements were actually progressing reasonably well along the normal path taken by past successful movements!"[129]

How do you cope with burn-out? First of all, keep in mind that capacity building, rectification of social injustice, strengthening community, and empowerment are long-term issues. There will always be ups and downs, victories and defeats. Prepare for the long haul, keeping in mind this advice: " 'It was not granted to you to complete the task,' said Rabbi Tarfon nineteen hundred years ago, 'and yet you may not give it up.' "[130]

Be careful not to take on too much too soon. Pace yourselves so that you or your organization does not become overwhelmed. Take on issues that will motivate and energize your organization. When you or your organization begin to become weary of the struggle, it may be time to take a break. Saul Alinsky says, for example, "A good tactic is one your people enjoy."[131]

Give yourself time to step away from the conflict and assess how far you have come. Then celebrate your successes together. Let yourselves enjoy what you have accomplished, and allow yourselves to feel renewed in one another's presence. Share your feelings of accomplishment and affirm one another's importance. Give recognition and reflect on your victories. Have fun and find rejuvenation in the relationships you have developed.

Solidifying Change

If you are successful in your organizing efforts, the unjust, harmful, dehumanizing systems or processes that have been exposed and broken up now need to be replaced with ones that are just, helpful, and humanizing. This is the "refreezing" stage of the change process. While confrontation tactics force opponents to pay attention and make short-term changes, political pressure tactics are intended to change laws and enforce regulations that preserve the short-term victories.[132]

To make lasting changes, organizational members need to think about ways to change laws, regulations, and levels of enforcement. Tenants can't demonstrate each time a landlord turns off the heat in a building. Instead, a tenants' organization needs to have a city code adopted and enforced that guarantees warm apartments. This means using political pressure tactics and asking for policy concessions in which the poor are protected against unequal treatment and unfair advantage, with the government acting as referee

of a new set of procedures, rules, or laws. Solidifying change may also take the form of establishing new agencies to oversee and enforce the laws.

Politics

Political tactics require detailed knowledge of laws and regulations, the power structure, special interest groups, and the political process. Organizers and community organization members must be active in the political arena, obtaining the political support of elected officials, such as local, county, and state legislators, judges, lawyers, lobbyists, and administrators of public agencies. Political strategies are discussed in chapter 14.

Policy

One way of generating action is to negotiate and bargain with public officials to obtain policy concessions. Your organization can mobilize the wider community to form an interest group that can lobby for legislative action. If the issues are large enough, you may have to move the political process in your favor by petitioning, developing referendums and initiatives, advocating changes in the law, or proposing new laws. For example, the civil rights movement resulted in the passage of the Civil Rights Act, the environmental movement brought about the Clean Air Act, and the labor movement, the National Labor Relations Act.

Establishing an Agency

If your organization has been successful in obtaining policy concessions, develop an agency that will operate programs and propose legislation on your behalf. The Civil Rights Act established affirmative action agencies. Educators have a Department of Education to represent their interests; labor has the Department of Labor; veterans have the Veterans Administration. The Environmental Protection Agency provides a means by which environmental claimants can seek "tangible results in firm policy."[133]

Monitoring and Enforcement

Even with laws, policies, and agencies in place, the social action process is still not complete. There is no guarantee that the same social or cultural forces will not continue to work to undermine the new structures activists have created. For example, even though the Emancipation Proclamation freed the slaves and the Fourteenth Amendment guaranteed equality, racism continued to be practiced by means of the Black Codes, racist organizations such as the Ku Klux Klan, and the *Plessy v. Ferguson* Supreme Court decision, which institutionalized "separate but equal" facilities in the United States.

A mechanism of monitoring and enforcement needs to be instituted to ensure that social systems abide by the new behavioral constraints. Clear sanctions or punishments for those who refuse to live by the new, nonoppressive standards must be established. An agency, usually a regulatory commission, must be set up as a "watchdog" to ensure compliance with standards. The Equal Employment Opportunity Commissions and Affirmative Action Agencies, for example, were established to guarantee compliance with nondiscrimination in employment.

Appropriations of funds must follow the establishment of advocacy agencies and regulatory commissions so that the executive branch of government has resources to enforce the law. The governor or president must establish those regulatory agencies and then follow through in a way that meets the spirit and intent of the law, and there needs to be a commitment on the part of the executive branch of government to enforce the laws.

An unsympathetic executive can undermine social policy by simply not enforcing the regulations. In a more subtle fashion, the composition of the regulatory commission can be so arranged that the very perpetrators of injustice and oppression become the regulators. Instead of reform and regulation, regulatory agencies are transformed into systems that reinforce oppression. Finally, enforcement of the laws can be twisted, loopholes found, exceptions made, delays granted, and a host of obfuscating processes developed that destroy the gains that you and your community organization have worked hard to achieve.

Terminating the Activist's Role

There will come a time when a social activist's work is finished and he or she moves on to other communities, other issues, other problems. Si Kahn says, for example:

> By staying in the community past the time for him to leave, the organizer inhibits the development of community leadership and independence. It is important for poor people in a community to become free not only of their dependence on the power structure but also of their dependence on the organizer. It can be as harmful to a community for an organizer to stay after he has completed his job as for him to leave before he has finished it.[134]

One way of determining whether it is time to leave is to assess the extent to which you have reached your goals.

1. *Members.* Do community members identify themselves as victims and play a victim role or have they gained confidence, empowerment, and control over their destiny?
2. *Leadership.* To what extent have community leaders emerged? Do these leaders act on behalf of the community, encouraging broad participation or do they use their positions to oppress others?
3. *Organization.* Does the community organization operate independently? Are its members motivated? Is the organization's structure compatible with its goals? Are community members engaged in helping the organization grow and develop? Is the organization capable of eliminating community problems over the long haul?
4. *Accomplishments.* How many goals has the organization met? How effectively has it used its tactics? What defeats has the organization experienced and how has it handled those defeats?
5. *Politics.* How effectively does the organization work with elected officials? Has the organization participated in election campaigns, in proposing initiatives or referendums, in obtaining changes in policy?
6. *Power.* Is the power structure responsive to the organization and to its political strength? Does the power structure recognize the organization as effectively representing the needs of the community? How many organization members occupy positions of leverage in the power structure?

While your organization may not score high in all of these areas, you can leave knowing that it is strong enough to move in a positive direction.

When you feel that the time for you to leave is coming, you need to prepare the community. Engaging the community took time and was a systematic process; disengagement should also be done over a period of time and with deliberation. Meet with the organization and explain that you will be leaving and your strategy for disengagement. By this time, your leadership style should be a low task/low relationship facilitating style (described in chapter 3). Take less and less active involvement in meetings. Then, begin to distance yourself from meetings. Tell the members that you will be absent occasionally and then more frequently.[135]

Begin to terminate the relationships you have developed. Visit as many people as you can, "attend meetings of block clubs, committees, and organizations in the community"[136] to say goodbye. Visit members of the power structure—those who have supported your efforts and those who have opposed you. Si Kahn suggests letting them know that you may return if needed by the community to prevent plans for those in power to try to pressure the organization once you leave.[137]

Meet with the organization and present your assessment of the organization. In your assessment explain the condition of the community when you came. Review the history of the organization, and give an evaluation of its condition at present. Affirm the organization's strengths, and commend members for their victories. Let them know what areas you think they need to work on in the future to become a stronger organization.

Have a celebration in which you and your organization can enjoy a closure experience. Members need to express their feelings toward you, and you will have a chance to say your final goodbyes to them and share what the organizing experience has meant to you.

Leave in such a manner that you can always return if necessary. "The knowledge that [the organizer] is still available to help the community if it needs him will help give poor people the confidence to work so effectively that the organizer will never need to return."[138]

Conclusion

The role of a social activist is to renovate society, transforming and changing the order of things. While social activism is not appropriate for every kind of social change, it is appropriate when entrenched power has a vested interest in maintaining inequitable or socially destructive social conditions. Success in social action is measured by the achievement of specific goals and by the oppressed members of a community taking charge of their lives. Sometimes this means that the oppressed must, in the short run, endure even more suffering—financially, emotionally, and physically—in order to obtain their demands. Through working together, however, risk taking can be shared. With the empowerment that comes from striking a blow for self-determination and independence, conflict and confrontation can be strengthening and empowering. The results can be tangible policy concessions, better laws, and guarantees of people's rights.

KEY CONCEPTS

abolition movement
temperance movement
women's rights movement
settlement house movement
workers' rights movement
pacifism
civil rights movement
protest against the war in Vietnam
process of social action
unfreezing
move to action
refreeze
act out
get out
opt out
flake out
cop out
resistance to change
inertia
homeostasis
fear of the unknown

disruption of routine
threats to security
threats to power
life cycle of resistance to change
active non-cooperation
exposure of perpetrators
information campaign
challenging distortions
public relations
legal action
injunctions
discovery
lawsuits
performance suit
class action suit
procedural suit
satyagraha
confrontation
rally
moral demonstration
picketing
march
sit-in
boycott
symbolic demonstration
burn-out
terminating the activist role

QUESTIONS FOR DISCUSSION

1. Marilyn Ferguson said, "Eventually, anyone concerned with the transformation of the individual must engage in social action." What do you suppose she meant?

2. In Saul Alinsky's essay "Of Means and Ends," the "fourth rule of ethics of means and ends is that judgment must be made in the context of the times in which the action occurred and not from any other chronological vantage point."[140] This seems to imply that morality is fluid and that there are no value absolutes that govern action. On the other hand, it presupposes an objective viewpoint that action must be evaluated in terms of the values, culture, and historical context in which it occurred and not by standards or values external to that action. What are the implications of this for social action and for ethical macro social work practice? Does this notion allow us freedom to change the context of action? Does it imply that action can also change the morality by which that action is viewed?

ADDITIONAL READING

History of Protest

Allen, Robert. *Reluctant Reformers: Racism and Social Reform Movements in the United States.* Washington, DC: Howard University Press, 1983.

Anderson, Walter. *The Age of Protest.* Pacific Palisades, CA: Goodyear, 1989.

Walters, Ronald G. *American Reformers: 1815–1860.* New York: Hill and Wang, 1978.

Organizing Theory and Practice

Alinsky, Saul D. *Reveille for Radicals.* New York: Vintage Books, 1969.

———. *Rules for Radicals: A Pragmatic Primer for Realistic Radicals.* New York: Vintage Books, 1971.

Freire, Paolo. *Pedagogy of the Oppressed.* New York: Continuum, 1992.

Huenefeld, John. *The Community Activist's Handbook: A Guide to Organizing, Financing, and Publicizing Community Campaigns.* Boston, MA: Beacon, 1970.

Hurvitz, Eugene, and Sue Hurvitz. *Working Together Against Homelessness.* New York: Rosen, 1994.

Ingram, Catherine. *In the Footsteps of Gandhi: Conversations with Spiritual Social Activists.* Berkeley, CA: Parallax Press, 1990.

Kahn, Si. *How People Get Power: Organizing Oppressed Communities for Action.* New York: McGraw-Hill, 1970.

———. *Organizing: A Guide for Grassroots Leaders.* New York: McGraw-Hill, 1981.

King, Martin Luther, Jr. *Stride Toward Freedom: The Montgomery Story.* New York: Ballantine, 1958.

Perkins, John. *Let Justice Roll Down.* Glendale, CA: Regal Books, 1976.

Sinclair, Upton. *The Cry for Justice: An Anthology of the Literature of Social Protest.* New York: Lyle Stuart, 1964.

EXERCISES

EXERCISE 29:
Critiquing Fighting Ministers

The description of the fighting ministers at the beginning of this chapter tells of a social action effort that seemed to end in failure for the change agents.

1. Do you agree that the effort failed? Why or why not?
2. Did the fighting ministers follow the methods described in this chapter? Which did they use? Which did they not use?
3. Were their tactics successful or not successful?
4. What would you have done in their place?
5. The change effort shifted from the unemployed steelworkers to the church itself as a focus of social action. Was this appropriate? Would you have done if you had been a fighting minister?

EXERCISE 30:
Developing a Social Action Problem

Think about a social problem in your own community that may be appropriate for social action change methods. Write a short paragraph describing the problem and how you would use social action to address it. What strategies and tactics would you use? What if your efforts failed? How would you deal with resistance to change and the life cycle of resistance?

EXERCISE 31:
Rules for Radicals

Listed below are Saul Alinsky's thirteen tactical rules for overpowering the opposition. Look over the list. What is your perception of these rules? Can you apply them to social change? Can you apply them to other situations where you are encountering resistance to change?

- *Rule 1.* Power is not only what you have but what the enemy thinks you have.
- *Rule 2.* Never go outside the experience of your people.
- *Rule 3.* Wherever possible go outside the experience of the enemy.
- *Rule 4.* Make the enemy live up to their own book of rules.
- *Rule 5.* Ridicule is man's most potent weapon.
- *Rule 6.* A good tactic is one that your people enjoy.
- *Rule 7.* A tactic that drags on too long becomes a drag.
- *Rule 8.* Keep the pressure on with different tactics and actions.
- *Rule 9.* The threat is usually more terrifying than the thing itself.
- *Rule 10.* The major premise for tactics is the development of operations that will maintain a constant pressure upon the opposition.
- *Rule 11.* If you push a negative hard and deep enough, it will break into its counterside.
- *Rule 12.* The price of a successful attack is a constructive alternative.
- *Rule 13.* Pick the target, freeze it, personalize it, and polarize it.[139]

PART III

Social Work Practice with Organizations

We live in a society that is an organizational society.
—ROBERT PRESTHUS[1]

COMMUNAL ACTION

Community comes about, according to Max Weber, by means of "communal action," or *gemeinschaftshandeln*. "We shall speak of communal action," writes Weber, "wherever human action is related in terms of its subjective meaning to the behavior of other human beings."[2] In *community*, we relate to one another on the basis of shared meanings. It is our attachment to particular values and our activity in creating human life worlds that makes community what it is.

In spite of their importance, however, human communal systems are fraught with difficulty. For one thing, community is highly insular. It is difficult to move from one community to another because communities are, for the most part, based on tradition, personal relationships, and kinship ties. If you do not share the values, history, or relationships of a community it is difficult to become a part of it. Because in the past, the life world of an individual was totally included in a community, there was very little incentive for that individual to join another community. The result was little change, adaptability, or mobility.

Communities, in addition, tend to be small, and because of language and geographical boundaries, people of different communities would rarely communicate with one another. Distrust and suspicion were not uncommon at the boundaries of communities. The result was friction and miscommunication that often led to war.

Finally, people in a community relate to the outer world and to one another on the basis of personal, subjective feelings that mitigate against the objective evaluation of situations based on facts. The result is decision making trapped in and colored by emotion.

As long as people were limited to a community, the world was immersed in communal and religious struggles and consumed with the insular world of kinship, ritual,

205

and subjectivity. The inner world of myth and magic consumed people. There was little incentive to be concerned about external, objective reality.

SOCIETAL ACTION

Gradually, however, as people in community rubbed up against one another more and more often, another form of human relationship emerged—that of society. In society, subjective meaning must take account of other groups and communities. The meanings and values that are shared in a community may not be acceptable in the larger society where other meanings and values exist. The external world of others become factors that an individual must now take into account. "Action is 'social' insofar as its subjective meaning takes account of the behavior of others and is thereby oriented in its course."[3] In society, communally shared meaning becomes transformed into general rules for facilitating communication and interaction among various community groups.

Communal action, then, must be translated into social action. The way this naturally occurs is by means of mutual understanding, discourse, and engagement at the boundaries of community. Society, therefore, is simply an enlarged version of community. While people must take on roles, engage in a certain amount of specialization, and develop power relations shaping rules by which action is governed, individuals in society continue to insert meaning into social relationships. They try to understand one another. To a certain extent society allows for "objectifying" social relationships, allowing both I-You and I-It relationships.[4]

RATIONAL ACTION

By 1650, scientists such as Roger Bacon and Galileo discovered laws of physics and invented mechanisms and tools by which the physical world could be understood. Science based on reason and logic and the objective observation of empirical facts, without reliance on subjective, internal feelings, or even religion, revolutionized the Western world. In that year, Thomas Hobbes, looking at society and politics, conceived that society could also be viewed objectively. In fact, thought Hobbes, society itself was merely a human construct and thus, governed by observable and predictable laws just as any other empirical phenomenon.[5] Implied in this vision was the possibility people could subject society to the cold light of objective observation and shape systems based on the reality of individual self-interest, desires, goals, and logical calculation.[6] So powerful was the application of calculative logic to society that it shaped the political ideas of John Locke, who was one of the philosophical founders of democracy, and Adam Smith, who shaped the economic theories of capitalism. The ideas of these two men helped shape the American Constitution.[7] The world of "You"-relations was being transformed into the world of "It."[8]

THE ARTIFICIAL SOCIETY

Functional reason brought to people a new way of relating to one another. Modern society becomes an artifact in which "'institutionally commanded action' (*anstalt-shandeln*) gradually replaces communal action. . . . Individuals are expected to obey societies' rules even if they did not have a chance to contribute to their design."[9]

The world of "It" becomes dominant, in which people are conceived as objects and the actions of human beings are designed by others. The way this social transformation occurs is by means of a new social systems design—modern complex organization or bureaucracy. This is why Max Weber said that "bureaucracy is the means of transforming social action (action by which communities are formed) into rationally organized action"[10] (action based on formal, instrumental reason by which organizations are formed).

When rationally commanded action begins, natural social action inevitably gives way to it. With bureaucracy, an artificially contrived form of social relationship enters the picture, one that does not exist in a natural community or society. It is the primary role of bureaucracy to drive out substantive reason on which "communal" and "social" action is based, replacing it with neutral, impersonal, calculative rational action. "Bureaucracy replaces society."[11] When members of a community or society decide to enter the "modern" world, that is, become goal directed, rational, and technological, they devise complex organizations as the means by which such transformation will be accomplished.

Organizations are symbols and representatives of "modernity." They are a new form of social relationship, one that is unprecedented. It is organization that brings about the new age. Terryberry summarizes this development. "In modern industrial societies," she says,

> this evolutionary process has resulted in the replacement of individuals and informal groups by organizations as actors in the social system. Functions that were once the sole responsibility of families and communities are increasingly allocated to formal organizations; child rearing, work, recreation, education, health, and so on. Events which were long a matter of chance are increasingly subject to organizational control, such as population growth, business cycles and even the weather.[12]

Social relationships based on feelings, sentiments, and values are converted into power relations. The symbolic meanings to which individuals attached their communities are of little importance, and the natural social system is swallowed up and replaced by artificial, control mechanisms. It is one of the supreme virtues of organization that it is a "democratizing" force. People demand and eventually are treated equally and universally according to the same rules and regulations. The ultimate result is that everything comes under the control of organizations. "Under otherwise equal conditions, rationally organized and directed action (*Gesellschaftshandeln*) is superior to every kind of collective behavior (*Massenhandeln*), and also social action (*Gemeinshaftshandeln*) opposing it,"[13] said Max Weber.

Macro social workers need to be immersed in community work with its methods of community development and social action. But macro level social work is not only community social work. The increasing rational organization of our society means that natural communal social action is increasingly restricted. As a result, we need to understand how organization is transforming community into social structures that are completely new, and how complex organizations are changing the nature of our entire social and cultural milieu.

The social environment of America today, for example, is comprised of interlocking networks of organizations. Many of these are businesses ranging from neighborhood shops and stores, to gigantic multinational conglomerates such as General Motors. Governmental organizations, from city and county bureaucracies to massive federal administrations such as the Department of Agriculture, Internal Revenue Service, United States Army, and others, fill the public sector. These organizational systems amass power and resources. Furthermore, complex organizations attempt to shape their environments to meet their own needs and to ensure that their goals are being met.

In contrast, most communities have no organized power base with which to press for claims on the social environment. Unlike large complex organizations, communities have few if any concrete resources by which they can apply to system maintenance or social change. While organizations devote much energy to maintaining their structures and their long-term stability, communities have few if any mechanisms to ensure stability or control over membership. People are free to move into or leave communities at will.

Organizations have political and contractual legitimacy, can own and acquire property, and have legal status as if they were persons. Corporations can be sued, fined, and held accountable for their actions. Communities, on the other hand, have ambiguous legitimacy at best. Some community associations such as churches or neighborhood organizations are incorporated as not-for-profit organizations, but neighborhoods and most other communities are not set up as structures with legal boundaries. While complex organizations spend much effort acquiring information so that they can plan and anticipate changes in their social environment, communities tend to plan on a small scale and for narrow survival needs, not in response to or to change wider society.

Social workers, therefore, need to be prepared to relate to this more impersonal, more complex, more interrelated world. The same old problems persist—those of poverty, drug and alcohol abuse, child abuse, and so on—but new problems are becoming urgent—technological change, structural unemployment, decimation of the world ecosystem and other complex policy questions. Social work in the future will require not only skill as a therapist but also the ability to understand and to apply problem-solving skills to modern complex organizations. Social workers skilled in organizational leadership, and who have an ability to diagnose social problems and solve them, will be the more valued and capable members of our profession. Social workers need to understand how organizational systems work, design systems that are better, infuse those which are unethical with integrity and goodness, fix them when they become dysfunctional, and use them to solve our pressing social problems.

This section describes several kinds of social work with organizations. Chapter 9 explores the phenomenon of modern complex organizations. Social planning, described in chapter 10, is one of the more important arenas of macro social work. Social planners relate both to complex organizations and to natural communities. Social planning may be seen as a bridge between community and organizational social work. Chapter 11 describes program development, how to stabilize the change effort by creating a social agency or organization to carry out your purposes. An organization needs leadership; chapter 12 deals with the field of social work administration, and chapter 13 with the arena of organization development.

ADDITIONAL READING

Polanyi, Karl. *The Great Transformation: The Political and Economic Origins of Our Time.* Boston, MA: Beacon Press, 1944.
Ramos, Alberto Guerreiro. *The New Science of Organizations: A Reconceptualization of the Wealth of Nations.* Toronto: University of Toronto Press, 1981.
Weber, Max. "Bureaucracy." *From Max Weber: Essays in Sociology.* H. H. Gerth and C. Wright Mills, eds. New York: Oxford University Press, 1958.

CHAPTER 9

Modern Complex Organizations

Sometimes the bureaucratic red tape of complex organizations can tangle up the most simple and natural human activities.

Bureaucracy is *the* means of transforming social action into rationally organized action. . . . Bureaucracy develops the more perfectly, the more it is "dehumanized," the more completely it succeeds in eliminating from official business love, hatred, and all personal, irrational, and emotional elements which escape calculation . . . and this is apprised as its special virtue.

—MAX WEBER, "BUREAUCRACY"[1]

IDEAS IN THIS CHAPTER

Marriage and the INS

Getting married is one of the normal aspects of human life and, for the most part, has little to do with formal complex organizational rules and regulations. Sometimes, however, bureaucratic red tape intrudes even here. Lynne Thaxter became engaged on New Year's Eve, 1990. She and Chris Brown, her fiancé, planned to get married in Fresno, California, on May 26. Everything seemed to be going well until the U.S. Immigration and Naturalization Service stepped in.

Chris Brown is British, and because he wanted to meet his intended bride in April, he applied and received a visitor's visa. The plan was that he would enter the United States as a visitor, get married, and then apply for permanent resident status.

Upon arriving in the United States Chris discovered that his plan wouldn't work. Federal law states that a person must have a special visa to enter the United States for the purpose of getting married. So, back to England went Brown to reapply. This time, he claimed his intention of getting married and duly applied for a "fiancé visa." His request was denied. In true catch-22 fashion, government officials ruled that since he had lied about the purpose of his April trip to America, he was guilty of fraud. Brown was labeled an "excludable alien."

Several weeks of negotiations and communication ensued requiring high levels of political intervention, including that of a U.S. congressman and the Western Region Commissioner of INS, who worked with officials in both England and the United States to bend the rules. Finally, the red tape was cut, and on an August 11 Lynn and Chris got married. This time not even Uncle Sam's bureaucracy stood in their way.[2]

Introduction

Complex organizations are all around us, and most of us take them for granted. Because we are born into them, we assume that these organizations are natural phenomena and accept them as the way things are. However, organizations don't just happen. People plan and devise them. Second, society has not always been like it is today. In fact, complex organization is a fairly recent phenomenon, and the world itself is becoming more and more organized all the time.

This chapter explores why organizations are so important, develops a definition of what organizations are, and explains why they have come about. Modern theories of organization are also examined. Finally, an action model of organization is presented and how it relates to macro social work practice is discussed.

Our Organizational Society

Organizations are important today because they have been extremely successful. Wherever one turns, one encounters organizations. In addition, they are influential. Organizations affect the way we relate, the way we think, and how we act. Organizations dominate nearly every aspect of our lives.

Organizations Are Ubiquitous[3]

Organizations are the defining characteristic of our age. We are born in organizations, educated in organizations, and eat food that was grown, processed, packaged, transported and sold by complex organizations. We work in organizations, do business with organizations, and eventually we will be buried by still other organizations. The clothes we wear, the furniture we use, the housing that provides us with shelter are all manufactured by complex organizations. Whenever we ride in an automobile or take a bus we are being provided with machines that were designed, mass produced, and marketed by organizations.

The clothing, food, housing, and transportation industries are all regulated by governmental organizations. When we vote, pay our income taxes, collect Social Security, sign up for the Selective Service, get a drivers license, or use the library, we engage these organizations.

Our political decisions are made, whether we like it or not, by means of organizational politics. We receive spiritual nourishment often through organized religion. Even our social and recreational life is dominated by organizations.

While individual nations are separated by language, national boundaries, and cultural allegiances, organizations know few of these restrictions. Individual organizations leap across language and cultural barriers. Many companies are multinational in nature, one company operating in many different countries. McDonald's operates in Europe, Asia, and Africa. Coca-Cola is manufactured worldwide. The more multinational some firms become, the more they diversify. They buy and sell organizations.

Organizations are also transcultural and transnational. One Japanese firm may own many American companies, or an American company may have interests in different European and Asian concerns. Today, for example, there is probably no such thing as an "American" automobile. It is not uncommon for a car with an American name to have been manufactured in another country, or a car with a foreign name to have been manufactured in the United States. Many automobiles have engines or components that are designed by an organization in one country and assembled by a different company in another country using materials or parts obtained or purchased by organizations located in still other countries.

This phenomenon occurs in the public and non-profit arena as well. Today governments cooperate in many cross-cultural ventures. The United Nations is one such effort. The Olympics, the Peace Corps, the World Bank, and Interpol as well as international social welfare organizations such as the Red Cross, Boy Scouts, Lutheran World Relief, and International Children's Fund operate worldwide. The European Common Market will, in the decade ahead, eradicate national boundaries for purposes of commerce and trade.

What makes all this possible is that organizations can relate to other organizations because of common goals, structures, communication systems, and ways of thinking. Organizations are becoming a common referent that is uniting people in common tasks worldwide that were impossible before.

Organizations Are Influential

The success of modern organizations can be measured not only by their size or their pervasiveness but also by their accomplishments. Organizations have helped us achieve a level of prosperity unmatched in any other period of history. We owe our material wealth to organizations and the technologies they support, and because organizations are powerful systems for producing and accomplishing things, we have come to depend on them.

> Bureaucracies satisfy, delight, and satiate us with their output of goods and services. . . . They do [this for us] not so much in our role as members of one or more . . . organizations, but as members of a society that is truly an organizational society.[4]

We are beholden, therefore, to the organizational economy that, to a great extent, determines our life chances and provides us with employment and an increasing and rich array of possessions. Organizations exert an enormous amount of influence.

Organizations Provide Personal Identity

Organizations exert internal as well as external influence. "Organizations shape our understanding, expectations and hopes as well as any material services they may provide."[5] "They also shape our mentality, control our life chances, and define our humanity."[6] We tend to obtain our sense of ourselves, our identity, and meaning about our world from organizations.[7] Organizations have become our social environment.[8] They are our cultural, social, and interpersonal frame of reference.[9] They define our present and, to a great extent, determine our future.

Organizations Are Powerful

Organizations are important to us because of their pervasiveness and their influence and also their power. Max Weber (1864–1920), perhaps the most astute observer of organization,[10] claimed that "as an instrument of rationally organized authority relations, bureaucracy was and is a power instrument of the first order for one who controls the bureaucratic apparatus."[11]

Organizations provide individuals with personal power. "Those who control these organizations control the quality of our life, and they are largely self-appointed leaders. . . . The person who controls an organization has power that goes far beyond that of those lacking such control.[12]

Organizations generate social power:

> Because of its superiority as a social tool over other forms of organization, bureaucracy generates an enormous degree of unregulated and often unperceived social power; and this power is placed in the hands of very few leaders.[13]

These leaders socialize individuals to organizational values and premises. They freely induce individuals to give up their own value preferences for those of the owner[14] of the organization and exact conforming behavior in every area of organizational life.[15]

Organizations generate economic power. "The power of the rich lies not in their ability to buy goods and services but in their capacity to control the ends toward which the vast resources of large organizations are directed."[16]

We are dependent on organizations because of their decision-making power. Organizations are the most powerful decision-making control instruments ever devised. The "artificial [organizational] system could be defined, therefore, as a consciously designed control machine."[17]

The problem with organizations, however, is not only the amount of power they control but who controls organizations and the ends for which that power is used. Organizations inevitably concentrate power "in the hands of a few who are prone to use [it] for ends we do not approve of, for ends we are generally not aware of, and more frightening still, for ends we are led to accept because we are not in a position to conceive alternative ones."[18]

What Are Organizations?

Organizations are artificial, intentionally contrived social tools for accomplishing the goals of their owners and getting work performed. Let's expand on that definition and explore some of its key components.

Organizations Are Artificial

Victor Thompson says that "organizations are tools or instruments—closed systems, prescriptive plans—in other words, artificial systems."[19] In the television series *Star Trek*, there is a life-form called a cyborg, a gigantic living but artificial system. The cyborg is composed of thousands of part human, part machine creatures. They communicate instantaneously, live in a symbiotic relationship, work toward a common goal, and are directed by a central executor. The cyborg is a metaphor for modern complex organizations. Because organization combines characteristics of both humans and machines, these "cybernetic social tools" have vast superiority over other forms of human associated life.[20]

One of the reasons for this superiority is that organizations produce technology.[21] The organization is both the product of and the producer of technology. Because technology could create a machine-oriented world that was more efficient and more productive, humans invented the organizational machine to produce more and better kinds of technology. This organizational technological world is artificial. Weber said:

> The decisive reason for the advance of the bureaucratic organization has always been its purely technical superiority over any other form of organization. The fully developed bureaucratic apparatus compares with other organizations exactly as does the machine with the nonmechanical modes of production.[22]

The artificial mechanism drives out natural human association. "Bureaucracy is *the* means of transforming social action into rationally organized action."[23] Jacques Ellul, echoing Weber, said that

> [the technical world] destroys, eliminates or subordinates the natural world and does not allow this world to restore itself or even to enter into a symbiotic relation with it. The two worlds obey different imperatives, different directives, and different laws which have nothing in common.[24]

This artificial world is one in which everything becomes predictable and manageable.

Organizations Are Intentional

Organizations are not naturally occurring social systems that are inevitably present whenever people congregate, as are communities. Organizations come about because one or several persons have thought about a goal that they want to accomplish and have devised a system for accomplishing that goal. Organizations are intentionally created systems for the purpose of accomplishing the goal of their owners.[25]

Organizations Are Contrived

Organizations are artfully contrived systems—perhaps the most complicated and useful systems ever devised by mankind.[26] They are rational, goal-oriented, decision-making machines for accomplishing the purposes of their owners in the speediest and most efficient way possible.[27]

Organizations Are Social Tools

"Organizations," Charles Perrow says, "must be seen as tools."[28]

> A tool is something you can get something done with. It is a resource *if* you control it. It gives you power that others do not have. Organizations are multipurpose tools. There are a great many things that one can do with them.... *Organizations are tools for shaping the world as one wishes it to be shaped.* They provide the means for imposing one's definition of the proper affairs of men upon other men.[29] (Emphasis in original)

Organizations are social tools because they use people as their components.[30] The advantages of a human tool is that people can think and make decisions and they can learn. Humans naturally form into systems and communicate with one another. Most humans are goal-seeking creatures. They understand about having aspirations and working to accomplish goals.

Finally, people are malleable. They are adaptable, can take direction, and are able to suspend their own thinking and values in favor of the values of others.[31] All of these qualities make humans ideal material out of which to form organizations. People become the "interchangeable parts" of organizational social tools.[32]

Organizations Accomplish Goals

Tools do not have goals.[33] They are neutral instruments to accomplish the purposes of their owners. The owners of the organization establish its goals; and the organization, by means of its human resources, technology, leadership, decision processes, rules, tasks, and procedures carries them out.

Organizations Perform Work

Modern organizations are contrived by rational calculation in order to accomplish work that is arranged in specific tasks so that the smooth coordination of activities can be achieved. Organizational tools composed of human beings are extremely efficient and effective. When one harnesses people and develops an organizational structure to channel and direct their energies, an enormous amount of work can be performed.

> Precision, speed, unambiguity, knowledge of the files, continuity, discretion, unity, strict subordination, reduction of friction and of material and personal costs—these are raised to the optimum point in the strictly bureaucratic administration, and especially in its monocratic form. As compared with all collegiate, honorific, and avocational forms of administration, trained bureaucracy is superior on all these points.[34]

Organizations of people design, plan, manufacture, sell, and transport myriad products. More important, however, organizations and their owners are responsible for shaping and coordinating the goals and direction of our society.

Organization Theory and Organization Behavior

The organization has been shaped by historical conditions and ideologies and has gone through a process of evolution. Not only has our understanding of organizations changed, but also organizations have shaped our views of ourselves and our social world.

To the extent that we are an "organizational society," we build into organizations our dreams, plans, and hopes for the future. By examining our

Paperwork and files are raised to the optimum level in complex organizations.

ideas about organizations we can come to understand our own culture better and even may predict with some accuracy where we are headed.

There are four "schools" of organization theory: (1) the classical bureaucratic school; (2) the human relations school; (3) the decision-making school; and (4) the contingency school.

The Classical Bureaucratic School

By 1850, theorists and inventors in the United States and Europe were beginning to glimpse the potential that empirical thinking applied to understanding natural sciences could have in creating technological miracles. The steam engine was reshaping the world of work and transportation. The telegraph was speeding communication. Machinery was increasing manufacture, and factories and factory towns were springing up. These factories were responsible for an amazing amount of productivity.

> Twenty thousand miles of track were laid in a decade, most of it in the West, and transcontinentals were pushed across the plains and the mountains with dizzy speed. Telegraph lines were strung from city to city and soon crossed the continent; cables were laid across the Atlantic. . . . The great packing plants at Chicago and Cincinnati, the flour mills of the Twin Cities, and breweries of Milwaukee and St. Louis, the iron and steel mills of the Pittsburgh region, the oil refineries of Ohio and Pennsylvania, and a hundred others worked day and night to meet the orders that poured in on them.[35]

While "the United States of Lincoln's day was a nation of small enterprises, . . . a change had begun with the Civil War and went on with mounting speed after the seventies."[36]

> In the five years after Appomattox almost every industrial record was shattered. More coal, iron ore, silver, and copper were mined, more steel forged, more rails were laid, more lumber was sawed and more houses were built, more cotton cloth was woven, more flour milled, more oil refined than in any previous five years in our history. In the decades from 1860 to 1870, the total number of manufacturing establishments increased by eighty percent and the value of manufactured products by one hundred percent.[37]

The proliferation of the great manufacturing companies, the business corporations

> made possible large scale combination, centralized control and administration, and the elimination of less efficient units, the pooling of patents, and, by virtue of their capital resources, power to expand, to compete with foreign business enterprises, to bargain with labor, to exact favorable terms . . . and to exercise immense influence with politics, state and national.[38]

By 1880, industry was in full swing. Breakthroughs were being made in scientific and technological fields, particularly in electronics and communication. Between 1860 and 1900, no fewer than 676,000 patents were granted by the U.S. Patent Office,[39] among them the radio, the phonograph, and the electric light. The gasoline combustion engine and the automobile were to revolutionize transportation as the assembly line was revolutionizing production. By the turn of the century, the organization of production and distribution was nearly complete.

> The life of the average man, especially if he was a city dweller, was profoundly changed by this development. Almost everything he ate and wore, the furnishing of his home, the tools he used, the transportation he employed were made or controlled by complex organizational systems.[40]

In addition to the organization of the economy, the bureaucratization of government and political life was beginning to take hold, particularly with the passage of the Pendleton Act in 1883. This act rationalized the federal Civil Service, eliminating patronage, amicism (giving preferential treatment to friends in hiring), and nepotism (giving preferential treatment to relatives) in government.

The heart of productivity was machinery. The corporation and factory were nothing but gigantic human machines in which all the parts were to fit together smoothly and function together just like a clockwork mechanism. At the top was the boss, and at the bottom were the workers. Relationships were arranged in a hierarchy. Communication flowed from top to bottom in a one-way direction along a "chain of command." Decisions were made by means of linear reckoning and incremental thinking congruent with modern scientific method. "Science," says Schuman,

> does not really attack a huge problem, it only goes after small ones. Incrementally, a step at a time, discoveries are made and techniques are developed that will eventually add up to a fantastic enterprise. ("One small step for man; one giant step for mankind.") The world gets scientized—gets rationalized—just a little bit at a time.[41]

And in exactly the same way, an organization encroaches on its environment, building on past decisions and moving ahead little by little.

This organizational machine could not function if the parts pulled in different directions. The organizational mechanism has to be "monocratic"—it is aimed in one direction and has one overarching goal to be implemented, the goal and direction of the one in command—the operator or the driver.[42] The parts of the organization—the workers—do what they are told and fill a niche in the organization design. These parts are like cogs in a wheel. Because "personal factors of love or hate are irrelevant (almost), anyone with the needed technical skills can be placed in the role. People are largely interchangeable, making it easily possible to construct all the organizations we need."[43] These parts are not to have ideas or values of their own. They are to carry out their instrumental roles as prescribed by their superiors. The "managers" are those who use their "rationality" to plan, organize, direct, supervise, control, order, regulate, and budget.

If individuals have ideas or values, they are to give them up in favor of carrying out the mandates of the organization. This occurs by means of a contract. Individual employees agree to give up an amount of time, energy, and thought to the demands of the organization in return for a paycheck. This, in turn, guarantees the individual some measure of hope in achieving prosperity and security. This contract is tantamount to social exchange.[44]

The director or boss steers the organizational machine toward its destination in the most efficient way possible. Of course, in order to

> develop a machinelike organization, we must also develop the kind of individual who will fit into, work well with, and be able to function in an atmosphere of repetition, narrowness, and almost complete order. Machinelike organizations need machinelike people.[45]

One problem is individuals who, as Charles Perrow commented, "track all kinds of mud from the rest of their lives with them into the organization, and . . . have all kinds of interests that are independent of the organization."[46] The solution was conceived by Frederick Winslow Taylor, one of the great organization theorists of our time. Taylor described his idea of making management "scientific" in his book *Principles of Scientific Management*, published in 1911.

It was the goal of scientific management that "every single act of every workman can be reduced to a science."[47] It was the role of "efficiency experts" to scientifically determine the most effective way of performing tasks. Management was to supervise and teach. The functionaries themselves, if properly taught, would behave in a way that productivity could be enhanced with everyone benefiting.[48] Working together for a common purpose, the entire organization could be scientifically converted into a rational system.

Just as the worker was split off from thinking about and creatively investing himself in his work, the same division was occurring in the field of government. In public organizations, extraneous issues such as "politics," which diverted the organizational mechanism from its course, were to be strictly separated from "administration." Woodrow Wilson (1856–1922) wrote:

> The field of administration is the field of business. It is removed from the hurry and strife of politics. . . . It is part of political life only as the methods of the counting house are part of the life of society; only as machinery is part of the manufactured product. . . . Administration lies outside the proper sphere of *politics*. Administrative questions are not political questions. . . . Politics is thus the special province of the statesman, administration of the technical official.[49] (Emphasis in original)

Political bodies, particularly legislatures, were to provide for policy and goal formulation. Administration was reduced to a functionary level, carrying out policies in a technically efficient manner, impartially and impersonally. The public administrator was to operate "*sine ira et studio*,"[50] without sympathy or compassion, on norms of fairness, equality, efficiency, and effectiveness.

Individuals would be hired for government service based on their qualifications for the job rather than personal criteria, favoritism, or other non–job-related criteria. Employees would be sheltered from political pressure to give preference to politicians or political "cronies" when arranging for services or allocating resources, and they would be prevented from using the power of their administrative offices for political gain.

Based on norms of accountability, functional rationality, and efficiency, administration was an arm of morality in government. Bureaucracy, therefore, intentionally excluded from its purview any hint of personal bias or preferences and the expression of individual compassion or altruism that diverted resources from the prescribed goals.[51] Bureaucracy, operating strictly on the basis of the "public interest" and bolstered by rules and procedures, insured that private interests would no longer usurp the public will. Morality as rescued by organization and bureaucracy was the means by which fairness, equity, justice, and equality were to be implemented in contrast to amicism, nepotism, and spoils in government.[52]

The Human Relations School

In 1929, an event occurred that was to radically change the course of history and the role of social administration. The stock market crash and resultant Great Depression virtually brought this nation to its knees, destroying faith in a laissez-faire role of government in the economy. Gone was the belief that if left unchecked the economy would automatically and inevitably adjust itself so that in the aggregate everyone would gain.

The aphorism of greed counteracting greed reached the end of its exploitative cycle. Social Darwinism was proved insufficient. The super rich had fallen, showing themselves not to be the "fittest." Gigantic corporations were vulnerable to their own profiteering and were unable to provide for the well-being of the nation. Not even science was able to rescue a nation so bent on exploiting natural as well as human resources that it nearly destroyed itself in the process.

Government, under the direction of such leaders as Franklin D. Roosevelt and Harry Hopkins, asserted itself once again and developed a series of programs designed to provide for the public interest. The tool that government used for this purpose was a massive array of agencies, bureaus, and social administration to pump hope and prosperity into the populace.

The process of unionization that had been growing, albeit with major resistance from both business and government, finally received official recognition. Worker needs and their right to bargain collectively became legalized by means of the National Labor Relations Act (NLRA), and implemented by the National Labor Relations Board (NLRB).

In 1927, a series of experiments called the Hawthorne studies were conducted at the Western Electric Company by Elton Mayo and his assistant Fritz Roethlisberger.[53] They discovered that work groups tended to exert their own dynamics that diverged considerably from the goals of the organization. In an assembly line, workers may adjust their speed and productivity to that of the slowest member of the work group. Or, they may collude in deciding among themselves particular norms of productivity based on perceived fairness, or even as a means of sabotage or retaliation against supervisors or others who "played favorites to cover up and to discipline others."[54]

Along with the formal, functional components of organization, therefore, a secondary social system was recognized. This secondary system was the informal, natural social system formed out of the needs, interests, and feelings of the members of the organization. So powerful was this human element that it could disrupt or interfere with the effectiveness and efficiency of the organization. The result was the beginning of a healthy respect for the role that group cohesion, control, and conformity can play in interfering with productivity. The natural system of group interaction was a force to be dealt with.

The Hawthorne experiments marked the introduction of "social science into the study of organizations"[55] and gave birth to the "human relations school" of organization. So pervasive was this emphasis on the individual that the metaphor describing organization shifted away from the mechanistic, physical science, machine-tool model.

In sharp contrast to the bureaucratic school, which viewed organizations as "closed" systems, the human relations school looked on organizations as "open systems" that are adaptable to the world, can grow, think, and evolve, and are largely "natural" rather than "artificial." Organizations were seen as nothing but enlarged versions of a human being.

> The "living system" of an organization is viewed as an enlarged version of man. The organization is believed to have, on a large scale, all the qualities of the individual, including beliefs, modes of behaving, objectives, personality, and motivations. It has inputs, interaction, responses, and outputs. This theory assumes that all behavior is goal seeking, in individuals and in organizations. Improvement of the system, therefore, is aimed at increasing its effectiveness as a totality in order that it may reach its goals.[56]

Individuals in this gigantic humanlike organism were viewed as creatures who had *needs* that must be met by the organization to assure full productivity. The trick for administration was to understand what made individuals productive and what constituted contentment.[57] Individuals were induced by manipulation of needs, satisfactions, group dynamics, socialization, and a host of psychological factors to become more integral components of the organization tool.

Along with human motivation, other components of the human relations school tended to differ from the classical bureaucratic model. Change, for example, was considered to be appropriate under certain conditions. Conflict, too, could be expressed within certain constraints. Organizational politics were recognized as a reality to be dealt with and not separated from administration. Politics, in fact, was the "grease" that often smoothed the formal, and at times dysfunctional, organizational rules.

For all its emphasis on "participatory" management and democratizing the workplace, however, organizational humanization did not extend to deciding on organizational goals or premises. This remained firmly in the hands of the owners of the organization. What seemed to be a benign form of humanization was, in reality, an attempt to use sociological and psychological knowledge about human beings to make them become more adaptable to organizational tools.

One must raise the question, Can an artificial construction such as an organization become more human or be "humanized"? Or, is such "humanization" simply capitulation by managers to the humanity that people inevitably express in organizational systems?

The human relations school implies a subtle form of coercion and control. Charles Perrow, for example, notes:

> We reinforce these premises in our own work. For example, most effectiveness studies now assume that high morale is an indicator of one aspect of organizational effectiveness. But these morale studies ask how satisfied people are with their jobs, supervisors, career prospects, working conditions, and pay. It goes unremarked and unnoticed that the definition of morale is in terms of what the company assumes would be good for it. The unstated premise is that high morale means that people find it gratifying to do what the organization wants them to do.[58]

Theorists of the human relations school made an effort to "humanize" the oppressive and impersonal organizational mechanism, but they failed to recognize that organizations, at least in their formal sense, are not "human" at all. The idea that artificial systems such as organizations have attributes of humanity such as "behavior," "rationality," "decision making," "motivation," or "character," is a theoretical error called *reification*. Berger and Luckman define reification as "the apprehension of the products of human activity *as if* they were something else than human products—such as facts of nature, results of cosmic laws, or a manifestation of divine will."[59] When "the particular categories and schemes of classification" that organizations employ become reified, they are transformed from mere values, norms, and rules that people invent into "attributes of the world."[60] When an artificial human creation is reified, as occurred with the human relations school, human beings become categories of their own creations, and subservient to their own social inventions. Reification strips people of their humanity, destroys self-determination, and places systems beyond human control.

It must be kept in mind that organizations do not "behave," "think," or "make decisions." Organizations do not have "character." Only humans have these attributes.

The Decision-Making School

In 1941 an event occurred that was to change the course of history of the United States and greatly affect the way organizations were viewed. This event was the entry of the United States into the Second World War. Suddenly, the nation was mobilized for action and the effects of the Great Depression were over. War production stimulated the economy as nothing else could have done. A divided and forlorn nation was galvanized into action.

The recommendations of the "human relations" school, emphasizing group process, motivation, inducing the worker to produce, cultivating communication, participative management, democracy in the workplace, humanizing organizations, and being sensitive to worker's needs and feelings, were incompatible with accomplishing the goal of winning the war. A model of organization congruent with the requirements of a turbulent environment, a hierarchy of command, a tight structure, and organizational control was required to shape the nation into a gigantic war machine in a single-minded drive to save the Allied nations from destruction. What may seem to be an anachronistic organizational model—the classic bureaucratic machine tool—was dusted off and polished up to save the United States from defeat at the hands of the supremely efficient and effectively organized war machines of the Axis nations—Germany, Japan, and Italy.

The bureaucratic machine tool was congruent with the demands of the time. In war, the social environment is a hostile, uncertain, turbulent, and changing arena. Individual interests, needs, motivations, or satisfactions have little place. Complete obedience to commands is absolutely necessary. Leadership is authoritarian—directing and commanding. Individual survival and the survival of the fighting unit requires that everyone play prescribed roles in strict compliance with procedures and the orders of the commander. There is no room for discussion, communal interaction, dialogue, or disagreement. Structure is hierarchical. Communication is one way, from top down. Relationships are prescribed within the chain of command. Formal rules, roles, and procedures are the order of the day. Internal conflict is reduced to a minimum. All action is directed to accomplishing a single goal—winning the battle.

This lesson was not lost on organizational theorists of the time. In particular, theorist Herbert A. Simon, who later won the Nobel Prize, developed a theory described in his book *Administrative Behavior*[61] published in 1945, which was to change the way we looked at organizations. Max Weber's classic work on bureaucracy was translated for the first time into English at about this same time. The mechanism of bureaucracy now had two theorists who could adequately explain and expand on its principles.

It is not by accident that this new school of organization theory is called neoclassical, neo-Weberian, or the decision-making school. This new school of administration builds on and extends the insights provided by Max Weber in a way that is chilling, and it is current even today.

Simon, claiming to base his model on logical positivism and systems theory, challenged the conventional rule-of-thumb notions[62] about organization and administration of that day. He criticized the rational model on which classical bureaucracy was based. This model assumes that the decision-maker is a rational individual who knows all of his or her preferences. This allows him or her always to choose among the alternatives, to have access to perfect information, and to rank those alternatives in ways to make decisions. Finally, this rational individual encounters "no limits on the complexity of the computation he can perform in order to determine which alternatives are best."[63] In economizing terms, the ability to reach the decisions that are best means to optimize or maximize.[64]

For Simon, the classical bureaucratic model attributes a "preposterously omniscient rationality to man . . . which has little discernible relation to the actual or possible behavior of flesh and blood human beings."[65] Theorists of the human relations school who based decision making on people's feelings, emotions, needs, values, and other irrational sentiments, who attempt to "reduce all cognition to affect,"[66] are likewise unrealistic because decisions must have a rational element. Simon contends that the model he offers is one that places organization in a context of rational action and decision making "as we should expect actually to see it in real life."[67]

For Simon, organization is a tool, as Weber would have agreed. But it is ultimately a much more sophisticated tool than the classical machine model that sputters and chugs along, full of pulleys and gears. Instead, Simon views organization from a cybernetic perspective. This view was completely astounding for his day, because the computer was only in the very beginning stages of invention.[68] While Simon did not use cybernetic language, his conceptual scheme is a metaphor of the organization as a gigantic computer. Computers process information and solve problems faster, more efficiently, more effectively than any human being. They are calculating, processing, organizing, and decision-making machines.

Organizations perform the same functions. They are nothing more than massive decision-making tools. In fact, Simon declared, organizations are themselves "frozen decisions."[69] While the bureaucratic model viewed the individual as a part in the organizational machine, for Simon, the individual is much like a computer chip. Each individual may have a piece of information and may be able to process information to a certain extent. But no one individual is fully capable of processing or retaining all of the information needed by organization in making decisions.

That is why, for Simon, individuals, for all of their pretensions to full rationality, are only "intendedly" rational. Human reason is *limited*.[70] Therefore, Simon says, "administrative theory is . . . the theory of intended and bounded rationality—of the behavior of human beings who *satisfice* because they have not the wits to *maximize*.[71] Satisficing behavior, a term invented by Simon, means that individuals do not have the capacity to rationally evaluate each potential solution but take the first "good enough" solution that they find.[72]

Only when they are linked together in a gigantic chain of information processing, such as an organization, can individuals in coordination approach something like full rationality. "Organization," according to Simon, "is important because the organizational environment provides much of the force that molds and develops personal qualities and habits."[73] Organization creates a new human character amenable to the needs, demands, and milieu of organization. The organization "selects the individual's ends, . . . trains him in skills, and . . . provides him with information"[74] which he needs to make decisions correctly.[75] But even more than that, "organization . . . places the organization members in a psychological environment that will adapt their decisions to the organization objectives."[76]

In order to be fully rational, therefore, individuals must be integrated into, and take their premises from, the organizational context of which they are a part. The way such integration occurs is by means of value conversion and by arranging decisions in such a way that individuals automatically provide input and behave according to their programmed instructions.

For Simon, the individual is and must be totally included in the organization world. Each computer chip adds to communication, and as the electronic stream of information flows, the data that each individual possesses are added together. All of the bits and pieces are activated to produce more speed and accuracy than any one individual could produce alone.

Because they are highly discrete entities individuals are not capable of collective action.[77] Organizations perform the function of helping individuals transcend their isolation by transforming values into premises for them. Thus converted, organizational premises are objective values that apply to everyone and as such have ethical content. They become the shoulds and oughts by which people order their behavior and take direction. Value premises are the channels by which everyone must operate. "The decision-making process must start with some ethical premise that is taken as 'given.' "[78] For Simon, just as for Chester Barnard, the organization becomes a "moral" system that inculcates individuals and provides them with ethical character—qualities they would not have on their own.

Once value channels of organizations are established, there is no need to "motivate" individuals to "behave" according to organizational norms, as the human relations school would recommend. To "change individual behavior, you do not have to change individuals, in the sense of altering their personalities or teaching them human relations skills. Instead," says Simon, "you change the premises of their decisions."[79]

These premises are to be found in the "vocabulary" of the organization, the structure of communication, rules and regulations and standard programs—in short, the structural aspects.[80] Controlling the premises of decisions allows for what Perrow calls "unobtrusive control," namely, the control of the cognitive premises underlying action.[81]

Perrow claims that the "control of . . . the subordinate *voluntarily* restricts the range of stimuli that will be attended to . . . and the range of alternatives that would be considered."[82] These internalized premises induce an employee to be "well-controlled. . . . He or she can be trusted to make more of his or her own decisions."[83] But these decisions are always in the service of the owner's goals. Furthermore, states Perrow, we often look on such unobtrusive controls as benign, using such terms as "socialization, or culture, or community norms, thus making it both sanitary and somehow independent of the organization. But we could just as well label premise setting as indoctrination, brainwashing, manipulation, or false consciousness."[84]

In spite of the fact that one does not have to change individual behavior, however, organizations do just that. Organizations mold human character to conform to the premises of organizational decisions. These premises, says Simon,

> inject into the very nervous systems of the organization members the criteria of decisions that the organization wishes to employ . . . It enables him to make decisions by himself as the organization *would like him to decide*.[85] (Emphasis added)

What is astounding about Simon's insights is the conclusion he reached about the relationship between organization and reason. Not only does organization make decisions, but it reasons. It is the bearer of rationality. Individuals are granted their reason by organizations. Reason, then, is not an invariate attribute of the human psyche. Rather, reason is a component of *organization*. Reason can be acquired only by becoming a part of an organization and allowing oneself to be molded by its premises. It is organization, said Simon, and not something intrinsic to the human character "that permits the individual to approach reasonably near to objective rationality."[86]

Individual human beings who exist outside of an organization cannot be considered rational beings. "It is *impossible*," said Simon, "for the behavior of a single, isolated individual to reach any high degree of rationality" (emphasis added).[87] In other words, an individual outside of the environment of organizations that mold his character, provide him with the premises of decision, give him information, help him rank alternatives, channel communication,

and bestow the contexts in which decision making can occur will not be rational at all. "Human rationality," said Simon, "gets its higher goals and integrations from the institutional setting in which it operates and by which it is molded."[88]

It is in organizations that individuals can claim to be rational beings. "The behavior patterns that we call organizations are *fundamental* to the achievement of human rationality in any broad sense. *The rational individual is, and must be, an organized and institutionalized individual*" (emphasis added).[89]

But Simon makes it clear that *individual* humans will never become fully rational. Only organizations, because they are capable of converting subjective values into objective, factual premises and can process information so quickly and efficiently, and search for alternatives in a more complete fashion, are entities that embody *authentic* rationality. Simon says:

> The limits of rationality have been seen to derive from the inability of the human mind to bring to bear upon a *single decision* all the aspects of value, knowledge, and behavior that would be relevant. The pattern of human choice is often more nearly a stimulus-response pattern than a choice among alternatives.[90] (Emphasis added)

Individuals are not rational actors but "behave" much like animals whose behavior must take the form of the requirements of organizations.[91]

It should be clear by now that the aim of organization is the total integration and inclusion of individuals into its premises. Organization tends to assume more and more qualities of the human character and, according to Simon, even characteristics that transcend those of humanity. Organization becomes human culture. Organization no longer is a tool serving human ends; it is itself the end, and humans are the means by which organization functions. Organization has supplanted individuals, and to the extent that an organization forms a total social milieu, individuals for their own good must conform.

Simon was accurate about organizational systems. He saw them more clearly perhaps than anyone since Max Weber. In agreement with Weber, Simon concluded that *modernity* originated with the invention of complex organizations. If we conceive of modernity as the rationalization of social action, then we must mark the real advent of human rationality with the advent or organization. The problem with Simon's conclusions, however, is that he, unlike Weber, had little argument with the systems that he described so well. Reading Simon critically provides us with unusual insight. If we are alert to the dangers of organization, we can observe how organizations treat individuals as "things," as objects that "behave," and we can become aware of how people are induced to think and believe as organizations would have them do. We may understand why it is difficult for individuals to maintain their values, beliefs, or integrity once they become part of the organizational information processing system.

Finally, we must recognize the deceitful implications of Simon's observations. Organizations, in reality, cannot grant an individual his or her reason. To the extent that people allow artificial systems such as organizations to determine their values, premises, and decision-making ability, people confer rationality on organizations and rescind their own ability to be rational and ethical creatures.

Capitulation to organization, therefore, means the demise of individual reason in the classical sense of one's ability to impute meaning and ethics into one's decisions, the undermining of authentic human action, and the loss of real decision-making power. Humans become objects stripped of the characteristics of authentic humanity. They concede those characteristics or qualities to the artificial organizational machine and those in control of it.

The Contingency School

By the 1960s the United States had recovered from World War II and had entered an era of expansion, growth, and development. Technology, particularly sophisticated computers and "space age" materials, progressed rapidly. At the center of this progress were organizations. Many of the newer organizations in this "high tech" world oriented to research and development needed to be open to change, capable of fitting in to new market niches. Relationships between government and the economy were closer and more integrated.

Organizational theorists began using a social "ecological systems" theory of organizational design, borrowing concepts from biology to explain the organizational phenomenon. The organization is considered to be a living system that is adaptable to its environment. They are "open" systems that obtain inputs, use information, make decisions, have outputs, and interact freely with their environments. If any part of this organismic system becomes dysfunctional, according to this model, the entire organizational system can be expected to reflect this dysfunction.

Organizations vary or are *contingent* on a number of factors. It is from this notion that the contingency school takes its name. The answer to the question, What is the best structure, size, and leadership style for an organization? is, It all depends.[92] While all organizations have similarities, no two organizations are exactly alike, just as no two humans are exactly alike. Each must fit and adapt to the conditions in which it finds itself and find a niche in the wider organizational environment.

This ecological systems model is a dynamic one. Organizations are seen as artificial constructs as in the bureaucratic model, but they have the qualities of an organism, as in the human relations school. An organization is "rational," as in the decision-making school. But unlike the decision-making school, an organization is a growing entity that exploits resources, changes, and develops.

Contingency-oriented organizational theorists using social ecological metaphors are developing the building blocks for "anatomy" and "physiology" of organizational design. They are constructing an entirely new species of social "organism." For example, in 1967, James D. Thompson developed a number of propositions, or what he calls "a conceptual inventory," by which organizations operate.[93] In addition, a number of contingency-based theories of leadership in the past twenty years have been developed; many of these were described in chapter 4. Among them are Fred Fiedler's Contingency Theory, and Paul Hersey and Kenneth Blanchard's Situational Leadership.[94]

Stephen Robbins has developed some understandings of a contingency model of organizational design using theories developed by a number of organizational psychologists and behaviorists. For example, Robbins identifies eleven kinds of organizational structures, each of which has a different combination of complexity, formalization, and centralization.[95] Emery and Trist, working in the arena of organizational environments, discovered at least four subtypes of organizational environments: placid-random, placid-clustered, disturbed-reactive, and turbulent field.[96] Organization psychologists, among them Abraham Maslow, Fredrick Herzberg, and Douglas McGregor, to name just a few, have developed numerous theories of motivation.

Contingency theory is in its infancy, but ultimately may prove to be the strongest and most important organization theory. It will also be the most complex. For example, Rensis Likert, in his "science-based theory," lists "forty-two aspects of organizations and for each one he indicates its values under each of four systems."[97] Without much difficulty you could probably develop a list of twenty to thirty components of organizations. It is likely that many of these components have subcomponents. Any one of these factors can vary depending on the addition of another factor. The number of combinations and possibilities of variations given the differences in components of organizations is virtually infinite. To understand how each component varies in relation to other components and to develop a theory of organizational design appropriate to varying conditions is a monumental task.

Those who work in social administration are at a stage of discovering and standardizing its language, its components, and some of its interrelationships.[98] Ultimately, the computer will assist in providing a range of different organizational designs based on emerging understanding of organizational dynamics.

What Does It All Mean?

Bureaucratic organizations were orginally thought of as hierarchically structured closed systems or machine tools in which humans were "cogs." The human relations school helped us see that humans needed to be treated differently than simple parts or components. People have needs, values, and feelings that must be recognized. Organization was seen as an organic entity. While the human relations school never fully exploited the ramifications of the "organic" model, it firmly planted the concept that organizations were in a sense "alive." They were conceived of as enlarged versions of man, open systems adaptable to their environments.

Herbert Simon, using systems thinking, blended both bureaucratic and human relations models into a "computer" conception of organizations that are "rational," gather and process information, and make decisions. They are cognitive systems. Individuals are totally included in and receive their rationality from this gigantic information processing system.

The contingency school extends this model to its limits using an ecological approach. The organization not only "thinks," but also is a living organism in which individuals are viewed as cells. Organizations interact, adapt, grow, fill niches, expand, and evolve into complex, interlocking, interconnected living ecological systems.

While these theories increase our understanding of organizations, they have disguised and often unrecognized limitations that reinforce a destructive and self-fulfilling source of social control and power. We tend to be unaware that "organizations in today's market society are necessarily deceitful."[99]

Ralph Hummel observes, for example, that the process of reification leads to a "dwindling of consciousness to the point where humans forget they have made their world."[100] Theorists endow organizations with attributes more compelling and powerful than the human beings who compose them. In organizational life humans are denied "opportunities for engaging in full social relationships, in we-relationships, and in the mutual construction of new solutions to individual problems."[101] People become dependent upon organizations, and they are induced to believe that life would be unthinkable and survival impossible without them.[102] People are taught to "live comfortably within a contrived reality"[103] as if that reality were authentic and meaningful for human life.

Alberto Guerreiro Ramos adds to this critique by observing that "current organizational theory is naive."[104] Organization theories are "not necessarily wrong: they are simply insufficient."[105] For example, many organization theorists lead us to believe that modern organizational society is "historically typical,"[106] that is, human associated life has always been organized and rationalized. People often do not understand that modern society is unprecedented because "no other society uses the criterion of economizing as the standard of human existence."[107] In all social systems preceding our own "the economic order [was] merely a function of the social order in which it was contained. Neither under tribal, or feudal, or mercantile conditions was there . . . a separate economic system in society."[108] "It is only our Western societies that quite recently turned man into an economic animal."[109] Organization is the tool by which this transformation takes place, the means by which social action is converted into rationally organized action.

Organizations induce humans to become factors of production[110] who behave according to utilitarian constraints of modern organizational life. "Students become the 'products' of universities. Workers become the 'tools' of management, and individuals holding roles within an institution become subsystems performing functions within a system—functionaries."[111] Organizations

> deceive both their members and their clients, inducing them to believe not only that what they produce is desirable, but also that their existence is vital to the interest of the society at large.[112]

Where people have not been "socialized to adopt the collective orientation"[113] of organization, they "must be changed so that they will not only want more things, but will have the skills necessary to produce them."[114]

Modern complex organization requires a "new personality type" to meet its demands.[115] Organization attempts to create a new, inhuman personality without values, feelings, or independent action unless officially approved and recognized by the organizational processing system. This new personality type is "docile,"[116] as Simon asserts, "infinitely moldable if only the right organizational structures can be discovered, designed and applied."[117] "Modern man," advises Thompson, "needs to learn to be comfortable with impersonality."[118]

Modern organizational theory would lead us to believe that organizations are accountable to and are shaped by the larger society in which they exist. In this view, organization theory "goes astray."[119] In fact, says Perrow, "the most significant failure of all organization theory [is] its failure to see *society* as adaptive to organizations.[120]

> The dominant organizations . . . institutionalize on their own terms to create the environments they desire, shape the existing ones, and define which sections of [society] they will deal with.[121]

The organization must be seen today as "defining, creating and shaping its environment,"[122] not the other way around. They have a "protean ability to shape society."[123]

> Society is adaptive to organizations, to the large, powerful organizations controlled by a few, often overlapping leaders. To see these organizations as adaptive to a "turbulent," dynamic, ever-changing environment is to indulge in fantasy.[124]

According to Victor Thompson, people need to learn to become comfortable with impersonality.

In essence, organization becomes our society and forms the very culture in which we exist.[125] Organization, as Presthus has commented, *is* our social environment.

Because they are so much a part of our social world, and provide us with so many goods and services, organizational systems are inclined to be seen as beneficent and benign instruments for social good, neutral technological apparatus under the control of their owners.

In reality, organizations are not simply benign instruments. They are systems in which people become totally embedded and from which they take their higher norms and values. So overwhelming is the influence, power, and control inherent in complex organizational systems that ultimately they swallow up the individual. Not only does organization mold human personality, but it shapes society as a whole. People have become factors of production, who surrender authentic social action for the confines of artificial, impersonal organizational life.

Action Theory of Social Systems Design

Action theory of macro social work challenges the premises on which organizational theories are based in the light of social work values and principles: society has become a component of the economy, community has become a component of organization, and individuals have become functional parts of organization systems. An action theory recommends that societal systems be designed with the following components:

1. *Multidimensionality.* Unidimensionality is a specific type of socialization by which the individual deeply internalizes the market ethos and acts as if this ethos were the overarching normative standard of the entire spectrum of his or her interpersonal relations.[126] In contrast, humans have a variety of needs, values, interests, abilities, and personality functions. A multidimensional social system would take into account the variety of forms of human experience. Multidimensionality aims not only for productivity and utility but also for maximization of human potential.

2. *Scope.* Market-oriented organizational systems should continue to play an important role in society, but they need to be restricted in size, function, and utility to allow other forms of human associated life, including community, to take their legitimate places in the social environment.

3. *Multiplicity of system designs.* A multiplicity of social system designs including but not limited to complex market-oriented organizations need to be conceptualized and implemented to provide creative social options for people. Of importance is the development of a variety of social systems that provide for authenticity, human actualization, meaning, and self-expression. Human actualization, for example, "can never be undertaken in a single type of organization."[127] Communes, neighborhood arts and theater groups, cultural associations, cooperative organizations, self-help groups, and religious communities all provide models of different arrangements to be considered.

4. *Choice.* Mechanisms need to be devised to protect human integrity and self-determination so that people are not deprived of personal choice or relieved of humanity in exchange for the opportunity to earn a living.

5. *Actualization.* In modern organizational society, "the more the job is of an economizing nature, the less its operational prescriptions leave its holders room for personal actualization."[128] An action theory of social systems design would providing individuals with escape routes from unidimensionality by allowing training, education, and option creation.

6. *Control.* Systems must be devised to allow individuals to assert control over particular aspects of their organizational existence rather than capitulate to forces of organizational domination.

7. *Value-laden.* Values, as inherent and necessary components of the human psyche, need to be recognized and affirmed in social systems design. The right and importance of individual value expression in organizations as well as outside of organizational existence should be recognized.

8. *Communal precedence.* Community as a cher-

ished and necessary form of natural human association should take precedence over artificial, contrived, instrumental forms of association where the two interact. Organizations should be components of the human communities in which they reside, not the reverse, as occurs today.

9. *Two-way communication.* Organizations tend to recognize unidirectional communication from the top down. While one way communication is efficient, action social work theory asserts that multidirectional communication, particularly that in which mutuality, perception checking, feedback, and personal affirmation and validation are necessary. Ways in which two-way or multiple directional communication can be effective in organizations should be explored.

10. *Creativity.* Action theory affirms and respects the individual's capacity to shape and construct his or her social environment and the systems that compose that environment. Opportunities and mechanisms to create and design and experience a variety of social systems should be provided.

11. *Socially marginal.* Social work needs to be particularly concerned with those people who are unable to compete in today's utilitarian, technological society. These people "subsist at the fringe of a social system. They are normless, rootless, unable to shape their life according to a personal project."[129] They are the marginalized, indigent, mentally incapacitated, homeless, homebound elderly, and criminal offenders. They are dependent upon the social systems designed for them and must be treated with dignity and compassion. Insofar as they are capable, inclusion, and not exclusion, should be the norm.

12. *Public good.* The instrumental, utilitarian, rational character of complex organizations results in the achievement of predetermined ends. "Therefore, questions like the 'good' of man or society have no place in the area of rational debate. Rational man is unconcerned with the ethical nature of ends per se. He is a calculative being intent only on accurately finding adequate means to accomplish goals."[130] Action theory would release people from subservience to private systems and provide opportunity for consideration of wider public good and implementing social systems for a public purpose.

Conclusion

There is no doubt that modern complex organizations are among the most important phenomena of our time—both for good as well as for ill. The importance of modern organization does not lie only in the speed, efficiency, and the marvelous increase in productivity, communication, technology, and decision making of our world. Nor does the importance of organizations lie merely in the fact that our life chances, opportunities, standards of living, careers, and livelihood depend on complex organization.

The importance of bureaucracy as the "rationalization of social relationships" is a fundamental shift in the way we relate to one another, the way we think, and the way our lives are conducted. Organizations are countervailing systems of power, instruments of modern technology. They are shapers of our society and its future. Modern complex organization is, therefore, a common and unprecedented referent for human associated life today, and it is a social phenomenon that macro social workers cannot ignore.

Many of the struggles experienced by modern pluralistic and third world communities are due to the overwhelming countervailing power of organizations. It is against the established "power structure," a euphemism for the system of complex, interlocking organizations, that many of the struggles for human rights have been fought. Community developers and social activists, therefore, "organize" powerless groups because, in part, it is only by means of organization that those in control of business and political organizations respond. Individual laborers, civil rights activists, and women were ineffective until they became "organized." Social planners try to even out power relations, goal setting and inclusion of those who may have been left out of decision-making arenas by the use of organizations "with which they work not only to seek certain ends, but also to reproduce, or refashion, social and political relations"[131] in ways that are more equitable, just, and humane.

Organizations are also a means of providing and developing social welfare programs and services for people. Program developers serve the interests of those who are not well organized, who cannot articulate their goals, and who do not have powerful organizations to press their cases. Macro social workers administer social agencies, working by means of organizations to provide efficient and effective service delivery. Finally, social workers apply methods and skills to help dysfunctional organizations become healthier environments for employees and clients. It is vital, therefore, that every macro social worker understand as thoroughly as possible the dynamics and theory of organizational phenomena.

KEY CONCEPTS

ubiquitous
multinational
transnational
influential
personal identity
powerful
complex organization
artificial
intentional
contrived
social tools
accomplish goals
perform work
organizational society
bureaucratic school
scientific management
sine ira et studio
nepotism
amicism
favoritism
human relations school
Hawthorne experiments
reification
decision-making school
bounded rationality
satisfice
unobtrusive control
contingency theory
action theory
multidimensionality
unidimensionality
actualization

QUESTIONS FOR DISCUSSION

1. To what extent do you think we control organizations? To what extent are we controlled by them?
2. In the process of helping us achieve our goals, is there a danger that organizations will, at the same time, reduce our humanity?
3. While organizations have enabled our society to become massive and complex, to what extent will artificial, contrived social relationships become important in human life in the future?
4. What responsibility has an organization and those who own and operate it to those who work for it, to the community in which it resides, and to society at large?
5. Forester says that we can "generally expect that organizational actors will deter cooperative, well-organized community-based organizations that might press to meet social needs to the detriment of concentrations of private capital. They distract public attention from social needs and instead focus on the promotion of individual consumption."[136] What does this statement mean? What are its implications for macro social work practice?
6. Social work is a field that prizes altruism, compassion, self-actualization, authentic personal relationships, and two-way communication. Organizations, on the other hand, tend to eliminate altruism and compassion, require impersonal relationships, and use one-way communication. Will dilemmas occur as social workers insert personal feelings and values in an impersonal organizational system? What difficulties would you expect? How would you cope with these discrepancies?

ADDITIONAL READING

Barnard, Chester I. *The Functions of the Executive*. Cambridge, MA: Harvard University Press, 1938.

Etzioni, Amitai. *Modern Organizations*. Englewood Cliffs, NJ: Prentice-Hall, 1964.

Hummel, Ralph. *The Bureaucratic Experience*. New York: St. Martin's Press, 1977.

Katz, David, and Robert L. Kahn. *The Social Psychology of Organizations.* New York: Wiley, 1978.

Ott, J. Steven. *The Organizational Culture Perspective.* Homewood, IL: Irwin, 1989.

Perrow, Charles. *Complex Organizations: A Critical Essay.* 2d ed. Glenview, IL: Scott, Foresman, 1979.

Presthus, Robert. *The Organizational Society.* Rev. ed. New York: St. Martin's Press, 1978.

Ramos, Alberto Guerreiro. *The New Science of Organizations.* Toronto: University of Toronto Press, 1981.

Ruitenbeek, Hendrik M., ed. *The Dilemma of Organizational Society.* New York: Dutton, 1963.

Simon, Herbert. *Administrative Behavior.* New York: Free Press, 1976.

Slater, Philip. *The Pursuit of Loneliness: American Culture at the Breaking Point.* Boston, MA: Beacon Press, 1971.

Taylor, Frederick Winslow. *The Principles of Scientific Management.* New York: Norton, 1947.

Thompson, James D. *Organizations in Action: Social Science Base of Administrative Theory.* New York: McGraw-Hill, 1967.

Thompson, Victor A. *Bureaucracy in the Modern World.* Morristown, NJ: General Learning Press, 1976.

————. *Without Sympathy or Enthusiasm: The Problem of Administrative Compassion.* University: University of Alabama Press, 1975.

Weber, Max. "Bureaucracy." In Hans Gerth and C. Wright Mills, eds., *From Max Weber: Essays in Sociology.* New York: Oxford University Press, 1946.

Weiner, Norman. *Human Use of Human Beings: Cybernetics.* New York: Avon Books, 1967.

Whyte, William H., Jr. *The Organization Man.* New York: Doubleday Anchor, 1958.

EXERCISES

EXERCISE 32:
The Airline Dilemma

John H. Wills, a pilot for American Airlines, will turn sixty this month. He has been a senior pilot for the past twelve years, and is in excellent physical health. His eyesight is still sharp and he feels at the height of his ability. Several times he has averted a disaster that a younger, less experienced pilot might not have. He loves to fly and wants to continue to do the job that he is best at doing and one which he does well.

Yet, Captain Wills is being forced to end his job as a pilot. He has appealed the ruling, but rules are rules. He must retire, even though he has a few good years left, has logged thousands of flying hours, and has an impeccable record, better than the younger pilot who will replace him.

The reason is because on October 31, 1990, a three judge Federal Appeals Court upheld a thirty-year-old Federal Aviation Administration rule that forces commercial airline pilots to retire at age sixty, in spite of the Federal Government's stance against age discrimination.

The agency contends that older pilots face "skill deterioration" and greater risk of "physical incapacitation." Consequently, they are more likely to be involved in accidents, even though this may not be true in individual cases.

Many older pilots, and an increasing number of medical experts, on the other hand, maintain that aging pilots in their sixties often are in better physical and mental condition than some in their thirties, forties, or fifties.

However, the rules must be applied uniformly and impersonally across the board. Captain Wills will retire, not because he has become incompetent, but because the rules say so. While the FCC allows for exceptions, the agency has never granted one.

1. Is it appropriate to bar airline pilots from flying a large commercial airplane just because they have reached the age of sixty?
2. What is more important: the even application of rules that apply to all or taking individual differences into account?
3. Is the real issue passenger safety or can you think of other reasons for requiring airline pilots to retire at sixty?

EXERCISE 33:
Alternative Solutions

Four theorists, Charles Perrow, Alberto Guerreiro Ramos, Donald Shon, and Victor A. Thompson, propose solutions to the problem of organization in our modern mass society. Examine each of these positions. With which do you agree? With which do you disagree? What

EXERCISES

are the underlying premises of each alternative solution? Where do you think each solution would lead us in the future? What alternative solution can you think of that is better than those presented here? Might a combination of these or other ideas provide a solution?

Charles Perrow

Charles Perrow gives us a choice between changing the economic system in whose service complex organizations operate or dealing with the issue of who controls the organization.

> Critics, then, of our organizational society, whether they are radicals of the left emphasizing spontaneity and freedom, the new radical right demanding their own form of radical decentralization, or the liberal in between speaking of the inability of organizations to be responsive to community values, had best turn to the key issue of who controls the varied forms of power generated by organizations rather than flail away at the windmills of bureaucracy. If we want our material civilization to continue as it is, and are not ready to change the economic system along the drastic ways of, say, China, we will have to have large-scale bureaucratic enterprises in the economic, social, and governmental areas.[132]

Alberto Guerreiro Ramos

Alberto Ramos promotes a theory of "organizational delimitation." Recognizing that organizations are permanent institutions in our social landscape that our civilization cannot

do without, Ramos suggests that we restrict them to specific roles and to arenas where they are appropriate, and not let them encroach on the rest of society, thereby leaving space for authentic community, social action, and ethical reason in human life. Rather than allow one overarching social system to dominate every aspect of our existence, Ramos recommends that we develop several different forms of human associated life.

> We must learn to develop many kinds of micro-social systems within the overall social fabric. We must limit the role of conventional organization in our lives so as to leave room for authentic interpersonal transactions.[133]

Donald Shon

Donald Shon takes a systems approach to the problem of organizations. He assumes that every system is composed of various parts. When one component part is changed, the rest of the system will, of necessity, also change. The most important component of any system is its underlying premise, or its theory base. If one changes the theory base of the system, then one can change the system itself. Based on Shon's recommendation, social workers would need to develop an alternative theory of social systems design more congruent with the realities and needs of the human condition.

> The theory is a core dimension. When the theory is changed the organization may be critically disrupted in four ways. The change may affect (1) its self-interpretation, (2) its goals, (3)

the nature and scope of its operations, and (4) its transactions with its environment.[134]

Victor A. Thompson

Victor A. Thompson asserts that organization is a necessary human tool, one that we cannot do without. In fact, modern civilization is based on and is better off with organizations and the premises on which they are founded. Rather than attempt to disrupt or change organizations, the solution to the problem of impersonality and dehumanization is for people to give up their fantasy of "personal relations" and adopt the new, modern organizational system and all the benefits it offers.

> The individual needs to be socialized to adopt the collective orientation in all his dealing with economic and governmental organizations (actually with "bureaucratic" organizations). . . . Modern man needs to learn to be comfortable with impersonality. All this amounts to is giving a high value to instrumentalism, to the achievement of established goals. . . . I expect abstract systems (impersonal systems of rules, artificial systems) to become more acceptable. They will be the source of more reinforcements, comparatively, than the favors of families and other natural systems. . . . Man and his institutions will fit one another better. A perfect fit we can never expect short of genetic or behavioral engineering. Such engineering is a long way off. We have not yet decided how to select either the engineers or the designs.[135]

CHAPTER 10

Becoming a Social Planner:
Making the Good Society

The tragedy of the commons is a modern tragedy in which the rational pursuit of private self-interest resists planning and . . . overrides the public good—whether that good is land, the ocean, the air, or even people.

It is, indeed, obvious that our view can never reach far enough for us to be certain that any action will produce the best possible effects. We must be content . . . [that] even if we can never settle with any certainty how we shall secure the greatest possible total of good, we try at least to assure ourselves that probably future evils will not be greater than the immediate good.

—G. E. MOORE, *PRINCIPIA ETHICA*

The theory of planning must include some theory of the society in which planning is institutionalized.

—JOHN DYCKMAN[1]

The essence of dramatic tragedy is not unhappiness. It resides in the solemnity of the remorseless working of things.

—GARRETT HARDIN[2]

IDEAS IN THIS CHAPTER

The Tragedy of the Commons[3]

The tragedy of the commons happens in this way. It begins with a pasture open to all. Each herdsman may keep as many cattle on the commons as he or she wishes. Normally, such an arrangement works when tribal wars, poaching, and disease keep the numbers of cattle and people well below the ability of the land to contain them all. Finally, however, the day comes when technology equalizes the ability of the open pasture to carry the burden. Wars are negotiated, diseases are cured, and hardier strains of cattle are introduced. At this point, the effectiveness of the commons degenerates into tragedy.

As a rational actor, each herdsman wants to maximize his or her self-interest and asks, "What is the benefit to me of adding one more animal to my herd?" Since the herdsman receives all of the profits from the sale of an animal, he will receive a positive utility of +1. On the other hand, adding one more animal will result in the land being overgrazed. Because the effects of overgrazing are shared by all, however, the costs of overgrazing for any herdsman making this decision is only a fraction of −1. Therefore, for a rational decision-maker, it is only sensible to add another animal to his herd, and another, and another.

This conclusion is reached by each herdsman sharing the commons. Each rational actor is locked into a way of thinking that compels him or her, in a world that is limited, to add to his or her herd without limit. Therein lies the tragedy of the commons. "Ruin is the destination toward which all men rush, each pursing his own best interest in a society that believes in the freedom of the commons. Freedom in a commons becomes ruin to all."[4]

The tragedy of the commons is a modern tragedy in which the rational pursuit of private self-interest resists planning and, in a world of high technology, overrides the public good—whether that good is land, the ocean, the air, or even people.

Introduction

Macro social workers are vitally concerned about the tragedy of the commons, about preserving and protecting the public good and the public interest when that interest is trampled by private self-interest ruthlessly pursued. It is out of this concern that macro social workers become engaged in the arena of social planning.

This chapter begins by locating the major issue of whether or not to plan, and provides a short history of social planning in America. Next, planning in general and social planning in particular are defined and what social planners do is described. How social planners practice their method is explored, along with different ways to approach social planning. Several social planning techniques are explained. Because planning is fraught with controversy, an action theory of social planning is suggested.

To Plan or Not to Plan: A Short History of Social Planning in the United States

Planning is a "process of selecting and designing a rational course of collective action to achieve a future state of affairs."[5] It includes calculating contingencies, maximizing resources, minimizing costs, and achieving goals in the most efficient manner. Planning extends from planning a wardrobe, a daily activity, or a term paper to utopian planning of entire societies, cities, and communities.

To Plan . . .

When you think about what you want to do in any one day, you are planning. If you have a goal that you are trying to reach or something that you want to accomplish, you begin to plan for it. Things happen when you plan. All modern social systems exist by planning. Large business organizations expend a great deal of energy planning and forecasting. Businesses plan marketing and research strategies and new products. Governments develop water resources plans, environmental plans, and land use plans. They plan highway construction, strategic defense, and space exploration.

An example of international planning was the Marshall Plan, a means by which those nations that

experienced massive destruction during World War II rebuilt themselves. Today, the European Common Market develops cooperative economic plans regulating and providing fiscal arrangements for its member countries.

If social workers want to accomplish something for people, they need to plan. Macro social workers engage in the process of social planning to ensure that services are provided on behalf of those who are in need.

. . . Or Not to Plan

Planning is not the only way we conduct our affairs, however. Things also happen if we leave decisions to chance, taking whatever comes along, or if we act spontaneously. There is a great deal to say for *not* planning. In fact, while planning is a very human activity, to allow oneself to experience life unfettered by prearrangement is also what it means to be human. Life would be dull if everything were organized, systematized, and planned in advance. Leaving things unplanned is liberating and exciting.

In fact, there are many who advocate that not planning at all, especially in the economy, is the best way to operate. The economy should be free from governmental interference. Then, not only will the economy regulate itself automatically, but it will produce an optimal amount of goods and services in the most efficient way and at the least cost. In the aggregate everyone will be better off if the economy is allowed to be free from planning and government regulation.

Planning in America

American society is a combination of planning and freedom from planning. The founding fathers were the first people in history to plan a new nation from scratch. They were acutely aware that while plans provide a direction, once they are made and become binding, they tend to prescribe a course or path that eliminates other options.

As a result, many American settlers held the view that individual liberty was too important to be harnessed by a pre-ordained blueprint. The social plan we call our Constitution was actually a way of insuring that choice would not be limited by a few people who could impose their own plans or ideas onto the populace. It was a social plan that prevented the few who hold power to plan for everyone else. We call this the "balance of power."

Many other societies, in contrast, have opted for governments of limited choice. They have allowed autocrats, dictators, and tyrants to rule their society. Some of these leaders have been well-intentioned and have tried their best to move their countries toward their vision of good. Others have exploited their nations in their own self-interest. Whether these leaders have been benevolent or not, the results have been the same. The people were left without power, choice, or options. They could not plan their own destiny. They had to accept a social system that often told them what to believe, what was true or false, or what they could and could not do. We can all think of examples of such oppression. Nazi Germany before its defeat, the USSR before its collapse, and the Roman Catholic church before the Reformation are only three of a long list.

In the minds of the planners of our nation, therefore, there were three areas where people should be particularly free from oppression. First, people should be free from political oppression. Second, they should have the opportunity to pursue their own private economic interests rather than have a centralized authority determine what their interests ought to be. Third, people should not have a system of religious belief forced on them. Liberty was conceived in political, economic, and religious terms.

Instead of government holding a monopoly on political power, therefore, individual citizens were to hold power, and government was to be subject to the will of the populace. Government was intended to be a sort of referee ensuring that individuals could carry out their own legitimate economic interests. Finally, religion was to be forever separated from the state, preventing the state from imposing a belief system on the populace and ensuring that minority groups would not impose their beliefs on the public at large.

As America grew, the social and political environment evolved a new phenomenon unanticipated by the framers of the Constitution—a complex, modern system of interlocking organizations. After the Civil War, gigantic corporations acquired enormous wealth and unregulated power, eventually controlling the political process and dominating local, state, and even the federal government.

As organizations concentrated economic and political power during the Progressive Era in American history (1880 to 1910), macro social workers became concerned that economic freedom had become mere license of the rich and powerful to exploit the poor and powerless. The inability of government to adequately assess and develop plans for social welfare meant that social problems were unaddressed, social issues were unattended, and people failed to obtain needed services and programs.

Social Planning

Concerned that the common man would become crushed, macro social workers began to press government to develop *social plans* to organize and place the provision of social welfare services on a more rational and secure basis. They wished to ensure that the poor and disadvantaged would not be excluded and that equity and access to opportunity would be guaranteed.

The Charity Organization Society movement, for example, largely utilized methods and principles of social planning as a basis of action. Originating in 1877 "in response to rapid urbanization and industrialization and the effects of the Great Depression of 1873,"[6] the COS movement developed a "science of charity" based on "rationality, efficiency, foresight, and planning."[7] Committed to the principle that "poverty could be cured and prevented if its causes could be discovered and removed,"[8] it attempted "to achieve some rationality in social welfare by managing the entire voluntary system based on the most respected social science principles of the time."[9]

"Heavily influenced by nineteenth century moralism and by Social Darwinism, [the COS movement] was basically secular, optimistic, and rationalistic, believing in the capacity of persons to change and the obligation of persons to move themselves, others, and the society toward perfection,"[10] resulting in the "earliest professional community organization in social work."[11] "The origins of social work involvement with social planning . . . can [therefore] be traced to attempts at social welfare planning . . . in the early Charity Organization Societies,"[12] which are "generally credited with being the beginning of modern social work."[13]

From its inception, social work and social planning were seen as largely synonymous, having common roots and common methods. For example, through the organization of private charities and interagency coordination, the COS movement affirmed that a collective and cooperative approach to the problems of poverty could be made, avoiding duplication, and ensuring collaboration, resource coordination, and efficiency.[14]

A direct descendant of the planning efforts of the COS movement, "the first community welfare council was founded from these roots in 1908. . . . [Its] function was coordination of voluntary services."[15] This soon expanded to include serious planning efforts at the grassroots level. Arthur Dunham, for example, defines a community welfare council as

> a local association of citizens, agencies, or both which unites citizen interest and professional skill in planning for and action on social and health problems. It seeks to determine current and emerging health and welfare needs, develop plans to meet them, and carry these plans to fruition.[16]

Soon, councils of social agencies sprang up in many cities throughout the country, continuing the momentum toward coordination and planning initiated by the COS movement, emphasizing "efficiency, centralization, and specialization in the planning and delivery of services by private agencies within the community."[17]

By World War I, centralized fund-raising agencies called "Community War Chests," were developed to "centralize planning and administration and achieve greater efficiency in utilization of community resources."[18] These agencies placed "emphasis on rational planning for agency use of these funds . . . [and] efficiency, planning, and willingness to respond to community priorities."[19]

The community chest and council movements represented "early attempts to assess community needs and to argue for rational decision making in projecting the development and location of community agencies"[20] by citizen volunteers and professional social work planners. So important were these councils that the influential Lane Report of 1939 cited the community welfare council as the only urban community organization on the scene that organized resources to meet community needs.[21]

As important as they were in social planning, coordination, and private charity, the efforts of councils of social agencies and united fund raising were not sufficient to meet the massive relief needs created by the economic collapse of the nation during the Great Depression. With the New Deal of President Franklin Delano Roosevelt, "the federal government assumed a greater role in social planning"[22] and in the provision of relief and in the development of social programs. Social planning became one of the weapons in the federal government's arsenal of social programs such as the Social Security system, which "required a projection of the number of and size of beneficiary claims and revenues,"[23] and any number of programs involving cooperative and coordinated effort. Since then, social planning has assumed a larger and clearer role in governmental social service provision, with the social planner becoming a more central, if technically oriented, professional.[24]

Housing and Social Planning

The federal government first encouraged community planning, with the introduction of the Housing Act of 1949,[25] which included the idea of a "community master plan," a planning concept that achieved broad public support.[26] As planning was becoming a central tool of government in assessing need and developing social programs, it was seen as too important an endeavor to be left to professionals alone. As a result, the Housing Act was amended in 1954 requiring applicants to show evidence that urban renewal projects had fulfilled code enforcement, relocation of displaced residents, financing,[27] and most importantly citizen participation in the planning process.[28]

> This participation involved the appointment of a city-wide advisory committee, generally composed of civic leaders, to work with planners. Representation of the poor, who were usually most affected by renewal activities, was neither mandatory nor commonplace. As experience with resident opposition to renewal increased, agencies began to give greater consideration to the involvement of neighborhood residents, although . . . citizen participation in urban renewal was modest.[29]

The Housing and Community Development Act of 1974 continued to encourage social planning at the local level by requiring citizen participation. The beginning experience with citizen planning involvement with federal housing programs led to greater efforts to include grassroots citizens in social planning in other social arenas.

Social Planning for Mental Health

In the 1950s and early 1960s social work planners and community activists engaged in social reform efforts to improve the nation's mental health system.

> [While] much of it [occurred] in the voluntary sector, state planners played a critical role because of their delivery of mental health services. . . . They tirelessly worked as advocates to provide information about the need for mental health services and the rights of mental patients. They were also effective campaigners and social activists and viewed their roles as most effective when stimulating the public welfare sector to provide more and better services.[30]

Supported by President John Kennedy, these efforts paid off with the passage in 1963 of the Comprehensive Community Health Act, which encouraged planning and development of local mental health services, development of planning boards, and community consultation.[31] More importantly for community-based social work and planning, the Community Mental Health Centers Act of 1963 "made it possible to employ community organizers in service delivery settings,"[32] providing "the first major impetus for agency-based community social work practice in the field of mental health."[33] This was one of the major pieces of legislation that affected social work and social planning. The field of mental health had been restricted to psychiatric social workers providing casework in hospital settings. This act replaced institutional care with community-based care through the establishment of community mental health centers, revolutionizing clinical social work, and paving the way for private practice.

Implicitly in the philosophy of community-based mental health care was the importance of advisory councils, which "were to be comprised of providers and consumers of services, and together with the state agency, had the responsibility for inventorying state facilities for the mentally ill and developing state-wide plans for the creation of mental health centers throughout the state."[34] As a result, community organizers and planners were "enabled to work inside the mental health service delivery system . . . operating from a nonmedical model that sought to prevent mental illness through nonclinical services that reflected social goals rather than psychiatric ones."[35] Among these community-based social goals was the

> principle of reliance upon community groups to define issues and problems and to participate in developing services. This principle of citizen participation became the rationale and basis for much community work practice.[36]

Citizen involvement and participation in planning and organizing services "emphasized local and democratic control of social institutions as a means of buttressing the individual's sense of personal control,"[37] a therapeutic goal in and of itself. Empowerment of citizens in the mental health movement included:

> (1) protection of the mentally ill through advocacy; (2) reduction of anomie and social isolation; (3) development of social support systems for patients and families; and (4) the therapeutic effect of social well being.[38]

Among the services that social work mental health planners undertook were "reviewing existing service provisions in a community, identifying unmet needs and initiating actions to meet them, seeing where duplication exists, and trying to achieve a better match between needs and resources."[39] They also provided information, advice, consultation, and training,[40] they were involved extensively with coordinating and planning bodies,[41] and they provided "political action strategies which ranged from mediation or negotiation to advocacy and confrontation."[42] Through all of these organizing efforts, social work mental-health planners held fast to the strategy of citizen participation and empowerment in mental health planning and service delivery.

As a consequence of the Community Mental Health Centers Act, "planning grants were awarded in every state and some 1,500 catchment areas [a regional planning district] were created in the United States. . . . [However,] just as these numbers began to peak, Richard M. Nixon became president"[43] and began to dismantle social service programs. During the Nixon administration in the mid 1970s, "interest in participation had begun to subside on all levels" and in "1973 the 'drift' became a tiderace."[44] Citizen participation in the mental health movement and elsewhere went into remission "and is currently directed toward minimal or token change."[45] "The mental health system [became] essentially a closed one"[46] in which powerful, professional, primarily psychiatric, and bureaucratic institutions used the community mental center legislation to consolidate and expand their interests[47] rather than those of the citizenry at large.

In 1980, at the end of President Carter's administration, the Mental Health Systems Act was passed, which would have provided for more community-based services. "Community organization functions of coordination, representation, advocacy and development were identified in the legislation."[48] However, with the ascendance of Ronald Reagan to the presidency, the act was repealed. Instead, block grants were given to states for mental health, alcohol abuse, and drug abuse, taking initiative for planning away from local communities. In spite of financing cuts, however, community mental health centers remain intact today,[49] testimony to the role of advocacy-based social work planning in the field of mental health.

Planning the "Great Society"

Building on the impetus of citizen participation and community-based social care established by the community mental health movement, "President John F. Kennedy's Council of Economic Advisers began working on antipoverty proposals using recommendations by the President's Committee on Juvenile Delinquency, the Ford Foundation, and various cabinet-level departments"[50] as a guide. Carrying forward the proposals of these groups after President Kennedy's assassination, President Johnson undertook one of the most ambitious campaigns of social change since the New Deal of Franklin Roosevelt. Among them, the Comprehensive Employment and Training Act, National Health Planning and Resources Development Act, and the Economic Opportunity Act "carved out a role for new quasi-public bodies to assume a planning, coordinating role on a municipal or regional basis."[51]

The Economic Opportunity Act (EOA) passed in 1964, often called the War on Poverty, initiated numbers of programs "based on the idea that the economic well-being of the poor could lead to the abolition of poverty if only the poor would take advantage of the opportunities before them."[52]

> Planned by a task force of experts, including some of the nation's leading academics and social scientists, [the War on Poverty] was a make-do, crash program that left a good deal to be desired. However well intentioned, it was badly conceived and, in the opinion of many, bound to fail, primarily because it was designed not to change society but to change its victims. . . . It emphasized not adequate income and job creation . . . but rather education, manpower training, and various social services.[53]

One of these antipoverty programs that did involve community organization and planning was the Community Action Program (CAP). "Community Action Agencies (CAAs) were created to improve public services, mobilize resources, and ensure the contribution of the poor in planning programs which affected them and their neighborhoods."[54] CAAs provided "advocacy for welfare recipients, establishment of day-care and health care, and pressured welfare public housing and other agencies to respond more effectively and equitably to the poor."[55]

An important requirement of CAAs in improving inner cities was " 'maximum feasible participation' by the poor in planning, development, and execution of the programs that the CAAs coordinated or sponsored."[56] While this requirement became highly controversial, the CAAs represented the poor in dealing with bureaucracies, trained individuals for leadership, and "helped institutionalize citizen input concerning federal programs and agencies for all members of society, not just the poor."[57]

In addition to the CAAs, the Demonstration Cities and Metropolitan Development Act of 1966 (the Model Cities Program) was expected to bring "resident groups, business interests, and social welfare agencies together in a planning network for developing the physical and social aspects of the community"[58] as well as increasing the supply of

housing, enhancing the social environment, and improving delivery systems.[59] Cities that qualified in an
initial planning project were provided funds to
change the social environment of the target area
using a benefit/cost analysis and active engagement
of residents in planning and executing the programs.[60]

Planning for Older Americans

Along with planning in mental health and antipoverty programs, social planning was a mode of
social intervention with older Americans. The Older
Americans Act (OAA) of 1965 and its implementation ensured that services to the elderly became the
province of the expert planner.[61] Expert social planning, according to Monk, "emerged as the dominant
form of community practice"[62] with the elderly.

> [Social planning] was, in fact, the cornerstone of the
> aging "networks," a conglomerate of state agencies
> on aging mandated by the OAA and the nearly seven
> hundred Area Agencies on Aging (AAAs). These are
> the local operations more commonly designated as
> county or city departments of senior services.[63]

Under this arrangement, state agencies on aging
were to design programs, coordinate services, and
assess needs. At the local level, the AAAs were required to produce three-year plans, award grants for
services, contract with local providers, and monitor
the implementation and quality of services. "The
AAAs were consequently made responsible for
mounting a continuous process of planning, including definition of service priorities, and development
of a comprehensive system specially designed to improve delivery of services."[64]

Although, according to Monk, these administrative responsibilities

> did not encourage AAAs to engage in open class ad-
> vocacy, their advisory boards had enough latitude to
> become interest-group representatives. . . . Assisted
> by planners with a bent toward policy analysis, com-
> munity advisory boards took a stand on proposed
> legislation, lobbied on behalf of their constituents,
> and maintained a constant watch on trends in pro-
> gram funding.[65]

These efforts paid off in tangible benefits to the
elderly, so that "by the time of the 1971 White House

Conference on Aging the administration's request
for funds to finance the entire act . . . reached the
$30 million mark . . . [and] by 1980 the OAA fund-
ing exceeded $500 million."[66]

With the 1973 amendments to the Older Americans Act, citizen participation in planning gained
further ground when the government spearheaded
broad citizen participation, but five years later, the
1978 amendment signaled the end of an expansion-
ist era in social planning for the elderly and the beginning of a more cautious managerial mandate.[67]
Rather than advocacy and citizen involvement,

> social worker planners in state agencies and local
> AAAs became more involved in scrutinizing pro-
> gram compliance. Writing contracts in the language
> of management by objectives, measuring units of
> service, adjudicating purchase of service agreements,
> negotiating budgets, establishing quality central and
> quality assurance procedures, and evaluating pro-
> gram efficiency became the new expertise of the
> macro-oriented social work.[68]

Lessons to Be Learned

Social planning in the United States has seen a
variety of approaches and results. It has been one of
the major points of entry for macro social workers
into many social programs such as housing, mental
health, poverty, and social services with the elderly.
In addition, the organized efforts inherent in social
planning have provided a means of engaging citizen participation in ways that had not previously
occurred. Social planning has resulted in an expansion of effective social programs in many areas of
need.

In one of these areas, antipoverty, the hastily
planned and overly ambitious programs of the Great
Society failed and resulted in a backlash.[69] "More
than any other program of Johnson's so-called Great
Society, the war on poverty accentuated doubts
about the capacity of social science to plan, and the
government to deliver, ambitious programs of social
betterment."[70] As a result, the ideal of citizen participation, at least in the development of antipoverty
programs, lost much of its appeal.

In retrospect, the demise of antipoverty programs was not so much a failure of planning at the
local level or a reflection on the quality of citizen
participation as it was a result of insufficient plan-

ning and inattention to citizen participation processes that did not allow time for societal changes to take place. The victims of poverty were expected to bear the brunt of change. And, according to several observers, the programs were doomed to fail because of inadequate funding. "In fact," says Trattner,

> Congress appropriated less money each year to combat poverty across the country than was necessary to finance an adequate welfare program in any one of the nation's leading cities. During the first year of the [Economic Opportunity] act's operation, when Mayor John Lindsay said that New York City needed $10 billion annually for five years to solve its welfare problems, Congress allocated around $750 million for the entire nation.[71]

It is important to understand the politics of social planning if we are to be effective in meeting social planning goals. The expansion and contraction of much of the role of social planning in recent American experience can be seen as a result of ideological struggles between administrations that are pledged to greater social engagement and those that are dedicated to shrinking the role of government in social welfare. There continues to be an important role for social planners to advocate for those in need and to encourage citizen participation in the planning process. It is important for the social work profession to support social planning efforts during periods in which a laissez-faire approach to planning is in ascendancy.

What Is Social Planning?

Social planning is the "development, expansion, and coordination of social services and social policies" utilizing rational problem-solving conducted at both the local and societal levels.[72] Social planning is a means by which macro social workers carry out their responsibility to provide for the welfare of society—to ensure that social programs, policies, and services meet people's needs to the greatest extent possible. It is incumbent on social work planners, therefore, to insist that those people who have fewer resources, less power, and little influence be given the opportu-

nity to develop plans for their welfare that can compete on an equal footing—recognition, funding, and entitlement—with plans developed by powerful business and political interests.

Who Are Social Planners?

There are two kinds of social planners. Some social planners are staff specialists working in direct service agencies, case management, group work, and clinical services. Social work planners work closely with the agency executive. They analyze needs, assess services, write grant proposals, conduct research, and make recommendations to help the agency meet the needs of its clientele, adjust agency resources, and adapt services to a changing population.

Social work planners working in direct service agencies often begin their careers as clinicians or counselors, developing interest in social planning as they become involved in wider social work issues. They may have a variety of titles such as planning consultant, staff analyst, planning analyst, mental health or developmental disabilities specialist, or resource developer. Some analyst or planner positions require an MSW degree and some experience, usually in the agency in which they work.

A second type of social planner works for an organization that is exclusively dedicated to social planning. Social planning agencies assess needs, regulate the amount and kinds of services in their service jurisdiction, review and make recommendations for awarding governmental grants, assist in developing new services, and in some cases maintain quality control over services in their mandated arena. Social planning agencies interact with a variety of service providers, agencies, and client organizations, as well as ancillary service systems such as universities, governmental agencies, businesses, and community groups to develop comprehensive plans for their service areas.

Comprehensive health planning agencies, for example, assess health needs and control the number and kind of health related services in a regional area. Area developmental disabilities boards gather information and develop plans that become the bases for the provision of new services and the awarding of governmental grants. They oversee the provision of services and make funding recommendations. Area agencies on aging assess needs of the aged, make recommendations, and formulate plans for provision of services for the elderly.

County planning agencies, mental health advisory boards, human relations commissions, and city planning boards are also devoted to planning services for people. Social work planners in these agencies most often have a planning background or degree in public health or public administration in addition to an MSW degree.

What Do Social Planners Do?

Committed to finding the most rational and feasible solution to social problems, the social planner has a complex role involving gathering empirical facts, organizational politics, and compromise. "Effective planning is the management of change."[73] Social planners are "designers who match technical, rational, aesthetic, and systemic thinking with selected configurations of supporters [and] exercise choices."[74]

Social planners provide expert advice, make assessments, coordinate, and plan services, scanning the social environment of the community for gaps in service provision or areas where services are poorly, inequitably, or ineffectively provided. They attempt to discern where new needs may arise, develop new programs, and strengthen existing ones.

Planning Principles

Social planning includes citizen participation, democracy, and mobilizing values in a particular direction, and is future oriented.

Citizen Participation

Like social activists or community developers, social planners are intimately involved with community betterment through citizen participation in the planning process. Social planners view community members as capable of planning for their future. By engaging in a thoughtful and planned process of

Social planners provide expert advice, make assessments, coordinate, and plan new services where existing services are poorly, inequitably, or ineffectively provided.

change and working with and through political, business, and social institutions, citizens can have a substantial impact on their quality of life. Therefore, a guiding premise of social planning is:

> [In order for an] organized community to adapt to changes in its environment that may affect its survival, it needs to plan for changes in variables which impinge on its ability to grow and develop structures for meeting basic needs.[75]

While community development and social action as modes of intervention at the community level are important, it is social planning that has the greatest potential for empowering people in a community to take direction over their lives. Social planners are armed with rational planning techniques, mandates for citizen participation written into law, and substantive service and program goals in aging, mental health, housing, poverty, child welfare, developmental disabilities, and criminal justice. They can control and fund program services and have entree into economic and governmental systems that community developers and social activists rarely can match.

In addition to strengthening community bonds, "citizen participation in social planning is not only consistent with social work's emphasis on self-determination, but it also increases the number of social services offered and increases utilization."[76] For example, in a study of the impact of citizen participation in housing, Gulati found that it "increased the level of resources and services made available to tenants,"[77] and Aigner found that "citizen participation had a strong impact on amount of money raised through taxation and spent on social services."[78] Social planners

> shape not only documents but also participation; who is contacted, who participates, [and] who persuades whom. . . . Planners . . . shape which facts certain citizens may have, [and] shape the trust and expectations of those citizens. Planners organize cooperation, or acquiescence . . . of public attention: selectively shaping attention to options for action.[79]

Democracy

Social planners must have methods available by which the needs of a community are recognized.

They ensure that resources and services are equitably and fairly distributed.[80] Planners work in and through governmental agencies, commissions, and bureaus, evaluating, arranging for, and funding services on behalf of and in cooperation with community groups. Social planning exists in a milieu of democratic values and processes.

In such a milieu, social work planners and social agencies can be targets of a number of interest groups vying to influence the policy and programmatic outcomes of the planning process. Macro social workers must be skilled in understanding the dynamics of those organizations and their constituents who also seek access to the planning process and who stand to gain from those plans. Planners need to be aware of organized interests who attempt to use the planning process to their private advantage rather than for the public interest at large. A social work planner reaches for

> informed participation that recognizes the rights of others but is skeptical of the purported benevolence of established interests that stand to reap substantial private gains from proposed projects.[81]

Planners work to "anticipate and counteract pressures that stifle public voice, that manipulate democratic processes of consensus-building, and that ignore the many in need so that a few may prosper."[82] Planning must be carried out by means of a deliberative, substantive, and "transformative" democratic process.[83]

Mobilization of Values

Because social work planning is often at the center of competing interests, social workers must have particular values that will guide them in their decision-making efforts. The principles of good social work planning include values of equity, justice, fairness, ending inequality, and creating a vision of a good society.

Social planners "worry not only about efficiency but also about decent outcomes; . . . not only about satisfied customers but also about the food, housing, and jobs the perfect market promises and the actual market fails to provide."[84] Planning efforts can be considered effective to the extent that things are changed in a direction that is better.[85]

Future-Orientation

Social planners nurture emergent ideas. While planning must be grounded in present reality, it forecasts and shapes the future. Forecasting is a rational process involving social causation, prediction, and control over future events. Once a future is envisioned, the means by which it can be attained also needs to be conceived. "In short, we become credible inventors of the future, designers and analysts who are also involved in selecting supporters and mobilizing the implementation of plans."[86]

The Planning Process

Several commentators on planned social change have asserted that the process of social planning "corresponds closely to the problem-solving model."[87] This model includes (1) defining and conceptualizing the problem in the interest of the community at large; (2) building a structure or network of relationships; (3) mobilizing values in particular directions by formulating policy and laying out alternative strategies; (4) deciding on an arena of action; (5) implementing plans; and (6) monitoring feedback and evaluation.[88] Even though planning methods are rational and based on facts, arriving at a plan to achieve an ideal future state cannot always be routinized. There are too many unknowns, too many variables for planning to be caught in a rigid process or method. Methods need to be contingent on the particular situation that presents itself to the planner.

Defining the Problem

Defining a planning problem is a process that occurs from two different perspectives. On the one hand, the definition of the planning problem may come from the social agency responsible for the substantive service arena in which the social planner is employed. For example, the Area Agency on Aging (AAA) may define a problem as assessing the needs of Alzheimer's victims over the next five years and developing a comprehensive program model for meeting those needs.

On the other hand, the definition of the problem may come from community members themselves. A citizen's advisory council on developmental disabilities, for example, may define the problem as a lack of day programs for severely disabled adults. In response to these assessments, a social planner may decide to assist in mobilizing planning efforts.

Social planners are intimately involved with community betterment through citizen participation in the planning process.

Building a Structure or Network of Relationships

Social planners do not operate alone in developing solutions to social problems. There are numerous actors, vested interests, groups, organizations, and agencies that may be affected by, have information about, and have a stake in the outcomes of the problem. To be effective, a social planner needs to consider the range of inclusion and the kinds of roles that various members ought to play in orchestrating a response to the problem.

Assessing Alternatives and Deciding on a Course of Action

Social planners, just as all macro social workers, need to look at the variety of solutions and assess their effectiveness in achieving the goals and outcomes desired. Assessing alternatives in social planning can be highly technical and at times complicated. Social planners use a variety of decision-making and forecasting techniques, such as difference equations, Markov models, networks, linear programming, queuing, simulations, benefit/cost analysis, and decision analysis.

Implementation

Social planning agencies often have the power of a federal, state, or local mandated authority to implement plans, including determining the amount, location, quality, and direction of service provisions to carry out the planned strategies, actions, projects, or programs to a successful conclusion. In addition, social planning agencies often are funnels for funding for particular projects. A social planning agency such as an area agency on aging or an area developmental disabilities agency will often implement plans by contracting with or providing a grant to private agencies.

Monitoring and Feedback

The planning process is not complete until a plan for evaluation and feedback is accomplished. Often if a private agency is responsible for writing a grant and obtaining funding from a social planning organization a program evaluation component is a part of the grant proposal. The social planner will be active in analyzing the consequences of change, monitoring program effectiveness, providing consultation, and if needed, specifying adjustments needed and identifying new problems that may call for action and planning.[89]

Social Work Planning Skills

In order to accomplish tasks, social work planners need to have three kinds of skills: (1) technical skills, (2) people skills, and (3) skills in the use of the political process.

Technical Skills

Social work planners should be expert in the use of the rational problem-solving process, working step-by-step to obtain accurate and clear problem resolution. They need to be skilled researchers able to perform surveys, collect data, use statistics, analyze information, and prepare reports. In addition, however, they need to have a variety of other problem-solving techniques at their disposal and should be skilled in applying those techniques to the planning issues that confront them.

Planning Techniques

Because social planning can be highly rational, linking organizations, resources, and plans to future goals, social planners make use of a variety of forecasting techniques as aids to planning and decision making. Rational planning techniques, also called "management science" or "action research," are used by planners to make the best decisions, to anticipate what would happen if a decision were implemented, and to evaluate the project.

Social planners use models to help formulate their plans. A model is a "simplified representation of some aspect of the real world."[90] It may be an actual physical representation, such as a miniature replica, or a diagrammatic model, such as a roadmap. A flow chart is a model that traces a process from one category to another. A flow chart, for example, may trace the process by which a bill becomes a law or the process by which an individual, apprehended for a crime, passes through the stages of the criminal justice system.[91] Graphs, charts, and decision trees are diagrammatic models. A decision tree identifies stages in a complex process to help the decision-maker point to the best choice of alternative solutions.[92]

Another kind of model is a conceptual model, "a purposeful reduction of a mass of information to a manageable size and shape, and hence . . . a principal tool in the analyst's workbox."[93] Garret Hardin's model of the commons, for example, is a conceptual model of what occurs when people have the right to use a public good for their own private advantage, resulting in overuse or congestion that is costly to all. One can apply this model to population, pollution, housing, and health problems.

The simplest kind of model is one for which you know the outcome and have all the information you need in order to develop the model or plan. A model in which things are predictable and certain is called a deterministic model.

In the world of people, however, things are rarely certain. One often has poor information, and some solutions may work, while some may not. Models that help a planner understand the probabilities that one solution or alternative will be better than others are called probabilistic models.[94]

When faced with a complex problem, planners should ask if constructing a model would shed light on the subject. Stokey and Zeckhauser recommend that a planner "should develop the ability to construct simple models . . . relying on an expert to refine the model and develop empirical data as a problem becomes more technical."[95]

Planners should understand some of the more common models and be aware of their limitations. While many models are particularly useful in planning, they are also useful in other arenas of macro social work. An example is one of the most common techniques, benefit/cost analysis.

The next section describes some of the more common decision models and their uses. These models may be highly quantitative in nature, requiring complex mathematical formulations. While computers can reduce computations, using these techniques requires more information than can be given here.

Difference Equations

Suppose you are asked to help assess the ability of a mental health system to fund its programs over the next several years. In order to do this you need to project income and expenses over that time period to decide what programs to expand or reduce. A public hospital in an inner city is faced with severe overcrowding. One possible solution is to build an additional facility; another is to disperse services into community clinics. A local area agency on aging is asked to fund programs for Alzheimer's patients over the next ten years. In order to put together a budget, the AAA needs an estimate of the number of people who would use the day programs during the first two years.

All of these forecasting problems are issues that rely on difference equations. "Difference equations are tools for exploring the way things change over time."[96] They use rates of growth over a specific time period in the past to project growth rates during a specific period in the future.

Markov Models

Suppose you are a social planner in a low-income community with high unemployment. You want to plan programs to deal with unemployment, and you need to know not only how many unemployed people there are now, but how many people will be unemployed at any particular time in the future and how those numbers will vary given certain conditions. You need to know what percentage of the employed population will be unemployed two years from now. You also want to know what percentage of the unemployed population will be employed two years from now. If you can trace employment rates over time and within differing conditions, you can develop some solutions to unemployment that can impact the problem effectively.

One model that can help you with this is the Markov model. Markov models can help you trace changes in a system over time. Assume, for example, that you think up four different solutions to the problem of unemployment. One solution is to obtain federal funds to improve the job security of those already employed. Another is to establish a training program for unemployed. A third is to attract new industry through tax concessions, and a fourth solution is to increase unemployment compensation. Which alternative will gain the most employment? Markov models can help you chart how employment and unemployment will vary with each of these different solutions, which may help you decide which solution or combination of solutions would be most effective.

Markov models can also help you understand population flows within a system. Imagine, for example, that an institution for the mentally ill in a community is operating at full capacity. The mental-health planning board has decided to open a new wing. Should it be a facility for long-term patients or short-term patients? What size facility do they need to build? Markov models help predict how many new persons can be admitted to the new facility at, for example, three-month intervals and how many people will be in the facility two years hence. This kind of information can help the board decide whether they need a short-term or long-term facility and what size the facility should be.[97]

Networks

During World War I, Henry Gantt, a prominent efficiency expert, developed a model called a Gantt chart by which work flow through various departments in an organization could be charted. A manager could then "tell at a glance the status of both the projects that are under way and activities and performance of the operating departments."[98] Gantt charts were predecessors of PERT (Program Evaluation and Review Technique) and CPM (Critical Path Method), which are now used to chart the process of projects that involve many interrelated activities.

PERT was the major planning technique used in the Polaris missile program. "To build the Polaris missile, management developed an intricate plan that consisted of a series of interrelated steps, some of which could be implemented simultaneously and some of which had to be finished before others could begin."[99] PERT and CPM are nearly the same; but if time estimates are certain, CPM is used, and if time estimates are uncertain, PERT is used.

The Critical Path Method consists of "laying out or diagramming the flow of activities in a project to identify all possible sequences of steps from beginning to the end of the project. The longest sequence is the *critical path*, which determines the completion time of the project. Once it is known, managers can focus on those particular activities that are likely to delay the project."[100]

The steps in using CPM are: first, the planner identifies every significant event that must occur to complete the project. Then these events, called milestones, are arrayed in sequential order, and time is allocated to each event. All milestones are plotted on a chart. The total time is then calculated, and a model showing all the events with their timelines is charted, so that each event is performed in order.

Linear Programming

Linear programming is useful when the planner must allocate scarce resources to completing projects or objectives.[101] Stokey and Zeckhauser state, for example, that linear programming "can be an invaluable aid for making policy choices that range from allocating the budget for a small library to selecting the components of a gigantic hydroelectric plant."[102] In community development, a linear programming model "of the entire Ganges-Brahmaputra river system takes into account flood control, power production, irrigation, navigation, and salinity control.[103] Because of its power, linear programming is one of the most highly developed and widely used management science techniques.

Its usefulness, in many ways, occurs because it is an optimizing model. In other words, it is "concerned with choosing the best levels for various activities in situations where these activities compete for scarce resources."[104] It would be useful for example, when a center for developmentally disabled must develop a work schedule to use staff time efficiently, a neighborhood community center must determine expenditure level for various activities, and an administrator in a child protective service agency must allocate caseworker's time among various cases.

Sometimes the issues are straightforward, such as spending $100,000 or allocating 450 hours of casework service. Often, however, the problems are such that inequalities exist. For example, a manager may want to minimize the cost of a job training program but at the same time he or she may be willing to go over budget if particularly good jobs can be found or more people placed. Fortunately, "most high speed computers are routinely programmed to perform these kinds of calculations. We need only to formulate the problem in the appropriate form."[105]

Queuing

Waiting line analysis, or queuing, uses formulas developed in the early 1900s to reduce time lost by waiting in a line or the costs incurred by having an empty station with no one waiting. This is important particularly in agencies where establishing a waiting list for services is not appropriate or where there are specific time lines for service such as in child protective agencies. By calculating the average arrival time, the average time in the line, and how the lines are arranged, one can decide to either hire more workers, prioritize services such as a "triage" system used in emergency rooms, or develop strategies to reduce waiting time.

Simulations

Sometimes you may be faced with a complex situation, the outcome of which is not predictable by using existing techniques. In this case you develop a miniature or simulated model and manipulate it to discover how situations would work in the real world. Simulation "is a process of building, testing, and operating models of real world phenomena through the use of mathematical relationships that exist."[106] Simulations help you discover flaws in your solution so you can modify the solution before you expend energy and incur any expense.

Today the use of computers can help develop such simulations to determine the best course of action.[107] The process of developing a simulation includes defining the problem and constructing the simulated model including all the relevant steps, interactions, and decision rules. Then define all of the variables and boundaries within which the model must operate. Finally, run the simulation, evaluate the results, and refine and revise the model.[108]

People Skills

Social work planners are not mere value-neutral technicians. They plan for and with people and engage in a number of organizing efforts including networking, negotiating, coalition creation, and consensus-building.[109] They should have good communication skills, because an analysis not communicated well is "worse than useless—it can be counterproductive and damaging, just as it might also at other times deliberately serve to obfuscate important issues."[110] Social work planners must be able to present proposals and ideas in language that people can understand.

Political Skills

Social work planners get involved, talk, and argue, especially when confronted by misinformation, misrepresentation, disparities in power, and subversion of a process that gives advantages to only a few. They try to even the scales, balancing power misalignments so that truth will win out in the end, encouraging "democratically structured, publicly aired political argument, not covert wheeling and dealing."[111]

How do you engage in such political action? By "informing the 'affected but unorganized' earlier rather than later in the planning process,"[112] and by

> checking, double-checking, testing, consulting experts, seeking third-party counsel, clarifying issues, exposing assumptions, reviewing and citing the record, appealing to precedent, invoking traditional values (democratic participation, for example), spreading questions about unexplored possibilities, spotlighting jargon and revealing meaning, negotiating for clearly specified outcomes and values, working through informal networks to get information, bargaining for information, [and] holding others to public commitments.[113]

Moreover, you must "anticipate misinformation in time to use those strategies effectively, rather than looking back and saying, 'Well, what we should have done was. . . .' "[114] For example, a "good idea presented the week after a crucial meeting (or too late on an agenda, or on the wrong agenda) will no longer do any good."[115]

Even though most social planning is "rational," the political process is highly "irrational," fraught with emotion and dependent on compromise, bargaining, and negotiation. A planner who assumes that dominant interests are bound by policies, rules, or regulations will miss the point of organizational power and self-interest. You may present a very rational analysis to politicians, developers, citizen groups, and others using the forecasting or decision techniques you've learned only to find that no one seems to be listening, at least not to the merits of your case.[116] The merits of the case, if they are not in the interests of those in power positions, are beside the point. A social planner who assumes that those in control of the machinery of society are constrained by rules, rational arguments, facts, or figures will be out of touch with the real operating principles of planning.

Four Approaches to Social Planning

There are four different approaches to social planning:

1. Reactive planning: to restore the past
2. Inactive planning: to preserve the present
3. Proactive planning: to accelerate the future
4. Interactive planning (based on the action model of macro social work): to create a just society for the future.[117]

Reactive Planning

Much modern problem solving is reactive in nature. Reactive problem solvers spend a great deal of energy fixing what is broken in social systems by identifying problems and designing solutions that restore the system's stable state. Reactive planning or problem solving, therefore, engages in issues after the fact.

Reactivists tend to look to a simpler, less complicated past that becomes their operative reality. As a result, they may tune out significant aspects of the causes of social problems, pretending that by holding onto an imaginary past they can exclude the pain of the present and minimize the struggles of the future. Reactivists in the Old South, for example, contended that African Americans were happy and contented as slaves, and things should be left as they were.

"Reactivists try to re-create a previous state of the system they control by unmaking changes that have converted the system state into one that they find less desirable."[118] Reactive planning assumes that the current system function is simply in need of repair and ignores the fact that the social environment may have changed and that the solution is not repair but adaptation. The process of diagnosing a social problem long after its inception is often impossible. Correcting it after it has become entrenched in the social and cultural environment is not only costly but difficult and time consuming.

Harkening back to a purer, less complicated social reality, reactivists assume that behaviors of the present are the result of abandonment of values of the past. Assuming that the solution to social problems is the eradication of the social evil that contaminates society, reactivists entrench rather than eliminate them. Prohibitionists, for example, attempted to destroy saloons, cripple alcohol manufacture, outlaw alcohol consumption, and interdict illicit trafficking in alcohol. Rather than resolve the problem of alcoholism in the United States, prohibition ultimately resulted in the rise of organized crime and in criminalizing a large percentage of the American population.

Reactivists sometimes have blamed technology for less than desirable conditions. During the early years of the Industrial Revolution in England, the Luddites, for example, attacked new factories being built because they were convinced that they were destroying the quality of life.[119]

Is the return to a previous state needed or even desirable? When we concentrate only on getting rid of what we do not want and what does not work, or become suspicious of progress, we "may not get what we do want. We may, instead, get something much worse. . . . [The] removal or suppression of a cause in our present state does not guarantee a return to a previous state."[120]

In addition, reactivists tend to see social issues one-by-one as if they were highly discrete and operated independently of each other. They fail to see that just as social systems interact, social problems are the result of systems interactions as well. One cannot simply solve one problem and then go on to the next. Instead, "action taken to resolve one problem may render ineffective or harmful the actions taken to resolve another. . . . Because the treatments of problems interact, the focus of planning should be on their interactions, not just on their separate reactions."[121]

Inactive Planning

Inactivists face the future by putting on the brakes. "The inactive approach conserves the present by preventing change. The world may not be perfect, but it is good enough. Inactivists believe that meddling with the natural course of events creates most of our problems.[122]

Inactivism does not mean "not acting."[123] Inactivists work hard at keeping things the same and preventing change. A large number of people must be kept busy without actually accomplishing anything, or they must be kept busy keeping others from doing something.[124] Inactivist policymakers, for example, set up commissions and committees that study problems, then do nothing, giving the illusion of progress while delaying it at the same time. Inactivist administrators use bureaucracy to wrap processes in red tape, obfuscating and delaying decisions. Inactivist presidents use the veto to stop the work of Congress, delaying what may have taken Congressional committees and the joint action of the Senate and the House months of work. Inactivist politicians waste time by blaming others for problems and by engaging in endless and fruitless debates about what went wrong, the object of which is to diffuse the problem and to justify their own inaction.

Social Darwinism

Implicit in the inactivist approach is a kind of Social Darwinism that assumes that social systems naturally "evolve," letting "nature take its course." It is not only easier but actually better, so proponents claim, to leave things alone. Intervening actively only distorts natural social processes, as when the government interferes with the economy by regulation, taxation, and redistributing wealth. This laissez faire inactivist approach assumes that by allowing things to happen on their own, everything will work out for the best. Governmental interventions such as planning, regulating businesses, operating programs, or providing services should be kept to a minimum. Public schools, libraries, parks, and other public services are best provided by the private sector. Public

or common goods, much like a "commons," should be open to all to exploit in their own self-interest.

Social Deviance

Inactivist decision making operates on the basis of conventional norms because convention protects the status quo. As a result, inactivist decision-makers tend to allow unattended social problems to pile up to the point where they cannot be ignored. Burdened by the consequences of their perspective, many inactivists adopt a "social deviance" paradigm of social problems, blaming victims of social problems as the cause of those problems and those who protest social injustice as destroyers of the social fabric. Inactivist power figures tend to punish people who threaten the social or who act out defiantly. Strikebreaking corporate bosses, for example, accuse union leaders of being troublemakers who incited workers and fomented dissention, as if the unions and not hazardous working conditions, low pay, and unfair labor practices, which corporate leaders themselves created, were the cause of worker dissatisfaction and unrest.

Because inactivist decision-makers try to put off decisions, they tend to respond to serious threats by engaging in what has come to be known as "crisis management." Inactivist planners act when necessary for survival or stability but do no more than is required to "turn off the heat." "Crisis management focuses on suppressing symptoms rather than on curing ailments."[125] Inactivist politicians and policymakers tend to see social problems in simplistic and synoptic ways. Their perspective often limits them to "law and order" solutions in the form of more laws, harsher penalties for lawbreakers, larger police forces, increased military budgets, and larger and more numerous prisons. They tend to be incapable of recognizing that these remedies, rather than solving problems, may add to them and prevent solutions.

Inactivist leaders relegate social planning to a subsidiary maintenance role of "filling in the gap" where the market has failed. Rather than get at the roots of social problems, social planning from an inactivist perspective simply "picks up the pieces." The welfare system and social planners are expected to clean up the damage (unemployment and poverty) that the market economy has left behind. Inactivist social planners are seen as adjuncts to the economy, "balancing social welfare resources to meet social welfare needs"[126] to keep the system going.

Proactive Planning

Proactivist planners are not satisfied with reverting to a less complicated past (like reactivists) or keeping things as they are (like inactivists). Instead, they are forward looking and future oriented. Not wanting merely to satisfice or seek "good enough" solutions, proactivist planners want to do as well as possible to optimize. They try to solve rather than resolve,[127] accelerate movement into the future rather than slow it down, and encourage change instead of resisting it. For them, the future is filled with opportunity. Change is virtually synonymous with progress.

Proactive planners attempt to forecast alternative futures and spend considerable time researching and anticipating. They tend to ride a precarious wave of future events. Proactive planners approach the future by predicting and preparing. Of the two, the most crucial is prediction, because planners know that if their calculations are wrong, "then the preparation, no matter how good, is either ineffective or harmful. On the other hand, even if preparation for a correctly predicted future is less than perfect, one is likely to be better off with [the calculations] than without them."[128] Proactivist planners "try harder to avoid missing opportunities (acts of omission) than doing something wrong."[129] It is better, claim proactivists, to ask forgiveness than permission.

Children of modern technology, proactivists encourage and facilitate its use and development as a crucial weapon in the game and tend to be enamored with its possibilities. Proactivists also become excited by growth for its own sake. "Growth is the ultimate objective of proactivists: to become the largest, wealthiest, strongest.[130] Proactivist planners attempt to squeeze growth out of the economy, shaping its confines to political and social goals of survival and dominance, rather than let the economy shape the society as inactivists tend to do.

Proactivists as political "gamesmen" enjoy using social and political systems in contests of power and progress, quickly moving systems further into modernity. In the calculus of winning, proactive gamesmen focus on indicators such as the standard of living, wealth accumulation, acquisition of power, and reaching a goal first with the most. To the extent that social problems create a drag on the system, proactivists engage social problem solving with some gusto, engaging in progressive examination and active social experimentation, particularly if there is evidence of a clear payoff.

Interactive Planning: The Action Model of Social Planning

Interactive or action planning, unlike proactivist planning, takes into account that plans, even those based on technology, never work out exactly as expected. There are often unintended consequences of decisions, both good and bad. Implementation requires that the critical assumptions on which any plan is based be explicitly formulated and checked frequently. For example, as we move toward a vacation destination along a planned route, we often learn of a better way to get there and change directions.

Planning, therefore, must be flexible and innovative. It ought not be bound by constraints of rationality or technology that simply implement goals incrementally and in a linear fashion. For example, as we approach our vacation destination, we may find that we do not like the resort as much as we had expected and decide to revise our plans and go elsewhere. Our knowledge and our values change with experience.[131] Planning decisions, therefore, inevitably include values and ethics. Models such as benefit/cost analysis that are based on economic criteria that cannot take human considerations into account are helpful. But they need to be founded upon values and community-based decision making.

Planning must be morally acute, and the values implicit in planning must be sensitive to system change. In the 1850s, killing a whale was socially sanctioned, but now it is a morally contentious issue because technologically improved ways to kill whales, increased demand for whale products, and the near extinction of whale species have occurred. In another example, unlimited growth may have been a worthy goal at one point in our history. But unless mediated by other worthy ends, such as environmental quality, growth becomes self-defeating or even disastrous. Action-oriented social planners, therefore, desire growth only if it contributes to development of people and is consistent with welfare of the entire social milieu.

Action planners, therefore, utilize their intuition to "try to idealize."[132] Moving beyond simple prediction and preparation, action-oriented planners attempt to create and control the future, shaping not only its design but also its internal culture. Like proactivists, action planners design the most desirable future and invent ways of approximating it as closely as possible. Action-oriented planners seek technical solutions where possible. They also infuse rational decision making with value content, consciously using their feeling problem-solving functions, by continually scanning social systems and adjusting plans as the situation changes. Action-oriented planners aim to not only achieve a goal but also to make quality decisions. They do not seek to resolve problems as reactivists or to solve problems as proactivists. They want to *dissolve* problems. This requires changing the system that has the problem in such a way as to eliminate the issue.[133]

Like proactivists, action planners use quantification and experimentation; and like reactivists, they also use experience and qualitative judgment where quantification and experimentation are impossible or ineffective. They take morality into account (as do reactivists), manners (as do inactivists), and efficiency (as do proactivists), but they integrate these considerations by focusing on effectiveness.[134]

Action planning is based on the idea that

> all those who are intended to benefit from planning should be given an opportunity to participate in it . . . that more development takes place by engaging in planning than as a result of the implementation of plans. Therefore, it is better to plan for oneself, no matter how badly, than to be planned for by others no matter how well.[135]

Action planning is consonant with advocacy. Action planners understand that the milieu in which they work is large complex organizational systems that are procedural and incremental in nature. Because organizations are powerful systems there is always a tendency to allow previous decisions and sunk costs to determine future action. (Sunk costs are money, time, and effort sunk into projects.) Sometimes projects that have negative outcomes are continued just because of the amount of costs sunk into them. Furthermore, large organizations press planners for decisions and concessions that favor their interests. As a result, there is always pressure on social planners to divert their attention away from addressing the needs and concerns of the people whose interests should be their primary concern. Action-oriented planners, therefore, continually struggle to balance the tension between organizational demands and needs of people.

The action-oriented social planner is always an advocate on behalf of his or her clientele and resists the temptation to sacrifice their interests to expediency, procedural issues, or self-interests of others. An action model of social planning seeks the creation of a truly just society.

Such an action theory of planning will be guided by the following principles:

1. Every person is on a journey of self-discovery laden with uncertainty and error. In this social environment every person is of value, including those who have fewer resources or who seem to diverge from the norm. Those people, who may be on the margins of society, challenge us to remember parts of ourselves we may have forgotten. They require us to reach beyond our narrow self-interest, our own community, and our own values and become better than we are. It is the quality of social interaction, not simply the quantity of possessions that define who we are and what is important.

2. We must be open to change. We should reward risk and those who challenge conventional wisdom and values rather than keep things the same or avoid examining our assumptions and values. We should resist subordinating social and human systems to economic, utilitarian purposes. Instead, we should treat people always and in every way as ends and not as means only, as affirmed in Kant's categorical imperative.[136]

3. Community and society can be reflections of our highest aspirations and values, not merely places where we live or milieus which we inhabit. Communities can become arenas of living relationships that enhance our well-being and from which we receive our substance.

4. Politics is not just the manipulation of self-interested power, the resolution of conflict, or a

way of adding up the sum of individual preferences to arrive at a majority. Politics also can be a choice-worthy life-style in which people shape a social world that aims toward the achievement of a good society.

Conclusion

Social planning is one of the most important and potentially powerful means by which macro social work achieves its goals. It has been, from the beginning of the social work profession, a key factor in the inception and implementation of social programs. Social planning has provided macro social workers with an entree into social systems that may otherwise have not been as accessible to social change.

Social planning uses a variety of skills and techniques, such as rational decision making and political skills, which draw heavily on social workers' thinking and sensing functions, along with "people skills," which draw on their feeling and intuition functions.

Finally, social planning is a highly value-laden endeavor in which planners must continually balance the needs and interests of the people they are serving with those of the claimants who press planners for concessions. The recommendations of social plans are potentially powerful tools in the allocation of resources and the mobilization of community interests.

Social planning is the work of advocating for those who are removed from the mainstream of a society, equalizing the distribution of services, resources, and opportunities. Social work planners must be technically proficient, politically skilled, and compassionately humanitarian. They can wield a great deal of power and must use that power in ways that are just and equitable.

KEY CONCEPTS

Charity Organization Society
Community Welfare Council
Council of Social Agencies
Housing Act (1949)

Housing and Community Development Act (1974)
Comprehensive Community Health Act (1963)
Community Mental Health Centers Act (1963)
Economic Opportunity Act (1964)
Community Action Program (CAP)
Community Action Agency (CAA)
Demonstration Cities and Metropolitan
     Development Act (1966)
Older Americans Act (1965)
citizen participation
planning process
models
deterministic model
probabilistic model
management science
difference equations
Markov model
networks
Gantt chart
PERT
Critical Path Method (CPM)
linear programming
optimizing
queuing
simulation
reactive planning
inactive planning
proactive planning
interactive or action planning

QUESTIONS FOR DISCUSSION

1. If planning is a normal aspect of the human condition, why has there been so much controversy over planning, particularly in the field of social welfare?

2. Social planners advocating one or the other approaches to social planning assume that theirs is the one best way. For example, Friedrick Von Hayek, a Nobel prize winning economist, has written in his book, *The Road to Serfdom:*

> The dispute between the modern planners and their opponents is *not* a dispute on whether we ought to choose intelligently between the various possible organizations of society; it is not a dispute on whether

we ought to employ foresight and systematic thinking in planning our common affairs. It is a dispute about what is the best way of so doing.[138]

Do you agree that there is a best way to do social planning? On what principles do you base your answer? If there is a best way, which approach would you consider the best?

3. Proactive social planners rely on technology and growth. What are the implications of the "Tragedy of the Commons" for proactivist social planners?

4. One stance toward social planning is to assume that there is no one best way but that each social problem might be addressed by different approaches depending on the situation. This may be called a "contingency" approach to social planning, in which an approach is matched with the conditions or situation. Consider whether a contingency approach to social planning is appropriate or even possible. What "contingencies" or factors would you select to determine which approach should be used?

5. The action approach presented is normative (suggests a best way and gives suggestions) as well as ideological. Should social planning be infused with ideology or should it be value neutral?

ADDITIONAL READING

Friedman, Milton. *Capitalism and Freedom.* Chicago, IL: University of Chicago Press, 1962.

Galbraith, John Kenneth. *The New Industrial State.* 2d ed. Boston, MA: Houghton Mifflin Company, 1971.

Hayek, Friedrich A. *The Road to Serfdom.* Chicago, IL: University of Chicago Press, 1944.

Mayer, Robert R. *Policy and Program Planning: A Developmental Perspective.* Englewood Cliffs, NJ: Prentice-Hall, 1985.

Michael, Donald N. *On Learning to Plan and Planning to Learn.* San Francisco, CA: Jossey-Bass, 1973.

Rohe, William M., and L. B. Gates. *Planning with Neighborhoods.* Chapel Hill: University of North Carolina Press, 1985.

Rothman, J. *Planning and Organizing for Social Change: Action Principles from Social Science Research.* New York: Columbia University Press, 1974.

EXERCISES

EXERCISE 34: Presidents and Planning Approaches

Each president has developed a different approach to governmental planning. Review the leadership approaches of the following American presidents. What planning approaches do you feel characterize these presidents?

In class arrange yourselves in triads. Compare your assessments and discuss why you chose the planning approaches you did. After you return to the class as a whole compare your assessments and your rationales. Which presidents are reactive, inactive, proactive, or interactive? Which style do you think has been most effective? With which presidential style do you most identify?

1. Roosevelt (1933–1945)
2. Truman (1945–1953)
3. Eisenhower (1953–1961)
4. Kennedy (1961–1963)
5. Johnson (1963–1969)
6. Nixon (1969–1974)
7. Reagan (1981–1989)
8. Bush (1989–1993)
9. Clinton (1993–   )

EXERCISE 35: Social Problems and Planning

The following are examples of *solutions* to various social problems. Try to identify the planning approach they exemplify: (a) reactive; (b) inactive; (c) proactive; (d) interactive.

1. Controlling the use of handguns
2. Outlawing abortion
3. Developing a system of national health insurance
4. Abolition of slavery

EXERCISES

5. Allowing gays to serve in the military
6. Landing a man on the moon
7. Developing the human genome project—the book of life
8. Interdicting illegal drugs
9. Mandating English as our official language
10. Building a fence to prevent aliens from entering the country illegally
11. Requiring women on welfare who have been convicted of child abuse to use a birth control implantation device
12. Requiring corporations to contribute part of their profits to replenishing the resources in the physical or social environment
13. Capital punishment
14. Setting aside one million acres of land as a tall grass prairie national park
15. Allowing renters of apartments in low-income housing projects to buy their apartments for a low or nominal fee

After you have identified the planning approaches, share rankings in class. Was there general agreement in rankings? What criteria were used to decide?

EXERCISE 36:
The Tragedy of the Commons

Garrett Hardin suggested in the "Tragedy of the Commons" that there are social problems that have no technical solution. He defines a technical solution as one that requires a change only in the techniques of the physical or biological sciences, demanding little or nothing in the way of change in human values or ideas of morality. In fact, for some problems, modern science and technology actually make things worse. One example is the population problem. As science develops techniques for a healthier, longer-lived population, the resources available to support that population diminish.

Hardin is describing what is known in economics as a "public good" as opposed to private goods. Examples of a public good are the air, the ocean, the common good, political freedom, and national security. A public good is freely available to all. It cannot be divided into pieces and sold. It cannot be priced. Public goods are the purview of government. Private goods, however, are divisible and can be priced, bought, and sold. Private goods are the purview of the economy.

If a public good is used for private purposes, and these uses have spillovers, then disastrous results may occur. An example of a spillover is pollution. Pollution of the air or the ocean affects areas beyond the territorial boundaries of the company or state or nation producing it. If someone contaminates the ocean, the quality of that public good is diminished for all.

If a person or a company uses the air as a place to get rid of waste products of production, everyone who breathes the polluted air is paying a price and in a sense is subsidizing the profit of the manufacturer. The private use of a public good can have public consequences. What is your evaluation of Hardin's assessment? Are there potentially injurious effects of technological advances for which technology itself has no solutions? How can the public good be protected from overconsumption and spillovers?

EXERCISE 37:
An Enemy of the People[137]

The following is a summary of part of Henrk Ibsen's play *An Enemy of the People*. Read this excerpt (or better yet, read the entire play in its original form). Consider the questions that follow the summary as you engage in class discussion.

GREAT EXCITEMENT IS IN THE AIR. Dr. Thomas Stockman, a physician, planned a series of baths which were to increase the health of the community and could be used for a profit. While a different model of construction than the one recommended by Dr. Stockman was developed by the town fathers and the Baths committee, the town is beginning to anticipate their opening and the prosperity that is on the horizon. Peter Stockman, the doctor's elder brother, is the town mayor and chairperson of the Baths, a man of action who took the doctor's idea and made it into a practical reality. Peter is an administrator, one who enjoys doing things, turning ideas into tangible results, and manipulating people for power and profit. Dr. Stockman, on the other hand, is an imaginative, creative, and idealistic professional who chafes at the bureaucratic process that seems to contaminate ideas by compromise and hidden agendas.

The doctor has been conducting some tests on the water because of isolated cases of typhoid and other complaints. He discovers that the water, instead of being pure and healthy, is actually polluted by tanneries upstream. If the baths open, a serious public health problem would

(continued next page)

EXERCISES

EXERCISE 37 (continued)

occur—a major outbreak of illnesses. Seeking a sympathetic ear, Dr. Stockman tells the editor of a liberal newspaper, who agrees to print the doctor's findings. Immediately, Dr. Stockman sends a copy to his brother, expecting the mayor to shut down the Baths and praise him for saving the lives of people and the reputation of the community.

His realist brother, however, is not at all happy with this news. It would ruin the town's future as a health resort. Not only that, but the repairs the doctor recommends would take years to accomplish and would be extremely costly. The town has already invested a great deal of money, energy, and expectation on this project. The entire economy of the town is based on the success of the Baths. In addition, Peter Stockman rationalizes, there is no proof that people will really become ill, and if they do, it is the doctor's responsibility to treat them. Dr. Stockman, the mayor asserts, has a moral obligation to the town not to attribute any illnesses to the Baths. Moreover, the doctor himself is an employee of the Baths and should display loyalty as an employee. His brother, the mayor, as his boss, orders Dr. Stockman to keep quiet.

Shocked and indignant at his brother's insensitive and authoritarian response, Doctor Stockman refuses to back down. A shrewd strategist, the mayor talks to the leader of the tradespeople, telling them that if Dr. Stockman has his way, the mayor will be forced to raise taxes. Threatened with financial ruin as well, the editor of the newspaper decides not to print the doctor's report.

Seeing his support crumbling about him, the doctor decides to go directly to the citizens themselves. Dr. Stockman's brother, however, refuses to allow him to use a public building, so he decides to give his speech at the home of a friend.

The night of the speech, the behind-the-scenes bureaucracy surreptitiously has stacked the cards against the doctor. The chairperson permits the mayor to speak first. The mayor repeats how the Baths are the lifeblood of the community, turning the crowd against the doctor even before he speaks. But Dr. Stockman begins anyway, accusing the people themselves of being poisoned by their own greed. "A community that lives on lies deserves to be destroyed," he says. The crowd shouts, "He is an enemy of the people." The chair of the meeting makes this sentiment official. "I move that we embody this opinion in a resolution . . ." Dr. Stockman, the responsible planner, is now the official enemy.

1. Who is the real "enemy of the people"? Are there parallels today? For example, what about the Chernoble disaster or the Love Canal incident in which entire communities were exposed to toxic waste?

2. How would you characterize the ethical dilemma of planning the Baths?

3. We read about "whistleblowers" who expose corruption, waste, and fraud in government and industry. How are these people like Dr. Stockman?

4. How did bureaucracy affect the moral sensibilities of the administrators? Of community members? Is this a common danger we should be concerned about?

5. Are there lessons to be learned in social planning that the play uncovers? What might these be?

6. What would you have done if you were Dr. Stockman?

CHAPTER 11

The Social Worker as Program Developer

Frank Guecho demonstrated that a concerned individual who sees a need can develop a social program.

What would he say, that famous poor man the leaders of this country so often talk about, and so rarely talk with, if he were given the chance to speak?

That I needed a home, and you gave me Food Stamps
That I needed a job, and you got me on the Welfare
That my family was sick, and you gave us used clothes
That I needed my pride and dignity as a man, and you gave me surplus beans
—SI KAHN[1]

IDEAS IN THIS CHAPTER

Frank Guecho Starts a Home

Frank Guecho had just been evicted from an alcohol-abuse recovery home in October, and he knew he had two choices: Change his life or lose it. "I had spent twenty-two years as an alcoholic and drug user," he said. "I needed to get away from my old circle of friends. I had to have a clean, sober environment, but there was nothing like that for someone who had come out of an initial recovery house."

So, with $15,000 of his own money, the forty-one-year-old Hanford, California, resident started his own sober environment. He calls it Sobriety House. "It's a home for homeless people," Guecho said. "People who come out of the initial recovery homes after detox need a place to learn how to be responsible and live in society. We teach them job skills." In 1991, Guecho moved his program to larger quarters on Mary Street. "Sobriety House allows them to stay as long as they need to, until they feel they've grown strong enough to make it in society." He developed a board that oversees the program and monitors the staff. When he had more than twenty people receiving help, with the support of his board, friends, residents, and the community, he expanded, adding two more dwellings.

Guecho has a lot of volunteer help, including Fareed Mohammed, assistant director, and Stacy Roberts, director of women's activities. They teach home repair, painting, and housekeeping. "Nobody sits around," says Frank. "Everybody is busy all day long. About eighty merchants around Hanford have chipped in with supplies and materials to help. I don't know where all the help is coming from. All I know is that I'll keep trying with all my strength to make this work. I believe this is something God has sent me to do. I've gone 118 days without drugs or alcohol. I'll keep trying to make it work one day at a time."[2]

Introduction

Community development, social action, and social planning often result in a new service or program to meet people's needs. Program development is an exciting and creative process. It is a satisfying feeling to know that you, like Frank Guecho, have established something new that will serve people after you have moved on.

Program development has a long and rich history in the United States as well as in macro social work. Every social agency in existence had its beginning as a social worker or a group of citizens saw a need and extended themselves in the highest tradition of public service, acting together out of compassion and caring to do something to meet that need.

This chapter begins with a short history of program development efforts in the United States. How to translate a project into an agency-based program is explored, including identifying the need, engaging a board of directors, writing a mission statement, establishing the agency, arranging for staffing, obtaining funding, and evaluating the program.

The History of Program Development

The first social welfare program in the United States had its origin with the Dutch Reformed Church of New Amsterdam, a Dutch colony settled in 1609. Like early Christian groups,[3] the colony established a voluntary collection for the poor and distributed it to the needy.[4] This system was effective for over fifty years; then, in 1664, "its policies were transformed to conform to the English pattern—public assistance through compulsory taxation."[5]

The first almshouse in the American colonies was established at Rensselaerswyck, New York, in 1657.[6] Later, the Quakers, who, constrained by their pacifist beliefs, would not bear arms so established a program of relief designed to "deal with the hardships likely to arise from the impending struggle" even before the Revolutionary War broke out.[7] Even though they were persecuted for their beliefs, they raised several thousands pounds, which they distributed to those in need without respect to religious or political ideals.

Many private associations sprang up in Colonial America—nationality groups, fraternal societies, and social organizations—to aid the unfortunate. "The first, and in some ways most important, of these 'friendly societies'[7] was the Scots Charitable Society, organized in 1657 by twenty-seven Scotsmen living in Boston."[8] The society aided the poor, cared for the sick, and buried its dead. This society, still functioning today, became the model for countless others that sprang up in next two hundred years.[9]

Benjamin Franklin was one of the early community and program developers in Colonial America. "Believing in the importance of preventing poverty rather than relieving it, he worked hard to increase the opportunities of people for self-help."[10] Among Franklin's efforts were (1) starting a club for the mutual improvement of its members that later resulted in the establishment of a library; (2) founding a volunteer fire company; (3) formulating a scheme for paving, cleaning, and lighting the streets of Philadelphia; (4) formulating a plan for policing Philadelphia; (5) leading the effort to establish the Philadelphia Hospital; and (6) founding an academy that later became the University of Pennsylvania.[11]

> More than any other American before him, Franklin established the principle of improving social conditions and opportunities for the poor through voluntary associations and worked to apply the principle of self-help to the community as well as to the individual.[12]

The Ursuline Sisters in New Orleans founded a private institution for girls in 1729, the first institution for children in the United States,[13] and in 1790, the Charleston Orphan House, Charleston, South Carolina, the first publicly supported children's institution, opened its doors. By 1851 there were seventy-seven children's institutions in the United States, and an additional forty-seven were built prior to 1860.[14]

In 1811, state governments began to help private institutions by financial subsidies, the first of which was the Orphan Asylum of New York, in 1811. In 1824, in New York City, the House of Refuge for Juvenile Delinquents was founded with state funds, followed two years later by one in Boston. In 1847, the House of Refuge for Delinquent Boys was begun in Massachusetts, operated by the state. The first institution for mentally retarded was opened in 1848 and operated by Dr. Samuel Gridley Howe. The next decade saw institutions for developmentally disabled opened in Albany, Columbus, and Lakeville, Connecticut.[15]

Perhaps the most prominent program developer in American history was Dorothea Dix, who nearly singlehandedly paved the way for reform and establishment of facilities for the mentally ill and developmentally disabled in the United States. Beginning as a Sunday School teacher for women inmates in a Cambridge, Massachusetts, asylum, she was horrified by the treatment to which they were subjected, particularly those who were mentally ill.[16]

While a number of private hospitals for persons with mental illness had already been established, public facilities were few in number.[17] Working as an advocate for persons with mental illness, Dix successfully pressed the state legislature to expand its facilities. Then she carried her crusade to more than a dozen other states. In the tradition of competent macro social work practice, she began each campaign with patient, careful research and successfully established several institutions. Next, using the statistics she gathered and direct political tactics she was instrumental in introducing a bill, in 1848, asking "Congress to appropriate 10 million more acres to the states to help pay for the construction and maintenance of mental hospitals."[18] When the bill was ignored, she reintroduced it. But members of Congress were more interested in "using the remaining public domain land for their own and for land speculator's purposes than for the mentally ill."[19]

For the next five years, in and out of congressional corridors, she lobbied representatives and senators until finally in 1854 her bill passed both houses of Congress.[20] President Franklin Pierce vetoed it. In his opinion, the bill was illegal because no precedent had been established for the federal government to provide social services.[21]

In addition to developing institutional care for the poor, the mentally and developmentally disabled, and children, private benevolent associations dealing with problems of poverty began to spring up. These societies aimed "not at providing material aid to the needy but at uplifting them through improving their character."[22] In 1837, a financial panic and depression occurred causing hardship and straining these existing relief agencies beyond their capacities. The result was the development of groups that attempted to coordinate, on a more rational basis, the various efforts to reduce poverty. New Yorkers, for example, came together to examine the city's charities, and their report portrayed a disjointed system of relief with overlapping and poorly coordinated services. In 1843, the New York Association for Improving the Condition of the Poor (AICP) was established. This organization later was to employ Harry Hopkins at the beginning of his career in implementing relief during the Great Depression of the 1930s. Members of the AICP "approached the poor in a spirit of Christian benevolence tempered by fear and perhaps a pang of guilt."[23] Many similar organizations also appeared "that emphasized godliness and the salvation of character as a prerequisite to improvement in the condition of the poor.[24] In the 1840s social group work saw its beginnings in the Jewish Center movement when groups of young Jewish people began to establish literary societies.[25] Today Jewish community centers continue to be active and a focal point for Jewish culture in many cities.

In the mid-1850s community-based approaches to institutional care of children began to be developed. In 1853, for example, the Reverend Charles Loring Brace, a twenty-seven year old missionary in New York's notorious Five Points District founded the Children's Aid Society of New York, originating the idea of foster home placement for abandoned, homeless, orphaned, and runaway children. The children's aid movement quickly caught on with the development of the Church Home Society in Boston in 1855, the Henry Watson Children's Aid Society in Baltimore in 1860, the Home for Little Wanderers in New York in 1861, and others.

After the Civil War there was a great increase in the development of social programs. In March 1865, the Bureau of Refugees, Freedmen, and Abandoned Lands, the nation's first federal welfare agency, was instituted to assist African Americans and others displaced by the Civil War. While the program was soon abandoned because of political pressure from the South, the spirit of program development on many fronts continued.

America was a Christian nation with a charitable impulse and tradition that was too strong to be eliminated. . . . In fact, so rapidly did private agencies continue to multiply that before long America's larger cities had what to many people was an embarrassing number of them. Charity directories took as many as one hundred pages to list and describe the numerous voluntary agencies that sought to alleviate misery, and combat every imaginable emergency. In Philadelphia alone, in 1878, there were some eight hundred such groups of one kind or another in existence.[26]

In 1851, following in the footsteps of George Williams (1821–1905), who founded the Young Men's Christian Association (YMCA) in England, a retired sea caption established the first American YMCA in Boston.[27] Seventeen years later, the first YWCA was founded. In 1860, the first Boy's Club was started in Hartford, Connecticut, by a church women's group.[28] The New York Society for the Prevention of Cruelty to Children established the first child protective service agency in 1875.

The Salvation Army, founded in 1865 by William Booth (1829–1912) in England, was transplanted to the United States in 1880.[29] In 1881, Clara Barton helped organize the American Association of the Red Cross. A year later, President Chester Arthur signed a treaty providing for an American branch of the International Red Cross, and Clara Barton, at age sixty-one, became its first president.[30] The Reverend M. Van Buren Van Arsdale founded the American Aid Association in 1883. The Association's name was later changed to the Children's Home Society, the parent agency for the National Children's Home Society, a federation of children's home societies in twenty-eight states that is still active today.[31]

Among the social agencies that saw their beginnings during what is now called the Progressive Era in American history was the Charity Organization Society established in Buffalo, New York, by the Reverend Stephen Humphries Gurteen in December 1877. The first Social Settlement, the Neighborhood Guild of New York City, was founded by Dr. Stanton Coit in 1887. It was modeled after Toynbee Hall established in England in 1884 by the Reverend Samuel Barnett and was based on the principles of Residence, Research and Reform, the three R's of the movement.[32] While only four settlements were founded before 1890, their number increased rapidly. By 1900 there were about one hundred in existence, and by 1910 roughly four hundred were in operation.[33]

Saint Xavier Francis Cabrini (1850–1917), the first U.S. citizen to be made a saint by the Roman Catholic church, became involved with immigrants, primarily Italians. Through her efforts over sixty orphanages, schools, free clinics, hospitals, and other programs were instituted. Among these were Colum-

bus Hospital in New York City in 1892 and Columbus Hospital in Chicago in 1905.[34]

The son of William Booth, founder of the Salvation Army, established the Volunteers of America in 1896.[35] In 1902, Goodwill Industries was formed. The Boy Scouts of America, founded in England by Lord Robert Baden-Powell (1857–1941) was established in America in 1910. That year also saw the origination of Catholic Charities, and in 1911, the Family Service Association of America opened its doors.

Many of these social agencies still exist, and along with thousands more, provide services to and meet the needs of people in a variety of social situations. America, particularly her social workers and concerned citizens, can be proud of the rich outpouring of compassion that has resulted in the establishment of so many social programs and agencies, a phenomenon that continues with vigor today.

Identifying the Need

Every person who is involved and engaged in social work can come up with an idea for a new program or see a need that is not being met. All it takes to develop that program or fulfill that need is concern, ingenuity, and a will to mobilize people to see the process through.

Verifying the Need

If you have a vision of your own, the place to begin in developing a new program is to verify the need.[36] Hasenfeld suggests that you begin by examining "statistical reports such as census data, local Social Security office data, county government surveys, and health surveys."[37] If you are not familiar with the various services available in your community, obtain a directory of social agencies. This will help you identify public and private social agencies already involved in providing services in the area of your interest. Visiting these agencies and meeting with social workers will enable you to assess what is already being done and whether or not there is a legitimate need for a new program.[38]

Doing a needs assessment is a critical first

step[39] in the development of any social program. "The purpose of a needs assessment study is to verify that a problem exists within a client population to an extent that warrants the existing or proposed service."[40] Often social planning agencies will not validate or assist in funding programs for which an assessment has not been performed to verify the need.

There are two different kinds of needs. One may define need in *normative* terms or in terms of *demand*.[41] Rubin and Babbie state that "if needs are defined normatively, then a needs assessment would focus on comparing the objective living conditions of the target population with what society, or at least that segment of society concerned with helping the target population, deems acceptable or desirable."[42] For example, evaluating services for persons who are developmentally disabled may lead you to the conclusion that they lack equal access to educational services afforded others in a particular geographical area. The same may be true of dental care, medical care, or housing for the homeless. These populations may be in need of services even if they cannot or do not express the need or claim dissatisfaction with their current conditions. In this case a social worker may advocate for such "underserved" populations by means of developing "precise estimates of the number and distribution of individuals or social units exhibiting the problem [believed] to exist."[43]

Defining needs normatively can often be done by using existing data. For example, the numbers of developmentally disabled children who actually attend school may be compared with the number of disabled children in the population. If there is a significant difference, it might be concluded that more school programs need to be established.

When needs are defined in terms of *demand,* "only those individuals who indicate that they feel or perceive the need themselves would be considered to be in need of a particular program or intervention."[44] Demand data is helpful when mobilizing community support for a program, but if need is defined solely in terms of the number of individuals who press for a service or who express an interest in it, all those people who do not understand the service, who are not aware of its benefits, or who may actively resist it will not be included in determining the extent of need. Therefore, demand data

should often be combined with normative data to determine the extent to which those eligible for a particular program would actually use it. While normative data may show that there is a need for additional housing or shelters for persons who are homeless, for example, demand data would give an indication of the numbers who would actually use shelters.

Needs Assessments

There are five approaches to performing needs assessments: (1) social indicators approach; (2) rates under treatment approach; (3) focused interview or key informant approach; (4) focus groups or community forum approach; and (5) the survey approach.[45] While you may wish to develop your own needs assessment, many times you'll find that a needs assessment has already been performed by a social service agency or a planning agency. Social indicators such as data on crime, abuse, housing, health, and others, for example, can be gathered from public and private agencies concerned with these problems. Rates under treatment, the extent to which people demand or utilize services within a community over a period of time, can be obtained from many social agencies. For example, if you are interested in determining the need for a shelter for battered women in a community, you can study the utilization of shelters in communities of similar size and demographics to determine potential need for such a facility.

Needs can also be assessed by talking to key informants who are experts or are knowledgeable about the needs of a particular problem area. Rubin and Babbie state, however, that while the key informant approach is easy and quick, and can help build connections with key community resources, the information is not coming directly from the population, and the quality of information depends on the objectivity and depth of knowledge of the informants.[46] Likewise, while community forums or focus groups give indication-of-demand data, they are suspect from a scientific perspective.[47] "Those with vested interests or with a particular ax to grind may be overly represented,"[48] especially those who feel negatively or threatened about a proposed need. For example, in attempting to establish the need for a

Every social agency has its beginning as a social worker or group of citizens sees a need and acts out of compassion and caring to do something to meet that need.

home for mentally ill, developmentally disabled, or troubled youth, you may find that community members may oppose the idea because they do not want such a facility in their neighborhood—"NIMBY"—not in my backyard. While this will help you assess the political climate that a program may face, it will not assist in demonstrating need. In addition, strong social pressures may prevent some people from speaking or from expressing minority viewpoints at community forums.[49] One way to overcome these threats to the validity of data is to hold closed meetings, one for each preselected homogenous group of people.[50]

Community surveys using a representative random sample of a community or a sample of the target group can also give an indication of need. If you use mail out questionnaires, however, you must weigh the advantages and disadvantages of this method given the problems in accuracy associated with low response rates. Making person to person contacts, on the other hand, will often give you ideas for resources and help you recruit potential board members and obtain information from key community leaders and groups who can be of assistance to you.

Working with an Advisory Group or an Action Board

If you are working on your own it will soon become apparent that "it is extremely difficult to develop a new program without the existence and active support of a group in the community that is highly committed to its development."[51] Sooner or later you will need to develop a group of people who can help you.

If you work on a community development, social action, or social planning project with a community-based task group, developing a program will be the natural outcome of that process. As your task group performs needs assessments, interviews key informants, conducts surveys, assesses social indicators, or conducts community forums, the needs become clearer. More than likely, the program concept is refined as you explore alternative solutions and develop a change strategy. By this time, the development of a specific ongoing program is no longer a dream but becomes the next step in a change effort.

Redefining the Task Group

Once you and the task group make a firm decision to develop a program, you need a legal entity to establish the program—a board of directors. The task group members need to consider whether they wish to shift from being an "action" group making community change to a board that stabilizes the change effort into a more or less permanent social agency. If this occurs, you shift your role from being a social activist, community developer, or social planner to that of a program consultant, staff member, or director of the new program.

Establishing the Board of Directors

Composed of volunteers, the board is an association of individuals that has legal responsibility and ownership over the program. The board defines the purposes of the agency, sets policy, owns the assets of the program, and has ultimate authority to make decisions about services, structure, personnel, and the budget.

The first decision of a board is whether it wants to establish a for-profit enterprise or a not-for-profit enterprise. Once this decision is made, the board must develop a constitution, articles of incorporation, and by-laws.

For-Profit Agencies

Income from a profit-making enterprise becomes the property of the owners to dispose of as they wish and is taxable. If the income earned by the enterprise, (minus taxes, interest on loans, salaries, and overhead) will provide profit, then it is to the advantage of the board to incorporate as a small business enterprise.

To become a business, the board must file a "fictitious name" (the name of the business), obtain a tax number, and apply for licenses required to operate in the city or county. Profit-making enterprises often obtain start-up money by taking out small business loans, repaying them from income generated by the service. Many board and care homes, institutions, hospitals, foster homes, small care facilities, as well as counseling clinics, incorporate as profit-making agencies.

Not-for-Profit Agencies

Social service organizations tend to have clientele who cannot pay the full rate for services. To meet expenses, these organizations rely on donations, fund raising, a variety of governmental grants, subsidies, and charitable gifts, as well as fees. The federal government allows organizations of this kind to apply for tax-exempt status. Among the kinds of organizations that usually are tax-exempt are churches, labor unions, benevolent associations, foundations, private schools, and social welfare organizations.

Social agencies that incorporate as not-for-profit organizations must meet requirements of both federal and state laws for exemption from taxation. Tax-exempt agencies can acquire assets, own property, and pay staff a reasonable salary, just as profit-making organizations do. However, any profits that the agency makes must be used for the charitable purposes for which the organization has been formed and not for the personal profit of its owners. Finally, no substantial part of the corporation's assets may be used for partisan political purposes.

There are a number of incentives for social service agencies to incorporate as not-for-profit organizations. For example, nonprofit organizations can charge fees for service, contract for services with the government, and take out loans. In addition, they have sources of funding not available to profit-making businesses; among these are government and charitable foundation grants. Tax-exempt organizations may solicit donations from individuals and engage in joint fund-raising campaigns such as the United Way. Individuals may use these donations as charitable contributions for income tax purposes. And, of course, not-for-profit corporations do not pay taxes on income, property, or other assets as for-profit businesses must.

Incorporation

Incorporation means that an organization or agency is officially listed and legally recognized as a corporation. This is important for several reasons. Many agencies are subject to licensing requirements, particularly day programs, residential facilities, food service programs, health or medical treatment programs, and others that provide direct care to clients. A board that attempts to provide such services without formal approval is operating illegally.

Incorporation is necessary if your organization wants to apply for governmental grants or to contract with public agencies for fees. In addition, if the board wishes to become a not-for-profit organization it must be incorporated at the state level, apply for not-for-profit status with the federal government, as well as meet local or state licensing requirements.

The process for becoming incorporated is straightforward. First, write to the secretary of state in the state in which you wish to incorporate. The secretary of state will send you forms that can be filled out by anyone familiar with the organization. Usually, two separate documents are required: the articles of incorporation and the organization's constitution and by-laws.

1. Articles of incorporation. Many times stock paragraphs that apply to any corporation can be used, usually including the name of the corporation, date, names of officers, and a statement of purpose. Often the secretary of state provides samples of acceptable incorporation language that can be adopted for your organization. You may be tempted to hire a lawyer to draft the articles of incorporation. This is not necessary, and it is expensive. By following the instructions from the secretary of state you and your task group can devise an acceptable set of articles for your organization. See figure 11.1 for a sample of Articles of Incorporation from the state of California.

2. Constitution and by-laws. Standard language exists for constituions and by-laws of not-for-profit organizations such as resolutions pertaining to the rules of nonpolitical involvement and use of funds for charitable purposes. The purpose of the organization, its structure, the kinds of officers and their roles, the manner in which officers are elected, the place and times of board meetings, the mechanisms by which meetings are to be conducted, and rules for making decisions are usually contained in the constitution and by-laws.

Working on articles of incorporation, a constitution, and by-laws can be a helpful process in thinking through the details of the new organization.

Figure 11.1
Articles of Incorporation, California

I

The name of this corporation is _____

_____.

II

A. This corporation is a nonprofit PUBLIC BENEFIT CORPORATION and is not organized for the private gain of any person. It is organized under the Nonprofit Public Benefit Corporation Law for:

      ( ) public purposes.

    or ( ) charitable purposes.

    or ( ) public and charitable purposes.

B. The specific purpose of this corporation is to

_____.

III

The name and address in the State of California of this corporation's initial agent for service of process is:

    Name _____

    STREET Address _____

    City _____ State <u>CALIFORNIA</u> Zip _____

IV

A. This corporation is organized and operated exclusively for charitable purposes within the meaning of Section 501(c)(3), Internal Revenue Code.

B. No substantial part of the activities of this corporation shall consist of carrying on propaganda, or otherwise attempting to influence legislation, and the corporation shall not participate or intervene in any political campaign (including the publishing or distribution of statements) on behalf of any candidate for public office.

V

The property of this corporation is irrevocably dedicated to charitable purposes and no part of the net income or assets of this corporation shall ever inure to the benefit of any director, officer or member thereof or to the benefit of any private person. Upon the dissolution or winding up of the corporation, its assets remaining after payment, or provision for payment, of all debts and liabilities of this corporation shall be distributed to a nonprofit fund, foundation or corporation which is organized and operated exclusively for charitable purposes and which has established its tax exempt status under Section 501(c)(3), Internal Revenue code.

_____

(Signature of Incorporator)

_____

(Typed Name of Incorporator)

Establishing the Agency

The organization is the visible and tangible arm of the board; it is the tool or agent by which services are delivered and the board accomplishes its purposes. This is why the organization is called an agency. Establishing a mission, a structure, staffing, and funding for the organization are four tasks boards must accomplish in setting up an agency.

Defining the Agency's Mission

A mission statement explains the purpose, goals, operational objectives, and activities of the agency. First, state the purpose for which you have formed the new agency, including a statement of need, a description of the population,[52] the geographical area served, and importance of the issues that the agency is attempting to resolve.

Second, state the organization's goals and a

The board defines the purpose of the agency, sets policy, and makes decisions about services, structure, personnel, and the budget.

specific set of program objectives to reduce or ameliorate the problem. Board members need to ask themselves what sorts of outcomes they envision, arranging them in their order of importance or the sequence in which the agency will address them. Describe the activities or services you will be offering to meet the needs or resolve the problem.

For example, suppose you are concerned with the number of unwed teen parents in your locale. A mission statement would look something like this: Fresno County has one of the highest rates of unmarried teen pregnancies in California. The mission of the Fresno Teen Pregnancy Center, is first, to identify populations at risk, reduce the number of teen pregnancies by providing education and prevention programs to teens; second, for teenage girls who become pregnant, to provide a program of counseling, support, parenting, and medical care; third, to provide supportive counseling and education in parenting for teen fathers.

Developing the Agency's Structure

No one structure is good for all agencies. Instead, there should be an appropriate "fit" among the various components of the organization. Smaller agencies that have fewer subsystems and that do not rely on sophisticated technology often operate on a personal basis with few rules, unstructured roles, and open communication. This is because staff see each other often and accommodate the organizational structure to their own values, views, and styles. Figure 11.2 is an organizational chart for a small social agency.

The larger the organization, the more complex it becomes—more subsystems exist, and more linkages need to be built so that they are smoothly coordinated. Communication, rules, and procedures become formalized so that everyone in the organization knows his or her role.

Staffing the Agency

Board members need to think through the kinds of services they want to offer, what kinds of tasks are involved in providing those services, the support functions required, and the kind of leadership style

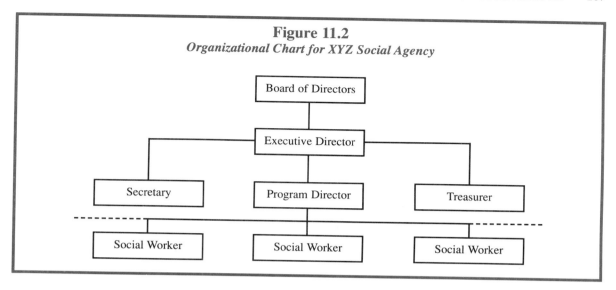

Figure 11.2
Organizational Chart for XYZ Social Agency

that will work best to coordinate staff and accomplish its purposes. Board members must decide on the kinds of skills needed and how many people to hire.

Usually, the first person hired is the executive director, who is the agency administrator. Boards delegate many of the service, staffing, and budgetary tasks to the executive who reports directly to the board. It is important, therefore, that the board members give a great deal of consideration to the role, tasks, qualifications, and personal qualities of the director.

Job descriptions need to be written. Job descriptions contain information about the tasks, roles, and responsibilities of the position. Information in the job description is translated to a job announcement, which describes the tasks but also includes the specific qualifications, salary, benefits, who to contact, application deadlines as well as a statement about nondiscrimination. Job announcements are often posted in social agencies, employment agencies, and personnel departments, and are advertised in newspapers, professional magazines, and newsletters.

Application forms need to be developed, including information about education, experience, skills, and abilities. It is important to remember that you are not allowed by law to ask for personal information such as race, sex, marital status, religion, and national origin.

After enough people have responded to the job announcement and have filled out the application forms, the executive and occasionally in smaller organizations members of the board interview potential staff. Often a second round of interviews are needed to narrow the list to the specific individuals who are the best candidates.

Recruiting Clients

The best source of clientele is referrals from other agencies in your area.[53] Most social agencies welcome having additional resources and are interested in knowing more about your services. One way to get the word out about your new program is by networking. Join the local council of social agencies or other social service networks in your area. Attend NASW meetings. Go to workshops and training programs where other professionals will be present. Visit agencies that will be the most likely referral sources. When you network or visit, carry a bunch of flyers or brochures, and hand them out to the people you tell about your new program. Invite them to visit. Your brochures should be clear and specific about your services, the kinds of clientele you can accept, fees, and geographic boundaries or other limitations of your service. There is nothing like face-to-face contact to spread the word about your program.

Television and radio spots are also helpful and often can be obtained free as a community service announcement. Have an open house to announce the opening of your program to community leaders, community agencies, and referral sources. This can be a gala affair with refreshments, a short presentation, and introduction of the board and those who have been instrumental getting the program established. Make sure that you maintain positive relationships with all the members of the community and that everyone understands the services you are providing.

Obtaining Funding

One of the more difficult aspects of beginning a new program is obtaining funding. However, it needn't be. Joan Flanagan, a skilled fund raiser says that people can "learn to raise money by doing it; they don't need any particular educational background, economic status, or writing skills. The only thing necessary to be a good fund raiser is the desire or will to raise money."[54]

Obtaining funding can occur in several ways. The board may take out a loan, solicit contributions from interested people or businesses, or assess membership dues. It may hold benefits or charge fees for service. If the board intends to operate on a nonprofit basis, it may apply for a grant. Grants are available from private foundations or from the government. Finally, your organization may contract with the government.

Solicitations

There are two kinds of solicitations. One is independent solicitation in which your program acts on its own behalf. The second is cooperative or coordinated solicitation.

INDEPENDENT SOLICITATION. According to Robert Geller, most charitable contributions come from individuals rather than foundations, government, or other sources.[55] There are several advantages in approaching individuals for money. First, it is quick. Unlike asking for money from foundations or the government, if you can sell someone on your program, you obtain funding immediately. In addi-tion to money, individuals may give you services or provide you with advice.[56] As you meet wealthy individuals you may be able to enlist them in your cause, and they may be able to provide you with other assistance or contacts.[57]

A potential drawback in asking individuals for money, however, is that, at times, money comes with "strings attached." It is one thing if the individual wants only recognition but quite another if the donor wants to dictate policy. You need to decide what you are willing to give up in return for the money.

In addition to asking a few wealthy individuals for contributions, you can also ask many less-wealthy persons for money. This often requires a well-thought-out campaign. Professional fund-raising organizations carry out these campaigns for a percentage of funds raised. Such fund raising can be very sophisticated with slick brochures, telephone solicitation, and television advertisements.

Other sources of contributions are businesses and corporations. Businesses obtain tax write-offs for making charitable contributions and are sometimes willing to make cash donations to worthy causes, particularly if they can obtain some publicity in return. In addition, a business may get behind a worthy project, involving its employees in fund-raising efforts and providing donations of material or support services. For example, a grocery store may donate food and a building supply company may donate lumber. Many businessmen are willing to serve on committees, give advice, or even donate services of staff to a worthy project.

COOPERATIVE SOLICITATION. So many charitable organizations exist today that people become overwhelmed with requests for money. As a result, social agencies make fund raising more efficient, effective, and equitable by means of organized, cooperative solicitation. Macro social workers have organized "councils of social agencies" such as United Way and United Charities. Organizations participating in United Way are released from the burden of spending their own staff time on fund raising and can devote their energy providing services. In addition, more money is raised collectively than if agencies competed with one another.

However, because United Way usually does not fund pilot projects or new, untested programs, they tend to take a limited number of new programs each year. Those they accept must often have an established track record. In addition, most United Way organizations have commitments to certain priorities or needs. If your agency does not meet these priorities, you may have difficulty obtaining this funding. Finally, many United Way organizations do not guarantee funding from year to year, nor do they guarantee a given amount of funding. If a program cannot show its effectiveness or is inefficient, its funding may be reduced or eliminated entirely.

Membership Dues

Membership dues are an important part of an organization or project. Churches, YMCA, YWCA, Boy Scouts, Girl Scouts, as well as neighborhood associations depend primarily on membership dues and member contributions. Dues are a source of funds and a way of developing commitment from a constituency.

As you engage in a membership drive, members will build support for the program. From your constituency, you can involve people on the board. When community members join and pay membership dues, they "own shares" in the project and have a stake in its outcome.

You can also use membership as a gauge of community support. A demographic assessment of membership lists can tell you where your primary support and involvement is coming from, where it is weakest or nonexistent, and therefore where you need to improve community relationships. By means of regular meetings with your members, social activities, and using members as volunteers, you and the members build community spirit, cooperation, and cohesion. Finally, members can become involved in fund-raising efforts such as organizing benefits.

Benefits

Many organizations depend on fund-raisers or benefits. Dinners, entertainment, dances, fairs, cookouts, raffles, auctions, theater productions, walk-a-thons, telethons, car washes, and yard sales are all ways that agencies make money for worthy projects. The Mennonite Central Committee raises most of its entire budget by means of an annual auction. The American Cancer Society and the Heart Association sponsor walk-a-thons. Lutheran Social Services sponsors boutiques and dinner dances. The Jerry Lewis Annual Telethon for Muscular Dystrophy is a national event, and the Girl Scouts are known for their annual cookie sale.

A number of side benefits attend such fund-raisers. First of all, the organization obtains publicity and community awareness. Second, a fund-raiser provides a good opportunity for community education about the project. Third, even the wider community becomes mobilized and involved in the project. Many times even people not connected directly with the organization will help out with a benefit. Finally, the benefit provides opportunity for the project staff, membership, and board to provide a service for the community. People who hate meetings will often show up at a benefit where they can meet one another, engage in social activities, and develop relationships.[58]

Benefits, however, are time consuming and involve a lot of hard, detailed work. They require skill in organization and often divert resources—particularly staff time—to the benefit. There are people, however, who are good at these kinds of projects and who enjoy organizing them. If you are lucky enough to have some of these people on your board or as members, they can make a real contribution to your organization.

Fees for Service

If your project is providing a service, you should consider charging a fee. Fees can be a significant source of funding. Counseling agencies typically charge a fee to help bear the cost of the service. Group work agencies charge fees, as do day-care services, alcohol and drug treatment programs, and recovery programs. Often fees are charged on a sliding scale according to a person's ability to pay. Frank Guecho, for example, charges $418 a month for residents at his Sobriety House. "But," he says, "most people can't pay. They can stay anyway, because we're like family here."

Fees are important for psychological reasons as well. People who pay a fee are more likely to respect the service and take it seriously. If a person is paying a reasonable fee, he or she will not tend to miss sessions and will tend to be more engaged in treatment than those for whom the service is free. They will also expect quality service from the agency if they are paying for it and will hold the staff accountable.

Private Foundation Grants

A private foundation is an organization set up as a charitable trust, and therefore it is not taxable. Many wealthy individuals use trusts as a way of reducing their taxable income while at the same time provide for worthwhile philanthropic purposes. College scholarships, for example, are educational grants, many of which are administered by a trust.

There are thousands of charitable foundations in the United States, each of which identifies specific purposes for which the grant money can be used. Among these are operating, community, general purpose, family, and corporate foundations.[59] An operating foundation is dedicated to only one project, organization, or program. Many times, for example, an organization will set up its own foundation, which then goes out and solicits money for that organization.

A second kind of foundation is a community foundation. "A community foundation serves a specific geographical area, usually a city or several counties."[60] Community foundations receive money from many different donors who are interested in the community but who have very specific stipulations. Community foundation staff administer the various trusts according to particular instructions. If you are applying to a community foundation, make sure that your project fits into one of the categories for which the trust was established.

General purpose foundations are usually large and heavily funded. They have broad areas of interest, often national in scope. Often they are established by wealthy individuals and have their own staff who administer the foundation funds and a board that makes funding decisions. These foundations usually carry the name of the founder, for example, the Carnegie Foundation, the Rockefeller Foundation, the Mellon Foundation, and the Ford Foundation. There is usually heavy competition for funds from these foundations.[61]

While a general purpose foundation is one whose original founders have died, a family foundation is one still controlled by the family members. Because the family members make funding decisions, people who have a personal contact or relationship with a member of the family have the best entree to these funds.

Finally, a corporate foundation usually gives its funds to arenas that will provide some benefit to the company's interests. Funds are often earmarked for the community projects in which the corporation does business, special interests of its employees, or areas of corporate concern. An example is Crown Zellerbach Foundation, which is located in San Francisco and provides funding for many local San Francisco social service organizations.

PROJECT AIMS TO TURN HOMELESS INTO PRODUCERS

In 1990, Joe Williams, Executive Director of the Fresno County Economic Opportunity Commission, decided to help break the cycle of criminal recidivism so prevalent among minorities. Aware that about 80 percent of California parolees are Hispanics or African Americans needing job training, education, as well as a residence to give them a start in a tight job market, Williams applied to the U.S. Department of Health and Human Services for a eighteen month pilot project to set up a Center for Homeless Parolees. According to Williams, "Parolees aren't able to cope with the outside. Sometimes they fly off the handle and lose their jobs if an employer says something negative. The next thing you know, they are back in the joint. Or they receive a few checks and get dirty and go back on drugs."

EOC came up with $30,000 in their own funds and about $510,485 in bank financing to buy and rehabilitate a twenty-five-bed residence on N. Howard Street in Fresno. Based on this funding, the U.S. Department of Health and Human Services awarded the EOC $290,000, the first time it has funded this kind of program. The California Department of Corrections also approved $292,000 in funds for the residential program which will be operated by the Third Floor, a substance abuse treatment center.

The residence center will offer crisis intervention, shelter, food, health care, counseling, career development, legal aid, recreation, transportation and referral services. Williams said the EOC expects to find permanent jobs each year for one hundred people surpassing the sixty-five people required by the contract.

Source: Pamela J. Podger. "Project Aims to Turn Homeless into Producers," *The Fresno Bee,* Dec. 31, 1991, p. B2.

Government Grants

Governmental organizations or agencies often have funds available for pilot projects, start-up grants, research grants, or ongoing funding grants. Many times governmental agencies may want to experiment with new and innovative approaches and will ask for proposals for such projects. The National Institute for Mental Health (NIMH), for example, often provides funding for pilot projects in the field of mental health.

At other times, governmental agencies may be established to assist small, struggling organizations or programs. The National Endowment for the Arts, for example, was specifically established to fund artists and to underwrite theater productions, writing, and music projects that would otherwise not be produced.

Finally, governmental agencies often do not want to establish a large bureaucracy but will provide grants to agencies instead. The Area Agency on Aging, for example, receives federal money to distribute to local agencies for provision of services to the elderly. In this way, local communities have input on the specific needs and can better allocate and provide services.

Obtaining a Foundation or Government Grant

There are two different approaches to obtaining money from foundations or from government funding agencies. The first is a reactive approach; the second is a proactive approach.[62] If you wait until grant announcements come to you and then you apply, you are using a reactive approach. This approach is most common with government grants. Using the proactive approach means actively searching for potential funding sources. Many boards use both reactive and proactive approaches to seeking grants.

CHOOSING THE SOURCE.   The process of applying for private foundation or government grants is much like applying for a job. Just as you would not apply for a job just because it is available, so you need to find a foundation or governmental grant that supports the kinds of things you want to do. Because foundations and government agencies are often very

specific about the kinds of projects they take on, it is usually a waste of time to take a "shotgun" approach. Finding a foundation that matches and supports your program mission gets you "in the ballpark."

INFORMATION RESOURCES.   There are a number of sources of information that can help you choose the right foundation. The Foundation Center "is an independent national service organization that has been established by foundations to provide a single authoritative source of information on foundation and corporate giving."[63] It provides annually updated directories and guides on small, medium, and large foundations including nine general foundation directories, thirteen subject directories, four grant directories, four guidebooks, and over twenty other publications covering grants and nonprofit funding.

If you are interested in a particular kind of government funding, you can get on the agency mailing list or subscribe to the *Federal Register*, a daily publication that provides information on federal government legislation and guidelines for new and revised grants. Most large public libraries subscribe to the *Federal Register.* You can also obtain the *Catalog of Federal Domestic Assistance,* which provides "basic information on federal resources, including a profile of each program, eligibility, deadlines, funding levels, and places to contact with telephone numbers."[64] The addresses of these resources are found in the additional reading at the end of this chapter.

IDEA STATEMENTS AND RFPs.   When you apply for funding to a private foundation, you must write an idea statement. Government agencies have a standardized process for applying for grants called RFPs, or "requests for proposals."

An idea statement gets you in the door of the foundation. It is a document that shows the foundation that you know what you want to do and that you have the ability to do it. An idea statement is two to four pages long and describes *what* you want to do, *how* you intend to do it, and *how much* it's going to cost.

An idea statement usually has the following components:

1. A summary or abstract of the entire proposal
2. An introduction to the idea statement

3. A need or problem statement
4. Goals of the project
5. Objectives (if they are different from goals)
6. The method by which you will accomplish the goals
7. The evaluation method you will use
8. Cost[65]

Make sure that your idea statement is neatly typed and is in the best writing style you can muster. Send it with a cover letter to the foundation you have chosen. If interested, the foundation will request a meeting, ask for further information, or ask you for a full grant proposal.

Government agencies send a request for proposal (RFP) to interested organizations. An RFP is an invitation to provide a proposal on a specific project and is usually distributed through state or regional social planning agencies that have the responsibility to administer grants at the local level. Sometimes RFPs are announced in newspapers.

If you are interested in applying for a government grant, you respond to the announcement and obtain application forms or documents. There may be a meeting for all applicants at which grant administrators provide specific information, distribute forms, and answer questions. Often, only applicants who attend the information session are permitted to apply.

WRITING A PROPOSAL.   Foundations and government agencies want to know not only that your project is a good one but also that your agency can perform the tasks for which you are requesting money. If you are invited to submit a proposal, you need to demonstrate your ability to perform the service requested, show that your agency is responsible, develop a budget for the project, set goals and objectives, and provide an evaluation component by which you measure how well your program meets its goals. Every grant proposal will require some kind of evaluation component as a condition of the grant. Many times the foundations will have a specific proposal outline of the kinds of information they require, which you use as a guide.

Because government agencies solicit applications for specific projects, they have a standardized guideline for funding proposals. Sometimes several organizations compete for these funds. Government agencies choose the proposal that offers the best program ideas at the least cost. Several sources on how to write grant proposals are listed in the Additional Reading section at the end of the chapter.

CARRYING OUT THE PROJECT.   Once you receive a grant, you must keep records and statistics on services provided, clientele, staff service hours, and other items. As an agency monitors its effectiveness, it will be able to pinpoint where it needs to improve, where it needs to grow, and areas where it is functioning well.

This information is invaluable in convincing funding agencies, foundations, constituents, members, and others who support the agency that their money has been well spent and that the agency deserves continued funding. Agencies that are unable to show that they are effective in carrying out their goals, that cannot account for meeting needs or making an impact in the arena of their service provision, cannot expect to receive ongoing support.

Contracting

Governmental agencies often contract with nonprofit agencies rather than administer their own programs. In some cases governmental agencies are specifically prohibited from being direct service providers. Agencies that typically contract for services are departments of social services, mental health, and probation. Departments of social services, for example, often contract with independent foster homes, small group homes, institutions, and counseling agencies. In California, regional centers for developmentally disabled contract with a wide variety of service providers called *vendors*. Regional centers contract with infant stimulation programs, speech therapists, day programs for adults, workshops, respite care programs, recreational programs, treatment centers, small family homes, group homes, and intermediate care facilities.

A program that provides a service for a county or state agency must meet county and/or state licensing requirements, fulfill the specific requirements of the funding agency, and accept the fees that are part of the contract.

Evaluating the Program

If the program that you have implemented is successful, others will want to know about it so that it can be replicated elsewhere. In particular, government agencies and foundations that provided the seed money to get you started will want to know how much impact the program has had on the problems that it was intended to remediate. This is important information, because if you can show that your program did what you intended it to do, you may be able to make a case for continuation or expansion of your program.

On the other hand, if your community project is not successful or fails, you need to be able to examine what went wrong so that you can learn from this experience and try a different approach the next time. Your clients also will want to be assured that they are receiving the best services that can be provided.

As a result, more and more program evaluation is automatically built into the process of obtaining funding from either government or private foundations. In other words, even before you begin a new program you must describe the needs that it is intended to meet or problem it attempts to ameliorate, how you will monitor the program's processes, and how you will assess the outcomes or impact of the program on the problem itself.

Program evaluation has a long history in macro social work. When Dorothea Dix advocated for an expansion of funding for public mental hospitals, for example, many hospital superintendents contributed to the movement by citing data on cure rates. Many claimed their programs were effective because they discharged 90 percent to 100 percent of their patients. While impressive, these figures tended to be misleading, because they failed to take into consideration relapses, rehospitalization, and the chronicity of many mental disorders.[66]

In 1917, there was a call for increased evaluation and the use of experimental approaches to solving problems. While the importance of program evaluation was recognized, the methodology for doing it was not available.[67] By the 1940s, several studies were conducted "examining the effects of work relief versus direct relief, the effects of public housing, and the effects of treatment programs on

juvenile delinquency,"[68] and program evaluation was beginning to come of age. In the 1950s program evaluation became widespread, with the result that, by the 1960s, textbooks, professional journals, and a professional association on evaluation research emerged.[69] "Concurrently, politicians, program administrators and social planners began to recognize the usefulness of evaluation research findings for developing social policy."[70]

The 1970s and 1980s witnessed an explosion of interest in program evaluation as politicians demanded that programs demonstrate their cost effectiveness and be accountable to the public.[71] In addition, because of the consumer movement, clients demanded quality services in many areas including social services.[72] As a result, program evaluation today "has become ubiquitous in the planning and administration of social welfare policies and programs."[73]

The purpose of program evaluation is to assess and improve the "conceptualization, design, planning, administration, implementation, effectiveness, efficiency, and utility of social interventions, and human service programs."[74] Carol Weiss says that program evaluation measures "the effects of a program against the goals it set out to accomplish as a means of contributing to subsequent decision making about the program and improving future programming."[75]

Types of Program Evaluation

There are three kinds of program evaluation: (1) input analysis, or needs assessments; (2) process analysis; and (3) impact or outcome analysis.

Needs Assessment

Needs assessment, discussed earlier, assists the program developer in program planning. The evaluator wants to know whether there is a need for a particular service or program and that the solution that the program offers has a reasonable chance of doing something about meeting that need or solving that problem.

Process Analysis

In process analysis, the evaluator examines the internal processes by which the program is being carried out.[76] Sometimes such a process analysis is performed by outside evaluators or consultants, but often agencies employ internal scanners who monitor the organization's effectiveness. Smaller agencies with limited resources leave monitoring to the agency administrator and top level managers to insure that the agency is functioning properly.

One way to conceptualize the internal system state of an agency is by means of "systems fit." Systems fit asserts that all the various components of an organization must fit together properly in order for the organization to function well. The key components of the system are the members of the organization, organizational processes, organizational structures and technologies, and organizational goals, strategies, and cultures.

For example, an organizational scanner will monitor organizational members' skills, attitudes, and values. He or she will ask such questions as: Do employee skills and training fit the job requirements? Are the best people attracted and retained by the rewards and advancement opportunities offered? Are professionals and others seeking autonomy and challenge assigned to less structured and less closely controlled jobs?[77] The evaluator may recommend improved recruitment and selection, counseling, stress management, and health maintenance programs.

The evaluator will look at processes of organizational decision making, leadership, and communication. He or she will ask such questions as: Does the decision-making process use all available resources and arrive at decisions that further organizational goals? Does organizational leadership create a sense of mission and identity among members? Is communication effective and efficient? Or, does it result in mixed messages, misunderstanding, or delay? The evaluator may recommend sensitivity training, team building, process consultation, third party interventions, or survey feedback techniques.

The evaluator assesses organizational structures and technologies by asking such questions as: Are those people who must work together closely grouped in units or otherwise linked structurally? Are procedures for coordinating work and information flow appropriate to the tasks and technology? Do members regard official rules and procedures as

fair and sensible? Do reward mechanisms encourage behavior compatible with organizational objectives?

The evaluator may recommend such techniques as job redesign, revised administrative procedures, reward mechanisms, redesigned divisions of labor, or new work procedures to improve effectiveness.

The evaluator may assess organizational goals, strategies, and cultures. He or she may ask whether procedures are supported by the organization's culture and norms. Are there power struggles or conflicts that prohibit achieving organizational objectives? The evaluator may recommend promoting goal clarification, coping with change through workshops and exercises, and changing the organizational culture.[78]

There are, in addition, more practical questions not directly connected with the systems processes that a program evaluator can ask that will help a social agency improve its usefulness. These kinds of questions "examine how best to implement as well as maintain the program."[79] For example,

1. Which fund-raising strategy yields the most funds?
2. What proportion of the target population is being served?
3. What types of individuals are *not* being reached by the program?
4. Why do targeted individuals refuse services?
5. Are clients satisfied with the service?
6. Why do clients drop out of the program prematurely?[80]

Outcome or Impact Analysis

Finally, the evaluator will be interested in examining system outputs, a process called impact analysis. Impact analysis attempts to measure the extent to which the program is achieving its goals. It assesses the outcomes of the program in terms of both quantity and quality.[81] Rubin and Rubin, for example, state that "impact evaluation measures the outcomes that affect the community."[82]

If the program made little or no difference in remediating the social ills for which it was designed, then one would question whether this approach was effective or should continue. On the other hand, if the program can be shown to be effective, then one may conclude that programs of a similar nature might be effective elsewhere.

Goals

A program evaluator must know what the goals of the program are. Often program goals are vague and nonspecific. For example, an organization may state in its mission that its goals are to "reduce crime" or "assist the homeless," or "strengthen and support victims of domestic violence." While worthy endeavors, these are not goals that can easily be assessed. Often the first task of a program evaluator, therefore, is to assist the board and administrator of a social agency to state their goals in clear, specific, and measurable terms.[83] Not only does defining goals more clearly assist in measurement but it also helps staff discover discrepancies between program goals and program content.[84]

Once the goals are clearly stated, the next task is to decide which of them to evaluate.[85] Weiss says that among the various criteria that can be used to decide which goals to evaluate are usability, practicality, and the relative importance that the staff gives to a goal.[86] It is important to assess those goals that are the most vital and not spend time evaluating goals that are of relatively little importance.

Sometimes goals are incompatible with one another. Weiss gives the example of a model cities program that sought to coordinate existing services while at the same time attempted innovative new programs. In this case, innovation is likely to weaken coordination, and coordination is likely to dampen the innovating spirit.[87] An evaluator must wrestle with deciding which of the two goals is more realistic and not treat the two as if they were independent and separate. Also, programs have short-term goals and long-term goals, and decisions need to be made about which are more relevant.[88]

An evaluator does not make these kinds of decisions independently, but must "thrash out the final selection of goals for study with decision makers and program managers."[89] Rubin and Babbie, for example, say that evaluators should "learn as much as possible about the *stakeholders*—those with vested interests in the evaluation whose beliefs, income status or careers and workload might be affected by the evaluation."[90] The evaluator should involve these stakeholders not only in the selection of goals and the design of the evaluation, but also at every step by "sharing mutual incremental feedback throughout all phases of the evaluation."[91]

Effectiveness Criteria

Once goals are decided on, the evaluator must put them in operational or measurable terms. A program may assess its effectiveness in terms of *quantity* of its outcomes. To assess quantity, one determines the volume, speed, or rate of services. For example, the goal of a probation department may be to maintain a certain rate of recidivism (the number of repeat offenses) made by offenders. The effectiveness criteria would be the specific number of offenses per offender in a period of time. Other effectiveness criteria may be number or hours of services provided, percentage of target group reached, number of people served, and number of people rehabilitated.

A program may also assess the effectiveness of its goals by the *quality* of the services it provides. How good were the services? For example, the goal of an in-home support service to the elderly may be to provide food preparation, visitation, transportation services. Evaluating the quality of the in-home support services would include determining how well food was prepared, the friendliness of the visitors, and the efficiency of transportation. Quality may be measured by assessing client satisfaction with services, the length of time treatment was effective, and the impact of services on the problem.

Measurements

Measurements are indicators of success or effectiveness. There are a number of scales, indices, tests, instruments, and measures that have already been developed and used for measuring organizations and groups. Among these are the Michigan Organizational Assessment Questionnaire, the Organizational Assessment Inventory, Group Effectiveness Survey, Organizational Diagnosis Questionnaire, and Job Diagnostic Survey.[92] You may also devise measures specifically for the program you are evaluating.

Often it is best if multiple measures are used. "By the use of a number of measures, each contributing a different facet of information, we can limit the effect of irrelevancies and develop a more rounded and truer picture of program outcomes."[93]

Just as an evaluator may develop multiple measures of assessing program effectiveness, he or she may also use multiple means of collecting data. The number and mix of sources of data are limited only by the ingenuity and imagination of the researcher. Possible sources are:

1. Interviews
2. Questionnaires
3. Observation
4. Ratings (by peers, staff, experts)
5. Psychometric tests of attitudes, values, personality, preferences, norms, and beliefs.
6. Institutional records
7. Government statistics
8. Tests of information, interpretation, and skills
9. Projective techniques
10. Situational tests presenting respondent with simulated life situations
11. Diary records
12. Physical evidence
13. Clinical examinations
14. Financial records
15. Documents (minutes of meetings, newspaper accounts, transcripts of trials)

Designing the Evaluation

Three kinds of designs are most useful in program evaluation research: pure experimental research, quasi-experimental research, and benefit-cost analysis.

Pure Experimental Research

Pure experimental social science research typically uses randomly selected subjects in controlled settings. For example, evaluating a new treatment program in a facility for juveniles addicted to drugs, using experimental research, would require randomly selecting a group of typical drug users from all drug users in the facility. The group would then be divided into two subgroups; one would be the control group and the other would be the experimental group. Next, the levels of drug abuse of each group would be assessed to get a baseline before treatment. The control group would receive conventional treatment or no treatment at all. The experimental group would receive the new treatment. After the treatment is completed, each group would be retested. The results would be compared. If the rate of drug use in the experimental treatment group is considerably less than that of the control group, one might conclude that the new treatment approach was effective.

While experimental research is fairly straightforward, you may already see why this "pure" experiment might not work in actual practice. For example, it may not only be impractical to exclude some juveniles from a treatment program but also illegal and/or unethical. In addition, because the offenders know who is receiving a treatment program, they may collude to interfere with its results. Success of the treatment program may be affected by any number of external factors that have nothing to do with treatment, such as the home, school, and peer relationships. Finally, organizations are notoriously turbulent settings and are continually changing. There is very little that a researcher can adequately control. People enter programs and leave them without notice. Staff come and go. People enter and grow independently of treatment in ways that may affect findings. As a result, pure experimental research may not be possible in organizational settings.

Quasi-Experimental Research

Quasi-experimental research provides ways to assess program effectiveness in the turbulent atmosphere of an organization and in community settings where many of the variables are less amenable to strict control. While there are many kinds of quasi-experimental research designs,[94] two that are useful in program evaluation are the time series and the nonequivalent control group designs.

TIME SERIES DESIGNS.   Time series designs attempt to account for events that give false indicators of success, such as changes in the program's environment, the life cycle of a program, or shifts in personnel. Sometimes what may seem to be an effect of a program may instead be due to changes in external conditions over time. For example, reduced drug abuse among juveniles in a group home may be due to heavy drug users leaving the group home, giving a false impression that treatment program was successful. Also, what may appear to be program effectiveness may only reflect improvement in staff capability in providing treatment. Finally, less capable staff may have been replaced with more competent people, and this improvement may give a false picture of program effectiveness.

Time series designs help correct these "threats" to the validity of results. Researchers using time series designs collect data at regular intervals over a period of time before the program is implemented to obtain a picture of the trends in a program's service pattern. As this information is assessed, the normal shifts in program activity can be accounted for. Then, when the new program being tested is instituted, it too is measured over time to allow for maturation of staff, adjusting to the new program routine, and changes in clients or staff. Finally, after enough evaluations are conducted that give an accurate picture of the new program's success rate, the time series before and during the program are compared to assess whether the new program is effective.

NONEQUIVALENT CONTROL GROUP DESIGNS. If it is impossible to divide a program into two groups for the purpose of program evaluation, it may be possible to find another group with similar characteristics with which the experimental group may be compared. For example, if you want to evaluate a new treatment program for youth in a residential facility, you could use residents of another residential facility that is receiving no treatment or a conventional treatment as a control group. Use a time series design to obtain a baseline on both the experimental group and the control group. Then, implement the treatment program with the experimental group while continuing to take measurements on both groups. After the treatment is over, test both groups and compare the results. If the experimental group improved in comparison to the control group, you may have some confidence that the outcome was the result of the treatment and not due to extraneous factors.

Benefit-Cost Analysis

Benefit-cost analysis is an extension of rational problem solving.[95] It is a way of looking at various program alternatives and estimating the benefit in dollars that each alternative will provide in comparison to its potential dollar costs. Once a benefit/cost ratio is established for each program alternative, the various benefit/cost ratios are compared. The one with the highest ratio, that is, the one that gives the best return, will often be selected. For example, if program A provides benefits of $200 and costs only $100, the benefit/cost ratio is 2/1 or 2. On the other hand, if program B provides the same benefits of $200 but costs $300, its benefit/cost ratio is 2/3 or .667. It is easy to see that if given a choice between the two programs, each of which is assumed to give equal benefits, the one that is least costly will give society the most return for each dollar spent.

The difficulty in benefit-cost analysis is accounting for all of the costs and benefits of a program and converting often highly intangible results into dollar figures. For example, what are the costs to a community if a child is abused or the benefits in dollars when the cycle of abuse is broken? How much is it worth to a community to empower its members to make decisions for themselves? Community empowerment may not be considered by some to be a benefit, because powerful groups may have a vested interest in keeping community members dependent on them. Some argue that trying to place dollar amounts on social costs is inappropriate, because activities like educating a mentally retarded child and providing needed specialized services ought to be done for humanitarian reasons even though the costs far outweigh any monetary benefits that will accrue.

In spite of these difficulties, benefit-cost analysis does have some ways of making decisions on fixing dollar amounts. One way, for example, is to set a "fixed level of benefits and assume that alternative programs are all attempting to reach the same goal."[96] The analyst then looks at the costs of all the programs to achieve the given level of benefit and chooses the one that costs the least.

While benefit-cost analysis is helpful in promoting efficiency and making rational decisions, it is most useful in the following kinds of situations:

1. When existing data or easily collected data give the scope and degree of program impact.[97]
2. When the main benefits can be reduced to dollar terms without extraordinary guesswork or neglect of crucial effects.[98]
3. When the indirect costs and spin-off costs of a social service program are easily and readily identifiable.
4. When the different measures of cost such as cost per case, cost per client, and cost per hour of service are calculable and can be compared to those of other agencies.

Hornick and Burrows recommend the following in applying benefit-cost analysis to social programs:

1. Compare only agencies with similar objectives and similar clients.
2. If the agency's records are inadequate, conduct a time budget study during a stable period of the study.
3. Use the same parameters or cost criteria for all agencies being compared.
4. Calculate the agency costs in as many ways as possible, such as cost per case, cost per client, and cost per hour of direct service to the client.[99]

Conclusion

Program development is a natural outcome of macro social work change. The process of developing a program includes obtaining a board of directors, writing a mission statement, funding the program, developing its structure, staffing the new agency, and developing a plan for evaluating the program's effectiveness. A macro social worker may feel proud and satisfied that the sometimes lengthy and time-consuming process that was begun with a needs assessment, progressed through a task group, problem-solving process involving community development, social action, or social planning has resulted in the development of a new agency, service, or program.

KEY CONCEPTS

institutional care
community-based care
normative needs
demand needs
needs assessment
social indicators approach
rates under treatment (RUT)
focused interviews
key informant
focus groups
community forum
surveys
board of directors
for-profit organization
not-for-profit organization
incorporation
articles of incorporation
constitution
by-laws
mission statement
agency structure
agency staffing
executive director
job description
job announcement
application form
independent solicitation
cooperative solicitation
United Way
membership dues
benefits
fees for service
private foundation grant
foundation
operating foundation
community foundation
general purpose foundation
family foundation
corporate foundation
government grant
reactive approach to grants
proactive approach to grants
sources of information
idea statement
RFP
grant proposal
contracting

vendor
program evaluation
program evaluation research
input analysis
process analysis
impact or outcome analysis
stakeholders
operational terms
measures
pure experimental research
quasi-experimental research
time-series design
non-equivalent control group design
benefit-cost analysis

QUESTIONS FOR DISCUSSION

1. What changes in purpose, structure, and roles do you think may be required of a task group as it moves from being a social or community action group to setting up an agency program?

2. You are thinking of setting up a small group home for persons who have mental illness problems. Discuss the benefits and disadvantages of being a profit-making organization and a not-for-profit organization, and make a decision about which way is best for your program.

3. Social agencies, businesses, as well as your college or university more than likely have articles of incorporation, constitutions, by-laws, and mission statements. Collect as many of these as you can. Compare the mission statements. What are their common characteristics? What do they tell you about an organization? Do they leave out anything you think is important? How could you improve them?

4. Compare the articles of incorporation, by-laws, and constitutions that you have collected. What are the similarities and differences?

5. Obtain an organizational chart from your college or university. Examine the staffing patterns. How is the organization structured? How many organizational layers are there? How wide is the structure dispersed horizontally? Would you characterize the organization as simple or complex? Formal or informal?

ADDITIONAL READING

Working with Boards and Staff

Devney, Darcy Campion. *Organizing Special Events and Conferences: A Practical Guide for Busy Volunteers and Staff.* Sarasota, FL: Pineapple Press, 1990.

Emenhiser, David. *Power Funding: Gaining Access to Power, Influence, and Money in Your Community.* Rockford, MD: Fundraising Institute, 1992.

Lawson, John D. *When You Preside.* 5th ed. Danville, IL: Interstate Printers and Publishers, 1980.

Whetten, Mary Bray, ed. *The Basic Meeting Manual: For Officers and Members of Any Organization.* Nashville, TN: Thomas Nelson, 1986.

Foundations

The following are publications of The Foundation Center, 79 Fifth Avenue, New York, NY, 10003. Each of these sources is updated and published annually.

The Foundation Directory. Contains profiles of the largest U.S. foundations—those that have at least $2 million in assets and disperse $200,000 or more annually. Includes information on 28,000 selected grants.

The Foundation Directory, Part 2: A Guide to Grant Programs $50,000 to $200,000. Data on over 4,200 mid-sized foundations including more than 28,000 recently awarded foundation grants.

Foundation Grants Index Annual. An index of grant subject areas. Within each subject area grant descriptions are listed geographically by state and alphabetically by foundation.

The Foundation 1000. Information on the one thousand largest foundations in the country responsible for 60 percent of all foundation grant dollars. Foundation 1,000 grantmakers hold over $100 billion in assets and award $6 billion in more than 190,000 grants to nonprofit organizations annually.

National Directory of Corporate Giving. Information on corporate foundations.

National Guide to Funding for Children, Youth and Families. Information on foundations and corporate direct-giving programs.

National Guide to Funding for the Economically Disadvantaged. Information on foundation for employment programs, homeless shelters, welfare initiatives, and others.

Governmental Funding Sources

Catalog of Federal Domestic Assistance. Superintendent of Documents. U.S. Government Printing Office. Mailstop SSOP. Washington, DC, 20402-9328.

Federal Register and *Federal Register Index.* Superintendent of Documents. P.O. Box 371954. Pittsburgh, PA, 15250-7954.

Contracting

Alson, F. M., et al. *Contracting with the Federal Government.* New York: Wiley, 1984.

Writing Grants and Proposals

Bauer, D. G. *The "How-to" Grants Manual.* New York: Macmillan, 1984.

Foundation Center. *The Foundation Center's Guide to Proposal Writing.* New York: Foundation Center, 1994.

Hall, Mary. *Getting Funded: A Complete Guide to Proposal Writing.* 3d ed. Portland, OR: Continuing Education Publications, Portland State University, 1988.

Read, Patricia. *Foundation Fundamentals: A Guide for Grantseekers.* 5th ed. New York: Foundation Center, 1994.

White, Virginia. *Grant Proposals That Succeeded.* New York: Plenum Press, 1984.

Program Evaluation

Bennet, Carl A., and Arthur A. Lumsdaine, eds. *Evaluation and Experiment.* New York: Academic Press, 1975.

Posavac, Emil J., and Raymond G. Carey. *Program Evaluation: Methods and Case Studies.* Englewood Cliffs, NJ: Prentice-Hall, 1985.

Rossi, Peter H., and Howard E. Freeman. *Evaluation: A Systematic Approach.* Beverly Hills, CA: Sage, 1982.

Tripodi, T. *Evaluative Research for Social Workers.* Englewood Cliffs, NJ: Prentice-Hall, 1983.

Weiss, Carol. *Evaluation Research.* Englewood Cliffs, NJ: Prentice-Hall, 1972.

Benefit-Cost Analysis

Thompson, M.S. *Benefit-Cost Analysis for Program Evaluation.* Beverly Hills, CA: Sage, 1983

EXERCISES

EXERCISE 38:
Developing a Program

You are a macro social worker with an inner-city task force on community development. The task force is particularly concerned about a number of problems that center on inner-city youth. These problems include dropouts, gangs, drug abuse, and crime. The lives of many inner-city youth are being wasted; they have few resources and opportunities. Recently, a young boy named Roy, one of the youth in your neighborhood, was killed in a gang fight.

The task force has named the project after Roy. Called Reclaiming Our Youth (ROY), the task force has decided on developing an innovative pilot program for job training, drug rehabilitation, education, counseling, recreation, and group work.

Form subgroups of six or seven persons. Decide on a chairperson and a recorder. Then decide how you will tackle the problem. Develop a plan for the program including a mission statement, goals and objectives, staffing, and a funding source. After your task group has finished, share your plan with the class.

EXERCISES

EXERCISE 39:
Developing an Idea Statement

This exercise gives you an opportunity to develop an idea statement and then experience the process of deciding among several different idea statements.

You decide that the ROY program (EXERCISE 38) will apply for a funding grant. In your community, there are about three hundred dropouts, at least fifty of whom are runaway youth. Among the ideas you have developed are to provide medical services, drug treatment, job finding, shelter, recreation, and counseling services as well as reunification services. Reunification helps families become reunited after children have been removed and placed in foster homes.

You are also interested in working with law enforcement to prevent sexual exploitation of youth. Your program would provide youth with financial assistance, alternative education to prevent dropping out of high school, job training, as well as legal services by which youth can become emancipated from their families of origin and live independently or in group settings.

Form groups of six or seven persons. These should be different groups than those in EXERCISE 38. Choose one of the ideas in this exercise or one that resulted from EXERCISE 38. Develop an idea statement that could be used for a grant proposal. The idea statement should be no longer than four pages and follow the outline presented in chapter 11.

The second part of this exercise gives you experience in deciding which idea statement should be asked for a full proposal. Form into several groups each one having a mixture of people from the previous groups. Each group plays the role of a foundation committee reviewing idea statements. Decide on the criteria that you will use in your group to evaluate the idea statements. Review each of the idea statements, then rank them in order according to your funding criteria. Criteria may include soundness of the idea, cost effectiveness, potential community impact, capability of implementation, long-range benefits, and others.

After your group has ranked the idea statements, share your ranking with the class. Discuss the rankings and the criteria committees used. Why did you decide on one idea statement rather than another? Spend time discussing what you learned about the process. What does it take to write a successful idea statement? Did deciding among rival idea statements help you discover what makes a good idea statement?

EXERCISE 40:
Designing a Program Evaluation

One of the components of the ROY program in which foundations and government agencies are particularly interested is the drug rehabilitation program. The program includes both a halfway house in-patient treatment program and an out-patient program. Each program offers counseling, medical care, and a twelve-step program. The counseling and medical care components use innovative treatment methods, and both foundations and governmental agencies are interested in assessing the effectiveness of these methods. The halfway house has space for six youths and includes recreation and life skills training. The ROY program has decided that it wants to assess the effectiveness of the counseling and medical care drug treatment services compared with other drug treatment programs. Second, it wants to measure the effectiveness of the in-patient drug treatment services in comparison with out-patient services to help in deciding which program should be refunded after the first year. Third, it wants an internal systems process analysis of the overall ROY program.

Form into teams of six persons. Develop a program evaluation design for each of the three components to be measured.

How would your team compare the effectiveness of the ROY program with other programs? How would your team measure the in-patient and the out-patient program and compare them? What internal systems state issues in the overall ROY program would you choose to monitor, and how would you monitor them?

In your research design describe (1) how you would decide on the goals of your research; (2) how you would operationalize your goals, i.e., what effectiveness criteria would you use; (3) what tests, scales, indices, or other measures you would use; (4) what methods of data collection you would use; and (5) what kinds of research designs you would choose. Would you use a pure experimental research design, a quasi-experimental design, or a benefit-cost analysis? After your group has developed its design, share it with other groups. What were the best features of the different designs? How could your design have been improved?

CHAPTER 12

The Macro Social Worker as Administrator

For Harry Hopkins, social administrator for President Franklin Roosevelt during the Depression, administration was not simply putting a policy into motion. It was deciding to do something, seeing it work, seeking new opportunities and acting on willingness to live in a stream of events that couldn't be predicted.

Now these are the last words of David.

He that ruleth over men must be just,
   ruling in the fear of God.
And he shall be as the light in the morning,
   when the sun riseth.
Even a morning without clouds,
   as the tender grass,
Springing out of the earth,
   by clear shining after rain.
     —II SAMUEL 23: 1A, 3B-5
      KING JAMES VERSION OF THE BIBLE

IDEAS IN THIS CHAPTER

Harry Hopkins, Macro Social Worker, Public Administrator

He wrote no books and gave few speeches. He never earned a large salary, and when he died he was nearly penniless. Rarely in good health, he was in pain much of his life. He was never elected to public office and did not earn advanced degrees. He was, throughout much of his career, vilified in the press and by many politicians. Yet, during the thirteen years that he remained in public service, he was recognized as the second most powerful man in America and had a profound impact on every major crisis from the international economic collapse to the dawn of the atomic age. Within five years of coming to Washington, he spent more money and employed more people than any other man in history. He directed programs that helped mobilize the nation for one of the greatest confrontations of the century and with that productivity paved the way for the defeat of the Axis powers. Emissary to two presidents, he forged the great alliance between the United States, the Soviet Union, and Great Britain, helping win World War II, and set the course for the postwar era.

He was Harry Lloyd Hopkins, macro social worker and public administrator. Born in 1890, he was the son of a gold prospector and championship bowler. His mother encouraged him in all his endeavors—"You were put on earth to serve others. Don't be afraid to take risks. What counts is not words but actions."

Hopkins attended Grinnell College where he majored in the new field of political science and was president of the senior class of 1912. He was an extrovert with acute powers of calculation and an ability to learn with speed and accuracy, his most remarkable attribute in later years. Hopkins had not made up his mind about a future career when he graduated and took a summer job at Christadora camp for poor children in New Jersey, an experience that was to change his life forever. After two months at the camp, he was, and would always remain, a zealous champion of the underprivileged.

He became a social worker at the Christadora House on New York's Lower East Side for room and board and $5 a month pocket money. The poverty and squalor of the city slums were to Hopkins alien and shocking. It was something he never forgot.

During his first winter in New York he asked for a job with the Association for Improving the Condition of the Poor (AICP) and was put on the payroll at $40 a month on a training basis. During the day he worked for Christadora House, and at night he went out on assignments for the AICP. Within two years this zealous social worker became the executive secretary of the New York City Board of Child Welfare.

He joined the Red Cross during World War I as director of the Gulf Division in New Orleans, and eventually he was overseeing all Red Cross activities in the southeastern part of the United States. After the war, Hopkins accepted a position as director of the Health Division of the AICP. He was charged with providing research into the health conditions of New York City. From there he became administrator of the New York Tuberculosis Association.

In 1928 Franklin Roosevelt was elected governor of New York. After the crash of 1929, he established the Temporary Emergency Relief Administration (TERA) and offered the position of deputy to young Harry Hopkins. TERA was the largest and most daring program for the relief of unemployment that had ever been undertaken by any state in the Union.[1] Within a year, he was appointed chairman, and by 1932, Harry Hopkins had given out $30 million in aid and helped over a million destitute people.

Shortly after Roosevelt was elected president, he invited Hopkins to head the Federal Emergency Relief Administration (FERA), which meant taking a reduction in pay from $15,000 to $8,000 to enter federal service. In his first two hours in office, Hopkins disbursed more than $5 million in aid to the states. But more than simply providing relief, Hopkins and Roosevelt were engineering a revolutionary change in the relationship between the American government and its citizens. Three-and-a-half weeks after he had entered federal government service, Hopkins spoke to the National Conference of Social Work and announced the principle that relief was an obligation of government, breaking with the tradition of nongovernmental intervention that had been in place for the previous seventy years.

At the end of his first year, Hopkins had helped in solving the vital problems of some 17 million people and spent $1.5 billion in aid with an organization consisting of only 121 people and a payroll of only $22,000 per month. Hopkins believed in jobs not welfare. He put together a program for putting people to work on governmental subsidized projects called the Civil Works Administration (CWA), one of the broadest programs ever instituted by the U.S. government, and none too soon. By 1933, 42,000 businesses had failed and 25 percent of the entire work force was unemployed. The country was near revolution. Nazism and communism were barking at the door.

"Get the money out fast, and get it out honestly," was Roosevelt's charge, and Hopkins did it with incredible zeal and at a terrific pace, putting 4 million people to work in the first thirty days of CWA's existence. In three-and-a-half months the CWA inaugurated 180,000 work projects. It built or improved 40,000 schools, laid 12,000,000 feet of sewer pipe, built 469 airports and improved 529 more, built 255,000 miles of road, employed 50,000 teachers, and built 3,700 playgrounds. Among the 4.26 million people for whom work was found were 3,000 writers and artists, the inception of the Federal Arts Program. "It is indefensible to allow the spirit of citizens to be crushed by squalor," he said.

While compassion drove Hopkins onward, it was his genius for problem solving that drove him upward. Administration was not simply putting a policy into motion. It was deciding to do something, seeing it work, seeking new opportunities, and acting on willingness to live in a stream of events that couldn't be predicted.

With the passage of the Work Relief Bill in 1934, Hopkins was put in charge of the Works Progress Administration (WPA). Told by Roosevelt, "Do something and do it quickly, and don't come back with problems," Hopkins eventually spent over $10 billion to create jobs mobilizing more men than both the army and the navy combined in World War I. By 1935 he had found jobs for over 18 million workers and reported to Roosevelt, "Well, they're all at work, just don't ask me what the hell they're doing." Hopkins organized medical care, housing, education, school hot lunch programs, adult literacy programs, day-care centers, rehabilitation for families, jobs, and direct relief. Washington became involved in almost every sector of American life.

Unimpressed by the pretensions of the rich and powerful, Hopkins refused to provide patronage for politicians and became a target for vilification. Yet he kept his office free from scandal. He asked for nothing but a commitment to serve. With Hopkins' efforts, unemployment was cut in half by 1936 and the cries for revolution were muted. Roosevelt was reelected to his second term.

During this period Hopkins was diagnosed with cancer of the stomach and given a 5 percent chance of survival. But survive he did with three quarters of his stomach removed. By 1939, at the end of his second term, Roosevelt began grooming Hopkins as a presidential candidate. Hopkins was appointed secretary of commerce to give him a role that was less controversial and had more status. But, shortly thereafter, he developed a mysterious ailment that prevented his body from absorbing food. The man who had fed millions was slowly starving to death. Fed intravenously and subsisting on vitamins and blood transfusions, he survived but became a semi-invalid.

Hopkins resigned from the cabinet and left public service, gaunt and worn after seven years of eighteen-hour days and constant pressure. Having no office, no position, and no title or salary, Hopkins was invited by his old friend Roosevelt to live as a guest at the White House. But world events would draw Hopkins back to even more important roles of public service.

When Winston Churchill became prime minister of Great Britain in May 1940, Britain was financially bankrupt and threatened with imminent destruction from Hitler's aerial attacks. Roosevelt sent Hopkins as his personal envoy to Churchill, who, desperate for American support and assistance, was not encouraged to learn that a social worker having no credentials or official standing was visiting him. Soon, however, he found in Hopkins a staunch ally. Against the cries of those who wanted the United States to remain neutral, Hopkins urged that America support Britain, arguing for a "Lend/Lease" program to arm the allies.

Harry Hopkins again was put in charge. With $7 billion to spend, Hopkins was directed to develop a program by which the United States could exceed the production of war goods of Germany, Italy, and Japan combined.[2] American war production was almost nonexistent. Having put millions of American people to work on any number of projects, Hopkins was skilled at breaking bottlenecks and red tape. Working from a card table in his bedroom at the White House, Harry Hopkins began the most massive undertaking of his career. Over a year later, on December 7, 1941, Japan attacked Pearl Harbor, bringing America into the war. Because of Hopkins, however, American war production was approaching full capacity, ready to arm and supply not only our own soldiers but those of our allies as well.

With the war effort well under way, Hopkins turned to diplomacy. Hopkins was convinced of the need for a closer relationship between Roosevelt and Churchill. Because of his close relationship with both men, he arranged a secret meeting between them in early August 1941. At about the same time, Hitler invaded Russia. While the German troops were approaching Moscow, Hopkins told Roosevelt that he needed to go to Russia to determine if Russia could hold and to assess the position of Stalin who once before had allied himself with Hitler. It was the most secret mission of World War II. Hopkins was convinced that Stalin was ruthless but in control. Hopkins returned to the United States and reported that Stalin would not forge an alliance with Hitler, convincing Churchill and Roosevelt to aid Russia, and establishing the foundation for the United Nations and the post–World War II order.

In 1943 Hopkins arranged the historic meeting between Churchill, Stalin, and Roosevelt in Teheran, forging the Grand Alliance. In 1944 Hopkins again collapsed, but Roosevelt inspired him once more to piece together the meeting of the Big Three at Yalta where the map of Europe was redrawn. Completely drained after Yalta, Hopkins was hospitalized. Roosevelt died three months later.

In 1945, with the fate of the United Nations in the balance, Truman convinced Hopkins to meet one more time with Stalin. Successfully negotiating a compromise, Harry Hopkins returned home a national hero. Soon after he died at age fifty-five.

Harry Hopkins, macro social worker and public administrator, the personal envoy of two presidents, empowered by the time he died to spend billions of dollars for the relief of others and billions more in Lend Lease, who guided America out of the Great Depression and whose foresight forged the Great Alliance, was a dedicated public servant and war hero. Public service was his creed, his life, his legacy. He had conviction without limit and was without a doubt one of the great humanitarians of our time. He died physically and financially broken, having spent every ounce of his strength in service to his country.

Introduction

People in charge of helping organizations function are administrators. Social workers who practice at either the micro or the macro level will have opportunities to work in a large, complex organization and experience the importance of administration in carrying out social work.

This chapter defines administration and describes several of the areas in which administration operates. The dilemmas that social work administrators face are explored so that you can be prepared, either as a micro or macro level practitioner, to understand and deal with them. Finally, an action model of social administration is proposed.

What Is Administration?

The word *administer* comes from the Latin *ad ministrare,* meaning "minister to" or "to serve." The word *administer* is used in this text to mean processes by which social work leaders meet social and personal needs, remediate social hurt, and create the conditions by which people's welfare can be improved by means of a social agency.[3] Administration is the "process that has to do with running an agency, and involves goals, policies, staff, management, services and evaluation."[4] Social workers and clients become partners in a mutual undertaking of making a better society for themselves and others. The social agency is the servant of the entire community in which it resides, a social tool for making a better world. Administrators include line supervisors, division or departmental managers, and the executive director. Much of the success of any social work program depends on the quality of its administrative leadership.

What Administrators Do

Social administration has several aspects. Luther Gulick, one of the foremost of early management theorists, described the functions of management as planning, organizing, staffing, directing, coordinating, reporting, and budgeting, for which he applied the acronym POSDCORB.[5] This listing has been repeated and modified by numerous authors.[6]

In this section, three of the most important of these functions are described. First is how social administrators use planning to facilitate social work. Second is budgeting, a form of planning that administrators must consider. Third is the staffing function, which today is called personnel administration. The section closes with a discussion about how socially conscious administrators engage in administrative decision making and some of the tools administrators use.

Planning

Social agencies are always in a state of change. There are new services to consider, new problems to solve, new contingencies to deal with, new issues in the agency's environment with which to interact, and new political and economic factors with which to contend. As a result, a good deal of social administrative effort on a day-to-day basis goes into planning. In fact, planning is probably one of the major tasks that an administrator accomplishes.[7] A responsible administrator will continually sift through the many issues confronting her or him and develop plans to deal with those issues. Rarely will he or she be caught off guard or unaware of problems in the agency's internal processes or external social environment.

Weinbach says that planning includes "those structures and activities that are used to shape future events in organizations."[8] Plans usually are written in some form that helps employees and clients orient themselves toward that direction. For example, the mission statement of a social agency tells people the purpose for which that agency has been established. "All other planning is shaped by the purpose or mission"[9] of the agency. The overall purpose of the social agency is most often decided by its board, the group that technically "owns" the social agency and defines its direction.

Planning also involves helping set goals and objectives for the agency and developing "work maps" showing how these goals and objectives can be accomplished.[10] Skidmore uses planning almost synonymously with rational problem solving in which the administrator and staff

1. select objectives
2. consider agency resources
3. enumerate alternatives
4. anticipate outcomes of alternatives
5. decide on the best plan
6. plan a specific program for action
7. are open to change.[11]

Among the kinds of plans that people in social agencies develop are internal policies, procedures, programs, and budgets. Koontz, O'Donnell, and Weinrich define policies as "general statements . . . which guide or channel thinking and action in decision making."[12] Policies, according to Herbert Simon, are the premises of decisions.[13] They include not only ways of thinking but also values.[14] Policies, therefore, determine to a large extent the direction that the social agency will take. It is important that a good deal of thought go into policies, because they shape the culture and determine the milieu of the agency. Procedures flow from policies, which are plans that help people work in a coordinated fashion and facilitate communication.

Administrators along with staff scan the social environment "for major discontinuities . . . that might provide opportunities or constraints"[15] and monitor "gradual changes in environmental indicators"[16] to plan for client needs and for ways that the social agency can meet those needs by developing new programs.

Budgeting

Both new and old programs are dependent upon and come from the most basic and important organizational plan, the agency's budget. Aaron Wildavsky says that "budgeting is translating financial resources into human purposes."[17] Because resources are finite and human desires are infinite, a budget can "never be just one thing, but must be many."[18] A budget "may be characterized as a series of goals with price tags attached,"[19] and when, "choices are coordinated so as to achieve desired goals, a budget may be called a plan."[20] A budget according to Gross is a " 'plan of action.' It represents the organization's blueprint for the coming months or years, expressed in monetary terms."[21] In addition to being plans of action, budgets "determine future states of affairs

through a series of current actions. Hence budgets are also predictions."[22] "Since funds are limited, a budget becomes a mechanism for allocating resources."[23] When an organization attempts to achieve its "desired objectives at its lowest cost, a budget may become an instrument for pursuing efficiency."[24]

"Once enacted, a budget becomes a precedent; the fact that something has been done once vastly increases the chance that it will be done again."[25] Budgets also become forms of power. When a "budget is used to keep spending within set bounds . . . it becomes a device through which some actors try to control the behavior of others."[26] Organizational budgeting, finally, is a "tool to monitor the financial activities [of an agency] throughout the year."[27]

How Budgeting Occurs

Budgeting is intended to be a rational process.

Making [budgetary] decisions depends on calculating which alternatives to consider and to choose. Calculation involves determining how problems are identified, [how they] get broken down into manageable decisions, . . . how choices are made as to what is relevant and who shall be taken into account.[28]

However, arriving at a budget is far from being a rational process. For one thing, people are limited in their ability to calculate, time is severely limited, and "the number of matters that can be encompassed in one mind at the same time is quite small."[29] As a result, people "simplify in order to get by. They make small moves, let experience accumulate, and use feedback from their decisions to gauge consequences."[30] In other words, people tend to make budgeting decisions incrementally.[31] Incremental decisions "proceed from an existing base."[32]

A number of factors intervene that affect incremental decision making. For one thing, many public social work agencies lack an accepted base. "Spending agencies do not know how much they will need; reviewing bodies do not know how much they should allocate. Requests for spending and actual appropriations fluctuate wildly."[33] If the social agency or program is new, the problem is compounded. Often a negotiated struggle takes place. Central funding sources, such as United Way, or in government agencies the county or state budget departments, will exert control knowing that agencies will push for increases as hard as they can.[34] The result is a game in which each attempts to maximize its position without regard for the other.

Added to this mix is the relative prestige among agencies[35] and the self-interested pursuit of power by the executives of agencies who see success in the budgeting arena as their "road to fortune."[36] Budgeting, therefore, at least in public or government social work agencies, and to a certain extent in private ones that depend on United Way funding, is a mixture of rationality and politics.[37]

Kinds of Budgets

Four budgeting models are used by social agencies. These are line-item budgeting, program budgeting, functional budgeting, and zero-based budgeting.

LINE-ITEM BUDGETING.   The line-item budget, the most commonly used form of budgeting in social agencies, is a description about revenue and expenditures on functional items such as salaries, rent, utilities, postage, office supplies, training, consultation, and so on. The line-item budgeting process is relatively easy to calculate and to understand. Since line items may cut across departments or divisions, each department calculates how much it spent on these various items in a given year. The budget planner adds up these line items, compares actual expenditures with last year's budget, and projects costs on those items into the next year.

An advantage of line-item budgeting is "simplicity and expenditure control. The categories are limited and fixed over time, and increases and decreases projected in any given line are usually determined as a small increment"[38] over the previous year. For example, assume that last year the agency spent $100 on paper products. Allowing for inflation, the board approved $110 for paper expenditure this year. However, because of increased demand for paperwork, the agency actually spends $120 dollars this year. Based on those figures, it would probably make sense for the board to budget $130 next year given increased need and increased costs.

Sometimes line-item budgets are developed by financial or accounting staff who often simply guess

how much cost projections might increase or decrease in the coming year. Then they ask the social work professionals what increases they expect to make. Based on those figures, the budget is submitted to the board who, without further information or understanding, is asked to approve it.[39]

As a result, line-item budgeting may not be efficient because it is based on previous expenditures that may or may not be accurate predictors of future needs. Furthermore, line-item budgets do not help an administrator plan agency change and innovation. Line-item budgets "encourage stagnant programs."[40] They tell nothing about the relative importance of budget items or whether they were in fact needed by the various departments or units. They "do not depict efficiency, effectiveness, priorities, or programs of the agency."[41]

FUNCTIONAL BUDGETING.   In functional budgeting the various organizational functions are placed into categories that can be examined and monitored. In small agencies, for example, the administrator may want to develop two different budget categories: one for program services and another for supporting or administrative services.[42] This allows the administrator to see what proportion of funds is being spent on these two areas. Large organizations may break a functional budget into functional systems such as fund raising, public relations, service programs, system maintenance (personnel, accounting), and support (clerical, facilities maintenance). Looking at these expenditures over time, the administrator can see if expenditures in one area are growing more quickly than others and whether the amounts allocated to these various functions are appropriate.

PROGRAM BUDGETING.   On August 25, 1965, President Lyndon Johnson announced that he was introducing "a very new and revolutionary system" of program budgeting that would produce the "most effective and least costly" way to accomplish national goals.[43] The idea of program budgeting is to "make budgetary decisions by focusing on end products and on gross categories of output such as governmental objectives" instead of on discrete line items such as personnel, equipment, or maintenance.[44] A program budget "is constructed by regrouping all line-item expenditures into their respective program areas . . . to reflect the various programs that these resources support."[45] For example, organizational administrators will ask themselves: (1) What do we do? (program); (2) Why do we do it? (objective); and (3) How are we doing? (output in relation to objectives, or results).[46]

A program budget will first define program objectives in terms that are capable of being analyzed; second, have specific time horizons for accomplishing objectives; third, measure program effectiveness; and fourth, develop and compare alternative ways of attaining objectives.[47] For example, if the goal of a program is to rehabilitate one hundred alcoholics in the coming year, the program administrator and staff calculate the resources needed to accomplish this goal. Immediately the meaning of "rehabilitation" may become an issue. The administrator and staff are challenged to develop an operational definition of "rehabilitation." It is best to make goals specific, measurable, and time limited. Particular treatment methods also need to be explored and assessed. The staff and program administrator will then try to project the costs of rehabilitating one hundred persons who are alcoholics.

At various points during the year the program and the budget are reviewed to assess the degree to which the program was successful in accomplishing rehabilitation. The review may also provide an opportunity to assess the effectiveness of various treatment modalities, to arrive at more realistic operational definitions, and to improve treatment effectiveness.

Program budgeting has an advantage over line-item budgeting and functional budgeting because it allows social workers to examine what they have done in the past year, providing a mechanism for planning a better program for the future. In addition, it involves everyone who is responsible for the program outcomes in the budgeting process, particularly the line staff. This makes budgeting an integral part of the treatment process, gives social workers increased control over their work, and provides incentives in goal accomplishment. Finally, it can be a tool in evaluating treatment and program effectiveness.

ZERO-BASE BUDGETING. Zero-base budgeting was developed at Texas Instruments during 1969 and was first adopted for use by the government by Jimmy Carter in the preparation of the 1973 budget.[48] The administrator and staff begin from scratch, look at the agency's operations, and have no commitments to prior budget amounts.

A zero-base budget calls for three major types of calculations: (1) justification of the need for agency activities and programs without reference to past practice; (2) justification of the requested level of expenditure based on needs; and (3) justification of the costs of needed programs from the ground up.[49]

Used with discretion, particularly during times of retrenchment or with particular programs where productivity is of concern, zero-base budgeting can be a "valuable performance enhancing tool."[50] However, zero-base budgeting is expensive and time consuming; if it is used exclusively it may not be worth the cost.[51]

Personnel

Because social agencies are composed of people and their business or reason for being is to enhance people's lives, the human side of organizational life is one of the most, if not *the* most, important aspects of social administration. Over the years, organizational life has become increasingly specialized and professionalized. Dealing with human workers has become known as "personnel administration," whose goal [is] influencing "the effectiveness of employees in the organization."[52]

Today, personnel administration has given way to another term, "human resources management."

> [which] refers to the use, development, assessment, reward, and management of individual organizational members or worker groups. It includes the design, implementation of systems for planning, staffing, and developing employees, managing careers, evaluating performance, compensating workers, and smoothing labor relations.[53]

While it is beyond the scope of this section to cover all of these personnel functions, in public organizations there are four principles of public personnel administration that have become important. These are the merit concept, the political reward concept, the need concept, and the preference concept. So pervasive are these ideas that they often apply to private and not-for profit social agencies as well as public agencies.

Merit

Merit means that "appointments, promotions, and other personnel actions should be made on the basis of relative ability."[54] This principle implies that organizations should always attempt to find the best person for the job, and that it is inappropriate and unfair to select someone merely because he or she is a relative or a friend.[55] Employers should be selected because of their ability and qualifications. The criteria on which selection is based should be "job related."

It is inappropriate to consider issues or qualities that have nothing to do with the job itself. Job selection should be fair, impartial, and without bias. The best way to ensure impartiality is to use competitive examinations. Other personnel decisions such as salary increases, reduction-in-force, and dismissals should also be done fairly and impartially according to merit.[56]

Political Reward

Political reward means that "government jobs should be awarded to those who have campaigned for or otherwise rendered valuable service to the party in power. This is often referred to as the spoils or patronage view of public employment."[57] While political patronage is rarely used to fill most Civil Service positions today, elected officials still see party loyalty and political support as being consistent with the "merit" principle. They will award staff positions to loyal followers since party affiliation and ideological commitment are legitimate job requirements for many politically appointed positions.

Need

Government jobs should go to those who are unemployed or underemployed.[58] A number of government programs beginning with the Works Progress Administration in the Roosevelt presidency up to the Comprehensive Employment and Training Act of 1974 (CETA) have provided public service employment to unemployed and underemployed persons, regardless of merit or political connections. Today this idea continues to be used with such plans

as "workfare" in which welfare recipients are placed in jobs as a condition for receiving public assistance.

Preference

Government jobs should be given to particular categories of people who deserve them because of service to the country or to redress past injustices. Beginning with the Colonial period to the present, veterans have been rewarded with jobs or with a "veterans' preference" in competition with nonveterans for Civil Service jobs.[59]

Today, proposals made to provide preferential treatment are seen as a way of redressing past injustices to members of disadvantaged groups who were previously discriminated against. "Preference for such persons is justified in terms of social justice."[60] Affirmative action, for example, is one way that "equal employment opportunity to minority groups and women is achieved."[61]

Personnel Principles and Social Work

Social workers may support one or more of these principles. For example, social workers support merit as a principle of hiring because merit implies hiring the best person for the job. They may give preference to women or persons who come from ethically diverse groups to provide a better mixture of employees. Sometimes, a person who is developmentally disabled may be hired because of the commitment of social work to the handicapped. Social workers may lobby for programs that assist unemployed or underemployed people obtain jobs. Today the Job Corps and Civilian Conservation Corps provide public service jobs to unemployed young people on the basis of need.

Decision Making

Administrators use a variety of techniques to make decisions in organizations. Techniques such as decision analysis, Markov models, linear programming, queuing, and decision-trees, for example, were described in chapter 10. Benefit-cost analysis was covered in chapter 11. These are common tools that administrators can use and with which they should be familiar.[62]

In addition to these quantitative methods, administrators use decision techniques with groups of staff members. There are three kinds of decision techniques that are common in meetings: (1) brainstorming, (2) reverse brainstorming, and (3) nominal group technique (NGT).

Brainstorming

Brainstorming allows a group to obtain the maximum amount of input in an orderly manner. Brainstorming reduces dominance by cliques and disruption by overassertive, excessively garrulous, or domineering individuals; eliminates group dependency on a single authority figure; and allows those who are generally silent to contribute. Brainstorming is useful when the solution to a problem requires the group's cumulative wisdom. It provides a means by which a number of ideas about a topic can be generated in a short amount of time.

When using brainstorming, explain the purpose and rules to ensure an orderly process, especially in the early stages of a group when members are still getting to know one another. The rules of brainstorming are:

1. *Expressiveness:* express any idea that comes to mind
2. *Nonevaluation:* no criticism allowed
3. *Quantity:* the more ideas the better
4. *Building:* try to build on one another's ideas[63]

Place the issue on a blackboard or on a sheet of newsprint. Explain that the purpose of brainstorming is to generate as many ideas as possible, not the quality of ideas. "The wilder the idea the better; it is easier to tame down than to think up."[64] Any idea, no matter how far-fetched, is appropriate. In fact, the wilder and more audacious the ideas the better, since the goal of brainstorming is to break through old ways of thinking and come up with new, innovative courses of action.

Stress that brainstorming should be fun, exciting, and interesting. Hopefully, ideas will be stimulated and members will build on one another's ideas or come up with new and different combina-

Brainstorming is useful when the solution to a problem requires the group's cumulative wisdom.

tions. During the course of idea generation, no comments, criticism, evaluation, or discussion is allowed. As ideas are generated, write them down as quickly as members can think of them. Shy or reluctant members should be especially encouraged to participate.

In order to make sure that everyone has a chance and that all of the ideas are elicited, you may limit members to one idea at a time. Once members have exhausted themselves, the group reviews all of the suggestions, prioritizes them, and votes for those that seem worthwhile.

While brainstorming is a popular technique, empirical evidence indicates that it might not be as helpful as it appears. Individuals working alone who were asked specifically to be creative tend to generate more solutions than brainstorming groups.[65] When individual scores are added together to yield group scores, individuals tend to outperform brainstorming groups.[66] Finally, training, practice, and allowing subjects to record ideas after the brainstorming session tend to improve the group's proficiency.[67]

Reverse Brainstorming

Reverse brainstorming looks at the costs of the decision rather than its benefits. After lists of various ideas have been generated and the task group is narrowing the list to the best ideas, ask task group members, "What might go wrong with this idea?" Looking at the negative consequences of ideas can help to eliminate unworkable ones.

Nominal Group Technique

Andre Delbecq and Andrew Van de Ven developed an approach that combined the benefits gained when a number of individuals worked alone in generating ideas (a group in name only, hence the label "nominal") with the group processing capacity of interacting groups. They called their technique the Nominal Group Technique or NGT. NGT differs from brainstorming in that individuals work alone in idea generation. The process is not freewheeling, but controlled and structured. While members may feel uncomfortable in using a highly structured process, discomfort usually diminishes after using the technique a time or two.

1. *Silent generation of ideas in writing.* The leader introduces the problem or issue in writing on a blackboard or newsprint pad, explains the theory of NGT and the procedure, and answers questions. Once everyone understands the process and the issue to be decided, each individual silently generates ideas about the issue in writing. Usually this takes ten to fifteen minutes.

2. *Round robin sharing.* Once everyone has finished generating ideas, each person in turn reads one idea from his or her list, and the leader writes it on the board or newsprint. If a member has an idea that is the same as one on the board, he or she moves to the next idea on his or her list. Members continue to read from their lists until all of the ideas are recorded.

3. *Discussion and clarification.* The leader and members look over the entire list to make sure that it is comprehensive, clear, accurate, and nonduplicative. The list is refined, but the merits of differing ideas are not commented upon, discussed, or debated.

4. *Voting.* Because a large number of items may be listed, decision making is best done by voting. Each person votes on his or her top three preferences, writing them on a small card and passing them to the leader. The leader then records the rankings. A first choice receives three points, a second choice, 2 points, and a third choice, one point. The points are added up, and the total is divided by the number of group members to obtain an average. The results are compared.

5. *Discussion (optional).* Because several ideas may receive the same scores, discussion may help the group understand why they voted the way they did.

6. *Revoting.* The voting process can be repeated for the top scoring items until a clear winner emerges.

Advantages of NGT

NGT protects individuals from group pressure, because anonymity is assured and discussion is not allowed. It also provides for face-to-face contact and interaction at an appropriate time and in a controlled atmosphere.

In the idea generation phase, each person is given the assurance that he or she will have opportunity to generate as many ideas as possible. This stimulates creativity and provides a quiet atmosphere in which everyone can give the problem their full concentration and attention. During the Round Robin phase, each person knows that all of his or her ideas will receive equal and legitimate attention. There is no competition to push one idea or another. Everyone will have a chance. The voting process provides for an explicit mathematical solution that fairly weighs all members' inputs.

Finally, there is opportunity for discussion in which members' subjective feelings, perceptions, and input can be factored into the final vote. Individuals understand that there will be joint group commitment to the final decision.

Dilemmas of Social Work Administration

Administration, it may be recalled, is a set of processes by which social work leaders meet needs, remediate social hurt, and create the conditions by which people's welfare can be improved by means of a social agency. Administrators facilitate interaction between employees and clients. They are not masters who command behavior, as are managers.[68] Management implies that techniques are applied *to* people as if they were passive objects, unable to manage themselves. It is "an activity that performs certain functions in order to acquire, allocate, and utilize human and physical resources to accomplish some goal."[69] Organization is a command instrument with premises, rules, and roles intended to produce the kind of behavior that management asserts is necessary for effective functioning.

> The essence of the manager's task is to organize the human and nonhuman resources available to the organization that employs him so as to improve its position in the marketplace. His role is to persuade, inspire, manipulate, cajole, and intimidate those he manages so that his organization measures up to criteria of effectiveness shaped . . . by the expectations of those in control of his organization—its owners.[70]

Management is based on a passive atomistic model of humankind, and organization is a system whose goals and premises supersede the persons who compose it.

Most organizational social work tends to take its premises in large part from managerial theory rather than social administration. As a result, administrative social work tends to have built-in contradictions that cause dilemmas for clients, social workers, and administrators.[71] These contradictions may cause a kind of "culture shock" for new social workers who begin their practice in large complex organizational systems.[72] They may create continual frustration for social workers who expect social agencies to be compassionate, personal systems in which mutuality in relationships and two-way communication are prized but find out that the opposite is true.[73] Social workers who have creative ideas for improving social conditions may find these ideas falling on unresponsive ears.

It is important to understand that these contradictions are not simply the failure of one agency or of one administrator. They are due to conditions implicit in organizations themselves and in theories of management that affect client, social worker, and administrator alike. The way to begin a truly social administrative practice, therefore, is to uncover the inherent discontinuities between social work practice on the one hand and management posing as social administration on the other. Once these contradictions are exposed, social workers can make decisions about how to respond to them.

Sociality

Organizations are artificially contrived tools. "Administrative action," says Victor Thompson, "in the modern world is impersonal and institutional. . . . It is expected to be (and usually is) objective, impersonal, unsentimental, occasioned by universalistic criteria rather than particularistic personal appeals or sympathies."[74] "Administration" says Lowi, "is the rationalization of social relations."[75]

Organizations are also "social" systems composed of human beings who "track all kinds of mud from the rest of their lives with them into the organization, and have all kinds of interests that are independent of the organization."[76] People are creatures of feeling and values, who impute meaning into existence and, by means of social action and mutual relationship, seek to overcome the alienation that separates individuals from each other.

Because organizations have both formal and informal elements and are both rational and social at the same time, they are often difficult to understand. While the "formal" components of the organization—the rules, roles, and processes—are the most obvious elements by which organizations operate, in reality, the organization depends on its informal, social aspects to function properly. The social elements are the glue that holds the organization together.

Organizations could not exist without cooperation, trust, sincerity, integrity, honor, friendliness, and the ability of individuals to establish mutual relations, to communicate, and to interact meaningfully with one another. "Instrumental output and the daily working environment both depend on good internal working relations in which staff insecurities, fears, and suspicions can be eased and where cooperation, pride in one's work, and innovation can be fostered."[77]

Social workers are usually people who are interested in promoting these kinds of healthy human relationships. The profession of social work is a means by which people can find meaning in life and a way to express their natural caring and love for others.

Organizations, however, including social agencies, not only do not promote natural social relationships but may war against them, particularly those qualities that make people authentically human.

> The impersonal, objective, institutional approach to action, while demanded by the norms of an industrial society, is somewhat at war with basic sociopsychological needs of individuals, most of whom have been socialized in primary groups where personal loyalty and action are stressed.[78]

One of the greatest challenges facing social administrators is how to make social agencies places in which people's sociality can be expressed without letting the formal, functional aspects dominate.

Functional Thinking

We often forget that scientific logic, as an all pervasive way of thinking, is a recent develop-ment. Alberto Ramos, for example, says that "in the age-old sense, reason was understood as a force active in the human psyche which enables the individual to distinguish between good and evil, false and genuine knowledge, and therefore, to order his personal and social life."[79] This kind of rationality today is called "substantive" or ethical thinking.

Substantive rationality was most highly developed by the ancient Greeks and by the scholastic tradition of such medieval philosophers as Thomas Aquinas, for whom "the life of reason in the human psyche was envisioned as a reality resisting being reduced to an historical and social phenomenon."[80] Substantive reason is an "invariant" characteristic of the human condition, beyond time or place. "Reason perceives in the organic processes of society a purposive activity which is rational in the sense that all things have a final end and moral in the sense that this end is objectively good."[81] It is the means by which humans impute meaning into relationships and social systems design, overpowering strictly empirical, calculative aspects of rationality.

The opposite of substantive rationality is "formal, functional rationality," or "modern reason," first articulated by Thomas Hobbes. "From Hobbes to Adam Smith and the modern social scientists in general, instincts, passions, interests, and sheer motivations replaced [substantive] reason as the referent for understanding and ordaining human associated life."[82] Formal, functional rationality is thinking by calculation, or reckoning. Reckoning is goal-directed thinking, shooting straight at a target, calculating all of the factors that impinge on reaching that goal in the shortest, quickest, most effective and efficient manner.

So pervasive has "modern" reason become that it is conventionally understood as reason at large. It replaced substantive or classical value-laden reason by which individuals sought to overcome those forces in the world that cause disruption and chaos. Functional reason is particularly compatible with the rise of capitalism, mass democracy, and modern complex organization, providing these systems with common characteristics and operating premises. It is the basis for rational problem solving, the generalist social work method, and administrative decision making.

Modern reason accepts ends as given and expects that administrators will induce workers to operate within those given frames of reference to achieve results, meet goals, and carry programs forward. Functional thinking, therefore, prescribes a process onto systems and people in which the areas of choice are restricted.

> By selectively restricting the information they make available organizations shape . . . what concerned citizens know about the conditions in their communities. . . . As organizations develop or restrict information, they shape others' knowledge and beliefs, and just as significant they shape others' abilities to act and organize.[83]

In addition, what has classically and historically been considered as the epitome of humanness—people's ability to value, to feel compassion and altruism, and to form personal relationships—has, under organizational rationality, become defined as "irrational." Irrational human emotions and values that escape calculation tend to be eliminated in organizational logic, as are faith, hope, and other "nonrational" sentiments. As a result, the organizational individual tends to be unable to function as a fully fledged human being. This "structure of objectivation (transforming life and person partly into a thing, partly into a calculating machine) penetrates all realms of life and all spiritual functions."[84] Machinelike qualities become part of the human psyche, and those actions that personalize individual action contrary to calculations that maximize the organization's goals become devalued.

When applied in social work organizational settings, functional reason can result in people being treated as categories rather than persons. Cases are "managed" and treatment is applied to people externally as if individuals were passive objects to be acted upon by the objective, technically oriented social work expert. This kind of treatment dehumanizes, isolates, and alienates the client from the social worker, and the social worker from him or herself.

The dilemma that modern organizational reason poses to the action-oriented social work administrator is how to use the generalist social work method and organizational problem solving in a way that recognizes subjective values and feelings rather than only calculation. Second, administrators are challenged to resist treating clients as "problem categories" to be solved rather than as unique individuals each of whom requires particular treatment.

Being Holistic

While social workers are skilled in viewing clients from a "holistic" perspective, organizations are, in general, not interested in the employee or client as a whole person. Because of the way services are structured, organizations may even require social workers to fragment services to the point of dealing with only one aspect of a client's functioning. Moreover, many social welfare organizations are charged with "fixing" people who are already damaged instead of getting at the root of solving social problems.

Social workers are fragmented in organizational life. An employee who is valuable to an agency is one who learns how to "fit in," to understand prescribed rules, structure, and the way the system operates. Valued employees are those who can smoothly transfer their skills to the milieu of the agency and apply themselves to that world in a conscientious way. An employee is most highly valued if he or she can put the personal aspects of life aside in favor of his or her task at hand. One becomes an "organizational man or woman," accepting the rules, roles, norms, and values as commanded. The less one questions agency dictates, the easier organizational life becomes. A result of this fragmentation is that the employee becomes alienated.

Organizational specialization and fragmentation create problems for social workers who want to treat clients with dignity and respect while at the same time work within the constraints that the organization imposes. Resolving this dilemma requires honoring one's own ethical and spiritual core while resisting the temptation to reduce clients to components of a social system. It requires bearing the tension between maintaining personal authenticity and wholeness on the one hand, while fitting into the prescribed rules, roles, and ways of organizational behavior on the other.

Personalized Treatment

In organizations, individuals do not need to like the people with whom they must work. Organization makes this easy, because people are expected to play formal roles and adhere to stereotyped behavior. People are not expected to relate personally. In fact, they are discouraged from doing so. Relating personally tends to distract people from getting work done, at least in some situations.

Instead, organization has provided a means by which social relationships are no longer tied to personal feelings or needs. Employees, as well as clients, should be treated "objectively"—impartially and impersonally. "Objective" discharge of business primarily means business according to calculable rules and "without regard for persons."[85] Those human elements that cannot be calculated should be eliminated. The "virtue" of organizational rules is the extent to which human beings become "dehumanized."[86]

The organization individual views him- or herself and colleagues as impersonally and unemotionally as possible. Clients become "cases" rather than persons, and the worker tries to conform to those expectations and behaviors required.[87] Individuals are "treated" or processed.

The bureaucratic machine imposes standardization and uniformity over its components. Individuals who bring in needs or goals other than those of the organization must be "induced to give up their own goals for the organization and accept those of the owner."[88] Bureaucracy "requires functionaries, people who do their organizational duty and who do what they are told in the interest of the owner's goal for the organization."[89] The employee is a mere functionary. The "boss" gives the orders and expects to be obeyed regardless of the particular interests or perceptions of the employee.

For some, accepting organizational roles may be a welcome relief from the demands of forging authentic social relationships. For those determined to insert meaning into life, however, organizations can impose severe conflicts and nearly impossible demands on the human psyche.

While it may be difficult, therefore, to transfer social work values, skills, and practice principles to large complex organizations, it is important to do so. It is even more important for the field of administra-

tion. As one moves up the administrative hierarchy into administrative positions, one is inculcated and socialized more and more to the norms of organizational life. The demands to surrender one's humanness become greater, and the personal skills that were necessary as a social work practitioner may become handicaps.

The ability of an administrator to transcend the dehumanization that organizations demand, however, can provide strength and support for others who fail to bear the tension and alienation that modern organization imposes. Authentic social work practice means confronting dehumanizing behavior in a responsible way so as not to participate in it.

Administrative Compassion

Social agencies are devoted to the "administration of compassion," attempting to assist the needy, the destitute, the hungry, and those who have been abused or are in emotional pain. In spite of the fact that the very heart of social work is compassion, the nature of organizations is to eliminate personal, compassionate, altruistic treatment of individuals.

Those who press for personalistic, compassionate treatment in organizations, according to Thompson, will find the "need for compassion is immature."[90] Furthermore, in the most highly developed bureaucracies, compassion is "illegal."[91]

> Compassion, as exceptional, special, nonlegitimate treatment is irrational in relation to the owner's goal, and it is also illegitimate—a form of theft or personal appropriation of administrative resources. . . . As far as bureaucratic legitimacy is concerned, compassion is theft.[92]

The stage is set for the condition that Nietzsche described as the "transvaluation of values." Compassion becomes defined as "corruption,"[93] and decision making according to valuational absolutes is relegated to the status of "bemusing illusions."[94] Ethics, by which individuals attempt to apprehend and mold their lives according to ideals of "the good" is transformed into mere rules and norms of behavior that conform to organizational goals. Employees are constrained from expressing or acting on altruistic feelings in making decisions for clients if those decisions contradict prescribed agency mandates.

One of the chief struggles of social workers in organizational settings, therefore, is how to maintain compassion and altruism in the face of the demands of organization to be impersonal and noncompassionate toward clients and other social workers. In the face of organizational impersonality, the challenge for the agency administrator is how to prevent the agency from developing a hardened, uncaring, and noncompassionate culture, and instead facilitate an atmosphere of concern, openness, and welcome for clients and staff alike.

Authentic Communication

Communication in normal social interaction is a means by which individuals express feelings and develop relationships. In organizational life, such communication is stripped of its significance. Communication becomes one-way and top-down.[95] Language becomes a matter of technical jargon, a secretive way of maintaining control and organizational channels. Meaning is transformed into the context of organizational understandings and not human communication.[96]

Social workers, however, prize the importance of two-way communication and are trained in the use of active listening, perception checking, paraphrasing, and giving feedback. Social workers who value interpersonal communication skills, such as the ability to express feelings and emotions, attending, genuineness, respect, and mutuality,[97] often become confused when those skills are ignored in organizational communication. In many cases, mutuality in communication is actually precluded and is seen as dysfunctional. One-way communication is expected by those at the very top of organizations.

Faced with these difficulties, social workers in organizational settings must separate authentic two-way communication when relating to clients and social work colleagues from functional, organizational modes of communication that are used in relating to the chain of command. In their need for speed, efficiency, and control, administrators in social agencies may tend to emphasize technical jargon and one-way, top-down communication as a universal mode of engaging people. The dilemma for social work ad-

ministrators is how to establish a milieu of authentic interpersonal communication without sacrificing the need for efficiency and effectiveness in accomplishing the goals of the organization. Social work agency administrators must be sensitive to the different uses of communication in organizations.

Administrative Innovation

Social workers are interested in social change and in helping people become fully human. Social workers also tend to be people who attempt to impute meaning into their lives and are committed to helping their clients do so as well. Organizations, on the other hand, tend to treat employees and clients alike in prescribed ways that detract from their uniqueness. They mitigate against change and demand conformity.[98] "Bureaucratic organizations . . . tend in time," says Victor Thompson, "to become rigid and routinized . . . rather than organizers of human creativity and innovativeness."[99] This organizational rigidity is "not due to personalities, poor leadership, lack of interpersonal skills, or administrative incompetence. It is due to their nature."[100]

In spite of organizational rigidity and resistance, change is the prerogative of administration.[101] While an administrator may be committed to seeking innovative solutions to social problems by using the resources of his or her agency, that administrator knows that this can happen only within prescribed boundaries. Just as any other employee, the administrator is constrained by the prescribed conditions that surround his or her office. The administrator's world is a vastly simplified and self-contained one,[102] a largely artificial world with its own set of rules and procedures. While administrators are important decision makers, they are limited in the discretion with which they can carry out their roles.

> The professional bureaucrat is chained to his activity by his entire material and ideal existence. In the great majority of cases, he is only a single cog in an essentially fixed route of march. . . . The individual bureaucrat is thus forged to the community of all the functionaries who are integrated into the mechanism. They have a common interest that the mechanism continues its functions and that the societally exercised authority carries on.[103]

Administrators, therefore, are often torn between the need to reach for creative solutions to problems using the organizational tool in innovative ways and the demand to work within the standard operating procedures of the organization, maintain organizational rules and boundaries, stay within a budget, and carry on business as usual.

As a result of the dilemma of innovation both workers and administrators are caught in a bind. Bureaucracy keeps the social worker from having control over or changing his or her own social environment, reduces the problem-solving ability of social workers, and creates difficulties in implementing organizational change, particularly if there are dysfunctions in the organizational system. The challenge for social administrators is how to keep the social agency adaptable to conditions in its environment, responsive to the needs of staff, and open to differing needs of its clientele while maintaining a stable, secure work environment.

Leadership

Leadership in social administration has tended to be reduced to "management" of individuals who must be "motivated" to behave in ways that are productive and efficient in organizational terms. Management in modern organizational society no longer has substantive qualities of hope and spirit, "personal sympathy and favor, grace and gratitude."[104] Instead, the manager is a "personally detached and strictly 'objective' *expert,*"[105] a value-neutral, impersonal nonentity. In Max Weber's terms, he or she is "a specialist without spirit, a sensualist without heart; [a] nullity that imagines it has attained a level of civilization never before achieved."[106] The manager oversees his or her office *sine ira et studio,* "without sympathy or enthusiasm."[107] The result is the avoidance of any personal responsibility for carrying out orders,[108] a perspective that carries through the entire organizational system. Organizational management "requires that human conduct be conditioned to obedience towards those masters who claim to be the bearers of legitimate power, [a form of] organized domination."[109] Rather than lead in a substantive sense, management applies techniques of overt control such as behavior modification and/or unobtrusive systems of rewards and inducements.

Management has little to do with the shared meanings of clients or staff, their relational or existential needs, or providing a vision of the agency's future.

Organization itself is a system of domination that transforms individual human beings into "things." This process, according to Paulo Freire, is a form of oppression. "The oppressed as objects, as 'things,' have no purposes except those their oppressors prescribe for them."[110] When an administrator imposes choice onto another and prescribes behavior, the administrator participates in the dehumanization of that person. The administrator becomes guilty of oppression.[111] The challenge to social work administrators is to become leaders that facilitate personal responsibility, individual choice, humanization, and independent action on the part of both clientele and social workers in the organization.

Coping with Dilemmas of Administration

Everyone in an organization is affected by the dilemmas that organizations create. Discrepancies between the role of the social worker and demands of the organization create stress. Social workers may respond in a number of ways to the stress of organizational demands. Individual strategies, while well intentioned, may lead to more stress and even to burn-out. Group strategies can lead to conflict and confrontation. It is important to understand how to cope with dilemmas that organizations create.

Individual Strategies

Among individual strategies a social worker can use are direct change efforts, blaming the system, take the blame him- or herself, and identify with the organization.

Direct Change Efforts

Often the first response of a social worker when he or she is exposed to a problem in organization is to "fire off memos, raise the issue at meetings, or discuss it with their superiors."[112] Social workers who are taught to face problems directly and seek resolution may be confused when his or her observations and suggestions are met not only with indifference but even with disdain by administrators or co-workers. Faced with "what is likely to be the repeated failures of such direct efforts at problem-solving the . . . worker begins to realize the extent to which organizational problems are endemic to professional life."[113]

Not only are organizational problems endemic, but by attempting to directly change the way an organization operates single-handedly pits the worker against an entire organization of interlocking subsystems all of which contribute to keep the system going. Furthermore, a worker may not often understand that his or her role is not to change the system but simply to do the job. Taking time away from task accomplishment to solve organizational problems may not be rewarded, but be discouraged.

Blaming the System

If administrators are unresponsive to the social worker and do not assist in helping resolve the discrepancies he or she feels, the worker may begin to blame the system, its policies, or administrators. The worker may question why administrators support, condone, or even develop the policies and procedures that the worker perceives as demeaning or antithetical to good social work practice. If the situation continues and administrators ignore, become resistant to, or punish the worker, she or he may feel alienated, resentful, and forced to condone a system that the worker may view as inherently oppressive. The worker may seek relief by pressing harder for organizational change or even the removal of a particularly oppressive and unresponsive administrator. This may be the only way that "will vindicate the worker who feels he has been forced into complicity with the agency's 'corrupt' practices."[114]

Taking the Blame

At this point the worker must deal not only with the original problem but also with his or her morale and feelings toward the agency. The focus of attention may shift from the issue at hand to the worker's attitude, which the administrator may feel is negative. Feeling victimized, the worker may perceive that his or her only option is to take the blame. The worker may become disenchanted, and demoralized, and feel defeated. At this point the worker may adopt one of several solutions.

1. *Accommodation.* Realizing that she or he is being blamed for a situation beyond his or her control, the worker gives up trying to resolve the issue and tries to recoup his or her losses. The social worker accepts that he or she is the problem, consciously changes his or her attitude, and accommodates to a system the worker cannot change. The social worker adapts to the organizational culture, accepting its limitations in order to keep the job. This accommodation solution has payoffs for the worker who shows that she or he is adaptable and "mature." The worker demonstrates that she or he is malleable, nonthreatening, and has potential to "fit in" to the organization.

2. *Alienation.* A second strategy is to appear to accommodate the organization while inwardly refusing to adapt to the norms of the organization. The worker separates him- or herself psychologically from the "dissonance" she or he feels, performing work, but is alienated from it at the same time. Workers who adopt an alienation stance maintain their integrity, keep their jobs, but become "numb or passive, involve themselves in paperwork, and do precisely as they are told."[115] This solution buys time for the worker. If the worker can bear the tension that working in an alienating environment causes, she or he may be able to survive. Given time the issue that brought on the alienation may even be resolved. On the other hand, the administrator may begin to document the worker's mistakes to build a case to eventually move him or her out of the agency.

3. *Avoidance.* A worker who is alienated will often insulate and isolate him- or herself from the dissonance she or he feels. The worker reduces engagement with others, particularly those who remind him or her of the dissonance. The worker will avoid sitting on committees because he or she sees these as not only a waste of time but also as painful reminders of the futility of organizational change. The ultimate result of avoidance is giving up and leaving the agency.

Identification

Another response is identification. Realizing that the way to succeed is not to buck the system, the worker gives up his or her values in favor of those of the organization. The worker identifies with the oppressor, in this case with the organization or its administrators. The worker adopts the culture, rules, procedures, and values of the organization as his or her own, becomes a protege of the administrator, takes the agency's side on issues, and is seen by the agency executives as someone who may be "management material."

Group Strategies

Group strategies for coping with administrative dilemmas allow social workers to form common solutions to organizational problems. An advantage of group strategies is that there is strength in numbers, less likelihood that any one individual will be scapegoated, and a feeling of empowerment. On the other hand, group strategies may lead to increased conflict and confrontation. Among group strategies are networking, organizational politics, group confrontation, and as a last resort, collective bargaining.

Networking

When a problem is perceived by a social worker, she or he will begin to talk about it with co-workers. This informal sharing, or networking, can help the aggrieved social worker let off steam in a friendly, nonthreatening way. Co-workers may have different perspectives on the problem and provide reality testing. If the social worker is naive, misperceives the situation, or lacks information, he or she will be able to obtain a clearer picture of the situation from others.

On the other hand, if co-workers share perceptions about a problem they can begin to process strategies for a solution. This may involve discussing it informally with the entire unit, developing joint strategies, and presenting the issue with solutions to administrators.

Organizational Politics

A problem may be seen as either too trivial to take joint action or may be too threatening to the administration. In either case, a group strategy that avoids direct group action is organizational politics, "greasing the wheel" or "sliding around the issue." For example, a particular work procedure may be getting in the way of accomplishing work. A rule may be outmoded, overly rigid, or inappropriate. The group jointly decides to ignore the procedure and accomplish their tasks in a way that they view as more effective. While the group is technically violating agency rules, members are using their initiative to jointly resolve the problem.

An advantage of organizational politics is that it resolves worker problems without bothering administrators. If administrators eventually raise a question, workers can ask forgiveness for breaking the rule but point out that they have solved a common problem independently. Often administrators will see that effectiveness has not been sacrificed, agree to the change, and even commend workers for their initiative. This strategy uses the maxim of proaction that states, "It is better to ask forgiveness than ask permission."

Confrontation

If administration is intractable and unwilling to listen to a group of social workers who network or use organizational politics, lines may be drawn and confrontation may take place. In this situation an organization developer may be helpful to both workers and administrators in coming to a resolution. Conflict resolution strategies are explored in chapter 13.

Collective Bargaining

If problems are long standing or are so great that conflict resolution has not been successful, social workers, like many other employee groups, may have little choice but to formally organize themselves into a collective bargaining unit or union. There are advantages and disadvantages in forming a union. On the one hand, unions provide legal power to employees. Contracts negotiated with management are binding on both parties. Often a formal grievance process is included in a union contract to assure employee rights. Unions protect workers who take direct action from reprisals. Unions can obtain concessions from management in the form of wages, benefits, and working conditions.

On the other hand, the process of unionization polarizes administrators and social workers. In one sense unions represent a defeat for social worker staff and administrators who ought to be able to settle disputes among themselves. In addition, unions are costly. While employees gain benefits, they must also support the union financially. If workers go on strike, they may suffer financial losses, at least temporarily. Sometimes union contracts themselves become so rigid by prescribing working hours or worker roles that they interfere with the process of providing services to clients. However, social workers may feel that the benefits of collective bargaining outweigh its costs.

Action Principles of Social Administration

A socially sensitive administrator will work to resolve issues so that workers do not have to strategize to solve administrative dilemmas. It is, after all, the role of the administrator to create an agency culture that is conducive to good work and to harmonious social relationships.

An action theory of social administration can help overcome dilemmas that administrators and social work staff often face. Following is a set of action principles that macro social workers can use to guide the practice of administrative leadership.

Social Orientation

The goals of a private business enterprise are growth, survival, and maximization of profit. But the mission of a social agency is to provide service to clients and community, remediate social problems, and meet social needs. Unlike a private corporation whose managers may experience little dissonance when they treat employees as if they are functionaries, the administrators of a social agency must be sensitive to the way employees and clients alike are treated. This concern does not come from utilitarian motives that assert that good

employee relations improve productivity or good customer service will result in increased profit for the organization.

An action oriented social administrator creates a healthy social environment because she or he is committed to helping people experience happy and productive lives. The social agency is a welcoming, caring social environment in which staff and clientele alike are treated with respect, genuineness, and honesty.

The social administrator works to insure that the social agency provides social relationships, decision-making methods, and personal practices are congruent with the values and principles of the social work profession. An action administrator resists allowing techniques, rules, or organizational procedures to overwhelm the social and personal relationships that are the heart of the services and the purpose for which the agency was formed. The social administrator devotes all his or her "knowledge, resources and talents to getting [this mission] done."[116]

Community Orientation

Action administrators see the agency as a servant of and extension of the community, not as separated from it. They work actively to become involved in the life of the community. They use the resources of the agency to strengthen the neighborhood in which it is situated, the community of clients it serves, and the wider network of social service agencies with which it is affiliated.

Administrators are advocates, representatives, buffers, symbols, and public relations officers all in one. They scan the community environment of the organization to help resolve issues before they become entrenched patterns. They link the agency with the community, deal effectively with claimants on the agency's resources, and bring benefits and protection to its clients and staff. Benefits consist of goodwill, funding, prestige, and relationships with political, business, and social organizations. Protection consists of preventing the individuals or organizations in the agency's social environment from making demands, violating agency norms, or interfering with getting the work of the agency accomplished.[117]

Substantive Thinking

Action administrators use their thinking function to rationally solve organizational problems and their sensing function to implement decisions efficiently and effectively. However, administrators understand that there is more to decision making than calculative rationality. The most expedient means may not always bring the best social ends. Before rational decision making takes place, action administrators examine the ends toward which decisions are aimed using their feeling function to ensure that they are good for clients, staff, and the wider community. Action administrators are visionaries and dreamers, using their intuition to grasp the wider dimensions of the agency's history, meaning, and values. They envision a future for the agency that will bring about a better social environment and stronger sense of community.

Holistic Approach

Action administrators understand and appreciate "all aspects of the agency's operations, its history, its relationships with the community, the idiosyncracies of the staff and anything else that is relevant to how the organization goes about its work."[118] This includes the technology, skills, and unique services that the organization brings to the community. Just as social administrators work holistically, they view clients

> as "whole" people; each individual has a life beyond the program, comprised of a variety of interests, relationships, histories. . . . People have strengths and can grow and change over time. This belief embraces the whole experience of a person and is not limited to defining the person as a "client" only. . . . From such a perspective, individuals are valued and respected for their ability to survive and adapt, and

Skilled administrators envision a future that will bring about a better social environment and a stronger sense of community.

there is a sense of hope regarding each person's capacity to continue to learn and develop over time in relationship with others.[119]

Personal Approach

Action administrators are personal rather than impersonal. They share parking and other perquisites with employees and do not insist on special, preferential treatment that separates them from other staff. They do not isolate themselves from staff or clients, but are accessible, supportive, and nurturing. Action administrators understand that the agency is a means to an end. The best administrators are those who maintain and consciously apply their own humanity in their organizational roles. Skilled administrators use their position to enhance, support, and encourage people to express their full humanity, not as a means of dehumanization or oppression.[120]

Open Communication

Action administrators develop a communication network that provides understanding and clarity. This includes one-way communication and two-way communication so that employees' and clients' ideas and responses are heard.[121] A good administrator is a good listener. He or she affirms people and their efforts and tries to understand the issues and complexities with which they are struggling.

Innovative Approach

Action administrators facilitate a structured system that provides understanding, stability, security, order, and ease of operation. They do not force people into hierarchial social arrangements or trap them in impersonal roles for convenience or efficiency, or to reinforce entrenched power positions.

While leadership may sometimes mean that decisions come from the top, whenever possible action administrators involve those who are directly affected by decisions, including clients, line workers, and first level supervisors.[122] Action administrators do not "deify existing practice interventions"[123] nor are they wedded to any one particular structure or to

"structuring" people. They engage and involve social workers as well as clients in the process of change.

Action administrators scan the social environment of the agency looking for ways to adapt the organization to better meet the needs of clients and the community in which it is located. Such administrators will be open to ideas of staff and clients in improving services and making the agency more compatible with the culture of its community.

The action administrator is aware of the natural desires of workers to improve and change their work environment. The action administrator helps workers redefine their jobs, their roles, and their interests, and choose the kinds of work they want to do. She or he understands the importance that social workers place in seeking meaning in their professional lives. He or she helps reduce the dissonance between the rules, structures, and impersonality of the organizational system. This means encouraging staff to "create oases of independent behavior . . . permitting somewhat more creative possibilities for themselves"[124] in shaping their social environment.

Finally, the action administrator works to recognize and provide incentives for suggestions and improvements that place clients and their needs over organizational rules and structures.

Action Leadership

Action administrators do not "manage" others. They provide direction rather than control, and assist employees by providing a milieu that is open and safe, accessible but with clear boundaries, and whose processes and methods are congruent with social work's professional values of honesty, trust, genuineness, and respect. They exemplify servanthood, emphasize importance of learning, are accessible, and maintain technical expertise.

1. *Servanthood.* An action administrative leader is not a "boss" but a "servant," the first among equals in a social agency. He or she is willing to pitch in and does not wait for a subordinate to do the work. She or he does not stand on ceremony or insist on using titles.

2. *Learning for a living.*[125] Action administrators are "challenged to continue learning more ef-

fective ways of helping people throughout their work lives. The ability and desire to self-assess and self-correct one's practice, on both individual and program levels, is central to professional practice."[126] Action administrators

are open to experimentation. They create learning environments for their staff by paying attention to client outcome data, by constantly putting the work of the program under a critical (but nonblaming) microscope, by encouraging contact with a diversity of people, and by providing support for risk-takers.[127]

3. *Accessibility.* Action administrative leaders are accessible. They spend a good deal of time interacting and initiating interactions. They keep their office door open and do not insist on appointments.

4. *Technical expertise.* Action administrative leaders must be skilled professionals. While not absolutely necessary, it is helpful if administrators are familiar with and have technical ability in the field in which the agency operates. Burton Gummer says, for example:

Research indicates . . . that successful managers have substantial knowledge of the business in which they are involved, including the specific products, competitors, markets, customers, technologies, unions, and governmental regulations associated with their respective industries.[128]

It is to the advantage of an administrator working in an agency for the mentally ill, for example, to be a knowledgeable clinician so that he or she understands the language, values, issues, problems, and dilemmas of that particular arena of practice. Such expertise enables an administrator to command the respect of the workers and clients on whose behalf she or he makes decisions.

Conclusion

Administration is one of the most important arenas of macro social work practice because nearly every aspect of social work service delivery depends on the quality of administrative leadership. Social workers must keep in mind that administration is fundamentally service. An administrator provides organizational services and resources to social workers so that they can provide social services to clients. Social administrators need to understand that their roles of planning, budgeting, caring for the human needs of staff, and making organizational decisions must be done in harmony with social work values.

Social administrators must not be naive, however, about the destructive aspects of the organizational tools that they control. Administrators must be aware of the dilemmas of social administration that are endemic to the organizational systems they lead. They must also be aware that social work staff are vulnerable to stresses that these dilemmas create. If administrators fail to deal adequately with those dilemmas, social workers may take individual action or develop collective strategies to resolve them. While there may be beneficial results to those strategies, worker action may involve conflict and even confrontation before stresses are resolved.

Social administrators need to work hard to ensure that social agencies do not let dilemmas of social administration undermine the provision of social services. Administrators as well as employees in social work organizations can apply an action model of administration to recapture the "social" component of organizations. Action administrators, in addition, provide a community orientation, a holistic, personal approach, open communication, and allow for innovation. An action model is one way by which social administrators can orient themselves to mediate or overcome dilemmas inherent in social organizations.

KEY CONCEPTS

administration
POSDCORB
planning
budgeting
incrementalism
line-item budget
functional budget
program budget
zero-based budget
personnel administration
merit
political reward

need
preference
brainstorming
reverse brainstorming
nominal group technique
dilemmas of social work administration
dilemma of sociality
dilemma of functional thinking
dilemma of holism
dilemma of personalized treatment
dilemma of administrative compassion
dilemma of administrative innovation
dilemma of leadership
individual strategies
direct change efforts
blaming the system
taking the blame
accommodation
alienation
avoidance
identification
group strategies
networking
organizational politics
confrontation
collective bargaining
action principles of social administration
social orientation
community orientation
substantive thinking
holistic approach
open communication
innovative approach
action leadership

QUESTIONS FOR DISCUSSION

1. Review the story of Harry Hopkins at the beginning of this chapter. What principles of social administration can you learn from his story? What qualities did he exemplify that are worthy of note. What were his weaknesses?

2. Comment on this quote by Max Weber from his classic essay on "Bureaucracy."

   When fully developed, bureaucracy also stands, in a specific sense, under the principle of *sine ira ac stu-*
dio (without sympathy or compassion). Its nature, which is welcomed by capitalism, develops the more perfectly the more the bureaucracy is "dehumanized," the more perfectly it succeeds in eliminating from official business love, hatred, and all purely personal, irrational, and emotional elements which escape calculation. This is the specific nature of bureaucracy and it is appraised as its special virtue.[146]

3. Review the various principles of public personnel administration. Controversy continues over giving special preference to selected groups, especially ethnic minorities, in public employment. Controversy also exists over awarding jobs on the basis of need to unemployed and underemployed. Should such principles as social justice or special need be used as justifying awarding jobs to some rather than to those who are equally or more qualified?

ADDITIONAL READING

Bellone, Carl J. *Organization Theory and the New Public Administration.* Boston, MA: Allyn and Bacon, 1980.

Berk, Joseph, and Susan Berk. *Managing Effectively: A Handbook for First-time Managers.* New York: Sterling, 1991.

Carter, R. *The Accountable Agency.* Beverly Hills, CA: Sage, 1983.

Fox, Elliot M., and L. Urwick. *Dynamic Administration: The Collected Papers of Mary Parker Follett.* New York: Hippocrene Books, Inc., 1977.

Glisson, C.A. "A Contingency Model of Social Welfare Administration," *Administration in Social Work,* 5 (1981): 15–30.

Harmon, Michael M. *Action Theory for Public Administration.* New York: Longman, 1981.

Kotter, John P. *A Force for Change: How Leadership Differs from Management.* New York: Free Press, 1990.

Maccoby, Michael. *The Gamesman: The New Corporate Leader.* New York: Simon and Schuster, 1976.

———. *The Leader: A New Face for American Management.* New York: Simon and Schuster, 1982.

Peters, Tom, and Nancy Austin. *A Passion for Ex-*

cellence: The Leadership Difference. New York: Random House, 1985.

Schuman, David. Bureaucracies, Organizations, and Administration: A Political Primer. New York: Macmillan, 1976.

Wildavsky, Aaron. Budgeting: A Comparative Theory of Budgetary Processes. Boston, MA: Little, Brown, 1975.

———. Politics of the Budgetary Process, 3d ed. Boston, MA: Little, Brown, 1979.

EXERCISES

EXERCISE 41:
The Ideal Administrator

Think of the various jobs that you have had or organizations such as a social agency, school, church, or business with which you have been involved. Think of the best administrator that you knew. What qualities elicited your admiration and respect? Make a list of the qualities you admire about an administrator.

Now think of the worst administrator that you have encountered. What qualities did that person exemplify? Make a list of these qualities. Compare both lists. Are there commonalities? Are there differences? What does this comparison say about the kinds of qualities that you think would make an ideal administrator?

Break into triads. Spend a few minutes sharing qualities that you admire in administrators. Share stories that illustrate those qualities and come to conclusions about what makes a good administrator. Review lists of those qualities that you saw as negative ones. Share stories that illustrate those qualities and come to a conclusion about them.

Return to the class as a whole and report on the conclusions reached by your triad. As you discuss your perceptions and experiences try to come to a consensus about what makes an ideal administrator.

Compare your class list with the action model of social administration presented in this chapter. Have you listed qualities that are similar to those described in the action model? Have you discovered others that are not listed? As a class draw conclusions about what makes a good social administrator.

EXERCISE 42:
Deciding on a Human Resources Model

Imagine yourself in the role of a newly hired human resources manager of a large social agency. Human resources management is responsible for personnel selection, training, and evaluation, and termination of employees. The chief executive officer (CEO) has told you that one of the first things you need to do is establish a perspective on personnel that will become the model reflected throughout the department and the agency as a whole. Your CEO has made things easy for you by having an assistant research four models in current management literature. While he has not reviewed these models he wants you to evaluate each of them and select the one that will help the organization meet its personnel needs according to the NASW Code of Ethics: "The social worker should work to improve the employing agency's policies and procedures and the efficiency and effectiveness of its services."[129] He has asked you to evaluate these models according to the two criteria of efficiency and effectiveness and report back to him with your recommendation.

Criteria

1. Effectiveness: Will the people selected using this model accomplish the agency's goals?
2. Efficiency: To what extent does the model take costs into consideration?

You decide to weigh each model according to the following scale:

5   very effective/efficient
4   moderately effective/efficient
3   adequately effective/efficient
2   somewhat effective/efficient
1   little effective/efficient
0   not effective/efficient

Model 1: The Functionary

People are considered to be "functionaries—individuals who do what they are supposed to do in pursuit of the organization's goal."[130] The human being is conceived of as a thing, an object to be used by the organization. "The human version of the cog is the functionary—a person who performs his function effectively regardless of its purposes."[131] The functionary "does his duty, applies his skills, performs his practiced

(continued next page)

EXERCISES

EXERCISE 42 (continued)

routines regardless of what goal or whose goal is involved. A screwdriver does not choose among goals of owners. It does what it is told."[132]

Model 2: Human Resource Extraction

People are seen by management as "human resources who along with financial, material, or time resources, contribute to the production of goods and services in an organization."[133] People are considered as factors of production on the same level as other organizational components. An effective organization has the ability "in either relative or absolute terms to exploit its environment in the acquisition of scarce and valued resources."[134]

The most visible external extraction function of public "personnel is the acquisition of human resources (male and female workers). . . . Hence, the staffing maintenance service provided by personnel offices and commissions is akin to that of a grocery store which maintains 'stocks' of goods purchased routinely by customers."[135]

While an organization extracts resources externally from its environment and maintains stocks of human material, organizations also utilize an internal extraction process. "The other side of the personnel administrator's role is to create conditions within the organization which improve its capacity to extract resources from its own members."[136] As human resources are extracted, stored, processed, and utilized, managers as well as staff must "concentrate on processes that contribute to goal accomplishment, *no matter what the goals are.*[137]

Model 3: Human Resources Accounting

The human resources accounting model, using modern functional reason, sees people as nothing other than pieces of equipment, such as business machines or furniture, that can be depreciated over time.

Accounting for human resources investment costs will make it possible to put rationality into the process of managing internal manpower movement (i.e., position turnover). Fully depreciated human resources can be given priority consideration for redevelopment investment. The moral choice between buying new (and usually young) talent and overhauling old (long service) people can be made explicit so that it can be regulated. . . . Where employees with low development and acquisition account balances have valuable skills which are not being used in their present jobs, reassignment becomes "profitable." . . . The costs of developing and redeveloping human resources would become an explicit, rational process constrained principally by economic considerations. . . . Depreciating human resources makes human resources accounting a meaningful and practical activity.[138]

A person, just as a desk, is acquired, used, renovated, transferred, or dispensed with depending on utilitarian considerations. A human is nothing more than a piece of equipment whose value lies entirely on the usefulness to which he or she can be put.

Model 4: Genetic Engineering

Genetic engineering is another possibility by which organizations can fill their human resource needs. Thompson, for example, asserts that managers cannot expect a perfect fit between man and organization "short of genetic engineering. Such engineering is a long way off. We have not yet decided how to select either the engineers or the designs."[139]

Thomas Gill moved this concept further toward actualization. "Cloning," says Gill, "is considered as a technique for filling human resource needs with individuals tailor-made to fit the needs of the organization."[140]

The biological sciences may be the most relevant discipline for management outside of the social sciences for contributions that we can apply in management theory. . . . In one sense, the biological revolution may only reinforce traditional or hierarchial management. The geneticist will clone a person or modify his genetic makeup to meet specific job requirements. . . . He can, by tinkering with genes, produce superhumans, subhumans, and hybrid human-animals to fill positions at all levels.

The new biology will force personnel administration to plan years ahead and to determine requirements for generations at a time. . . . Proper cloning would ensure getting workers with the proper natural talent and save on training costs. There would be almost no dropouts.[141]

EXERCISES

Calculating and Deciding on a Model

Calculate scores for each model. Which model was most effective? Which was most efficient? Which model would you recommend to your manager? After you have decided on your own recommendation, form groups of four or five persons. Compare scores. Come to a group decision about which model to recommend to management.

Discussion

In your group, discuss the following questions and their implications of this process for social administration. Then return to the class as a whole and share your perspectives.

Administrators often use rational calculation (a numerical ranking system) based on efficiency/effectiveness criteria to arrive at decisions.

1. Was ranking these models according to effectiveness/efficiency criteria appropriate? Why or Why not?
2. What other criteria could you have used?
3. What kind of a cultural milieu would result from implementing the model you recommended?
4. What are the ethical implications of the process used in this exercise?

EXERCISE 43:
Leaders or Managers

This chapter has asserted that there is a difference between management and leadership. Managers are charged with achieving organizational goals,

and power is a means for facilitating that achievement. Managerial power "focuses on tactics for gaining compliance." Exerting power in organizations "does not require goal compatibility, merely dependence." Leadership, in contrast, "requires some congruence between the goals of the leader and the led."[142]

Warren Bennis describes the difference between leadership and management this way: "Leaders are people who do the right thing; managers are people who do things right. Both roles are crucial, but they differ profoundly."[143] According to Bennis, American organizations are "underled and overmanaged. They do not pay enough attention to doing the right thing, while they pay too much attention to doing things right."[144] Bennis argues that one antidote for the managerial dilemma is to train people for "leadership," which means doing the morally right thing, rather than training people to be managers who apply administrative power to exact people's compliance to achieve organizational goals.

Break into small groups and discuss the following questions. Return to the class as a whole and share your conclusions with the others.

1. Is Bennis correct in his distinction between management and leadership?
2. Is it possible to be an administrator in a bureaucracy and not "manage" people?
3. Does social work need more managers or more leaders? Why?

EXERCISE 44:
Equal Treatment Dilemma

Review the following quote from Victor A. Thompson, *Without Sympathy or Enthusiasm: The Problem of Administrative Compassion*. Think about how this comment relates to the provision of social welfare services. Discuss your opinion with your classmates, and try to come to some conclusion.

The modern administrative norm, which made efficient administration possible, was the rule that everyone in the same problem category should be treated equally. The result of the norm was to strip away the uniqueness of individuals and to turn administration into an efficient mass processing of cases within each problem category. This resulted in an enormous lowering of unit costs plus other valuable consequences, such as predictability. Thus the norm was a necessary prerequisite of modern, mass-democratic government. . . .

Nearly all administrative organizations . . . apply the norm of equality. Even in nondemocratic governments of industrial nations, the norm is applied to everyone but the political elite. The "rule of law" in this sense is an administrative necessity in an industrial country. . . . Though it is too late for industrialized and industrializing nations, there are countries that still can choose between personalized, individualized, compassionate administrative

(continued next page)

EXERCISES

EXERCISE 44 (continued)

treatment of at least some of the population . . . and administrative efficiency. For us it is simply too late.[145]

What is your opinion of Thompson's assessment? Does this apply to the provision of social casework services in social welfare organizations? Do we want to abandon the "rule of law" in our organizational arrangements in favor of personalistic treatment of people? What would happen if we did? Do you agree with Thompson that even if we wanted to do this, it is too late for us?

CHAPTER 13

Becoming an Organization Developer

The stress of case loads in a social service agency contributed to a self-defeating attitude among the staff until an organization developer helped to reopen communication and rework relationships.

If you ask me how I do it, sometimes I don't know. All I know is I take a lot of behavioral science, throw it all together, get in a room, and try to create an authentic environment where something positive happens. Community building is in line with my belief about what has to happen. I call it team building. It is creating an environment where inspiration takes place, where there is energy in the collective "weness." I just tap into it and let it happen.

—TOM JONES, ORGANIZATION DEVELOPER

311

IDEAS IN THIS CHAPTER

Jean Carlyle Takes a Stand

For the past ten years, Wells County has experienced a high level of growth. While welcome, growth has also produced traffic congestion, increased gangs, drug use, and crime, and as a result, a rise in the case loads of the Wells County Probation Department (WCPD). Several years ago probation officers with the WCPD were generalists, each person handling all the persons in a geographical area. As some areas grew more rapidly than others, however, continual shifting of boundaries became necessary. East county, which contained many immigrant and low income populations, experienced a large amount of growth and a greater degree of crime as well. Case loads in the East Side unit grew more rapidly, but the crimes were of a different nature, necessitating more work. A vicious cycle developed. The more work, the less time there was to monitor cases, and the more likely the clients would repeat offenses. Not only was work more difficult, but social work success rates were far lower than those of other units whose work loads were lighter and whose clients were far less difficult to work with.

The East Side unit had younger, more inexperienced workers as well as some who were older and "burned out." It also had acquired some of the less competent workers. Many more assertive and capable workers, having obtained valuable experience, transferred to other units or were promoted to specialist positions. As a result, the unit began to think of itself as the "Siberia" of the probation department—victim of an unjust system.

In an effort to balance case loads, Ms. Jean Carlyle, supervisor of the East Side unit, had to change assignments often. With each change, work loads became even more backed up. While Jean did everything possible to develop equity, many members of the unit did not feel they had the resources to adequately supervise their clientele. The six supervisors in other geographical areas where there was less growth, however, resisted shifting boundaries, because they did not want to absorb more work for themselves and their workers, cause confusion in their units, or risk their success rates. Supervisory meetings often ended in heated arguments in which supervisors of units with smaller case loads defended their territory against Jean, who staged what she considered a one person battle and often felt discriminated against.

Jean, however, did not give up on the East Side office, because she wanted to make it into one of the best units in the agency and because of her commitment to serving Spanish speaking and African-American populations on the East Side. Located physically away from the central office, the East Side staff had some status and privilege, resulting in greater cohesion. In addition, they had private offices, unlike workers at the Central unit who were all located in one large pool with workers separated only by 5-foot-high cloth barriers. However, being isolated from Central, they were "out of the loop" of information and power.

Because of growth, the entire agency moved into new headquarters. The East Side office merged with the Central unit in the new building. The members of the East Side office lost what little special status they had, and what was worse, in the new arrangement, they were deprived of their individual offices. Mr. Thompson, a new probation chief, began putting pressure on all units to meet demands from the state for accountability. His style was simply to apply pressure and weed out workers who were incompetent.

Farthest behind and with poorer success rates, Jean was under the gun to crank out more work from staff who were already overwhelmed with more difficult loads and who now had to travel farther to visit clients. The members of the unit blamed Jean for what they believed was her inability to adequately represent the needs of the unit in agency meetings, for the increased work load, for losing their private offices, and now for putting more pressure on them, a demand that Jean had sheltered her workers from in the past but could no longer do.

Stress levels in the unit rose higher. Conversations, that previously could be private were now heard by everyone. Members had little opportunity to blow off steam with one another. As a result, East Side unit members began to take longer lunches, sometimes leaving on prolonged "home visits," not returning until the next day. Meeting behind closed doors, members of Jean's unit became openly hostile to her. "Wimp" could be heard whispered in corridors when she walked by. Morale in the unit plummeted. Distrust, miscommunication, and conflicts were developing. In spite of all Jean's attempts at gaining the confidence of the unit, several of the less capable members became increasingly stressed.

One day, in the middle of a conversation, one of her workers started shouting at Jean. Jean was stunned, as were the rest of the probation officers, as the worker's screaming voice echoed through the agency. Jean went to Mr. Thompson, who only berated her for being ineffective. In spite of what Jean considered to be heroic measures to advocate for her workers, even they had turned on her. Jean felt helpless, alone, and stressed.

The county had recently hired Kathy Herbert, a social work organization developer who had visited the Probation Department and explained her services. With no one else to turn to, Jean called Kathy, and they met over coffee. Jean began for the first time to pour out the frustrations that had built up over years of being a buffer between her unit and the rest of the agency. Her feelings were deep and painful, and it was embarrassing for her to express her grief. She felt that her battles to help her unit, her concern for their welfare, and her compassion were being thrown back at her in the form of resentment and anger. She felt blamed for the very situations she had fought against.

Kathy provided a listening ear, and over the course of several weeks helped Jean work through her anger, loss, and hurt. Together they began to problem-solve and work on different approaches to the problem. She met with Jean and her unit and together they engaged in mutual problem solving. Gradually, the unit began to see that they were in a self-defeating cycle, and while they were under stress and blaming Jean, their own attitudes and work habits were contributing to their low morale and lack of self-esteem. Jean also realized that she needed to be much more directive and began to make some changes in how she related to her unit. Her self-confidence began to return, and she began to feel in control once again, developing a proposal for redistributing work loads for all units on a more equitable basis.

As the East Side unit members began to take responsibility for themselves and stopped blaming the supervisor for issues beyond her control, Jean and her unit began to work together as a team once again. Jointly, they began to strategize for solutions. While the external pressures of work did not ease up, Jean and her unit were communicating on a regular basis and reworking their relationships.

Introduction

It is probably safe to say that there is no organizational system without defects. Everyone who works for organizational systems will, at times, find themselves under stress and experience burn out, or have their lives thrown into turmoil. They may become demoralized, in conflict with those with whom they work, or experience job dissatisfaction. In addition, if the organization experiences financial problems, they may find themselves out of work and their lives in disarray. These problems can affect the provision of quality services to clients. Clients of social agencies may experience inefficient or ineffective services, rigid or inflexible responses to their needs, or an organizational system fraught with "red tape."

Because organizations affect people's lives in so many ways, therefore, macro social workers are increasingly turning their attention to these important social systems, finding that the methods, skills, and processes they use in healing families, groups, or communities also work with helping dysfunctional organizations.

This chapter will acquaint you with the emerging field of organization development and with a number of techniques by which macro social workers help organizational systems improve their functioning.

Types of Organization Developers

Macro social workers who work with dysfunctional organizational systems are called organization developers. There are two kinds of organization developers. An internal organization developer is an employee of a direct service social agency, such as a county social services department, regional center for developmentally disabled, hospital, or mental health facility, who works exclusively with the employees, supervisors, and administrators inside that agency. Internal consultants may tend to be cautious and more thoughtful in their recommendations because they must live with the changes that they recommend.[1]

An external organization developer works either as a private consultant or as a member of an organization development firm and provides management consultation, training, and problem solving to many different organizations and agencies. While external consultants can offer objective perspectives, because they are from the outside, they often do not have an intimate understanding of the history, culture, goals, and procedures of the organization. As a result, external consultants may have a tendency to institute drastic changes because they do not have to live with the results.[2]

What Is Organization Development?

Organization development is an "emerging behavioral science discipline that provides a set of methodologies for systematically bringing about organization change, improving the effectiveness of the organization and its members."[3] The environment of the organization developer is change. There are a number of factors that impel organizations toward change and factors that cause organizations to resist change. Organization developers must understand both of these forces in order to devise strategies that enable organizations to respond positively to the need for change.

Forces for Change

Robbins tells us that there are at least six forces that are "increasingly creating the need for change—the changing nature of the work force, technology, economic shocks, changing social trends, the 'new' world politics and the changing nature of competition."[4] Because of this "increasingly complex environment, it becomes even more critical for management to identify and respond to forces of social and technical change."[5] Those organizations that adapt to changing circumstances will survive. Those that fail to adapt will not.[6]

Forces Against Change

Organizations are social tools that accomplish a specific goal or solve a problem.[7] As a result, "organizations are not necessarily intended to change."[8] In fact, there are any number of factors that contribute to organizations resisting change. Among these are (1) the psychology of the owner; (2) the system's state; (3) size; (4) structure; (5) chain of command; (6) subordinate positions of workers; and (7) the organizational culture.

The attitude of the owner of the organization can determine whether or not it will be receptive to change. While organizational problems may be obvious to line workers, they may go unrecognized by the owner for long periods of time. The owner and administrators may not want to hear about problems or may themselves have contributed to them. Thompson says that "in a monocratic administrative system—a bureaucracy—the external owner has all the rights. He alone can innovate. Therefore, innovation will depend upon the psychology of the owner—his mood, confidence, faith and so forth."[9]

The tendency of an organization to maintain a stable systems state will work against change. An organization is "a set of interrelated and interdependent parts arranged in a manner that produces a unified whole"[10] and as such has inherent mechanisms to maintain homeostasis or stability.[11] Organizations exhibit inertia, which means that they tend to keep moving in the same direction.[12]

An organization's size will affect its receptivity to change. Smaller systems are more malleable and adaptable to change. The larger the system, the more difficult it is to shift its direction. More people are involved in a change, any one of whom can cause resistance. More subsystems must be integrated into the change effort, be coordinated, and be linked together.

The organization's structure creates problems for change.

> The hierarchy promotes delays and sluggishness; everything must be kicked upstairs for a decision either because the boss insists or because the subordinate does not want to take the risk of making a poor decision. All this indecision exists at the same time that superiors are being authoritarian, dictatorial, rigid, making snap judgments which they refuse to reconsider, implementing on-the-spot decisions without consulting with their subordinates, and generally stifling any independence or creativity at the subordinate levels. . . . The hierarchy promotes rigidity and timidity.[13]

Change must proceed up and down the chain of command. And, in general, it will be resisted at each level, particularly when organizations are composed of highly trained professionals.[14]

> Subordinates are under constant surveillance from superiors; thus they often give up trying to exercise initiative or imagination and instead suppress or distort information. Finally, since everything must go through channels, and these are vertical, two people at the same level in two different departments cannot work things out themselves, but must involve long lines of superiors.[15]

Because workers are functionaries who do what they are told, it may be seen as inappropriate to suggest changes and it may even be self-defeating for them to do so. Individuals at lower levels of organizations may be reluctant to complain to their supervisors out of fear of causing trouble. They may not want to appear disgruntled because this could reflect badly on their performance evaluations. Those who call attention to problems may even be subject to reprisal.

> Subordinates are afraid of passing up bad news, or of making suggestions to change. (Such an action would imply that their superiors should have thought of the changes and did not.) They are also more afraid of new situations than of familiar ones, since with the new situations, those above them might introduce new evils, while the old ones are sufficient.[16]

Sometimes a culture develops in organizations in which people pretend that problems do not exist. When an organization changes, its culture must also change.

> The culture of the organization becomes a part of the people who perform the work. In changing these old patterns, people must alter not only their behavior, but also their values and their view of themselves. The organization structure, procedures and relationships continue to reinforce prior patterns of behavior and to resist the new ones.[17]

As a result of these factors, "almost any change, . . . will be psychologically painful."[18] bringing with it "upheaval and dissatisfaction."[19] "Organizations," as Robbins says, "by their very nature are conservative. They actively resist change."[20]

Two Strategies for Change

There are two strategies in dealing with change that an organization developer can choose. One is to let nature take its course. The second is to control the forces of change.

Sometimes forces in the organization's environment are beyond the control of its owners. Change in the environment of the organization often just happens. When change just happens, organization staff tend to be *reactive*. They simply try to accommodate themselves to situations that have already occurred. For example, the state legislature may decrease funding for social welfare programs. A hiring freeze may be instituted or staff laid off. Policies that affect how agencies operate may be changed. Affirmative action policies, for example, may be reversed. Grants for special projects, such as programs for pregnant teenagers may not be renewed. All of these kinds of changes beyond the control of a local agency may mean that services are curtailed and the agency reorganized.

While every event in the organization's environment may not always be under the agency's control, administrators can have a major impact on the way an organization responds to external conditions. The best way of managing change is to plan for it in advance by being forward looking and purposeful rather than react to situations after the fact.[21] Planning for change is called being *proactive*. "Planned organizational change is a deliberate attempt to modify the functioning of the total organization or one of its major parts in order to bring about improved effectiveness."[22]

Organization staff can anticipate and plan for change. Administrators can develop contingency or back-up plans, seek alternative sources of funding, or innovative ways of using available resources. Organization developers help organizational members plan for and carry out change.

The Organization Development Process

Organization development is a process of engaging in change that is

(1) planned, (2) organization wide, (3) managed from the top, (4) to increase organization effectiveness and health, (5) through planned interventions in the organization's processes (6) using behavioral science knowledge.[23]

Planned change first "seeks to improve the ability of the organization to adapt to changes in its environment. Second, it seeks to change employee behavior."[24] If one is to be proactive in planning an "effective intervention, one needs some kind of comprehensive change theory."[25]

Approaches to Organization Development

Organization developers can take several approaches in planning for change. In one approach, the organization developer sees the system as a process of inputs, throughputs, outputs, and feedback. The change strategy could occur at any point in this process continuum. A change in one part of the system could create changes in other parts of the system.

The social ecology approach views an organization as an open system that is continually interact-

Organization developers are concerned about employees who experience work-related personal problems.

ing with and adapting to its environment. A dysfunctional organizational system is one that has failed to adapt. A system design that may at one time have been appropriate or workable has become outmoded or incongruent with the new conditions. A once flexible organization has become rigid, unable to scan its environment or cope with tensions or stresses that its environment presents. The organization developer tries to help the administration and staff anticipate changes and initiate strategies for adapting to them.

Another way of conceptualizing the change process is to see the problem as a matter of different "levels of analysis." The organization developer might focus on the level of individual effectiveness, examining morale, absenteeism, or productivity. She or he could focus at the level of the group or unit in the organization, improving conflict resolution, communication, or coordination. The organization developer could concentrate on the effectiveness of the organization as a whole, making sure its overall goals are being met and that the organization's culture is healthy.[26]

A fourth way of approaching organizational change is to see the organization as the sum of its component subsystems. The organization developer focuses on one or more subsystems in the organization. For example, the organization developer could begin with improving the reward system in the hope that improving compensation or benefits will improve organization effectiveness. He or she might examine the communication system, improving information flow between units. The decision-making system may be examined to improve the decision quality and quantity. The fiscal budgeting system could be a focal point, improving efficiency and cost-effectiveness, and reducing waste.[27]

Another way to approach organization development is contingency theory. Contingency theory, you may recall, says that systems are composed of a variety of components, which must fit together harmoniously in order for the system to function effectively. The organization developer looks at the relationship of all of the parts of the organization and attempts to discover which of the parts do not fit well with the others. Once the dysfunctional components are located, they are adjusted so that all the parts of the organization work smoothly together.

A final approach to organization development is therapeutic. In this approach, the organization developer is much like a therapist or physician, whose clients are dysfunctional organizations. Just as a social work clinician uses personality theory to diagnose psychopathology, an organization developer will use organization theory and a variety of theories of human behavior, group dynamics, and organization behavior to diagnose organizational problems. While a social work therapist decides if a problem is at the level of the individual, couple, or family; the organization developer focuses on the individual, group, or organization as a whole. Both develop a treatment plan and provide an intervention to restore the system to better functioning. Finally, both evaluate the treatment to ensure its success.

The approach taken here is one that combines these various aspects of organization development.

Steps in Organization Development

Michael Harrison describes the steps in organization development in this way:

1. Scouting—The consultant and client get to know each other. . . . The consultant seeks to determine how ready and able the client and other members of the organization are to follow through on a project and to change their behavior and their organization.
2. Entry—The consultant and the client negotiate about their expectations for the project and formalize them in a contract specifying the timing and nature of the consultant's activities.
3. Diagnosis—The consultant gathers information about the nature and sources of organizational problems and analyzes this information, examines possible solutions, considers ways to improve effectiveness, and provides feedback to clients.
4. Planning—Consultants and clients jointly establish objectives for the project's action phase and plan any steps (interventions) to be taken to solve problems and improve effectiveness.
5. Action—Clients implement these plans with the help of the consultant.
6. Evaluation—Clients and consultant assess the impacts of the action phase and consider further

actions. Under ideal conditions an independent researcher evaluates project outcomes.

7. Termination—The project terminates if no further action is planned. The project may break off earlier if clients or consultants become dissatisfied with it.[28]

You probably recognize this model as an adaptation of the generalist social work method or the rational problem solving process described in chapter 3. In the discussion that follows, the generalist social work model is used. It includes problem recognition, problem identification, identifying symptoms, diagnosing the problem, developing a treatment plan, and implementing the plan.

It is important to understand that these steps do not always happen in a rigid, lockstep fashion. Several of them may occur almost simultaneously. For example, as you engage the staff and clientele of an agency, you use your feeling function to develop a relationship. As you engage people, you begin to understand the problem and its location, and you will already be thinking of a diagnosis. Using your intuition, you imagine how things could be better, and a treatment plan suggests itself to you. As you begin to work on a solution using your sensing function, you may discover other problems and symptoms and may need to review your treatment plan. You will need to use all your thinking, sensing, feeling, and intuitive functions and be adaptable to the changing milieu of the organization.

Problem Recognition

If you feel ill, you know that something is wrong with you. You may experience discomfort or pain, have a fever, feel listless, or develop a rash. In the same way, people in a dysfunctional organization experience a number of symptoms. They may lack motivation, display decreased morale, or be prone to stress and burn out. Dysfunctions may show up in inter-unit rivalry, miscommunication, or conflict. The symptoms may manifest themselves in lessened organizational effectiveness, inefficiency, or poor adaptability to the organization's environment.

In spite of attempts to avoid or deny the existence of organizational problems, if they are to be solved, the administrator must ultimately admit that there is some dysfunction in the organization. The administrator may attempt to solve the problem alone or with his or her group of top assistants. If the attempt fails, and the problem continues, he or she may recognize that an organization developer is needed.

Problem Identification

When a person is ill, he or she goes to a physician. The physician asks "Where does it hurt? What are your symptoms?" In the same way, the organization developer needs to obtain an idea of the administrator's perception of the problem. Where in the organizational system does it seem to be located? How is the problem manifesting itself?

If you are an internal organization developer, begin addressing the problem by exploring with the administrator your initial impressions. Then describe a process for solving the problem and means of accountability in resolving it.

If you are an external organization consultant, talk to the organization's board of directors. They are the legal owners of the organization, and the ones who set policy and who are ultimately responsible for any changes that are made. When you talk to these people, try to assess whether the problems they have identified are ones that you have the skills and capabilities of addressing. In addition, be clear that the system and solutions you propose are ethically congruent with your professional and personal commitment to bring about a better social environment. Give the administrators or board an idea of the time, resources, cost, and agency commitment to bring about the changes that the organization leaders want to achieve so they can decide whether they are able and willing to undertake the process. At the same time, assess for yourself the extent to which the organizational leaders are open, accessible, and willing to invest the time and energy in the process of change. Ultimately, you must decide whether or not you can be of help to the organization and the extent to which the administration is serious about wanting to change.

Be clear about the methods you plan to use and the extent to which you may need access to employees, agency records, and files. Stress the need for confidentiality and your expectation that the agency protect employees, clients, and the administration from reprisal or breaches of trust, which would irreparably damage the change process. Finally, should you decide to proceed, you may want to formalize these agreements and understandings in the form of a written contract.

Gathering Information

After a physician has asked a patient some initial questions, she or he examines the patient and, depending on the symptoms, focuses on the particular area in the patient's system where the problem is occurring. The physician has a number of methods and instruments to help gather information. Furthermore, as a physician examines the patient, she or he distinguishes between a healthy system state and an unhealthy one. The physician gathers facts and tries to better understand the illness process.

In the same way, an organization developer spends considerable time examining an organization. An organization developer can choose from a number of information gathering methods and tools. And he or she has a concept of a healthy system state by which to judge the extent of the dysfunctions. The criteria that an organization developer uses to distinguish between a healthy and dysfunctional system are called effectiveness criteria.

Tools and Techniques

When you enter an organizational system, begin your diagnosis by asking questions, gathering facts, and performing a variety of tests. For example, observe the organization's milieu as a participant observer, gather information by means of questionnaires, or examine agency records. Most of these tools and techniques are part of the research skills used by all macro social workers, described in chapter 6.

Most important of all, however, talk to people. Try to get an idea of where the problem is located, understand the kind of symptoms displayed, and identify the extent of the problem more clearly.

Talking to People

When you talk to people, use focused or semi-structured interviews. Begin with the administrator and his or her key staff, because they are the ones who will implement changes and to whom you will report your findings. Then talk to other people in the organization. Just as a social work psychotherapist offers an opener to a client, such as "Tell me what brings you here," you can ask, "Tell me your story." Establish rapport and communicate a caring attitude. Make sure that you talk to as many people in the organization as you can, at all levels. Even if you are concerned with only one unit or part of an organization, reach out beyond that unit's boundaries because what affects one unit will often affect other units in the organization.

Participant Observation

In addition to interviewing people directly, use yourself as a research instrument by means of participant observation. Engage the day-to-day life of the organizational system, observing its culture and interactions. Listen to the gossip, participate in staff meetings, talk with employees as they gather around the coffee pot, chat with the receptionist and secretaries. Immediately after you make an observation, take time to record the details as objectively as possible. A good participant observer will watch for signs of stress, tension, conflict, avoidance, poor performance, and communication problems.[29]

Questionnaires

Talking individually to people and using yourself as a participant observer will help you pinpoint specific questions. You can then devise a questionnaire and distribute it to all employees or to a random sample if the organization is large. Questionnaires can be helpful because of their anonymity, the speed by which information can be collected, their ease of tabulation, and their ability to reduce bias.

Existing Data

Existing data from the organization's files, records, budgets, and personnel information can help you obtain a clearer picture of the problem.

System Effectiveness

An organization developer gets an idea of an organization's health by the effectiveness with which its components work together.[30] Michael Harrison describes three effectiveness criteria that you can use to evaluate the current state of "systems fit" in an organization: (1) the effectiveness of the organization's output: output goals include the quantity and quality of organizational productivity; (2) its internal systems state: organizations need people who have effective interpersonal relationships, agree on goals and procedures, and express a level of work satisfaction; and (3) its effectiveness in adapting to its social environment and its ability to use resources: public service organizations need to be adaptable to an environment over which they often have little control.[31]

A fourth component, not mentioned by Harrison, is the organization's culture. The culture of an organization consists of

> shared values, beliefs, assumptions, perceptions, norms, artifacts, and patterns of behavior. It is the unseen and unobservable force that is always behind organizational activities. Culture is to the organization what personality is to the individual—a hidden, yet unifying theme that provides meaning, direction, and mobilization.[32]

The organization's culture must be strong and clear.

Output Goals

Output goals are "targets toward which members strive."[33] For example, a social welfare department may have as an output goal the remediation of family breakdown, enhancing the safety and welfare of children, or protecting children from abuse. A way of assessing the effectiveness of an organization's output goal is to see the extent to which it is meeting the goal. How well, for example, is a child protective agency hindering child abuse? How effective is a family service agency in remediating family dysfunction?

Other output criteria are the quantity and quality of outputs. For example, if a case work agency is effective in the quantity of its outputs, it will process a sufficient number of clients per month. One that is less effective will have a waiting list or backlog of clients.[34]

Output quality describes the level of services a social agency provides. For example, a recent study of child care programs conducted by a team of researchers from several universities, titled "Cost, Quality and Child Outcomes in Child Care Centers,"

> rated just one in seven as being of good quality where children enjoyed close relationships with adults and teachers focused on the individual needs of the children. . . . The level of quality at most U.S. childcare centers, especially in infant/toddler rooms does not meet children's needs for health, safety, warm relationships, and learning the study concluded.[35]

In this case the quality of output goals of many child-care centers would be considered poor.

Internal System State

The internal system state is determined by those components of the organization that affect how the goals will be reached. Questions you could ask, for example, might be: How efficient is the agency in providing services? What is the ratio of service units to their cost? How much waste or downtime occurs in service provision?

Examine how satisfied the employees are. Be on the lookout for the extent to which members of an organization experience emotional pain and discomfort related to work stress. Employees may be absent or late more often than seems warranted, morale may be low, and work-related injuries may be high. The organization may experience a great deal of employee turnover.

Also examine internal relationship processes. For example, you may ask: What is the extent to which the members of the agency are engaged in destructive conflicts? How cohesive and cooperative are workers? Is there a smooth flow of information among people? How high is employee participation in decision making?[36]

Agency Adaptation

Adaptation of the agency to its wider environment is an important indicator of organizational health. Is there adequate financial support for the agency? Does it have enough human resources at its disposal? How proactively does it scan its environment and anticipate problems? How positive are its relationships with private, public, and not-for-profit agencies in its environment? What is its reputation in the community?[37]

Organization Culture[38]

The organization's culture is composed of its values, the meanings that people attach to the organization, and the underlying premises and beliefs that an agency represents. An organization developer will attempt to examine signs of a weak or fragmented culture. People in an agency with a strong culture will have a clear sense of its mission and believe that the mission is important and that the agency provides necessary and needed services. They are committed to that mission because there is congruence between what the agency does and what staff want to accomplish. The agency will be a place that helps employees do their best for their clients.

On the other hand, an agency with a weak culture has a vague sense of its purpose, and often there is a discrepancy between what it says about itself and what it actually does. People lack idealism, energy, and a sense of enthusiasm about the agency and what it does. People simply "put in their time" because they know that their efforts will not pay off, be recognized, or may even be discouraged. There may be an underlying sense that what people do or think doesn't matter.

A weak culture occurs when staff have little idea about the history or philosophy of the agency. They lose sight of who the heroes of the agency are and the values those heroes represent. Agencies with weak cultures give vague or conflicting messages about what is important or how to succeed in the agency. For example, an agency where the implicit message is "it's not what you know, but who you know" is one that encourages people to spend more time appeasing others than getting the job done. An agency with a weak culture spends little time recognizing employee achievements and organizational successes. It will resist celebrations as if the time spent is a detraction from getting the work of the agency accomplished or actually interferes with the agency's goals.

The culture of an organization is weak or fragmented when employees in some units or work sites are given preferential treatment or when different classes of employees are treated differently. When a culture is weak or in trouble people get frightened. This shows up in emotional outbursts such as denouncement of an agency policy in the workplace and visible displays of anger, or through personal problems such as a wave of divorces or alcohol abuse.

Diagnosing the Organization's Problems

After a physician has gathered enough information, a pattern or "syndrome" will appear. The physician recognizes this pattern as a particular disease process and gives it a label. "You have measles," the doctor says. The physician has diagnosed the problem.

In much the same way an organization developer will develop a diagnosis of the organization's dysfunctions. After you have gathered information, examine it for patterns, themes, and common indicators that will tell you where in the system the problem is located and what the sources of the problem are. This becomes a tentative diagnosis. Following are several diagnostic indicators of problems in organizations.

The Sound of "If Onlys"[39]

People are expressing hopelessness, alienation, and powerlessness in an organization where you hear things like: "If only I could work with that so and so . . . ," "If only this could be changed . . . ," or "If only people would listen to me."

Dualism

When a company operates on the basis of either/or dichotomies organizational managers demand employees commit themselves by asking "Are you for it or against it?" The implied message is acquiescence to the manager's ideas or policies. Employees understand that they need to "toe the line." Questioning decisions or offering alternative ideas is seen as disloyalty or disagreement.

Unchallenged Ambiguity

If we leave things vague enough, we can't be challenged or held accountable. "We'll do that as soon as possible," "We're working on it," or "I'll get around to it" are typical responses to problems that never get resolution.

Inconsistencies

Supervisors or workers are given double messages that leave them in a position of trying to second guess administrators. When this happens, workers or supervisors either take literally what administrators say and risk making a mistake, or they ignore administrators, use their own judgment, and risk going against the administrators' demands.

For example, an administrator tells supervisors to tighten services because of budget problems, but gives no guidelines. Attempting to comply, a supervisor applies rules more strictly but fairly, angering a client who complains to the director. The supervisor is threatened with termination if clients complain again.

"Let George Do It"

People in the organization see things going wrong and do nothing about it. Nobody volunteers. Mistakes and problems are habitually hidden or shelved.[40]

No Problem Here[41]

One level of organization dysfunction occurs when ambiguities or inconsistencies cannot be discussed. A sign of greater dysfunction is when the fact that they can't be discussed cannot be discussed. "Don't talk, don't feel, don't think" rules become unspoken policy. People begin to say, "This is a place that's not prepared to address the issues" or "We can't challenge statements, decisions, or assumptions." Instead of confronting discrepancies directly, people express their feelings indirectly by complaining, griping, and sniping over coffee.

Too Hot to Handle

Workers tend to stay away from a conflict when its source is their own supervisor or interaction between supervisors. If those in authority demand that workers take sides in these disputes, and workers are caught in the middle, they are in an untenable position.

Unresolved Conflicts

"Conflict is mostly covert and managed by office politics and other games, or there are interminable and irreconcilable arguments. When there is a crisis people withdraw or start blaming one another."[42]

Triangulation

Two people won't talk with each other, so they go through a third party who gets stuck with the problem. If the person can solve the problem, he or she becomes a hero or heroine. If not, he or she becomes the "stuckee." Stuckees tend to be rescuers who cannot say no. Triangulators are people who refuse to take responsibility or who avoid direct communication.

The Sorry Circle

Sometimes triangulation expands to include several people. One person, for example, is offended or blocked by another worker. Instead of talking to the offender directly, the person goes to his or her supervisor. Rather than bring together the two who are in conflict, the supervisor continues the process, complaining to the supervisor of the alleged offender. Instead of bringing everyone together, the second supervisor assumes the offender is guilty and reprimands the alleged offender. If enough time is allowed to elapse until the alleged offender is made aware of the problem, he or she may have completely forgotten the incident and be totally confused.

A perpetrator of the sorry circle may operate even more subtly by sending a formal memo of complaint to supervisors and the administrator without sending a copy to the alleged offender. Left out of the communication loop, the alleged offender is presumed guilty without knowing he or she has been accused.

Overcontrol

"People at the top try to control as many decisions as possible. They become bottlenecks and make decisions with inadequate information and advice. People complain about the manager's irrational decisions. . . . The manager tightly controls small expenditures and demands excessive justification. He allows little freedom for making mistakes."[43]

"Nero Fiddled While Rome Burned"

During times of great organizational stress, administrators may tend to work hard at solving insignificant issues while the agency is crumbling about them. For example, the director and top management of a social agency were being accused of incompetence, its board was under siege, and the state was threatening to take over the agency's operation. Workers were demoralized, services had nearly ground to a halt, clients were up in arms, and the budget was in a shambles. The director called a strategy meeting of all top management staff. It dealt with a procedure on how to answer phone calls from clients.

Scapegoating

Staff anger, frustration, and anxiety may get "pinned" onto one individual or sub-unit of the organization. The individual or unit ends up with the most difficult assignments, usually with fewer resources, and then is blamed when things go wrong. Ultimately, the individual or the unit becomes the vehicle for system dysfunction. "One more mistake and you're out."[44]

"I Get No Respect"

When administrators are under stress they sometimes demand blind allegiance based on their position in the organization rather than on their leadership style or quality of decisions. Staff are expected to support and offer deference to shore up the administrators' sagging self-esteem, compromising their own integrity in the process.

"Do as I Say, Not as I do"

In this dysfunctional game, managers assume that they are a "species apart" and not liable for the same behaviors or procedures for which they hold others accountable. Considering themselves beyond reproach, and dispensing favors or punishment with impunity, a culture of favoritism is set in motion. Double standards become the norm. People are treated progressively as objects the farther down they are positioned in the hierarchy. For example, while holding investigators accountable to the highest moral standards, J. Edgar Hoover, founder and for over thirty years head of the FBI, was a gambler whose debts were written off by organized crime. This resulted in a "hands off" policy toward investigating the crime syndicate. Hoover also used his agency files to blackmail politicians including several presidents.

I'm All Alone Here

The ultimate result of "I get no respect" and "Do as I say and not as I do" is that administrators feel alone in trying to get things done. Somehow, orders, policies, and procedures don't get carried out as intended.[45] The administrator or worker becomes increasingly isolated, frustrated, and without support.

The Party Line

Overly stressed administrators stop listening to internal and external organizational reality, failing to adequately scan the organization. Instead, they fall back on rules, roles, procedures manuals rather than what is required to meet changing conditions. When in doubt, they pull out the procedures manual as an authority to buttress their decisions.

Lack of Trust

"The judgment of people lower down in the organization is not respected outside the narrow limits of their jobs. People compete when they need to collaborate. They are very jealous of their area of responsibility. Seeking or accepting help is felt to be a sign of weakness. Offering help is unthought of. They distrust each other's motives and speak poorly of one another."[46] Lack of trust flows into the culture of the entire organization.

Playing Politics

While a certain amount of slippage is important in any organization to "grease the wheels," if organizational politics becomes the normal way of operating, the organizational culture operates not on what you know, but who you know. Those who are "in" are listened to rather than those who raise disquieting questions; supervisors operate on the basis of "cya—cover your ass"; and the agency itself may be seen as a place in which maneuvering to get ahead is the norm.

"We Have Always Done It This Way"

People may be reluctant to admit that things are not going well because it may reflect on them and on their own performance. Because they are immobilized and cannot change, they resist seeing that current practices no longer fit changing circumstances and display blindness to problem situations. Instead of adapting to change, they say, "we have always done it this way."

Helplessness

"People swallow their frustrations: 'I can do nothing. It's *their* responsibility to save the ship.'"[47]

Burn Out and Get Out

"People feel locked into their jobs. They feel stale and bored but constrained by the need for security. Their behavior in staff meetings is listless and docile. It's not much fun."[48] Ultimately, people become so burned out that they end up getting out of the organization.

Developing a Treatment Plan

Just as a physician gives a patient a "prescription" and specific treatment instructions, you must develop a prescriptive plan to cure the organizational dysfunction. Organizational treatment is often com-plex and involves intensive work. Depending on your diagnosis of where the problem is located, you can treat the system at the individual level, the group level, the intergroup level, or the organization level.

Organization developers have devised a number of treatments. While you need to be aware of these solutions, they may or may not work in the particular setting in which you are seeking answers. The field of organization development is a young one, and solutions are still in the process of development. In addition, a solution developed for one organization may not fit another. Adjust any prescriptive solution to the particular situation you face. This may mean developing an entirely new and innovative solution.

Organization Development at the Individual Level

People bring into organizations not only skills but also feelings, values, and personal problems. In addition, staff are affected by the general dysfunctions, stresses, and culture that organizations themselves create. Problems at the individual level usually begin to be expressed in lowered job performance and effectiveness, erratic attendance, increasing tardiness, or excessive absenteeism. An employee may have a "negative attitude," become physically ill, or accident prone.

Work-Related Personal Problems

Personal-life stresses such as divorce, death, marriage, or giving birth often affect individual job performance. Personal behavior problems such as alcohol and drug abuse, compulsive eating disorder, or gambling can impact work effectiveness. Many people are victims of emotional disorders such as chronic depression, bipolar psychosis, obsessive compulsive disorders, or phobias that affect their jobs. Workaholism is one such disorder that is particularly common in organizations.

TREATING WORK-RELATED PERSONAL PROBLEMS.   When problems are of a purely personal nature, make an assessment and either provide short-term counseling or make a referral to a clinical social worker, usually one practicing in an Employee

Assistance Program (EAP). Employee assistance programs provide diagnosis, counseling, and referral for individuals under personal or job-related stress.

Sometimes organizational leaders and workers bring into their positions dysfunctions carried over from their childhood. Workers and managers who come from abusive, alcoholic, or addictive homes often use the organization as a source of their own addictions. Overworking because of a compulsion rather than for enjoyment is an addiction common in organizations. People who are workaholics or who work under a workaholic boss are ultimately less rather than more productive. The driven workaholic introduces stress to the work place. "Because they don't take care of themselves, they frequently feel a lot of anger and resentment,"[49] eventually displaying physical symptoms such as headaches, backaches, ulcers, and irritable bowel syndrome. Exhibiting denial, they operate by "don't think, don't feel, don't talk" rules. While "work addiction can be just as unhealthy as substance abuse, the majority of U.S. corporations not only tolerate it, they actually reward it."[50]

System-Wide Individual Problems

Organization developers are concerned with how organization systems contribute to individual well-being. When system-wide patterns of organizational dysfunction cause stress-related burn-out, interpersonal conflicts, or emotional and health problems you should become personally involved in the treatment process.

STRESS. One of the most common work-related problems is stress. Everyone experiences stress. In fact, a certain amount of stress is necessary for life. There are two kinds of stress: positive stress and negative stress. Positive stress includes experiences that are perceived as challenging, exciting, and stimulating. For example, for some people, speaking to a group is a personally affirming and enhancing opportunity.

Negative stress is physically and emotionally damaging. For some people, speaking to a group is so painful and threatening that the person may become physically ill, forget what he or she was to say, and afterward have a feeling of shame or embarrassment. Organizations often contain negative stressors

that affect people. Excessive routine may lead to boredom for some, while for others excessive change can lead to stress and burn-out. Exposure to danger may be a positive stressor for persons in certain occupations such as fire and police work. Overexposure to danger, however, can create personal dysfunction, such as post-traumatic stress disorder.

On the other hand, according to a 1988 study by the American Medical Association,

> jobs causing the most problems were *not* those with a great deal of pressure to work hard and fast such as high-powered executive jobs often associated with heart attacks. Instead, the types of jobs causing increases in blood pressure were lower-level jobs. These were jobs where there were high psychosocial demands coupled with little control over the workplace and little use of skills.[52]

As a result, "an employee who is experiencing a high level of stress may develop high blood pressure, ulcers, irritability, difficulty in making routine decisions, loss of appetite, accident proneness, and the like."[51]

Work-related stressors have become major health problems. A study by the California Worker's Compensation Institute states that the "increase in work-related mental stress claims in the 1980s was phenomenal." Claims of mental stress resulting in lost work time increased from 1,178 incidents in 1979 to 9,368 in 1988, a total of 540 percent. Even these figures could be undercounted by as much as 30,000. Job pressures caused mental stress 69 percent of the time, followed by harassment, 35 percent, firing, 15 percent, discrimination, 7 percent, demotion, 2 percent, and other grievances, 11 percent. The authors of the report recommend that "we should start thinking about job design, about moving toward enhancement of skills, about better job training, and increasing worker participation in decision making."[53]

BURN-OUT. Burn-out is an occupational hazard that leaves people "vulnerable to doubt, disillusionment, and an eventual exhaustion of energy."[54] People who are experiencing burn-out may also have physical symptoms such as "ulcers, headaches, backaches, frequent colds, [and] sexual problems."[55] Edelwich says that while burn-out can occur in any kind of involvement, "it does not occur with anything like the same regularity or carry with it the same social costs in business as it does in the human services, where it takes on a special character and special intensity."[56] Burn-out may occur as a result of individual or system deficiency.[57]

Edelwich has developed a four-stage system of diagnosing burn-out in the helping professions.

- *Stage 1: Idealistic enthusiasm.* While those who enter a helping profession do so with a sense of altruism and idealism, some may develop near euphoria; they lose themselves in their helping role, leading to unrealistic expectations in their work. For example, social workers may expect that their presence will make all the difference in the world to their clients, that the job will work a miracle in their own lives, that success and its rewards will be immediate, automatic, and universal, and that clients will be highly motivated and respond with appreciation to the workers' omniscience and omnipotence.
- *Stage 2: Stagnation.* When these expectations go unrealized, social workers may lose the "momentum of hope and desire that brings a person into the helping field."[58] The job does not meet all of their personal needs, such as the need to earn a decent living, to be respected, to have satisfying family and social relationships, or have the leisure to enjoy them.[59] A worker who gives all of his or her energy to clients during the day and has little left over may retreat from his or her family or from the sources of rejuvenation that are available. The small world of the agency becomes the major means of identification and meeting the worker's needs, but in reality the agency sucks the worker dry.
- *Stage 3: Frustration.* Being bogged down and losing one's energy and enthusiasm leads to frustration, disappointment with oneself and others, and disillusionment about one's role and about the social work profession. Symptoms of frustration are emotional outbursts, exhaustion, depression, and illnesses such as headaches and colds.[60]
- *Stage 4: Apathy.* If unrecognized and untreated, frustration leads to apathy, the final stage of burn-out. Apathy exhibits itself in detachment, boredom, indifference, and retreat. The job is no longer exciting or fulfilling.[61]

TREATMENT FOR JOB-RELATED STRESS. A number of relaxation techniques such as biofeedback, meditation, and stress management training, as well as physical examinations and physical exercise are available to treat individual stress. Companies often provide counseling services, memberships to fitness clubs, and even gyms to help employees cope with job-induced stress.[62] Johnson and Johnson Company, for example, has developed a Live for Life (LIL) program. LIL is a "total immersion" approach that includes fitness, smoking cessation, moderation of drinking, good nutrition, weight control, blood pressure control, and stress management.[63] By the third year of the program involving eight thousand employees, LIL showed enough profit in time and money saved by reducing absences and illnesses to pay back expenses incurred the first year.[64]

Agencies can treat burn-out by reducing the amount of time (per day, per year, and per career lifetime) that the social worker spends working directly with clients. One way this can be accomplished is a form of job rotation in which a worker shifts after a number of years from direct service to administrative or educational roles. Other possibilities are the provision of support groups or peer counseling groups.[65] These groups, however, may reinforce burn-out rather than alleviate it. The best form of treatment is prevention by helping workers at the beginning of their careers to establish realistic expectations. If stages of burn-out occur, assessment, education, and making personal and/or job related changes can be implemented.[66]

QUALITY OF WORKING LIFE PROGRAMS. Overspecialization, rigid rules and roles, and formalized procedures can make jobs routine and lacking in challenge. Quality of working life programs, or QWLs, such as job rotation, work modules, job enlargement, and job enrichment can make work more meaningful and increase worker motivation.

1. *Job rotation.* Rotating jobs is a way of providing employees who are no longer challenged with their assignments with increased variety. By diversifying activities, workers learn new skills and management obtains more flexibility in scheduling work. On the other hand, rotating jobs can mean increased training costs, job dis-

ruption, and increased inefficiency because of lag time in job changeover.[67]

2. *Work modules.* Undesirable jobs may be spread among everyone in a unit rather than assigning them permanently to only a few people. At the beginning of a workday, employees request a set of job modules that constitute a day's work, changing jobs as often as three or even four times per day. Work modules allow individuals greater autonomy over work, take into account workers' job preferences, and build skill variety into the workday.[68]

3. *Job enlargement.* Job enlargement increases the number of different operations required in a job, thereby increasing its diversity. Expanding assignments by adding a variety of interesting, meaningful tasks helps employees identify with and make the project their own. If, however, the enlarged job merely adds more boring or meaningless tasks to existing ones, the value of job enlargement will be lost.[69]

4. *Job enrichment.* Job rotation, work modules, and job enlargement deal with increasing the number of operations of a job. Job enrichment involves the content of the work, expanding functions to include decision making, planning, executing, and inspecting the work. Successfully enriched jobs add not only increased responsibility but also autonomy, independence, self-reliance, and self-esteem. The worker is trusted to perform an entire job and is provided feedback so that he or she may correct his or her own performance.[70]

Organization Development at the Group Level

While groups are powerful systems for accomplishing work, they can also create difficulties if they become dysfunctional. Communication problems, interpersonal relationship problems, poor leadership, undefined tasks or roles, intra-unit rivalry or conflict—all are issues that you may confront.

Organization developers and theorists have developed a number of techniques for improving group effectiveness. Among these are T-groups, integrated work teams, project management, quality circles, team development, and group conferences.

T-Groups

T (training)-groups, also known as sensitivity, encounter, or growth groups, were developed in 1946 by Kurt Lewin at the National Training Laboratory for Group Development, Bethel, Maine. He and his associates discovered that feedback of data about group interaction was a rich learning experience. It helped people to develop self-awareness, communication skills, and interpersonal effectiveness.[71]

T-groups usually begin with a structured activity, such as a "trust walk," or "nonverbal communication" exercise aimed at generating interpersonal feelings. After the exercise, members share their feelings. The leader is intentionally nondirective to promote member interaction and ensure that the group develops its own leadership.

By the late 1970s most organization developers moved away from using T-groups even though they can be a source of rejuvenation, particularly for staff and administrators who live "drab and muted lives."[72] Team-building and group discussions and conferences aimed at organizational problem solving replaced the T-group movement.[73]

Integrated Work Teams

One way you can increase job satisfaction among individuals is to transform functional work groups into integrated work teams. Instead of several groups performing a single role independently of one another, assign several tasks to a team. The team decides on the specific member assignments and is responsible for rotating jobs as tasks require. Many work crews operate as integrated teams. For example, in cleaning a large building a supervisor will identify tasks but allow workers as a group to choose how the tasks will be allocated. Road work crews, outside maintenance crews, or construction crews often distribute work this way.[74]

Project Management

Project management is another way to structure teams for effective work accomplishment. Individuals from several departments or units are pulled together and assigned to work on a specific project. Because project teams are generally temporary, a

Integrated work teams, such as this group of employees at East Wind Nutbutters, a cooperatively run company, decide on specific member assignments and the responsibility for rotating jobs.

leader needs to know how to build a team quickly, adapt his or her leadership style to the situation, and help the group become a functioning unit. The leader must help members understand and accept their new role assignments.

If not organized correctly, a project management team has potential for role or task conflict. You can be helpful in assisting a new project management leader or the organizational manager think through these issues before the project team is developed.

Quality Circles

A quality circle is made up of workers, often a normal work unit, who have a shared area of responsibility. They meet together weekly on company time and on company premises to discuss their qual-

ity problems, investigate causes of problems, recommend solutions, and take corrective action. Members not only take responsibility for solving problems but also generate and evaluate their own feedback. Part of a quality circle's success means developing trust, sharing, and good communication skills, much as occurs in a T-group.[75]

Team Development and Group Conferences

A team is a "group of individuals who depend upon one another to accomplish a common objective."[76] Team building and team development are used to assist work group members who are either unfamiliar with one another or experience difficulty in working together. A goal of team development is to improve the communication, cooperation, and cohesiveness of units to increase their effectiveness.[77] Team development is an ongoing process occurring simultaneously with the work itself.[78]

This process is also appropriate for engaging two departments that are experiencing inter-unit rivalry. Bring them together to consider how to better attain organizational objectives. A meeting of two or more units is called a group conference.

There are six steps in the team development/group conference process:

- *Step 1: Establish the need for a team* or a team development process.
- *Step 2: Diagnose the problem.* You may give out questionnaires and/or have a meeting with the team to formulate a diagnosis of the level of team development and to establish an agenda of issues.
- *Step 3: Planning.* Give feedback to the team members on the issues, establish a set of objectives, and develop a group contract with the team asking for a commitment to work on specific issues over a certain span of time.
- *Step 4: Treatment process.* Ideally the team meets for several days away from the office. Begin by restating the objectives and laying out the issues. The team members form an agenda ranking the issues in order of importance. A technique for prioritizing is to have members write down the five problems they consider to be detrimental to the group's functioning and task accomplishment and then rank the prob-

lems from 1 to 5, 1 being the most serious problem. Next, make five columns, ranking each column in order of importance or urgency, the first column being most urgent or important and the last column not urgent:

(1) *Most Urgent* (needs immediate response)
(2) *Very Urgent* (needs response within the week)
(3) *Urgent* (needs response within the month)
(4) *Less Urgent* (can wait more than one month)
(5) *Not Urgent* (can be put off for the immediate future)

Place the all problem issues that members ranked 1, or most serious, under the heading "Most Urgent." When everyone has finished with their highest priority problems draw a line and rank the problems that members consider second highest priority and so on until the five problem issues are ranked. Once group members are satisfied with the completeness of the listing, they can easily visualize their priority rankings in terms of most urgent to least urgent as well as examine the range of problem areas.

Members next determine "ease" and "speed" of arriving at solutions. For each first-priority problem in the "Most Urgent" column rate the ease of solution: E for easy, MD for moderately difficult, and H for hard. Then indicate the amount of time it will take to reach resolution. Speed can be indicated by Q for quick, A for average, and L for lengthy. Participants can then see which issues are most important and most urgent, and how difficult it will be to solve them. If needed this process can be continued with second priority problems in the most urgent column, third priority problems, and so on.

With this new information, group members can decide which problems to tackle first. Sometimes a very important problem may appear to have a fairly easy solution. On the other hand, the team may decide on dealing with problems that can easily be resolved even though they may not be the most important ones.
- *Step 5*: Help members reach an agreement to work in new ways, to restructure roles, and to develop time lines to test out new processes.

The means by which the group works on its own internal problems can be a beginning for restructuring the group's internal dynamics. For example, if the leadership is identified as a major problem, assign the unit supervisor or division chief to an observer or recorder role and appoint someone else to lead the group. This will enable the leader be objective and involved, and will also insure that he or she listens to the group and hears what is said about administrative leaders without defending him- or herself.

If there are subgroup rivalries within the group, break the subgroups apart and place the members in different subgroups to promote interaction with others. If communication problems or conflicts exist between particular members, ask them to get together in dyads or triads to work together for a common issue. One person tells his or her perceptions while the listener reflects them back to the speaker. Then the message sender and receiver exchange roles so that communication and listening is practiced. During these exchanges, work closely with each subgroup, listening and facilitating the process, modeling, coaching, giving feedback, and structuring activities to help members work more closely together.

Once members have resolved interpersonal issues, they may be ready to deal with task related issues. The goal is to arrive at specific action plans, to which all members can commit themselves, to promote better working relationships, communication, and cohesion. "Before the meeting ends, the team should list action items to be dealt with, who will be responsible for each item, and a time schedule.[79]
- *Step 6: Evaluation.* Develop criteria for evaluating whether the team has been effective, provide training in the new processes, and, if needed, make periodic re-assessments and adjustments.

Organization Development at the Intergroup Level

Organizational problems often exist at the boundaries between subunits in organization where different groups, units, or departments interact, communicate, and relate.

Problem-Solving Task Forces

A problem-solving task force is a short-term conference group made up of two departments that have trouble coordinating their work. Robert Blake, Herbert Shepard, and Jane Mouton developed a technique called intergroup team building.[80] The following process is a modification of this technique.

During group discussion, bring out as many symptoms as possible to get a clear picture of the performance problems and uncover its dynamics. Then ask each unit to go to separate rooms. Using information developed in the discussion phase, assign them the task of developing a list of problems that interfere with the coordination and performance of the units.

After the lists are complete, the units meet together and record their lists on a board for all to see. Facilitate a process of narrowing the lists to specific underlying issues or causes. Next, divide the group into several subgroups, each having equal representation from the two units. Ask them to arrive at solutions to the problems they have identified.

Finally, the subgroups return to the larger group to report on solutions and reach a consensus. Develop a mutual contract in which both units commit themselves to the joint solution, and agree to assess its effectiveness and report back to evaluate on a specific date.

Problem-solving task forces are useful in solving problems that have reached a crisis point. For longer term solutions, however, you may need to develop ongoing coordination task forces composed of representatives from various units whose role is to monitor, assess, and propose solutions to coordination problems, resolve disputes, and facilitate planning between units.

Boundary Spanning

Boundary spanners are trouble shooters who are on the lookout for problems and who work to ensure that the relationships between units are smooth. They coordinate efforts between units, teams, or task forces by bringing them together for problem solving. Boundary spanners help resolve conflicts between supervisors, facilitate integration and work flow, listen to complaints, and in general make sure that communication and integration of the units occur.[81]

Inter-Unit Conflict Resolution Strategies

The Chinese word for change contains two parts—one means danger and the other, opportunity. While change can create opportunity, it is not without risk. One of the darker aspects of change is conflict in which one person achieves but at the expense of another, who perceives him- or herself as being blocked. Conflict is common in organizations, especially when there is a great deal of interdependency, creating rivalry, communication, and performance problems.[82] An important role of an organization developer is to help manage conflict constructively.

The Conflict Cycle[83]

- *Stage I: Tension development.* A minor conflict occurs. At first the issue may seem insignificant, but it creates discomfort. While this is the best time to deal with the irritation, people tend to avoid recognizing or confronting the situation, hoping it will pass or not repeat itself.
- *Stage II: Role dilemma.* As conflicts continue, a dilemma is created and tension builds, causing confusion. A feeling that things are not supposed to be like this occurs, and issues become more urgent. There is an increased sense of powerlessness and helplessness. In order to resolve the confusion and reach equilibrium, people try to understand who is at fault, pinpoint the cause of the problem, and attach it to an incident, issue, event, or person. The injured parties try to get out of the dilemma by asking themselves, "What am I doing to cause this tension?" "What is the other person doing?" "What is happening here?" "Who's in charge?" "What's wrong?" Because individuals struggle alone with the issue, it is difficult to break into the cycle.
- *Stage III: Injustice collecting.* People begin to attach blame. Hurts multiply, piling up with each new confrontation. People begin to nurse their wounds; participants inventory injustices,

dwelling on their own injuries. Each party feels justified in his or her anger, actively blaming the other parties. Those involved are unconsciously preparing for battle. At this point, the cycle may be broken by having the parties face each other and talk about the issue. But because individuals have withdrawn into themselves, cataloging their injuries, communication tends to be tense and difficult.

- *Stage IV: Confrontation.* By this time, the original problem may have been forgotten or swallowed up in the accumulated hurts each person feels. The focus of the conflict is now on getting even, obtaining revenge, or restitution. Trading hurts, however, only exacerbates injuries, further damaging relationships, blocking communication, and further separating the parties from understanding or resolving the issue. Conflict at this stage is often destructive.

If the people involved remain inflexible at this stage, one of two different results may occur. In the first scenario, as tension continues to build, one injured party resolves not to "take it" any more and waits for another incident to occur. When the injury occurs, he or she "explodes," causing the conflict to surface. Conflict between the parties escalates out of control, ending in a "fight."

In the second scenario, people withdraw from battle in a continuing pattern of avoidance—refusing to face the issue. Sometimes there is a frozen silence. The hurts are so deep that injured parties refuse to interact at all, and in a passive way try to punish one another by withdrawal.

If the individuals are able to stop trading verbal punches or to open themselves up to one another it is still possible to trace the conflict back to the original problem and work toward resolution.

- *Stage V: Adjustments.* If the parties have chosen to either fight or withdraw, they are locked in a standoff. In families this leads to separation and divorce, and in international conflict, to an open

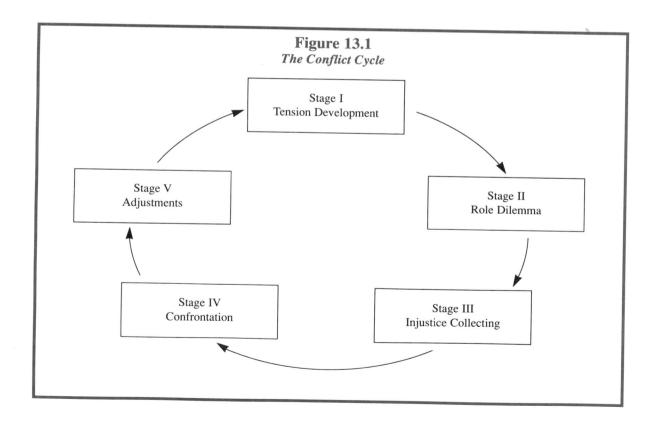

Figure 13.1
The Conflict Cycle

Stage I
Tension Development

Stage II
Role Dilemma

Stage III
Injustice Collecting

Stage IV
Confrontation

Stage V
Adjustments

battle or a "cold war." In organizations, it can prompt an employee to ask for a transfer or to quit, rival units to refuse to work on common projects, and labor unions to go on strike. If, however, the parties are able to engage one another, adjustments may still be made, but this cannot be done without the help of an intermediary such as a third-party peacemaker.

Conflict Resolution

Jumping into the content of a dispute without laying the groundwork often only escalates the conflict and produces negative results. It is important to help parties declare their intentions to make a commitment to be constructive. The best resolutions come about when each party makes an unconditional commitment to be constructive; to do only those things that will be good both for the relationship and for themselves, whether or not the others reciprocate.[84] The following list is an expansion and adaptation of ideas derived from "Unconditionally Constructive Strategy" developed by Roger Fisher and Scott Brown of the Harvard Negotiating Project.[85]

1. I will commit myself to make things right, even if I may not be sure of how that may occur or how committed others may be at the moment. I will declare my intention to resolve the conflict and work toward reconciliation even if others' commitments seem to waver.
2. I will work at expressing and owning my negative feelings so that what caused them can be worked through and resolved.
3. I will balance reason and emotion even if other parties are acting only emotionally or only logically.
4. I will work at understanding. Even if they misunderstand me, I will try to understand them.
5. I will work at good communication. Even if others are not listening, I will listen to them and consult with them on matters that affect them.
6. I will be reliable. Even if others are trying to deceive me, I will neither offer blind trust nor try to deceive them.
7. I will use persuasion rather than coercion. Even if they are trying to coerce me, I will be open to persuasion, and I will try to persuade them.

8. I will work at acceptance. Even if others reject me and my concerns as unworthy of their consideration, I will accept others as worthy of consideration.
9. I will be open to learning. Even if others seem to be unbending, I will be accessible and committed to my own growth and learn from this experience.
10. I will relate with respect. I will respect ideas, feelings, and perceptions even if they differ from my own. I will respect my own perceptions and expect that others will offer me respect.

Three different processes can be used in resolving conflicts. Mediation is a preferred process if the problem involves healing a personal injury or an injustice that resulted in broken personal relationships. If the problem is resolving an issue external to each party, reaching agreement in a dispute, or arriving at a settlement to which both parties must agree, then the appropriate strategy is negotiation. Finally, mutual problem solving is the preferred strategy if the conflict is one of restoring or resolving a breach in a working relationship.

MEDIATION. Mediators are advocates for both parties in a disagreement. Mediators help those involved recognize injustice, restore equity, regain the relationship, and commit to future resolution.

1. *Recognize the injustice.* Begin by having both parties describe how they became involved in the conflict. Ask party A to describe the conflict, including both facts and feelings. Ask party B to listen and take notes. When party A is finished, ask party B to summarize the main facts and feelings until party A can say, "Yes, that is what I said."

    The process is repeated with party B describing the conflict while party A listens, takes notes, and then summarizes what party B said.
2. *Restore equity.* Explain that this stage is to restore what was broken or bring balance back to the relationship. Using the following "four R's," ask each party to suggest what would be needed to restore equity: (a) *related* to the hurt, (b) *reasonable*, (c) *respectful*, and (d) *restorative*. You, as mediator, make sugges-

tions and help parties formulate alternatives. After all of the suggestions are expressed, help both parties see commonalities and areas of agreement. Each suggestion is handled in turn until both parties agree that the solutions will restore the broken relationship. If there are still unspoken or unresolved hurts, these need to be expressed.

3. *Regain the relationship*. The parties contract to implement the mutually agreed upon solutions.

4. *Commit to future resolution*. Finally, ask both parties what behaviors or actions will they use to prevent future conflicts. What agreements need to be made to build trust? How will accountability be dealt with? Write a summary and have each party sign an agreement. Schedule a follow-up meeting to check on what each party is doing to keep the contract, follow their agreements, and/or make adjustments.

NEGOTIATION.   Negotiation is a universal process in which an issue or dispute affecting two parties is settled and a mutual agreement is reached. People negotiate every day over many issues.[86] The most successful negotiation is one that ends in a win/win situation. Both parties get something they want, and each will be willing to negotiate again. However, there are also win/lose, lose/win, and lose/lose outcomes. Negotiators work hard to prevent one or both sides from losing.

1. *Preparation*. Prepare yourself by examining the situation in which both parties find themselves, including the background, culture, and reasons why each party takes the position he or she does. Ask for or gather information from both parties about their positions and what each is willing to give up to reach a solution.

    You need to be clear about the issues and the demands that each party is making. You cannot negotiate what one party is not capable of or not authorized to give. Asking for the impossible will only result in a deadlock or a lose/lose situation.

2. *Presentation of demands*. Meet with both parties. Choose a neutral setting in which both parties are comfortable and a time when neither will be rushed. Ask each party to present his or her position and formally lay out demands. The demands should be specific, clear, and measurable. Plan an agenda.

3. *Negotiating rounds*.
    a. Round 1. Meet with party A, the most inflexible party, and obtain as many concessions as you can that will come close to what you know party B will accept. Explain what you think the chances of success are. Tell A which areas and in what amounts he or she may need to consider giving up.
    b. Round 2. Meet with party B and present the concessions of party A. Depending on your assessment of party B's position, you may offer only part of party A's demands. Try to come to agreement on as many issues as possible. On those areas where party A's concessions are not acceptable, extract from party B a compromise that will come as close as possible to what you know party A will accept.
    c. Round 3. As party B considers his or her position and strategy, meet again with party A and present the items on which you have obtained agreement, pressing A to make concessions on the remaining issues to obtain as much as B's demands as possible.
    d. Continuing rounds. Continue to negotiate until a compromise is reached. If either party becomes inflexible, try to understand why and problem solve, helping to arrive at creative solutions. Then present those solutions to the other party, asking him or her to consider alternative solutions until an acceptable compromise is reached.

Mutual Problem Solving

Mutual problem solving relies on "seeking fundamental points of difference rather than on determining who is right, who is wrong, who wins, or who loses."[87] This technique requires that you bring the conflicting parties together and encourage them to face the underlying causes of their conflict. The purpose is to solve the problem through collaboration rather than to accommodate different points of view, as with negotiation.[88]

First, each party defines the problem, and both parties commit themselves to a resolution. Ask each party to privately make a list of concerns and the reasons for taking a particular position. Combine each party's listings, rewording the concerns in a positive manner. For example, "One concern I have is that I don't want to have to put up with your reneging on our agreements" becomes "Keeping our agreements is important." Write down the reworded lists in full view on a board or sheet of newsprint.

Each party silently writes down possible solutions to the problems that have been listed. Collect and place all the solutions in plain view next to the list of problems. Participants assess the solutions in terms of their particular interests and goals. Modify, shape, combine, adapt, or change the solutions until both parties adopt one or possibly a series of solutions that are acceptable.

Develop a contract in which each conflicting party is held mutually accountable for the solution. If a solution does not work because one or the other has violated the contract, bring the parties together again to air grievances and renegotiate the contract. If each party tries the solution in good faith, but it does not work, bring the parties together again to review why the approach did not work. Adjust the solution to accommodate the issues that continue to get in the way.

Organization Development with the Organization as a Whole

Organization developers frequently work with an organization as a whole. One method of increasing organizational effectiveness is management by objectives (MBO). MBO is a process whereby each unit of an organization develops long-range goals and short-term objectives.[89]

MBO begins with the administrator formulating long-range goals and strategic plans. These plans are broken down into specific overall organization objectives. Objectives are statements of measurable results the organization is to achieve within a specific time period. Each department of the organization applies the organizational objectives, setting departmental or subunit objectives. Then, within each work unit, line supervisors develop specific job objectives for each worker.

Next, action plans are developed that contain the sequence of tasks, key activities, and budgets required to accomplish the objectives. Managers develop methods for ensuring the accomplishment of the objectives for which they have responsibility. The action plans are implemented, and individuals are assigned responsibility for specific tasks.

Usually a strategy for behavior reinforcement and motivation is developed to strengthen performance through training, compensation, or other techniques. Periodic progress reviews provide feedback for adjusting objectives, action plans, and control methods.[90]

Action Model of Organization Development

This chapter has presented a model and techniques for helping an organization system engage in a planned change effort. However, some qualifications need to be addressed. Social work organization development is not simply a matter of implementing managerial or organizational change no matter what direction the change. In an action model of organization development, the social worker acts in ways congruent with the norms and values of the social work profession. Frank Lowenberg and Ralph Dolgoff describe these values as:

1. Regard for individual worth and human dignity . . . furthered by mutual participation, acceptance, confidentiality, honesty, and responsible handling of conflict.
2. Respect for people's right to choose, to contract for services, and to participate in the helping process.
3. Contribute to making social institutions more humane and responsive to human needs.
4. Demonstrate respect for and acceptance of the unique characteristics of diverse populations.[91]

A social worker as organization developer may be placed in a situation where the demands of the organization and the action model of social work values are in conflict. For example, because management uses the force of command, there may be an implied or overt message that employees must participate in a change process whether they want to or not. Change can be imposed on people even if it is against their own wishes. In this case, greater autonomy and worker participation is sacrificed for organizational control. EXERCISE 45 will help you explore employee

EXERCISES

EXERCISE 45:
How to Reduce Resistance
to Change

Read the following extract on how to reduce resistance to change, particularly those parts in italics. Answer the questions that follow. Then form into triads and compare answers. Return to the larger group and discuss your conclusions.

> As most organizational change can be expected to generate resistance, it can also be postulated that *the greater the participation of staff in the change process, the more likely that they will have an opportunity to coalesce and organize against the change.* This is especially true when major system change is at stake. In such cases, use of power and authority may be required to effectively initiate the change.[92]

1. Compare the advice in this excerpt with the ethical principles cited by Lowenberg and Dolgoff. With which principles is the excerpt congruent? With which principles does the excerpt conflict?
2. The excerpt postulates that the greater the staff participation in the change, the more likely staff will organize against change in organizations. What assumptions about employees are implicit in this statement? Is the reverse true? That is, the less staff participate in the change process, the less likely they will organize against change? What does your knowledge about unions and labor relations tell you about this assumption? Do you think people will tend to resist change if they are involved in the process?
3. The excerpt asserts that when major system change is at stake, power and authority may be required to bring about change.

What assumptions about the use of power and authority are implicit in these statements? Do you think that using power and authority facilitates change or hinders it?
4. If you, as an organization developer, were asked by management to force change onto workers and were given power and authority to do so, would you comply? Why or why not? Are there any circumstances under which organizational change should be forced onto employees against their wishes? What circumstances might these be?
5. The advice in the excerpt places organizational goal achievement over employee self-determination. What would you, as an organization developer, do if you were asked by management to facilitate a change process that might weaken mutual participation, interfere with the right of employees to choose, or participate in the helping process?

---

self-determination, mutual participation, and people's right to choose in organizational change.

Principles of Organization Development as Action Therapy[93]

In addition to the values and ethical norms of the social work profession, a model of organization development as action therapy is based on the following principles:

1. When deciding whether to begin or to continue a relationship with a client organization, action therapists must determine for themselves the degree to which the overall purposes of the organi-

zation are compatible with their personal values and the norms of the social work profession.[94]
2. The action therapist must begin his or her involvement by developing a sense of the organization staff members' subjective appreciation of the organization, despite whatever critical stance the therapist may later take toward the organization.
3. The action therapist must be frank in revealing his or her own values and assumptions, explain his or her goals, and describe the techniques and processes he or she will use to achieve them.[95]
4. The action therapist will discern and critically assess moral-ethical aspects of the organization's processes. While the action therapist will not impose his or her values on the organiza-

tion, the therapist has an obligation to create a climate in which moral-ethical issues may be critically evaluated, and may even play an active part in that criticism.

5. An action therapist will not regard his or her activities as merely a series of instrumental techniques for the attainment of increased worker productivity, efficiency, or effectiveness at the expense of justice, fairness, and worker rights, but will work to bring about shared responsibility, worker involvement, and mutual engagement in task accomplishment and problem solving.[96]

6. The action therapist will explore the extent to which the imposition of formal authority (1) helps or hinders the creation and transmittal of shared meanings and (2) facilitates cooperative, responsible, and accountable human action. He or she will work to bring about an institutional culture compatible with human dignity and self-determination.

7. The action therapist will clarify the effects of organizational norms and processes of social interaction upon the achievement of organizational ends and will attempt to bring about processes that humanize those ends.

8. The action therapist will maintain his or her responsibility to determine the compatibility of an organization's structure, processes, and projects with the general stated purposes of the organization and bring about changes in either its ends or its means to achieve a healthier setting for both employees and clientele.[97]

9. The action therapist will understand that social agencies are in the service of meeting the human needs of a community of people. The board, staff, clientele, and wider community are mutually accountable to one another. Everyone has a stake in the effective and efficient provision of services.

Conclusion

Organization developers are therapists to dysfunctional organizational systems who use social work skills at the individual, group, intergroup, and organizational level to bring a dysfunctional organization back to effective functioning. An action model of organization development uses techniques developed to help change organizational systems, but always in the service of means and ends that are ethically good. Although the therapist's role avoids imposing specific value prescriptions onto organizational systems, it inevitably and necessarily involves the therapist as a self-conscious and intentional moral actor.

KEY CONCEPTS

organization development
internal organization development
external organization development
forces for change
forces against change
reactive
proactive
planning organizational change
approaches to organizational development
the systems process approach
social ecology approach
levels of analysis approach
sum of subsystems approach
contingency theory approach
therapeutic approach
steps in organization development
problem recognition
problem identification
gathering information
systems effectiveness
output goals
internal system state
adaptation to social environment
culture
syndrome
EAP
stress
burn-out
work-related personal problems
system-wide individual problems
quality of work life (QWL)
job enlargement
job enrichment
job rotation
job modules
t-groups

team building
group conference
integrated work team
project management
quality circle
problem-solving task force
boundary spanning
conflict cycle
conflict resolution
mediation
negotiation
mutual problem solving
management by objectives (MBO)
action model of organization development
action therapy

QUESTIONS FOR DISCUSSION

1. How are the role, skills, and process of an organization developer similar to those of a psychotherapist?
2. How is the role of an organization developer similar to or different from that of a community developer?
3. Organization developers are charged with improving the effectiveness of the organization with which they have contracted. Are there situations in which an organization developer may find his or her social work values in conflict with helping the organization become more effective? What are some ethical conflicts organization developers might encounter?
4. An action model of organization development prescribes to the action therapist a role as moral actor. Is this role appropriate or inappropriate? What limitations or dangers are implicit in this role for action therapists? Is being a moral actor a role with which you would feel comfortable in carrying out organization development? Why or why not? What information would you need if you were serious about being a moral action therapist?
5. Most organizations are prescriptive systems, which means that their ends are predetermined. In fact, organizations are tools for implementing the predetermined ends of the owners. Does an organization developer have a right to question those ends? Why or why not? Would an external organization development consultant ever find work if he or she questioned the ends to which client organizations were directed?

ADDITIONAL READING

Conflict Resolution and Negotiation

Fisher, Roger, and Scott Brown. *Getting Together: Building a Relationship That Gets to Yes.* Boston, MA: Houghton Mifflin, 1988.

Fisher, Roger, and William Ury, with Bruce Patton, ed. *Getting to Yes: Negotiating Agreement without Giving In.* 2d ed. New York: Penguin, 1991.

Organization Development

Beckhard, Richard. *Organization Development: Strategies and Modes.* Reading, MA: Addison-Wesley, 1969.

Bennis, Warren, et al. *The Planning of Change,* 4th ed. New York: Harcourt Brace College Pubs., 1985

French, Wendell, and Cecil H. Bell, Jr. *Organization Development: Behavioral Science Interventions for Organization Improvement.* 2d ed. Englewood Cliffs, NJ: Prentice-Hall, 1978.

Kanter, Rosabeth Moss. *The Change Masters.* New York: Simon and Schuster, 1983.

Peters, Tom, and R. Waterman. *In Search of Excellence: Lessons from America's Best Run Companies.* New York: Harper and Row, 1982.

Management Consultation

Goodstein, L. *Consultation with Human Service Systems.* Reading, MA: Addison-Wesley, 1978.

Lippitt, G. "A Study of the Consultation Process," *The Journal of Social Issues,* 15 (1959): 43-50.

Lippitt, G., and R. Lippitt. *The Consulting Process in Action.* La Jolla, CA: University Associates, 1978.

Schein, Edgar A. *Process Consultation: Its Roles in Organization Development.* Reading, MA: Addison-Wesley, 1969.

EXERCISES

EXERCISE 46:
Conflict Resolution

The purpose of this exercise is to discover alternative ways of resolving conflicts in an agency setting. Silently read the following scenario and then rank the twelve alternatives. After everyone has finished his or her individual rankings, break into random groups of four to eight people each. Sit far enough apart so that you can work without disturbing one another. Discuss your individual rankings and come to a group consensus. Record the group ranking. Then, return to the class as a whole. Compare group rankings. What were the most preferred solutions? What were the least preferred? Why were these solutions chosen? How did the individual rankings compare to the group rankings?

Scenario

You are a manager of the program development section of a relatively young, innovative private vocational rehabilitation agency engaged in the competitive world of providing case management, training, education, counseling, advocacy, and legal services for a variety of clients who are SSI (Supplemental Security Income) recipients. Services are up, and the company is expanding. You report to the chief of research and development. Your section is a key one because of the need for envisioning services to meet needs in new and innovative ways.

The chief of research and development has decided to establish a team that would oversee each new program service. The team would do research, planning, program development, case management, and person-

nel and would be responsible for overseeing a new program idea from its conception through the research, planning, funding, and implementation stages. The representative from case management has been appointed as chair of the team.

Recently, a promising new program idea has been devised that will create a new market niche. At a planning team meeting, you present the new program idea, including demographics, needs, existing services, cost, and a proposed time schedule. Of special interest, you think, is the introduction of a new computerized system of record keeping that would provide better quality client services, efficiency, accountability, and save time, as well as aid communication among staff, since any staff could immediately access client files. While there would be considerable cost savings in the long run, the short-term costs of installing computers and software and training people in the use of the new equipment would be considerably greater than using the current method of recording—handwritten notes.

During the meeting, the planning manager voices serious objections. He is interested in getting the new program implemented soon, and the delay in time caused by setting up and training people in the use of computerized equipment, he says, would lose the company's competitive edge, overcoming any long-term cost savings. As manager of program development, you disagree and note that the new computerized record-keeping equipment could be useful in all of the agency's programs and services, and its long-term uses would outweigh short-term savings.

Arguments on both sides become heated. The head of case man-

agement sides with you, but the personnel manager sides with the planning manager. The result is a stalemate. After the meeting you reflect on what you consider to be a personal loss. You also realize, however, that your own department agrees with your position and that the Planning Department is behind the short-term consideration. Because this is an important issue, you try to figure out what your alternatives are. As you think about it, you see them in the following way:

1. You can have a meeting with the planning representative and stress the positive aspects of your idea, indicating that the equipment will make the company the most innovative and foremost vocational rehabilitation provider in the state.
2. You can rework your plan to go along with the objections of the planning representative, doing the best you can with the long-term cost considerations of the plan.
3. You can send a letter to the president resigning your position on the team.
4. You can tell the planning representative that if he goes along with your position now, you will give full support to his new agency reorganization plan that is to be presented to the team in the near future.
5. You can go to the chief of Research and Development and request that he intercede for your position.
6. You can ask the planning representative to meet with you for a full day next week in order to work out your differences and

EXERCISES

come up with an alternative solution.

7. You can ask a member of the chief of Research and Development's staff to sit in on all team meetings and act as the new chairperson and arbitrator of all problems.

8. You can send the planning representative a letter (with copies to all team members, the chief of Research and Development, and the president) indicating that opposition to your plan is holding up a potentially profitable project.

9. You can ask the chief of Research and Development to attend the next team meeting in order to stress the importance of this project to the continued growth of the company.

10. You can immediately walk into the planning representative's office and ask him to justify his position to you.

11. You can ask for the intervention of a third-party negotiator.

12. You can complain to your unit and urge them to campaign for your position to the rest of the agency, hoping to sway opinion your way.

PART IV

Societal Social Work

If anyone else still has illusions about this country, it's not the poor. They know that this country will spend $20 billion to put a man on the moon, but will not spend $20 to put a man on his feet. They know it will spend more to keep weevils from eating the cotton than to keep rats from eating the fingers of a baby in Harlem. They know it will pay a U.S. senator over $100,000 a year not to plant cotton, but will not pay $1 to the families on his plantation not to raise hookworms in the stomachs of their own children.
—SI KAHN

Societal-level social workers engage social problems that affect large groups of people through the political process and social policy. Social policies become operating premises of societies. Social policy analysts pursue goals that move us toward a good society. Societal-level social work is based on the engagement and mobilization of social values. Social policies need to be aimed toward values that are ethically good.

Social ethics is problematic in our individualistic, self-interested, and impersonal society. It is because of the social values on which our society is based that we have difficulty solving some of our most pervasive social problems. Social work as a profession sometimes has failed to chart a new direction in part because it too is captured by some of these values.

If macro social work is to become a meaningful and viable arena, and effectively overcome social problems, we need to develop a clear understanding of values and ethics. We also need to examine the role of social work for the future and develop reconstructed models by which social work can attack social problems more successfully.

Chapter 14 deals with societal social work and chapter 15 with social values and ethics and examines some issues facing a reconstructed macro social work for the future. Exercises in each of these chapters and additional reading will help you in examining the ideas more fully.

CHAPTER 14

Social Work at the Societal Level:
Social Policy and Politics

Joan Claybrook is a persistent policy advocate at the national level.

Every gun made, every warship launched, every rocket fired signifies, in the final sense, a theft from those who hunger and are not fed, those who are cold and not clothed.

This world in arms is not spending money alone. It is spending the sweat of its laborers, the genius of its scientists, the hopes of its children.

—PRESIDENT DWIGHT D. EISENHOWER

IDEAS IN THIS CHAPTER

Joan Claybrook: Policy Advocate[1]

The tall bespectacled woman at a makeshift lectern in a Capitol Hill hearing room doesn't look particularly fierce. Her face is scrubbed, her shoes sturdy, her smile ready. In a brightly colored suit and pearls, she looks like an aging version of the Junior Leaguer she once was. But make no mistake; consumer advocate Joan Claybrook is no pussycat.

As president of Public Citizen, the consumer-advocacy group founded by Ralph Nader in 1971, Claybrook has a point of view on just about every issue affecting the public good from health care to insurance, from legal rights to banking. But there are two things that really get to her: automobile safety and campaign finance. For weeks in May 1992 she hammered away at how much public money President Bush took in during his presidential and vice presidential campaigns ("over $420 million by the end of 1992," she says), while he said he would veto any campaign-finance reform bill that provided for public funding of congressional elections or restricts spending on them. In early May 1992, a bill doing just that landed on his desk, and Joan Claybrook was one of the people who pushed it there. As she sees it she represents the interests of the people, and the people deserve to win.

"It's important to approach people in the best way that you can," says Claybrook. "We think very hard about that. What is the best way to communicate the message?" She goes about it by studying the issues, learning their history, including previous congressional votes. And she works the media: staging press conferences, writing opinion pieces, sending letters to the editor.

Claybrook was reared to be a social policy analyst. At her parent's house, dinner conversations were about politics. Her father, a bond attorney and Baltimore City Council member, stalwart of the local civil rights movement in the 1950s, was a founder of the Maryland Americans for Democratic Action.

Her mother, a homemaker, was a natural organizer who believed that their three children ought to be encouraged to do anything they wanted, even if they failed. After her parents died, Joan's attitude changed. "I never thought about having to achieve either before or after their deaths, but I realized that

I was the older generation now, and that I had a lot to give."

One of the original Nader's Raiders, Claybrook became a consumer advocate even earlier. She came to Washington in 1965 as a fellow of the American Political Science Association, the first time the program included women. Required to work for a member of Congress, Claybrook signed on with James MacKay, a Southern Liberal Democrat who asked her to work on auto safety. She had just read an amazing book, *Unsafe at Any Speed*, by Ralph Nader. When MacKay decided to introduce an auto-safety bill, the first regulatory bill for the auto industry, he asked Claybrook to draft it. As Claybrook followed the bill through Congress, she was introduced to lobbying Nader-style. "I saw Ralph in operation—how he manipulated, maneuvered, pushed and pulled, how he used disclosures to shock people," she recalls. "It was an incredibly fast education."

The following September, the bill—which established safety standards for motor vehicles—was enacted into law. At the end of her fellowship, Claybrook moved to the National Traffic Safety Bureau (NTSB) where she became assistant to the director. She stayed there until 1970 when she joined Nader. In 1973 she founded and directed Congress Watch, Public Citizen's congressional lobbying group, and when Jimmy Carter was elected president, she was asked to head the NTSB. She pushed to require automobile makers to provide air bags or at least passive seat belts. In 1980, she was back in the trenches of the consumer movement as president of Public Citizen. "I have a love of battle," she says. "I work on issues I care deeply about and get paid enough to live on. Who could ask for anything more?"

Introduction

Macro social workers practice in the arena of policy and politics. While *public* policies are operating principles by which governmental systems carry out their goals, *social* policies are operating premises developed to provide direction in the solution of social problems. Social policy issues, for example, include such questions as: Should U.S. citizens have the right to possess handguns? Should women have a right to abortion, and should the federal govern-

ment subsidize abortions for poor women who cannot afford them? Should people who are gay be afforded the same rights and protection of the laws as other citizens? Should people who are terminally ill be allowed the choice to terminate their own lives with the assistance of a physician? Should capital punishment (execution) be permitted in the United States? Answering policy questions such as these provide positions that guide us in problem resolution and provide directions for developing legislation.

Theories or models of social policy describe how systems, groups, and people influence local, state, and federal governments to achieve policy preferences. Who determines what our policies are in relation to difficult social questions? Do social policies emerge out of grass-roots democracy or are they the result of the intersection of competing interest groups? Are policies set by legislative bodies at the local, state, or national levels or are they actually determined by large governmental bureaucracies that must make day-to-day decisions about what is best and right? Are social policies established by the "power elite"—corporate executives and influential politicians such as state governors, Cabinet members, or the president or do they come about by a rational decision-making process? Before you can have impact on social policy, you need to understand who makes social policy. This chapter describes seven models or theories of social policy making.

In addition to understanding the real world of policy making, you need to be able to critically assess social policies in terms of their effectiveness in achieving the welfare of the people they are intended to benefit—whether these policies are "good, right, or rational for society."[2] If a social policy actually creates harm, for example, it needs to be criticized and changed. You need to be able to explore what is wrong with current social policy, understand how social policies can be made better, and be able to decide among competing policy preferences. The policy analysis process is presented for thinking through difficult policy issues.

Social change comes about when proposals are enacted into tangible policy outcomes in the real world. The chapter explores how policy proposals must be implemented to make changes in people's lives.

Finally, social policies deal with value questions and affect people's lives in very real ways. Social work policy analysts need a model that is congruent with the practice principles and values of the social work profession. Such a model is contained in an action theory of social policy, described at the end of this chapter.

Theories and Models of Policy Making

There are a number of ways of describing who decides on the social policies that social workers carry out. Among these are (1) the elite model; (2) the institutional model; (3) the interest-group model; (4) the rational-actor model; (5) the administrative-actor model; (6) bargaining and negotiation; and (7) the systems model.[3]

Elite Theory

Elite theory asserts that policy is in the hands of a few individuals who pull the strings of government, business, and other powerful systems in public affairs, arranging the rules according to their preferences and values.[4] Individuals who control massive amounts of wealth and large organizational systems tend to have far more influence and access to policy arenas than others who lack such resources.[5] Those who control massive corporations use government as a resource to exact policy preferences in their favor.[6]

John Kenneth Galbraith says that "the public bureaucracy . . . can be effectively and durably influenced only by another organization. And between public and private organizations there can be a deeply symbiotic relationship."[7] The elite have prerogatives and access that others do not have. For example, "the president of General Motors has a prescriptive right, on visiting Washington, to see the president of the United States. The president of General Electric has a right to see the secretary of defense and the president of General Dynamics to see any general."[8] These corporate elites use these prerogatives to "impose their values on the society and the state."[9]

Many of these individuals may not have been elected by the people but are often appointed to high

level policy-making or Cabinet level posts in government. Elites often shift from running large business corporations to running massive federal bureaucracies and vice versa. They exert enormous influence by imposing their own policy preferences on the agencies they direct.

"The power," says Galbraith, of this elite system "rests on its access to belief." What is good for General Motors is good for America. By submerging their prerogatives to decide into the general will of mass corporate and public bureaucracy, people can co-opt themselves into the belief that they are serving not only the national interest but their own interests as well. Elitists believe a model of policy making is best because "the masses are largely passive, apathetic, and ill-informed."[10] "Public policy," therefore, does "not reflect demands of 'the people' so much as it does the interests and values of elites."[11]

Institutional Model

The institutional model of policy making claims that policy is the purview of the formal institutions of government. Officially the legislatures in both state and federal governments are the policy-making bodies that make laws that give direction to government and become the responsibility of the executive branch to carry out. Congress, for example, develops laws governing water usage, standards for the use of public lands, the safety of food and drugs, and so on. These policies become the responsibility of federal agencies such as the Bureau of Water Resources, the Bureau of Land Management or the Food and Drug Administration to carry out. Likewise, state legislatures mandate policies for state departments of Education, Transportation, Health, Social Services, Developmental Disabilities, Corrections, Mental Health, and others.

The same kind of arrangement occurs with county boards of supervisors who set policies regulating county sheriffs, departments of social services, mental health, probation, public works, and public health. At the local level policy is developed by city councils over city agencies. School boards determine policies by which school districts operate.

Policy analysts need to understand the ways that governmental institutions make policies and carry them out. The process by which an idea becomes a law is a complex one. At the federal level, for example, a legislator becomes convinced of an issue needing resolution. Policies are often suggested by interest groups that press the legislator for action. The legislator gives the issue to staff to research and draft a proposal, which is then printed in the *Congressional Record*.

It is not uncommon for several legislators to develop proposals on issues that reflect their own perspective on a problem or the particular perspectives of interest groups or their constituents. As the various proposals are reviewed, one proposal, often a synthesis of several, is presented as a policy alternative.[12] Several legislators may be asked to sign as cosponsors of this coalesced proposal, and it is officially introduced and assigned to a committee for review. Hearings are held, and the policy is "marked up" to reflect the concerns of committee members who have heard public testimony.

If the proposed policy receives the endorsement of the committee, it is forwarded in its revised state to the full membership of the legislative body, the House or Senate, in which it originated. Often a similar bill will have already been introduced into the other chamber as well. If both House and Senate versions are approved, the differences between them are worked out in a conference committee.

Once the compromise version is approved by both houses, it becomes law after it is signed by the chief executive. If the president vetoes the bill, it goes back to the full legislature, which must approve it by a two-thirds vote of each chamber. Because of the complexity of this process, only about 5 percent of the bills introduced eventually become law.[13]

Within the context of this model, government and its internal processes is the arena in which policy is officially formed. Thomas Dye asserts that three principles give credibility to the institutional model. First, policy is the official purview of government, and only the institutions of government can create public and social policies and lend legitimacy to them.[14] Second, only government includes everyone within its jurisdiction, and no one is excluded. In this way public policies are universal.[15] Finally, government operates with publicly sanctioned power of enforcement or coercion. Only government can compel people to comply with policies by threat of fines or imprisonment.[16]

Interest-Group Theory

While the legislative process may be the means by which policy becomes governmentally legitimized, "government institutions have accepted interest-group liberalism as the official public philosophy"[17] by which policy is actually conceived and created. According to Theodore Lowi, "interest-group liberalism . . . is the official contemporary public philosophy [which] provides the standards, the frame of reference, by which Americans view the appropriateness of policy proposals."[18]

Government institutions operate within a milieu of intersecting interest groups and a political culture of pluralism, both of which determine the direction of public policy in America.

> Pluralism refers to the existence of a mutual balance of power among religious, ethnic, economic, and geographical groups, with overlapping membership, all of which participate in policy making through mutual adjustment of conflicting goals within policy arenas.[19]

Pluralism is the outcome of the way that politics was conceived by the founding fathers. James Madison, one of the authors of the Federalist Papers, for example, was highly suspicious of a government of elites making policy. "It is essential," he said, "to such a government that it be derived from the great body of the society, not from an inconsiderable proportion of or a favored class of it."[20] Madison saw the polity in a democratic state as a "multiplicity of interests"[20] among which are "a landed interest, a manufacturing interest, a mercantile interest, a moneyed interest."[22] Because the natural propensity of these interests "is to vex and oppress each other [rather] than to co-operate for their common good,"[23] government offices should be divided and arranged "in such a manner that each may be a check on the other and that the private interest of every individual may be a sentinel over public rights."[24]

The role of government is not to impose an ideal or unitary policy onto the populace but rather to design political institutions so as to "manage social conflict" among these contending interest groups.[25] Government carries out its conflict management function by (1) establishing rules of the game, (2) arranging compromise and balancing interests, (3) enacting compromises in the form of public policy, and (4) enforcing these compromises.[26] The outcome of such conflict management is an equilibrium in which people's "ambition must be made to counteract ambition."[22]

In this classical pluralistic model, social problems are supposed to

> work their way to decision-making arenas for action. Individual involvement in group politics helps generate loyalty to the system, with the result that society remains relatively stable, . . . and policies that ultimately emanate from group interaction represent a consensus of diverse opinion.[28]

Advocates of the classical pluralist model claim that because of the fundamentally pluralistic nature of the American political environment, policy making occurs as various interest groups press for policy outcomes on both the institutional as well as agency structures of government. Policy making is a reflection of the success or failure of these groups in having their particular preference schedules enacted into legislation.

Businesses, for example, continually lobby government for favorable legislation. Corporations bargain for preferential policy treatment in the form of subsidies, price supports, tax breaks, tariff protection, loans, contracts, the free use of public land, and other benefits. Social policy analysts may work for or against these interest groups, all of which compete with one another for scarce resources. Social policy advocates, for example, work at organizing the poor and disenfranchised groups in pressuring government for policy outcomes in their favor. Welfare rights organizations, consumer advocacy groups, those advocating for mental health services, and others lobby the government to enact policies that will advance their cause.

Interest groups exert their influence by means of political action committees, or PACs. PACs sponsor particular viewpoints and perspectives on legislation and exert their influence by funneling campaign contributions to candidates whom they hope will vote for legislation in their favor. While many PACs are established by the corporate sector, other PACs are established by social action, environmental, and social welfare advocacy groups. For example, the National Association of Social Workers

PAC is the Political Action for Candidate Election (PACE), which makes contributions to candidates "who profess positions similar to those of the social work professional association."[29]

A problem with the pluralist paradigm of policy making is not that it is an inaccurate description of the way policy making works but that its outcomes have become distorted from the original intention of the founding fathers. E. E. Schattschneider, for example, once remarked that "the flaw in the pluralist heaven is that the heavenly chorus sings with a strong upper-class accent."[30] Interest groups that most often have access to policy concessions and win out in the struggle over resources are the powerful, organized interests headed by "well-educated experienced leaders [who] are the controlling forces within the groups. Elites appear as leaders of groups and compete with other elite-led groups for policy rewards."[31] Interest-group theory, therefore, results not in actors who operate on a level playing field but rather in unequal struggles of powerfully entrenched organized elites using groups to press for policy prizes.

Rational-Actor Model

The rational-actor model is based on the same premises as rational problem solving (see chapter 3).[32] According to Graham Allison, *"Rationality refers to consistent, value-maximizing choice within specified constraints."*[33] *Within this model a rational actor defines his or her goals and objectives and ranks "in order of preference each possible set of consequences that might result from a particular action."*[34] *The rational actor chooses among alternative actions according to those whose "consequences rank highest in the decision-maker's payoff function."*[35]

Edwards and Sharkansky define the rational policy process as (1) identifying a problem, (2) clarifying and ranking goals, (3) collecting all relevant options for meeting the goal, (4) predicting the consequences of each alternative, and (5) selecting the alternative that comes closest to achieving the goal.[36]

Those who claim that policy making is rational assume that a particular group or even the entire nation acts out of self-interest, which that group or nation attempts to maximize by means of a set of value preferences. In this case, a group or the nation-as-a-whole acts as if it were an individual competing for scarce resources or attempting to reach a prescribed goal in an environment of other like-minded, competitive, maximizing, self-interested rational actors. This "concept of rationality is important mainly because if a person acts rationally, his behavior can be *fully* explained in terms of the goals he is trying to achieve."[39]

The question as to why nations engage in seemingly "irrational" activities such as war can, therefore, be understood in terms of rational action. Each "national" actor is in competition with every other actor to maximize its national interest. These interests have to do with appropriating resources, maintaining the integrity of boundaries, developing "spheres of influence," obtaining markets for goods, and such intangibles as maintaining national pride and honor. Policies are the outcomes of the expression of the preferences of such actors who rationally attempt to maximize those group or national interests.

Sometimes social planners or social policy analysts attempt to rationally convince political actors about the necessity of programs based on needs, values, facts, or even human concern or compassion and become confused when those arguments fall on deaf ears. As a social policy analyst you need to understand that political actors often operate primarily out of their own rational self-interest. You must appeal to that interest if you are to be successful.

Administrative Actor Model

While the legislature may set broad policies, it is organizational actors and agencies that interpret, implement, and decide on policy at the local level where it really counts.[38] Public agency administrators give policy concessions, impose rules, and propose laws in favor of claimants and their constituents. It is the organizational actor who controls and makes policy.

For example, Morrow states that "when public administration agencies are either organized or reorganized, the expectation is that the structure and jurisdiction of these agencies will facilitate the legitimization of some values at the expense of others."[39] This is the role of administrative organizations. Public organizations become targets of vested

interest groups who seek to maximize their value preferences by capturing agencies or by influencing the policy outcome expressed by those agencies. Those interest groups that are able to obtain policy concessions in the form of an administrative agency have a powerful tool in their hands that they can use to extract additional policy concessions. They constitute what Morrow calls "intrabureaucratic lobbies for certain biases" or particular value preferences.[40] The Department of Agriculture, for example, reflects and responds to the particular needs and preferences of the farming industry, particularly the American Farm Bureau Federation (AFBF). So successful has the AFBF been that in 1995 it won $10 billion per year in federal crop subsidies for farmers.[41]

In the same way, the Department of the Interior reflects voices of conservationists. And the Defense Department "is subjected to claimant pressure from the various branches of the armed forces, each of which seeks to amplify its own role within the defense establishment."[42]

Public organizations come into being as a result of problem areas and policy agitation. The staff of these organizations relate to their constituents, provide services, address needs, bargain with claimants for the organization's resources, develop expertise on the policy arena they are mandated to address, arrange interorganizational alliances, scan their environment for resources, and predict consequences of current conditions.

The staff and administration of many of these governmental bureaus have watched politicians and political administrations come and go while they continue to exert influence and carry out their routine at the grass-roots level. Organizational bureaucrats, therefore, collect an immense amount of experience, wisdom, and information over the years with which to address problems. Much of this information is extremely useful in policy debates on the reality of one or another solution to a problem.

In addition to staying power and information, another reason for the power and stability of administrative organizations in policy making is their tendency to move ahead in small, incremental steps, scanning the horizon of the political environment and responding marginally to pressures. Administrative organizations build on past decisions, plan, and forecast on a short-term yearly basis from a budget that has sunk costs and past program commitments.

These organizations are often impervious to the demands of politicians, who may attempt to divert or utilize organizational resources on behalf of their own interests or ideology. Allison observes, for example, that "government behavior relevant to any important problem reflects the independent output of several organizations, partially coordinated by government leaders. Government leaders can substantially disturb, but not substantially control, the behavior of these organizations."[43]

Bargaining and Negotiation

The Environmental Protection Agency (EPA) was established as a result of intense lobbying by environmentalists, and the Bureau of Land Management was lobbied for by ranchers and miners who wanted an agency to protect their interests. Often these groups conflict. The outcome is frequently determined by "bargaining among groups and their spokesmen in legislatures and administrative agencies."[44]

Bargaining implies that there is an exchange in which claimants press for advantage and a bargain is struck among agencies or organizations as they deal with one another. This bargaining "nearly always results in compromise among the numerous interests, with each making concessions in the interests of securing at least a portion of its goals."[45] Policy is the result of compromises that "represent the most practical view of the "common good" or "public interest."[46]

Systems Theory

The systems model is possibly the most comprehensive policy model available because it includes many of the other models already described.[47] The policy process is seen as a total system in which the variety of political actors such as legislatures, administrative agencies, political parties, interest groups, elected executives, and private citizens all operate in various ways to determine policy.

This model suggests that the policy-making process is a closed system in which claimants to policy preferences provide inputs to the policy process. These inputs are processed by the political decision-making arena, resulting in outputs that impact the political, social, and economic environment. A feed-back loop is then created in which the subsystems in the political environment react to policy outputs and generate new inputs. The outputs of one policy decision create material for the inputs to a new decision.

The systems model of policy making, therefore, assumes a self-contained, self-regulatory, self-adjusting process. Several policy processes work together to form a complex intermixture of activities, each playing a role in the ultimate formulation of a policy. Politics becomes much like a "servo mechanism" that moves of its own volition. Social policy analysts who are familiar with systems thinking and the systems model, however, can intervene at salient points in the systems process and use the system to achieve policy ends.

The Policy Analysis Process

This section provides a tool, derived from a variation of rational problem solving, that you can use in developing and designing social policy. It includes defining the policy problem, getting the facts, finding the real problem, relabeling, finding the solution, choosing among alternatives, and ranking alternatives.

Defining the Problem

In order to develop policy alternatives you need to define the problem. Ask yourself what part of the policy problem you want to resolve. Are you looking at symptoms or are you looking at causes? Are you interested in certain aspects of the issue, or should you try to tackle the problem as a whole? How do you define a policy problem in such a way that it is solvable, given the limitations on your resources—time, manpower, funding, and expertise? All of these are questions with which one must struggle in defining a social policy problem. Individuals and groups need to be able to accept working through the process systematically. This means putting aside the tendency to reach for what may seem obvious and immediate solutions before the problem has been completely defined.

As you work to define the problem there are a number of initial pitfalls you should avoid. One of these is "premature labeling." Another is a "solution in search of a problem" or "accepting the leader's definition" of a problem. A final pitfall is relying on personal influence.

Premature Labeling[48]

A policy issue cannot be worked on until it is identified and labeled. A label is shorthand for a range of issues and concepts that have meaning to you. Labeling helps you to see the policy in a clear way, restricts the range of choices, and identifies what is, as well as what is not, to be considered. Labeling a problem too early in the process, however, may prevent you from considering the problem in its most complete aspect. For example, "one definition for a problem rather than another may lead the analyst to be concerned with symptoms rather than causes, with causes when symptoms are all that realistically can be treated, or with the wrong problem entirely.[49] At the beginning of policy analysis, therefore, leave options open until the real problem emerges clearly.

The Solution in Search of a Problem

You come armed with a full repertoire of solutions gleaned from articles, journals, meetings, research, and your own experience and values. You encounter a condition that one of these ready-made solutions might fix. You phrase the problem so that your solution is the best and most logical remedy.[50] If you are lucky, your solution will fit the problem, but more than likely, the situation is more complicated and, having already made up your mind, you may have closed the door to other possibilities.

Task groups also tend to arrive at solutions early and then look for problems to fix. Solutions often seem to be obvious. Each person may phrase the problem to fit his or her preconceived solution, resulting in a jumble of solutions posing as problems. Each of the definitions of the problem may appear logical and to the individuals proposing them, necessary. The squabbling that ensues is a "battle of solutions" in which each group member attempts to persuade the group that his or her solution is best.

If you and/or the group continually seem to focus on solutions, you are playing the "solutions in search of a problem" game. This process is almost always destructive. It rarely leads to effective solu-

tions because the problem has not been clearly defined based only on its characteristics. The process has, more than likely, led to the group accepting a statement with which most, if not all, are uncomfortable. While those whose ideas prevail may "win," it is at the expense of the others. Those who "lose" may feel that they were forced to capitulate or compromise. They may go along but not be committed to the solution.

Accepting the Leader's Definition

If you are a social work policy analyst who has a highly developed intuitive sense, you may have a knack for putting your finger on the crux of the problem.[51] Allowing your intuitive sense to dominate the problem identification process, however, may work some of the time, but it won't work all of the time.

The group may accept your version of the problem because of your expertise, your track record, or your power position. None of these is a valid reason for deciding on a problem definition. If you happen to be wrong one time, you will have wasted valuable time and tarnished your own reputation. Therefore, if you have a hunch about what the real problem is, and know that you tend to be right, it is best to wait, watch, and use the group process to confirm your intuition rather than make a pronouncement. Keep in mind that you need to help the whole group work through a process in which all can learn. You are not helping if you move too far ahead of your group.

Personal Influence

Finally, those who are most persuasive, influential, or assertive may have their version of the definition accepted by the group. Parts of different problem perceptions may be pieced together or a compromise may be reached among dominant members. The result is a problem statement based on the personalities and personal influence of the members and not the real problem.

Getting the Facts

The facts you need to gather concern the nature, scope, magnitude, perpetrators, victims, and consequences of the problem. Once you have a grasp of the problem as it currently exists, you find out about its origins and history. Knowing the antecedents of a problem will help you understand the variety of factors that led to the present situation, the length of time the problem has been in existence, and its extent and severity. In addition, knowing what has been tried in the past will help you avoid dead-end solutions or blind alleys. Knowing what has worked will keep you from reinventing the wheel. Ask yourself: When? Who? Why? What? Where? and How? This will get you started on being "objective" about the problem situation.

When did the problem first appear? Through what historical events or circumstances has the social problem evolved to the present state of affairs? Did it come about suddenly or does it have a long history?

Who are the major actors? These may be decision-makers, agency or organizational administrators, various interest groups, community leaders, or legislators. Who has contributed to the problem? Are there groups of perpetrators or potential targets that may have caused or added to the policy issue? Who are the prime victims of the policy problem? Who has the most to gain by solving the problem? Who has the most to lose?

Why did the policy problem come about? What events or conditions led to the current state of affairs? Are there particular cycles or trends that reveal the kinds of factors that are causally related to the problem?

What are some of the major consequences of the policy problem? This question deals with symptoms of the problem. What are the economic, social, and political effects of the problem? What social situations or social conditions have contributed to the continuance of the problem or added to its complexity? A second question deals with solutions. What kinds of policy solutions have been tried in the past? How effective were these policy solutions? Have the social policies themselves changed or been modified?

Where is the problem located? Is the policy problem generalized throughout the community or are particular areas affected more than others? If you are working within an organization, is the problem localized in one unit or in several units? Obtaining an idea of where the problem is located will give you an idea of where to start.

How important is the problem? How widespread is it? How many people are affected by it?

Gathering Information

Bring together those representatives who have a stake in the problem to help define the problem from their perspective and ask them the questions you have prepared. These may be politicians, planners, community leaders, agency administrators, victims, and service providers. Assume, for example, that your group has decided to work on the problem of violence in your neighborhood. Gather together politicians, city council representatives, judges, and police in a focus group. Invite leaders of youth organizations, school officials, and parents. Meet with representatives of firearms lobbies such as the local chapter of the National Rifle Association, Citizens Committee for the Right to Keep and Bear Arms, or the Second Amendment Foundation. Speak with representatives of groups advocating the restriction or control of firearms, such as members of the Center to Prevent Handgun Violence. Educational Fund to End Handgun Violence, Handgun Control, Inc., and the National Coalition to Ban Handguns. Talk with gun manufacturers, gun shop merchants, owners of sporting goods stores and sports groups who use firearms. Add to your list neighborhood associations, neighborhood watch groups, and groups who advocate for victims of crimes. Discuss the issue with people who have been personally victimized by violence, and if possible those who are perpetrators of violence, such as gang members or persons convicted of various kinds of violence. Finally, read and gather statistics on violence, such as the National Center for Health Statistics or Bureau of Census statistics on deaths attributed to violence.

As you meet with individuals or groups, keep in mind the principles of focused interviewing and focus groups described in chapter 6. Be alert for persons who are interested enough to want to work on the solution after the problem has been identified sufficiently.

If you are not able to bring together or interview actors representing the various elements of the policy problem, then simulate those points of view. One way of doing this is to role play the various positions so that a complete format of alternatives can be generated.

Defining the "Real" Problem

After you have gathered information on the problem from key actors or your simulation group, your perception of the "problem" may bear little resemblance to the issue you initially formulated.[52] This is to be expected because your perceptions of the problem are refined, clarified, and shaped by the new information you have developed.

At this point it is important to remember that even though there may be many perspectives on the problem, you have control over the way you define the problem. There is no one best problem statement nor is there only one "real" problem. "Each problem situation contains within its boundaries—however vague and fuzzy those boundaries might be—numerous potential "real" problems."[53] Most problems are laden with subjective perceptions and values. For example, as your group explores its concern about violence in your neighborhood any number of issues may occur to you. Does the problem concern the availability of handguns, assault rifles, or hunting weapons? Is the problem the large number of shop owners who sell guns? Or, does the problem lie in the laws that permit easy access to weapons? Are you concerned about violence on TV or about specific kinds of violence such as domestic violence and rape, or violence used in the commission of robberies? Are you concerned about youth-oriented violence such as youth gangs?

Choose a problem definition that is meaningful and valid for you and your constituents. Certain problems will speak to you intuitively. Look at the scope of the problem, for example. Some problems may seem so large or unwieldy that they appear unsolvable. You may have to break them down into smaller, more manageable pieces. On the other hand, you may see patterns of smaller problems that you want to group together into a larger one.

One criteria of choice may be whether the problem is one that you can actually do something about. It doesn't make sense to try to fight violence in general, but you might choose the family aspect (domestic violence is on the rise), the youth aspect (gang violence is killing innocent people), or the legal aspect (allowing people to carry concealed weapons should be outlawed). You could narrow your focus to a particular neighborhood (the number of shootings in North Town is excessive) or location (violence at Lincoln School is too high).

Relabeling

Finally, relabel the problem and come up with a working problem statement from which you will continue the problem-solving process. For example, using our hypothetical problem, your group may redefine the problem to focus on controlling access to handguns in North Town.

Finding the Solution

After a problem has been identified and labeled, and a problem statement developed, you can devise possible solutions or interventions. As you look over your problem statement it may occur to you that some aspects of the problem will not change no matter what you do. There are also, more than likely, a number of conditions that can be changed.[54]

Locating Points of Change

Determine which issues can be changed and which cannot. Eliminate all those issues about which you can do nothing. For example, in considering the problem of controlling access to handguns you decide that the manufacture of guns or the importation of guns into the community are issues you cannot change. Try to be conservative when deciding on issues you feel you cannot change. Things that may at first appear unchangeable may turn out to be amenable to change after all.

After you eliminate items that you cannot do anything about, you are left with those elements of the problem over which you have some control. For example, you may be able to change people's attitudes about gun ownership. You may be able to impact the legality of handguns. You may be able to affect gun safety and training in the use of guns. You may examine interdicting weapons or providing gun-free areas where weapons are excluded. These are windows of opportunity where changes can be made. Let's call these "change points."

Solutions

The purpose of designing an intervention or problem solution is to manipulate the change points to eliminate or ameliorate the problem. Karger and Stoesz suggest that the following questions should be asked about policy alternatives:[55]

1. How is the policy intended to work?
2. What are the resources or opportunities the policy is expected to provide (i.e., power, cash economic opportunity, in-kind services, status redistribution)?
3. Who will be covered by the policy and how (universal versus selective entitlement, means testing)?
4. Who will pay for the policy?
5. How will payments be arranged (subsidies, taxes, fines)?
6. Who will be responsible for implementing the policy once it becomes law?
7. What kinds of administrative arrangements will be necessary (i.e., roles of private sector, community membership, local/state/federal government)?
8. Under whose jurisdiction/auspices will the policy fall?
9. What guarantees are there that the policy will be carried out as intended (i.e., how will you control for quality control, fraud, misappropriation, misinterpretation)?
10. How long will the policy be in existence?
11. How will the effectiveness of the policy be evaluated and over what time span?

One way to develop a policy solution is called iteration; you systematically combine various change points to open up ideas that you may have never thought of. The way of going about iteration is, first, choose several change points and arrange the most important ones in columns under labels that will help you focus your solutions. For example, in seeking solutions to the issue of gun control you will need to consider (1) the agent responsible for controlling access to guns, (2) what action to take, and (3) who will pay for controlling access. List all the possible agents in one column, all of the actions in another, and who will pay in a third.

Agent	Action	Who Pays
police	buy	taxpayers
judges	tax	criminals
citizens	destroy	businesses
volunteers	outlaw	gun owners
special agency	incentives	gun dealers
federal officers	permits	NRA
city council	subsidize	manufacturers
	fines	

Then "iterate" to form potential solutions by choosing one item from each column, for example, "*police* will *buy* guns paid for by *taxpayers*" would be your first potential solution. "*Police* will *buy* guns paid for by *criminals*" is the second solution, and so on. Some of these solutions will make no sense at all. You eliminate these. What you are left with are solutions that might be considered. Continue iterating until you have made all of the possible combinations from the columns. In addition to the solutions you discover through iteration, always consider obvious or favored alternatives. Leaving things just the way they are is an option that should always be considered.

Choosing among Alternatives

You should now have a number of interesting and viable solutions to your policy problem. One or two of the alternatives may meet your policy goals better than others. In the best of all worlds you would choose the policy alternative that you think is the best one. However, a good policy alternative may not be politically or economically feasible. You now decide which of your most highly ranked alternatives have the best chance of being implemented.

Political Feasibility

Many actors will have a stake in the outcome of any policy. Each of these individuals or groups has a preferred solution that will compete with yours in the political arena. If there is strong political opposition to your solution, you will not go far in implementing it. Politicians may be interested in your policy solution to the extent that it affects their constituency. They may also be interested because it

Table 14.1
PRINCE Political Accounting System
Alternative: Establish a special agency to restrict handguns

Actors	Issue Position	x	Power	x	Salience	=	Total Support by Actors
Mayor	-1	x	2	x	2	=	-4
City Council	+1	x	3	x	3	=	9
NRA	-3	x	2	x	3	=	-18
Taxpayers Association	+1	x	1	x	1	=	1
Handgun Control Inc.	+3	x	1	x	3	=	9
Police Chief	+1	x	1	x	3	=	3
						Net Score	0

may enhance or detract from their chances for re-election. They may have strong personal opinions one way or another on the policy issue. If you intend to implement a project, then political actors—those who hold power—and their influence are important for you to consider.

One way to assess the amount of support various alternatives can expect from key political decision-makers is the PRINCE political accounting system developed by O'Leary and Coplin.[56] PRINCE requires scoring each political decision maker in areas of issue position, power, and salience. By comparing the total support scores of each alternative solution you can see which alternatives are most politically feasible.

For example, assume that one solution that your group favors is to establish a special agency paid for by taxpayers that would restrict the number of handguns in North Town. First, determine who are the political actors that would be involved in the decision. The political actors in this case are the mayor, the city council, a local chapter of the National Rifle Association, the local taxpayers association, a local chapter of the Handgun Control, Inc., and the chief of police. Table 14.1 illustrates how the PRINCE model works.

The first variable to be considered is issue position. Score issue position with a range from +3 to -3; a plus indicates support and a minus indicates opposition. A "3" is assigned if the political actor is unequivocally in favor of or opposed to the alternative. A "1" or a "2" is assigned if the decision maker is

less clearly in favor of or opposed to the alternative. A "0" is assigned if the actor is neutral.

The second variable is the amount of power possessed by the actor to act on the alternative. If the actor has maximum influence to decide on the issue, a "3" is assigned. A "1" or "2" is assigned for moderate influence and a "0" is given for no capability of influencing at all.

The third variable is salience, the degree to which the actor cares about and pays attention to the alternative. It measures how high the issue is on the actor's agenda of important things. (This is different from issue position, which indicates how strong the person's preference is for this particular alternative. For example, violence may be very salient for an actor who cares deeply about it, but she or he may have little preference or low issue position for a particular alternative solution.) A "3" for salience indicates that an issue is of major importance on the actor's agenda, a "1" or "2" indicates it is of moderate salience, and a "0" indicates it is of no importance at all.

After you estimate the three variables multiply across the rows to determine each actor's support of the alternative. Then add up the final product of the scores to obtain a net score on the alternative. The larger the positive number, the more likely that political support for the alternative will be positive. The closer the net score to zero, the more likely the alternative will be politically contentious. The larger a negative score, the more likely the issue will be politically unfeasible.

Economic Feasibility

The most economically beneficial alternative can be determined by using a benefit-cost analysis (described in chapter 11). Given two proposals each of which will meet your goals, the one that has the highest benefit/cost ratio will often be more appealing to decision-makers. Generally speaking a benefit/cost ratio that approaches or exceeds 1 will tend to attract attention because the benefits of that alternative will equal or exceed costs.

Before you expend a lot of energy on a policy proposal, make sure that funding is available and that costs are not prohibitive. You may need to consider innovative ways of funding such as combinations of private, public, and membership sources of income.

Force Field Analysis

You now have three different measures that you can use to gauge your alternatives: (1) ranking alternatives according to what you consider best; (2) political feasibility; and (3) economic feasibility. You may think of other criteria as well. Now you must choose a solution. One technique to help you make this choice is force field analysis.

Force field analysis, described in chapter 11, is based on the idea that with every decision for change there are forces impelling change and those resisting change. Consider each alternative solution according to positive and negative factors. First, what are the negative factors that detract from its acceptance? For example, a solution may be politically contentious, low on your preference list, time consuming, or have a low benefit/cost ratio. Write down an estimated weight for the negative or constraining forces of each alternative solution.

Then ask yourself what are the positive factors that add to its attractiveness? A solution may be politically attractive, have a positive benefit/cost ratio, be high on your preference list, be easy to implement, or take little time to put into place. Write down an estimated weight for the positive or impelling forces.

Subtract the sum of the combined weights of the impelling forces from the sum of the combined weights of the restraining forces for each alternate solution. The alternative with the highest positive score has the best chance of being successful in meeting

---

ENDANGERED SPECIES ACT: A LAUGHABLE FAILURE

We are fond of proclaiming that ours is a government of laws. But there are times when we expect too much of laws and not enough of ourselves. This explains the depressing failure of the Endangered Species Act. An example, according to Tom Wolf, an environmental advocate who has worked for the Nature Conservancy, is the Mexican wolf, or lobo. There are, he says, about 40 lobos left in captivity in the United States. The center of its former range is in southwest New Mexico, the Gila National Forest. Today this forest resembles Kuwait before the Persian Gulf war: It is ringed by heavily armed ranchers who graze their cattle at below-market prices on public lands. "Shoot, shovel and shut up" is the final rancher solution to the lobo problem.

The last wild lobo in the United States bit the dust around mid century, after the New Mexico Stock Growers Association decided to get serious about its competition. The growers evoked a time-honored tradition. They "asked" the federal government for help. Unlike New Mexico's Indians and Latinos, who settled near the rivers, these Anglo ranchers marched into lobo land (protected from the Apaches by federal troops), where they felled the forests, shot the deer that were the wolf's prey and brought in as many sheep and cattle as they could. What was not worth taking became public land.

The dust from this disaster bred conservationists like Teddy Roosevelt and Aldo Leopold, the father of wildlife management. The next time anybody bothered to look, America had a series of national forests ringed by private ranches on the best, lowest lands. Political deals were made, with grazing fees for the perpetual and exclusive use of the adjacent public lands set laughably low. A lobo population that never exceeded 1,500 became an easy target. The lobo's highly developed social system made systematic slaughter simple. Taxpayer's strychnine, poison gas, traps, and guns did the dirty work.

This federal program, called Animal Damage Control, continues today, targeting whatever 26,000 public lands ranchers consider a threat to the sacred cow. Such is the genius of our Western way of politics. One hand of the federal government kills everything wild. Another "recovers" species. Another pays ranchers and loggers to make sure "recovery" fails. Once the lobo was "listed" as an endangered species in 1976, the Fish and Wildlife Service moved as slowly as possible to obey the law. Now it may be too late.

Source: Tom Wolf, "Endangered Species Act: A Laughable Failure," *The Fresno Bee*, May 10, 1991, p. H1.

your change requirements. After you have scored each alternative according to force field analysis, rank your alternative proposals from best to worst.

Implementing Policy: The "Real" World of Politics

Once you decide on a policy proposal, the next step is to develop methods for getting it noticed by those who can help implement it. There are a number of ways of getting your policy proposal before interested persons.

1. *The case conference.* One place to start is "through a conference that includes the agencies that logically should be offering a service. Even in large federal programs, changes have been made as the result of recognizing that what is dysfunctional for one client may be dysfunctional for many."[57]
2. *Fact gathering.* Having the right information in the form that can be used properly gives you leverage and influence for change.
3. *Position taking.* By "issuing a statement or a report [you] have gone on public record as a participant . . . in a change process. Taking a position draws the lines of the contest. It clarifies one's own objectives and provides a point of identification."[58]
4. *Committee work.* "Committees, whether they are local, state, or national in scope, are a step in the decision-making process. . . . By providing a forum for the public discussion of ideas, committees of various kinds serve to publicize potential alternatives, and get them into the decision-making process. Social workers can serve on such committees or act as consultants to committees on which they are not eligible to serve as regular members."[59]
5. *Petitions.* Petitioning "serves to proclaim public support . . . for a policy alternative. It informs decision-makers that there are people out there who have a stake in the decision."[60]
6. *Media campaigns.* The use of radio, television, and newspapers can be an important part of the policy change process. Publicity, stories, and pictures bring issues to public attention and create a climate in which change is possible.[61]

Political Pressure Tactics

Confrontation tactics, described earlier, are "vital for getting the attention of authorities and showing them the power of the community organization. Confrontations are social explosions that yell 'Pay Attention! There is a problem here!' "[62]

Political pressure tactics are different from confrontation tactics. "To make lasting changes, organization members need to think about ways to change laws, regulations, and levels of enforcement. . . . Political pressure tactics are intended to change laws and enforce regulations that preserve the short-term victories."[63] Organization members play by the rules of politics and pressure others to abide by laws and regulations that have already been set up by means of legal tactics. The game shifts to working within

Petitioning serves to proclaim public support for a policy alternative.

the system to make the changes a permanent part of the social and political landscape.

Effective social action campaigns are built by skillfully blending confrontation, legal actions, and political pressure. If the goal of your organization is to increase the city's commitment to open housing, for example, representatives of your organization might lobby to get a strong open-housing ordinance on the books (a political pressure tactic). At the same time, they seek a court injunction to halt the city's receipt of state development funds until its housing profile improves (a legal tactic) and conduct demonstrations in the plaza in front of city hall to publicize the difficulties facing the poor in finding housing.

Political Strategies

In addition to these strategies you need to work directly within the political system. First, you can lobby elected representatives to support policy proposals that you want to get onto the political agenda. You may be called upon to give expert testimony before a legislative body. If lobbying or expert testimony fails, you and members of your community organization may become directly involved in the political process by running for political office, sponsoring referendum and initiative campaigns, or serving on citizen and neighborhood advisory or political boards.[64]

Lobbying

Lobbying means persuading elected officials to consider and to press for policy considerations that your organization feels are important. "In the real world of political processes, decisions are influenced and made by those who work the system in their favor."[65] Politicking or lobbying is a fundamental part of the American system of government "constructed on the notion of pluralism."[66] In other words, our government "was designed to encourage and accommodate the expression of conflicting views, group conflict, negotiating, bargaining, and compromise."[67]

While large business corporations work in their own self-interest to influence policy in their favor, social workers lobby governmental officials in the public interest. "The social work profession's special interest is . . . a concern for individuals, groups, and communities who cannot lobby for themselves."[68]

Our mandate is to equalize the power balance and ensure that the poor and community groups are represented in the political bargaining process. "The main reason for lobbying is to provide needed services for people."[69]

The political process "requires and even demands that some individuals speak on behalf of others and that opposing groups resolve conflicts. The very nature of the political process is one of individual interaction, and this clearly implies the importance of social work skills."[70]

Social workers can also ally themselves with legislators in helping promote the public welfare by taking the pulse of the community and interest groups. Social workers and politicians can be allies in seeking the public good and furthering the public interest. Social workers compete by means of moral power, citizen representation, and facts and figures. After all, it is not business interests that mobilize mass rallies and marches or organizations of community citizens to press for policy concessions.

The Lobbying Process

Haynes and Mickelson give the following guidelines for successful lobbying:

The key to offering successful testimony is preparation. Richard Codd, president of the American Planning Association, testifies before Congress, February 1995, against H.R. 925, the Private Property Protection Act.

1. Know your issue thoroughly. Anticipate the opposition's claims and formulate persuasive counterarguments. Be prepared to provide technical information that will be useful to the politician(s) involved.
2. Identify a core group of committed and effective workers who will lead a coalition of interested groups and individuals who can be called on to write letters, lobby, or publicize the issue.
3. Locate a lawmaker who is sympathetic to your issue and is likely to be effective in advancing the cause, and continue to work with him or her for the duration of the process.
4. Be familiar with the formal legislative structure and procedural steps a bill must take to become a law.
5. Spend as much time as possible at the capitol, both to answer legislative questions and to be in a position to intervene effectively at the critical moment by offering advice or information before decisions have been made.[71]

Finally, Patti and Dear note that a lobbyist must be able to acknowledge the merits of competing proposals. Even though you may be lobbying for your own proposal, if you are unable or unwilling to acknowledge strengths of alternative proposals or weaknesses of your own, you may be seen as a propagandist and your credibility may be damaged.[72]

Face-to-Face Lobbying

When meeting with a legislator or legislative aide, keep in mind that the representative needs your information and assistance. Be prepared. Make sure you have your facts in hand. It is important to "be honest and factual whenever a legislator or legislative aide is contacted.[73]

Straightforward presentations with data are generally the most persuasive approach. Be able to answer two critical concerns of legislators: (1) what will the proposed legislation cost, and (2) what the social impact of this bill will be. Provide written and supportive documents, making sure that this material is as succinct as possible. Thank the legislator for the appointment and for open-mindedness. Follow up with a thank-you letter that includes a synopsis of the position taken by that legislator during the meet-

ing. Follow through with anything that you have agreed to do.[74]

Letter Writing

Letters are an effective way of getting your point across. Letters are often read carefully, particularly if they come from constituents. Letters to legislators should be short, to the point, and credible, one or two pages at most.[75] Describe your position exactly and provide documentation. State the action you want the legislator to take. For example, be specific about whether you want him or her to vote yes or no on legislation or to co-sponsor legislation.

Avoid form letters. The more personal the letter, the more effective. Clearly written letters on your own stationery are the most effective.[76] End your letter with a short thank you for considering your proposal or request.

Telephoning

While there is no substitute for a personal letter, phone calls, usually forty-eight hours before a legislative vote, will signal a legislator which way the wind is blowing on a piece of legislation and may swing those who are undecided. When calling, state who you are and the message you wish to convey. For example, "I would like to urge Representative Smith to vote yes on Bill 33 because. . . ." Leave your name, address, and phone number to confirm that you are a constituent.

Testifying

Often when legislation is considered, a committee will want to gather as much information as possible from a wide variety of viewpoints. You may be asked to testify. The key to offering successful testimony is preparation.[77] For example, the Child Welfare League of America provides the following information in its *Washington Workbook for Child Advocates*:

1. Briefly introduce yourself. Tell who you are and what program you are representing. Acknowledge your appreciation for considering your testimony, give an idea of how many people you represent, and your qualifications.

2. State your goal and outline your main points.

3. Talk about the problem. Discuss the significance of the issue and try to relate it to the district in which the legislators before you represent.

4. Talk about current efforts to resolve the problem—what solutions have been tried; which ones have worked; which have failed. Explain why current efforts are insufficient and how they can be improved.

5. Offer specific recommendations. What can the legislator do to help solve the problem at hand?

6. Summarize your main points, thank the panel or committee and tell them you would be happy to answer questions.

7. Keep your presentation to ten minutes or less. Never read your statement, but make it interesting and conversational.[78]

Action Model of Social Policy

Each of the policy models described in this chapter contains some truth. It is true, for example, that policy emanates from the institutions of government, and that those who hold power by virtue of wealth or position are often influential actors who determine policy out of self-interest. Interest groups in our pluralistic society mobilize values in the direction that they desire and in the process use bargaining and negotiation to achieve their ends. Public agencies such as the Departments of Agriculture, Commerce, and Defense react to those special interests by establishing and implementing policy to benefit their constituencies. All of these components form a complex interacting policy-making system.

The elites, professionals who hold the key to bargaining and negotiation, wealthy interest groups, executives of large government, and corporate organizations all have considerable influence on the policy-making process and pursue their own individually determined goals. The advantage of modern politics is that citizens are freed from the responsibility of grappling with complex and time-consuming public issues. That is the responsibility of elected or appointed officials. These officials, however, become easy targets of powerful corporation officers, lobbyists, and vested interest groups who

exploit governmental agencies and social policy to their own advantage. As a result, government becomes an arena in which private interests gain concessions in the form of social policies. Politics becomes the purview of professionals who attempt to maintain power by satisfying the conflicting interests as they perceive them. As long as these professionals and the systems designed by them allocate resources and provide decision-making arrangements that satisfy the interests of the populace as a whole, the system may be said to be working.

The average citizen may not object to having little, if any, direct input on policy issues because representative democracy does provide benefits. However, a large number of citizens do not share equally in these benefits. These are the poor, the marginalized, and the handicapped. Furthermore, these groups tend to be unrepresented because "the lack of influence on the part of lower socioeconomic groups in the social policy process is virtually built into governmental decision making."[79] The absence of decision-making power is called non-decision making.[80]

Many groups have been subject to non-decision making in the American political process. African Americans, Native Americans, and women were legally excluded from decision-making prior to emancipation and suffrage, for example. Often disadvantaged groups such as the poor are not represented on boards or agencies mandated to aid them. As a result, social policy carried out by those involved in the policy system may reflect the "assumptions about the human condition that may be reasonable to the upper socioeconomic groups that make them, but bare little resemblance to the reality of the lower socioeconomic groups that are supposed to be beneficiaries."[81] This policy-making process is not only "irregular and irrational, it is also unrepresentative."[82]

A theory of policy and politics that resists taking the assumptions of conventional policy-making for granted is called a *normative* theory of policy-making. Normative policy theory is less concerned about describing how policy actually takes place than exploring how it ought to occur.[83] While a normative theory of politics and social policy was not clearly articulated by the social reformers of the Progressive Era, when social work progressives and populists attempted to reshape the political landscape, it was, nevertheless, implicit in the work of activists such as Lillian Wald and Jane Addams and politicians such as "Fighting Bob" La Follette, Eugene V. Debs, and Woodrow Wilson who attempted to reform politics and political practices.

In addition to activists and progressive politicians, muckrakers "exposed the inequalities of business, romanticized labor, and denounced corruption"[84] in such works as *The Shame of the Cities* (Lincoln Steffans), *The Octopus* (Frank Norris), and *The Jungle* (Upton Sinclair). Reformers like Frederic C. Howe who wrote *Confessions of a Reformer* in 1907 and *The Modern City and Its Problems* in 1915 sensitized the nation to problems in the political and policy arenas. Theologian Walter Rauschenbusch revitalized Christian consciousness with his books *Christianity and The Social Crisis* and *Christianity and the Social Order*. In 1913, economist Charles A. Beard scandalized the conservative world with *An Economic Interpretation of the Constitution of the United States*.

These social reformers believed that every person has a role and responsibility to make democracy work and had a vision of the formation of a good society for all. Theodore Roosevelt, for example, in an article in McClure's magazine entitled "Reform though Social Work" wrote, "No hard-and-fast rule can be laid down as to the way in which such work [reform] must be done; but most certainly every man, whatever his position, should strive to do in some way and to some degree."[85]

Normative policy theory underlies an *action model* that casts the self as a political actor, and is based on a belief in grass-roots democracy, community politics, value-based education, and a vision of the state as a good society.

The Self as Political Actor

The action model of social policy asserts that people ought to be active in shaping policy that affects their lives. Social policy ought to be the purview of the citizens themselves, not social elites, governmental institutions, administrative decision makers, or the political system as a whole. Policy is best made when people engage one another in a "face-to-face-situation or encounter."[86] In order for people to become authentic political actors, there-fore, individual citizens need direct access to the policy-making processes through deliberation and voting on policy matters that affect their lives.

Grass Roots Democracy

Representative democracy was practical and efficient in early America when great distances and poor communication meant that direct democracy was impossible. Representative democracy was functional because community was still a living social system and politicians often were truly "representative" of the culture and values of the communities that elected them.

Today, no one representative can adequately speak for all. Massive cities and the increasingly pluralistic and complex nature of our society make representative democracy increasingly dysfunctional. Modern technology, however, has made politics accessible to each person. Television, computers, and the "information highway" make distance no barrier to communication and decision making.

An action model of public policy envisions a "populist" or people's orientation to democracy, often termed "grass roots" democracy, in which social and political decisions are made at the level of the community, not in legislative chambers or in the board rooms of multinational corporations. In an action model of politics, the citizens' role in the political process is more than choosing officials, providing arrangements by which the system can function, or providing the means by which individuals or interest groups can pursue their own private interests. Instead, politics and policy-making would occur as a daily and normal role of all citizens who exert their sense of what is good and right in mutual interaction and problem solving. If each citizen were to view him- or herself as a political actor, then carrying out political processes would become a worthwhile endeavor in and of itself.

By taking direct charge of those processes that affect their lives, individuals and communities can enhance their sense of destiny, their self-reliance, and their purpose as well as create a stronger, more cohesive nation. Government would be truly "of the people, by the people, and for the people" rather than of the elites, by the Congress, and for interest groups as it exists today.

Community Politics

Grass roots democracy and populist policy-making are dependent on a renewed conception of community as a center of politics and the political process. In the same way that modern technology makes direct grass roots democracy a reality, it also enables communities to once again become political realities rather than mere social artifacts. The information super highway, E mail, and computer networks can link people together in ways never before possible. Communities, in fact, take on new forms that are only now being imagined.

An action model of social policy opts for highly decentralized decision-making arrangements while maintaining a committed centralized federal core. Today, decentralization favors the owners of large, complex business corporations, which tend to usurp and dominate political decision making. This is why powerful business interests tend to favor minimal government and work to weaken strong centralized federal governmental structures.

An action model anticipates that organizations assume restricted but important roles in society. As communities acquire political power, social and economic organizations take on different roles. Rather than dominating the social landscape, complex organizations become responsive to the communities in which they reside. Instead of exploiting the community for human "resources," tax breaks, and other incentives, complex organizations work in a truly interactive fashion with the community as a whole for its benefit. A decentralized political process with community as its base is not only egalitarian but also serves public rather than private interests. For community-based, decentralized democracy to be effective, a strong, centralized federal governmental policy-making body is needed to ensure that everyone has equal access to decision making and that communities are not overwhelmed by organizational systems.

Value-Based Education

Value thinking, a language of discourse about values, and a theory of values is required as part of an action orientation to social policy. Values that infuse each community's history and culture are rec-ognized. Policies are seen as ways that communities define and implement social values in the lives of citizens. When communities interact, policies are established for ever larger political units.

Education in values and in value decision making are important components of civic and social consciousness. Value education is an important way of instilling the history and culture of a particular community and is an alternative to functional, empirically-based education as currently taught in public schools.[87]

Closely allied with value education is character education. Early group social work was identified as a method of character education, character building, and citizenship.[88] A revitalized group social work providing value and character education prepares citizens for value-centered decision making, the ability to activate their own sense of what is good and right and to deal with difficult value questions.

Participation in democratic processes and exercising one's values are fundamental to the role of every citizen. Values as shaped by the community and the larger society are actively pursued and included as a part of political or government decisions. In an action oriented policy process politics of virtue, not expedience; the public good, not private interests; and social worth, not economic profit, guide policy decisions.[89]

The State as a Good Society

In the action model, the state is composed of a variety of pluralistic communities each of which develops its own cultural milieu by means of value education and interaction with other communities. The ethnic, historical, and cultural diversity of these communities is recognized and honored as building blocks of the social order. Society is not seen as an aggregation of individual interests, tastes, or opinions that compete in the policy arena on an equal level. Instead, there are certain overarching ideals toward which the society ought to move. Within the policy arena, some values will be subordinated to those ideals. For example, where public interests and private interests conflict, public interests will generally supersede purely private self-interest. Privilege and position will give way to equalizing opportunity of the less privileged and less powerful. Encouraging accumulation of wealth will receive less policy recognition than assisting those who lack means of survival.

Conclusion

The process of social change that begins with social work research, community development, and social action often results in social policy proposals that can be enacted into law. Social policy occurs as institutional political actors, competing interest groups, government agencies, and business corporations bargain for policy concessions in an interlocking system of decision making.

Social workers need to be engaged in thinking about and actively immersed in this policy arena. This means proposing policies that can improve society. To abdicate this role inevitably means leaving the field of policy and politics to those who wield power at the highest levels of influence.

Macro social workers need to understand theories of policy-making and the methods for deciding on, proposing, and getting policy implemented. But more than understanding and working within the political system as it currently exists, macro social workers also need to have a vision of a normative process of politics and social policy that helps move America toward a vision of what it could become in today's highly technological, fast-paced world. An action theory of social policy is a normative theory providing a vision of the self as a political actor, a belief in grass-roots democracy, community politics, and value-based education, and a vision of the state as a good society.

KEY CONCEPTS

public policy
social policy
policy-making models
elite model
institutional model
interest group model
pluralism
PAC

rational actor model
rationality
rational policy process
administrative actor model
bargaining and negotiation
systems model
policy analysis process
defining problems
solution in search of a problem
getting facts
role playing
relabeling
change points
iteration
political feasibility
PRINCE
economic feasibility
benefit-cost analysis
force field analysis
case conference
position taking
committee work
petitions
media campaigns
political pressure
tactics
political strategies
lobbying
face-to-face lobbying
letter writing
telephoning
testifying
action model of social policy
non-decision making
normative policy-making
self as political actor
grass-roots democracy
community politics
value education
state as a good society

QUESTIONS FOR DISCUSSION

1. In this chapter the point was made that modern technology has made politics accessible to each person in ways never before conceived possible. Computers, television, and the "informa-

tion highway" make distance no barrier to communication and decision making. Do you think that technology will make politics and social policy processes more accessible to people, increasing the quality and representativeness of policy solutions?

2. A proposal was made in this chapter for direct citizen access to policy and politics rather than leaving politics to professionals such as elected and appointed officials and lobbyists. What are the advantages of this proposal? What are its disadvantages? Given the fact that often less than 50 percent of those eligible to vote actually exercise this right, is it realistic to expect that citizens will want to become more directly involved in politics even if they have the opportunity?

3. DiNitto and Dye assert that "social policy is a *continuing political struggle* over . . . conflicting goals and objectives, competing definitions of problems, alternative approaches and strategies, multiple programs and policies, competing proposals for reform, and even different ideas about how decisions should be made."[90] Discuss the following questions:

   a. If this is an accurate statement about social policy, can decisions that are good in themselves ever be made about social issues?

   b. Can policies be made on any other basis than conflict resolution or on a set of majoritarian decision rules?

   c. If resolving policy disputes by bargaining or voting are the only options available, is there any assurance that policies will be developed that rise above dominance by those groups that have the most power or the most votes?

4. Can you think of a different model of politics that would be an appropriate one for our highly mobile, technological society?

ADDITIONAL READING

Elite Model

Domhoff, G. William. *Who Rules America?* Englewood Cliffs, NJ: Prentice-Hall, 1967.

———. *The Higher Circles: The Governing Class in America.* New York: Random House, 1970.

———. *The Powers That Be: Processes of Ruling-Class Domination in America.* New York: Random House, 1979.

Mills, C. Wright. *The Power Elite.* New York: Oxford University Press, 1956.

Galbraith, John Kenneth. *Economics and the Public Purpose.* Boston, MA: Houghton Mifflin, 1973.

Institutional Model

Truman, David B. *The Governmental Process.* New York: Knopf, 1971.

Rational Actor Model

Allison, Graham T. *The Essence of Decision: Explaining the Cuban Missile Crisis.* Boston, MA: Little, Brown, 1971.

Edwards, George C., III, and Ira Sharkansky. *The Policy Predicament: Making and Implementing Public Policy.* San Francisco, CA: Freeman, 1978.

Stokey, Edith, and Richard Zeckhauser. *A Primer for Policy Analysis.* New York: Norton, 1978.

Interest Group Model

Lowi, Theodore. *The End of Liberalism.* New York: Norton, 1969.

Administrative Actor

Morrow, William L. *Public Administration: Politics and the Political Process.* New York: Random House, 1975.

System Model

Easton, David. *A Framework for Political Analysis.* Englewood Cliffs, NJ: Prentice-Hall, 1965.

———. "An Approach to the Analysis of Political Systems." *World Politics* 9 (1957): 383-400.

Social Policy and Social Work

Dye, Thomas R. *Understanding Public Policy.* 2d ed. Englewood Cliffs, NJ: Prentice-Hall, 1975.

Galper, Jeffrey H. *The Politics of Social Services.* Englewood Cliffs, NJ: Prentice-Hall, 1975.

Glazer, Nathan. *The Limits of Social Policy.* Cambridge, MA: Harvard University Press, 1988.

Haynes, Karen S., and James S. Mickelson. *Affecting Change: Social Workers in the Political Arena.* New York: Longman, 1991.

Harrington, Michael. *The Other America: Poverty in the United States.* New York: Macmillan, 1962.

Meenaghan, Thomas M., and Robert O. Washington. *Social Policy and Social Welfare.* New York: Free Press, 1980.

Pierce, Dean. *Policy for the Social Work Practitioner.* New York: Longman, 1984.

Prigmore, Charles S., and Charles R. Atherton. *Social Welfare Policy Analysis and Formulation.* 2nd ed. Lexington, MA: Heath, 1986.

EXERCISES

EXERCISE 47: Social Policy

Listed below are a series of social policy problems. Break into groups of six or seven. Choose one of these problems.

- Should drugs be legalized?
- Should a system of national health insurance be developed?
- Should the welfare system be revised?
- Should the death penalty be abolished?
- Should the Equal Rights Amendment for women be ratified?
- Should the remaining old-growth forests in the United States be protected?

- Should prayer be allowed in public schools?
- Should affirmative action programs be eliminated?

Gather facts about the problem, asking who, why, what, where, and how. Gather information and decide on the "real" problem to be worked on by role playing. Decide on several solutions by locating change points and iteration. Rank your solutions according to those you think are the ones that will solve the policy problem.

Present your policy problem to the rest of the class, describing how you selected the problem, the problem definition your group decided on, and at least three solutions. Compare the process each group used. Was the process effective or ineffective? How could your problem solving process be improved?

EXERCISE 48: Using PRINCE to Test Political Feasibility

Choose at least four actors who have control over the policy problem you worked on in EXERCISE 47. For each of the three alternative solutions you have chosen, use the PRINCE political feasibility model to decide on the issue position, power, and salience and total support of the actors. Calculate the scores, rate each solution, and rank the alternative solutions.

Did the PRINCE ranking turn out as you expected?

CHAPTER 15

The Future of Macro Social Work

By his acts of resistance, Gordon Hirabayashi held America accountable to its principles of equality and justice before the law, and he was willing to pay the price for those principles, acts which were eventually to provide vindication of the entire Japanese-American population.

The Categorical Imperative

We ought always and in every way treat mankind and every other rational being as an end and never merely as a means only.

—IMMANUEL KANT, *GROUNDWORK OF THE METAPHYSIC OF MORALS*

Social work's mission should be to build a meaning, a purpose, and a sense of obligation for the community. It is only by creating a community that we establish a basis for commitment, obligation, and social support. We must build communities that are excited about their child-care systems, that find it exhilarating to care for the mentally ill and the frail aged, and make demands upon people to behave, to contribute, and to care for one another. Psychotherapy will not enable us to do that, and the further down the psychotherapeutic path social workers go, the less effective they will be in achieving their true mission.

—HARRY SPECHT AND MARK COURTNEY, *UNFAITHFUL ANGELS*[1]

IDEAS IN THIS CHAPTER

Gordon Hirabayashi Takes a Stand

Members of a small Christian religious movement called Myu Kyo Kai, which preached social responsibility and pacifism, Gordon Hirabayashi's parents were out of place in their overwhelmingly Buddhist and increasingly militant Japanese homeland. Like the Pilgrims, they came to America seeking freedom to practice their religious faith and opportunity to live out the principles of tolerance and justice in the new land. Settling in Seattle, they became hard working, thrifty farmers, started a family and, like hundreds of thousands of American immigrants before them, instilled in their children values of honesty, integrity, respect, and honor before the law.

Dedicating themselves to helping their children succeed, they sent their son Gordon to the University of Washington, where he majored in sociology and was elected vice president of the campus YMCA. Gordon joined the Quaker faith and became active in the American Friends Service Committee, an organization dedicated to nonviolence and promoting justice for the oppressed.

On December 7, 1941, with the bombing of Pearl Harbor, Hawaii, Gordon's life and that of all other Japanese Americans changed as a wave of hysteria swept over the Pacific states. Almost immediately the U.S. Treasury Department froze the assets of everyone who had a Japanese last name, citizens and noncitizens alike. Nine days later, Lieutenant General John L. DeWitt recommended to Washington that "action be initiated at the earliest practical date to collect all alien subjects . . . and remove them to the Zone of the Interior."[2] "A Jap's a Jap," General DeWitt reported. "They are a dangerous element. . . . There is no way to determine their loyalty. . . . It makes no difference whether he is an American citizen; theoretically he is still a Japanese, and you can't change him."[3]

Supported by letters from congressmen and senators from the three Pacific Coast states, leaders of hundreds of organizations demanded that President Roosevelt intern all Americans of Japanese ancestry.[4] In response, the FBI indiscriminently closed Japanese-owned businesses just before Christmas and began rounding up Japanese Americans who seemed "suspicious."[5] The movement to strip Americans of Japanese ancestry of their money, possessions, businesses, homes, livelihood, and jobs swelled like a rising tide. On February 19, 1942, Executive Order 3906 was signed, giving the secretary of war authority to exclude "any or all" persons of Japanese ancestry from certain "military areas."

Over the next few months, the process of uprooting every person of Japanese ancestry who resided in the three Pacific Coast states, and many of those living in Hawaii, and shipping them to inland concentration camps gathered momentum. On March 24, 1942, while the relocation process was proceeding, General DeWitt ordered an 8:00 P.M. to 6:00 A.M. curfew for all persons of Japanese ancestry, citizens and aliens alike, as well as German and Italian aliens.[6] An American citizen by birth, Gordon was now required by law to rush back to his dorm room every evening to insure that he would not engage in treasonous or subversive activities, the only student on campus so restricted. Feeling the impact of the curfew's innate unfairness, Gordon soon began to ignore the curfew, placing himself in danger of criminal prosecution. While technically breaking the law, it did not occur to Gordon that anything would actually happen to him. "We are American citizens. They can't do this to us," he argued with his Issei (first generation Japanese American) relatives. But as more and more Japanese Americans were rounded up, the more cynical began to argue, "You will be there with us."[7]

The men were relocated first; their wives and families were left to dispose of homes, furniture, and other possessions in only a few days. Gordon stopped attending college and plunged into work with the Friends Service Committee, translating, explaining, counseling, moving, transporting, and helping make arrangements to ease the burden of relocation on these families.

During this period, Gordon and his roommate, Bill Makino, wrestled with the implications of the evacuation order, eventually agreeing that in spite of overwhelming pressure to conform, they "had an obligation as Americans to challenge the injustice."[8] Writing out a statement to clarify his thinking, Gordon concluded "that if he was going to uphold principles vital to the rights of Americans, he could not accept orders that discriminated against him because of his ethnic background."[9]

If I were to register and cooperate . . . I would be giving helpless consent to the denial of practically all of the things which give me incentive to live. I must maintain the democractic standards for which this nation lives. Therefore, I must refuse this order for evacuation. . . . I am objecting to the *principle* of this order which denies the rights of human beings, including citizens.[10]

"I was confronted," he said, "with certain values that I held high, the principles of American citizenship, what we considered fair play and justice. If I were to go along with the order, I would have to restructure all of those values and develop a new philosophy of life. . . . So I decided to hold to those values and disobey the law."[11]

Makino's sense of responsibility to his elderly parents, however, ultimately took precedence, and he decided to comply with the evacuation order. Gordon's parents were relatively young and he felt they would be supportive of his decision to resist the order. While his mother agreed with his ideals, she was distraught. Defiance of the government was unthinkable, and she feared that Gordon would be mistreated, even tortured, if he resisted. His parents were afraid they would never see him again. Gordon's concern, on the other hand, was for his parent's safety. Ultimately he decided that he had to do what he knew to be right, even though it might cost his freedom and his future.

Of all the 112,353 Japanese Americans who obeyed the order out of loyalty and to prove their patriotism, only Gordon and one other Nisei, Minoru Yasui, resisted the forced relocation on principle. In response, a group of Gordon's Caucasian friends formed what came to be known as the Gordon Hirabayashi Defense Committee. One of the leaders, Mary Farquharson, a Washington state senator and wife of a university professor, asked Roger Baldwin, executive secretary of the ACLU in New York to help. Not wanting to impede the war effort, the board of the ACLU refused the case, but Baldwin contributed money to help meet court costs.[12]

On Saturday, March 30, 1942, about a week before the university district was to be evacuated, Gordon Hirabayashi, accompanied by Arthur Barnett, fellow Quaker and Defense Committee attorney, went to the Seattle FBI to officially refuse the evacuation order and turn himself in. Not knowing what to do, several agents escorted Gordon to a Maryknoll mission school where the Japanese were being registered and urged him to sign up. Gordon refused. Taking him to another registration station, Gordon again declined on principle. Finally they escorted him to the King County jail where he remained for nine months awaiting trial. During this delay, "Mary Farquharson and her committee—ministers, businessmen, professors—raised funds and spoke before countless groups about the injustice being done."[13]

Gordon's case was finally heard by Judge Lloyd L. Black. The government's case simply rested on proving that Gordon was of Japanese descent. To do this Judge Black had Gordon's parents brought under guard from Tule Lake Relocation Camp and held in a Seattle jail as witnesses against their own son. Because his father could not speak English, Gordon was commanded to translate his father's testimony that Gordon was present and of Japanese ancestry. After only a few minutes deliberation, the jury found Gordon guilty of being of Japanese descent and sentenced him to a jail term of forty-five days for curfew violation and forty-five days for failure to report for evacuation. Gordon spent four months in jail before the authorities let him return to Spokane on February, 1943, to await the results of an appeal to the state supreme Court. Free for the first time in over a year, Gordon continued working for the American Friends Service Committee.

In September, however, Gordon was in court again. This time he refused to fill out the special Selective Service questionnaire for persons of Japanese ancestry, which he felt was discriminatory. "It was," he believed, "an outright violation of both the Christian and American principles of justice and democracy."[14] Gordon also refused to report for his preinduction physical examination because, as a Quaker, he objected to serve in the military on religious grounds.[15] Gordon was found guilty of refusing to serve in the military and sentenced to an additional twelve-month term at McNeil Island federal penitentiary.

On June 21, 1943, the U.S. Supreme Court ruled on both the Gordon Hirabayashi and Min Yasui cases. Agreeing with the military that Japanese Americans were by nature disloyal to the United States, the Court unanimously upheld both their convictions for curfew violation, but declined to consider the legality of the evacuation order.[16] Condemned by the Supreme Court, Gordon Hirabayashi was branded a criminal and traitor.

After serving his prison term, Gordon resumed his college education, earning a Ph.D. in sociology and rising to chair the Department of Sociology at the University of Alberta, Edmonton, Canada, where he continued in his Quaker faith and was active with the Friends Service Committee.

Forty-two years later, attorney Peter Irons and a group of young Sansei (third generation Japanese Americans) lawyers whose parents had been imprisoned in the relocation camps reopened the cases of Gordon Hirabayashi and Min Yasui on behalf of all those who were interned during the war, filing a rarely utilized writ of error, *corum nobis*. The sansei lawyers had found evidence that high government officials and U.S. government lawyers had conspired against the entire Japanese-American population by misstating facts, lying, suppressing, altering, destroying, and withholding crucial evidence from the U.S. Supreme Court regarding the loyalty of Japanese Americans. While the government had alleged numerous acts of sabotage, treason, and espionage by Japanese Americans, there was, in fact, "not a single solitary instance of sabotage or espionage by over 127,000 Americans of Japanese ancestry" during the war.

On January 19, 1983, the *corum nobis* team filed suit. Not wanting to admit it was wrong, and because the government's own lawyers had concocted evidence against Japanese American citizens, the U.S. government brought the full force of its power against the Sansei lawyers. On November 10, 1983, however, Judge Marilyn Hull Pattel found there was unequivocal evidence that no military necessity had existed for the relocation of Japanese Americans. Asserting that the evacuation order was "politically, legally, and morally indefensible," Judge Pattel overturned the convictions of Min Yasui and Gordon Hirabayashi. A bill was then introduced in Congress for reparation payments to all those interned, which, in spite of numerous obstructions and delays, including a presidential veto by George Bush, was finally passed in 1988.

In the era of the 1940s any act of resistance to the war effort was considered un-American. For a Japanese American to resist not only appeared treasonous but also was in direct conflict with the Japanese culture. In spite of appearances, however, Gordon Hirabayashi's acts of resistance were heroically ethical. By his acts of resistance, Gordon held America accountable to its principles of equality and justice before the law, and he was willing to pay the price for those principles. His actions eventually provided vindication of the entire Japanese American population.

Introduction

If you are like many others you are drawn to the profession of social work by a "passion for social justice and a desire to help those most in need."[17] It is because of such idealism and concern for making our society a better place that macro social work took root. More than ever, our society is desperate for people of stature, vision, and resolve who can help solve our most pressing social problems. "Almost everyone agrees today that American society has reached a critical point."[18] This crisis consists of social problems that "seem well nigh insoluble."[19] As a result, these "unattended social problems" appear to be "structural and, quite likely, permanent features of the political landscape."[20]

Our inability to solve many of our most pressing social ills is due to the incapability of Americans of all social classes to understand the causes of or to conceive solutions to social problems. "The social failures of American political institutions," says Frank Coleman, "are not like an oversight, corrected after a second look but are a permanent blindness fixed in the nature of the institutions and the social philosophy used to design them."[21] The social philosophy to which Coleman refers is contained in the ideas and social ideologies that have shaped "the consciousness of a whole people through our national inheritance."[22]

Because social problems grow out of fundamental principles in the social order, we have a difficult time recognizing and solving them. The result is that many people are "unable to identify matters of major social importance and to apply available resources to their solution."[23]

Social workers, however, struggle to develop solutions to the social problems that plague us. But in that struggle, many of the remedies social workers use aim to change the character of people who are victims of problems rather than remake the social order itself. Psychotherapy, for example, focuses on helping individuals adapt to social situations or become reconciled to seeking happiness from within. "To the extent that these reforms prescribe individualistic remedies for collective grievances"[24] they overlook the general deterioration of social life and are in keeping with American social denial.

If the recommendations about curing our social ills offered by the social work profession are to be effective, they must change the ideologies that form the premises of our social order. Such a task may be difficult because social workers who propose to "reverse the trend of urban decline would have to challenge the most cherished norms of American life."[25] But difficult as it may be, social workers must understand that "the ailments [of American life] cannot be cured without a profound change in thought and in values."[26]

This chapter begins with a theory of values that a reconstructed model of social work may take as a base. Three underlying value presuppositions of American society are described: individualism, self-interest, and impersonality. These ideologies result in a variety of social problems for which macro social workers struggle to find solutions. Three strategies have been implemented with varying degrees of success: The existentialist solution, the accommodation solution, and the activist solution. Sometimes these strategies are in conflict with one another and at other times may tend to entrench the very problems that they intend to solve. Social workers in general, and macro social workers in particular, need to re-examine their operating premises and develop a unified strategy with a consistent theory base that can bring us closer to a good society. The chapter closes with an examination of the action model of social work as a strategy for such a reconstructed social work.

A Theory of Values and Ethics

The world of science and technology is consumed with understanding facts. Facts comprise nearly everything around us. They are the raw material out of which we derive understanding about the world.

Facts are data that we gather by means of our senses. Facts exist as objects in space and time. They are independent of people and their intentions.

> [Facts] are not things that are so because someone has decreed that they should be so, or because men have become accustomed to so regarding them; they are so everywhere, no matter what any man might think or do. They are not relative, then, to customs, laws, opinions, or conventions; they are things that are true by nature.[27]

Facts tell us about a state of affairs or about something that exists; they are tangible, observable, and empirical. When scientists come to understand universal patterns or laws by examining facts they uncover truth about the physical or biological world. Facts are consistent and true regardless of time or place. We can predict and control many events by understanding facts.

So compelling is the search for empirical truth and the power of prediction and control that it offers that we rarely take the time to consider that facts are only part of the real world. There is another way of looking at reality that is not factual at all. This is the world of values.

Values are not tangible, directly observable, or clearly identifiable. In spite of this we all know they exist. Values do not exist in space and time. They are qualities by which facts are ordered. It is the pattern, the order of the facts that scientists observe, that give facts their power. When we say "ought" to physical phenomena, we are implying that there is more to facts than "is." "Because things are as they are does not prove that they are as they should be or that they should be different from what they are."[28]

In the human realm, the connection between values and facts becomes important. Because of our ability to evaluate things and make value choices we are not completely constrained by facts. Values allow us to impose an "ought" onto the facts of our social existence. If we were bound by facts alone we would live a completely determined existence.

Values are the qualities, meanings, and intentions by which we order our lives. They are premises and assumptions upon which we base our choices, decisions, and ideas. While we construct the content of our choices out of facts, the choices themselves are driven by our values. We are who we are because of our values. The ability to value is a large part of what makes us human. We choose our life-style, career, and marriage partner on the basis of those things we cherish and hold high.

Because we are valuing creatures, we can create a social world based on those qualities we consider important: honor, integrity, compassion, justice, altruism, caring, and so on. And it is by means of values such as these that our social lives acquire meaning. The values of a society, are reflected in its social policies and the way it embodies values in its social structures.

Values allow people to rise above the facts of their existence. In the ugliest of conditions, they can find beauty, and in the most desperate of circumstances, hope. Victor Frankl, for example, demonstrated how compassion for others allowed him to survive appalling conditions in World War II concentration camps.[29]

Macro social work is an intensely value-laden enterprise. We make choices for the public good and in the public interest. Social workers need to understand how to consciously use values but they also need a theory that helps them understand what values to use. Just as we think rationally and order facts, so too we think valuationally and order our values so as to use them effectively. The three levels of values are: subjective values, objective values, and ethical values.

Subjective Values

While all people have the same perceptual apparatus, each person perceives reality from his or her particular point of view. While we may agree on facts, we make those facts our own as we impute meaning to them. Several people who look at the same facts will often come to different conclusions about what those facts mean.

The meanings we attach to our sense perceptions are the result of values that operate at the subjective level. In aesthetics, for example, subjective values are a matter of personal taste. In the arena of truth, subjective values take the form of personal opinion, and in the arena of goodness, they are desires, wants, or interests. Because my perceptions of the world are uniquely my own, my subjective values are not open to dispute. They are valid for me even though they may not be for anyone else.

I have, for example, my own taste in clothing and food based on what appeals to me and what I like. While there are those who claim to have better taste than me, no one can dictate my taste. I like what I like. These likes are uniquely my own and are a matter of personal preference. The world of economics operates at the subjective level of taste and is based on trying to decipher people's tastes and cater to them.

I form my own attitudes and opinions based on my perception of the world, and I have opinions about things even though no one else may agree with me. American politics is based on subjective opinion.

> Each individual is entitled to his or her own "bit of space" and is utterly free within its boundaries. In theory, at least this civil and psychic right is extended to everyone, regardless of their race, ethnicity, or value system, insofar as their exercise of this right does not infringe on the right of others to do likewise.[30]

Finally, I seek those things that I perceive as being good for me. They become my desires, wants, or self-interests and come out of my self-perceived needs. What may be good and life enhancing for me may not be so for others. While no one can make me want something that I perceive as not good for me, ultimately I must decide what is in my own self-interest. I have a right to pursue those self-interests as long as that pursuit is lawful. It is the role of government to protect my rights to pursue my lawful interests.

Objective Values

While the tastes, opinions, and interests of one individual usually have little impact on others, we must take the preferences of others into account. As subjective values of people are added together, they become standards by which society can take direction. Subjective values become "objective" when they cease to be items that apply only to me and, either informally or formally, become standards by which my behavior can be evaluated. Subjective values need to be converted to objective ones so that society has a common standard by which to operate.

Objective values are those that are held by large groups in society. Subjective values, once aggregated, become objective values and can be treated as facts by social scientists. They can be operationally defined, observed, counted, and used as social indicators by researchers. Social scientists routinely take public opinion polls on any number of issues, giving us an objective view of the content of people's values, ranging from who is most likely to be elected to public office to attitudes about gun control, abortion, and others.

People's sense of taste is the object of the clothing, music, and food industries. When these industries take my taste into account and cater to it, along with that of others, standards of taste become translated from the particular to the general. As the fashion industry discovers or orchestrates trends, it captures or dictates what is fashionable and develops standards by which people's taste is judged. What is fashionable today, however, may be out of fashion tomorrow.

In the same way, my opinions together with the opinions of others become objective means by which we give direction to our government. When we vote we express our subjective opinions, which then are translated into decisions about who is elected or the fate of policy propositions. Our society schedules voting at regular intervals to account for the fact that people's political preferences change over time.

Finally, the free market economy as a whole is driven by aggregated individual desires and wants; people express preferences, giving signals to the economy about what to produce or not produce. The "law of supply and demand" assumes that when many people express preferences, more of a commodity will be produced, and prices will drop. Businesses perform marketing surveys to find out people's preferences about products before they invest money in them. The market, therefore, responding to people's preferences is generally determined by the operation of the aggregation of people's subjective desires.

If enough people agree on values and hold themselves accountable to them, subjective values can be converted into objective values or laws.[31] Once this occurs, objective values have morality imputed to them. Morality occurs when common standards, arising out of subjective values, exist in a form by which behavior can be said to be good or bad and right or wrong, and can be applied to everyone.

For example, norms of behavior for using automobiles are established because the expression of one person's unfettered desires to reach a goal may interfere with the similar interests of others. Rules are established to promote smooth traffic flow and they apply to everyone equally. They are objective standards of behavior. If someone breaks a traffic rule, she or he may be subject to fines or some other punishment. Traffic rules, therefore, carry moral weight. We ought to obey traffic laws because they allow people to meet their needs while preventing them from hurting or harming others in the pursuit of their interests.

We establish norms or rules by voting. When one value preference receives at least 51 percent of the vote, this preference becomes converted into a law that carries moral significance and applies to everyone. While voting is one way that people establish morality in society, formal institutions of society become the arbiters of morality. These institutions are legislatures in the public arena and large, complex organizations, both public and private. Morality can be commanded by those who have power, such as managers of organizations or government officials.

Conventional values are those that apply to community or society.[32] When something is conventionally good, a number of people in the society have agreed to it. It is good only insofar as it expresses the tastes, opinions, and interests of the people who adopted it.

Morality does not require a person to be ethically good, just, or truthful. It simply requires that a person not act in ways that break the rules. As long as a person acts lawfully, she or he is considered moral, but if a person breaks a rule or operates outside of standard conventional behavior, then he or she may be subject to correction. Morality tends to operate, therefore, at a level of social maintenance requiring little except an appropriate behavioral response.

Conventional values may apply in one society and not in another. Until recently, for example, it was illegal and therefore immoral in South Africa for a black person to marry a Caucasian. Other cultures do not consider such conduct immoral at all. Debates in the United Nations on any number of social issues extending from human rights abuses, hunting endangered species, and the decimation of rain forests are examples of how nations express differing conventional values. Conventional moral values, therefore, even if adopted by an entire nation, are not universal, absolute, or even necessarily good in and of themselves. They are dependent on the subjective values inherent in the interests, needs, and desires of nations or cultures.

Macro social workers deal for the most part with the conventional moral values of society. We need to understand that these values arise out of the presuppositions of our society. When we work to reform social systems, we try to change not only the outcomes of conventional values, that is, the social policies, social programs, or social plans, but also the processes and social structures by which those values become implemented. This means working in the political and organizational arenas where conventional values and rules are generated.

Ethical Values

If a person attempts to go beyond conventional morality and look at the quality of things or consider what is good in and of itself, then that person is beginning to ask questions about ethics. While the absence of moral behavior may be evidence of a lack of ethics, moral behavior is not necessarily equivalent to ethical action. While ethics may include morality, it is not coincidental with morality.

One may be a completely moral person but have little or no conception of ethics. Conversely, one may not act according to the moral conventions of a particular society but be highly ethical. Social activists, for example, often refuse to act according to the moral conventions of a society that they perceive as unethical. Many college students in the late 1960s refused to participate in the war in Vietnam, acting on their conscience and against social norms. Gordon Hirabayashi was charged with treason and imprisoned because he acted on his belief that the government was acting unjustly.

When a society attempts to do more than simply reach for a majority consensus about subjective opinion and become a society that is good in and of itself, it is infusing ethics into is social values. It is only then that we can talk about social ethics rather than moral conventions. In contrast with mere convention, therefore, ethics attaches itself to values that transcend the individual or society and that reach for absolute significance.

The ancient Hebrews had a vision of justice (*mishpat*), righteousness (*tsedekah*), and harmony, peace, wholeness, and beauty (*shalom*) in social relationships. The classical Greeks determined that there are only three ultimate ethical values to which all others may be attached: Truth, Good, and Beauty.

Ethical values such as these are universal because they transcend time and place and apply to all societies. They are absolutes because they are ends in themselves and cannot be reduced to any other value. While value absolutes cannot be apprehended in their ultimate form, if people want to be ethical as well as moral they must make the attempt to engage them on a personal level and institutionalize them in society.

An individual may attach his or her subjective opinions, preferences, tastes, and interests to ethical absolutes that are true or just, good or righteous, and express beauty or *shalom*. When a person does this, he or she transcends his or her personal values and converts them into ones that are of lasting and ultimate worth.

Bravery is such a value. We all admire someone who is brave. But bravery is good only to the extent that it is infused with something beyond itself, something good on which it depends. For example, if I act bravely to fulfill my own individual self-interest or defend my opinions or preferences, bravery devolves to a subjective value. It is called having guts, being macho, or having chutzpa. One braves adversity to prove a point, as a test of dominance, to gain respect, or to reach a goal. There is nothing intrinsically good or necessarily bad about these expressions of bravery.

But, if someone takes a risk for something ultimately good beyond him- or herself, bravery is converted to courage. The word *courage* comes from the French *le coeur*, which means "having heart." By heartening yourself, you take a risk for a person or issue beyond yourself, not knowing what the outcome will be, and you display courage. Courage is an ethically good value because it is attached to something good beyond the self.

Purpose is another value that may be ethically good depending on whether it is attached to a value absolute. At the subjective level, one's purpose is self-interest. Self-interest that does not take into account the interests of others is called selfishness. Purposive acts that are selfless and in the interests of others, aiming toward the good, are called noble. We recognize that someone who acts nobly has a purpose larger than him- or herself.

Ethically good or true values are important because they require people to conform not only their outward behavior but also their inner being to values beyond themselves. In the same way, social ethics are found by transforming socially conventional values through a higher purpose that transcends the immediate and expedient. What may be seen as "national interests," for example, may be recast into the "public good," conventional opinion may be converted into a truth of society.

Japanese Americans, for example, now well established and financially secure, display ethical action in their efforts to improve the quality of life of other Asian Americans. Each year since 1983, for example, the Nisei Student Relocation Commemorative Fund has awarded scholarships to Southeast-Asian refugee high school students. Since the Nisei were helped by church and civic groups to attend college and restore their lives after internment in concentration camps during World War II, they now feel an obligation to help recent Asian immigrants who are less fortunate.[33] Just as they were helped, they willingly help others. Altruism such as this demands that individuals make ethical choices.

No one can force a person to be ethical. Ethics comes from a sense of compassion, caring, concern, and obligation that transcends oneself. Ethical intentions occur only when one understands the importance and value of others in community. Morality is the coinage of values in civil society and in organizations. Ethics is the coinage of values in community.

Values in American Life

The political tradition of early America was formed by selecting from the larger world of values those congenial to its development—radical individualism and ruthless self-interest. By the turn of the twentieth century complex bureaucracy in both private and public arenas created a technological society in which impersonality became an overriding force. So powerful was the legacy of individualism, self-interest, and impersonality in American society that they became a "total ideology which could not be challenged or even questioned."[34] Today these values manifest themselves "in characteristic and unvarying ways related to the American constitutional philosophy"[35] blocking "the emergence of alternative social policies."[36]

In order to fully understand why social problems in our society seem impervious to permanent resolution, an understanding of these ideologies needs to be developed. This section describes individualism, self-interest, and depersonalization and their consequences for American life.

Individualism

The basic ideology of American life is individualism. "Individualism lies at the very core of American culture."[37] It is the cornerstone of our political and economic systems and determines, to a large extent, the way we view ourselves.

We cherish the individual rights that our Constitution upholds, especially the right to freely express our opinions. The values of dignity, self-reliance, independence, and self-determination are rooted in our tradition of individualism. Our form of government itself is founded "in the principle of liberal democracy . . . that the sole source of right is the absolute will of the individual."[38] The kind of individualism that this kind of freedom inspires is "expressive individualism," the notion that each "person has a unique core of feeling and intuition"[39] that expresses his or her individuality. Expressive individualism enriches social and cultural life. As each individual gives political expression to his or her values and opinions, the polity finds its locus and direction. The content of public life is the result of expressive individualism.[40]

Private enterprise operating in a free market is based on "the individual as the ultimate entity in society."[41] The kind of individualism on which the economy depends is called "utilitarian individualism." Our economy would not exist if each person did not have the freedom to exert his or her own self-interests and freely pursue them. The wealth of

material goods that exist today is the result of utilitarian individualism in the economic sphere. So crucial is this kind of individual freedom that "most arguments against the free market [grow out of] a lack of belief in freedom itself,"[42] according to Milton Friedman. The political and economic strength of our society depend on the values inherent in utilitarian individualism.

While individualism forms the foundation of our culture it is not without drawbacks. "Some of our deepest problems, both as individuals and as a society, are closely linked to our individualism."[43] While individualism presupposes autonomy and freedom, in some contexts it also "weakens the very meanings that give content and substance to the ideal of individual dignity,"[44] resulting in obedience and conformity.[45] The "immersion in private economic pursuits undermines the person as a citizen."[46] While individualism guarantees the expression of human values, it paradoxically destroys the basis of social values themselves.

The Empty Self

Individualism has, in reality, contributed to emptiness of the self. "The ideal self in its absolute freedom is completely "unencumbered."[47] Individualism claims that "every person should be unencumbered by the rest of society in terms of how he or she conducts behavior within such areas as religion, government, and economy."[48]

> "Values" turn out to be the incomprehensible, rationally indefensible thing that the individual chooses when he or she has thrown off the last vestige of external influence and reached pure, contentless freedom.[49]

This results in an absence of any "objectifiable criteria of right and wrong, good or evil in American society. The self and its feelings become our only moral guide."[50] But, if selves are

> defined by their preferences, and those preferences are arbitrary, then each self constitutes its own moral universe, and there is no way to reconcile conflicting claims of what is good in itself. All we can do is refer to chains of consequences and ask if our actions prove useful or consistent in the light of our own "value-systems."[51]

Without an external guide, people become "limited to a language of radical individual autonomy . . . [and] cannot think about themselves or others except as arbitrary centers of volition. They cannot express the fullness of being that its actually theirs."[52] The unencumbered self becomes rootless, alienated, and empty.[53]

Under these premises, society has no natural or organic bases, but "is an abstraction [in which] only isolated individuals exist."[54] People find themselves "thinking of man as an empty vessel, without emotion or commitment to ideals, into which are poured the traditions and requirements of society."[55]

This is especially true of professionals such as social workers who have been trained to withhold their own values and to treat themselves and others objectively. For psychotherapists, in particular, individualism is "the notion of pure, undetermined choice, free of tradition, obligation, or commitment as the essence of the self"[56] The atomistic professional "stands apart from what [he or she] does. . . . Commitments remain calculated and contingent on the benefits they deliver."[57]

Conformity

Radically free, unencumbered selves live in a world that has an "absence of social life," and they have such a "frequently expressed hunger for binding relationships"[58] that they look to organizational systems to provide them with the sociality they desire. The "artificial system, prescriptive laws, . . . the orders of a conscious, organizational, decision-making process, therefore, presume a free individual."[59] Malleable, dependent, and capable of adaptation to almost any kind of circumstance, the docile,[60] valuationally unencumbered self presents exactly the conditions necessary "to succeed in an impersonal world of rationality and competition."[61]

Destruction of Public Life

While individualism has allowed freedom, it has also resulted in "the doctrine that all evaluative judgments, and more specifically all moral judgments, are *nothing but* expressions of preference, expressions of attitude or feeling."[62] Ultimate values are defined out of existence as a means by which society orders itself. "Good and bad, right and wrong,

justice and injustice are not eternal verities independent of the intelligence of particular man"[63] but are contingent on whatever subjective values are conventionally viable at the time.

Because "there are as many opinions as to what constitutes 'right reason' as there are men,"[64] values can be defined only in terms of the interests and needs of highly discrete individuals. Devoid of overarching ideals to which the citizenry is obliged to conform, therefore, American "political institutions . . . cannot and should not seek to impose an ideal pattern on the life of a man, simply because there is none."[65] While individuals are left with their subjective values as a basis for understanding social problems and policy in American life, the "passive, nondynamic view of man's psyche fails to acknowledge the role of values in human affairs."[66] As a result, Americans tend to be unable to see beyond subjective personal opinion to larger social issues. People not only fail to recognize social problems but also are incapable of developing solutions to them.

Self-Interest

One of the basic premises of American constitutional philosophy is that everyone should "be committed to the rational pursuit of self-interest."[67] The individual has an absolute right to be "his own authority on all points which affect his conscience and self-interest"[68] independent of the restraints of any "higher law" or "right reason."[69] Self-interest has become a dominant motivating force in the economy as well as in public affairs. In the economy, acquisitive self-interest is a recognized trait of American character, the "driving force of modern productive work"[70] and a mandatory value on which the market system is based. The market channels self-interest "as the energy to thrust the economy forward, to speed up production and generate rapid economic growth."[71] Self-interest is a necessary means of "organizing individual citizens to achieve a high standard of living."[72]

Self-interest is also the focal point of public affairs. The basis of American constitutional philosophy, "in the absence of any norm of public rectitude," was to establish "the private interest of every individual 'as a sentinel over the public rights.' "[73] Politics is "sustained by the intersection of interests of independently situated political actors. These actors identify the good for themselves in radically different ways and ruthlessly pursue it."[74]

The intersection of different interests in the political marketplace automatically gives indicators for the direction of the social order.[75] When aggregated, these political preferences provide, if not a common good, at least a public interest that is supposed to reflect the desires of the people at any one time. Self-interest enlightened by social concern and altruism also endows society with a means by which social policies can be addressed and "is viewed as the proper remedy for social ills."[76]

In spite of its effectiveness and utility, however, self-interest is not socially benign or altruistic even when aggregated to form the "public interest." At its base it is a pernicious ideology that destroys public spirit, denies the public good, undermines community, and sets individuals against one another. Reinhold Niebuhr pulled no punches when he said:

> Evil is always the assertion of some self-interest without regard to the whole, whether the whole be conceived as the immediate community, or the total community of mankind, or the total order of the world.[77]

Rejection of Public Good

Self-interest results in "rejecting the notion of conforming private interests to a public purpose,"[78] depriving the populace "of an adequate ideal of civilization in terms of which the members of society may be organized."[79] Thomas Hobbes, one of the philosophical founders of modern society, "rejected the cardinal assumption that rights and duties, the good of the individual, and the good of society are harmonious and coincident."[80] Higher ethical values such as altruism, compassion, and justice are neglected when common or public decisions are at stake. Not only is personal idealism undermined, but

> the unity of society is destroyed when one does not think of the long-term effects of economic exploitation or of consistently placing private above public interests. If such actions become universal, society would fly apart by centrifugal force. It is shared values that hold society together.[81]

Conflict Management

In American society, questions of the public good are left to the pulling and hauling of conflicting self-interests as individuals and groups compete for concessions in the policy arena.[82] The game of American politics, reduced to conflict resolution between contending actors, "is corrupt, sterile, and deprived of purpose."[83] Government is deprived of any substantive role and has largely become, as John Locke recommended, a function of umpire policing the rules of the game "by settled and standing Rules, indifferent and the same to all Parties."[84] This view is echoed by Milton Friedman, who asserts that "government is essential both as a forum for determining the 'rules of the game' and as an umpire to interpret and enforce the rules decided upon."[85]

Public goods are up for grabs by acquisitive private interests out to exploit the public sector for their own advantage. Having only his innate desires and preferences as his guide, the self-interested individual "will maximize his net welfare if he takes advantage of the public good at minimum cost to himself."[86]

Even public service is open to exploitation. Morrow calls this a "bazaar" model of politics in which organized interest groups bargain in the public arena for goods, services, and policy concessions. Government is simply a vendor or provider of opportunity for those who exploit its resources to increase their power and influence at public expense.

> [Public] agencies plan their marketplace strategies with virtually a deaf ear to any notion of the "common good" or "public interests." . . . Agencies spend little time on the question of what is intrinsically good. Instead, they tend to be willing accomplices to those whose interests control most of their resources in the private marketplace, and in effect, extend the private marketplace into public arenas.[87]

Policy-making is a process of bargaining and negotiating between the various organized interests groups who act in the political arena. Having reduced politics to subjective personal opinion and decision making to the summing up of those opinions,

> the public order is largely artificial and contrived out of the intersection of conflicting interests of individual men, and in rational, technological society, the "competitive struggle for dominance."[88]

Ethically rational discourse tends to be eliminated in American public affairs.

Education

Education is likewise deprived of a purpose other than creating technologically skilled individuals who can easily accommodate to the needs of complex organizational systems and to the utilitarian goals to which both individual and organizations are directed. The idea that "the public good is implemented through educating men to regard themselves as selfless instruments of a social purpose"[89] is an illusory dream.

Community

When self-interest is a guiding premise of society, "an explicit concern for community is dispensed with."[90] Social relationships are translated into utilitarian group processes culminating in the "absence of social life . . . intimated by a frequently expressed hunger for binding relationships"[91] and the capacity of American communities "to complete the lives of its members is denied."[92] Community is not sought for its own sake but as another arena in which utilitarian self-interests can be met.[93]

In summary, while unfettered self-interest provides people with freedom and opportunity, it leaves no ultimate values beyond the self on which to base society, politics, education, or authentic community.

Dehumanization

In modern, self-interested, individualistic society, "each person treats the other primarily as a means to his or her end . . . to seek to make him or her an instrument of one's purposes by adducing whatever influences or considerations will in fact be effective."[94] Atomistic individuals are replaceable parts in the overall social mechanism. People are largely interchangeable, making it possible to construct all the systems society needs.[95] For many social theorists this "objectification" and dehumanization of individuals is the culmination of the destructiveness of modernity.

Social dehumanization does not have to occur by coercion: it can occur by unobtrusive controls. Individualism and self-interest have provided the basic ingredients for these controls:

> Western technical society has produced methods of adjusting persons to its demands in production and consumption which are less brutal but in the long run more effective than totalitarian suppression. They depersonalize not by commanding but by providing [that which] makes individual creativity superfluous.[96]

Max Weber put the matter in the clearest and starkest of terms. Complex organization "develops the more perfectly the more the bureaucracy is 'dehumanized.' . . . This is the specific nature of bureaucracy and is appraised as its special virtue."[97] Dehumanization not only is the supreme value by which bureaucracy operates but also becomes "virtuous." What was once considered horrific—the process of making a person into an empty thing devoid of humanity—has become inverted into the opposite, just as compassion has become corruption and altruism has become an indicator of immaturity.[98]

Responses to American Ideology

Because of radical individualism people are left with only their subjective opinions to guide them. Deprived of a rich social life, they are lonely and disaffected. Lacking authentic community, they are alienated from themselves and others.

Having rejected any absolute ethical values as a guide to behavior, the individual is left with only acquisitive self-interest as a primary motivation. The ultimate value in life is "grabbing and holding on unlimitedly."[99] The result is dehumanization.

Into this social malaise, social critics and social work reformers have attempted to restore the humanity, sociality, and ethical values that have been lost. The three main strategies offered by these groups are (1) the existentialist response, (2) the accommodation response, and (3) the activist response.[100]

Existentialist Response

The transformation of radically free, self-interested individuals into passive objects was observed by existentialists Soren Kierkegaard, Jean Paul Sartre, and Friedreich Nietzsche, who urged people "to resist a world in which everything was transformed into a thing, a means, an object of scientific calculation, psychological and political management."[101] The common enemy of these existentialist philosophers "was and is the objectifying, depersonalizing power of technical society."[102]

Kierkegaard fought against adjusting to social dehumanization. Instead, he "asks the individual to break away from this society in order to save his existence as a person."[103] For Kierkegaard, the inability to impute meaning into one's life is a sickness.[104] This sickness results in alienation, in which people live a surface existence.

People may speculate on life's meaning or experience immediate sensory satisfactions but rarely do they allow themselves to go beyond subjective sense perceptions. Lacking recognition of ethical values beyond the self, modern individuals experience only half of their humanity. Kierkegaard recommends taking a leap of faith into authentic existence and resisting the nothingness that the loss of ethical absolutes has caused.[105]

Jean Paul Sartre also asks individuals to separate from the dehumanization of society, but unlike Kierkegaard, he rejects the idea of ethical absolutes on which the person should base his or her existence. Instead, Sartre "tries to save the person by asking him to create himself without norms, laws, and principles, without anybody or anything else . . . the willing self, the decision decided for the sake of deciding and not for the sake of content, the freedom maintaining itself by the rejection of any obligation and devotion."[106]

Friedreich Nietzsche's main concern was "nihilism," the depersonalization of mass technological society that "destroys the creative power in life. Man becomes . . . a cog in the all-embracing machine of production and consumption."[107] Nietzsche's recommendation was the adoption of heroic acts of self-affirmation, which he called the will to power.

> Only a new beginning of the will which wills itself can save life from complete disintegration. This will . . . is the self-affirmation of life as life against everything which transforms it into an object, a thing, a tool.[108]

These existentialists attempted to preserve human freedom while maintaining authenticity in the face of the degrading depersonalization of modern organizational society. However, their solutions tend to present the person as defenseless and vulnerable to the very forces against which he or she is supposed to protect him- or herself. The self is left alone in heroic self-affirmation, bereft of abiding relationships in a cold and impersonal society, while attempting to find meaning in emptiness and absurdity.

Accommodation Response

In contrast to the heroic self standing alone, accommodationists recommend that people become adjusted to the modern world. Accommodationists tend to have few complaints about the premises on which modern society is based. Allying themselves with social systems and social ecological theory, accommodationists assert that defects in society arise because of stresses in adjusting to growth and to the fast pace of changes. Accommodationists are committed to enhancing the "progress" modern society has made, correcting those aspects that are dysfunctional. Rather than wishing to change society or its premises, accommodationists support the status quo.

The first accommodation strategy is a managerial response. The accommodationist as social manager uses organizational systems to increase productivity, provide services, and keep the machinery of society moving. The second accommodation solution is offered by clinical social workers who focus on individuals who have been unsuccessful in managing themselves in organizational society.

Managerial Accommodation

The manager accepts the view that the "individual needs to be socialized to adopt the collective orientation in all his dealings with economic and governmental organizations . . . [and] be comfortable with impersonality."[109] Rather than human virtues of compassion or altruism, the primary values of management are efficiency and effectiveness. "Effectiveness" is defined as the extent to which the premises, rules, roles, and procedures of organizational life have been inculcated into a person's psyche.[110] It is management's responsibility to train, educate, socialize, and motivate individuals to accept organizational goals and ensure that they are carried out efficiently and effectively.[111]

By increasing the organization and rationalization of society, the manager contributes to its improvement. By means of picking up the pieces of economic dislocation, redistributing resources in the form of welfare, rehabilitating offenders and addicts, sheltering the homeless, and providing other social services, the defects of modern society are managed, if not corrected.

However, as social work management has uncritically accepted organizational behavior as its operating premises, it has become another component in the armamentarium of social conformity rather than social reform. Public social service organizations and their constituents are merely one more special interest group in the burgeoning number of claimants on public resources.

Therapeutic Accommodation

In the therapeutic view, people in society who suffer alienation because of rampant individualism, who fail to muster appropriate competitive self-interest, or who cannot adjust to organizational impersonality have failed to mature and may need therapy.[112] The psychotherapies "enhance and empower the self to relate successfully to others in society and achieve a kind of satisfaction without being overwhelmed by [its] demands."[113] They attempt to heal ineffectively socialized individuals, helping them accept individualism, become skilled in the self-interested pursuit of success, and adapt to impersonality as necessary components of modern organizational life.[114]

Many people are in need of counseling and psychotherapy at some time in their lives, and therapists find many rewards in helping individuals, couples, and families overcome dysfunctional behaviors. Social work therapists help people break cycles of abuse, codependency, and addiction as well as treat depression, anxieties, and other emotional and behavioral disorders. Psychotherapy works at healing personal problems one by one rather than solving social problems that give rise to individual hurts. While there is much good accomplished through psychotherapy, there are limitations as well.

The individualistic premises on which psychotherapy is based raise questions about its useful-ness in healing those who are damaged by organizational society. Paul Tillich, for example, says that "more and more psychotherapists have discovered that the conflicts of their patients are partly and often largely conditioned by the social situation in which they live."[115]

The psychotherapeutic endeavor is so "radically individualistic"[116] that it exacerbates the atomism and ultimately the alienation of the person, and unwittingly reinforces the very impersonality it attempts to cure. In its "relentless emphasis on self-interest . . . the very language of therapeutic relationship seems to undercut the possibility of other than self-interested relationships."[117]

> The therapist takes the functional organization of industrial society for granted as the unproblematic context of life. The goal of living is to achieve some combination of occupation and "life-style" that is economically possible and psychically tolerable, that works. The therapist, like the manager, takes the ends as they are given; the focus is upon effectiveness of the means.[118]

Stripped of any ethical norm not congruent with self-interested goal-achievement, therefore, values are reduced to utilitarian functions. For the therapist, "the only morality that is acceptable is the purely contractual agreement of the parties: whatever they agree to is right."[119]

> Just as the notion of an absolutely free self led to an absolutely empty conception of the self, complete psychological contractualism leads to the notion of an absolutely empty relationship. And this empty relationship cannot possibly sustain the richness and continuity that the therapeutically inclined most want, just as they want not empty but rich and coherent selves.[120]

Psychotherapists "Band-Aid" social problems by treating those who have already been damaged but do not extend the same amount of energy and thought to eradicating the conditions that caused the damage in the first place. To the extent that social work expends its energy in privatized clinical psychotherapeutic treatment valuable social resources are diverted from solving the causes of social problems. Psychotherapy is reactive rather than proactive and is incapable of conceptualizing broad social remedies or preventing people's lives from social disruption.

Psychotherapists tend to abandon one of the concepts on which the social work profession was founded and which has made it a relevant and a powerful voice. They have difficulty understanding and making use of community. "For the therapeutically inclined, community is something hoped for, something yearned for, something sadly missing most of the time, and, when found . . . something that therapeutic language cannot really make sense of."[121] Privatized psychotherapy, in addition, is expensive and is often beyond the reach of the most vulnerable people in society—the marginalized, the poor, the young, the elderly, and the homeless.

Critique of Accommodation

Accommodation solutions reflect American existence today. "Between them, the manager and the therapist largely define the outlines of twentieth century culture."[122] They neither question nor struggle against the underlying individualistic, self-interested norms of American society, but rather accept them as its operating premises. The accommodation solutions

> proffer a normative order of life, with character ideals, images of the good life, and methods of attaining it. Yet it is an understanding of life generally hostile to older ideas of moral order. Its center is the autonomous individual, presumed able to choose the roles he will play and the commitments he will make, not on the basis of higher truths but according to the criterion of life-effectiveness as the individual judges it.[123]

Accommodation responses tend to uncritically accept the devaluation of community in deference to a contrived, economizing mode of human existence. They try to improve the existing order, support existing ideologies and policies, change individuals, or fine tune the social ecosystem to meet needs. Both managers and therapists believe that the individual must learn to become comfortable with impersonality.[124]

For the manager and the therapist being good in such a value-neutral, contractual world has lost its substantive ethical content and "becomes a matter of being good *at things*."[125] A good employee is one who does his or her job effectively, efficiently, and impersonally. A good person is one who is good at adjusting to different roles, balancing demands, and choosing one of numerous life-styles in an effort at finding realization and self-fulfillment. There is a severe limit to the power of managerial and the psychotherapeutic remedies to solve social problems.

Social Change Response

Another group of social workers who attempt to heal the dysfunctions of society do not accept the social or political arrangements as given or expect individuals or groups to accommodate themselves to the premises of the social order. Communalist social workers change the direction of society at the community level. Activist social workers "demand social transformation for the sake of the person"[126] at the societal level. These social workers, who base their practice on social change, explicitly reject "the managerial-therapeutic ethos"[127] of accommodationists.

The Communalist Perspective

Communalist social workers are "motivated by a desire to hold onto the last vestiges of the autonomous community and its ideal of the independent citizen."[128] They see in community a means by which social relationships can thrive. By giving people goals that transcend the individual and seeking higher purposes, community transcends ruthless self-interest. It allows cooperation, commonality, and value expression as a way of life. For communalist social workers, community is not

> a collection of self-seeking individuals, not a temporary solution, like Parents without Partners, that can be abandoned as soon as a partner has been found, but a context within which personal identity is formed, a place where fluent self-awareness follows the currents of communal conversation and contributes to them.[129]

Communalists are "committed to helping communities adjust to new challenges in ways that do not rupture tradition or destroy democractic participation."[130] Communalist social workers make a good society at the grass-roots level, build relationships, solve social problems, and meet needs wherever they are found, much in the tradition of the Settlement House Movement.

Communalist social workers believe that "community social work *is* social work."[131] They have a mission to resurrect the

> yet unfulfilled mission of social work: to deal with the enormous social problems under which our society staggers—the social isolation of the aged, the anomie experienced by youth, the neglect and abuse of children, homelessness, drug addiction, and the problems of those who suffer from AIDS.[132]

For communalists, "psychotherapy is useless in dealing with these great social problems."[133] Instead, social work accomplishes its mission by developing a new vision of society with community at its center.

The Activist Perspective

Social work activists are "motivated by a desire to transform the whole society, and particularly the economy, so that a more effectively functioning democracy may emerge."[134] They get involved

> wherever social patterns become visible, by which persons are treated as means or transferred into things, deprived of their freedom to decide and create, or [are] thrown into anxiety, or bitterness, or tragic guilt.[135]

Social activists oppose organizational systems and managerial ideologies that foster oppression. They emphasize values of community over the impersonal, bureaucratic power of organizational systems that "do not understand, and are not answerable to local community feeling."[136] Because individualism disadvantages those who are not constituted by temperament, circumstance, or intelligence to actively compete in modern society, social activists organize people to equalize opportunity.

Critique of Social Change Strategies

Critics of the communalist perspective assert that community cannot sustain the kind of social processes that communalists want. While one may grieve its loss, community is an outmoded social system. Given our increasingly mobile, technologi-

cal, and materialist society, resurrecting community as a substantive social form is an unrealistic dream. While communalist solutions to social problems may have been effective at the turn of the twentieth century, they ignore the political and social realities at the turn of the twenty-first century.

Critics of the activist perspective argue that social action is reactive rather than proactive. Activists tend to become engaged where oppression and injustice are fully entrenched using confrontation tactics to fix a system that is already broken rather than prevent injustice in the first place. Other critics argue that confrontation tactics only create conflict and social disruption, exacerbating social discontent and fostering social problems.

While necessary as a countervailing effort against large complex organizations, social action plays the same game that organizations play but for limited stakes. While broad social justice issues, such as peace or violence capture the attention of social activists, most social action tends to have limited short-term objectives such as forcing a slumlord to be responsive to tenants' rights, confronting a company that is polluting the water supply, or protesting a nuclear power site. Activists may force one organization to be more socially responsible, but the infrastructure of economic and political organizations perpetuates the system of dehumanization and oppression. By attacking injustices one by one, activists may win battles but lose the war.

Finally, critics of communalist and social action solutions assert that it is unrealistic and ultimately self-defeating to expect oppressed people to rescue society from the dysfunctions brought about by the rich and powerful.

Action Approach to Macro Social Work

Solving the great social problems of our day cannot be accomplished by choosing one of these strategies over another, but requires a reformulation of each solution into one consistent model of social work. By integrating and reconstituting these solutions, the action approach can help social workers rediscover a central role for social work in the transformation of society.

Action Approach and Existentialism

Conventional social work relies primarily on systems and social ecological thinking. These perspectives are "dominant exactly because they play a support role for today's dominant organizations."[137] They reinforce a passive view of the human condition as if humans were parts of larger systems into which clients and social workers alike must fit. Systems and ecological perspectives contribute to impersonality, contrived relationships, and human behavior structured to accomplish goals that are external to people. Because they do not include higher ethical values, systems and social ecology perspectives uncritically accept the underlying premises of social systems and fail to assess the ends to which they are driven.

In contrast, symbolic interactionism derived from existentialist philosophy forms the basis for an action orientation to social work. Symbolic interaction provides action-oriented social work the premises of sociality, personalism, community, substantive thinking, and dualistic transcendence.

Sociality

Chapter 9 described the emergence of a modern society in which "the criterion of economizing becomes the standard of human existence."[138] This artificial, impersonal societal system[139] presents "itself to its members as an expression of the order of the universe."[140] It is composed primarily of one dominant social form—that of complex organization. Organization aims at mass uniformity and unidimensionality; it imposes social control in the name of economic freedom over almost all aspects of social life. Today, many of society's members "experience their existence as being in tune with such an order."[141] They learn to become "comfortable with impersonality"[142] and "give high value to instrumentalism, to the achievement of established goals."[143]

In contrast, "symbolic interactionists assume that society is essentially social"[144] rather than economic or material. Society is the context in which humans impute meaning to their existence; it is not the "determinant of that action."[145] As a result, symbolic interactionists propose a "multi-centric" society. Instead of one dominant, overpowering social form, a variety of social forms exist each of which is deliberately contrived to fill different human needs. Among these are forms "suited for personal actualization, convivial relationships, and community activities of citizens."[146]

Personalism

Existentialist philosophy stands against individualism by offering personalism as a model of the self. Personalism asserts that a person does not exist as a unitary self.

> We exist only as part of a world—in combination with something. There is no such thing as a self; only self-in-world. There is no life without the hyphen! To be a human being we "hyphen" with other human beings.[147]

A person always exists, therefore, in a dyadic relation. There are two forms of this dyadic relation. One is the combination I-Thou; the other is the combination I-It.[148]

Individualism exists in the I-It relation. When an individual "hyphens" him- or herself to things such as functions, structures, or artificial systems, the self becomes a category of those things. The individual becomes impersonal and takes on the qualities of the object. This is why individualism is compatible with organization. The relations in organization are impersonal, I-It relations. In organization, the individual treats others as objects to be used, things to do what she or he requires or behave as he or she wishes. The other is an "It." To the extent that an individual engages the other as I-It, she or he also becomes an object, a category, a tool. An individual is treated in the I-It relationship as a fragment, an alienated part.[149] For this reason the combination "I-It can never be spoken with the whole being."[150]

Personalism,[151] on the other hand, exists in the I-Thou relationship. A "Thou" is a presence that a person experiences in the here and now. When a person relates to the other as a subject, the person enters into a complexity of aliveness and depth that she or he experiences by means of feelings, values, and intuition, as well as thinking and sensing. A person experiences the I-Thou by invitation to relationship, not by treating the other as a thing to use that will do as one wants or behave as one desires. A person experiences the I-Thou in fullness and wholeness. For this reason the combination "I-Thou can only be spoken with the whole being."[152]

Action social workers cherish personalistic I-Thou relationships because they are the authentic means of becoming human and whole. To the extent that social work devolves to maintaining individualistic I-It relations, social workers alienate, fragment, and destroy the humanity of others.

Community

Individualism expanded into a societal form is collectivism.[153] Collective artificial systems such as organizations are aggregations that "give birth to a new species of inhuman beings,"[154] the I-It. Both individualism and collectivism violate true community: individualism because it "understands only a part of man"; collectivism because it "understands man only as a part."[155]

In contrast, community gives birth to the self, the I-Thou. "True personal being [is] fulfilled, not in isolation, but in community."[156] Community is the source in which personalism, the I-Thou relation, flourishes.[157] There is no self, the I-Thou, that is not born of community. "Community involves mutual relation of man with man, rather than a system of external institutions in which the self is diminished and distorted."[158]

Psychotherapy as an exclusively private endeavor can result only in enhancing I-It functional behavior. In action social work, in contrast, workers understand that the healing of the self, the I-Thou, cannot occur in isolation from community. "No individual exists without participation, and no personal being exists without communal being. The person as a fully developed individual self is impossible without other fully developed selves."[159] Psychotherapy that attempts to help people develop the I-Thou must do it as a part of community, not apart from it.

Multiple Ways of Knowing

Modern reason tends to be a unitary, monolithic way of thinking. Its usefulness as rational problem solving is transferred to social work as the generalist social work method. This method is linear, sequential, calculative, and value neutral. It gives privi-

leged status to cognitive thinking and sensory application. With modern reason, "questions like the 'good' of man or society have no place."[160]

Symbolic interaction, however, questions the assumption that instrumental reason and empirical investigation are the only correct modes of knowledge. The symbolic interaction perspective "relies on the principle that there are multiple ways of knowing."[161] Understanding the human condition in all its complexity, for example, is impossible without the ability to apprehend noncalculable feelings and emotions. Discovering how to make a good society requires nonempirical ethical thinking. Apprehending feelings and values depends on intuition, which transcends cognition and provides insight that functional reason is incapable of understanding.

Symbolic interaction, therefore, recognizes that other noncalculable, nonempirical, and value-laden forms of reason need to be recognized. One such form is a "force active in the human psyche"[162] that "moves the individual toward a continuous, responsible, and arduous effort to subdue his passions and inferior inclinations."[163] This kind of rationality, called substantive reason, assists the "individual to distinguish between good and evil, false and genuine knowledge"[164] and thereby "achieve that excellence of character [moral virtue] which is potential to [his or her] nature."[165] Substantive reason validates the centrality of ethics in thinking. Ethics comes from accepting inner necessity, not outward conformity. This inner necessity provides for critique of the lived world in which people exist.

> Ethics introduces a radical kind of doubt into the everyday world. It questions the adequacy with which social forms embody the moral intentionality of the culture; moreover, it questions the goodness of these cultural intentions, setting the cultural horizon of meaning within a more universal and ultimate context.[166]

It is by means of such critique that social problems can be understood and recognized, a task that modern functional reason is incapable of doing. Action social work methods based on symbolic interaction honor immediate experience as a valid form of knowledge as well as value-laden understanding. It accepts the reality of intuition, feelings, and ethics.

Dualistic Transcendence

By helping bear the tension between I-It functional existence and authentic I-Thou substantive existence, symbolic interaction can help transcend dehumanization and impersonality. The way that symbolic interaction deals with this tension is dualistic transcendence. A person who lives in dualistic transcendence consciously recognizes the dual nature of existence and lives with the tension it creates.

Dualistic transcendence is implicit in the idea of "two-ness," which African Americans use to survive oppression in a land of freedom. Wynetta Devore asserts that dualistic transcendence or "two-ness" can be the basis for a new model of social work.[167]

"Two-ness" is lived out in the daily life of each immigrant as she or he struggles to maintain identity with his or her primary culture while at the same time adopt the language and means of survival in the new environment. Anyone who attempts to maintain the central core of one's being in the midst of the impersonality created by modern organizational society can identify with "two-ness."

Dual allegiance means holding to what is good and right, what is important, while living in a world that rejects many of those values. By recognizing the alienation brought on by organizational society, social workers can devise strategies to help people bear the tension and even transcend it rather than give up their inner personal core of values, adapt, or accommodate themselves to the world of I-It.

In summary, symbolic interaction, which forms the basis of action social work, advocates a society in which community is the central social form, personalism as a model of the self, multiple ways of knowing, particularly the validation of ethical thinking, and dualistic transcendence as a way of maintaining the self in an impersonal society.

A Renewed Accommodation Solution

Two of the most powerful weapons in the arsenal of action social work are social administration and the psychotherapies. Before these strategies can be fully utilized to help build a transformed society, they must be renovated so that they no longer inculcate people further into individualism, self-interest, and impersonality.

Social Administration

Social agencies are the instruments by which social workers deliver social services. Social agencies provide power bases by which poor, marginalized, and oppressed people may press for recognition and assert their interests in the political process. Agencies are tools that social workers use to mobilize resources, influence, and expertise on behalf of their clients.

The challenge of social administration goes beyond "making minor adjustments such as 'humanizing' management [or helping people]' psych out' the job in order to keep it."[168] Instead, social work must develop an action model of leadership (chapter 4), social organization (chapter 9), and social administration (chapter 12) based on principles of existential symbolic interaction.

An action model of administration doesn't use language and thinking that might link it to "management." It resists treating people as objects or means to organizational ends.[169] Mission statements affirm that social agencies are tools for the enhancement of both employees and clientele. The social agency intentionally becomes a component of the community it serves by including clients and staff in all aspects of the agency's functioning. Clients and community members volunteer as members of agency boards of directors and are enlisted as partners in service provision. Employee unions are not seen as threats to administrative control; rather, employees are encouraged to form associations that ensure engagement of employees in areas that affect their work lives. The use of employee decision-making groups, such as quality circles and work modules, is fostered.

In cases where bureaucracy has already taken its toll, therapeutic measures may be taken to restore community. If employee attitudes have hardened or people have succumbed to impersonality, the judicious use of T groups under competent leadership may help soften feelings, renew enthusiasm, and restore personal relationships. Where bureaucracy promises more speed, the virtues of slowness and deliberation are extolled. If communication has been reduced to one-way technical jargon, more personal face-to-face interaction can be encouraged. If bureaucracy demands efficiency at the expense of relation-ships, production lags and even occasional break-downs may be built in to the process to give people time to breathe and rethink whether they really need to do what is being done. If clients are treated as cases or reduced to objects, they can be honored and seen as partners in the process of social renewal. If paper-work, filling out forms and keeping records are more important than client services, an examination of the purpose for forms and paperwork can be carried out and a conscious effort made to eliminate them. If bu-reaucracy vows to clean politics out of administration, citizens groups, commissions, participatory councils, politically appointed watchdogs, and ombudsmen can restore decision making to communities.[170]

Psychotherapy

Action psychotherapy rejects individualism and embraces personalism. It reestablishes a theory of the social self as a person-in-relation rather than person-in-the-environment that ignores the social as-pect. Action-oriented psychotherapy reexamines its philosophical and theoretical roots, joining with so-cial care rather than individualist psychology.

Action psychotherapy rejects the development of specialization and privatization. Specialization isolates the person and fragments services. Privati-zation of treatment is in conflict with the social na-ture of social work and removes treatment from those most in need of it. Privatization denies the communal roots of the healing process.

Action psychotherapy integrates individual so-cial repair into generalist social work practice at the community level. It unites community and therapy to heal the social and emotional ills that people face and rejects the perception that

> all forms of popular psychotherapy are fundamen-tally and inherently in conflict with communally-based kinds of interventions. Therefore, it is not possible to integrate the practice of individual psy-chotherapy with the practice of communally-based systems of social care. There is an inherent conflict between the altruism that is required to build a com-munity-based system of social care and the amoral individualism of psychotherapy.[171]

A new awareness that community itself is a source of social and emotional health and well-being offers the psychotherapies a meaningful context for practice. Native Americans and other populations have understood this principle all along, that "the problems of one are the concerns of all" and "the healing of one is the healing of all."[172]

In this renewed action model of psychotherapy, social work therapists develop joint communal and psychotherapeutic solutions to human problems and work to prevent people from re-entering the systems that caused the social and personal problems in the first place. Action psychotherapy locates psy-chotherapeutic interventions in community clinics where the whole person and families can be in-volved in healing processes. It is aimed at strength-ening the self to bear the tension of dehumanization in the world, not accommodation to organizational society.

Finally, action psychotherapy rejects the duality of purpose that social work has had for decades: clinical practice versus social reform.[173] It aligns with renewed models of social change in an effort to bring about a good society, not just healthy individuals.

Renewed Models of Social Change

The two most powerful models of macro social work are those advocated by communalists and so-cial activists. A renewed model of social change in-tegrates both into a joint approach to creating a new society.

Communal Social Work

The communal social work model recognizes community as a central mode of social healing. It challenges the social work profession to an increased commitment to community work, a process that be-gins with a conviction that through the healing power of community people can live meaningful and productive lives.

Action communal social work recognizes that America has a unique opportunity to preserve its di-verse communal forms. If community is to survive today it will be because ethnic populations have pre-served community against the encroachments of modern life. Their links with community are often strong and personal, and have provided support, nur-turance, and identity. Rivera and Erlich call these

Those involved in social work recognize community as a primary place of social healing.

communal forms "neogemeinshaft" communities. They are

> examples of communities becoming and evolving within a hostile environment. Their survival skills, which often relate to their ethnic history, add to their uniqueness, thereby requiring a reconsideration of the concept of community.[174]

The action communal social work model casts the community as a place of refuge, a reminder of roots, and a place where language, foods, rituals, and relationships provide meaning and substance. Renewed communal social work stands in solidarity with these populations to maintain and enhance their traditions and culture on their own terms.

A second new model of communal social work is the community-based model developed by Specht and Courtney. In this model, we begin

> with the assumption that the community itself has the capacity to deal with most individually experienced problems through classes, self-help groups, social clubs, recreation groups, special interest groups, and community service organizations. Moreover, we assume that working with community groups is the pre-

ferred way to meet social needs because, in addition to solving the individual's problems, we increase the community's overall problem-solving ability.[175]

In addition to these two communal forms, social work planners, community developers, organization developers, program developers, and social administrators can form "think tanks" and coalitions with communally sensitive people to explore other modes of community. Such groups consider how to blend various skills and perspectives, develop alternative models, and conceptual schemes that preserve community and transform it in ways that will meet people's social needs in the increasingly hi-tech and organizational twenty-first century.

A Renewed Social Activism

One of the first and most important roles of renewed social activism is to engage in a thorough critique of modern, technological, organizational society. Such a critique should be based on a theory of social ethics. The macro social worker as ethicist is "the conscience of a community" or even the "conscience of society."[176]

> [The activist] together with all movements for social justice . . . shows how the competitive society produces patterns of existence which destroy personality because they destroy community . . . [and] must pursue, in spite of political and social odds against it, the tradition of social criticism.[177]

The role of renewed social activism is to recommend alternative modes of social living and solutions to social problems at the political and societal levels.[178] While renewed social activism may at times work for specific short-term gains, social critiques and social policy solutions are developed for longstanding, fundamental changes in the premises on which the social order is based. Renewed social activism works at changing the political system not simply using it for obtaining policy concessions for particular interest groups. In making fundamental recommendations, social activism works on behalf of marginalized, oppressed populations. Julio Morales, for example, says that "the collective humanism of Puerto Rican society is also a culturally sanctioned pattern that enhances community organizing. It appeals to a sense of justice and fairness, an important guiding principle for community social work practice."[179]

As professional social work identifies and links itself closely with ethnically diverse people in our society, it repositions itself as champion of the oppressed. From this alliance a renewed social activism reflects the spirit of liberty and justice, with new models, new methods, and a new sense of its true mission. In the words of Noam Chomsky:

> It would be tragic if those who are fortunate enough to live in the advanced societies of the West were to forget or abandon the hope that our world can be transformed to a world in which the creative spirit is alive, in which life is an adventure full of hope and joy, based rather upon the impulse to construct than upon the desire to retain what we possess or seize what is possessed by others.[180]

Renewed social activism works at changing the individualistic, self-interested, and dehumanizing premises on which our society is based and offers a means by which it can move toward a personalist, communally based society that values people as ends and not as means.

Conclusion

While devotion to the individual has grown in professional social work, active participation in solving social problems has tended to shrink, diverting "social work from its original mission and vision of the perfectibility of society."[181] Social work's growing emphasis on clinical psychotherapy has diluted its commitment to community and society-wide social issues. Acceptance of systems and social ecological approaches has reinforced social work's ideological identification with individualism, self-interest, and impersonality.

In spite of these trends away from macro-oriented practice, the field of social work has a unique opportunity to reclaim its heritage as the profession committed to community enrichment and conceiving a society that is ethically good as well as economically prosperous.

This chapter has described a theory of values and an action approach of social work based on symbolic interaction. This approach recommends a multicentric society, personalism, multiple ways of knowing, and a strategy of dualistic transcendence. The action approach recommends renewed accommodation solutions in the areas of administration and psychotherapy and renewed social change in the areas of communal social work and social action.

KEY CONCEPTS

facts
values
subjective values
objective values
morality
rules of convention
ethics
individualism
expressive individualism
utilitarian individualism
self-interest
conflict management
"bazaar" politics
dehumanization
existentialist response
nihilism
accommodation solutions
managerial accommodation
therapeutic accommodation
social change solutions
communalist perspective
activist perspective
multicentric society
personalism
I-Thou
I-It
multiple ways of knowing
substantive reason
dualistic transcendence

QUESTIONS FOR DISCUSSION

1. Review the case of Gordon Hirabayashi at the beginning of this chapter. Reflect on the following questions:

a. What values were expressed by Gordon's resistance to internment?

b. Were they subjective, objective, or ethical values?

c. How would you characterize his response? Was it an existentialist response, an accommodation response or a social change response? Was it a combination of these responses?

d. What conclusion can you arrive at about the importance of taking an ethical stance?

2. The National Rifle Association has successfully carried the battle of upholding the right of people to bear arms. The result has been little gun control legislation in this country. Some people assert that the Second Amendment provides a moral, if not legal, right to own handguns. Are there ethical values that override this moral and legal right? If so, what does that higher good consist of?

3. Kant's categorical imperative says: "We ought always and in every way treat mankind and every other rational being as an end and never merely as a means only." How does this apply to macro social work? How does it apply to the role of a community social worker, an organizational social worker, and a societal level social worker?

4. Simon and Aigner state that

social work is neither pro capitalism nor pro socialism. As they presently exist, both capitalist and socialist political economies fail to provide the conditions necessary for all members to meet their basic needs, accomplish their life tasks, and realize their values and aspirations. There are oppressed, victimized, and neglected groups in all societies.[185]

Do you agree or disagree that both capitalism and socialism fail to provide for people's needs? If you agree that capitalism has built-in market failures, does social work have a responsibility to help correct those market failures and help people meet needs, accomplish life tasks, and realize their aspirations? What solutions can you recommend?

5. A renewed social activism recommends longstanding, fundamental changes in the premises on which the social order is based. A renewed social activism works at changing the political system not simply using it for obtaining policy concessions for particular interest groups. This recommendation tends to fly in the face of mainstream political processes that intentionally close debate on the fundamental premises of American society. Kariel, for example, says that

the range of politics—public action, public life—is *objectively* delimited. Politics is properly kept from interfering with what is presumed closed and settled. Economic, cultural, and spiritual enterprises are expected to remain private matters, not to be publicly debated and changed. . . . Politics consists not of the perpetual reexamination and reconstruction of fundamentals but of working within the system.[186]

Do you agree or disagree that there is little hope of reconstructing the fundamentals of the American political system? If the political system itself is flawed and denies the opportunity for "reexamination and reconstruction of fundamentals," what chances exist for making any substantive changes in American society?

6. Do you think that the role of macro social work has declined in recent years? What do you think the role of macro social work should be in the future?

7. An action model of social work has informed the theoretical content of this book. What is your perception of this model? What are its strengths? What are its limitations?

8. The journey of a macro social worker does not end with formal education. Instead, it is only the beginning of a journey that may well last a lifetime. What role do you see for yourself in the field of macro social work?

ADDITIONAL READING

Existentialism

Barrett, William. *Irrational Man: A Study in Existential Philosophy*. Garden City, NY: Doubleday, 1958.

Berdyaev, Nikolai. *Slavery and Freedom*. New York: Scribner's, 1944.

Buber, Martin. *I and Thou*. 2d ed. New York: Scribner's, 1958.

Frankl, Viktor E. *Man's Search for Meaning: An Introduction to Logotherapy*. New York: Washington Square Press, 1963.

Kierkegaard, Soren. *Fear and Trembling and the Sickness unto Death*. Trans. Walter Lowrie. Garden City, NY.: Doubleday, 1954.

Social Critique

Berger, Peter, and T. Luckman. *The Social Construction of Reality*. Garden City, NY: Doubleday, 1967.

Ellul, Jacques. *The Technological Society*. New York: Vintage Books, 1967.

Horkheimer, Max. *The Eclipse of Reason*. New York: Oxford University Press, 1947.

Mannheim, Karl. *Man and Society in an Age of Reconstruction*. New York: Harcourt, Brace and World, 1940.

Marcuse, Hebert. *One-Dimensional Man: Studies in the Ideology of Advanced Industrial Society*. Boston, MA: Beacon Press, 1964.

Neibuhr, Reinhold. *The Children of Light and the Children of Darkness*. New York: Scribner's, 1944.

Niebuhr, Reinhold. *Moral Man and Immoral Society: A Study in Ethics and Politics*. New York: Scribner's, 1960.

Polanyi, Karl. *The Great Transformation*. Boston, MA: Beacon Press, 1957.

Ramos, Alberto Guerreiro. *The New Science of Organization: A Reconceptualization of the Wealth of Nations*. Toronto: University of Toronto Press, 1981.

Rauschenbusch, Walter. *A Theology for the Social Gospel*. Nashville, TN: Abingdon, 1945.

Reich, Charles A. *The Greening of America*. New York: Bantam Books, 1970.

Slater, Philip. *The Pursuit of Loneliness: American Society at the Breaking Point*. Boston, MA: Beacon Press, 1971.

Toffler, Alvin. *The Third Wave*. New York: Morrow, 1980.

Voegelin, Eric. *The New Science of Politics: An Introduction*. Chicago, IL: University of Chicago Press, 1952.

Wilson, H.T. *The American Ideology: Science, Technology and Organization as Modes of Rationality in Advanced Industrial Societies*. London: Routledge and Kegan Paul, 1977.

Weisskopf, Walter. *Alienation and Economics*. New York: Dell, 1971.

Value Theory

Baier, Kurt. *The Moral Point of View: A Rational Basis of Ethics*. New York: Random House, 1965.

Bronowski, J. *Science and Human Values*. Rev. ed. New York: Harper and Row, 1965.

Kant, Immanuel. *Groundwork of the Metaphysic of Morals*. Trans. H. J. Paton. New York: Harper and Row, 19964.

Kant, Immanuel. *Prolegomena to Any Future Metaphysics*. Introduction by Lewis White Beck. Indianapolis, IN: Bobbs-Merrill, 1960.

MacIntyre, Alisdair. *After Virtue*. Notre Dame, IN: University of Notre Dame Press, 1984.

Means, Richard L. *The Ethical Imperative: The Crisis in American Values*. Garden City, NY: Doubleday, 1969.

Roubiczek, Paul. *Ethical Values in the Age of Science*. Cambridge, MA: Cambridge University Press, 1969.

Winter, Gibson. *Elements for a Social Ethic: The Role of Social Science in Public Policy*. New York: Macmillan, 1966.

Winter, Gibson. *Social Ethics: Issues in Ethics and Society*. New York: Harper and Row, 1968.

EXERCISES

EXERCISE 49:
A Renewed Ethical Code

One of the hallmarks of a macro social work is its substantive ethical base. Write down at least five of the most important ethical values that you think the profession of macro social work ought to have. Form triads and share your lists. Come up with a composite list. In class compare your lists with the one that follows. Then, develop an ethical code that can guide the field of macro social work.

A Proposed Ethical Code

Macro social workers have a vision of creating a society that seeks truth and justice, and becomes good. As we seek those values, we are guided by a number of principles.

1. Macro social workers challenge and push society to be everything that it can become while living with the reality of conditions as they are.
2. Macro social workers have the courage and the will to challenge those forces that condone, perpetuate, and cause human suffering.
3. Macro social workers speak for those who cannot speak for themselves, advocate for those who have no voice, and seek empowerment for the powerless and well-being for those whose lives are deprived.
4. When required, macro social workers stand outside the social consensus, shatter norms, and challenge the status quo. They may refuse to participate in social processes or systems that

are destructive to the human condition.
5. Macro social workers value and seek to rekindle in the life of society a sense of authentic community, a substantive conception of democracy, economic justice, and a way of ethical reason in which individuals realize their potential.
6. Macro social workers are committed to society's future. They work to bring about the best that society can become, even when it actively resists becoming that best.
7. Macro social workers are against violence and destruction. They fight against oppression of people and of the human spirit wherever they occur. They are against greed and avarice, compulsive exploitation, ruthless competition, and mindless individualism.
8. Macro social workers are against deception that saps the human spirit. They fight against denial in any of its forms and question conventional wisdom when it promotes injustice, poverty, inequality, powerlessness, and helplessness.

EXERCISE 50:
Cancer Ward

According to Simon and Aigner, "social work demands a pledge to social justice and humanitarian values, with the structure of a just society flowing inductively from this value stance." Read the following excerpt from Cancer Ward[182] by Aleksandr Solzhenitsyn. Break into small groups and reflect on the questions that follow.

Then, after reforming into the larger class come to conclusions about the role of macro social work in bringing about social and economic justice.

> (SULUBIN:) We have to show the world a society in which all relationships, fundamental principles, and laws flow directly from ethics and from them *alone*. Ethical demands must determine all considerations: how to bring up children, what to train them for, to what end the work of grown-ups should be directed, and how their leisure should be occupied. . . . We should consider one criteria only: How far is it ethical.
> (KOKSTOGLOTOV:) . . . Where is the material basis for your scheme? There has to be an economy, after all, doesn't there? That comes before everything else.
> (SHULUBIN): Does it? . . . an economy could and should be built on an ethical basis.[183]

1. Do you agree or disagree that the one important question to be asked is, "How far is it ethical"? Why or why not?
2. What are the components of an ethical society?
3. What role, if any, should macro social workers play in bringing about such a society?
4. Do you believe that the important questions of society are practical issues such as how to arrange for the production and distribution of goods and services? If so, what recommendations would you make about how to arrange for the production and distribution of goods?

EXERCISES

5. What role, if any, should macro social workers play in arranging for production and distribution of goods?

EXERCISE 51:
Critiquing Social Work's Mission

Specht and Courtney make a claim about what they believe ought to be the mission of social work that places community at its center. They state:

Social work's mission should be to build a meaning, a purpose, and a sense of obligation for the community. It is only by creating a community that we establish a basis for commitment, obligation, and social support. We must build communities that are excited about their child-care systems, that find it exhilarating to care for the mentally ill and the frail aged, and make demands upon people to behave, to contribute, and to care for one another. Psychotherapy will not enable us to do that, and the further down the psychotherapeutic path social workers go, the less effective they will be in achieving their true mission.[184]

This statement implies that the profession of social work is on the wrong path, and that its current emphasis on clinical treatment is inappropriate. Form into triads and discuss this statement. In your triad reflect on the following questions. After the class reassembles, come to some conclusion about social work's mission and the roles of macro social work and micro social work.

1. What are the strengths of Specht and Courtney's argument?
2. What are its limitations?
3. Do you agree with Specht and Courtney's assessment of the mission of social work? If not, what do you think the mission of the social work profession ought to be?
4. What role do you think communal social work ought to play in the social work profession?
5. What role do you think psychotherapy ought to play in social work?

Macro Social Work: A Profession of Heroes

I don't know what your destiny will be, but one thing I do know: the only ones among you who will be really happy are those who have sought and found how to serve.

—ALBERT SCHWEITZER[1]

Nothing that is worth doing can be achieved in our lifetime; therefore, we must be saved by hope. Nothing which is true or beautiful or good makes complete sense in any immediate context of history; therefore, we must be saved by faith. Nothing we do, however virtuous, can be accomplished alone; therefore, we are saved by love. No virtuous act is quite as virtuous from the standpoint of our friend or foe as it is from our standpoint. Therefore, we must be saved by the final favor of love which is forgiveness.

—REINHOLD NIEBUHR[2]

IRENA SENDLER: SOCIAL WORKER RESCUER[3]

In 1940, Nazis confined 500,000 Polish Jews in the Warsaw Ghetto to await their deaths. Most people in Warsaw turned their backs but not Irena Sendler. A Warsaw social worker, Sendler decided to invest herself in this community and wangled a permit to check for signs of typhus, a disease that the Nazis feared.

Sendler decided to do something about what she saw. Joining Zegota, a tiny underground cell dedicated to rescuing the Jews, she took on the code name "Jolanta." Because the deportations of Jews had already begun, it was impossible to save the adults, so Sendler began smuggling children out in an ambulance. Over the next three years, Sendler successfully transported almost twenty-five hundred Jewish children to safety, giving them temporary new identities. In order to keep track of the children's real names, she carefully placed their identities in bottles, which she buried in her garden.

It was difficult for Sendler to find people who were willing to help these children. However, after much effort, she did find families and developed a network of churches and convents that were willing to help. "I have clothing for the convent," she would write, and the nuns would come and pick up the children.

In 1943, the Gestapo arrested and tortured Sendler, and sentenced her to die. However, her colleagues in the Polish underground bribed a prison guard to free her at the last minute, listing her as "executed" on the official form. In hiding, Sendler continued her work of rescuing children. After the war, she dug up her bottles and began searching for the parents of the children she had rescued. She could find only a few because most had died in Nazi concentration camps.

Years later, when Irena Sendler was honored for her rescue work and her picture appeared in a newspaper, "a man, a painter, telephoned me," Sendler said. "I remember your face," he said. "It was you who took me out of the Ghetto." Sendler had many calls like that.

MACRO SOCIAL WORK: A PROFESSION OF SERVICE

Macro social work is *the* profession that aims itself at social transformation, social reform, community betterment, and making a good society. We need social workers of vision, commitment, and courage who see a future in which social relationships among people are as important as technological improvement; in which community solidarity and engagement are prized as much as organizational efficiency and effectiveness; in which heroes and heroines of social justice and community development are revered as much as the flamboyant entertainment celebrities or sports figures.

This text opened with the observation that the trend in social work for the last several decades has been away from macro social concerns and toward micro social work practice. Counseling and psychotherapy is needed, and there are many rewards in treating individuals, couples, and families and helping people change their lives and overcome personal troubles. Much good is being done helping people break cycles of abuse, co-dependency, and addictions as well as treating depression, anxieties, and other emotional and behavioral disorders.

As important as micro social work is, the extent to which we focus our professional energies on individual problems rather than the social conditions that may have brought them about, the more we tend to ignore the wider and more fundamental social problems.

Macro social work is a field that works to bring about social change and an end to social problems by means of social research, community development, social action, social planning, program development, social administration, organization development, and social policy.

Macro social workers are among the most outstanding Americans our country has produced. They are people of the stature of Saint Elizabeth Ann Seton, Charles Booth, Dorothea Dix, The Reverend Samuel Barnett, The Reverend Charles Loring Brace, Clara Barton, Sojourner Truth, Mary Parker Follett, Mary Simkhovitch, Grace and

As a social worker, you can help overcome oppression, exploitation, and suffering, and make the world a better place for the generations to come.

Edith Abbott, Clifford Beers, Harriet Tubman, Lord Robert Baden-Powell, Sir George Williams, Lilian Wald, Dorothy Day, the Reverend William Booth, Jane Addams, Harry Hopkins, Mary McLeod Bethune, Saint Frances Cabrini, W.E.B. Dubois, Michael Harrington, and others. The contributions of these macro social workers have changed the direction of our nation and improved the quality of our lives.

Others, while not identified as macro social workers, have likewise devoted themselves to macro social work concerns and have been leaders in the process of social transformation. The Reverend Dr. Martin Luther King Jr., The Reverend John Perkins, Saul Alinsky, Si Kahn, The Reverend Jesse Jackson, and Caesar Chavez have been prominent activists and social reformers in our time. We need to remember these heroes and their accomplishments. They form a "cloud of witnesses" who surround our efforts today and on whose shoulders we ride. From these heroes we can learn about compassion in a world that is often uncaring, altruism in a world of selfish consumption, sacrifice in a world of self-interest, and humanity in a world rife with dehumanization. A list of books written by and about many of these macro social workers follows:

Jane Addams (1860–1935)

Addams, Jane. *Philosophical and Social Progress.* New York: Crowell, 1893.
Addams, Jane. *The Spirit of Youth and the City Streets.* New York: Macmillan, 1909.
    Reprint. Champaign: Univ. of Illinois Press, 1989.

Addams, Jane. *The Long Road of a Woman's Memory*. New York: Macmillan, 1916.

Addams, Jane. *Twenty Years at Hull House*. New York: Macmillan, 1938.

Addams, Jane. *The Second Twenty Years at Hull House*. New York: Macmillan, 1930.

Aloise, Frank E. *Jane Addams*. New York: Crowell, 1971.

Davis, Allen. *American Heroine: The Life and Legend of Jane Addams*. New York: Oxford Univ. Press, 1973.

Farrell, John C. *Beloved Lady: A History of Jane Addams' Ideas on Reform and Peace*. Baltimore, MD: N.p., 1967.

Kittredge, Mary. *Jane Addams: Helper of the Poor*. New York: Chelsea House, 1988.

Meigs, Cornelia Lynde. *Jane Addams: Pioneer for Social Justice*. Boston, MA: Little, Brown, 1970.

Tims, Margaret. *Jane Addams of Hull House, 1860–1935*. New York: Macmillan, 1981.

Edith Abbott (1876–1957)

Abbott, Edith. *The Tenements of Chicago, 1908–1935*. 1936. Reprint. New Salem, NH: Ayer, 1970.

Abbott, Edith. *Women in Industry*. New York: Appleton, 1910. Reprint. New Salem, NH: Ayer, 1969.

Abbott, Edith. *Some American Pioneers in Social Welfare*. Chicago, IL: Univ. of Chicago Press, 1937.

Grace Abbott (1878–1939)

Abbott, Grace. *The Immigrant and the Community*. 1917. Reprint. Englewood, NJ: Ozer, 1971.

Costin, Lela B. *Two Sisters for Social Justice: A Biography of Grace and Edith Abbott*. Champaign: Univ. of Illinois Press, 1983.

Robert Baden-Powell (1857–1941)

Jeal, Tim. *The Boy-Man: The Life of Lord Baden-Powell*. New York: Morrow, 1990.

Reynolds, Ernest Edwin. *Baden-Powell: A Biography of Lord Baden-Powell of Gilwell*. London: Oxford Univ. Press, 1943.

Clarissa (Clara) Harlowe Barton (1821–1912)

Barton, Clara. *The Story of the Red Cross: Glimpses of Field Work*. 1904. Reprint. New York: Airmont, 1968.

Covert, Jeannette. *The Story of Clara Barton of the Red Cross*. New York: J. Messner, 1941.

Fishwick, Marshall W. *Clara Barton*. Morristown, NJ: Silver Burdett, 1966.

Hamilton, Leni. *Clara Barton*. New York: Chelsea House, 1988.

Sloate, Susan. *Clara Barton: Founder of the American Red Cross*. New York: Fawcett, 1990.

Clifford Beers (1876–1943)

Beers, Clifford. *A Mind That Found Itself*. New York: Longman, Green, 1909.

Dain, Norman. *Clifford W. Beers: Advocate for the Insane*. Pittsburgh, PA: Univ. of Pittsburgh Press, 1980.

Mary McLeod Bethune (1875–1955)

Holt, Rackham. *Mary McLeod Bethune: A Biography*. New York: Doubleday, 1964.

Peare, Catherine O. *Mary McLeod Bethune*. New York: Vanguard, 1951.

Charles Booth (1840–1916)

Simey, T. S., and M.B. Simey. *Charles Booth: Social Scientist*. Westport, CT: Greenwood Press, 1980.

Rev. William Booth (1829–1912)

Collier, Richard. *The General Next to God: The Story of William Booth and the Salvation Army*. New York: Dutton, 1965.

Ervine, St. John. *God's Soldier: General William Booth*. New York: Macmillan, 1935.

Rev. Charles Loring Brace (1826–1890)

Brace, Charles Loring. *The Dangerous Classes of New York and Twenty Years among Them*. 1880. Reprint. Silverspring, MD: National Association of Social Workers, 1978.

St. Frances Cabrini (1850–1917)

Borden, Lucille Papin. *Francesca Cabrini*. New York: Macmillan, 1945.

Di Donato, Pietro. *Immigrant Saint: The Life of Mother Cabrini*. New York: St. Martin, 1991.

Dorothy Day (1897–1980)

Coles, Robert. *Dorothy Day: A Radical Devotion*. Redding, MA: Addison-Wesley, 1989.

Day, Dorothy. *The Long Loneliness: Autobiography of Dorothy Day.* San Francisco, CA: Harper, 1981.

Day, Dorothy. *Little by Little.* New York: Knopf, 1983.

Day, Dorothy. *Loaves and Fishes.* San Francisco, CA: Harper, 1983.

Miller, William D. *A Harsh and Dreadful Love: Dorothy Day and the Catholic Worker Movement.* New York: Liveright, 1973.

Miller, William D. *Dorothy Day: A Biography.* San Francisco, CA: Harper, 1982.

Dorothea Lynde Dix (1802–1887)

Malone, Mary. *Dorothea L. Dix: Hospital Founder.* Champaign, IL: Garrard, 1968.

Marshall, Helen E. *Dorothea Dix: Forgotten Samaritan.* Chapel Hill: Univ. of North Carolina Press, 1937.

Wilson, Dorothy Clarke. *Stranger and Traveler: The Story of Dorothea Dix, American Reformer.* Boston, MA: Little, Brown, 1975.

William Edward Burghardt Du Bois (1868–1963)

Broderick, Francis L. *W.E.B. Du Bois: Negro Leader in a Time of Crisis.* Stanford, CA: Stanford Univ. Press, 1959.

Du Bois, W.E.B. *The Autobiography of W. E. B. Du Bois.* Reprint. New York: International Publishers Co., 1968.

Hamilton, Virginia. *W. E. B. Du Bois: A Biography.* New York: Harper-Row, 1972.

Homer Folks (1867–1963)

Trattner, Walter I. *Homer Folks: Pioneer in Social Welfare.* New York: Columbia Univ. Press, 1968.

Harry Hopkins (1890–1946)

Adams, Henry Hitch. *Harry Hopkins: A Biography.* New York: Putnam, 1977.

Kurzman, Paul. *Harry Hopkins and the New Deal.* Fairlawn, NJ: Burdick, 1974.

McJimsey, George. *Harry Hopkins: Ally of the Poor and Defender of Democracy.* Cambridge, MA: Harvard Univ. Press, 1987.

Searle, Charles F. *Minister of Relief: Harry Hopkins and the Depression.* Syracuse, NY: Syracuse Univ. Press, 1963.

Florence Kelley (1859–1932)

Goldmark, Josephine. *Impatient Crusader: Florence Kelley's Life Story.* Champaign: Univ. of Illinois Press, 1953.

St. Elizabeth Ann Seton (1774–1821)

Dirvin, Joseph I. *Mrs. Seton: Foundress of the American Sisters of Charity.* New York: Farrar, Straus and Giroux, 1975.

Feeny, Leonard. *Mother Seton: Saint Elizabeth of New York.* Cambridge, MA: Ravengate Press, 1991.

Power-Waters, Alma. *Mother Seton: First American-Born Saint.* New York: Pocket Books, 1976.

Mary Simkhovitch (1867–1951)

Simkhovitch, Mary K. *The City Worker's World in America.* 1917. Reprint. New Salem, NH: Ayer, 1971.

Simkhovitch, Mary K. *Neighborhood: My Story of Greenwich House.* New York: Norton, 1938. Reprint. New Salem, NH: Ayer, n.d.

Simkhovitch, Mary K. *Twenty Five Years at Greenwich House: 1902–1927.* New York: Greenwich House.

Graham Taylor (1851–1938)

Taylor, Graham R. *Chicago Commons Through Forty Years.* Chicago, IL: Univ. of Chicago Press, 1936.

Wade, Louise C. *Graham Taylor: Pioneer for Social Justice.* Chicago, IL: Univ. of Chicago Press, 1964.

Sojourner Truth (1797–1883)

Bernard, Jacqueline. *Journey Toward Freedom: The Story of Sojourner Truth.* New York: Norton, 1967. Reprint. New York: Feminist Press, 1990.

Fauset, Arthur H. *Sojourner Truth: God's Faithful Pilgrim.* 1938. Reprint. Chesapeake, VA: ECA Assoc., n.d.

Washington, Margaret. *The Narrative of Sojourner Truth.* New York: Vintage Books, 1993.

Harriet Tubman (1820–1913)

Bradford, Sarah H. *Harriet Tubman: The Moses of Her People.* Magnolia, MA: Peter Smith, n.d.

Petry, Ann. *Harriet Tubman: Conductor on the Underground Railroad.* New York: Crowell, 1955.

Sterling, Dorothy. *Freedom Train: The Story of Harriet Tubman.* Mahwah, NJ: Troll Associates, 1985.

Lilian Wald (1867–1940)

Dufus, Robert. *Lilian Wald: Neighbor and Crusader.* New York: Macmillan, 1938.

Wald, Lilian. *The House on Henry Street.* New York: Holt, 1915. Reprint. New Brunswick, NJ: Transaction, 1990.

Wald, Lilian. *Windows on Henry Street.* Boston, MA: Little, Brown, 1934.

George Williams (1821–1905)

Hodder-Williams, J. E. *The Life of Sir George Williams: Founder of The Young Men's Christian Association.* New York: Association Press, 1915.

ADDITIONAL READING

Bach, George, and Laura Torbet. *A Time for Caring.* New York: Delacourte, 1982.

La Pierre, Dominique. *The City of Joy.* Garden City, NY: Doubleday, 1985.

Luks, Allen, and Peggy Payne. *The Healing Power of Doing Good.* New York: Fawcett, 1992.

Meltzer, Milton. *Who Cares? Millions Do: A Book about Altruism.* New York: Walker, 1994.

Oliner, Samuel P., and Pearl M. *The Altruistic Personality: Rescuers of the Jews in Nazi Europe.* New York: Free Press, 1988.

Schon, Donald. *The Reflective Practitioner: How Professionals Think in Action.* New York: Basic Books, 1985.

Zimmerman, Richard. *What Can I Do to Make a Difference? A Positive Action Source Book.* New York: Plume, 1991.

APPENDIX

How to Get Involved

There are numerous organizations and agencies in which you can volunteer to obtain experience in macro social work. There is no substitute for experience. Before you start your social work internship you should have some kind of social work experience. Call a social agency in your local community or one of the volunteer agencies listed here.

Chapter 1—Introduction to Macro Social Work

Action
The Federal Domestic Volunteer Agency
1100 Vermont Ave. NW
Washington, DC 20525
202–634–9108

Action programs include the Foster Grandparent Program (FGP), the Retired Senior Volunteer Program (RSVP), the Senior Companion Program (SCP), Volunteers in Service to America (VISTA), AmeriCorps, the Student Community Service Program, and the ACTION Drug Alliance.

Campus Outreach Opportunity League (COOL)
386 McNeal Hall
University of Minnesota
St. Paul, MN 55108
612–624–3018

Community Volunteer Services Commission of
    B'nai B'rith International (CVS)
1640 Rhode Island Ave. NW
Washington, DC 20036
202–857–6582

Four-One-One
7304 Beverly St.
Annandale, VA 22003
703–354–6270

Goodwill Industries Volunteer Services
9200 Wisconsin Ave.
Bethesda, MD 20814
301–530–6500
(or call your local Goodwill chapter)

Holiday Project
2029 Vista Lane
Petaluma, CA 94594
707–763–5621

National Assembly of National Voluntary Health
    and Social Welfare Organizations
1319 F St. NW
Suite 601
Washington, DC 20004
202–347–2080

Next Door Foundation
3046 W. Wisconsin Ave.
Milwaukee, WI 53208
414–931–7708

Partners in Friendship
508 N. 1st St.
Sarell, MN 56377
612–252–5857

Peace Corps
P-301
Washington, DC 20526
800–424–8580

Points of Light Foundation
1737 H St. NW
Washington, DC 20006
202–223–9186

SCI-International Voluntary Service
Route 2, Box 506
Crozet, VA 22932
804–823–1826

United Way
Voluntary Action Center
402 Ordean Building
Duluth, MN 55802
218–726–4776

Volunteer—The National Center
1111 North 19th St.
Suite 500
Arlington, VA 22209
703–276–0542

Volunteers in Asia
Box 4543
Stanford, CA 94309
415–723–3228

Volunteers in Service to America (VISTA)
1100 Vermont Ave. NW
Suite 8100
Washington, DC 20525
202–606–4845

Volunteers of America, Inc. (VOA)
3813 North Causeway Blvd.
Metairie, LA 70002
504–837–2652

Volunteers Under Thirty
P.O. Box 1987
Denver, CO 80201
303–277–5968

Winant and Clayton Volunteers
109 E. 50th St.
New York, NY 10022
212–751–1616

Youth Service America
810 18th St. NW
Suite 705
Washington, DC 20006
202–783–8855

Chapter 2—Social Problems: The Challenge of Being a Macro Social Worker

The following represents only a small number of the social work and social welfare organizations in the United States dedicated to eradicating social problems.

Child Welfare
American Humane Association
63 Inverness Drive East
Inglewood, CO 80112
303–792–9900

Big Brothers/Big Sisters of America
230 N. 13th St.
Philadelphia, PA 19107
215–567–7000

Child Welfare League of America
440 1st St. NW
Suite 310
Washington, DC 20001
202–638–2952

Children, Inc.
P.O. Box 5382
Richmond, VA 23220
804–359–4562

Children's Aid Society
150 E. 45th St.
New York, NY 10017

Children's Defense Fund
25 E. 45th St. NW
Washington, DC 20001
202–628–8787

Christian Children's Fund
Box 26511
Richmond, VA 23261
804–644–4654

Father Flanagan's Boys Home
14100 Crawford St.
Boys Town, NE 68010
402–498–1111

Save the Children Federation
50 Wilton Rd.
Westport, CT 06880
203–221–4000

Group Work
Boy Scouts of America
1325 Walnut Hill Lane
P.O. Box 152079
Irving, TX 75015
214–580–2000

Boys and Girls Club of America
12330 W. Peachtree St.
Atlanta, GA 30309
404–815–5700

Camp Fire, Inc.
4601 Madison Ave.
Kansas City, MO 64112-1278
816–756–1950

Community Youth Group Gang Services
144 S. Fetterly Ave.
Los Angeles, CA 90022
213–232–7685

Girl Scouts of the USA
830 3rd Ave.
New York, NY 10022
212–940–7500

YMCA-USA
101 N. Wacker Drive
Chicago, IL 60606
312–977–0031

YWCA of the USA
726 Broadway
New York, NY 10003
212–614–2700

Poverty
Catholic Charities
1731 King St.
Suite 2200
Alexandria, VA 22314
703–549–1390

Jewish Welfare Board
15 E. 25th St., 14th Fl.
New York, NY 10010
212–532–4949

Salvation Army National Headquarters
799 Bloomfield Ave.
Verona, NJ 07044
201–239–0606

The Elderly
National Association for Hispanic Elderly
2727 W. 6th St.
Suite 270
Los Angeles, CA 90057
213–487–1922

National Association of Area Agencies on Aging
    (NAAAA)
1112 16th St. NW
Suite 1000
Washington, DC 20036
202–296–8130

Family Services
Jewish Board of Family and Children's Services
120 W. 57th St.
New York, NY 10019
212–582–9100

Family Service America
1700 W. Lake Park Dr.
Milwaukee, WI 53224
800–221–2681

Hunger
Food for the Hungry
7729 E. Greenway Rd.
Scottsdale, AZ 85260
800–2HUNGER

Heifer Project International
P.O. Box 808
Little Rock, AR 72202
501–376–6836

The Hunger Project
Global Office
One Madison Ave.
New York, NY 10010
212–532–4255

Interfaith Hunger Appeal (IHA)
470 Park Ave. South
New York, NY 10016
212–689–8460

Love Is Feeding Everyone (LIFE)
310 N. Fairfax Ave., 2nd Fl.
Los Angeles, CA 90036
213–936–0895

Meals for Millions
1644 Da Vinci Court
P.O. Box 2000
Davis, CA 95617

Share Our Strength (SOS)
733 15th St. NW
Suite 700
Washington, DC 20005
800–222–1767

Homelessness
Coalition for the Homeless
500 8th Ave.
Room 910
New York, NY 10018
212–695–8700

Habitat for Humanity
Habitat and Church Streets
Americus, GA 31709-3498
912–924–6935

The National Coalition for the Homeless
1621 Connecticut Ave. NW
Suite 400
Washington, DC 20009
202–265–2371

Other
National Organization of Travelers Aid Societies
512 C St. NE
Washington, DC 20002
202–659–9468

Chapter 6—Becoming a Macro Social Work Researcher

A number of organizations exist whose goals are to further research on social problems. You can contact one of these organizations to get more information about the specific problems they investigate, become involved in the social issues with which they are concerned, or learn about becoming a social work researcher.

National Association of American Community
        Organizations
18900 Schoolcraft
Detroit, MI 48223

Regional Institute of Social Welfare Research
P.O. Box 152
Athens, GA 30603

Social Legislation Information Service
440 1st St. NW
Suite 310
Washington, DC 20001
202–638–2952

Society for the Study of Social Problems
906 McClung Tower
University of Tennessee
Department of Sociology
Knoxville, TN 37996-0490
615–974–3620

U.S. Association for the Club of Rome
1359 SW 22nd Terrace, 2nd Fl.
Miami, FL 33145
305–858–0167

Welfare Research, Inc.
112 State St.
Albany, NY 12207
518–432–2563

Chapter 7—Becoming a Community Developer

Social workers should get involved in strengthening and improving communities. Listed below are organizations devoted to community development efforts in the United States as well as internationally.

Domestic Community Development

Breakthrough Foundation
1952 Lombard St.
San Francisco, CA 94123
415–673–0171

Chums, Inc.
9815 S. Parnell
Chicago, IL 60628

Federation of Egalitarian Communities
c/o East Wind Community, Inc.
Route 3, Box 6B2
Techumseh, MO 65760
417–679–4682

Institute for Local Self-Reliance
2425 18th St. NW
Washington, DC 20009
202–232–4108

National Association for Community Leadership
200 S. Meridian St.
Suite 340
Indianapolis, IN 46225
317–637–7408

National Association of Neighborhoods
1651 Fuller NW
Washington, DC 20009
202–332–7766

National Center for Urban Ethnic Affairs
P.O. Box 20, Cardinal Station
Washington, DC 20064
202–319–5129

National Community Action Foundation
2100 M St. NW
Suite 604
Washington, DC 20037
202–775–0223

National People's Action
810 N. Milwaukee Ave.
Chicago, IL 60622
312–243–3038

National Training and Information Center
810 Milwaukee Ave.
Chicago, IL 60622
312–243–3035

International Community Development

Afghanistan Relief Committee
667 Madison Ave., 18th Fl.
New York, NY 19921
212–355–2931

Alliance for Communities in Action
P.O. Box 30154
Bethesda, MD 20824
301–229–7707

AmeriCares
161 Cherry St.
New Canaan, CT 06840
203–966–5195

ASHOKA: Innovators for the Public
1700 N. More St.
Suite 1920
Arlington, VA 22209
703–527–8300

CARE
Worldwide Headquarters
660 1st Ave.
New York, NY 10016
212–686–3110

Counterpart Foundation
910 17th St.
Suite 328
Washington, DC 20006
202–296–9676

Direct Relief International
P.O. Box 30820
Santa Barbara, CA 93130
805–687–3694

Grassroots International
48 Grove St., #103
Someville, MA 02144
617–628–1664

International Rescue Committee
386 Park Ave. South
New York, NY 10016
212–679–0010

Oxfam America
115 Broadway
Boston, MA 02116
617–482–1211

Overseas Development Network (ODN)
2940 16th St., #110
San Francisco, CA 94103
415–431–4204

Peace Corps
P-301
Washington, DC 20526
800–424–8580

United Nations Disaster Relief Fund
Secretariat Building, Room 2395
1 United Nations Plaza
New York, NY 10037

United Nations International Children's Emergency
    Fund (UNICEF)
3 United Nations Plaza
New York, NY 10017
212–326–7000

*Religious Community Development and
Relief Organizations*
American Friends Service Committee
1501 Cherry St.
Philadelphia, PA 19102
215–241–7000

American Jewish World Service
15 W. 26th St., 9th Fl.
New York, NY 10010
212–683–1161

Church World Service
775 Riverside Drive
New York, NY 10015
212–870–2061

Heifer Project International
P.O. Box 808
Little Rock, AR 72202
501–376–6836

Lutheran World Relief
360 Park Ave.
New York, NY 10010
212–532–6350

Mennonite Central Committee
P.O. Box 500
Akron, PA 17501
717–859–1151

Presiding Bishop's Fund for World Relief
    (PBFWR)
815 2nd Ave.
New York, NY 10017
212–867–8400

World Vision
P.O. Box 5002
Monrovia, CA 91016-9918

Chapter 8—Becoming a Social Activist

Getting involved in social action means bringing about a more just society. There are many organizations today that are dedicated to bringing about justice and an end to oppression.

Social Action Organizations

Association of Community Organizations for
  Reform Now (ACORN)
1024 Elysian Fields Ave.
New Orleans, LA 70117
504–943–9944

Interreligious Foundation for Community
  Organization
402 W. 145th St., 3rd Fl.
New York, NY 10031
212–926–5757

National Association for the Southern Poor (NASP)
712A 3rd St. SW
Washington, DC 20024-3104
202–554–3265

National Office of Jesuit Social Ministries
  (NOJSM)
1424 16th St. NW
Suite 300
Washington, DC 20036
202–462–7008

Operation PUSH
930 E. 50th St.
Chicago, IL 60615
312–373–3366

Training and Consultation in Social Change

Center for Organizational and Community
  Development
University of Massachusetts
School of Education
377 Hills St.
Amherst, MA 01003
413–545–2038

Institute for Social Justice (ISJ)
1024 Elysian Fields Ave.
New Orleans, LA 70117
504–943–5954

Midwest Academy (MA)
225 Ohio St.
Suite 250
Chicago, IL 60610
312–645–6010

Organize Training Center (OTC)
422-A Vicksburg
San Francisco, CA 94114
415–821–6180

*Human Rights and Social Justice
Organizations*

American Civil Liberties Union
132 W. 43rd St.
New York, NY 10036
212–944–9800

Amnesty International, USA
322 8th Ave.
New York, NY 10001
212–807–8400

Anti-Defamation League of B'nai B'rith
823 United Nations Plaza
New York, NY 10017
212–490–2525

Center for Third World Organizing
3861 M. L. King, Jr. Way
Oakland, CA 94609
415–654–9601

Clergy and Laity Concerned
198 Broadway
New York, NY 10038
212–964–6730

Commission for Racial Justice
700 Prospect Ave., 7th Fl.
Cleveland, OH 44115
216–736–2100

Congress of Racial Equality (CORE)
1457 Flatbush Ave.
Brooklyn, NY 11210
718–434–3580

Disability Rights Center
2500 Q St. NW
Suite 121
Washington, DC 20007
202–337–4119

Equal Rights Advocates
1370 Mission St., 3rd Fl.
San Francisco, CA 94103
415–621–0505

Gay and Lesbian Alliance Against Defamation
(GLAAD)
99 Hudson St., 14th Fl.
New York, NY 10003
212–966–1700

Gay Rights Advocates
540 Castro St.
San Francisco, CA 94114
415–863–3622

Gray Panthers Project Fund
311 S. Juniper St.
Suite 601
Philadelphia, PA 19107
215–545–6555

Handgun Control, Inc.
1225 I St. NW
Suite 1100
Washington, DC 20005
202–898–0792

Human Rights Watch
1522 K St. NW
Suite 910
Washington, DC 20005
202–371–6592

Japanese American Citizens League
1762 Sutter St.
San Francisco, CA 94115
415–921–5225

Leadership Conference on Civil Rights
2027 Massachusetts Ave. NW
Washington, DC 20036
202–667–1780

The League of Women Voters USA
1730 M St. NW
Washington, DC 20036
202–429–1965

League of United Latin American Citizens
(LULAC)
900 E. Karen St.
Suite C215
Las Vegas, NV 89109
702–737–1240

Mexican American Legal Defense and Education
Fund (MALDEF)
1101 2nd St., 2nd Fl.
San Francisco, CA 94105
415–543–5598

National Association for the Advancement of
Colored People (NAACP)
4805 Mt. Hope Drive
Baltimore, MD 21215
301–358–8900

National Council of La Raza
810 First St. NE, 3rd Fl.
Washington, DC 20002
202–289–1380

National Council of Negro Women, Inc. (NCNW)
1211 Connecticut Ave, NW
Suite 702
Washington, DC 20036
202–659–0006

National Organization for Women (NOW)
1000 16th St. NW
Washington, DC 20036
202–223–3915

National Right to Life Committee
419 7th Ave. NW
Suite 500
Washington, DC 20004
202–626–8800

National Urban League
500 E. 62nd St.
New York, NY 10021
212–310–9000

Native American Rights Fund
1506 Broadway
Boulder, CO 80302
303–447–8760

Planned Parenthood Federation
810 7th Ave.
New York, NY 10019
212–785–3351

Simon Wiesenthal Center
9760 W. Pico Blvd.
Los Angeles, CA 90035
213–553–5486

Southern Christian Leadership Conference (SCLC)
334 Auburn Ave. NE
Atlanta, GA 30303
404–522–1420

Women's Defense Fund
2000 P St. NW
Washington, DC 20036
202–887–0364

Hunger
End Hunger Network
222 N. Beverly Drive
Beverly Hills, CA 90210
213–273–3179

End World Hunger
1460 W. McNab Road
Fort Lauderdale, FL 33309
303–977–9700

National Student Campaign Against Hunger and
    Homelessness (NSCAHH)
29 Temple Place
Boston, MA 02111
617–292–4823

Peace
Bikes Not Bombs
P.O. Box 5638
Brightwood Station
Washington, DC 20011
202–589–1810

Concerned Educators Allied for a Safe
    Environment (CEASE)
P.O. Box 44-456
Somerville, MA 02144
617–628–9030

Grandmothers for Peace
909 12th St.
Suite 118
Sacramento, CA 09814
916–444–5080

Chapter 10—Becoming a Social Planner: Making the Good Society

Social planning is an important part of macro social work. Listed below are some of the planning organizations that you can contact for more information about the field of planning.

American Planning Association
1776 Massachusetts Ave. NW
Suite 400
Washington, DC 20036
202–872–0611

American Society of Consulting Planners
1776 Massachusetts Ave. NW
Suite 400
Washington, DC 20036
202–872–1498

National Association of Area Agencies on Aging
    (NAAAA)
1112 16th St. NW
Suite 1000
Washington, DC 20036
202–296–8130

National Planning Association
1424 16th St. NW
Suite 700
Washington, DC 20036
202–265–7685

United Way
701 N. Fairfax St.
Alexandria, VA 22314-2045
703–836–7100

Chapter 11—The Social Worker as Program Developer

The following represents some of the social work programs mentioned in chapter 11 as well as other well-known and long-established social work programs. There are thousands more active social agencies across the United States. If you are interested in beginning a program, social workers in these organizations can give you valuable information about what they do and how their organizations work, and put you in touch with others who can help you get started.

American Red Cross
National Headquarters
Washington, DC 20006
202–737–8300

Big Brothers/Big Sisters of America
230 N. 13th St.
Philadelphia, PA 19107
215–567–7000

Boys and Girls Clubs of America
12330 W. Peachtree St. NW
Atlanta, GA 30309
404–815–5700

Boy Scouts of America
1325 Walnut Hill Lane
P.O. Box 152079
Irving, TX 75015
214–580–2000

Camp Fire, Inc.
4601 Madison Ave.
Kansas City, MO 64112-1278
816–756–1950

Catholic Charities
1731 King St.
Suite 2200
Alexandria, VA 22314
703–549–1390

Children's Aid Society
150 E. 45th St.
New York, NY 10017

Family Service America (formerly Family Service Association)
1700 W. Lake Park Drive
Milwaukee, WI 53224
800–221–2681

Girl Scouts of the USA
830 3rd Ave.
New York, NY 10022
212–940–7400

Legal Aid Society
15 Park Row, 22nd Fl.
New York, NY 10038
212–577–3340

National Organization of Travelers Aid Societies
512 C St. NE
Washington, DC 20002
202–659–9468

Salvation Army National Headquarters
616 Slates Lane
P.O. Box 269
Alexandria, VA 22313
703–684–5500

YMCA-USA
101 N. Wacker Drive
Chicago, IL 60606
312–977–0031

YWCA of the USA
726 Broadway
New York, NY 10003
212–614–2700

Chapter 12—The Macro Social Worker as Administrator

Listed below are organizations that social work administrators have formed or associate with to better develop the field of administration. To learn more about what social work administrators are doing in your area, contact one of these organizations or join the American Society for Public Administration (ASPA).

American Society for Public Administration
(ASPA)
1120 G St. NW
Suite 700
Washington, DC 20005
202–393–7878

American Society for Public Administration
Section for Women in Public Administration
1120 G St. NW
Suite 700
Washington, DC 20005
202–393–7878

Conference of Minority Public Administrators
1120 G St. NW
Suite 700
Washington, DC 20005
202–393–7878

Institute of Public Administration
Luther Halsey Gulick Building
55 W. 44th St.
New York, NY 10036
212–730–5480

National Council of Local Public Welfare
Administrators
810 1st St. NE
Suite 500
Washington, DC 20002
202–682–0100

National Council of State Human Service
Administrators
810 1st St. NE
Suite 500
Washington, DC 20002
202–682–0100

National Forum for Black Public Administrators
777 N. Capitol St. NE
Suite 807
Washington, DC 20002
202–408–9300

National Network for Social Work Managers
6501 Federal Highway
Suite 5
Boca Raton, FL 33487
407–997–7576

Chapter 13—Becoming an Organization Developer

Organization development is a growing field in macro social work. Listed below are some organizations that you can contact if you want more information about this field.

Black Affairs Center for Training and
Organizational Development (BACTOD)
10918 Jarboe Court
Silver Spring, MD 20901
301–681–9827

Center for Human Services (CHS)
7200 Wisconsin Ave.
Suite 600
Bethesda, MD 20814
301–654–8338

Institute for Dispute Resolution (formerly Center
for Public Resources)
366 Madison Ave., 14th Fl.
New York, NY 10017–3122
212–949–6490

Center for Organizational and Community
    Development (COCD)
University of Massachusetts
School of Education
377 Hills St.
Amherst, MA 01003
413–545–2038

Independent Community Consultants (ICC)
P.O. Box 141
Hampton, AR 71744
501–798–4510

National Staff Development and Training
    Association (NSDTA)
810 1st St. NE
Suite 500
Washington, DC 20002–4267
202–682–0100

Chapter 14—Social Work at the Societal Level: Social Policy and Politics

Only a few of the many social policy advocacy organizations in the United States are listed here. If
there is a policy issue that interests you, contact one
of these organizations. They will tell you how you
can become active in working for social change, provide you with information, and tell you what efforts
are being made in your local community. Your local
NASW chapter also can help you discover areas in
which you can make a difference.

The Elderly
American Association of Retired Persons (AARP)
1909 K St. NW
Washington, DC 20049

Gray Panthers
1424 16th St. NW
Suite 602
Washington, DC 20036

National Committee to Preserve Social Security
    and Medicare
2000 K St. NW
Suite 800
Washington, DC 20006
202–822–9459

National Council on the Aging, Inc.
600 Maryland Ave., SW
West Wing 100
Washington, DC 20024
202–479–1200

Homelessness
National Alliance to End Homelessness
1518 K St. NW
Suite 206
Washington, DC 20005
202–638–1526

National Law Center on Homelessness and Poverty
918 F St. NW
Suite 1006
Washington, DC 20005
202–662–1530

National Low Income Housing Coalition
1012 14th St. NW Suite 1006
Washington, DC 20005
202–662–1530

National Resource Center on Homelessness
    and Mental Illness Policy Research
    Associates, Inc.
262 Delaware Ave.
Delmar, NY 12054
800–444–7415

Hunger
Bread for the World
802 Rhode World Island Ave. NE
Washington, DC 20018
202–269–0200

Center on Budget and Policy Priorities
777 N. Capitol St. NE
Washington, DC 20002
202–408–1080

Food First—The Institute for Food and
  Development Policy
145 9th St.
San Francisco, CA 94103
415–864–8555

Food Research and Action Center
1875 Connecticut Ave. NW
Suite 540
Washington, DC 20009
202–986–2200

Results
245 2nd St. NE
Washington, DC 20002
202–543–9340

Child Welfare
Child Welfare League of America (CSLA)
440 1st St. NW
Suite 310
Washington, DC 20001
202–638–2952

Children's Defense Fund
Box 26511
Richmond, VA 23261
804–644–4654

National Committee for the Prevention of Child
  Abuse
332 S. Michigan Ave.
Chicago, IL 60604
312–663–3520

Gun Control
Center to Prevent Handgun Violence
1225 I St. NW
Suite 1100
Washington, DC 20005
202–289–7319

Educational Fund to End Handgun Violence
110 Maryland Ave. NE
Box 72
Washington, DC 20002
202–544–7227

Handgun Control, Inc.
1225 I St. NW
Suite 1100
Washington, DC 20005
202–898–0792

National Coalition to Ban Handguns
100 Maryland Ave. NE
Washington, DC 20002
202–544–7190

Peace
The Arms Control Association
11 Dupont Circle NW
Washington, DC 20036
202–797–4526

Council for a Livable World
20 Park Plaza
Boston, MA 02116
617–542–2282

Peace Action
1819 H St. NW
Suite 640
Washington, DC 20006-3603
202–862–9740

World Policy Institute
777 United Nations Plaza, 5th Fl.
New York, NY 10017
212–490–0010

World Watch Institute
1776 Massachusetts Ave. NW
Washington, DC 20036
202–638–6300

The Environment
Center for Environmental Education (CEE)
1725 DeSales St. NW
Suite 500
Washington, DC 20036
202–429–5609

Conservation International
1015 18th St. NW 10th Fl.
Washington, DC 20036
202–429–5660

Environmental Defense Fund
257 Park Ave. South
New York, NY 10010
212–505–2100

Environmental Research Foundation
P.O. Box 3461
Princeton, NJ 08543

Friends of the Earth
218 D St. SE
Washington, DC 20003
202–544–2600

Sierra Club Legal Defense Fund
730 Polk St.
San Francisco, CA 94115
415–567–6100

Wilderness Society
900 17th St. NW
Washington, DC 20006
202–833–2300

Zero Population Growth
1400 16th St. NW
Suite 320
Washington, DC 20036
202–332–2200

Others

Mothers Against Drunk Driving (MADD)
511 East John Carpenter Freeway
Suite 700
Irvin, TX 75062

Chapter 15—The Future of Macro Social Work

You can become involved with professional social workers and learn more about what social work is doing to promote a better society. Several social work organizations are listed below. Join one today. You will meet macro social workers and find out more about this important arena of social work. By attending conferences, you can get on the cutting edge of the profession and even help move it into the future.

American Public Welfare Association
810 1st St. NE
Suite 500
Washington, DC 20002-4267
202–682–0100

National Association of Puerto Rican Hispanic
    Social Workers
P.O. Box 651
Brentwood, NY 11717
516–864–1536

National Association of Social Workers (NASW)
750 1st St. NE
Suite 700
Washington, DC 20002-2441
202–408–8600
(or contact your local chapter)

National Network for Social Work Managers
6501 Federal Highway
Suite 5
Boca Raton, FL 33487
407–997–7576

North American Association of Christians in Social
    Work (NACSW)
Box 7090
St. Davids, PA 19087-7090
610–687–5777

NOTES

Preface

1. Anne Wilson Schaef, *When Society Becomes an Addict* (San Francisco: Harper and Row, 1987), p. 3.

Chapter 1: Introduction to Macro Social Work

1. Adapted from Alex Pulaski, "A difficult death in a strange land," *The Fresno Bee,* Feb. 16, 1993, pp. A1 and A18.
2. Ibid.
3. Robert Presthus, *The Organizational Society,* rev. ed. (New York: St. Martin's Press, 1988), and Hendrik M. Ruitenbeek, ed., *The Dilemma of Organizational Society* (New York: Dutton, 1963).
4. Isaiah 1:17, James 1:27, Lev. 19:33, Deut. 10:19. King James Version of the Bible.
5. Harry Specht and Mark Courtney, *Unfaithful Angels: How Social Work Has Abandoned Its Mission* (New York: Free Press, 1994).

Part I: Solving Social Problems and Making Social Change

1. Harry Specht and Mark E. Courtney, *Unfaithful Angels: How Social Work Has Abandoned Its Mission* (New York: Free Press, 1994), p. 27.
2. Charles Zastrow, *The Practice of Social Work,* 3d ed. (Homewood, IL: Dorsey Press, 1989), p. 217.
3. Ibid., pp. 13-15.
4. Augustus Y. Napier with Carl A. Whitaker, *The Family Crucible: One Family's Therapy—an Experience That Illuminates All Our Lives* (Toronto: Bantam Books, 1978), p. 47.
5. Zastrow, *Practice,* p. 216.
6. Allen Pincus and Anne Minahan, *Social Work Practice: Model and Method* (Itasca, IL: Peacock, 1973), p. 54.
7. Ibid., p. 56.
8. Ibid., p. 59.
9. Ibid., p. 61.
10. Zastrow, *Practice,* p. 223.
11. Napier, *Family Crucible,* pp. 44-58.
12. Gibson Winter, *Elements for a Social Ethic: The Role of Social Science in Public Policy* (New York: Macmillan, 1966), p. 9.

13. Herbert Simon, *Administrative Behavior,* 3d ed. (New York: Free Press, 1976), pp. 101, 102.
14. Charles Perrow, *Complex Organizations: A Critical Essay* (Glenview, IL: Scott, Foresman, 1979), p. 6.
15. For a readable and insightful perspective on existentialist philosophy, see William Barrett, *Irrational Man: A Study in Existential Philosophy* (Garden City, NY: Doubleday Anchor, 1962).
16. Winter, *Elements,* p. 18.
17. George Herbert Mead, *Man, Self, and Society* (Chicago, IL: University of Chicago Press, 1934).
18. Morton Deutsch and Robert M. Krauss, *Theories in Social Psychology* (New York: Basic Books, 1965), pp. 183.
19. Winter, *Elements,* p. 20.
20. Ibid., p. 18.
21. Michael M. Harmon, *Action Theory for Public Administration* (New York: Longman, 1981), pp. 24-41, and Michael Harmon, "Toward an Active Social Theory," in Carl J. Bellone, ed., *Organization Theory and the New Public Administration* (Boston, MA: Allyn and Bacon, 1980), pp. 186-91.
22. Eric Voegelin, *The New Science of Politics* (Chicago, IL: University of Chicago Press, 1952), p. 27.
23. Harmon. "Toward an Active Social Theory," p. 186.
24. Winter, *Elements,* p. 97.
25. Ibid., p. 21.
26. Felix G. Rivera and John L. Erlich, *Community Organizing in a Diverse Society* (Boston, MA: Allyn and Bacon, 1992), p. 11.
27. Winter, *Elements,* p. 20.
28. Michael Heus and Allen Pincus, *The Creative Generalist: A Guide to Social Work Practice* (Barneveld, WI: Micamar, 1986), pp. 47-65, 108-26, 271.
29. Harmon, *Action Theory,* pp. 4, 5.
30. Ibid., p. 6.

Chapter 2: Social Problems: The Challenge of Being a Macro Social Worker

1. Si Kahn, *How People Get Power: Organizing Oppressed Communities for Action* (New York: McGraw-Hill,), p. 124.
2. Alan Nevins and Henry Steele Commager, *A Pocket History of the United States,* 5th ed. (New York: Washington Square Press, 1966), p. 5.
3. Ibid., p. 6.

4. Beulah Compton, *Introduction to Social Welfare and Social Work* (Homewood, IL: Dorsey Press, 1980), p. 178.

5. Nevins and Commager, *Pocket History*, p. 180.

6. Ibid.

7. Ibid.

8. Ibid., p. 181.

9. Compton, *Introduction to Social Welfare*, p. 221.

10. Ibid., p. 227.

11. Clinton Rossiter, *The First American Revolution* (New York: Harcourt, Brace and World, 1956), p. 148.

12. Ibid.

13. Ibid., p. 149.

14. Ronald G. Walters, *American Reformers 1815-1860* (New York: Hill and Wang, 1978), p. 78.

15. Ibid., p. 80.

16. Ibid.

17. Ibid., p. 85.

18. Ibid., p. 78.

19. Charles D. Garvin and Fred M. Cox, "A History of Community Organizing since the Civil War with Special Reference to Oppressed Communities," in Cox et al., *Strategies of Community Organization* (Itasca, IL: F.E. Peacock, 1987, p. 30.

20. Delmatier, Royce; McIntosh, Clarence; and Waters, Earl, G., *The Rumble of California Politics: 1848-1970* (New York: Wiley, 1970), p. 59.

21. Ibid., p. 33.

22. Ibid., p. 59.

23. Garvin and Cox, *History*, p. 30.

24. Delmatier, et al., *Rumble of California Politics*, p. 71.

25. Ibid., p. 72.

26. Ibid., p. 87.

27. Garvin and Cox, *History*, p. 30.

28. Delmatier, et al., *Rumble of California Politics*, p. 184.

29. Ronald C. Frederico, *Social Welfare in Today's World* (New York: McGraw-Hill, 1990), p. 294.

30. H. Wayne Johnson, *The Social Services: An Introduction*, 3d ed. (Itasca, IL: F. E. Peacock, 1990), p. 24.

31. C. Wright Mills, *The Sociological Imagination* (London: Oxford University Press, 1959), p. 8.

32. Thomas J. Sullivan and Kenrick S. Thompson, *Introduction to Social Problems* (New York: Macmillan, 1988), p. 3.

33. Charles Zastrow, *Social Problems: Issues and Solutions* (Chicago, IL: Nelson-Hall, 1988), p. 6.

34. Robert K. Merton and Robert Nisbet, *Contemporary Social Problems*, 2nd ed. (New York: Harcourt, Brace, 1966), p. 799.

35. Richard L. Means, *The Ethical Imperative: The Crisis in American Values* (New York: Anchor Books, 1970), p. 8.

36. Ritchie P. Lowry, *Social Problems* (Lexington, MA: D. C. Heath, 1974), p. 93.

37. Ibid., p. 204.

38. Jerome G. Manus, *Analyzing Social Problems* (New York: Praeger, 1976), pp. 74-76.

39. Lowry, *Social Problems*, p. 205.

40. Alvin Toffler, *Future Shock* (New York: Random House, 1970).

41. Gibson Winter, *Elements for a Social Ethic* (New York: Macmillan, 1966), p. 15.

42. Henry S. Kariel, *Beyond Liberalism: Where Relations Grow* (New York: Harper & Row, 1978), p. 5.

43. Frank M. Coleman, *Hobbes and America: Exploring the Constitutional Foundations* (Toronto: University of Toronto Press, 1977), p. 3, 4; Kariel, *Beyond Liberalism*, p. 5.

44. See, for example, Frank M. Coleman, *Hobbes and America: Exploring the Constitutional Foundations* (Toronto: University of Toronto Press, 1977) for a discussion of the legacy of Thomas Hobbes, John Locke, and James Madison on American politics.

   The Federalist Papers by Alexander Hamilton, James Madison, and John Jay (New York: The New American Library, 1961) is a primary source of the philosophical underpinnings which informed the writing of the Constitution. Federalist 10, 39, and 51 are of special importance, all written by James Madison.

   Also of interest is Charles A. Beard's seminal *An Economic Interpretation of the Constitution of the United States* (New York: MacMillan, 1941).

45. Kariel, *Beyond Liberalism*, p. 5.

46. Coleman, *Hobbes*, pp. 55, 77, 121, 144, 145, and Robert N. Bellah, Richard Madsen, William M. Sullivan, Ann Swidler, and Steven M. Tipton, *Habits of the Heart: Individualism and Commitment in American Life* (New York: Harper & Row, 1985).

47. Coleman, *Hobbes*, p. 142.

48. Kariel, *Beyond Liberalism*, p. 6.

49. Lawrence Haworth, "The Good Life: Growth and Duty," in *Social Ethics: Issues in Ethics and Society*, Gibson Winter, ed. (New York: Harper & Row, 1968), p. 174.

50. Coleman, *Hobbes*, p. 17.

51. Ibid., p. 16.

52. Kariel, *Beyond Liberalism*, p. 11.

53. Frederico, *Social Welfare*, p. 297.

54. Jim Detjen and Susan Fitzgerald, "Gun-Related Violence Compared to a National Health Crisis," *Fresno Bee*, June 10, 1992, p. A6.

55. Michael Wolff, Peter Rutten, Albert F. Bayers III, and the World Rank Research Team, *Where We Stand: Can America Make It in the Global Race for Wealth, Health, and Happiness?* (New York: Bantam Books, 1992), p. 289.

56. James, Rowley, "Rapes, Assaults Spur Crime Rates," *Fresno Bee*, April 20, 1992, pp. A1 and A9.

57. Christi Parsons, "Domestic—Violence Sign Miss Medical Detection: Experts See Need for Patient Advocates," *Fresno Bee*, Aug. 26, 1990, p. B1.

58. Wolff, et al., *Where We Stand*, p. 294.

59. Ibid., p. 294.

60. Ibid.

61. Ibid.

62. Detjen and Fitzgerald, "Gun-related Violence," p. A6.

63. Ann C. Roark, "Times Tough on the Young, Study Finds," *Fresno Bee*, March 23, 1992, p. A1.

64. Ibid.

65. California Teachers Association, "Teacher Views," May 1991.

66. Walter I. Trattner, *From Poor Law to Welfare State: A History of Social Welfare in America* (New York: Free Press, 1989), p. 95.

67. Ibid., p. 87.
68. William Ryan, *Blaming the Victim* (New York: Pantheon Books, 1971).
69. Jerome G. Manus, *Analyzing Social Problems* (New York: Praeger, 1976), p. 16.
70. Dean Pierce, *Social Work and Society: An Introduction* (New York: Longman, 1989), p. 153.
71. Charles Perrow, *Complex Organization: A Critical Essay,* 2d ed. (Glenview, IL: Scott, Foresman, 1979), pp. 189-92.
72. Lowry, *Social Problems,* pp. 218-24.
73. Perrow, *Complex Organizations,* p. 190.
74. Victor A. Thompson, *Without Sympathy or Enthusiasm: The Problem of Administrative Compassion* (University: University of Alabama Press, 1975), pp. 90-94.
75. Charles Hampden-Turner, *From Poverty to Dignity* (Garden City, NY: Anchor Books, 1975), p. 106.
76. C. Wright Mills, *The Sociological Imagination* (New York: Oxford University Press, 1959), p. 8.
77. Eric Berne, *Transactional Analysis in Psychotherapy: A Systematic Individual and Social Psychiatry* (New York: Grove Press, 1967), pp. 104, 105.
78. Coleman, *Hobbes,* p. 21.
79. Felix G. Rivera and John L. Erlich, *Community Organizing in a Diverse Society* (Boston: Allyn and Bacon, 1992), p. 2.
80. Noam Chomsky, *Language and Responsibility* (New York: Pantheon Books, 1977), pp. 4, 5.
81. Fresno Bee, editorial, "Babies—The Future—At Risk," April 26, 1990, p. B4.
82. Marjie Lambert, "Protecting Our Children: The System Just Isn't Working," *The Fresno Bee,* June 13, 1993, p. A1.
83. Ibid.
84. U.S. Bureau of the Census, *Statistical Abstract of the United States: 1994,* 114th ed. (Washington, DC: U.S. Government Printing Office, 1994).
85. Doug Hoaglund, "Teenage Suicide: Tragic and Sometimes Preventable," *The Fresno Bee,* June 12, 1994, p. F5.
86. Donald L. Bartlett and James B. Steele, "Middle Class Is Squeezed as Rich Get Richer and Poor Poorer," *Fresno Bee,* Oct. 27, 1991, p. A8.
87. Stefan Fatsis, "Recession Aside, Majority of Rich Are Getting Richer," *Fresno Bee,* Oct. 21, 1991, pp. A1, A12.
88. Bartlett and Steele, "Middle Class," p. A8.

Chapter 3: Methods of Solving Social Problems

1. Thomas Hobbes, *Leviathan: or the Matter, Forme, and Power of a Commonwealth Ecclesiastical and Civil,* Frederick J. E. Woodbridge, ed. (New York: Scribner's, 1930), ch. V, pp. 174-75.
2. Ibid., ch. XIII, p. 252.
3. Ibid., ch. XIII, p. 253.
4. Ibid., Introduction, p. 136.
5. Thomas Hobbes, *Leviathan: or the Matter, Forme and Power of a Commonwealth Ecclesiastical and Civil,* Michael Oakeshott, ed. (New York: Collier Books, 1962), author's introduction, p. 19.
6. Ibid., p. 42.
7. Ibid., p. 41.
8. Ibid., ch. 22, p. 169.
9. Barry G. Sheckley, "Adult Experiential Learning: A Grasping and Transforming Process," mimeographed manuscript, undated, unpaged.
10. Ronald L. Simons and Stephen M. Aigner, *Practice Principles: A Problem Solving Approach to Social Work* (New York: Macmillan, 1985), pp. 7-10; Louise C. Johnson, *Social Work Practice: A Generalist Approach,* 2d ed. (Boston, MA: Allyn and Bacon, 1986), p. 17.
11. Simons and Aigner, *Practice Principles,* pp. 25-29.
12. Simons and Aigner, (ibid., p. 25) point out that "this approach has been given various labels by authors who have contributed to it: the problem-solving model (Compton and Gallaway, 1979), the planned change method (Pincus and Minahan, 1973), an objective framework (Klenk and Ryan, 1974), and a problem-focused model (Spitzer and Welsh, 1969). In addition to Simons and Aigner's review, it is called the generalist social work method by Johnson (1986), a problem-solving approach by Charles Zastrow (1989), the problem-solving process by Macht and Quam (1986, pp. 49-55), and has been reformulated into a task centered approach by Laura Epstein in 1988 and Hepworth and Larsen in 1990. Bloom calls this the "generic problem-solving approach" (1990, p. 105). Skidmore, Thackery, and Farley call it the "casework process" (1991, p. 62), DiNitto and McNeece call it the "generalist model" (1990, p. 63), and Grinnell (1988) and Smith (1988) apply it directly to social work research.
13. Ronald Lippitt, Jeanne Watson, and Bruce Westley, *The Dynamics of Planned Change* (New York: Harcourt, Brace and World, 1958), pp. 131-43; Alan Pincus and Anne Minahan, *Social Work Practice: Model and Method* (Itasca, IL: Peacock, 1973), pp. 90-91. Compare Charles Zastrow's Problem-Solving Approach:
   1. Identify as precisely as possible the problem or problems
   2. Generate possible alternative solutions
   3. Evaluate the alternative solutions
   4. Select a solution or solutions to be used and set goals
   5. Implement the solution(s)
   6. Follow up to evaluate how the solution(s) worked
   Charles Zastrow, *The Practice of Social Work,* 3d ed. (Chicago, IL: Dorsey, 1989), p. 16.
14. Simons and Aigner, *Practice Principles,* p. 26.
15. B.R. Compton and B. Gallaway, *Social Work Processes,* 2nd ed, (Homewood, IL: Dorsey, 1979), p. 232.
16. John Dewey, *How We Think,* rev. ed. (Lexington, MA: Heath, 1933).
17. Herbert Simon, *Administrative Behavior: A Study of Decision-Making Processes in Administrative Organization,* 3d ed. (New York: Free Press, 1945), pp. 80-81.
18. Graham T. Allison, *The Essence of Decision: Explaining the Cuban Missile Crisis* (Boston, MA: Little, Brown, 1971), pp. 10-36. Allison calls the model the "classical" or "rational actor" model. His description is succinct and noteworthy. Classic or rational decision making is based on an economic model of man who makes optimal choices in narrowly constrained, neatly defined situations.

   In these situations rationality refers to an essentially Hobbesian notion of consistent, value-maximizing *reckoning* or adaption within specified constraints. In economics, to choose rationally is to select the most efficient alternative, that is, the alternative that maximizes output for a given input or minimizes input for a given output. Rational consumers purchase the amount of goods, A, B, and C, etc., that maximizes their utility (by choosing a basket of goods on the highest possible indifference curve). Rational firms produce at a point that maximizes profits (by setting marginal costs equal to marginal revenue).

In modern statistical decision theory and game theory, the rational decision problem is reduced to a simple matter of selecting among a set of given alternatives, each of which has a given set of consequences; the agent selects the alternative whose consequences are preferred in terms of the agents utility function which ranks each set of consequences in order of preference. (P. 29)

Also see Edith Stokey and Richard Zeckhauser, *A Primer for Policy Analysis* (New York: Norton, 1978), pp. 3-44.

19. C. West Churchman, *The Systems Approach* (New York: Dell, 1968), pp. 146-76.
20. Allison, *Essence of Decision*, pp. 29, 30.
21. Michael M. Harmon, *Action Theory for Public Administration* (New York: Longman, 1981), p. 178.
22. Victor A. Thompson, *Without Sympathy or Enthusiasm: The Problem of Administrative Compassion* (University: The University of Alabama Press, 1975), p. 10.
23. Ronald Toseland and Robert Rivas, *An Introduction to Group Work Practice* (New York: Macmillan, 1984), p. 269.
24. Bobby R. Patton and Kim Giffin, *Problem Solving Group Interaction* (New York: Harper and Row, 1973), pp. 155-60.
25. Kurt Lewin, "Frontiers in Group Dynamics: Concept, Method and Reality in Social Science; Social Equilibria and Social Change," *Human Relations* 1 (1) (June 1947): 5-41.
26. The Action Model of social work is based on Max Weber's theories of social action and derived from the work of symbolic interaction school of sociology, particularly George Herbert Mead and Alfred Schutz. This model is in specific contrast to and not to be confused with the Action Theory of Talcott Parsons, a structural functionalist model that is aligned with a social systems perspective.
27. Harmon, *Action Theory*, p. 5.
28. Ibid., pp. 4, 5.
29. Ibid., p. 69.
30. Proverbs 29:18, King James Version of the Bible.
31. Otto Pollak, *Human Behavior and the Helping Professions* (New York: Spectrum, 1976), p. 10.
32. Earl Babbie, *Social Research for Consumers* (Belmont CA: Wadsworth, 1982), pp. 21-26.
33. Gibson Winter, *Elements for a Social Ethic: The Role of Social Science in Public Policy* (New York: Macmillan, 1966), p. 186.
34. Ibid.
35. Harmon, *Action Theory*, p. 126.
36. Ibid., p. 6.
37. Richard M. Grinnell, Jr., *Social Work Research and Evaluation*, 3d ed. (Itasca, IL: Peacock, 1988), pp. 11-13.

38. Harmon, *Action Theory*, p. 125.
39. Ibid., p. 126.
40. Thompson, *Without Sympathy or Enthusiasm*, p. 1.
41. Simon, *Administrative Behavior*, pp. 80-83.
42. Ibid., p. xxvii.
43. Ibid., p. xxviii.
44. Ibid., p. xxx.
45. Ibid., p. 82.
46. Ibid., p. 102.
47. Aaron Wildavsky, *The Politics of the Budgetary Process*, 2d ed., (Boston, MA: Little, Brown, 1974); William L. Morrow, *Public Administration: Politics and the Political System* (New York: Random House, 1975).
48. Robert Formaini, *The Myth of Scientific Public Policy* (New Brunswick, NJ: Transaction, 1990), p. 1.
49. Ibid., p. 5.
50. Ibid., p. 95.
51. Ibid., p. 96.
52. Simon, *Administrative Behavior*, pp. 80-83.
53. Wildavsky, *Politics*.
54. Morrow, *Public Administration*.
55. Formaini, *Myth*, p. 1.

Chapter 4: Leadership: The Hallmark of Macro Social Work

1. Daniel Levine, *Jane Addams and the Liberal Tradition* (Westport, CT: Greenwood Press, 1971), p. ix.
2. Ibid., p. xi.
3. Ibid., p. 42.
4. Ibid., p. 129.
5. Ibid., p. 179.
6. Ibid.
7. Ibid., p. xi.
8. Ibid., p. 181.
9. Ibid., p. x.
10. Hans Falck, *Social Work: The Membership Perspective* (New York: Springer, 1988), p. 161.
11. Elenore L. Brilliant, "Social Work Leadership: A Missing Ingredient?" *Social Work*, 31 (5) (Sept.-Oct., 1986): 326.
12. Burton Gummer, *The Politics of Social Administration: Managing Organizational Politics in Social Agencies* (Englewood Cliffs, NJ: Prentice-Hall, 1990), p. 122.
13. Chauncey Alexander, "Professional Social Workers and Political Responsibility," in Maryann Mahaffey and John W. Hanks, eds., *Practical Politics: Social Work and Political Responsibility* (Silverspring, MD: National Association of Social Workers, 1982), p. 15.
14. Gummer, *Politics of Social Administration*, p. 123.
15. Ibid.
16. Stephen P. Robbins, *Essentials of Organizational Behavior*, 3d ed. (Englewood Cliffs, NJ: Prentice-Hall, 1992), p. 136; Paul Hersey and Kenneth H. Blanchard, *Management of Organizational Behavior: Utilizing Human Resources*, 5th ed. (Englewood Cliffs, NJ: Prentice-Hall, 1988), pp. 88-90.
17. Eugene E. Jennings, "The Anatomy of Leadership," *Management of Personnel Quarterly*, 1 (1) (Autumn 1961).

18. Charles Perrow, *Complex Organizations: A Critical Essay,* 2d ed. (Glenview, IL: Scott, Foresman, 1979), p. 102.

19. Douglas McGregor, *The Human Side of Enterprise* (New York: McGraw-Hill, 1960).

20. Ibid., pp. 33-44.

21. Ibid., pp. 45-57.

22. Charles Perrow, *Complex Organizations: A Critical Essay* (Glenview, IL: Scott, Foresman, 1972), p. 98.

23. Paul Hersey and Kenneth H. Blanchard, "Changing Patterns of Leadership: 3-D Leader Effectiveness Theory," paper prepared for the Leadership Workshop Conference, U. S. Military Academy, June 25-27, 1969.

24. Hersey and Blanchard, *Management of Organizational Behavior,* p. 93; Robbins, *Essentials,* p. 139.

25. Hersey and Blanchard, "Changing Patterns of Leadership."

26. Hersey and Blanchard, *Management of Organizational Behavior,* pp. 91, 92; Robbins, *Essentials,* p. 138.

27. Hersey and Blanchard, "Changing Patterns of Leadership," p. 5.

28. Robert R. Blake and Jane S. Mouton, *The Managerial Grid* (Houston, TX: Gulf, 1964).

29. Hersey and Blanchard, "Changing Patterns of Leadership," pp. 6-9.

30. Abraham K. Korman, " 'Consideration,' 'Initiating Structure' and Organizational Criteria—A Review" *Personnel Psychology,* 19 (4) (1966): 349-61.

31. Hersey and Blanchard, *Management of Organization Behavior,* p. 142

32. Fred E. Fiedler, *A Theory of Leadership Effectiveness* (New York: McGraw-Hill, 1967).

33. Ibid. Perrow, *Complex Organizations,* p. 106.

34. Ibid.

35. Hersey and Blanchard, *Management of Organization Behavior,* p. 142.

36. Edgar H. Shein, *Organizational Psychology,* 3d ed. (Englewood Cliffs, NJ: Prentice-Hall, 1980), p. 116.

37. Hersey and Blanchard, *Management of Organizational Behavior,* pp. 116-22.

38. Ibid., pp. 172-81.

39. Ibid., pp. 177-81.

40. R. W. Toseland and R. F. Rivas, *An Introduction to Group Work Practice* (New York: Macmillan, 1984), p. 91.

41. Adapted from B. Tuckman "Developmental Sequence in Small Groups, *Psychological Bulletin,* 63 (1963): 384–99.

42. Hersey and Blanchard, *Management of Organizational Behavior,* p. 151.

43. Toseland and Rivas, *Introduction to Group Work Practice,* p. 301.

44. Ibid., p. 300.

45. Ibid., p. 307.

46. Hersey and Blanchard, *Management of Organization Behavior,* p. 179.

47. Adapted from Armand Lauffer, *Assessment Tools for Practitioners, Managers and Trainers* (Beverly Hills, CA: Sage, 1982), p. 9.

48. Ibid., p. 12.

49. Ibid.

50. David C. McClelland, *Power: The Inner Experience* (New York: Irvington, 1975), p. 260.

51. Ibid.

52. Michael Harmon, *Action Theory for Public Administration* (New York: Longman, 1981), p. 43.

53. Ibid., p. 35.

54. Ibid., p. 36.

55. Ibid., p. 36.

56. Gummer, *Politics of Social Administration,* p. 132.

57. James M. Kouzas and Barry Posner, *The Leadership Challenge: How to Get Extraordinary Things Done in Organizations* (San Francisco: Jossey-Bass, 1987), p. 7.

58. Ibid., p. 187.

59. Henry Kissenger, in Charles A. Rapp and John Poertner, *Social Administration: A Client Centered Approach* (New York: Longman, 1992), p. 281.

60. Warren Bennis and Burt Nanus, *Leaders: The Strategies for Taking Charge* (New York: Harper and Row, 1985), p. 3.

61. Theodore Hesburgh, in Rapp and Poertner, *Social Administration,* p. 281.

62. Kouzas and Posner, *Leadership Challenge,* p. 83.

63. Ibid., p. 19.

64. Ibid., p. 83.

65. Ibid., p. 115.

66. Ibid., p. 113.

67. Bennis and Nanus, *Leaders,* p. 3.

68. Ibid., p. 110.

69. Kouzas and Posner, *Leadership Challenge,* p. 222.

70. Ibid., p. 162.

71. Ibid.

72. Ibid., p. 184.

73. Adapted from, "Adjectives Feedback," Exercise 168 in *Structured Exercises,* University Associates, submitted by John E. Jones.

Part II: Social Work Practice with Communities

1. Si Kahn, *How People Get Power: Organizing Oppressed Communities for Action* (New York: McGraw-Hill, 1970), pp. 123-24.

2. Herbert J. Rubin and Irene S. Rubin, *Community Organizing and Development,* 2d ed. (New York: Macmillan, 1992), p. 3.

3. Thomas M. Meenaghan, Robert O. Washington, and Robert M. Ryan, *Macro Practice in the Human Service: An Introduction to Planning, Administration, Evaluation, and Community Organizing Components of Practice* (New York: Free Press, 1982), p. 97.

4. Wynetta Devore, "The African American Community in 1990: The Search for a Practice Method," in Felix G. Rivera and John L. Erlich, ed. *Community Organizing in a Diverse Society* (Boston, MA: Allyn and Bacon, 1992), p. 83.

5. Hans S. Falck, *Social Work: The Membership Perspective* (New York: Springer, 1982), p. 158.

6. Ibid., p. 160.

7. John Forester, *Planning in the Face of Power* (Berkeley: University of California Press, 1989).

8. Felix G. Rivera and John L. Erlich, *Community Organizing in a Diverse Society* (Boston, MA: Allyn and Bacon, 1992), pp. ix, x.

9. Meenaghan, Washington, and Ryan, *Macro Practice*, p. 98.

Chapter 5: Communities

1. Robert N. Bellah, Richard Madsen, William M. Sullivan, Ann Swidler, and Steven M. Tipton, *Habits of the Heart* (New York: Harper and Row, 1985), p. 28.
2. Excerpted and adapted from the "Weapons of the Spirit," a film by Pierre Sauvage Productions and Friends of Le Chambon, Inc., 1988.
3. Antonia Pantoja and Wilhelmina Perry, "Community Development and Restoration: A Perspective," in Felix G. Rivera and John L. Erlich, *Community Organizing in a Diverse Society* (Boston, MA: Allyn and Bacon, 1992), p. 237.
4. Bellah et al, *Habits of the Heart*, p. 333.
5. Ibid., p. 72.
6. Ibid., p. 73.
7. Ibid., p. 162.
8. Ibid., p. 50.
9. Ibid., p. 226.
10. Ibid., p. 333.
11. Ibid., p. 227.
12. Robert A. Nisbet, *The Sociological Tradition* (New York: Basic Books, 1966), p. 47.
13. Carel B. Germain, "The Place of Community Work within an Ecological Approach to Social Work Practice," Samuel H. Taylor and Robert W. Roberts, eds., *Theory and Practice of Community Social Work* (New York: Columbia University Press, 1985), p. 34.
14. Carel B. Germain, ed., *Social Work Practice: People and Environments—An Ecological Perspective* (New York: Columbia University Press, 1979), p. 7.
15. Ibid., p. 35; Phillip Fellin, *The Community and the Social Worker* (Itasca, IL: Peacock, 1987).
16. Germain, "The Place," p. 36.
17. Ibid.
18. Fellin, *The Community*, p. 23.
19. Germain, "The Place," p. 41.
20. Fellin, *The Community*, p. 24.
21. Germain, "The Place," p. 42.
22. Ibid., p. 43.
23. Ibid., p. 45.
24. Ibid.
25. Fellin, *The Community*, p. 3.
26. Ibid., p. 24.
27. Ibid., p. 25.
28. Armand Lauffer, *Assessment Tools for Practitioners, Managers, and Trainers* (Beverly Hills, CA: Sage, 1982), p. 20.
29. Ibid., p. 14.
30. Germain, "The Place," p. 39.
31. Ibid.
32. Ibid., p. 37.
33. Ibid.
34. Fellin, *The Community*, p. 25.
35. Bronislaw Malinowski, "Anthropology," *Encyclopaedia Britannica*, Supplementary vol. 1, pp. 132-133.
36. Roland Warren, *The Community in America* (Chicago, IL: Rand McNally, 1963), p. 208.
37. Ibid., p. 208.
38. Fellin, *The Community*, p. 31.
39. William Graham Sumner, *Folkways* (1906; New York: Dover, 1959).
40. Gibson Winter, *Elements for a Social Ethic: The Role of Social Science in Public Policy* (New York: Macmillan, 1966), pp. 7, 8.
41. Germain, "The Place," p. 40.
42. Michael M. Harmon, *Action Theory for Public Administration* (New York: Longman, 1981), p. 59.
43. Ibid., p. 59.
44. Winter, *Elements*, p. 8.
45. Ralph P. Hummel, *The Bureaucratic Experience* (New York: St. Martin's, 1977), pp. 34, 35.
46. Antonio Pantoja and Wilhelmina Perry, "Community Development Restoration: A Perspective," in Rivera and Erlich, *Community Organizing*, p. 227.
47. Winter, *Elements*, p. 9.
48. Thomas Hobbes, *Leviathan: Or the Matter, Forme, and Power of a Commonwealth Ecclesiastical and Civil*, introduction by Richard S. Peters, ed. Michael Oakeshott (New York: Free Press, 1947).
49. Winter, *Elements*, pp. 7-9.
50. Ibid., p. 10.
51. Ibid.
52. Harmon, *Action Theory*, pp. 36-40.
53. Bellah et al., *Habits of the Heart*, p. 142.
54. Thomas Hobbes, "Introduction" to *Leviathan*, in *Hobbes: Selections*, F.J.E. Woodbridge, Ed. (New York: Charles Scribners's Sons, 1958), p. 138.
55. Bellah, et al., *Habits of the Heart*, p. 143.
56. Hans S. Falck, *Social Work: The Membership Perspective* (New York: Springer, 1988), p. 16.
57. Harmon *Action Theory*.
58. Harry Specht and Mark Courtney, *Unfaithful Angels: How Social Work Abandoned Its Mission* (New York: Free Press, 1994), p. 76.
59. Ibid., p. 138.
60. Ibid., pp. 106-30.
61. Bellah et al., *Habits*, p. 104.
62. C. Meyer, *Social Work Practice—A Response to the Urban Crisis* (New York: Free Press, 1970), p. 126.
63. Falck, *Social Work*, p. 14.
64. Carel B. Germain and Alex Gitterman, *The Life Model of Social Work Practice* (New York: Columbia University Press, 1980).
65. Falck, *Social Work*, p. 15.
66. Ibid., p. 16.
67. Ibid., p. 20.
68. Ibid., pp. 15, 16.
69. Ibid., p. 16.
70. Harmon, *Action Theory*, p. 49.
71. Ibid., p. 50.
72. Pantoja and Perry, "Community Development," p. 228.
73. Ibid., p. 227.
74. Lawrence Haworth, "The Good Life: Growth and Duty," in

Gibson Winter, *Social Ethics: Issues in Ethics and Society* (New York: Harper and Row, 1968), p. 186.

75. Patricia Martin and Gerald G. O'Connor, *The Social Environment: Open Systems Applications* (New York: Longman, 1989), p. 231.

76. Roland Warren, *Social Change and Human Purpose toward Understanding and Action* (Chicago, IL: Rand-McNally, 1977), p. 208.

77. Germain, "The Place," pp. 34, 35.

78. Bellah et al., *Habits,* p. 69.

79. Warren, *Social Change,* p. 208.

80. Haworth, "The Good Life," p. 184.

81. Ibid., pp. 178-79

82. Bellah et al., *Habits,* p. 68.

83. Ibid., p. 76.

84. Haworth, "The Good Life," p. 168.

85. Harmon, *Action Theory,* p. 59.

86. Sheldon Wolin, "Political Theory as a Vocation," *American Political Science Review,* 63 (Dec. 1969): 1,078.

87. Ibid.

88. Mancur Olson, *The Logic of Collective Action* (Cambridge, MA: Harvard University Press, 1965), p. 2. Also see James M. Buchanan and Gordon Tullock, *The Calculus of Consent: Logical Foundations of Constitutional Democracy* (Ann Arbor: University of Michigan Press, 1962).

89. F. Clemenger, "Review of the Life Model of Social Work Practice by C.B. Germain and A. Gitterman," *Journal of Education for Social Work,* 16 (3) (1980):122.

90. Thomas M. Meenaghan, Robert O. Washington, and Robert M. Ryan, *Macro Practice in the Human Services: An Introduction to Planning, Administration, Evaluation, and Community Organizing Components of Practice* (New York: Free Press, 1982), p. 104.

91. Victor A. Thompson, *Bureaucracy and the Modern World* (Morristown, NJ: General Learning Press, 1976), p. 2.

92. R. M. MacIver, *Society* (New York: Macmillan, 1937).

93. Bellah et al., *Habits,* pp. 71-75, 335.

94. Ibid., p. 72.

95. Ibid., p. 74.

96. Ibid., p. 72.

97. Harmon, *Action Theory,* p. 59.

98. Falck, *Social Work,* pp. 14-17.

99. Harmon, *Action Theory,* p. 52.

100. Bellah et al., *Habits,* p. 136.

101. Ibid., p. 138.

102. F. A. Hayek, *The Counter-Revolution of Science: Studies on the Abuse of Reason* (New York: Free Press, 1964), pp. 32-33.

103. Bellah et al., *Habits,* p. 69.

104. Warren, *Social Change,* p. 68.

105. Ibid., p. 207.

106. Max Weber, "Bureaucracy," in *Economy and Society: Outline of Interpretive Sociology,* 3 Vols., ed. Guenter Roth and Claus Wittich, trans. Ephraim Fischoff, et al. (Berkeley: University of California Press, 1978), p. 987.

107. Hummel, *The Bureaucratic Experience,* p. 32.

108. Ibid., p. 35.

109. Ibid., p. 36.

110. Ibid.

111. Warren, *Social Change,* p. 207.

112. Martin and O'Connor, *The Social Environment,* p. 238.

113. Bellah et al., *Habits,* p. 116.

114. Ibid.

115. Ibid., p. 153.

116. Ibid.

117. Ibid.

118. Ibid.

119. Ibid., p. 162.

120. Haworth, "The Good Life," p. 173.

121. Ibid., p. 173.

122. Ibid., p. 171.

123. Ann Schaef, *When Society Becomes an Addict* (San Francisco, CA: Harper and Row, 1987).

124. Interview with Carter Camp, *Akwesasne News,* published by the Mohawk Nation, early Autumn 1973, as quoted in Shirley Jenkins, *The Ethnic Dilemma in Social Services* (New York: Free Press, 1981), p. 16.

125. Robert K. Greenleaf, *Servant Leadership: A Journey into the Nature of Legitimate Power and Greatness* (New York: Paulist Press, 1977), p. 36.

126. Veroff, Kulka, and Douvan, quoted in Bellah et al., *Habits,* p. 121.

127. Sam Roberts, "America on the Move: How Mobile a Nation Is It?" *The Fresno Bee,* Dec. 12, 1994, p. A1.

128. Ibid.

Chapter 6: Becoming a Macro Social Work Researcher

1. T. S. Simey and M. B. Simey, *Charles Booth; Social Scientist* (Westport, CT: Greeenwood Press, 1980), p. 5.

2. Ibid., p. 247.

3. Ibid., p. 242.

4. Ibid., p. 4.

5. Ibid., p. 1.

6. Ibid., p. 243.

7. Ibid., p. 36.

8. Ibid., p. 40.

9. Ibid., p. 41.

10. Ibid., p. 62.

11. Ibid., pp. 47, 48.

12. Ibid., p. 4.

13. Ibid., p. 110.

14. Ibid., p. 190.

15. Ibid., p. 42.

16. Ibid., p. 183.

17. Ibid., p. 184.

18. Ibid., p. 264.

19. Ibid., p. 3.

20. Richard M. Grinnell, Jr., *Social Work Research and Evaluation,* 3d ed. (Itasca, IL: Peacock, 1988), p. 14.

21. Allen Rubin and Earl Babbie, *Research Methods for Social Work* (Belmont, CA: Wadsworth, 1979), p. xxiv.

22. Ibid., p. 79.

23. Walter I. Trattner, *From Poor Law to Welfare State: A His-*

tory of Social Welfare in America, 4th ed. (New York: Free Press, 1989), p. 62.

24. Ibid.

25. Ibid.

26. June Axinn and Herman Levin, *Social Welfare: A History of the American Response to Need,* 2d ed. (New York: Longman, 1982), p. 146.

27. Ibid., p. 147.

28. R. Brown, *Explanation in Social Science* (London: Routledge & Kegan Paul, 1963), p. 24.

29. Rubin and Babbie, *Research Methods,* p. xxiii.

30. Grinnell, *Social Work Research,* p. 14; Rubin and Babbie, *Research Methods,* p. xxvii.

31. Grinnell, *Social Work Research,* p. 10.

32. Peter Leonard, "The Contribution of the Social Sciences: Ideology and Explanation," in Catheriane Briscoe and David N. Thomas, eds., *Community Work: Learning and Supervision,* National Institute Social Services Library No. 32 (London: George Allen & Unwin, 1977), p. 71.

33. Herbert Rubin and Irene S. Rubin, *Community Organizing and Development,* 2d ed (New York: Macmillan, 1992), pp. 156, 157.

34. Ibid., p. 156.

35. Armand Lauffer, *Assessment Tools for Practitioners, Managers and Trainers* (Beverly Hills, CA: Sage, 1982), p. 8.

36. Norman J. Smith "Formulating Research Goals and Problems," in Grinnell, *Social Work Research,* pp. 91, 92.

37. Rubin and Rubin, *Community Organizing,* p. 158.

38. Michael Harmon, *Action Theory for Public Administration* (New York: Longman, 1981), p. 30.

39. Ibid., p. 31.

40. Ibid., p. 41.

41. Ibid., p. 42.

42. Ibid.

43. Leonard, "Contribution," p. 71.

44. John Lambert, "Putting Things into Perspective: Research Methods and Community Work," in Catherine Briscoe and David N. Thomas, eds., *Community Work: Learning and Supervision,* National Institute Social Services Library No. 32 (London: George Allen & Unwin, 1977), p. 104.

45. Rubin and Rubin, *Community Organizing,* p. 156.

46. Lauffer, *Assessment Tools,* p. 8.

47. Rubin and Rubin, *Community Organizing,* p. 156.

48. Ibid., p. 256.

49. Grinnell, *Social Work Research,* p. 11.

50. John Lofland, *Analyzing Social Settings* (Belmont, CA: Wadsworth, 1971), p. 2.

51. Leonard, "Contribution," p. 74.

52. Lambert, "Putting Things into Perspective," p. 115.

53. Leonard, "Contribution," p. 71.

54. Grinnell, *Social Work Research,* p. 15.

55. Ibid., pp. 16-18.

56. Adapted from ibid., p. 19.

57. Rubin and Babbie, *Research Methods,* p. 503.

58. Ibid.

59. George J. Wahrheit, Robert A. Bell, and John J. Schwab, "Selecting the Needs Assessment Approach," in Fred M. Cox, John L. Erlich, Jack Rothman and John E. Tropman,

eds., *Tactics and Techniques of Community Practice* 2nd ed. (Itasca IL: Peacock, 1984), p. 49.

60. Quoted in Earl Babbie, *Social Research for Consumers* (Belmont, CA: Wadsworth, 1982), p. 222.

61. Rubin and Babbie, *Research Methods,* p. 503.

62. Rubin and Rubin, *Community Organizing,* p. 157.

63. F. A. Fear, K. A. Carter, and M. Thullen, "Action Research in Community Development: Concepts and Principles," *Research in Rural Sociology and Development,* 2 (1985):199.

64. Rubin and Rubin, *Community Organizing,* p. 158.

65. J. Steven Ott, *The Organizational Culture Perspective* (Homewood, IL: Irwin, 1989), p. ix.

66. Ibid.

67. This section on how to diagnose organizational and community culture is adapted from Terrance E. Deal, *Corporate Culture* (New York: Addison-Wesley, 1982), pp. 130-39.

68. Robert N. Bellah, Richard Madsen, William M. Sullivan, Ann Swidler, and Steven M. Tipton, *Habits of the Heart: Individualism and Commitment in American Life* (New York: Harper and Row, 1985), pp. 71-75.

69. Ibid., p. 335.

70. Wahrheit, Bell, and Schwab, "Selecting the Needs Assessment Approach," p. 41.

71. Ibid.

72. Harvey L. Gochros, "Research Interviewing," in Grinnell, Jr., *Social Work Research,* p. 275.

73. Ibid., p. 272.

74. Ibid., p. 269.

75. Ibid., p. 276.

76. Ibid., p. 269; Rubin and Rubin, *Community Organizing,* p. 159.

77. Wahrheit, Bell, and Schwab, "Selecting." p. 42.

78. Ibid., p. 43.

79. Rubin and Rubin, *Community Organizing,* p. 160.

80. Rebecca F. Guy, Charles E. Edgley, Ibtihaj Arafat, and Donald E. Allen, *Social Research Methods: Puzzles and Solutions* (Boston, MA: Allyn and Bacon, 1987), p. 220.

81. Rubin and Rubin, *Community Organizing,* p. 160.

82. Guy et al., *Social Research Methods,* pp. 191-97.

83. Ibid., p. 197.

84. Ibid., p. 245.

85. For more information on conducting interview surveys, see Rubin and Babbie, *Research Methods,* pp. 322-28; Grinnell, *Social Work Research,* pp. 283-297; Guy et al., *Social Research Methods,* pp. 244-48.

86. Rubin and Babbie, *Research Methods,* p. 322.

87. Ibid.; Guy et al., *Social Research Methods,* p. 245.

88. Guy et al., *Social Research Methods,* p. 243.

89. Rubin and Babbie, *Research Methods,* p. 320.

90. Guy et al., *Social Research Methods,* p. 243.

91. Ibid., p. 242.

92. Ibid., p. 248.

93. Rubin and Babbie, *Research Methods,* p. 329.

94. Ibid.

95. Ibid., p. 162.

96. Guy et al., *Social Research Methods,* p. 231.

97. Rubin and Babbie, *Research Methods,* p. 324.

98. Guy et al., *Social Research Methods,* p. 235.

99. Julio Morales, "Community Social Work with Puerto Rican Communities in the United States: One Organizer's Perspective," in Felix G. Rivera and John L. Erlich, *Community Organizing in a Diverse Society* (Boston, MA: Allyn and Bacon, 1992), p. 106. Reprinted by permission.

Chapter 7: Becoming a Community Developer

1. Marilyn Ferguson, *The Aquarian Conspiracy* (Los Angeles, CA: J. P. Tarcher, 1980), p. 207.
2. Si Kahn, *How People Get Power: Organizing Oppressed Communities for Action* (New York: McGraw-Hill, 1978), p. 105.
3. Antonia Pantoja and Wilhelmina Perry, "Community Development and Restoration: A Perspective," in Felix G. Rivera and John L. Erlich, eds., *Community Organizing in a Diverse Society* (Boston, MA: Allyn and Bacon, 1992), p. 240.
4. Jack Rothman with John E. Tropman, "Models of Community Organization and Macro Practice Perspectives: Their Mixing and Phasing," in Fred M. Cox, John L. Erlich, Jack Rothman, and John E. Tropman, eds., *Strategies of Community Organization,* 4th ed. (Itasca, IL: Peacock, 1987), p. 5.
5. Walter I. Trattner, *From Poor Law to Welfare State: A History of Social Welfare in America,* 4th ed. (New York: Free Press, 1989), pp. 33, 34.
6. Quoted in Beulah R. Compton, *Introduction to Social Welfare and Social Work: Structure, Function, and Process* (Homewood, IL: Dorsey, 1980), pp. 278-79.
7. Ibid., p. 279.
8. Ibid., p. 290.
9. Ibid., p. 418.
10. Linda Ruth Pine, "Demonstration Cities and Metropolitan Development Act 1966," in Patricia M. Melvin, ed., *American Community Organizations: A Historical Dictionary.* (New York: Greenwood, 1986), p. 45.
11. Ibid., pp. 45, 46.
12. Linda Ruth Pine, "Economic Opportunity Act (EOA) 1964," in Melvin, ed., *American Community Organizations,* pp. 53-56.
13. Compton, *Introduction,* p. 460.
14. Ibid.
15. Linda Ruth Pine, "Housing and Urban Development Act, 1968," in Melvin, ed., *American Community Organizations,* p. 83.
16. Susan Redman-Rengstorf, "Neighborhoods U.S.A. (NUSA) 1975," in Melvin, ed., *American Community Organizations,* pp. 131-32.
17. Susan Redman-Rengstorf, "Neighborhood Reinvestment Corporation (NERC) 1978," in Melvin, ed., *American Community Organizations,* p. 129.
18. Robert R. Fairbanks, "Housing and Community Development Act (HCDA) 1974, in Melvin, ed., *American Community Organizations,* p. 81.
19. Ibid., p. 82.
20. Ibid., p. 83.
21. Patricia M. Melvin, ed., "National Neighborhood Policy Act 1977," in Melvin, ed., *American Community Organizations,* p. 127.
22. Ibid.
23. Ibid., p. 128.
24. Ibid., p. 129.
25. Lynne Navin, "Neighborhood Self-Help Development Act, 1978," in Melvin, ed., *American Community Organizations,* p. 130.
26. J. F. X. Paiva, "A Conception of Social Development," *Social Service Review,* 51 (2) (1977): 327-36.
27. David G. Gill, "Social Policies and Social Development: A Humanistic-Egalitarian Perspective," *Journal of Sociology and Social Welfare,* 3(3) (1976): 242-63.
28. Quoted in Rothman and Tropman, "Models," p. 5.
29. S. K. Khinduka, "Community Development: Potentials and Limitations," in *Strategies of Community Organization: Macro Practice,* 4th ed., Fred M. Cox, John L. Erlich, Jack Rothman, and John E. Tropman, eds. (Itasca, IL: Peacock, 1987), p. 353.
30. Kahn, *How People Get Power,* p. 5.
31. Felix G. Rivera and John L. Erlich, eds., *Community Organizing in a Diverse Society* (Boston, MA: Allyn and Bacon, 1992), p. 10.
32. Ibid., p. 11.
33. Ibid.
34. Ibid.
35. Ibid., pp. 11, 12.
36. Ibid., p. 12.
37. Pantoja and Perry, "Community Development," p. 237.
38. Kahn, *How People Get Power,* p. 11.
39. Steve Burghardt, *Organizing for Community Action* (Beverly Hills, CA: Sage, 1982), p. 20.
40. Kahn, *How People Get Power,* p. 34.
41. Ibid., p. 26.
42. Ibid., p. 21.
43. Ibid., p. 22, 23.
44. Ibid., p. 24.
45. Ibid., p. 25.
46. Ibid., p. 48, 49.
47. Rothman and Tropman, "Models," p. 34.
48. Kahn, *How People Get Power,* p. 12.
49. Ward H. Goodenough, *Cooperation in Change: An Anthropological Approach to Community Development* (New York: Russel Sage Foundation, 1963), pp. 19-20.
50. Kenneth L. Chau and Peter Hodge, "The Practice of Community Social Work with Third World Countries" in Samuel H. Taylor and Robert W. Roberts, eds., *The Theory and Practice of Community Work* (New York: Columbia University Press, 1985), p. 388.
51. Ibid.
52. Ibid.
53. Ibid., p. 389.
54. Roland Oliver, *The Missionary Factor in East Africa* (London: Longmans, 1952), p. 180.
55. Chau and Hodge, "Practice," p. 389.
56. Ibid., p. 392.
57. Ibid.
58. Colonial Office, *Education Policy in British Tropical Africa*

(London: HMSO, 1925), in Chau and Hodge, "Practice," p. 392.

59. International Missionary Council, "Report of the Jerusalem Meeting of the International Missionary Councils," *The Christian Mission in Relation to Rural Problems,* vol. 6 (London: Oxford University Press, 1928), in Chau and Hodge, "Practice," p. 420.

60. United Nations, Community Development and Economic Development, Part 1: *A Study of the Contribution of Rural Community Development Programs to National Economic Development in Asia and the Far East* (Bangkok: UN Economic Commission for Asia Land the Far East, 1960), in Chau and Hodge, "Practice," p. 397.

61. Peter R. Baehr and Leon Gordenker, *The United Nations in the 1990's* 2d ed. (New York: St. Martin's, 1994), p. 130.

62. Ibid., pp. 130, 131.

63. Ibid., pp. 133, 134.

64. Ibid., p. 136.

65. Ibid.

66. Ibid., p. 142.

67. Evan Luard, *The United Nations: How It Works and What it Does* (New York: St. Martin's, 1979), p. 57.

68. Ibid., p. 70.

69. Baehr and Gordenker, *United Nations,* p. 133.

70. Timothy Luke, *Social Theory and Modernity: Critique, Dissent, and Revolution* (Newbury Park, CA: Sage, 1990), p. 191.

71. Chau and Hodge, "Practice," p. 398.

72. Kahn, *How People Get Power,* p. 26.

73. Khinduka, "Community Development," p. 353.

74. Ibid.

75. Harry Specht and Mark Courtney, *Unfaithful Angels: How Social Work Has Abandoned Its Mission* (New York: Free Press, 1994), pp. 152-75.

76. Ibid., p. 153.

77. Ibid.

78. Ibid., p. 152.

79. Ibid.

80. Ibid.

81. Ibid., p. 154.

82. Ibid., p. 150.

83. Ibid., p. 148.

84. Ibid., p. 155.

85. Ibid.

86. Ibid., p. 159.

87. Ibid., p. 156.

88. Ibid.

89. Ibid., p. 158.

90. Ibid., p. 161.

91. Ibid.

92. Ibid., p. 27.

Chapter 8: Becoming a Social Activist

1. Marion Wright Edelman, *The Measure of Our Success: A Letter to My Children and Yours* (Boston, MA: Beacon Press, 1992), pp. 59, 60.

2. Marilyn Ferguson, *The Aquarian Conspiracy* (Los Angeles, CA: Tarcher, 1980), p. 191.

3. Gustavo Gutierrez, "Notes for a Theology of Liberation," *Theological Studies* (Baltimore, MD: Waverly Press, 1970), p. 254.

4. Ibid., p. 247.

5. George Lakey, *Strategy for a Living Revolution* (San Francisco, CA: Freeman, 1973), p. xiii.

6. Saul D. Alinsky, *Rules for Radicals: A Pragmatic Primer for Realistic Radicals* (New York: Vintage Books, 1974), p. 3.

7. Donald B. Kraybill, *The Upside Down Kingdom* (Scottsdale, PA: Herald Press, 1978), p. 23.

8. June Axinn and Herman Levin, *Social Welfare: A History of American Response to Need,* 2d ed. (New York: Longman, 1982), p. 47.

9. Ibid., p. 48.

10. Ibid., p. 47.

11. Ibid.

12. Ibid., p. 46.

13. Ibid., p. 141.

14. Ibid.

15. Ibid., p. 143.

16. Ibid., p. 301.

17. Jane Addams, *Twenty Years at Hull House* (New York: New American Library, 1938), p. 158.

18. Ibid., pp. 227-29.

19. Ibid., pp. 126-27.

20. Allen F. Davis, "Settlement Worker in Politics, 1890-1914," in Maryann Mahaffey and John W. Hands, eds., *Practical Politics: Social Work and Political Responsibility* (Silverspring, MD: National Association of Social Workers, 1982), p. 85.

21. Ibid., pp. 36, 37.

22. Ibid., p. 38.

23. Ibid.

24. Addams, *Twenty Years,* pp. 148-49.

25. Axinn and Levin, *Social Welfare,* p. 147.

26. Ibid., p. 148.

27. Charles Garvin and Fred Cox, "A History of Community Organizing," in Fred M. Cox, John L. Erlich, Jack Rothman, and John E. Tropman, *Strategies of Community Organization,* 4th ed. (Itasca, IL: Peacock, 1987), p. 35.

28. Axinn and Levin, *Social Welfare,* p. 248.

29. Foster Rhea Dulles, *Labor in America: A History,* 3d ed., (New York: Crowell, 1966), p. 22.

30. Ibid., p. 30.

31. Ibid., p. 166-68.

32. Ibid., p. 171.

33. Ibid., p. 172.

34. Ibid., p. 209-10.

35. Ibid., p. 263.

36. Ibid., p. 264.

37. Ibid., p. 275.

38. Ibid.

39. Ronald G. Walters, *American Reformers: 1815-1860* (New York: Hill and Wang, 1978), p. 113.

40. Ibid., p. 113.

41. Herbert J. Rubin and Irene S. Rubin, *Community Organizing*

and Development, 2d ed. (New York: Macmillan, 1992), p. 245.

42. Ibid., p. 245.
43. Warren C. Haggstrom, "The Tactics of Organization Building," in Cox et al., *Strategies,* p. 406.
44. Ibid., p. 406.
45. Alinsky, *Rules,* p. 12.
46. Ibid., pp. 12, 13.
47. Si Kahn, *How People Get Power: Organizing Oppressed Communities for Action* (New York: McGraw-Hill, 1978), p. 2.
48. Haggstrom, "Tactics," p. 406.
49. Ibid., pp. 406, 407.
50. Ibid., p. 407.
51. Ibid.
52. Ibid., p. 408.
53. Saul D. Alinsky, *Reveille for Radicals* (New York: Vintage Books, 1969), p. 90.
54. Julio Morales, "Community Social Work with Puerto Rican Communities," in Felix G. Rivera and John L. Erlich, ed., *Community Organizing in a Diverse Society* (Boston, MA: Allyn and Bacon, 1992), p. 96. Reprinted by permission.
55. Ibid., p. 97.
56. Ibid., p. 101.
57. Ibid.
58. Ibid., p. 97.
59. Haggstrom, "Tactics," p. 407.
60. Ibid., p. 411.
61. Ibid., p. 410.
62. Rubin and Rubin, *Community,* p. 226.
63. Haggstrom, "Tactics," p. 409.
64. Ibid.
65. Ibid.
66. Donald F. Harvey and Donald R. Brown, *An Experiential Approach to Organization Development* (Englewood Cliffs, NJ: Prentice-Hall, 1991), pp. 208-10.
67. Rubin and Rubin, *Community,* p. 308.
68. Ibid., p. 307.
69. Ibid., p. 308.
70. Ibid.
71. Harvey and Brown, *An Experiential Approach,* pp. 199-200.
72. Rubin and Rubin, *Community,* p. 245.
73. Ibid., p. 246.
74. Ibid., p. 266.
75. Alinski, *Rules for Radicals,* p. 128.
76. John Forester, *Planning in the Face of Power* (Berkeley: University of California Press, 1989), p. 46.
77. Ibid., p. 47.
78. Rubin and Rubin, *Community,* p. 296.
79. Ibid.
80. Ibid., p. 298.
81. Ibid., p. 297.
82. Ibid.
83. Ibid., p. 298.
84. Ibid.
85. Ibid.
86. Quoted in Marilyn Ferguson, *The Aquarian Conspiracy* (Los Angeles, CA: Tarcher, 1980), p. 199.

87. Haggstrom, "Tactics," p. 406.
88. Ibid., p. 412.
89. Rubin and Rubin, *Community,* p. 264.
90. Ibid.
91. Forester, *Planning,* p. 46, 47.
92. Ibid., p. 45.
93. Rubin and Rubin, *Community,* p. 320.
94. Ibid., p. 302.
95. Ibid., p. 313.
96. Ibid., p. 313, 314.
97. Ibid., p. 303.
98. T. Branch, *Parting the Waters: America in the King Years 1954–1963* (New York: Simon and Schuster, 1988), p. 438.
99. Ibid., pp. 471-72.
100. Alinsky, *Rules for Radicals,* pp. 127-30.
101. Rubin and Rubin, *Community,* p. 313.
102. Ibid., p. 304.
103. Alinsky, *Rules for Radicals,* p. 130.
104. Rubin and Rubin, *Community,* p. 264.
105. Ibid., p. 318.
106. Ibid.
107. Ibid.
108. Ibid., p. 265.
109. Ibid.
110. Ibid.
111. Saul Alinsky, *Rules for Radicals,* pp. 127-30.
112. Haggstrom, "Tactics," pp. 412-13.
113. Rubin and Rubin, *Community,* p. 309.
114. Ibid.
115. Ibid., p. 312.
116. F. D. Ginsberg, *Contested Lives: The Abortion Debate in an American Community* (Berkeley: University of California Press, 1989), p. 95.
117. Rubin and Rubin, *Community,* pp 312, 313.
118. Ibid., p. 313.
119. Ibid., p. 314.
120. Ibid.
121. Ibid.
122. Ibid., p. 316.
123. Ibid., p. 317.
124. R. Lawson and M. Naison, eds., *The Tenant Movement in New York City, 1904-1984* (New Brunswick, N.J.: Rutgers University Press, 1986), pp. 227-28.
125. Rubin and Rubin, *Community,* p. 256.
126. Ibid., p. 257.
127. Ibid., p. 265.
128. T. Gitlin, *The Sixties: Years of Hope, Days of Rage* (New York: Bantam, 1989), p. 424.
129. B. Moyer, *The Movement Action Plan: A Strategic Framework Describing the Eight Stages of Successful Social Movements* (San Francisco, CA: Social Movement Empowerment Project, 1987), p. 1.
130. Gitlin, *The Sixties,* p. 438.
131. Alinsky, *Rules for Radicals,* pp. 127-30.
132. Rubin and Rubin, *Community,* p. 266.
133. William L. Morrow, *Public Administration: Politics, Policy, and the Political System,* 2d ed. (New York: Random House, 1980), p. 125.

134. Kahn, *How People Get Power,* p. 116.
135. Ibid., p. 120.
136. Ibid., p. 121.
137. Ibid.
138. Ibid.
139. Alinsky, *Rules for Radicals,* pp. 127-30.
140. Ibid., p. 30.

Part III: Social Work Practice with Organizations

1. Robert Presthus, *The Organizational Society,* rev. ed. (New York: St. Martin's, 1978).
2. Ralph Hummel, *The Bureaucratic Experience* (New York: St. Martin's, 1977), p. 33.
3. Max Weber, *The Theory of Social and Economic Organization,* trans. A.M. Henderson and Talcott Parsons, Talcott Parsons, ed. (New York: Free Press, 1947), p. 88.
4. Martin Buber, *I and Thou,* trans. Walter Kaufmann (New York: Scribner's, 1970).
5. Thomas Hobbes, *Leviathan: Or the Matter, Forme, and Power of a Commonwealth Ecclesiastical and Civil,* Introduction by Richard S. Peters, Michael Oakeshott, ed. (New York: Collier, 1962).
6. Ibid.
7. Frank M. Coleman, *Hobbes and America: Exploring the Constitutional Foundations* (Toronto: University of Toronto Press, 1977).
8. Buber, *I and Thou.*
9. Hummel, *Bureaucratic,* p. 33.
10. Max Weber, "Bureaucracy," *Economy and Society: An Outline of Interpretive Sociology,* 3 vols., Guenther Roth and Claus Wittich, eds. (New York: Bedminster Press, 1968), p. 987.
11. Hummel, *Bureaucratic,* p. 45.
12. Shirley Terryberry, "The Evolution of Organizational Environments," *Administrative Science Quarterly,* 12 (4) (1968): 601.
13. Weber, "Bureaucracy," p. 987.

Chapter 9: Modern Complex Organizations

1. Max Weber, "Bureaucracy," *Economy and Society: An Outline of Interpretive Sociology,* 3 vols., Guenther Roth and Claus Wittich, eds., E. Fischoff, et al., tran. (New York: Bedminster Press, 1968), p. 987.
2. Adapted from Guy Keeler, "Uncle Sam's 'blessing' will join couple separated by red tape," *The Fresno Bee,* June 26, 1990, p. A 11.
3. James D. Thompson, *Organizations in Action* (New York: McGraw-Hill, 1967), p. 3.
4. Charles Perrow, *Complex Organizations: A Critical Essay,* 2d ed. (Glenview, IL: Scott, Foresman, 1979), p. 6.
5. John Forester, *Planning in the Face of Power* (Berkeley: University of California Press, 1989), p. 23.
6. Perrow, *Complex Organizations,* p. 6.
7. Herbert A. Simon, *Administrative Behavior: A Study of Decision-Making Processes in Administrative Organization,* 3d

ed. (New York: Free Press, 1976), pp. xvi, xix, 79, 101. See also Perrow, *Complex Organizations,* p. 6.
8. Robert Presthus, *The Organizational Society* (New York: St. Martin's, 1978).
9. Ralph Hummel makes this point in a lucid description of bureaucracy as the "new society" and as the "new culture." Ralph P. Hummel, *The Bureaucratic Experience* (New York: St. Martin's, 1977), pp. 20–91.
10. David Schuman asserts that "Max Weber was the first modern—and possibly the most brilliant—theorist of society and organization. . . . It is Weber who supplies the foundation of modern organization thought." David Schuman, *Bureaucracies, Organizations and Administration: A Political Primer* (New York: Macmillan, 1976), p. 54.
11. Weber, "Bureaucracy," p. 987.
12. Perrow, *Complex Organizations,* pp. 6, 13.
13. Ibid., p. 7.
14. Victor A. Thompson, *Without Sympathy or Enthusiasm: The Problem of Administrative Compassion* (University: The University of Alabama Press: 1977), p. 10.
15. Simon, *Administrative Behavior,* p. 103.
16. Perrow, *Complex Organizations,* pp. 6, 13.
17. Victor A. Thompson, *Bureaucracy and the Modern World* (Morristown, NJ: General Learning Press, 1976), p. 10.
18. Perrow, *Complex Organizations,* p. 7.
19. Thompson, *Bureaucracy,* p. 3.
20. Perrow, *Complex Organizations,* p. 6; Thompson, *Bureaucracy,* p. 8.
21. Schuman, *Bureaucracies,* p. 23.
22. Weber, "Bureaucracy," p. 973.
23. Ibid., p. 987.
24. Jacques Ellul, *The Technological Society* (New York: Vintage Books, 1976), p. 79.
25. Thompson, *Bureaucracy,* pp. 10, 15.
26. Thompson, *Without Sympathy,* p. 9, 13.
27. Thompson, *Bureaucracy,* pp. 25, 26.
28. Perrow, *Complex Organizations,* p. 13; Thompson, *Bureaucracy and the Modern World,* pp. 3, 9, 10, 15, 33.
29. Perrow, *Complex Organizations,* p. 13.
30. Thompson, *Without Sympathy,* p. 15.
31. Simon, *Administrative Behavior,* p. 85. Simon uses the term *docility.* Docility, according to Simon, is used in its proper dictionary sense of "teachability," a characteristic, he says, which "can be observed in the behavior of individuals and in the behavior of organizations" as well as in higher animals (p. 86).
32. Thompson, *Without Sympathy,* p. 28.
33. Thompson, *Bureaucracy,* pp. 25, 26.
34. Weber, "Bureaucracy," p. 973.
35. Alan Nevins and Henry Steele Commager, *A Pocket History of the United States,* 5th ed. (New York: Washington Square Press, 1966), p. 247.
36. Ibid., p. 168.
37. Ibid., p. 248.
38. Ibid., p. 268.
39. Ibid., p. 258.
40. Ibid., p. 270.
41. Schuman, *Bureaucracies,* p. 72.
42. Thompson, *Bureaucracy,* p. 8.

43. Thompson, *Without Sympathy,* p. 28.

44. Thompson, *Bureaucracy,* p. 17.

45. Schuman, *Bureaucracies,* p. 57.

46. Perrow, *Complex Organizations,* p. 4.

47. Frederick Winslow Taylor, *The Principles of Scientific Management* (New York: Norton, 1967), p. 64.

48. Ibid., pp. 69, 70.

49. Woodrow Wilson, "The Study of Administration," *Political Science Quarterly,* 2 (June 1887): 197-222.

50. Max Weber, "Politics as a Vocation," in H.H. Gerth and C. Wright Mills, eds., *From Max Weber: Essays in Sociology* (New York: Oxford University Press, 1946), p. 95.

51. Thompson, *Without Sympathy,* pp. 13, 18, 58, 66, 67.

52. Ibid., p. 20.

53. F. J. Roethlisberger and W. I. Dickson, *Management and the Worker* (Cambridge, MA: Harvard University Press, 1947).

54. Perrow, *Complex Organizations,* p. 93.

55. Schuman, *Bureaucracies,* p. 86.

56. The Conference Board, *Behavioral Science: Concepts and Management Application* (New York: National Industrial Conference Board, 1969), p. 8.

57. Much of the human relations school has been concerned with such issues as human motivation. Among the most prominent theorists are Abraham Maslow, Douglas MacGregor, Frederick Herzberg, Chris Argyris, and Rensis Likert.

58. Perrow, *Complex Organizations,* p. 153.

59. Peter L. Berger and Thomas Luckman, *The Social Construction of Reality* (Garden City, NY: Anchor Books, 1967), p. 189.

60. J. March and H. Simon, *Organizations* (New York: Wiley, 1958), p. 165.

61. Herbert A. Simon, *Administrative Behavior: A Study of Decision-Making Processes in Administrative Organization,* 3d ed., (New York: Free Press, 1976).

62. Ibid., p. xxx.

63. Ibid., p. xxvii.

64. Ibid., p. xxix.

65. Ibid., p. xxvii.

66. Ibid.

67. Ibid.

68. Ibid., xxv. Simon writes, "The first edition of this book was published shortly after the first modern digital computer came into the world and some years before the computer found even the most prosaic applications in management."

69. Ralph Hummel makes the same observation. He says, "Bureaucracies and specifically their organizational structures are such routines frozen into permanently repeated patterns; that is, they are institutions." *The Bureaucratic Experience* (New York: St. Martin's Press, 1977), p. 35.

70. Simon, *Administrative Behavior,* p. xxviii.

71. Ibid.

72. When an individual "satisfices," he or she accepts the first solution that he or she arrives at by means of a sequential or incremental search. In other words, the way organizational managers really decide is to search until the first acceptable solution that meets their goals is reached and then stop, as opposed to optimizing, which means that they would continue the search indefinitely until they reach the best possible solution.

73. Simon, *Administrative Behavior,* p. xvi.

74. Ibid., pp. 79, 80.

75. Ibid., p. 79.

76. Ibid.

77. The failure of self-interested, rational individuals to be able to work collectively, even for causes that serve their own self-interest, is described in Mancur Olson, *The Logic of Collective Action* (Cambridge, MA: Harvard University Press, 1965), p. 2.

78. Simon, *Administrative Behavior,* p. 50.

79. Ibid., p. xii, 79.

80. Perrow, *Complex Organizations,* p. 149.

81. Ibid., pp. 149-53.

82. Ibid., p. 151.

83. Ibid.

84. Ibid., p. 152.

85. Simon, *Administrative Behavior,* p. 103.

86. Ibid., p. 80.

87. Ibid., p. 79.

88. Ibid., p. 101.

89. Ibid., p. 102.

90. Ibid., p. 108.

91. Simon says that there is, in fact, no "qualitative" difference between humans and animals in their ability to generalize. It is merely a matter of degree rather than kind (ibid., n. p. 86).

92. Harvey Sherman, *It All Depends: A Pragmatic Approach to Organization* (University: University of Alabama Press, 1966).

93. Thompson, *Organizations.*

94. Stephen P. Robbins, *Essentials of Organization Behavior,* 3d ed. (Englewood Cliffs, NJ, 1992), pp. 140-50.

95. Stephen F. Robbins, *Organization Theory: The Structure and Design of Organizations* (Englewood Cliffs, NJ: Prentice-Hall, 1983), p. 61.

96. Fred E. Emery and Eric L. Trist, "The Causal Texture of Organizational Environments," *Human Relations,* Feb. 1965, pp. 21-23.

97. Perrow, *Complex Organizations,* pp. 115, 116.

98. Thompson, *Organizations,* p. vii.

99. Alberto Guerreiro Ramos, "A Substantive Approach to Organizations," in Carl J. Bellone, ed., *Organization Theory and the New Public Administration* (Boston, MA: Allyn and Bacon, 1980), p. 158.

100. Hummel, *Bureaucratic Experience,* p. 42.

101. Ibid., pp. 42-43.

102. Ibid., p. 42.

103. Ramos, "Substantive Approach," p. 158.

104. Ibid., p. 140. See also Alberto Ramos, *The New Science of Organization: A Reconceptualization of the Wealth of Nations* (Toronto: University of Toronto Press, 1981), pp. 3, 4.

105. Michael M. Harmon, *Action Theory for Public Administration* (New York: Longman, 1981), p. 52.

106. Ramos, "Substantive Approach," p. 146.

107. Ibid., p. 149.

108. Karl Polanyi, *The Great Transformation* (Boston, MA: Beacon Press, 1971), p. 71.

109. Marcel Mauss, in G. Dalton, ed., *Primitive, Archaic, and Modern Economies: Essays of Karl Polanyi* (Boston, MA: Beacon Press, 1971), p. ix.

110. Ramos, "Substantive Approach," p. 147.
111. Hummel, *Bureaucratic Experience,* p. 42.
112. Ramos, "Substantive Approach," p. 158.
113. Thompson, *Without Sympathy,* p. 90.
114. Ibid., p. 67.
115. Hummel, *Bureaucratic Experience* pp. 133-37.
116. Simon, *Administrative Behavior,* pp. 85-87.
117. Hummel, *Bureaucratic Experience,* p. 136.
118. Thompson, *Without Sympathy,* p. 91.
119. Perrow, *Complex Organizations,* p. 201.
120. Ibid., p. 194.
121. Perrow, *Complex Organizations,* pp. 194, 196.
122. Ibid., p. 994.
123. Perrow, quoted in Ramos, "Substantive Approach," p. 142.
124. Perrow, *Complex Organizations,* p. 194.
125. Hummel, *Bureaucratic Experience,* pp. 45-50, 83-88.
126. Ramos, *New Science,* p. 123.
127. Ibid., p. 124.
128. Ibid., p. 125.
129. Ibid., p. 128.
130. Ibid., p. 106.
131. Forester, *Planning,* p. 72.
132. Perrow, *Complex Organizations,* pp. 55, 56.
133. Ramos, *New Science,* p. 160.
134. Donald Shon, *Beyond the Stable State* (New York: Random House, 1971), pp. 33-38.
135. Thompson, *Without Sympathy,* pp. 90, 91, 92, 94.
136. Forester, *Planning,* p. 79.

Chapter 10: Becoming a Social Planner: Making the Good Society

1. John W. Dyckman, "The Practical Uses of Planning Theory," *Journal of the American Institute of Planners,* 35 (Sept. 1969): 300.
2. Garrett Hardin, "The Tragedy of the Commons," *Science,* 162 (Dec. 1968): 1243. Copyright 1963 American Association for the Advancement of Science. Used with Permission.
3. Adapted from Ibid., pp. 1243-1248.
4. Hardin, "Tragedy," p. 1244.
5. Robert R. Mayer, *Policy and Program Planning* (Englewood Cliffs, NJ: Prentice-Hall, 1985), p. 4.
6. Paul A. Kurzman, "Program Development and Service Coordination as Components of Community Practice," in Samuel H. Taylor and Robert W. Roberts, eds, *Theory and Practice of Community Social Work* (New York: Columbia University Press, 1985), p. 97.
7. Walter I. Trattner, *From Poor Law to Welfare State: A History of Social Welfare in America,* 4th ed. (New York: Free Press, 1989), p. 88.
8. Margaret E. Rich, *A Belief in People: A History of Family Social Work* (New York: Family Service Association of America, 1956), p. 13.
9. Kurzman, "Program Development," p. 97.
10. P. Nelson Reid, "Community Organization," in Arthur E. Fink, Jane H. Pfouts, and Andrew W. Dobelstein, *The Field of Social Work,* 8th ed. (Beverly Hills, CA: Sage, 1985), pp. 226, 227.
11. Ibid., p. 227.
12. Michael Jacobson, "Working with Communities," in H. Wayne Johnson, ed., *The Social Services: An Introduction,* 3d ed. (Itasca, IL: Peacock, 1990), p. 395.
13. Beulah H. Compton, *Introduction to Social Welfare and Social Work: Structure, Function and Process* (Homewood, IL: Dorsey Press, 1980), p. 162.
14. Kurzman, "Program Development" p. 97; Reid, "Community Organization," p. 227.
15. Kurzman, "Program Development," p. 97.
16. Arthur Dunham. *The New Community Organization* (New York: Crowell, 1970), p. 438.
17. Diana M. DiNitto and C. Aaron McNeece, *Social Work: Issues and Opportunities in a Challenging Profession* (Englewood Cliffs, NJ: Prentice-Hall, 1990), p. 72.
18. Ibid.
19. Kurzman, "Program Development," p. 98.
20. Jack Rothman and Mayer N. Zald, "Planning Theory and Social Work Community Practice," in Taylor and Roberts, *Theory and Practice,* p. 130.
21. Kurzman, "Program Development," p. 99.
22. Rothman and Zald, "Planning Theory," p. 142.
23. Ibid., p. 131.
24. Ronald L. Simons and Stephen M. Aigner, *Practice Principles: A Problem Solving Approach to Social Work* (New York: Macmillan, 1985), p. 208; and Neil Gilbert and Harry Specht, "Who Plans?" in Fred M. Cox, John L. Erlich, Jack Rothman, and John E. Tropman, *Strategies of Community Organization,* 3d ed. (Itasca, IL: Peacock, 1979), p. 347.
25. Simons and Aigner, *Practice Principles,* p. 208.
26. Gilbert and Specht, "Who Plans?" p. 347.
27. Simons and Aigner, *Practice Principles,* p. 208.
28. Ibid., p. 209.
29. Gilbert and Specht, "Who Plans?" p. 347.
30. Madelene R. Stoner, "The Practice of Community Social Work in Mental Health Settings," in Taylor and Roberts, *Theory and Practice,* p. 285.
31. Rothman and Zald, "Planning Theory," p. 131.
32. Stoner, "Practice," p. 285.
33. Ibid., p. 290.
34. Ibid., p. 294.
35. Ibid., p. 291.
36. Ibid., p. 293.
37. Ibid., p. 291.
38. Ibid.
39. Ibid., p. 297.
40. Ibid., p. 298.
41. Ibid., p. 300.
42. Ibid., p. 301.
43. Ibid., pp. 307, 308.
44. Gilbert and Specht, "Who Plans?" p. 348.
45. Stoner, "Practice," p. 305.
46. Ibid.
47. Ibid.
48. Ibid., p. 309.
49. Ibid.
50. Linda Ruth Pine, "Economic Opportunity Act (EOA) 1964," in Patricia Mooney Melvin, ed., *American Community Organizations* (New York: Greenwood Press, 1986), p. 54.

51. Kurzman, "Program Development," p. 100.
52. Trattner, *From Poor Law,* p. 293.
53. Ibid.
54. Pine, "Economic Opportunity Act," p. 54.
55. Ibid.
56. Ibid.
57. Ibid., pp. 55, 56.
58. Neil Gilbert. "The Design of Community Planning Structures," *Social Service Review,* 53 (1979): 647.
59. Linda Ruth Pine, "Demonstration Cities and Metropolitan Development Act, 1966," in Melvin, *American Community Organizations,* p. 45.
60. Ibid., p. 46.
61. Abraham Monk, "The Practice of Community Social Work with the Aged," in Taylor and Roberts, *Theory and Practice,* p. 268.
62. Ibid.
63. Ibid.
64. Ibid., p. 269.
65. Ibid., p. 270.
66. Ibid., p. 269.
67. Ibid., p. 272.
68. Ibid., pp. 268-72.
69. Trattner, *From Poor Law,* p. 293.
70. James T. Patterson, *America's Struggle Against Poverty, 1900–1985* (Cambridge, MA: Harvard University Press, 1986).
71. Trattner, *From Poor Law,* p. 294.
72. Armand Lauffer, "The Practice of Social Planning," in Neil Gilbert and Harry Specht, eds., *Handbook for Social Services* (Englewood Cliffs, NJ: Prentice-Hall, 1981), p. 583.
73. Guy Benveniste, *Mastering the Politics of Planning: Crafting Credible Plans and Policies that Make a Difference* (San Francisco, CA: Jossey-Bass, 1989), p. 264.
74. Ibid., p. 263.
75. Simons and Aigner, *Practice Principles,* p. 210.
76. Ibid.
77. P. Gulati. "Consumer Participation in Administrative Decision Making," *Social Service Review,* 56 (1982): 72-84.
78. Steven M. Aigner, "Social Development and Mass Society," *Iowa Social Service Review,* 56 (1982): 375-92.
79. John Forester, *Planning in the Face of Power* (Berkeley: University of California Press, 1989), p. 28.
80. Armand Lauffer, *Social Planning at the Community Level* (Englewood Cliffs, NJ: Prentice-Hall, 1978), p. 9.
81. Forester, *Planning,* p. 40.
82. Ibid., p. 137.
83. Alan Walker, *Social Planning: A Strategy for Socialist Welfare* (Oxford: B. Blackwell, 1984), p. 2.
84. Forester, *Planning,* p. 4.
85. Walker, *Social Planning,* p. 2.
86. Benveniste, *Mastering the Politics,* p. 264.
87. Simons and Aigner, *Practice Principles,* p. 212, cite Armand Lauffer, *Social Planning at the Community Level* (Englewood Cliffs, NJ: Prentice-Hall, 1972) along with R. Perlman and A. Gurin, *Community Organization and Social Planning* (New York: Wiley and Council on Social Work Education, 1972).
88. This model is an adaptation of Simons and Aigner, *Practice Principles,* pp. 212, 213.
89. Ibid., p. 213.
90. Edith Stokey and Richard Zeckhauser, *A Primer for Policy Analysis* (New York: Norton, 1978), p. 8.
91. Ibid., p. 9.
92. Ibid., p. 10.
93. Ibid., p. 8.
94. Martin J. Gannon, *Management: An Integrated Framework,* 2d ed. (Boston, MA: Little, Brown, 1982), p. 138.
95. Stokey and Zeckhauser, *A Primer,* p. 21.
96. Ibid., p. 47.
97. Ibid., pp. 98-114.
98. Gannon, *Management,* p. 144.
99. Ibid., p. 145.
100. Ibid., p. 146.
101. Ibid., p. 142.
102. Stokey and Zeckhauser, *A Primer,* p. 177.
103. Ibid.
104. Ibid.
105. Ibid., p. 179.
106. Gannon, *Management,* p. 151.
107. Ibid.
108. Ibid., pp. 152, 153.
109. Forester, *Planning,* p. 28.
110. Ibid., p. 5.
111. Ibid., p. 40.
112. Ibid.
113. Ibid.
114. Ibid., p. 41.
115. Ibid., p. 5.
116. Ibid.
117. Jamshid Gharajedaghi in collaboration with Russell L. Ackoff. *A Prologue to National Development Planning* (New York: Greenwood Press, 1986), p. 27.
118. Ibid., p. 28.
119. Ibid.
120. Ibid., p. 29.
121. Ibid.
122. Ibid.
123. Ibid., p. 30.
124. Ibid., p. 29.
125. Ibid.
126. Robert R. Mayer, *Social Planning and Social Change* (Englewood Cliffs, NJ: Prentice-Hall, 1972), p. 17.
127. Gharajedaghi, *A Prologue,* p. 31.
128. Ibid.
129. Ibid., p. 30.
130. Ibid.
131. Ibid., p. 37.
132. Ibid., p. 35.
133. Ibid., p. 36.
134. Ibid.
135. Ibid.
136. Immanuel Kant, *Groundwork of the Metaphysic of Morals,* trans. H. J. Paton (New York: Harper and Row, 1956), Sect. 67, p. 96.
137. Adapted from Henrik Ibsen, "Enemy of the People," in *Four Great Plays by Ibsen* (New York: Bantam Books, 1959), pp. 130-215.
138. Friedrich A. Hayek, *The Road to Serfdom* (Chicago, IL: University of Chicago Press: 1944), p. 35.

Chapter 11: The Social Worker as Program Developer

1. Si Kahn, *How People Get Power: Organizing Oppressed Communities for Action* (New York: McGraw Hill, 1970), p. 124.
2. Adapted from Mark Grossi, "Sobriety House Offers Road Back to Society," *The Fresno Bee,* Dec. 31, 1991, p. B2.
3. Acts 2:44, 45.
4. Walter I. Trattner, *From Poor Law to Welfare State: A History of Social Welfare in America* (New York: Free Press, 1989), p. 17.
5. Ibid., p. 17.
6. Beulah R. Compton, *Introduction to Social Welfare and Social Work: Structure, Function, and Process* (Homewood, IL: Dorsey Press, 1980), p. 197.
7. Trattner, *From Poor Law,* p. 33.
8. Ibid.
9. Ibid.
10. Compton, *Introduction,* p. 176.
11. Ibid.
12. Ibid.
13. June Axinn and Herman Levin, *Social Welfare: A History of the American Response to Need,* 2d ed. (New York: Longman, 1982), p. 58.
14. Ibid., p. 58.
15. Ibid., p. 59.
16. Trattner, *From Poor Law,* p. 60.
17. Ibid., p. 61.
18. Ibid., p. 62.
19. Ibid.
20. Ibid., p. 63.
21. Ibid.
22. Ibid.
23. Ibid., p. 65.
24. Ibid., pp. 63, 64.
25. Compton, *Introduction,* p. 288.
26. Trattner, *From Poor Law,* pp. 84, 85.
27. Compton, *Introduction,* p. 287.
28. Ibid., p. 288.
29. Ibid.
30. Ibid., p. 358.
31. Ibid., p. 298.
32. Trattner, *From Poor Law,* p. 154.
33. Ibid., p. 158.
34. Matthew A. Fitzsimons and Fulton J. Sheen, "Saint Frances Xavier Cabrini," *World Book Encyclopedia* (Chicago, IL: World Book, 1985), vol. 3, p. 9.
35. Compton, *Introduction,* p. 288.
36. Yeheskel Hasenfeld, "Program Development," in Fred M. Cox, John L. Erlich, Jack Rothman, and John E. Tropman, eds., *Strategies of Community Organization,* 4th ed. (Itasca, IL: Peacock, 1987), p. 142.
37. Ibid.
38. Ibid.
39. Joseph P. Hornick and Barbara Burrows, "Program Evaluation," in Richard M. Grinnell, Jr., ed., *Social Work Research and Evaluation,* 3d ed. (Itasca, IL: Peacock, 1988), p. 402.
40. Ibid., p. 402.
41. Allen Rubin and Earl Babbie, *Research Methods for Social Work* (Belmont, CA: Wadsworth, 1989), p. 500.
42. Ibid., p. 500.
43. Hornick and Burrows, "Program Evaluation," p. 403.
44. Rubin and Babbie, *Research Methods,* p. 500.
45. Ibid., p. 501.
46. Ibid., p. 502.
47. Ibid.
48. Ibid.
49. Ibid.
50. Ibid.
51. Hasenfeld, "Program Development," p. 155.
52. Ibid., p. 145.
53. Hasenfeld, "Program Development," p. 151.
54. Joan Flanagan, "How to Ask for Money," in Fred M. Cox, John L. Erlich, Jack Rothman, and John E. Tropman, eds., *Tactics and Techniques of Community Practice* 2d ed. (Itasca, IL: 1984), p. 310.
55. Robert Geller, "Successful Grant Writing," in Cox, Erlich, Rothman, and Tropman, *Tactics,* p. 298.
56. Flanagan, "How to Ask," p. 311.
57. Ibid.
58. Ibid., p. 313.
59. Geller, "Successful," p. 300.
60. Ibid.
61. Ibid.
62. Ibid., p. 297.
63. *The Foundation Directory* (New York: Foundation Center, 1995), p. xxiii.
64. Geller, "Successful," p. 302.
65. Ibid., p. 304.
66. Rubin and Babbie, "Research Methods," p. 481.
67. Hornick and Burrows, "Program Evaluation," p. 400.
68. Rubin and Babbie, "Research Methods," p. 482.
69. Ibid.
70. Hornick and Burrows, "Program Evaluation," p. 401.
71. Ibid., Rubin and Babbie, "Research Methods," p. 482.
72. Hornick and Burrows, "Program Evaluation," p. 402.
73. Rubin and Babbie, "Research Methods," p. 482.
74. Peter H. Rossi and Howard E. Freeman, *Evaluation: A Systematic Approach* (Beverly Hills, CA: Sage, 1982).
75. Carol H. Weiss, *Evaluation Research: Methods of Assessing Program Effectiveness* (Englewood Cliffs, NJ: Prentice-Hall, 1972), p. 4.
76. Herbert J. Rubin and Irene S. Rubin, *Community Organizing and Development,* 2d ed. (New York: Macmillan, 1992), p. 411.
77. Michael I. Harrison, *Diagnosing Organizations: Methods, Models and Processes* (Newbury Park, CA: Sage, 1987), p. 77.
78. Ibid., pp. 6, 78.
79. Rubin and Babbie, "Research Methods," p. 499.
80. Ibid.
81. Harrison, *Diagnosing,* p. 34.
82. Rubin and Rubin, *Community,* p. 412.
83. Weiss, *Evaluation,* p. 26; Rubin and Babbie, "Research Methods," p. 496.
84. Weiss, *Evaluation,* p. 28.
85. Ibid., p. 30.

86. Ibid.
87. Ibid., p. 31.
88. Ibid.
89. Ibid.
90. Rubin and Babbie, "Research Methods," p. 488.
91. Ibid.
92. Harrison, *Diagnosing,* pp. 139, 140.
93. Weiss, *Evaluation,* p. 36.
94. See, for example, Donald T. Campbell and Julian C. Stanley, *Experimental and Quasi-Experimental Designs for Research* (Chicago, IL: Rand-McNally, 1963) for a description of three pre-experimental designs, three true experimental designs, and ten quasi-experimental designs.
95. I use the term "benefit-cost" analysis rather than the more common "cost-benefit" analysis because ratios of benefits to costs are normally expressed as benefit/cost rather than the reverse. For more information on benefit-cost analysis, see E. J. Mishan, *Economics for Social Decisions: Elements of Cost-Benefit Analysis* (New York: Praeger, 1972).
96. Weiss, *Evaluation,* p. 86.
97. Ibid., p. 88.
98. Ibid.
99. Hornick and Burrows, "Program Evaluation," p. 416.

Chapter 12: The Macro Social Worker as Administrator

1. Robert E. Sherwood, *Roosevelt and Hopkins: An Intimate History,* rev. ed. (New York: Harper, 1950), p. 32.
2. Ibid., p. 281.
3. Sue Spencer, *The Administration Method in Social Work Education* (New York: Council on Social Work Education, 1959), pp. 22-25.
4. Rex A. Skidmore, *Social Work Administration: Dynamic Management and Human Relationships,* 2d ed. (Englewood Cliffs, NJ: Prentice-Hall, 1990), p. 12.
5. Luther Gulick, "Notes on the Theory of Organization," in Luther Gulick and Lyndall Urwick, eds., *Papers on the Science of Organization* (New York: Institute of Public Administration, 1937), pp. 3-13.
6. Harold Koontz, Cyril O'Donnell, and Heinz Weinrich, *Essentials of Management* (New York: McGraw-Hill, 1986), p. 4, lists planning, organizing, staffing, leading, and controlling. Arthur G. Bedeian, *A Standardization of Selected Management Concepts* (New York: Garland, 1986) uses planning, organizing and controlling. Henry Mintzberg, *The Nature of Managerial Work* (Englewood Cliffs, NJ: Prentice-Hall, 1980), pp. 86-98, lists organizing, coordinating, planning, and controlling. Rex A. Skidmore, *Social Work Administration: Dynamic Management and Human Relationships* 2d ed., (Englewood Cliffs, NJ: Prentice-Hall, 1990), p. 17, cites planning, organizing, staffing, directing, and controlling. Paul Hersey and Kenneth H. Blanchard, *Management of Organizational Behavior: Utilizing Human Resources,* (Englewood Cliffs, NJ: Prentice-Hall, 1988), p. 6., lists planning, organizing, motivating, and controlling. Robert W. Weinbach, *The Social Worker as Manager: Theory and Practice* (New York: Longman, 1990), p. 18, asserts that social work management functions are planning, organizing, staffing, leading, and controlling.
7. Weinbach, *Social Worker,* p. 75.
8. Ibid.
9. Ibid., p. 78.
10. Hersey and Blanchard, *Management,* p. 6.
11. Skidmore, *Social Work,* p. 44.
12. Koontz, O'Donnell, and Weinrich, *Essentials,* p. 20.
13. Herbert Simon, *Administrative Behavior: A Study of Decision-Making Processes in Administrative Organization,* 3d ed. (New York: Free Press, 1976), pp. xvii, xxxvii.
14. Ibid., pp. 48-52; see also John P. Flynn, *Social Agency Policy: Analysis and Presentation for Community Practice* (Chicago, IL: Nelson-Hall, 1987), pp. 133-72.
15. Robert H. Miles, *Macro Organizational Behavior* (Santa Monica, CA: Goodyear, 1980), p. 322.
16. Ibid., p. 323.
17. Aaron Wildavsky, *Budgeting: A Comparative Theory of Budgetary Processes* (Boston, MA: Little, Brown, 1975), p. 3.   The same quote also appears in Wildavsky, *Politics of the Budgetary Process,* 2d ed., (Boston, MA: Little, Brown, 1974), p. 1.
18. Wildavsky, *Budgeting,* p. 3.
19. Wildavsky, *Politics,* p. 2.
20. Ibid., Wildavsky, *Budgeting,* p. 4.
21. Malvern J. Gross, "The Importance of Budgeting," in Simon Slavin, ed., *Social Administration: The Management of the Social Services* (New York: Haworth, 1978), p. 233.
22. Wildavsky, *Budgeting,* p. 4.
23. Ibid.
24. Ibid.
25. Wildavsky, *Politics,* p. 3.
26. Wildavsky, *Budgeting,* p. 4.
27. Gross, "Importance of Budgeting," p. 233; Skidmore, *Social Work,* p. 68.
28. Wildavsky, *Budgeting,* p. 5.
29. Ibid. See also Simon, *Administrative Behavior,* pp. xxviii, xxx.
30. Wildavsky, *Budgeting,* pp. 5, 6.
31. Wildavsky, *Budgeting,* p. 6; and Burton Gummer, *The Politics of Social Administration: Managing Organizational Politics in Social Agencies* (Englewood Cliffs, NJ: Prentice-Hall, 1990), p. 51.
32. Wildavsky, *Budgeting,* p. 6.
33. Ibid.
34. Ibid., p. 7.
35. Ibid.
36. Ibid.
37. Gummer, *Politics,* pp. 50-51.
38. Charles A. Rapp and John Poertner, *Social Administration: A Client-Centered Approach* (New York: Longman, 1992), p. 219.
39. Roderick K. Macleod, "Program Budgeting in Nonprofit Institutions," in Simon Slavin, *Social Administration: Management of the Social Services* (New York: Haworth Press and Council on Social Work Education, 1968), p. 251.
40. Rapp and Poertner, *Social Administration,* p. 219.
41. Skidmore, *Social Work,* p. 69.
42. Rapp and Poertner, *Social Administration,* p. 219.

43. Wildavsky, *Budgeting,* p. 275.
44. Ibid.
45. John J. Stretch, "Seven Key Managerial Functions of Sound Fiscal Budgeting: An Internal Management and External Accountability Perspective," *Administration in Social Work,* 3 (Winter 1979), 447.
46. Wildavsky, *Budgeting,* p. 297.
47. Ibid.
48. Peter A. Pyhrr, "The Zero-Base Approach to Government Budgeting," in Fremont J. Lyden and Ernest G. Miller, eds., *Public Budgeting: Program, Planning and Evaluation,* 3d ed. (Chicago, IL: Rand McNally, 1978), p. 253.
49. Wildavsky, *Budgeting,* p. 282.
50. Rapp and Poertner, *Social Administration,* pp. 221-22.
51. Ibid., p. 221.
52. Herbert G. Heneman, III, Donald P. Schwab, John A. Fossum, and Lee D. Dyer, *Managing Personnel and Human Resources* (Homewood, IL: Dow Jones–Irwin, 1981), p. 2.
53. Judith R. Gordon, *Human Resource Management: A Practical Approach* (Newton, MA: Allyn and Bacon, 1986), p. 5.
54. Felix A. Nigro and Lloyd G. Nigro, *The New Public Personnel Administration,* 2d ed. (Itasca, IL: Peacock, 1981), p. 2.
55. Joseph N. Cayer, *Public Personnel Administration in the United States* (New York: St. Martin's Press, 1975), p. 31.
56. Nigro and Nigro, *New Public,* p. 2.
57. Ibid., p. 3.
58. Ibid.
59. Ibid.
60. Ibid., p. 4.
61. Ibid.
62. Martin J. Gannon, *Management: An Integrated Framework,* 2d ed. (Boston, MA: Little, Brown, 1982), pp. 137-57.
63. Bobby R. Paton and Kim Giffin, *Problem-Solving Group Interaction* (New York: Harper and Row, 1973), p. 163.
64. Ibid.
65. Donelson R. Forsyth, *An Introduction to Group Dynamics* (Monterey, CA: Brooks/Cole, 1983), p. 166.
66. Ibid.
67. Ibid., pp. 166-67.
68. Charles A. Rapp and John Poertner, in *Social Administration: A Client-Centered Approach,* for example, assert that this approach is a "new metaphor" in which the traditional organizational chart is inverted so that "the pinnacle of the chart is the client and all organizational personnel are subservient. In fact, supervisors are subservient to frontline workers, and the 'boss' is subservient to supervisors and frontline workers," p. 277.
69. Martin J. Gannon, *Management: An Integrated Framework,* 2d ed. (Boston, MA: Little, Brown, 1982), p. 10.
70. Robert N. Bellah, Richard Madsen, William M. Sullivan, Ann Swidler, and Steven M. Tipton, *Habits of the Heart* (New York: Harper and Row, 1985), p. 2.
71. See, for example, such recent books as Robert W. Weinbach, *The Social Worker as Manager: Theory and Practice.* Even the otherwise enlightened book by Charles A. Rapp and John Poertner, *Social Administration: A Client-Centered Approach* talks about administration as the form of "client-centered management," an oxymoron that symbolizes the current ideological confusion inherent in social administration. See, for example, p. 17 in which administrators are to "promote the idea that clients are heroes," while on p. 6, clients are "a resource to be acquired." The idea of a client as a hero is congruent with an active-social model of man, while the idea of clients as resources is an example of a passive-atomistic model.
72. Ralph P. Hummel, *The Bureaucratic Experience* (New York: St. Martin's, 1977), p. 8.
73. Bernard Neugeboren, *Organization, Policy and Practice in the Human Services* (New York: Longman, 1985), p. 105.
74. Victor A. Thompson, *Without Sympathy or Enthusiasm: The Problem of Administrative Compassion* (University: University of Alabama Press, 1975), pp. 3, 4.
75. Theodore J. Lowi, *The End of Liberalism* (New York: Norton, 1969), p. 30.
76. Charles Perrow, *Complex Organizations,* 2d ed. (Glenview, IL: Scott, Foresman, 1979), p. 4.
77. John Forester, *Planning in the Face of Power* (Berkeley: University of California Press, 1989), p. 69.
78. Thompson, *Without Sympathy,* p. 4.
79. Alberto Guerreiro Ramos, *The New Science of Organizations: A Reconceptualization of the Wealth of Nations* (Toronto: University of Toronto Press, 1981), p. 4.
80. Ibid., p. 5.
81. Frank M. Coleman, *Hobbes and America: Exploring the Constitutional Foundations* (Toronto: University of Toronto Press, 1977), p. 47.
82. Ramos, *New Science,* p. 5.
83. Forester, *Planning,* p. 140.
84. Paul Tillich, "The Person in a Technical Society," in John A. Hutchison, *Christian Faith and Social Action* (New York: Scribner's, 1953), pp. 150-51.
85. Max Weber, "Bureaucracy," in *Economy and Society: An Outline of Interpretive Sociology,* 3 vols. eds. Guenther Roth and Claus Wittich, trans. E. Fischoff, et al. (New York: Bedminster Press, 1968), p. 975.
86. Ibid.
87. Hummel, *Bureaucratic,* p. 21.
88. Victor A. Thompson, *Bureaucracy and the Modern World* (Morristown, NJ: General Learning Press, 1976), p. 113.
89. Ibid., p. 115.
90. Ibid., p. 110.
91. Ibid., p. 112.
92. Ibid., p. 114.
93. Victor Thompson, in *Bureaucracy and the Modern World,* correctly states that "in the modern industrial period, *compassion is illegal* (emphasis in the original), p. 112. In addition, in his book, *Without Sympathy or Enthusiasm,* Thompson observes that "in fact, a caring relation between the incumbent of a role in a modern organization and a client is regarded as unethical..." (p. 17). Ralph Hummel in *The Bureaucratic Experience* further examines this inversion of what social workers normally consider among their highest values.

> Managers who "humanize" or "personalize" some of their relationships with their hierarchy . . . are not simply stepping on the toes of some people who will be jealous . . . they are, in fact, subverting the basic struc-

ture of modern organization; they are opening up to question the taken-for-granted values system . . . and factually and legally engaging in "corruption" in the true sense of the word by propagating emotional relationships that threaten death to rationalistically legitimated ones. (P. 16)

94. Thompson, *Without Sympathy,* p. 86.
95. Hummel, *Bureaucratic,* p. 144.
96. Ibid., pp. 150-55.
97. Gerard Egan, *You and Me: The Skills of Communicating and Relating to Others* (Monterey, CA: Brooks/Cole, 1977).
98. Thompson, *Bureaucracy,* pp. 77-107.
99. Ibid., p. 77.
100. Ibid., p. 101.
101. George Brager and Stephen Holloway, *Changing Human Service Organizations: Politics and Practice* (New York: Free Press, 1978), p. 1.
102. Herbert Simon, *Administrative Behavior,* 3d ed. (New York: Free Press, 1976), p. xxix.
103. Max Weber, "Bureaucracy," in *From Max Weber: Essays in Sociology,* trans. H. H. Gerth and C. Wright Mills (New York: Oxford University Press, 1946), pp. 228-29.
104. Ibid., p. 216.
105. Ibid.
106. Max Weber, *The Protestant Ethic and the Spirit of Capitalism,* trans. Talcott Parsons (New York: Scribner's, 1958), p. 182.
107. Max Weber, "Politics as a Vocation," in *From Max Weber,* p. 215.
108. Ibid., p. 95.
109. Ibid., p. 80.
110. Paulo Freire, *A Pedagogy of the Oppressed* (New York: Continuum, 1992), p. 46.
111. Ibid., p. 31.
112. Brager and Holloway, *Changing,* p. 15.
113. Ibid.
114. Ibid.
115. Ibid.
116. Rapp and Poertner, *Social Administration,* p. 19.
117. Brager and Holloway, *Changing,* p. 15.
118. Gummer, *Politics,* p. 133.
119. Rapp and Poertner, *Social Administration,* p. 17.
120. Skidmore, *Social Work,* p. 25.
121. Ibid.
122. Ibid.
123. Rapp and Poertner, *Social Administration,* p. 24.
124. Naomi Gottlieb, *The Welfare Bind* (Columbia University Press 1974), p. 130.
125. Rapp and Poertner, *Social Administration,* p. 23.
126. Ibid.
127. Ibid., p. 24.
128. Gummer, *Politics,* p. 133.
129. NASW Code of Ethics, 1979. The section from which this mandate was taken is:

IV. The Social Worker's Ethical Responsibility to Employers and Employing Organizations

L. Commitments to Employing Organization. The Social worker should adhere to commitments made to the employing organization.

1. The social worker should work to improve the employing agency's policies and procedures, and the efficiency and effectiveness of its services.
130. Thompson, *Bureaucracy,* p. 34.
131. Ibid., p. 17.
132. Thompson, *Without Sympathy,* p. 10.
133. Gordon, *Human Resource Management,* p. 5.
134. Stanley E. Seashore and Ephraim Yuchtman, "A System Resource Approach to Organizational Effectiveness," *American Sociological Review,* 32, (6) (Dec. 1967): 891-903.
135. Nigro and Nigro, *New Public,* p. 37.
136. Ibid., p. 59.
137. Ibid., p. 31. Emphasis in original.
138. Glen A. Bassett, "Employee Turnover Measurement and Human Resources Accounting," *Human Resources Management* (Fall 1972), pp. 29, 30.
139. Thompson, *Without Sympathy,* p. 94.
140. Thomas W. Gill. "Brave New Planet," *Personnel Administration* (May-June 1970), p. 39.
141. Ibid., p. 40.
142. Stephen P. Robbins, *Essentials of Organizational Behavior,* 3d ed. (Englewood Cliffs, NJ: Prentice-Hall, 1992), pp. 156-57.
143. Warren Bennis, *Why Leaders Can't Lead* (San Francisco, CA: Jossey-Bass, 1989), p. 18.
144. Ibid.
145. Thompson, *Without Sympathy,* p. 41. Copyright © 1975 Univ. of Alabama Press. Reprinted by permission.
146. Weber, "Bureaucracy," pp. 215, 216.

Part IV: Societal Social Work

1. Si Kahn, *How People Get Power: Organizing Oppressed Communities for Action* (New York: McGraw-Hill, 1978), p. 124.

Chapter 13: Becoming an Organization Developer

1. Stephen Robbins, *Essentials of Organization Behavior,* 3d ed. (Englewood Cliffs, NJ: Prentice-Hall, 1992), p. 276.
2. Ibid.
3. Donald F. Harvey and Donald F. Brown, *An Experiential Approach to Organization Development,* 4th ed. (Englewood Cliffs, NJ: Prentice-Hall, 1992), pp. ix, 5.
4. Robbins, *Essentials,* p. 270.
5. Harvey and Brown, *Experiential,* p. 13.
6. Ibid., p. 39.
7. Victor A. Thompson, *Bureaucracy and the Modern World* (Morristown, NJ: General Learning Press, 1976), p. 2.
8. Harvey and Brown, *Experiential,* p. 10.
9. Thompson, *Bureaucracy,* p. 84.
10. Stephen P. Robbins, *Organization Theory: The Structure and Design of Organizations* (Englewood Cliffs, NJ: Prentice-Hall, 1983), p. 9.
11. Ibid., p. 13.
12. Ibid., p. 14.
13. Charles Perrow, *Complex Organizations: A Critical Essay,* 2d ed. (Glenview, IL: Scott, Foresman, 1979), p. 34.

14. Thompson, *Bureaucracy,* p. 96.
15. Perrow, *Complex Organizations,* p. 34.
16. Ibid.
17. Harvey and Brown, *Experiential,* p. 41.
18. Thompson, *Bureaucracy,* p. 96.
19. Harvey and Brown, *Experiential,* p. 41.
20. Robbins, *Organization Theory,* p. 266.
21. Robbins, *Essentials,* p. 276.
22. Harvey and Brown, *Experiential,* p. 57.
23. Richard Beckhard, *Organization Development: Strategies and Models* (Reading, MA: Addison-Wesley, 1969, p. 9.
24. Robbins, *Essentials,* p. 276.
25. Edgar H. Schein, *Organizational Psychology,* 3d ed. (Englewood Cliffs, NJ: Prentice-Hall, 1980), p. 243.
26. Harvey and Brown, *Experiential,* p. 57.
27. Robbins, *Essentials,* pp. 288-95.
28. Michael I. Harrison, *Diagnosing Organizations: Methods, Models, and Processes* (Newbury Park, CA: Sage, 1987), p. 5.
29. For a good description of the use of participant observation, see John Lofland, *Analyzing Social Settings: A Guide to Qualitative Observation and Analysis* (Belmont, CA: Wadsworth, 1971).
30. Ibid., p. 33.
31. Ibid., pp. 33-35.
32. J. Steven Ott, *The Organizational Culture Perspective* (Homewood, IL: Irwin, 1989), p. ix.
33. Harrison, *Diagnosing,* p. 33.
34. Ibid., p. 34.
35. Barbara Vobejda, "Most Child-Care Centers Inadequate, Study Says," *The Fresno Bee,* Feb. 6, 1995, p. A1.
36. Harrison, *Diagnosing,* p. 35.
37. Ibid.
38. Many of the ideas for this section were adapted from Terrence E. Deal, *Corporate Culture* (Addison-Wesley, 1982), pp. 130-39.
39. Tom Jones, Organization developer, Worx, Inc., personal interview, Dec. 22, 1993, Fresno, CA.
40. Robert W. Weinbach, *The Social Worker as Manager: Theory and Practice.* (White Plains, NY: Longman, 1990), p. 316.
41. Jones, personal interview.
42. Weinbach, *Social Worker,* p. 318.
43. Ibid., pp. 317, 318.
44. Ibid., p. 318.
45. Ibid., p. 317.
46. Ibid.
47. Ibid., p. 319.
48. Ibid., p. 318.
49. Rebecca Jones, "Workaholic Women Suffer When They Put Boss First," *The Fresno Bee,* May 14, 1991, p. A 10.
50. Ibid.
51. Robbins, *Essentials,* p. 286.
52. Harvey and Brown, *Experiential,* p. 306.
53. Ibid., p. 307.
54. Jerry Edelwich with Archie Brodsky, *Burn-Out: Stages of Disillusionment in the Helping Professions* (New York: Human Sciences Press, 1980), p. 15.
55. Ibid.
56. Ibid.
57. Bernard Neugeboren, *Organization, Policy, and Practice in the Human Services* (New York: Longman, 1985), p. 114.
58. Edelwich, *Burn-Out,* p. 71.
59. Ibid., p. 72.
60. Ibid., p. 156.
61. Ibid., pp. 164-82.
62. Harvey and Brown, *Experiential,* p. 308-12.
63. Ibid., p. 309.
64. Ibid., p. 309, 310.
65. Edelwich, *Burn-Out,* p. 243.
66. Ibid., p. 145.
67. Robbins, *Essentials,* p. 64; Robbins, *Organization,* p. 252.
68. Robbins, *Essentials,* p. 65.
69. Robbins, *Organization,* p. 254.
70. Ibid., p. 255.
71. Schein, *Organizational,* pp. 162-63.
72. Perrow, *Complex Organizations,* p. 109.
73. Harvey and Brown, *Experiential,* pp. 293-96. See also Paul Hersey and Kenneth H. Blanchard, *Management of Organizational Behavior: Utilizing Human Resources,* 5th ed. (Englewood Cliffs, NJ: Prentice-Hall, 1988), pp. 149-51.
74. Robbins, *Essentials,* p. 67.
75. Harvey and Brown, *Experiential,* pp. 452-58; Robbins, *Essentials,* pp. 68, 69.
76. Harvey and Brown, *Experiential,* p. 336.
77. Ibid., pp. 337, 338.
78. Ibid., p. 349.
79. Ibid., p. 351.
80. Robert R. Blake, Herbert Shepard, and Jane S. Mouton, *Managing Intergroup Conflict in Industry* (Houston, TX: Gulf, 1964). See also Robert R. Blake and Jane S. Mouton, *Solving Costly Organizational Conflicts: Achieving Intergroup Trust, Cooperation, and Teamwork* (San Francisco, CA: Jossey-Bass, 1984).
81. Robert H. Miles, *Macro Organizational Behavior* (Santa Monica, CA: Goodyear, 1980), pp. 339-48.
82. Ibid., p. 131.
83. Adapted from, and used by permission of, Ronald Claassen, Director, Center for Conflict Resolution and Peacemaking, Fresno Pacific College, Fresno, California. A form of the conflict cycle appeared in Norman Shawchuck, *How to Manage Conflict in the Church: Understanding and Managing Conflict* (Indianapolis, IN: Spiritual Growth Resources, 1983), and an earlier form in Jerry Robinson and Roy Clifford, *Managing Conflict in Community Groups* (Champaign-Urbana: University of Illinois, 1974).
84. Roger Fisher and Scott Brown, *Getting Together—Building a Relationship That Gets to Yes* (Boston, MA: Houghton Mifflin, 1988), p. 37.
85. Ibid., p. 40.
86. This section was adapted from Freda Gomes, "How to Be a Winning Negotiator," *The Toastmaster,* June 1984, pp. 15-19.
87. Robbins, *Organizational Theory,* p. 303.
88. Ibid.
89. Ibid., p. 24.
90. Harvey and Brown, *Experiential,* pp. 417-23.
91. Frank Lowenberg and Ralph Dolgoff, *Ethical Decisions for Social Work Practice,* 2d ed. (Itasca, IL: Peacock, 1985), p. 14.

92. Neugeboren, *Organization*, p. 182.
93. Michael M. Harmon, *Action Theory for Public Administration*, (New York: Longman, 1981) states that "for want of a better label, the term 'action therapist,' roughly an amalgam of sympathetic critic, therapist and 'process' consultant, will be used to designate the prototype of the applied theorist's role suggested by the Action paradigm" (p. 178).
94. Ibid., p. 181.
95. Ibid.
96. Ibid., p. 184.
97. Ibid., p. 180.

Chapter 14: Social Work at the Societal Level: Social Policy and Politics

1. Excerpted from Judith Weinraub *(Washington Post)*, "Consumer Advocate Doesn't Back Down from a Good Fight," *The Fresno Bee,* June 21, 1992, p. F5.
2. William L. Morrow, *Public Administration: Politics and the Political Process* (New York: Random House, 1975), p. 10.
3. Thomas R. Dye, *Understanding Public Policy,* 2d ed. (Englewood Cliffs, NJ: Prentice-Hall, 1975), pp. 17-39.
4. Ibid., p. 24.
5. John Kenneth Galbraith, *Economics and the Public Purpose* (Boston, MA: Houghton Mifflin, 1973), p. 46.
6. See, for example, C. Wright Mills, *The Power Elite* (New York: Oxford University Press, 1956); G. William Domhoff, *Who Rules America?* (Englewood Cliffs, NJ: Prentice-Hall, 1967); and G. William Domhoff, *The Powers That Be* (New York: Random House, 1979).
7. Galbraith, *Economics,* p. 46.
8. Ibid.
9. Ibid., p. 66.
10. Dye, *Understanding,* p. 25.
11. Ibid.
12. Howard J. Karger and David Stoesz, *American Social Welfare Policy: A Structural Approach* (New York: Longman, 1990), p. 59.
13. Ibid.
14. Dye, *Understanding,* p. 18.
15. Ibid.
16. Ibid.
17. Morrow, *Public,* p. 170.
18. Ibid. See Theodore J. Lowi, *The End of Liberalism* (New York: Norton, 1969).
19. Morrow, *Public,* p. 50.
20. James Madison, Federalist No. 39, in Alexander Hamilton, James Madison, and John Jay, *The Federalist Papers,* Introduction by Clinton Rossiter (New York: New American Library, 1961), p. 221.
21. Ibid., Federalist No. 51, p. 324.
22. Ibid., Federalist No. 10, p. 79.
23. Ibid.
24. Ibid., Federalist No. 51, p. 322.
25. Frank M. Coleman, *Hobbes and America: Exploring the Constitutional Foundations* (Toronto: University of Toronto Press, 1977), pp. 128-29. See also Thomas Dye, *Understanding,* p. 21.
26. Dye, *Understanding,* p. 21.
27. Madison, Federalist No. 51, p. 322.
28. Morrow, *Public,* pp. 50, 51.
29. Karger and Stoesz, *American,* p. 60.
30. E. E. Schattschneider, quoted in Morrow, *Public,* p. 51.
31. Morrow, *Public,* p. 51.
32. Diana M. DiNitto and Thomas R. Dye, in *Social Welfare: Politics and Public Policy* (Englewood Cliffs, NJ: Prentice-Hall, 1983), for example, describe the policy-making process as having the following steps: (1) Identifying Policy Problems, (2) Formulating Policy Alternatives, (3) Legitimizing Public Policy, (4) Implementing Public Policy, and (5) Evaluating Policy.
33. Graham T. Allison, *Essence of Decision: Explaining the Cuban Missile Crisis* (Boston, MA: Little, Brown, 1971), p. 30.
34. Ibid., p. 29.
35. Ibid., p. 30.
36. George C. Edwards, III, and Ira Sharkansky, *The Policy Predicament: Making and Implementing Public Policy* (San Francisco, CA: Freeman, 1978), p. 7.
37. John Harsanyi, "Some Social Science Implications of a New Approach to Game Theory," in Allison, *Essence,* p. 31.
38. Morrow, *Public,* pp. 63-66.
39. Ibid., p. 79.
40. Ibid., p. 63.
41. Michael Doyle and Jim Boren, "Dooley Harvested Subsidies," *The Fresno Bee,* March 29, 1995, p. A1.
42. Morrow, *Public,* p. 64.
43. Allison, *Essence,* p. 67.
44. William L. Morrow, *Public Administration: Politics, Policy, and the Political System,* 2d ed. (New York: Random House, 1980), p. 90.
45. Ibid.
46. Ibid.
47. Ibid., p. 95.
48. Christopher Bellavita and Henrik L. Blum, "Problem Analysis: An Analytical Tool for Policy Analysts and Planners," unpublished manuscript, Sept. 1, 1981.
49. Ibid.
50. Ibid.
51. Ibid., p. 6.
52. Ibid., p. 12.
53. Ibid., p. 13.
54. Ibid., p. 14.
55. Karger and Stoesz, *American,* pp. 26, 27.
56. William D. Coplin and Michael K. O'Leary, *Everyman's PRINCE: A Guide to Understanding Your Political Problems,* 2d ed. (North Scituate, MA: Duxbury Press, 1976).
57. Charles S. Prigmore and Charles R. Atherton, *Social Welfare Policy: Analysis and Formulation,* 2d ed. (Lexington, MA: D. C. Heath, 1986), p. 195.
58. Ibid.
59. Ibid., p. 196.
60. Ibid.
61. Ibid.
62. Herbert J. Rubin and Irene S. Rubin, *Community Organizing and Development,* 2d ed. (New York: Macmillan, 1992), p. 266.

63. Ibid.
64. Ibid., p. 274.
65. Karen S. Haynes and James S. Mickelson, *Affecting Change: Social Workers in the Political Arena,* 2d ed. (New York: Longman, 1991), p. 64.
66. Ibid.
67. Ibid.
68. Ibid.
69. Ibid., p. 66.
70. Ibid., p. 65.
71. Michigan Sea Grant Advisory Service, "How Citizens Can Influence Legislation in Michigan" (Lansing: Michigan State University Cooperative Extension Service, 1981).
72. Haynes and Mickelson, *Affecting Change,* p. 72.
73. Ibid., p. 71.
74. Ibid., pp. 73-74.
75. Ibid., p. 74.
76. Ibid.
77. Ibid., p. 76.
78. Ibid., p. 76-77.
79. Karger and Stoesz, *American,* p. 63.
80. Peter Bachrach and Morton S. Baratz, *Power and Poverty* (New York: Oxford University Press, 1979), p. 7.
81. Ibid.
82. Ibid.
83. For some critics of modern political and policy theory, see Eric Voegelin, *The New Science of Politics* (Chicago, IL: University of Chicago Press, 1952) and Sheldon Wolin, *Politics and Vision* (Boston, MA: Little, Brown, 1960).
84. Henry Steele Commager, *The American Mind* (New York: Bantam, 1950), p. 252.
85. Theodore Roosevelt, "Reform Through Social Work," *McClure's Magazine,* (March 1901), p. 454, in Richard Hofstadter, *The Age of Reform* (New York: Vintage Books, 1955), p. 207.
86. Michael M. Harmon, "Toward an Active Social Theory of Administrative Action: Some Empirical and Normative Implications," in Carl Bellone, *Organization Theory and the New Public Administration* (Boston, MA: Allyn and Bacon, 1980), p. 197.
87. For an alternative educational model congruent with the action approach, see Paulo Freire, *Pedagogy of the Oppressed* (New York: Continuum, 1991).
88. Kenneth E. Reid, *Social Work Practice with Groups: A Clinical Perspective* (Pacific Grove, CA: Brooks/Cole, 1991), pp. 26-27. See also K. Reid, *From Character Building to Social Treatment: The History of the Use of Groups in Social Work* (Westport, CT: Greenwood Press, 1981).
89. For a perspective on a value-centered theory of politics see Stephen Salkever, "Virtue, Obligation, and Politics," *Political Science Review,* 68: 78, 91.
90. DiNitto and Dye, *Social Welfare,* p. xiv.

Chapter 15: The Future of Macro Social Work

1. Harry Specht and Mark E. Courtney, *Unfaithful Angels: How Social Work Has Abandoned Its Mission* (New York: Free Press, 1994), p. 27.
2. Bill Hosokawa, *Nisei: The Quiet Americans: The Story of a People* (New York: Morrow, 1969), p. 258.
3. Ibid., p. 260.
4. Steven Okazaki, *Unfinished Business: The Japanese American Internment Cases,* Mouchette Films Production, 1984.
5. Hosokawa, *Nisei,* p. 252.
6. Bill Hosokawa, *JACL in Quest of Justice: The History of the Japanese American Citizens League* (New York: Morrow, 1982), p. 172.
7. Okazaki, *Unfinished Business.*
8. Hosokawa, *JACL,* p. 177.
9. Ibid., p. 177.
10. Gordon K. Hirabayashi, "Why I Refused to Be Evacuated," in Audrie Girdner and Anne Loftis, *The Great Betrayal: The Evacuation of the Japanese-Americans During World War II* (London: Macmillan, 1969), p. 204.
11. Okazaki, *Unfinished Business.*
12. Hosokawa, *JACL,* pp. 177, 178.
13. Ibid., p. 178.
14. Girdner and Loftis, *Great Betrayal,* p. 328.
15. Ibid., p. 328.
16. Hosokawa, *JACL,* pp. 276-78.
17. Specht and Courtney, *Unfaithful Angels,* p. x.
18. Richard L. Means, *The Ethical Imperative: The Crisis in American Values* (Garden City, NY: Anchor Books, 1970), p. 1.
19. Ibid.
20. Frank M. Coleman, *Hobbes and America: Exploring the Constitutional Foundations* (Toronto: University of Toronto Press, 1977), p. 30.
21. Ibid., p. 17.
22. Ibid., p. 6.
23. Ibid., p. 4.
34. Ibid., p. 28.
35. Ibid., p. 18.
26. Walter A. Weiskopf, *Alienation and Economics* (New York: Dell, 1971), p. 16.
27. Richard Taylor, *Good and Evil: A New Direction* (New York: Macmillan, 1970), p. 21.
28. Weiskopf, *Alienation,* p. 27.
29. Viktor E. Frankl, *Man's Search for Meaning: An Introduction to Logotherapy* (New York: Washington Square Press, 1963).
30. Robert N. Bellah, Richard Madsen, William M. Sullivan, Ann Swidler, and Steven M. Tipton, *Habits of the Heart: Individualism and Commitment in American Life* (New York: Harper and Row, 1985), p. 76.
31. Herbert Simon, *Administrative Behavior: A Study of Decision-Making Processes in Administrative Organization,* 3d ed. (New York: Free Press, 1976), pp. 5, 50, 53.
32. Taylor, *Good and Evil,* pp. 17-31.
33. Kenji Murase, "Organizing the Japanese-American Community," in Felix G. Rivera and John L. Erlich, *Community Organizing in a Diverse Society* (Boston, MA: Allyn and Bacon, 1992), p. 178.
34. Coleman, *Hobbes,* p. 121. Richard Hofstadter adds this observation: "However much at odds on specific issues, the major political traditions have shared a belief in the rights of property, the philosophy of economic individualism, the

value of competition . . . and the natural evolution of self-interest and self-assertion, [as] staple tenets of the central faith in American political ideologies." Richard Hofstadter, "Woodrow Wilson: Democrat in Cupidity," in Arthur Mann, ed., *The Progressive Era: Liberal Renaissance or Liberal Failure* (New York: Holt, Rinehart and Winston, 1963), p. 71.

35. Coleman, *Hobbes,* p. 16.
36. Henry S. Kariel, *Beyond Liberalism: Where Relations Grow* (New York: Harper and Row, 1977), p. 11. Emphasis in original.
37. Bellah et al., *Habits,* p. 142.
38. Coleman, *Hobbes,* pp. 55, 59.
39. Bellah et al., *Habits,* p. 334.
40. Ibid., p. 45.
41. Milton Friedman, *Capitalism and Freedom* (Chicago, IL: University of Chicago Press, 1962), p. 5.
42. Ibid., p. 15.
43. Bellah et al., *Habits,* p. 142.
44. Ibid., p. 144.
45. Ibid., p. 143.
46. Ibid., p. 38.
47. Ibid., p. 80.
48. Thomas M. Meenaghan and Robert O. Washington, *Social Policy and Social Welfare: Structure and Applications* (New York: Free Press, 1980), p. 89.
49. Bellah et al., *Habits,* p. 80.
50. Ibid., p. 76.
51. Ibid.
52. Ibid., p. 81.
53. Ibid., p. 139.
54. Meenaghan and Washington, *Social Policy,* p. 89.
55. Means, *Ethical Imperative,* p. 73.
56. Bellah et al., *Habits,* p. 152.
57. Bellah et al., *Habits,* p. 69.
58. Coleman, *Hobbes,* pp. 13, 14.
59. Victor A. Thompson, *Without Sympathy or Enthusiasm: The Problem of Administrative Compassion* (University: University of Alabama Press, 1975), p. 97.
60. Simon, *Administrative Behavior,* pp. 85, 86.
61. Bellah et al., *Habits,* p. 153.
62. Alasdair MacIntyre, *After Virtue,* 2d ed. (Notre Dame, IN: University of Notre Dame Press, 1984), pp. 11, 12.
63. Coleman, *Hobbes,* pp. 59, 60.
64. Ibid., p. 60.
65. Ibid., p. 61.
66. Means, *Ethical Imperative,* p. 72.
67. Kariel, *End of Liberalism,* p. 5.
68. Coleman, *Hobbes,* p. 125.
69. Ibid., p. 59.
70. MacIntyre, *After Virtue,* p. 227.
71. Elbert V. Bowden, *Economic Evolution* (Cincinnati, OH: Southwestern, 1981), p. 193.
72. Charles L. Schultze, *The Public Use of Private Interest* (Washington, DC: The Brookings Institution), p. 18.
73. James Madison, Alexander Hamilton, and John Jay, *The Federalist,* No. 51, introduction by Edward Mead Earle (New York: Random House, n.d.).
74. Coleman, *Hobbes,* p. 10.

75. Bellah, et al., *Habits,* p. 33.
76. Coleman, *Hobbes,* p. 77.
77. Reinhold Niebuhr, "The Children of Light and the Children of Darkness," in Gibson Winter, *Social Ethics: Issues in Ethics and Society* (New York: Harper and Row, 1968), p. 148.
78. Coleman, *Hobbes,* p. 116.
79. Ibid., p. 99.
80. Ibid., p. 59.
81. Means, *Ethical Imperative,* p. 31.
82. Coleman, *Hobbes,* pp. 127-31.
83. Ibid., p. 38.
84. John Locke, *The Second Treatise of Government,* Thomas P. Peardon, ed. (New York, Liberal Arts Press, 1952), Sect. 87, p. 49.
85. Milton Friedman, *Capitalism and Freedom* (Chicago, IL: University of Chicago Press, 1962), p. 15.
86. Vincent Ostrom and Elinor Ostrom, "Public Choice: A different Approach to the Study of Public Administration," *Public Administration Review,* March/April 1971, p. 206.
87. William L. Morrow, *Public Administration: Politics, Policy, and the Political System,* 2d ed. (New York: Random House, 1980), p. 83.
88. Kariel, *Beyond Liberalism,* p. 10.
89. Coleman, *Hobbes,* p. 116.
90. Kariel, *Beyond Liberalism,* p. 6.
91. Coleman, *Hobbes,* pp. 13, 14.
92. Ibid., p. 14.
93. Bellah et al., *Habits,* pp. 134-35.
94. MacIntyre, *After Virtue,* pp. 23, 24.
95. Thompson, *Without Sympathy,* p. 28.
96. Paul Tillich, "The Person in a Technical Society," in Gibson Winter, ed., *Social Ethics: Issues in Ethics and Society* (New York: Harper and Row, 1968), p. 134.
97. Max Weber, "Bureaucracy," in *From Max Weber: Essays in Sociology,* trans. H. H. Gerth and C. Wright Mills (New York: Oxford University Press, 1946), pp. 215, 216.
98. Thompson, *Without Sympathy,* pp. 1-7.
99. Coleman, *Hobbes,* p. 121.
100. Bellah et al., *Habits,* p. 50.
101. Tillich, "The Person in a Technical Society," p. 121.
102. Ibid., p. 126.
103. Ibid., p. 122.
104. Soren Kierkegaard, *Fear and Trembling,* in *Fear and Trembling and the Sickness unto Death,* trans. Walter Lowrie (Garden City, NY: Doubleday, 1958), p. 145.
105. Tillich, "The Person in a Technical Society," p. 121.
106. Ibid., p. 127.
107. Ibid., p. 125.
108. Ibid.
109. Thompson, *Without Sympathy,* pp. 90, 91.
110. Paul Hersey and Kenneth Blanchard, *Management of Organizational Behavior: Utilizing Human Resources,* 5th ed. (Englewood Cliffs, NJ: Prentice-Hall, 1988), pp. 127-43.
111. Ibid., pp. 249-62.
112. Bernard Neugeboren, *Organization, Policy, and Practice in the Human Services* (New York: Longman, 1985), p. 96.
113. Bellah et al., Habits, p. 47.
114. Bellah et al. comment that "we have, in fact, seen that ther-

apeutic understandings of interaction work best in bureaucratic and market situations where individuals are under
pressure and need to coordinate their activities with preci-
sion." *Habits,* p. 139.

115. Tillich, "The Person in a Technical Society," p. 128.
116. Bellah et al., *Habits,* p. 135.
117. Ibid., pp. 135, 139.
118. Ibid., p. 47.
119. Ibid., p. 139.
120. Ibid.
121. Ibid., p. 138.
122. Ibid., p. 47.
123. Ibid.
124. Thompson, *Without Sympathy,* p. 91.
125. Bellah et al., *Habits,* p. 60.
126. Tillich, "The Person in a Technical Society," p. 128.
127. Bellah et al., *Habits,* p. 50.
128. Ibid.
129. Ibid., p. 135.
130. Ibid., p. 51.
131. Hans S. Falck, *Social Work: The Membership Perspective*
(New York: Springer, 1988), p. 158.
132. Specht and Courtney, *Unfaithful Angels,* p. 27.
133. Ibid.
134. Bellah et al., *Habits,* p. 50.
135. Tillich, "The Person in a Technical Society," p. 137.
136. Bellah et al., *Habits,* p. 51.
137. Ralph P. Hummel, *The Bureaucratic Experience* (New York:
St. Martin's, 1977), p. 214.
138. Alberto Guerreiro Ramos, *The New Science of Organizations: A Reconceptualization of Wealth of Nations* (Toronto:
University of Toronto Press, 1981), p. 110.
139. Thomas Hobbes, "Introduction," *Leviathan* (New York:
Collier Books, 1961).
140. Ramos, *New Science,* p. 109.
141. Ibid.
142. Thompson, *Without Sympathy,* p. 91.
143. Ibid.
144. Ramos, *New Science,* p. 111.
145. Ibid., p. 111.
146. Ibid., p. 135.
147. Ross Snyder, *On Becoming Human: Discovering Yourself
and Your Life World* (Nashville, TN: Abingdon, 1967), p. 84.
148. Martin Buber, *I and Thou* (New York: Scribner's, 1958).
149. Nikolai Berdyaev, *Slavery and Freedom* (New York: Scribner's, 1944), p. 135.
150. Buber, *I and Thou,* p. 3.
151. Berdyaev, *Slavery,* pp. 130-38.
152. Buber, *I and Thou,* p. 3.
153. Berdyaev, *Slavery,* p. 135.
154. Hummel, *Bureaucratic Experience,* p. 2.
155. Martin Buber, "What Is Man," in *Between Man and Man*
(New York: Macmillan, n.d.), p. 200.
156. Will Herberg, ed., *Four Existentialist Theologians* (Westport, CT: Greenwood, 1975), p. 4. Reprint of 1958 edition.
157. Ibid., p. 9.

158. Ibid., p. 4.
159. Paul Tillich, *Systematic Theology,* Vol. 1 (Chicago, IL: University of Chicago Press, 1951), p. 176.
160. Ramos, *New Science,* p. 106.
161. Ibid., p. 110.
162. Ibid., p. 4.
163. Ibid., p. 17.
164. Ibid., p. 4.
165. Ibid., p. 82.
166. Gibson Winter, *Elements for a Social Ethic: The Role of Social Science in Public Policy* (New York: Macmillan, 1966),
p. 219.
167. Wynetta Devore, "The African-American Community in
1990: The Search for a Practice Method," in Felix G. River
and John L. Erlich, *Community Organizing in a Diverse Society* (Boston, MA: Allyn and Bacon, 1992), pp. 79-80.
168. Hummel, *Bureaucratic Experience,* p. 16.
169. The challenge of critiqueing functional rationality has been
taken on by Karl Mannheim in *Man and Society in an Age
of Reconstruction* (New York: Harcourt, Brace and World,
1940); theorist Max Horkheimer, *The Eclipse of Reason*
(New York: Oxford University Press, 1947); and his associates, including Herbert Marcuse, Theodor Adorno, Erich
Fromm and Jurgen Habermas of the Frankfurt School of the
Institut fur Sozialforschung. More recently, this task has
been revisited by Alberto Guerreiro Ramos and by Eric
Voegelin, *The New Science of Politics* (Chicago, IL: University of Chicago Press, 1952). Another fruitful arena of reformulation is the redefinition of administration by theorists
of the "new public administration," particularly Carl Bellone
and Michael Harmon.
170. Hummel, *Bureaucratic Experience,* p. 202.
171. Specht and Courtney, *Unfaithful Angels,* p. 170.
172. E. Dan Edwards and Margie Egbert-Edwards, "Native
American Community Development," in Felix G. Rivera
and John L. Erlich, *Community Organizing in a Diverse Society* (Boston, MA: Allyn and Bacon, 1992), p 46.
173. Specht and Courtney, *Unfaithful Angels,* p. 163.
174. Devore, "African American Community," p. 83.
175. Specht and Courtney, *Unfaithful Angels,* p. 155.
176. Ibid.
177. Tillich, "Person in a Technical Society," p. 137.
178. Ibid., p. 136.
179. Julio Morales, "Community Social Work with Puerto Rican
Communities in the United States: One Organizer's Perspective," in Rivera and Erlich, *Community Organizing,* p. 98.
180. Noam Chomsky, quoted in Rivera and Erlich, p. 64.
181. Specht and Courtney, *Unfaithful Angels,* p. 27.
182. Ronald L. Simon and Stephen M. Aigner, *Practice Principles: A Problem-Solving Approach to Social Work* (New
York: Macmillan, 1985), p. 23.
183. A. Solzhenitsyn, *Cancer Ward* (New York: Bantam, 1969),
pp. 429-44.
184. Specht and Courtney, *Unfaithful Angels,* p. 27.
185. Simon and Aigner, *Practice Principles,* p. 21.
186. Kariel, *Beyond Liberalism,* p. 8.

Epilogue: Macro Social Work—A Profession of Heroes

1. Quoted in Richard Zimmerman, *What Can I Do to Make a Difference: A Positive Action Source Book* (New York: Plume, 1991), p. 2.

2. Reinhold Niebuhr, quoted in Marian Wright Edelman, *The Measure of Our Success: A Letter to My Children and Yours* (New York: Harper Collins, 1993), p. 59.

3. Adapted from *U.S. News and World Report,* March 21, 1994, p. 58.

AUTHOR INDEX

SUBJECT INDEX

Photo Credits